The Court and the Charter

Leading Cases

Second Edition

Thomas M.J. Bateman
St. Thomas University

Janet L. Hiebert
Queen's University

Rainer Knopff
University of Calgary

Peter H. Russell
University of Toronto

emond ▪ Toronto, Canada ▪ 2017

Emond Montgomery Publications Limited
60 Shaftesbury Avenue
Toronto ON M4T 1A3
http://www.emond.ca/highered

Printed in Canada.

We acknowledge the financial support of the Government of Canada. Canadä

Publisher: Mike Thompson
Managing editor, development: Kelly Dickson
Senior editor, production: Jim Lyons
Production supervisor: Laura Bast
Copy editor: Cindy Fujimoto
Typesetter: Christopher Hudson
Proofreader: Nancy Ennis
Cover designers: Stephen Cribbin & Simon Evers
Back cover photo: Mike Thompson

Library and Archives Canada Cataloguing in Publication

Bateman, Thomas Michael Joseph, 1962-, author
     The Court and the Charter : leading cases / Thomas M.J. Bateman, Janet L. Hiebert, Rainer Knopff, Peter H. Russell. — Second edition.

Includes bibliographical references and index.
ISBN 978-1-77255-175-4 (softcover)

     1. Canada. Canadian Charter of Rights and Freedoms—Cases.   2. Canada. Supreme Court—Decision making—Cases.   3. Judgments—Canada—Cases.   4. Civil rights—Canada—Cases.   I. Hiebert, Janet, 1960-, author   II. Knopff, Rainer, 1948-, author   III. Russell, Peter H., author   IV. Title.

KE4381.5.B38 2017   342.7108'5   C2017-900399-2   KF4483.C5.B38 2017

Contents

A. The Pre-Charter Era

B. Fundamental Freedoms

C. Democratic Rights

D. Legal Rights

E. Evolving Scope of Section 7

F. Equality Rights

G. Language Rights

H. Remedies

Appendix

Preface

This collection of leading Supreme Court of Canada Charter of Rights decisions stems from successful collections of edited Supreme Court decisions first published in 1965. Peter Russell's *Leading Constitutional Decisions* became the standard reference for undergraduate political science students of Supreme Court decision-making. Not a few law students used it to prepare for their exams as well. It underwent several successful editions and culminated in *Federalism and the Charter: Leading Constitutional Decisions*, published in 1989 with the collaboration of F.L. Morton and Rainer Knopff.

In that year, the court had five years' experience with the Charter and was only beginning to settle some fundamental interpretive issues raised by the Charter and by the expectations set for it by litigants, interest groups, governments, and other commentators. But it was clear by then that the Supreme Court would apply the Charter with enthusiasm and vigour, boldly going where the pre-Charter court had feared to tread. By 1989, several major pieces of legislation had been struck down. Perhaps the most spectacular exercise of judicial review was the court's January 28, 1988 decision to declare null and void Canada's *Criminal Code* provisions restricting access to abortion. Newspaper headlines the next day blared that the court advanced a woman's right to abortion. The decision was praised and pilloried. If the Charter made little impression on Canadians before then, the *Morgentaler* decision would henceforth change popular opinion about the Charter and the power of courts.

In some respects, we have a clear idea of how the Charter is to be understood and can readily identify some basic interpretive doctrines developed by the court. In other respects, we are as uncertain as ever about the meaning of the Charter. Many Charter decisions reveal deep divisions among justices. The Canadian court experiences a rather high rate of turn-over (particularly in comparison to the United States Supreme Court, whose justices are appointed for life rather than until 75 years of age as in Canada) and this contributes to doctrinal uncertainty. The court has also shown that it is willing to reconsider and reverse its earlier Charter decisions. As new issues come up, the court is often faced with situations that neither it nor the drafters of the Charter had anticipated.

The Charter enjoys the affection of Canadians, especially young Canadians. So keen are they about their rights that they often think the Charter is the Constitution. They are wrong on this point, of course, and they are often unclear about the purposes of the Charter or how Charter decisions are made. Undergraduate students, for example, generally associate the Charter with all things good and just. They commonly know that the courts have enforced the Charter's legal rights protections vigorously in favour of those charged with crimes and those subject to national security policies. They are also likely to know that the Supreme Court has advanced the rights of gays and lesbians and may applaud the court for doing so.

They are often surprised, however, to learn that the Supreme Court has struck down legislation limiting tobacco companies' right to advertise their products; that it had allowed some forms of child pornography to be produced in Canada; that it forbade the minister of Justice from surrendering a murder suspect (who was later convicted) to the United States in the absence of assurances that the death penalty will not be administered upon conviction; that it denied a claim for public payment for autism treatments; and that extreme drunkenness, according to a 1994 decision, can diminish one's guilt in sexual assault cases.

Students are often distressed to learn that justices are divided on the merits of controversial Charter decisions and that judicial opinions both for and against a result are highly persuasive. They are surprised to learn that Supreme Court decisions are difficult to understand and much more complex than media reports suggest. They are often perplexed by the court's (sometimes selective) use of non-legal evidence in its decision-making. More broadly, they are unsettled by the fact that rights cannot be enjoyed absolutely and that rights often conflict with one another.

We hope that this collection of Charter decisions continues to unsettle students, because only in this way can they confront and correct received opinion on the nature and consequences of Charter review in Canada. While the secondary literature on the Charter is massive and rich, there is no substitute for reading the primary data of the Supreme Court—its decisions. Wrestling with the decisions stimulates an appreciation for the complexity of the issues, the indeterminacy of Charter provisions, the different views of justices, the strategic calculations of litigants and interveners, and the way in which decisions are translated by the media for public consumption.

This collection contains a small but, we hope, representative sample of the hundreds of Supreme Court Charter decisions that have been rendered since 1984. We have selected cases for inclusion on the basis of three criteria: (1) Does the decision break new and enduring doctrinal ground? For example, *R. v. Oakes* (1986) was included because it set the template for applying the section 1 reasonable limits clause to legislative violations of Charter rights. (2) Does the case reveal a particularly difficult issue that divides justices and also requires the court to weigh evidence that stretches its institutional capacity? On this basis, *Gosselin v. Quebec* (2002) and *Sauvé v. Canada* (2002) are obvious candidates for inclusion. (3) Does the case either stimulate or proceed from political controversy? On this criterion, *R. v. Mills* (1999) and *Carter v. Canada* (2015) are instructive examples.

This book is a companion to another volume of cases, *The Court and the Constitution*, also published by Emond. While *The Court and the Constitution* covers federalism, constitutional change, Aboriginal rights, and the Charter (and thus a broader sweep of history), this volume zeroes in on the Charter. We follow a similar format in both volumes, editing the decisions to manageable length and providing introductory editors' notes to set each decision in political and legal context. In both volumes, each decision is preceded by discussion questions to test understanding and probe issues further.

Constitutional jurisprudence is a moving target and any decision has the potential to alter the course of constitutional law. For this reason, both books are supplemented by a website containing edited Supreme Court decisions and introductory editors' notes (see below).

Our project is made possible by the enthusiastic support of Emond Publishing, and particularly Mike Thompson. Many thanks to him and the staff. The authors and the publisher also wish to thank the following people for providing their comments and suggestions during the development of this book: Dave Snow, University of Guelph; Peter McCormick, University of Lethbridge; Kelly Saunders, Brandon University; Bahaa Sunallah, Carleton University; Matthew Hennigar, Brock University; and Alison Braley, University of Toronto.

Website

This book is supplemented by an extensive password-protected website containing intro-
ductions and edited decisions for many additional Supreme Court of Canada cases not
included in this book: see emond.ca/charter2e. Instructors who have selected this book for
course use can contact an Emond representative at 1-888-837-0815, or visit emond.ca/
contact-us.

About the Authors

Thomas M.J. Bateman is Associate Professor of Political Science at St. Thomas University.
Janet L. Hiebert is Professor of Political Studies at Queen's University.
Rainer Knopff is Professor of Political Science (Emeritus) at the University of Calgary.
Peter H. Russell is Professor of Political Science (Emeritus) at the University of Toronto.

Introduction

The entrenchment of the *Canadian Charter of Rights and Freedoms* into the Canadian Constitution on April 17, 1982 is among the most significant developments in Canadian constitutional history. While the Charter is only part of the Canadian Constitution, which has both written and unwritten components, and was merely a part of the package of changes entrenched when the Constitution was patriated from Britain in 1982, in the popular mind the Charter towers over other pillars of Canadian constitutionalism. While federalism and parliamentary government continue to pervade our constitutional self-understanding and the actual workings of the country, Canadians increasingly articulate their values and their political demands as rights. Supreme Court justices travel the lecture circuit. Supreme Court nominees now appear before Parliament prior to appointment. Canadian life is very different in the post-Charter era. This introduction explores the changes that the Charter has produced.

Is the Charter the cause of change in Canada or the effect of change? Alan Cairns, one of Canada's most insightful students of constitutional politics, has argued that the Charter has not only produced institutional changes that elevate the status of courts and litigation in Canada but has also activated a variety of groups and identities whose interests and rights can now be advanced through the rhetoric of rights that the Charter has spawned. The Charter, in his view, has produced Charter Canadians.[1] Others argue that the Charter is an institutional consequence of deep cultural changes taking shape in the post-war era. The shift from materialist values, stressing economic growth and physical security, to post-materialist orientations, emphasizing egalitarianism, environmentalism, gender, sexual and ethnic identities, and the general ideal of self-fulfillment, generated political conditions favourable to entrenched citizen rights.[2] While debates about the causal influence of the Charter on Canadian political life will continue for a long time, it is a fact that the Canadian Charter was entrenched in the swirl of larger forces, and itself has led to important changes in Canadian politics and government.

ROOTS OF THE CHARTER

The inclusion of a bill of rights in Canada's Constitution was not even considered at the time the country was founded. The Fathers of Confederation were mid-Victorian British colonials. The Constitution they revered was not the American, but the British. The British

---

1 Alan C. Cairns, *Reconfigurations: Canadian Citizenship and Constitutional Change*, Douglas E. Williams, ed. (Toronto: McClelland & Stewart, 1995).

2 Neil Nevitte and Ian Brodie, "Evaluating the Citizens' Constitution Theory" (1993) 26 *Canadian Journal of Political Science* 235.

Constitution most certainly did not contain a bill of rights. Its first and highest principle was parliamentary sovereignty.[3]

This did not mean that Canada's founders were hostile to rights. Indeed, as Janet Ajzenstat has shown, the founding debates were full of claims about rights and rights protection.[4] Although it may sound strange to modern ears, Canada's founders believed that rights were better protected by the British parliamentary system than by the U.S. institutional system, including the latter's constitutionally entrenched bill of rights. During the Confederation debates in the Canadian legislature, for example, David Christie, quoting the American *Declaration of Independence* virtually word for word, maintained that both the British and American Constitutions rest "on the same great principle"—"that life, liberty and the pursuit of happiness are the unalienable rights of man, and that to secure these rights, governments are instituted among men, deriving their just powers from the consent of the governed."[5]

Although Canada's founding Constitution, the *British North America Act* (in 1982, renamed the *Constitution Act, 1867*), did not explicitly entrench civil liberties based on philosophical theories of human rights, it did secure some practical, historical rights aimed at protecting the interests of the English Protestant minority in Quebec and the French-Catholic minority outside Quebec. Section 93 guaranteed Quebec Protestants the right to denominational schools that Roman Catholics at that time enjoyed in Ontario. Section 133 ensured that English could be used in the Quebec legislature and French in the Canadian Parliament, that both languages could be used in the courts of Canada and Quebec, and that the laws of Canada and Quebec would be published in both languages. Inclusion of these minority rights in the Constitution was a crucial part of the Confederation bargain.

At the time of Confederation, and for a long time thereafter, Canada did not have a well-established practice of citizens using courts to challenge violations of their rights by governments. Section 93 invited minorities to appeal to the federal government for remedial action against deprivations of their school rights by provincial governments. In the 1890s Manitoba school crisis, Charles Tupper's Conservative government proposed to use its remedial power under section 93 to protect the rights of Manitoba's French-Catholic minority. The Tupper Conservatives were defeated in the 1896 general election by Wilfrid Laurier's Liberals, who favoured provincial rights over minority rights. This was the last time any federal government considered using its section 93 remedial power. French-Catholic minorities outside Quebec fared no better when they tried to secure their rights through the courts. Canada's highest court, the Judicial Committee of the Privy Council, was anything but activist in interpreting the ambit of section 93 rights. When lower courts ruled that legislation in 1890 that made English Manitoba's official language violated the

---

3 Donald Creighton, *The Road to Confederation: The Emergence of Canada, 1863-1867* (Toronto: Macmillan, 1964), and Peter H. Russell, *Constitutional Odyssey: Can Canadians Become a Sovereign People?*, 3rd ed. (Toronto: University of Toronto Press, 2004) ch. 2.

4 Janet Ajzenstat, *The Canadian Founding: John Locke and Parliament* (Montreal and Kingston: McGill-Queen's University Press, 2007) ch. 3.

5 Janet Ajzenstat, Paul Romney, Ian Gentles, and William D. Gairdner, *Canada's Founding Debates* (Toronto: Stoddart, 1999) at 191.

constitutional rights of francophones, Manitoba's governments simply ignored the decisions—and got away with it until the late 1970s.[6]

The Second World War marked the turning point in Canadian attitudes toward civil liberties and human rights. Canada's participation in the war and the post-war settlement heightened awareness of the need to protect fundamental rights and liberties against all governments, including democratically elected governments. Canada took a leading role in the founding of the United Nations and the adoption of the Universal Declaration of Human Rights. These developments created significant public interest in Canada's adoption of its own charter of fundamental rights and freedoms. Between 1947 and 1950, two joint parliamentary committees and a Senate committee considered proposals for a constitutional bill of rights.[7] At this point, leaders of the governing Liberal Party opposed a constitutional charter on the grounds that it would undermine parliamentary sovereignty and provincial rights. Nonetheless there was now a growing body of opinion in Canada, across the political spectrum, seeking stronger protection of rights and freedoms.

The removal and dispossession of west-coast Japanese Canadians during the war, followed after the war by the Gouzenko espionage inquiry's gross violation of basic civil rights, broadened support for a charter among Canadian civil liberties organizations. A series of court cases in the 1950s focused attention on the use of the courts to thwart the repressive policies of the Duplessis regime in Quebec. In seven cases between 1953 and 1959 the Supreme Court of Canada, now Canada's highest court, upheld challenges by religious and political minorities to Quebec laws and policies.[8] These Supreme Court decisions were based on a variety of grounds, including common law, the constitutional division of powers, and a doctrine first put forward in 1938 by Chief Justice Duff that the *British North America (B.N.A.) Act* contained an implied constitutional bill of rights that at least protected the right of free public discussion essential for the proper working of the parliamentary system of government.[9]

The implied bill of rights was invoked by a number of Supreme Court justices in the Quebec civil liberties cases decided by the court in the 1950s, but never gained the support of a majority of the judges. While civil libertarians were pleased with the immediate results of the Quebec cases, the decisions strengthened their determination to secure legal protection for civil liberties in a stronger form than that afforded by the vague and uncertain implied bill of rights doctrine.

It took the election in 1957 of a Conservative government under the leadership of John Diefenbaker to put a Canadian bill of rights proposal back on the political agenda. Diefenbaker had been an ardent advocate of a bill of rights for many years and his support for such a measure was an important factor in his rise to political prominence. The *Canadian*

---

6 For a discussion of these developments, see the introduction to *Mahe v. Alberta,* case 31.

7 For an account, see Christopher MacLennan, *Toward the Charter: Canadians and the Demand for a National Bill of Rights, 1929-1960* (Montreal and Kingston: McGill-Queen's University Press, 2003).

8 For a discussion of these cases, see the introduction to *Saumur v. Quebec and Attorney General of Quebec,* [1947] S.C.R. 492 (the case report for *Saumur* can be found in the instructor's supplements package).

9 *Reference re Alberta Statutes,* case 1.

Bill of Rights was not an addition to the Constitution of Canada. It was passed as an ordinary act of Parliament.[10] As such, it is not entrenched and can be set aside by future parliaments, and it has no application to the provinces. The Bill has two main clauses. Section 1 declares that in Canada certain fundamental rights and freedoms "have existed and shall continue to exist without discrimination by reason of race, national origin, colour, religion or sex." It identifies as fundamental rights the right to life, liberty, security of the person and the enjoyment of property, and the right not to be deprived thereof except by due process of law; the right to equality before the law and the protection of the law; and freedom of religion, speech, assembly, association, and the press. Section 2 provides that unless the *Bill of Rights* is explicitly set aside, every federal law shall "be so construed and applied as not to abrogate, abridge or infringe" the rights and freedoms set out in the Bill.

The *Canadian Bill of Rights* remains part of Canadian law to this day, but it has been almost totally eclipsed by the *Canadian Charter of Rights and Freedoms*, which became part of the Constitution in 1982. This is not only because of the statutory bill's limited contents and non-constitutional status, but also because the Supreme Court of Canada gave it little force. In a handful of cases, the court used the *Bill of Rights* as a basis for interpreting a federal law in a liberal way, but on only one occasion did the court rule a federal law inoperative because it conflicted with the Bill. This was in the 1970 *Drybones* case,[11] where the Supreme Court, in a 6-to-3 decision, ruled inoperative a section of the *Indian Act* restricting Indians' access to alcohol on the ground that the section violated their right to equality before the law. Four years later, in *Lavell and Bédard*,[12] the Supreme Court drew back from *Drybones*, when a majority reduced equality before the law to a procedural right and upheld the section of the *Indian Act* that denied an Indian woman who married a non-Indian her Indian status, while allowing Indian men who marry non-Indians to retain their status.

The very ineffectiveness of the *Canadian Bill of Rights* added momentum to the drive for a constitutional bill of rights. By the time the Diefenbaker bill of rights was adopted, the Liberal Party had reversed its position on protecting rights and freedoms. The Liberals now contended that nothing but an entrenched constitutional bill of rights would do. In the 1960s, they found a strong champion of that cause in Pierre Elliott Trudeau. When Trudeau became justice minister in the Pearson Liberal government in 1967, he made a Canadian charter of human rights the centrepiece of a federal constitutional counterattack against the constitutional changes Quebec was proposing that aimed at strengthening provincial powers so that the Québécois could be "*maîtres chez nous.*"[13] The core of what became known as the Trudeau vision was a constitutional charter of rights expressing the values shared by all Canadians that would serve as a common bond of Canadian citizenship. It was its potential as an instrument of national unity, more than its civil libertarian values,

---

10 S.C. 1960, c. 44.

11 *The Queen v. Drybones*, [1970] S.C.R. 282 (the case report for *Drybones* can be found in the instructor's supplements package).

12 See *Attorney General of Canada v. Lavell and Bédard*, case 3.

13 Pierre Elliott Trudeau, *A Canadian Charter of Human Rights* (Ottawa: Queen's Printer, 1968).

that made the Charter Trudeau's "magnificent obsession."[14] In his final parliamentary speech on the Charter, Trudeau emphasized its nation-building aspect.[15]

Trudeau became prime minister in 1968; from then until the end of the 1970s he was engaged in a continuing struggle with Quebec and the other provinces over patriating and reforming the Canadian Constitution. Throughout this struggle, a constitutional charter of rights was the first priority of Trudeau and his government. In Victoria in 1971, Trudeau and the provincial first ministers seemed to have reached a resolution of their differences when they signed the Victoria Charter.[16] Taking pride of place at the top of the proposed amendment package was a mini-charter of rights. It included the fundamental rights of conscience, expression, association, and assembly and such basic rights of parliamentary democracy as universal suffrage, annual sessions of Parliament, and elections every five years. English and French language rights, so crucial to the Trudeau government's national unity objective, were included but applied to the provinces on a checkerboard basis according to each premier's willingness to opt in. The Victoria Charter died when Quebec's Liberal premier, Robert Bourassa, under attack for getting so little for Quebec, withdrew his support.

The Quebec election of 1976 brought to power the Parti Québécois, headed by René Lévesque, whose constitutional objective was a sovereign Quebec that was loosely associated with Canada. The constitutional battle heated up. The Trudeau government was now convinced that renewal of the federation required nothing less than an entirely new constitution. In 1977, it appointed the Pepin-Robarts Task Force on National Unity to tour the country and bring forward ideas and initiatives on the question of Canadian unity. Trudeau did not wait for the National Unity Task Force to complete its work. In 1978, he published a booklet entitled *A Time for Action* that set out a two-stage process of constitutional renewal, the first stage to be completed unilaterally by the federal government and Parliament, the second stage with the provinces.[17] A charter of rights would be included in the first stage, but it would apply only at the federal level. Details of the first phase were set out in a *Constitutional Amendment Act* (Bill C-60).

By this time, the constitutional landscape was littered with proposals from provincial governments, Aboriginal organizations, political parties, and private groups that were pushing for everything from Senate reform to replacing the monarchical head of state. A charter of rights did not figure prominently in these proposals or in the final report of the Task Force on National Unity. The Task Force emphasized recognition of Canada's regional divisions and its linguistic and cultural diversity as the most effective recipe for national unity.[18] In the fall of 1978, amid this frenzy of new constitutionalism, Trudeau and the

---

14   Stephen Clarkson and Christina McCall, *Trudeau and Our Times, Volume 1: The Magnificent Obsession* (Toronto: McClelland & Stewart, 1990).

15   Quoted in Peter H. Russell, "The Political Purposes of the Canadian Charter of Rights and Freedoms" (1983) 61 *Canadian Bar Review* 30 at 36.

16   Peter H. Russell, *Constitutional Odyssey: Can Canadians Become a Sovereign People?*, 3rd ed. (Toronto: University of Toronto Press, 2004) at 85-91.

17   Prime Minister's Office, *A Time for Action: Toward the Renewal of the Canadian Federation* (Ottawa: Government of Canada, 1978).

18   Task Force on National Unity, *A Future Together: Observations and Recommendations* (Ottawa: Supply and Services Canada, 1979).

provincial first ministers returned to constitutional negotiations. To no one's surprise, with so many crosscutting proposals on the table, those talks ended in failure in February 1979.[19]

Three months later, Trudeau and his government were defeated by Joe Clark's Conservatives in the May 1979 federal election. Constitutional renewal was not a priority of the Clark government. In November 1979, Trudeau announced his retirement from politics. This might have marked the end of the road for a charter of rights, at least for quite a long time, had it not been for a remarkable reversal in the political fortunes of the federal Liberal Party and Pierre Trudeau. In December, the Clark minority government was defeated on a vote of no confidence. In the ensuing election, Pierre Trudeau, who had come back from the political dead, led his party to victory. He immediately girded for battle in the Quebec referendum organized by the Lévesque government to secure a popular mandate for negotiating Quebec sovereignty and association with Canada. In the May 1980 referendum, Trudeau's leadership was crucial in defeating the sovereignty-association proposal by a margin of 60 to 40 percent. In the referendum campaign, Trudeau promised that, if his side won, he would lead a process of constitutional renewal.

Trudeau's promise of constitutional renewal was vague and did not highlight a charter of rights. Soon after the referendum, his government resumed negotiations with the provincial governments on a broad range of proposals, including a constitutional charter of rights. Once again, these efforts to reach agreement among federal and provincial leaders failed. Following this failure, Trudeau broke dramatically with the traditional, elite-accommodation approach to constitutional reform. On the evening of October 2, 1980, in a televised address to the country, he announced that his government intended to proceed unilaterally with patriation and a few constitutional changes, dubbed "the people's package." The people's package contained an all-Canadian Constitution-amending formula, a charter of rights and freedoms, and constitutional recognition of the principle of fiscal equalization. In a startling political move, Trudeau indicated that the federal government would request that the British Parliament give these radical reforms legal effect, with or without the provinces' consent. At this stage, only two provinces (Ontario and New Brunswick) supported them.[20]

This federal threat of unilateral action had unexpected consequences that weakened the opposing provinces' capacity to oppose the Charter. One consequence was the role that parliamentary committee hearings would play in promoting the popularity of the Charter. Although the Trudeau government had hoped the proposals would gain quick approval in the House of Commons, public interest extended the duration of hearings and also boosted public support for the proposed Charter.[21] A second consequence was that the unilateral threat provoked constitutional litigation in which the Supreme Court's savvy and politically expedient ruling compelled the provincial and federal governments to return to the bargaining table and ultimately find a way to secure agreement.[22]

---

19 Roy Romanow, John Whyte, and Howard Leeson, *Canada ... Notwithstanding: The Making of the Constitution, 1976-1982* (Toronto: Carswell/Methuen, 1984).

20 *Ibid.*

21 James B. Kelly, *Governing with the Charter: Legislative and Judicial Activism and Framers' Intent* (Vancouver: University of British Columbia Press, 2005) at 63-64.

22 *Re: Resolution to Amend the Constitution*, [1981] 1 S.C.R. 753 (*Patriation Reference*), case 14 in the companion book to this volume, *The Court and the Constitution* (Toronto: Emond, 2017).

MAKING THE CHARTER

The draft Charter that the Trudeau government submitted to Parliament in October 1980 was considerably bolder and more comprehensive than either the mini-charter it had proposed in Victoria in 1971 or the charter that was part of its 1978 time-for-action plan. Added to the political and democratic rights from earlier proposals was a more comprehensive set of rights: an equality-rights section aimed at overcoming the inadequacies of the *Canadian Bill of Rights* and adding age to the prohibited categories of discrimination, language-of-government rights that were no longer on a provincial opt-in basis, and new minority-language education rights and mobility rights aimed at strengthening the unity of the country.

But the federal government's draft was still fundamentally a blue rights charter, emphasizing negative rights that limit what government can do. Absent were the red or positive rights that require action by the state to enhance citizens' opportunities and well-being—rights that Trudeau in his 1968 pamphlet on a charter of human rights said "are desirable and should be an ultimate objective for Canada."[23] The political left could take some solace from the absence of any protection of property rights, as well as from a clause in the equality-rights section permitting affirmative action programs to ameliorate the conditions of disadvantaged groups. The general limiting clause that emerged through the exchange of draft charters in the intergovernmental meetings held in the summer of 1980 no longer focused on national security and emergencies as the justification for encroachments on rights. But the limiting clause designed to secure provincial support made compatibility with parliamentary government the test of acceptable limits on rights and freedoms. The new wording seemed to expose constitutional rights to easy override by legislatures. The 1980 meetings with the provinces similarly led to language in the legal-rights sections that would restrict rights to what is available under existing law—a qualification of legal rights strongly advocated by Ontario.

On November 7, 1980, Jean Chrétien, minister of justice in the Trudeau government, opened the proceedings of the Joint Parliamentary Committee on the Constitution. The committee was made up of 15 members of Parliament (MPs) and 10 senators (15 Liberals, 8 Conservatives, and 2 New Democratic Party (NDP) members). The joint committee held 106 meetings in 56 hearing days. It heard from 6 governments, 93 groups, and 5 individuals and received over 1,200 submissions and letters.[24] All committee hearings were televised. The parliamentary committee was an unprecedented opening up of the constitutional process in Canada and an integral part of Trudeau's effort to go over the heads of provincial leaders and engage the public directly in the constitutional reform process. While, in principle, the joint committee dealt with all the components of the people's package, the focus was very much on the Charter, especially for the many interest groups who made submissions. Most of these groups were intent on strengthening the Charter. There was little interest in what a strong, judicially enforced Charter might mean for the policy-making role of courts or for parliamentary democracy more generally.

---

23   Trudeau, *supra* note 13 at 27.

24   Romanow et al., *supra* note 19 at 247-48.

The changes in the Charter that resulted from the joint committee's hearings and deliberations came about through governmental interaction with the committee. Jean Chrétien attended committee meetings to explain the thinking behind the government's draft and participated in discussions of proposed changes. On January 12, 1981, Chrétien put an amended version of the Charter before the committee. The amendments responded to criticisms of the government's draft and incorporated a number of suggested amendments. On February 13, 1981, the government submitted a slightly amended version of its January 12th draft to the committee. This is the version of the Charter that the committee approved and that, save for two later additions, is the basis of the Charter we now have.

The most important change made by the joint committee, in terms of how the Charter would be applied by the courts, was to the general limiting clause at the beginning of the Charter. Instead of requiring that acceptable limits on rights be compatible with the parliamentary system of government, the amended limiting clause requires that they be "demonstrably justified in a free and democratic society." Another important change is that limitations on rights must be prescribed by law, and cannot simply occur through the course of police conduct or the actions of other public authorities working on behalf of the state. These changes put the burden of proof on government to justify laws that encroach on Charter rights and freedoms. As is evident in many of the cases included in this volume, the wording of section 1 opens the door wide to judicial appraisal of government policy. Just as important as the revision of section 1 was the strengthening of legal rights and the addition of a remedial provision to strengthen the enforcement of these rights. Section 24(2) of the Charter requires the exclusion of evidence obtained in a manner that violates Charter rights if a court determines that its inclusion "would bring the administration of justice into disrepute." This provision of the Charter has made judicial scrutiny of police conduct an important phase of criminal trials. Other important changes made in response to submissions to the parliamentary committee were the addition of mental or physical disability to the explicitly prohibited grounds of discrimination listed in section 15; section 27, requiring that the Charter be interpreted "in a manner consistent with the preservation and enhancement of the multicultural heritage of Canadians"; and section 16(2), making English and French the official languages of New Brunswick.

Though generally supportive of proposals to strengthen and broaden the Charter, the parliamentary committee stage by no means led to the adoption of all such proposals. For example, an amendment put forward by Conservative committee members to include a right to property was first accepted by the government. But when NDP leader Ed Broadbent said that his party would withdraw its support for the Trudeau government's constitutional proposals if constitutional protection of private property were included, the government dropped the property right proposal. At this point in the constitutional political struggle, the Liberals, knowing the Conservatives were opposed to Trudeau's unilateralism, needed NDP support to broaden the political base for their constitutional plan. Advocacy groups for gays and lesbians were also unsuccessful in having sexual orientation added to the list of unconstitutional grounds of discrimination in section 15. However, members of the committee suggested that judicial interpretation of section 15 might evolve to protect gays and lesbians from state discrimination.

A major addition to the rights provisions of the people's package that occurred through the committee hearings was a new section of the package, outside the Charter, giving constitutional recognition to "the aboriginal and treaty rights of the aboriginal peoples of Canada." With one change, this became section 35 of the *Constitution Act, 1982*. The Aboriginal rights addition to the people's package was dropped entirely when Trudeau met with the provincial premiers in November 1981 to secure their support for his patriation package. However, in response to public demonstrations across the country, it was quickly restored, with one change—the addition of the word "existing" before "aboriginal and treaty rights."[25] This word was added to gain support for the section from Alberta's Premier Peter Lougheed. As it turns out, the qualification of Aboriginal and treaty rights by the word "existing" has not prevented the courts from rendering a generous and liberal interpretation of these rights.[26] Although Aboriginal rights were not themselves included in the Charter, section 25 of the Charter was inserted to ensure that Charter rights and freedoms are not construed so as to derogate from Aboriginal or treaty rights or other rights of Aboriginal peoples recognized through the *Royal Proclamation of 1763* or that may be secured through modern land claims agreements.

The *Canadian Charter of Rights and Freedoms* was basically complete when it emerged from the joint parliamentary committee in February 1981. Only a few changes would be made after this. The first occurred when the Charter came before the House of Commons for approval as part of the revised package of proposed constitutional amendments in the early spring of 1981. In the final days of the House debate, as a result of intense lobbying by women's organizations, section 28 was added to the Charter, stating that "[n]otwithstanding anything in this Charter, the rights and freedoms referred to in it are guaranteed equally to male and female persons."[27] Though the battle to obtain this addition to the Charter was waged with great fury and passion, it has not played a significant role in Charter interpretation. This is also true of another change accepted at this time—a reference to the "supremacy of God" in the Charter's preamble.

The final changes to the Charter occurred in November 1981 when Canada's Constitution makers returned to the traditional process of elite accommodation—a first ministers meeting. This meeting was a direct consequence of the Supreme Court of Canada's ruling in September 1981 on the constitutional validity of the Trudeau government's unilateral approach to constitutional reform and patriation. Two provinces, New Brunswick and Ontario, supported Trudeau's approach, but the other eight did not. Three of the dissenting provinces, Manitoba, Newfoundland, and Quebec, referred the question of the constitutionality of Trudeau's unilateral approach to their provincial courts of appeal. The decisions of these courts (Manitoba's and Quebec's courts deciding federal unilateralism was constitutional, Newfoundland's that it was not) were appealed to the Supreme Court of Canada. In the *Patriation Reference* opinion, the court found that a new constitutional

---

25 For an account, see Douglas E. Sanders, "The Indian Lobby" in Keith Banting and Richard Simeon, *And No One Cheered: Federalism, Democracy, and the Constitution Act* (Toronto: Methuen, 1983) at 301-32.

26 For some of the key judicial decisions on Aboriginal and treaty rights, see Part III of the companion book, *The Court and the Constitution*.

27 See Penny Kome, *The Taking of Twenty of Twenty-Eight: Women Challenge the Constitution* (Toronto: Women's Educational Press, 1983).

amending formula and a charter of rights would affect the powers and role of the provinces, but nonetheless ruled 7 to 2 that there was no legal requirement that the federal government secure the consent of the provinces before requesting the U.K. Parliament to enact these amendments to Canada's Constitution. However, the Supreme Court balanced this finding with another that held 6 to 3 that the federal government would be violating an unwritten convention of the Constitution if it requested such constitutional changes without "a substantial degree of provincial consent."[28]

Prime Minister Trudeau decided to respect the Supreme Court's opinion on constitutional convention and invited the provincial premiers to the Ottawa Conference Centre in the first week of November 1981 to see whether he could secure their support for his package of constitutional proposals. At this meeting, with the country watching every move on television, Trudeau and the premiers of nine provinces agreed on the basis for proceeding with the revised package of constitutional reforms. Only Quebec's premier, René Lévesque, refused to commit his province to the agreement.

To obtain provincial support, Trudeau had to make two major concessions. One was to accept the amending formula favoured by the provinces and scrap his own formula, which included a referendum as a deadlock-breaking device. The other was to add a legislative override clause, section 33, to the *Charter of Rights and Freedoms*. This section empowers the federal Parliament and provincial legislatures to declare that a law shall operate "notwithstanding" certain sections of the Charter. This section applies to the more universal rights in the Charter—the political freedoms in section 2, the legal rights in sections 7 to 14, and the equality rights in section 15. It does not apply to the parliamentary democracy rights or the language and mobility rights that were central to Trudeau's national unity aims. Legislation using the notwithstanding clause, or "override," is, in effect, insulated from Charter review. The provision can also be invoked to set aside the effects of a judicial ruling. Either use of the notwithstanding clause can be in force for five years and can be renewed.

The notwithstanding clause was placed in the Charter to meet the concerns of several premiers, notably Allan Blakeney, the NDP premier of Saskatchewan, and Sterling Lyon, the Conservative premier of Manitoba, to balance the judicial protection of rights with parliamentary democracy. Advocates of the clause thought the override should be available for those rare occasions when Charter-based judicial review goes against the strongly held views of an elected legislature. In essence, it was designed to be a democratic safety valve. The legislative override has been used infrequently[29] and remains highly controversial.[30] Its most

---

28   See case 14 in the companion book, *The Court and the Constitution*.

29   See Tsvi Kahana, "The Notwithstanding Mechanism and Public Discussion: Lessons from the Ignored Practice of Section 33 of the Charter" (2001) 44:3 *Canadian Public Administration* 255.

30   See John D. Whyte, "On Not Standing for Notwithstanding" (1990) *Alberta Law Review* 347; Peter H. Russell, "Standing Up for Notwithstanding" (1991) *Alberta Law Review* 293; and Janet L. Hiebert, "Compromise and the Notwithstanding Clause: Why the Dominant Narrative Distorts Our Understanding" in James B. Kelly and Christopher P. Manfredi, eds., *Contested Constitutionalism: Reflections on the Canadian Charter of Rights and Freedoms* (Vancouver: University of British Columbia Press, 2009) at 107.

dramatic use was by Quebec, in 1988, in response to a Supreme Court decision overturning its French-only sign law.[31]

The First Ministers meeting produced one other modification of the Charter—an affirmative action rider to the mobility rights allowing provinces with below-average employment rates to protect jobs from out-of-province job seekers. This change was made primarily to meet the concerns of Newfoundland.

The Charter was now almost complete. When the amended draft emerged from the First Ministers meeting, and it appeared that the guarantee of gender equality in section 28 was not protected from the legislative override, all hell broke loose. The government and Parliament quickly agreed to restore the words "[n]otwithstanding anything in this Charter" at the beginning of section 28. Thus the Charter has two notwithstanding clauses and provides no guidance as to what should happen if they ever collide with each other. The text of the Charter was now in its final form.

It still remained for the Charter to become part of Canada's constitutional law. In early December 1981, a resolution supporting the revised package of constitutional amendments passed in both Houses of the Canadian Parliament. In the House of Commons, 247 members supported the motion and only 24 members—17 Conservatives, 5 Liberals, and 2 NDP—opposed it. The next step was to ask the U.K. Parliament, for the last time, to enact an amendment to Canada's Constitution. This it did by passing the *Canada Act 1982*, which enacted the *Constitution Act, 1982* and stated that the U.K. Parliament would never again legislate with respect to Canada. The *Constitution Act, 1982* was attached to the *Canada Act 1982* as a schedule. It contains all the constitutional amendments that make up the revised people's package, including a made-in-Canada Constitution-amending formula and the *Canadian Charter of Rights and Freedoms*. In March 1981, the *Canada Act 1982* was passed by both Houses of the U.K. Parliament. On April 17, 1982, in a signing ceremony on Parliament Hill, Queen Elizabeth proclaimed the *Canada Act 1982* in force. The Charter was now Canadian law.

THE CHARTER GOES TO COURT

It is important to understand all the conditions that make Charter litigation possible. Certainly the existence of an entrenched charter of rights is a necessary condition. But it is not a sufficient condition. A receptive political culture of rights-consciousness also contributes to rights-based litigation, but this too is insufficient. Political scientist Charles Epp argues that a supportive resource infrastructure is also necessary for the Charter to go to court:

> [C]ases do not arrive in supreme courts as if by magic. … [T]he process of legal mobilization— the process by which individuals make claims about their rights and pursue lawsuits to defend or develop those rights—is not in any simple way a direct response to opportunities by constitutional promises or judicial decisions, or to expectations arising from political culture. Legal mobilization also depends on resources, and resources for rights litigation depend on a support structure of rights-advocacy lawyers, rights-advocacy organizations, and sources of financing.[32]

---

31 See *Ford v. Quebec (Attorney General)*, case 5.

32 Charles R. Epp, *The Rights Revolution: Lawyers, Activists, and Supreme Courts in Comparative Perspective* (Chicago: University of Chicago Press, 1998) at 18.

In Canada, such an infrastructure was in the making even before the Charter was entrenched and is now a highly developed part of post-Charter Canada. Some litigation support organizations have enjoyed public support, but different governments have taken different views on the merits of public funding of organizations dedicated to the use of the Charter to promote legal change.[33]

A DISTINCTIVE CANADIAN JURISPRUDENCE

Prior to the adoption of the Charter, the Supreme Court had been inconsistent in its willingness to interpret rights as constraints on state actions. Despite a brief period of civil-liberties activism in the 1950s, based on federalism and common law principles, the Supreme Court took a decidedly restrained approach to the 1960 statutory *Bill of Rights*. Of 34 Supreme Court cases engaging the *Bill of Rights*, in only four did the rights claimant win, and in only one decision did the court strike down a provision of a federal law.[34] The Supreme Court was unsure of its ability to use an act of Parliament to strike down other acts of Parliament and it remained stolidly under the influence of the constitutional doctrine of parliamentary sovereignty.

When the Supreme Court was first faced with a case involving a Charter challenge, it dispelled doubts that it would interpret the new Charter vigorously. *Law Society of Upper Canada v. Skapinker*[35] was not the most propitious of cases in which to break new ground. It involved a lawyer seeking to practise law, but who was prohibited from doing so because he was not a Canadian citizen. Of greatest use to him was the section 15 equality rights provision, but that section would not come into force until April 1985.[36] Instead, he argued that the citizenship requirement was contrary to his mobility rights protected by section 6. Skapinker lost the case based on the court's highly legalistic reading of section 6. But the court's *obiter* was telling. "We are here engaged in a new task, the interpretation and application of the *Canadian Charter of Rights and Freedoms*," wrote Justice Estey. With the *Constitution Act, 1982*, of which the Charter is a central part, comes "a new dimension, a new yardstick of reconciliation between the individual and the community and their respective rights."[37] Estey's liberal attitude toward rights and the role of the Supreme Court pervaded many early decisions of the court, consigning the deferential record of the pre-Charter court to fading memory.[38]

---

33 For a critical account of legal resource mobilization structures in Canada, see F.L. Morton and Rainer Knopff, *The Charter Revolution and the Court Party* (Peterborough, Ont: Broadview Press, 2000).

34 Christopher P. Manfredi and James B. Kelly, "Misrepresenting the Supreme Court's Record? A Comment on Sujit Choudhry and Claire E. Hunter, 'Measuring Judicial Activism on the Supreme Court of Canada'" (2004) 49 *McGill Law Journal* 741.

35 [1984] 1 S.C.R. 357.

36 We know that section 15 was the most useful provision in a challenge like this because a similar challenge to the citizenship requirement, made years later and based on section 15, succeeded. See *Andrews*, case 27.

37 *Law Society of Upper Canada v. Skapinker, supra* note 35 at paras. 10 and 11.

38 Perhaps the most brazen example of judicial activism in this period is *R. v. Therens*, [1985] 1 S.C.R. 613.

As part of its new activism, the Supreme Court was at pains to disavow the "frozen concepts" approach to constitutional interpretation that had characterized much of its jurisprudence under the 1960 *Bill of Rights*. According to this view, the *Bill of Rights* protected rights and freedoms as they existed at the time of its passage. This meant, for example, that the Bill's protection of religious freedom must be read in the light of the longstanding federal *Lord's Day Act*—that is, that this act was compatible with the kind of religious freedom protected by the Bill.[39] Very early in its Charter jurisprudence, the Supreme Court rejected this approach and made it clear that it would treat the Charter as a "living tree" instead. Thus, while the court had upheld the *Lord's Day Act* under the *Bill of Rights*, it struck the *Lord's Day Act* down under the Charter (see *The Queen v. Big M Drug Mart Ltd.*, case 4).

If the meaning of the Charter was not to be frozen by existing law and practice at the time of its passing, neither would it be constrained by the framers' intent. In another early Charter case (*Re B.C. Motor Vehicle Act*, case 20), the Supreme Court, speaking through Justice Lamer, warned that judicial fidelity to original intent or understanding would "freeze" the meaning of the Charter, making it incapable of "growth, development and adjustment to changing social needs."[40]

While the Supreme Court minimized the intent or purposes of the Charter's framers as a guide to its interpretation, it did not reject the relevance of "purpose" altogether. Indeed, in a number of early Charter decisions, Chief Justice Dickson emphasized a "purposive" approach that would read Charter provisions in the light of the interests or purposes they were meant to protect. These purposes were to be discovered not in the intentions of the framers, however, but in our evolving liberal democratic tradition. That tradition, of course, contained laws, such as the federal *Lord's Day Act*, that the court wanted to strike down. The essence of the purposive approach was thus to discover the principled direction in which the tradition was evolving in order to identify the anachronistic policies that had to be left behind.

As it turned out, the court's purposive approach often led to a broad (or "large and liberal") reading of Charter rights and freedoms. Ironically, it was aided in this expansive interpretation by the fact that the Charter's first section explicitly recognizes that its rights can be subject to limits where these are demonstrably justified, prescribed by law, and consistent with a free and democratic society. Virtually everyone agrees that rights and freedoms cannot be absolute, that they must be subject to sensible limitations. Where, as in the United States, there is no explicit clause recognizing limits on constitutional rights, courts have often achieved the necessary limits by defining rights restrictively. Thus, the U.S. Supreme Court has excluded obscenity from the ambit of the First Amendment's guarantee of freedom of speech and press. In Canada, by contrast, the explicit recognition of rights limitations in section 1 has allowed our Supreme Court to establish a two-stage process of Charter interpretation that separates the question whether a right has been infringed from the question whether that infringement can be justified as a "reasonable limit in a free and democratic society." This Charter "two-step" enables the Supreme Court of Canada to interpret rights broadly, thus making it relatively easy to establish a *prima facie* violation,

---

39   *Robertson and Rosetanni v. R.*, [1963] S.C.R. 651.

40   *Re B.C. Motor Vehicle Act*, [1985] 2 S.C.R. 486 at para. 53.

leaving to a second stage of analysis the question whether the challenged law can be justified under section 1. Thus, the Canadian Supreme Court, unlike its American counterpart, has found that "obscenity" enjoys the Charter's freedom-of-expression guarantee in principle, but has nevertheless upheld censorship of obscenity as a "reasonable limit" on constitutional freedom.

Once the Supreme Court rules that legislation violates a right, the government has the responsibility and burden of persuasion to satisfy the court that the impugned legislation is both reasonable and constitutionally valid. The test for this was first outlined in *R. v. Oakes*[41] (case 14), which remains, with modifications, the general standard that governments must meet. The test asks two main questions. The first is whether the legislative objective is sufficiently "pressing and substantial" to warrant restricting a right. The second is whether the legislative means are "proportional" to the objective. The proportionality test has three components: (1) there must be a "rational connection" between the legislative means and their objective—that is, the means must be non-arbitrary and actually achieve the objective; (2) the legislative means must impair the right as little as possible (known as the "minimal impairment" requirement); and (3) the deleterious nature of the rights infringement must be proportionate to the beneficial purposes of the legislation.[42]

Rarely does the Supreme Court rule that the Charter prevents Parliament or a provincial legislature from pursuing outright a specific legislative goal. The court has become extremely deferential to Parliament and the provincial legislatures on the first element of its section 1 test—that is, whether legislation is important enough to restrict rights. Only rarely do governments fail at this stage. However, this has meant that the court must depend on the second aspect of this section 1 test, the proportionality criteria, to determine whether the impugned legislation is valid even though it restricts rights.

The Charter two-step has generated considerable controversy. In the early days of the Charter, some scholars argued against the idea of an explicit two-stage approach to interpreting Charter rights, suggesting that the limitation clause simply acknowledges the obvious fact that rights are not absolute and that judicial review should define their scope restrictively as in the American example. One argument in favour of imposing such definitional limits on rights is that it reduces the frequency of judicial oversight of legislation, particularly in circumstances where legislation does not implicate a fundamental right. In this view, to interpret rights so broadly or abstractly that their judicial meaning is divorced from a theory or understanding of the function and role of rights in a liberal democracy would result in judicial review of legislation even in circumstances where the rights claim is peripheral to why a democratic community would accept constraints on duly enacted legislation.

A broad interpretation of rights in the first stage of judicial review encourages protracted and costly litigation, in the hope, often vain, that a judicial finding of a rights violation will result in the invalidation of the disputed legislation. The Charter two-step also puts governments in the unattractive position of appearing to be against rights, since they are

---

41   [1986] 1 S.C.R. 103.

42   This last component was mentioned in *Oakes, ibid.*, but elaborated on in *Dagenais v. Canadian Broadcasting Corporation*, [1994] 3 S.C.R. 835.

defending legislation that the court has ruled to be a restriction on Charter rights. Sometimes the government argues that it is necessary to restrict one Charter right to protect another right. However, more often, the crux of the government's argument is not that it is necessary to restrict a specific Charter right to protect another right, but that it is necessary to restrict a Charter right to promote a justifiable and compelling public interest. What makes the latter argument difficult to defend, politically, is that most people reflexively believe that rights should trump interests.

This raises an interesting quandary for the court. How strict should the court be when determining whether the government has discharged its burden for demonstrating the justification of its legislation? The danger of an onerous justificatory burden is that governments may not be able to prove that society would be harmed if the legislation were not allowed. This is because it is often difficult to predict or measure what effects legislation (or the absence of legislation) will have on society. But there is also a danger if the court does not demand strong justification for legislation that restricts rights. If it is too easy for governments to restrict rights, the Charter will cease to represent an effective constraint on rights-offending legislation, and governments will no longer worry about ensuring that legislation is sensitive to Charter rights.

The Supreme Court's post-Charter turn to judicial activism is evident in the fact that it upheld the Charter claim in nine of the first 15 Charter cases it decided, striking down five pieces of legislation (two provincial, three federal) in the process.[43] In addition, all but two of the court's first 15 Charter decisions were unanimous. This early enthusiasm did not last, however. Greater caution and disagreement soon emerged. Three trends, in particular, succeeded the early activist period.

First, the Supreme Court became somewhat more restrained in its application of Charter rights as time went on. One early indication was how the court relaxed the minimal-impairment component of the *Oakes* test.[44] As originally formulated, the test implied that legislatures must choose the very least restrictive legislative way of achieving their objective. In a federal system, this might mean that provinces addressing similar issues within their jurisdictions would have to converge on the legislative approach of the least rights-restrictive province. This is precisely the kind of federal homogenization feared by many of the provinces during the Charter-making period. Instead of confirming these fears, the court, soon after *Oakes*, in *Edwards Books*,[45] tweaked its minimal-impairment test, suggesting that a law need impair a right "as little as reasonably possible" in order to pass the section 1 test. Another indication of judicial caution occurred in *Morgentaler v. The Queen*;[46] here, the court struck down Canada's *Criminal Code* provision regulating access to abortion, but a majority of justices did so on the narrowest procedural terms possible, while only Justice Wilson asserted an expansive interpretation of Charter rights to invalidate the law.

---

43   One of the federal laws that was overturned was the *Lord's Day Act*; see *Big M Drug Mart*, case 4.

44   *R. v. Oakes, supra* note 41.

45   *R. v. Edwards Books and Art Ltd.*, [1986] 2 S.C.R. 713.

46   The case report for *Morgentaler v. The Queen*, [1976] 1 S.C.R. 616 can be found in the instructor's supplements package.

The following factors contribute to a government's success in defending legislation. First, the Supreme Court has been more inclined to strike down laws that were passed in the pre-Charter environment than to strike down laws passed after the Charter was enacted. The most striking example of an old law ripe for invalidation was Parliament's *Lord's Day Act* of 1906. What had helped this law withstand challenge under the 1960 *Bill of Rights*—its age—now made it vulnerable to Charter attack.[47] Moreover, the court struck down this old law precisely because it had an unconstitutionally religious purpose, as reflected in its name. By contrast, when the court invalidated more recently passed legislation, it rarely took issue with legislative objectives, but instead quarrelled with the means the legislature used to achieve them. An example is the court's invalidation of most of Canada's 1988 tobacco-advertising-control law.[48]

Second, as James Kelly explains, judicial norms are regularly integrated into legislative decision-making processes. Not only do government lawyers advise relevant departments and their ministers about the level of risk that legislation could be constitutionally challenged and defeated, they also make recommendations on how to draft laws in a manner that reduces the risk of judicial invalidation.[49]

Despite the increased focus in legislative decision-making processes on issues of Charter compatibility, judges are not necessarily willing to uphold legislation. Between 1984 and 2012, the Supreme Court invalidated 45 acts of the federal parliament (along with 27 provincial acts).[50]

Despite an early pattern of judicial unanimity, this pattern gave way to one of judicial uncertainty, which became evident in high levels of dissent and separate concurrences. However, in recent years, the court has demonstrated higher levels of agreement—revealing an ebb and flow in the similarity in how judges view the relevant Charter issues and arguments.[51]

Many commentators consider disagreement to be a healthy sign of intellectual vigour on the part of the court and also a hint at future directions in which the law may develop. These benefits compete, however, with the institutional imperative that the court's decision-making should resolve disagreement about the meaning of the law for the benefit of present and future litigants as well as all others bound by the law. A basic function of the court is to state what the law is and give guidance to those bound by it. Thus, there is pressure for consensus among the justices as to the result and the reasons for the result.[52]

The degree of disagreement among justices leads to questions about the basis of disagreement. Why do learned judges disagree with one another when they are exposed to the

---

47   See *The Queen v. Big M Drug Mart Ltd.*, case 4.

48   See *RJR-MacDonald Inc. v. Canada (Attorney General)*, case 7.

49   Kelly, *supra* note 21, at 222-57.

50   Janet L. Hiebert and James B. Kelly, *Parliamentary Bills of Rights: The Experiences of New Zealand and the United Kingdom* (Cambridge, UK: Cambridge University Press, 2015) at 73.

51   Peter J. McCormick, *The End of the Charter Revolution: Looking Back from the New Normal* (Toronto: University of Toronto Press, 2015) at 207-14.

52   For discussion of the importance of consensus on high courts, see Jeffrey Rosen, "Roberts's Rules" (2007) 299 *Atlantic Monthly* 104.

same facts, the same law, and the same arguments? The traditional legal or "formalist" model of judicial decision-making suggests that legal problems are amenable to legal solutions; legal criteria yield a single correct answer to legal disputes. However, the fact that judges so often disagree on the appropriate resolution of a case suggests that the legal model is far too simplistic. Other explanations include the personal-attribute model, according to which certain traits or attributes of judges—for example, their religion, professional experience, place of birth, and upbringing—influence their decision making.[53] Scholars have also developed the powerful attitudinal model, according to which judges are understood to possess public policy preferences. They advance those preferences by picking from particular cases those precedents and interpretive principles that support their preferred results in a persuasive, legally acceptable manner.[54] Related to the attitudinal model is the strategic model of judicial decision-making, according to which judges will vote strategically, sometimes against their deeply felt preferences, in order to maximize the chances that those preferences will be reflected in the policies of other institutional actors in other branches of government.[55] Strategic behaviour may operate in the manner in which justices decide to grant or deny leave to appeal to the court. For example, a judge who favours the lower court result in a case being appealed to the Supreme Court may vote to deny leave if she thinks that her colleagues would vote to reverse on the merits. It also undoubtedly operates in the negotiations among justices and in the drafting of opinions to attract votes to convert either dissenting or plurality judgments into a majority ruling. James Gibson's pithy characterization of the factors that shape judicial judgments straddles both the attitudinal and strategic camps. According to Gibson, "Judges' decisions are a function of what they prefer to do, tempered by what they think they ought to do, but constrained by what they perceive is feasible to do."[56] Emmett Macfarlane builds on this multi-varied perspective. His study of the Supreme Court, which includes interviews with many of the justices themselves along with their clerks, emphasizes the importance of the ideas and norms that shape how judges approach their role. Thus, while policy preferences, values, and ideologies matter in

---

53   See Donald R. Songer and Susan W. Johnson, "Judicial Decision Making in the Supreme Court of Canada: Updating the Personal Attribute Model" (2007) 40 *Canadian Journal of Political Science* 911.

54   The classic text on the attitudinal model is Jeffrey A. Segal and Harold J. Spaeth, *The Supreme Court and the Attitudinal Model Revisited* (New York: Cambridge University Press, 2002). For a review of early Canadian work on this topic, see Thaddeus Hwong, "A Review of Quantitative Studies of Decision Making in the Supreme Court of Canada" (2004) 30 *Manitoba Law Journal* 353. For more recent work, see C.L. Ostberg and Matthew E. Wetstein, *Attitudinal Decision Making in the Supreme Court of Canada* (Vancouver: University of British Columbia Press, 2007).

55   The classic works here are Walter F. Murphy, *Elements of Judicial Strategy* (Chicago: University of Chicago Press, 1964), and Lee Epstein and Jack Knight, *The Choices Judges Make* (Washington: Congressional Quarterly Press, 1998). For Canadian work in this field, see Manfredi and Kelly, *supra* note 34.

56   James L. Gibson, "From Simplicity to Complexity: The Development of Theory in the Study of Judicial Behavior" (1983) 5 *Political Behavior* 1 at 9.

understanding judicial behaviour, it is also important to recognize that what judges think about how they ought to approach their work is also a fundamental factor.[57]

THE CHARTER AND CANADIAN DEMOCRACY

The foregoing discussion makes clear that Charter review entangles the courts, particularly the Supreme Court, in policy-making. The court frequently insists that it refrains from pronouncing on the merits or wisdom of particular policies or laws and that it merely measures laws and policies against a constitutional standard, but its assurances do not entirely succeed. The constitutional standards are vague and the evidence of actual judicial decision-making indicates that there is more discretion available to judges, especially high court judges, than a superficial impression suggests. As Christopher Manfredi has argued, judicial review highlights a paradox of liberal democratic constitutionalism. Liberal democracy is constitutional democracy—democracy subject to certain principled limits contained in the Constitution and applied by courts. Courts should be independent of the political departments of government so that law can be applied, and seen to be applied, impartially. But if judicial review is inescapably "political"—that is, entangling courts in public policy decisions made by the representative chambers of government—then such independence becomes as problematic as it is salutary. Liberal constitutionalism requires that independent courts impartially enforce the law. Democratic principles require that courts be accountable for the policy-laden decisions they render. Charter review puts courts in an awkward relation to the representative institutions of democratic government.[58]

Three issues flow from the paradox of liberal constitutionalism. First, civil society actors routinely and systematically attempt to use Charter review to achieve policy objectives they cannot or will not obtain in the representative chambers of government. Second, observers have inquired whether the Charter has produced a "juristocracy"[59] in Canada, in which the judges are the philosopher-kings. Third, the paradox has stimulated some political actors to reform the judicial appointment process in Canada, making more transparent and democratically accountable a process that has until recently escaped most Canadians' attention.

The Charter provides strong incentives for interest groups to pursue their policy objectives through the courts rather than through lobbying elected politicians and public servants. The classic argument for this is that majoritarian institutions are inherently insensitive to minoritarian rights claims and that courts, as "forums of principle," act on arguments of principle regardless of how many legislators support them. But this argument assumes that there is a bright line distinguishing claims of right and claims of policy interest. Such bright lines rarely exist. More common is the pursuit of policy objectives articulated as Charter

---

57   Emmett Macfarlane, *Governing from the Bench: The Supreme Court of Canada and the Judicial Role* (Vancouver: University of British Columbia Press, 2012) at 7-10.

58   Christopher P. Manfredi, *Judicial Power and the Charter: Canada and the Paradox of Liberal Constitutionalism*, 2nd ed. (Toronto: Oxford University Press, 2001).

59   Ran Hirschl, *Towards Juristocracy: The Origins and Consequences of the New Constitutionalism* (Cambridge, Mass: Harvard University Press, 2004).

rights claims by means of litigation strategies.[60] Is this an abuse of the judicial process? Individuals or groups that can make a plausible rights-based claim and have standing before a court are limited only by their available resources and prospects of success. If courts are receptive to rights-based arguments with significant policy implications, why should groups or individuals not be permitted to litigate? On the other hand, to the extent that interest groups ask courts to advance policy objectives, they ask judges to do what judges disavow and what courts are institutionally unfit to do. The long-term public reputation of courts as independent and impartial tribunals may suffer.

The second issue concerns what role legislatures have with respect to Charter review. Are they now impotent observers of the politics of rights, increasingly passed over in favour of policy-making by the courts, and without recourse themselves? The Charter, of course, does contain the section 33 notwithstanding clause, but politicians have become extremely wary of invoking it. The popularity of the Charter and citizens' greater confidence in judges' versus legislators' judgments about the meaning of the Charter[61] all militate against its use. Although the notwithstanding clause has been used more than a dozen times, many of the uses of this power occurred in the early years of the Charter.[62] Moreover, most uses of the clause did not set aside judicial decisions but pre-empted judicial review and protected policy distinctions before it was clear how the Supreme Court would rule.[63] However, the notwithstanding clause has become so politically contentious that it has been rendered, in one commentator's eyes, a "paper tiger."[64]

What else can governments do? In an influential study, Peter Hogg and Allison Thornton have argued that, in fact, there is an active and fruitful dialogue between the courts and legislatures on Charter issues even when section 33 is not invoked.[65]

Not everyone accepts dialogue theory, however. Critics argue that a more accurate metaphor to describe the institutional relationship between courts and legislatures under the

---

60 The classic work on the litigation strategy of the American National Association for the Advancement of Colored People is Richard Kluger, *Simple Justice: The History of Brown v. Board of Education and Black America's Struggle for Equality* (New York: Knopf, 1975). In the Canadian context, see M. Elizabeth Atcheson et al., *Women and Legal Action: Precedents, Resources, and Strategies for the Future* (Ottawa: Canadian Advisory Council on the Status of Women, 1984).

61 Nik Nanos, "The Charter Values Don't Equal Canadian Values: Strong Support for Same-Sex and Property Rights" (2007) 28 *Policy Options* 50.

62 Kahana, *supra* note 29.

63 This interpretation is drawn from a review of all uses of this power, as compiled by Kahana, *ibid.*

64 Howard Leeson, Paul Howe, and Peter H. Russell, *Judicial Power and Canadian Democracy* (Montreal and Kingston: McGill-Queen's University Press, 2001) at 297.

65 See Peter Hogg and Allison Thornton, "The Charter Dialogue Between Courts and Legislatures (Or Perhaps the Charter Isn't Such a Bad Thing After All)" (1997) 35 *Osgoode Hall Law Journal* 7.

Charter is monologue[66] or ventriloquism[67] because courts generally dominate the conversation, leaving Parliament only the option of replicating judicial suggestions, rather than making independent choices.

Noting that courts normally strike down laws based on the proportionality criteria outlined in *Oakes* is not a complete answer to concerns about the political power of courts. One concern with this emphasis on proportionality criteria is that it stresses the particular aspect of judicial review—the evaluation of the quality of how a legislative goal is being pursued—that challenges the skills and expertise that judges reasonably possess. It is rarely possible to identify precisely how best to achieve a particular legislative goal because those developing legislation do so in a policy environment of competing data about whether identified policy means will be effective when addressing the policy objective and uncertainty about whether and how the policy goals will affect the behaviour, attitudes, and expectations of those who are affected. Nevertheless, the Supreme Court's approach ensures that it will regularly have to don the hat of the policy analyst in assessing whether the way Parliament or a provincial legislature pursues its intended goals compares favourably with some other hypothetical policy scheme.[68]

But there is another important implication for the dialogue thesis of the Supreme Court's approach to section 1 of the Charter. As discussed above, one manifestation of this Charter-oriented focus on policy is a new requirement that Charter issues be anticipated and certain associated risks identified as part of the process for securing approval before an initiative can go to Cabinet for consideration. Consequently, the policy governing the Memorandum to Cabinet was changed in 1991 to include Charter analysis in terms of "an assessment of the risk of successful challenge in the courts, the impact of adverse decisions, and possible litigation costs."[69] This emphasis on Charter compatibility, which is equated with consistency with judicial section 1 considerations, has enhanced significantly the influence of governmental lawyers in the policy process, whose role has changed from being the provider of "a technical review of legislation to a substantive role in the development of new policy," so much so that other departments now regularly rely on its advice in the course of developing legislation.[70] Many provincial governments have also adopted procedures to identify and redress Charter concerns before legislation is introduced to the legislature.[71]

---

66   F.L. Morton, "Dialogue or Monologue?" in Leeson et al., *supra* note 64 at 111.

67   Christopher P. Manfredi and James B. Kelly, "Six Degrees of Dialogue: A Response to Hogg and Bushell" (1999) 37 *Osgoode Hall Law Journal* 513.

68   Janet L. Hiebert, *Charter Conflicts: What Is Parliament's Role?* (Montreal and Kingston: McGill-Queen's University Press, 2002) at 58.

69   Mary Dawson, "The Impact of the Charter on the Public Policy Process and the Department of Justice" in Patrick Monahan and Marie Finkelstein, eds., *The Impact of the Charter on the Public Policy Process* (Toronto: York University Centre for Public Law and Public Policy, 1993) at 53.

70   James B. Kelly, "Bureaucratic Activism and the Charter of Rights and Freedoms: The Department of Justice and Its Entry into the Centre of Government" (1999) 42 *Canadian Public Administration* 494.

71   Kelly, *supra* note 21 at 214.

Yet not all political actors believe this emphasis on Charter compatibility necessary leads to better policy. As one former provincial attorney general states:

> In my experience, *Charter* compliance in the legislative process is inherently reactive, rather than proactive, as it requires government to approach policy-making from the perspective of risk analysis rather than from the perspective of broader social and economic priorities or the balancing of differing societal interests. In other words, although the question "is this legislation Charter-compliant?" often leads to a different answer than the question "is this legislation good public policy?," the former question often takes precedence in public policy analysis. As a result, risk management becomes the driver of the analysis.[72]

CONCLUSION

Studying the life and times of Canada's *Charter of Rights and Freedoms* shows how difficult it is to separate the realms of law and politics. Eliminating the political context in which the Charter came into being and the political forces with which it interacts would make it impossible to understand its unfolding meaning in Canadian life. And yet, although we readily acknowledge this, we also insist that the Charter and its interpretation by the courts are not simply an undifferentiated part of the political process. Citizens in a constitutional democracy have expectations of non-partisan rationality and—dare we say it?—justice in the decisions of the judicial arbiters of their constitutional rights, expectations that they do not apply to the avowedly political branches of government. The challenge for the judges and for those who assess their work is to ascertain how such expectations are best satisfied.

---

72 Geoffrey Plant, "Governing in the Shadow of the Charter" (2007) paper presented at the Canadian Bar Association Conference, Calgary, June 1, 2007 (unpublished).

A. THE PRE-CHARTER ERA

1

Reference re Alberta Statutes (Alberta Press Case), 1938

Until 1982, the Canadian Constitution, unlike that of the United States, did not contain a comprehensive bill of rights protecting a list of fundamental civil liberties from legislative encroachment. The enactment of the *Canadian Bill of Rights* in 1960 did not change that situation. The *Canadian Bill of Rights* was simply a federal statute, not an amendment to the *B.N.A. Act*. As such, it did not apply to the provinces and, even at the federal level, could be set aside by ordinary federal legislation. Besides, as the *Lavell and Bédard*[1] case shows, the Supreme Court was reluctant to give much weight to its provisions.

The absence of a comprehensive charter of rights in the *B.N.A. Act*, however, did not mean that no entrenched constitutional rights could be found there. The mistake was often made of stating that the powers of self-government had been exhaustively distributed between the two levels of government provided for in the *B.N.A. Act*. According to this "exhaustion theory," the only constitutional limitation on legislative supremacy in Canada prior to 1982 was the division of legislative powers. But this theory was a slight exaggeration. Sections 93 and 133 of the *B.N.A. Act* enshrine minority education and language rights[2] that it would appear cannot be diminished by either federal or provincial legislation without a constitutional amendment. In addition, constitutional safeguards of more fundamental rights may be implied by some of the institutional provisions of the *B.N.A. Act*. For instance, section 99, providing security of tenure for the judges of Superior Courts (Canada's trial courts for the most serious civil and criminal cases), restricts the legislative powers not only of the provinces but of the federal Parliament as well.[3]

In the *Alberta Press* case, constitutional protection of another cluster of rights of fundamental importance to the practice of liberal democracy was first suggested in the reasons given by Chief Justice Duff and Justice Cannon for declaring Alberta's *Accurate News and Information Act* unconstitutional. The federal government had asked the Supreme Court to examine the constitutional validity of this Act along with two other Social Credit Bills enacted by the Alberta Legislature in 1937. The other two Acts concerned some of the regulations and institutions required for a Social Credit system of credit and exchange. The *Accurate News and Information Act* was designed to ensure that newspaper presentation of Social Credit policy satisfied the government's criterion of accuracy. The Supreme Court

---

1 See case 3.

2 See the introduction to case 31.

3 See *McEvoy v. Attorney General for New Brunswick*, [1983] 1 S.C.R. 704.

unanimously found all three Acts *ultra vires.* Only its decision on the *Bank Taxation Act* was appealed to the Privy Council.

Chief Justice Duff's opinion, with which Justice Davis concurred, characterized the *Accurate News and Information Act* as legislation affecting the "right of free public discussion of public affairs." This right, he maintained, is essential for the proper working of the parliamentary system of government called for by those sections of the *B.N.A. Act* vesting legislative power at the national level in a federal parliament and by the reference in the *B.N.A. Act*'s preamble to "a constitution similar in Principle to that of the United Kingdom." He considered provincial legislation abrogating this right to be unconstitutional. While he stated that the federal Parliament was empowered to protect this right, he did not suggest that it was beyond Ottawa's power to restrict it. While Justice Cannon also held that the Alberta legislation should be struck down because it interfered with the freedom of discussion essential to a democratic state, he based his opinion on a more conventional division-of-powers ground. Legislation curtailing freedom of the press was traditionally part of the criminal law and therefore could be enacted only by the federal Parliament under its exclusive criminal law power.

If one looks only at the court's prior decisions, the invocation of an implied bill of rights by three of its members is somewhat surprising, especially since it was unnecessary to invalidating the legislation. As Carl Baar notes, "[t]he Court had no record of support for civil liberties," and Justice Duff himself, a British Columbian, "had written opinions in previous years that reflected the anti-oriental sentiments of the Canadian west coast."[4] The answer to this riddle appears to lie in the political context in which the decision was made. The federal government had already disallowed earlier Social Credit legislation in Alberta and disallowance was seriously considered in this case. One argument in favour of disallowance was that it could be justified on the broad ground of protecting freedom of speech and press, while judicial invalidation was likely to focus on narrow jurisdictional considerations. On the other hand, too frequent resort to disallowance could be seen as an attack on the province by a heavy-handed central government. Ottawa chose a legal reference, but its own factum clearly invited an implied-bill-of-rights interpretation. In addition, most of the public criticism of the Press Bill was based on civil libertarian considerations. Given the widespread consensus on the importance of a free press, "it was both politically safe and politically heroic for the Supreme Court to defend civil liberties."[5] It was an inviting context for a new departure. ∿

Discussion Questions

1. On what parts of the Constitution did Chief Justice Duff base his finding of an implied right to free public discussion?

2. What is the "exhaustion theory" of the Canadian Constitution? How does Chief Justice Duff's opinion depart from it, and how is Justice Cannon's opinion consistent with it?

3. To what extent was Chief Justice Duff's doctrine of implied rights followed by the Supreme Court in subsequent cases?

4. What are the limitations of an implied rights doctrine?

---

4 Carl Baar, "Using Process Theory to Explain Judicial Decision Making" (1986) 1 *Canadian Journal of Law and Society* 73.

5 *Ibid.* at 74.

REFERENCE RE ALBERTA STATUTES
[1938] 2 S.C.R. 100

Hearing: January 11, 12, 13, 14, 17, 1938; Judgment: March 4, 1938.

Present: Duff C.J. and Cannon, Crocket, Davis, Kerwin, and Hudson JJ.

DUFF C.J.:

[The Chief Justice first examined the constitutional validity of the *Bank Taxation Act* and the *Credit of Alberta Regulation Act* and concluded that both of these bills were *ultra vires.*]

We now turn to Bill No. 9.

This Bill contains two substantive provisions. Both of them impose duties upon newspapers published in Alberta which they are required to perform on the demand of "the Chairman," who is, by the interpretation clause, the Chairman of "the Board constituted by section 3 of [t]he *Alberta Social Credit Act.*"

The Board, upon the acts of whose Chairman the operation of this statute depends, is, in point of law, a non-existent body (there is, in a word, no "board" in existence "constituted by section 3 of [t]he *Alberta Social Credit Act*") and both of the substantive sections, sections 3 and 4, are, therefore, inoperative. The same, indeed, may be said of sections 6 and 7 which are the enactments creating sanctions. It appears to us, furthermore, that this Bill is a part of the general scheme of Social Credit legislation, the basis of which is [t]he *Alberta Social Credit Act*; the Bill presupposes, as a condition of its operation, that [t]he *Alberta Social Credit Act* is validly enacted; and since that Act is *ultra vires*, the ancillary and dependent legislation must fall with it.

This is sufficient for disposing of the question referred to us but, we think, there are some further observations upon the Bill which may properly be made.

Under the constitution established by [t]he *British North America Act*, legislative power for Canada is vested in one Parliament consisting of the Sovereign, an upper house styled the Senate, and the House of Commons. Without entering in detail upon an examination of the enactments of the *Act* relating to the House of Commons, it can be said that these provisions manifestly contemplate a House of Commons which is to be, as the name itself implies, a representative body; constituted, that is to say, by members elected by such of the population of the united provinces as may be qualified to vote. The preamble of the statute, moreover, shows plainly enough that the constitution of the Dominion is to be similar in principle to that of the United Kingdom. The statute contemplates a parliament working under the influence of public opinion and public discussion. There can be no controversy that such institutions derive their efficacy from the free public discussion of affairs, from criticism and answer and counter-criticism, from attack upon policy and administration and defence and counter-attack; from the freest and fullest analysis and examination from every point of view of political proposals. This is signally true in respect of the discharge by Ministers of the Crown of their responsibility to Parliament, by members of Parliament of their duty to the electors, and by the electors themselves of their responsibilities in the election of their representatives.

The right of public discussion is, of course, subject to legal restrictions; those based upon considerations of decency and public order, and others conceived for the protection of various private and public interests with which, for example, the laws of defamation and sedition are concerned. In a word, freedom of discussion means, to quote the words of Lord Wright in *James v. Commonwealth* [[1936] A.C. 578, at 627], "freedom governed by law."

Even within its legal limits, it is liable to abuse and grave abuse, and such abuse is constantly exemplified before our eyes; but it is axiomatic that the practice of this right of free public discussion of public affairs, notwithstanding its incidental mischiefs, is the breath of life for parliamentary institutions.

We do not doubt that (in addition to the power of disallowance vested in the Governor General) the Parliament of Canada possesses authority to legislate for the protection of this right. That authority rests upon the principle that the powers requisite for the protection of the constitution itself arise by necessary implication from [t]he *British North America Act* as a whole (*Fort Frances Pulp & Power Co. Ltd. v. Manitoba Free Press Co. Ltd.* [[1923] A.C. 695]); and since the subject-matter in relation to which the power is exercised is not exclusively a provincial matter, it is necessarily vested in Parliament.

But this by no means exhausts the matter. Any attempt to abrogate this right of public debate or to suppress the traditional forms of the exercise of the right (in public meeting and through the press) would, in our opinion, be incompetent to the legislatures of the provinces, or to the legislature of any one of the provinces, as repugnant to the provisions of [t]he *British North America Act*, by which the Parliament of Canada is established as the legislative organ of the people of Canada under the Crown, and Dominion legislation enacted pursuant to the legislative authority given by those provisions. The subject matter of such legislation could not be described as a provincial matter purely; as in substance exclusively a matter of property and civil rights within the province, or a matter private or local within the province. It would not be, to quote the words of the judgment of the Judicial Committee in *Great West Saddlery Co. v. The King* [[1921] 2 A.C. 91, at 122], "legislation directed solely to the purposes specified in section 92"; and it would be invalid on the principles enunciated in that judgment and adopted in *Caron v. The King* [[1924] A.C. 999 at 1005-6].

The question, discussed in argument, of the validity of the legislation before us, considered as a wholly independent enactment having no relation to the *Alberta Social Credit Act*, presents no little difficulty. Some degree of regulation of newspapers everybody would concede to the provinces. Indeed, there is a very wide field in which the provinces undoubtedly are invested with legislative authority over newspapers; but the limit, in our opinion, is reached when the legislation effects such a curtailment of the exercise of the right of public discussion as substantially to interfere with the working of the parliamentary institutions of Canada as contemplated by the provisions of [t]he *British North America Act* and the statutes of the Dominion of Canada. Such a limitation is necessary, in our opinion, "in order," to adapt the words quoted above from the judgment in *Bank of Toronto v. Lambe* [(1887), 12 A.C. 575] "to afford scope" for the working of such parliamentary institutions. In this region of constitutional practice, it is not permitted to a provincial legislature to do indirectly what cannot be done directly (*Great West Saddlery Co. v. The King* [[1921] 2 A.C. 91 at 100]).

Section 129 of [t]he *British North America Act* is in these words:

> 129. Except as otherwise provided by this *Act*, all Laws in force in Canada, Nova Scotia or New Brunswick, at the Union, and all Courts of Civil and Criminal Jurisdiction, and all legal Commissions, Powers, and Authorities, and all Officers, Judicial, Administrative, and Ministerial, existing therein at the Union, shall continue in Ontario, Quebec, Nova Scotia, and New Brunswick respectively, as if the Union had not been made; subject nevertheless (except with respect to such as are enacted by or exist under *Acts* of the Parliament of Great Britain or of the Parliament of the United Kingdom of Great Britain and Ireland), to be repealed, abolished, or altered by the Parliament of Canada, or by the Legislature of the respective Province, according to the Authority of the Parliament or of that Legislature under this *Act*.

The law by which the right of public discussion is protected existed at the time of the enactment of [t]he *British North America Act* and, as far as Alberta is concerned, at the date on which the *Alberta Act* came into force, the 1st of September, 1905. In our opinion (on the broad principle of the cases mentioned which has been recognized as limiting the scope of general words defining the legislative authority of the Dominion) the Legislature of Alberta has not the capacity under section 129 to alter that law by legislation obnoxious to the principle stated.

The legislation now under consideration manifestly places in the hands of the Chairman of the Social Credit Commission autocratic powers which, it may well be thought, could, if arbitrarily wielded, be employed to frustrate in Alberta these rights of the Crown and the people of Canada as a whole. We do not, however, find it necessary to express an opinion upon the concrete question whether or not this particular measure is invalid as exceeding the limits indicated above.

The answer to the question concerning this Bill is that it is *ultra vires.*

CANNON J.:

[Justice Cannon first examined the *Bank Taxation Act* and the *Credit of Alberta Regulation Act* and concluded that both were *ultra vires.*]

The third question put to us is the following:

> Is Bill No. 9, entitled *An Act to ensure the Publication of Accurate News and Information*, or any of the provisions thereof and in what particular or particulars or to what extent *intra vires* of the legislature of the province of Alberta?

… The preamble of the bill, which I will hereafter call the "Press bill" recites that it is

> expedient and in the public interest that the newspapers published in the Province should furnish to the people of the Province statements made by the authority of the Government of the Province as to the true and exact objects of the policy of the Government and as to the hindrances to or difficulties in achieving such objects to the end that the people may be informed with respect thereto.

Section 3 provides that any proprietor, editor, publisher or manager of any newspaper published in the province shall, when required to do so by the Chairman of the Board constituted by section 3 of the *Alberta Social Credit Act*, publish in that newspaper any statement furnished by the Chairman which has for its object the correction or amplification of any statement relating to any policy or activity of the government of the province published by that newspaper within the next preceding thirty-one days.

And section 4 provides that the proprietor, etc., of any newspaper upon being required by the Chairman in writing shall within twenty-four hours after the delivery of the requirement

> make a return in writing setting out every source from which any information emanated, as to any statement

contained in any issue of the newspaper published within sixty days of the making of the requirement and the names, addresses and occupations of all persons by whom such information was furnished to the newspaper and the name and address of the writer of any editorial, article or news item contained in any such issue of the newspaper.

Section 5 denies any action for libel on account of the publication of any statement pursuant to the *Act.*

Section 6 enacts that in the event of a proprietor, etc., of any newspaper being guilty of any contravention of any of the provisions of the *Act,* the Lieutenant-Governor-in-Council, upon a recommendation of the Chairman, may by order prohibit,

> (a) the publication of such newspaper either for a definite time or until further order;
> (b) the publication in any newspaper of anything written by any person specified in the order;
> (c) the publication of any information emanating from any person or source specified in the order.

Section 7 provides for penalties for contraventions or defaults in complying with any requirement of the *Act.*

The policy referred to in the preamble of the Press bill regarding which the people of the province are to be informed from the government standpoint is undoubtedly the Social Credit policy of the government. The administration of the bill is in the hands of the Chairman of the Social Credit Board who is given complete and discretionary power by the bill. "Social Credit," according to sec. 2(b) of ch. 3, 1937, second session, of [t]he *Alberta Social Credit Amendment Act* is

> the power resulting from the belief inherent within society that its individual members in association can gain the objectives they desire;

and the objectives in which the people of Alberta must have a firm and unshaken belief are the monetization of credit and the creation of a provincial medium of exchange instead of money to be used for the purpose of distributing to Albertans loans without interest, per capita dividends and discount rates to purchase goods from retailers. This free distribution would be based on the unused capacity of the industries and people of the province of Alberta to produce goods and services, which capacity remains unused on account of the lack or absence of purchasing power in the consumers in the province. The purchasing power would equal or absorb this hitherto unused capacity to produce goods and services by the issue of Treasury Credit certificates against a Credit Fund or Provincial credit account established by the Commission each year representing the monetary value of this "unused capacity"—which is also called "Alberta credit."

It seems obvious that this kind of credit cannot succeed unless every one should be induced to believe in it and help it along. The word "credit" comes from the latin: *credere*, to believe. It is, therefore, essential to control the sources of information of the people of Alberta, in order to keep them immune from any vacillation in their absolute faith in the plan of the government. The Social Credit doctrine must become, for the people of Alberta, a sort of religious dogma of which a free and uncontrolled discussion is not permissible. The bill aims to control any statement relating to any policy or activity of the government of the province and declares this object to be a matter of public interest. The bill does not regulate the relations of the newspapers' owners with private individual members of the public, but deals exclusively with expressions of opinion by the newspapers concerning government policies and activities. The pith and substance of the bill is to regulate the press of Alberta from the viewpoint of public policy by preventing the public from being misled or deceived as to any policy or activity of the Social Credit Government and by reducing any opposition to silence or bring upon it ridicule and public contempt.

I agree with the submission of the Attorney-General for Canada that this bill deals with the regulation of the press of Alberta, not from the viewpoint of private wrongs or civil injuries resulting from any alleged infringement or privation of civil rights which belong to individuals, considered as individuals, but from the viewpoint of public wrongs or crimes, i.e., involving a violation of the public rights and duties to the whole community, considered as a community, in its social aggregate capacity.

Do the provisions of this bill, as alleged by the Attorney-General for Canada, invade the domain of criminal law and trench upon the exclusive legislative jurisdiction of the Dominion of this regard?

The object of an amendment of the criminal law, as a rule, is to deprive the citizen of the right to do that [which], apart from the amendment, he could lawfully do. Sections 130 to 136 of the *Criminal Code* deal with seditious words and seditious publications; and sect. 133(a) reads as follows:—

> No one shall be deemed to have a seditious intention only because he intends in good faith,—
>
> (a) to show that His Majesty has been misled or mistaken in his measures; or
>
> (b) to point out errors or defect in the government or constitution of the United Kingdom, or of any part of it, or of Canada or any province thereof, or in either House of Parliament of the United Kingdom or of Canada, or in any legislature, or in the administration of justice; or to excite His Majesty's subjects to attempt to procure, by lawful means, the alteration of any matter of state; or

(c) to point out, in order to their removal, matters which are producing or have a tendency to produce feelings of hatred and ill-will between different classes of His Majesty's subjects.

It appears that in England, at first, criticism of any government policy was regarded as a crime involving severe penalties and punishable as such; but since the passing of *Fox's Libel Act* in 1792, the considerations now found in the above article of our criminal code that it is not criminal to point out errors in the Government of the country and to urge their removal by lawful means have been admitted as a valid defence in a trial for libel.

Now, it seems to me that the Alberta legislature by this retrograde Bill is attempting to revive the old theory of the crime of seditious libel by enacting penalties, confiscation of space in newspapers and prohibitions for actions which, after due consideration by the Dominion Parliament, have been declared innocuous and which, therefore, every citizen of Canada can do lawfully and without hindrance or fear of punishment. It is an attempt by the legislature to amend the *Criminal Code* in this respect and to deny the advantage of sect. 133(a) to the Alberta newspaper publishers.

Under the British system, which is ours, no political party can erect a prohibitory barrier to prevent the electors from getting information concerning the policy of the government. Freedom of discussion is essential to enlighten public opinion in a democratic State; it cannot be curtailed without affecting the right of the people to be informed through sources independent of the government concerning matters of public interest. There must be an untrammelled publication of the news and political opinions of the political parties contending for ascendancy. As stated in the preamble of [t]he *British North America Act*, our constitution is and will remain, unless radically changed, "similar in principle to that of the United Kingdom." At the time of Confederation, the United Kingdom was a democracy. Democracy cannot be maintained without its foundation: free public opinion and free discussion throughout the nation of all matters affecting the State within the limits set by the criminal code and the common law. Every

inhabitant in Alberta is also a citizen of the Dominion. The province may deal with his property and civil rights of a local and private nature within the province; but the province cannot interfere with his status as a Canadian citizen and his fundamental right to express freely his untrammelled opinion about government policies and discuss matters of public concern. The mandatory and prohibitory provisions of the Press Bill are, in my opinion, *ultra vires* of the provincial legislature. They interfere with the free working of the political organization of the Dominion. They have a tendency to nullify the political rights of the inhabitants of Alberta, as citizens of Canada, and cannot be considered as dealing with matters purely private and local in that province. The federal parliament is the sole authority to curtail, if deemed expedient and in the public interest, the freedom of the press in discussing public affairs and the equal rights in that respect of all citizens throughout the Dominion. These subjects were matters of criminal law before Confederation, have been recognized by Parliament as criminal matters and have been expressly dealt with by the criminal code. No province has the power to reduce in that province the political rights of its citizens as compared with those enjoyed by the citizens of other provinces of Canada. Moreover, citizens outside the province of Alberta have a vital interest in having full information and comment, favourable and unfavourable, regarding the policy of the Alberta government and concerning events in that province which would, in the ordinary course, be the subject of Alberta newspapers' news items and articles.

I would, therefore, answer the question as to Bill No. 9 in the negative.

[Justice Davis concurred with Chief Justice Duff. Justices Kerwin, Crocket, and Hudson all concluded that the three bills were *ultra vires*. However, their conclusion that the Press Bill was *ultra vires* was based not on the considerations regarding freedom of the press advanced by Chief Justice Duff and Justice Cannon, but on the much narrower ground that the *Act* was ancillary to and dependent on the *Alberta Social Credit Act*, which was itself *ultra vires*.]

Roncarelli v. Duplessis, 1959

On December 12, 1946, guests at Frank Roncarelli's high-end licensed restaurant, Quaff-Café in Montreal, were interrupted by a police confiscation of all of the establishment's liquor and the cancellation of the restaurant's liquor licence. Roncarelli was later informed that the revocation was indefinite. Six months later, and after 34 years in business, the restaurant closed and Roncarelli suffered significant financial losses.

Roncarelli was a member of a Christian sect called the Jehovah's Witnesses whose members believe in an imminent end to the world and their exclusive rapture. The Witnesses were at that time virulently anti-Catholic, preaching that the Pope was the anti-Christ. Such messages did not go over well in the deeply Catholic Quebec of the day and tensions were made worse by the duty discharged by Witnesses to proselytize on the streets of the province. There were instances of civil unrest as a result. Montreal police reacted by jailing Witnesses for peddling wares on the streets without a licence, impeding pedestrian traffic, and so on. But the objective was clear: silence the sect.

Roncarelli did not engage in street proselytism but he did assist by posting property bonds almost 400 times so that Witnesses could get out of jail pending trial. In so doing, he frustrated the objectives of the police who wanted to rid the streets of the Witnesses. In November 1946, Montreal authorities changed the rules to require cash deposits of $400 for bail. Roncarelli discontinued his practice, but the Witnesses responded by printing thousands of copies of a pamphlet declaring that the government was persecuting Christians. These pamphlets were stored in a church building leased for the group by Roncarelli. Roncarelli's lucrative restaurant business gave him the means to support the cause.

When the police discovered Roncarelli's link to the pamphlets, the chairman of the Quebec Liquor Commission, Edouard Archambault, was notified. Archambault contacted Maurice Duplessis, the autocratic premier of Quebec who was also attorney general. Here is the key factual issue in the case—Duplessis either advised or told the chairman to revoke the liquor licence and never issue another to Roncarelli.

Roncarelli had trouble finding a francophone lawyer to take his case. Eventually, Frank Scott, one of the country's premier constitutional scholars (who incidentally was a famous poet and co-founder of the Cooperative Commonwealth Federation), agreed, although he had never pleaded a case before a court before and at the time was unsure whether he was even a member of the Quebec bar.[1] Suits against Archambault or the commission required the attorney general's consent, but this, obviously, was not forthcoming. So Roncarelli's team decided to sue Duplessis directly, in his personal capacity, arguing that he had acted

---

1   Allan C. Hutchinson, *Is Eating People Wrong? Great Legal Cases and How They Shaped the World* (New York: Cambridge University Press, 2011) ch. 3.

without legal authority to inflict harm on the plaintiff. This was a tort action, not a civil liberties claim.

Roncarelli won at trial but lost on appeal. He was vindicated at the Supreme Court by a 6-to-3 decision that went to the foundations of constitutionalism, holding that the key to decent, limited, humane government is that holders of political power must have lawful warrant for their conduct.[2] The majority's reasons are also memorable for the discussion of the nature and limits of discretion in the discharge of legal authority by administrative officers. Such comments were in a strict sense irrelevant to the decision, however, because the majority held that the issue was the usurpation of authority by the premier rather than the misuse of lawful authority possessed either by him or the chairman of the Quebec Liquor Commission.[3]

If the decision was so celebrated, how could other learned justices dissent? Three arguments were persuasive to the dissenters. First, the key factual finding was the nature of the communication between the premier and Archambault: was it merely advice or was it an order? The dissenters held that the decision was ultimately Archambault's. Second, article 88 of Quebec's *Code of Civil Procedure* required that one month's notice be given to public officials before actions could commence against them. No such notice was given to Duplessis. For two dissenters this was determinative. The majority rejected the article 88 argument, writing that it applies to officials who are sued in the performance of their duties, and not Duplessis, who acted outside his legal capacity. Third, for Cartwright C.J., the Quebec Liquor Commission was an administrative body that made decisions based on matters of policy, not on rights and liabilities. Its decisions, being purely administrative, were not reviewable and its discretion was unfettered. Given that the liquor law did not specify the grounds on which licences could be revoked, it was thus entitled to revoke Roncarelli's licence for the reasons submitted by Duplessis.

In this case, the principle of the rule of law stands in for the freedom of religion, a civil liberty that was not entrenched in Canadian constitutional law at the time. *Roncarelli* is a good example of how common law principles in the Canadian constitution can be used to protect rights. It is perhaps important to note that all but one of the justices finding against Roncarelli in the Court of Appeal and the Supreme Court were francophones. ∼

Discussion Questions

1. How could the Quebec government have complied with the principle of the rule of law described by the majority and still silence the Witnesses?

2. Justice Rand wrote that the rule of law requires that the exercise of discretion be limited by the objects or purposes of the law being administered. How can these purposes or objectives be discerned? Are some methods preferable to others?

---

2   This point was amplified in *Re Manitoba Language Rights*, [1985] 1 S.C.R. 721.

3   Claude-Armand Sheppard, "Roncarelli v. Duplessis, Art. 1053 Revolutionized" (1960) 6 *McGill Law Journal* 2 at 90.

RONCARELLI v. DUPLESSIS
[1959] S.C.R. 121

Date: 1959-01-27

PRESENT: Kerwin C.J. and Taschereau, Rand, Locke, Cartwright, Fauteux, Abbott, Martland, and Judson JJ.

The judgment of Rand and Judson JJ. was delivered by

RAND J:

[Rand recounts the circumstances leading to the decision to revoke Roncarelli's liquor licence.]

At no time did he take any part in the distribution of the tracts: he was an adherent of the group but nothing more. It was shown that he had leased to another member premises in Sherbrooke which were used as a hall for carrying on religious meetings: but it is unnecessary to do more than mention that fact to reject it as having no bearing on the issues raised. Beyond the giving of bail and being an adherent, the appellant is free from any relation that could be tortured into a badge of character pertinent to his fitness or unfitness to hold a liquor licence.

The mounting resistance that stopped the surety bail sought other means of crushing the propagandist invasion and among the circumstances looked into was the situation of the appellant. Admittedly an adherent, he was enabling these protagonists to be at large to carry on their campaign of publishing what they believed to be the Christian truth as revealed by the Bible; he was also the holder of a liquor licence, a "privilege" granted by the Province, the profits from which, as it was seen by the authorities, he was using to promote the disturbance of settled beliefs and arouse community disaffection generally. Following discussions between the then Mr. Archambault, as the personality of the Liquor Commission, and the chief prosecuting officer in Montreal, the former, on or about November 21, telephoned to the respondent, advised him of those facts, and queried what should be done. Mr. Duplessis answered that the matter was serious and that the identity of the person furnishing bail and the liquor licensee should be put beyond doubt. A few days later, that identity being established through a private investigator, Mr. Archambault again communicated with the respondent and, as a result of what passed between them, the licence, as of December 4, 1946, was revoked.

In the meantime, about November 25, 1946, a blasting answer had come from the Witnesses. In an issue of one of the periodicals, under the heading "Quebec's Burning Hate," was a searing denunciation of what was alleged to be the savage persecution of Christian believers. Immediately instructions were sent out from the department of the Attorney-General ordering the confiscation of the issue and proceedings were taken against one Boucher charging him with publication of a seditious libel.

It is then wholly as a private citizen, an adherent of a religious group, holding a liquor licence and furnishing bail to arrested persons for no other purpose than to enable them to be released from detention pending the determination of the charges against them, and with no other relevant considerations to be taken into account, that he is involved in the issues of this controversy.

The complementary state of things is equally free from doubt. From the evidence of Mr. Duplessis and Mr. Archambault alone, it appears that the action taken by the latter as the general manager and sole member of the Commission was dictated by Mr. Duplessis as Attorney-General and Prime Minister of the province; that that step was taken as a means of bringing to a halt the activities of the Witnesses, to punish the appellant for the part he had played not only by revoking the existing licence but in declaring him barred from one "forever," and to warn others that they similarly would be stripped of provincial "privileges" if they persisted in any activity directly or indirectly related to the Witnesses and to the objectionable campaign. The respondent felt that action to be his duty, something which his conscience demanded of him; and as representing the provincial government his decision became automatically that of Mr. Archambault and the Commission. ...

In these circumstances, when the *de facto* power of the Executive over its appointees at will to such a statutory public function is exercised deliberately and intentionally to destroy the vital business interests of a citizen, is there legal redress by him against the person so acting? This calls for an examination of the statutory provisions governing the issue, renewal and revocation of liquor licences and the scope of authority entrusted by law to the Attorney-General and the government in relation to the administration of the Act.

[Rand then discusses the provision of the *Act Respecting Alcoholic Liquor.*]

... Section 35 prescribes the expiration of every permit on April 30 of each year. Dealing with cancellation, the section provides that the "Commission may cancel any permit at its discretion." Besides the loss of the privilege and without the necessity of legal proceedings, cancellation entails loss of fees paid to obtain it and confiscation of the liquor in the possession of the holder and the receptacles containing it. If the cancellation is not followed by prosecution for an offence under the Act, compensation is provided for certain items of the forfeiture. Subsection (5) requires the

Commission to cancel any permit made use of on behalf of a person other than the holder; s. 36 requires cancellation in specified cases. The sale of liquor is, by s. 42, forbidden to various persons. Section 148 places upon the Attorney-General the duty of

1. Assuring the observance of this Act and of the Alcoholic Liquor Possession and Transportation Act (Chap. 256), and investigating, preventing and suppressing the infringements of such acts, in every way authorized thereby;
2. Conducting the suits or prosecutions for infringements of this Act or of the said Alcoholic Liquor Possession and Transportation Act. R.S. 1925, c. 37, s. 78a; 24 Geo. V, c. 17, s. 17.

The provisions of the statute, which may be supplemented by detailed regulations, furnish a code for the complete administration of the sale and distribution of alcoholic liquors directed by the Commission as a public service, for all legitimate purposes of the populace. It recognizes the association of wines and liquors as embellishments of food and its ritual and as an interest of the public. As put in Macbeth, the "sauce to meat is ceremony," and so we have restaurants, cafés, hotels and other places of serving food, specifically provided for in that association.

At the same time the issue of permits has a complementary interest in those so catering to the public. The continuance of the permit over the years, as in this case, not only recognizes its virtual ncessity [sic] to a superior class restaurant but also its indentification [sic] with the business carried on. The provisions for assignment of the permit are to this most pertinent and they were exemplified in the continuity of the business here. As its exercise continues, the economic life of the holder becomes progressively more deeply implicated with the privilege while at the same time his vocation becomes correspondingly dependent on it.

The field of licensed occupations and businesses of this nature is steadily becoming of greater concern to citizens generally. It is a matter of vital importance that a public administration that can refuse to allow a person to enter or continue a calling which, in the absence of regulation, would be free and legitimate, should be conducted with complete impartiality and integrity; and that the grounds for refusing or cancelling a permit should unquestionably be such and such only as are incompatible with the purposes envisaged by the statute: the duty of a Commission is to serve those purposes and those only. A decision to deny or cancel such a privilege lies within the "discretion" of the Commission; but that means that decision is to be based upon a weighing of considerations pertinent to the object of the administration.

In public regulation of this sort there is no such thing as absolute and untrammelled "discretion," that is that action can be taken on any ground or for any reason that can be suggested to the mind of the administrator; no legislative Act can, without express language, be taken to contemplate an unlimited arbitrary power exercisable for any purpose, however capricious or irrelevant, regardless of the nature or purpose of the statute. Fraud and corruption in the 'Commission may not be mentioned in such statutes but they are always implied as exceptions. "Discretion" necessarily implies good faith in discharging public duty; there is always a perspective within which a statute is intended to operate; and any clear departure from its lines or objects is just as objectionable as fraud or corruption. Could an applicant be refused a permit because he had been born in another province, or because of the colour of his hair? The ordinary language of the legislature cannot be so distorted.

To deny or revoke a permit because a citizen exercises an unchallengeable right totally irrelevant to the sale of liquor in a restaurant is equally beyond the scope of the discretion conferred. There was here not only revocation of the existing permit but a declaration of a future, definitive disqualification of the appellant to obtain one: it was to be "forever." This purports to divest his citizenship status of its incident of membership in the class of those of the public to whom such a privilege could be extended. Under the statutory language here, that is not competent to the Commission and *a fortiori* to the government or the respondent: ... . There is here an administrative tribunal which, in certain respects, is to act in a judicial manner; ... : what could be more malicious than to punish this licensee for having done what he had an absolute right to do in a matter utterly irrelevant to the *Liquor Act*? Malice in the proper sense is simply acting for a reason and purpose knowingly foreign to the administration, to which was added here the element of intentional punishment by what was virtually vocation outlawry.

It may be difficult if not impossible in cases generally to demonstrate a breach of this public duty in the illegal purpose served; there may be no means, even if proceedings against the Commission were permitted by the Attorney-General, as here they were refused, of compelling the Commission to justify a refusal or revocation or to give reasons for its action; on these questions I make no observation; but in the case before us that difficulty is not present: the reasons are openly avowed.

The act of the respondent through the instrumentality of the Commission brought about a breach of an implied public statutory duty toward the appellant; it was a gross abuse of legal power expressly intended to punish him for an act wholly irrelevant to the statute, a punishment which inflicted on him, as it was intended to do, the destruction of his economic life as a restaurant keeper within the province. Whatever may be the immunity of the Commission or its member from an action for damages, there is none in the respondent. He was under no duty in relation to the appellant and his act was an intrusion upon the functions of a statutory body. The injury done by him was a, fault engaging liability within the principles of the underlying public law of Quebec: *Mostyn v. Fabrigas* [98 E.R. 1021], and under art. 1053 of the *Civil Code*. That, in the presence of expanding administrative regulation of economic activities, such a step and its consequences are to be suffered by the victim without recourse or remedy, that an administration according to law is to be superseded by action dictated by and according to the arbitrary likes, dislikes and irrelevant purposes of public officers acting beyond their duty, would signalize the beginning of disintegration of the rule of law as a fundamental postulate of our constitutional structure. An administration of licences on the highest level of fair and impartial treatment to all may be forced to follow the practice of "first come, first served," which makes the strictest observance of equal responsibility to all of even greater importance; at this stage of developing government it would be a danger of high con-sequence to tolerate such a departure from good faith in executing the legislative purpose. It should be added, however, that that principle is not, by this language, intended to be extended to ordinary governmental employment: with that we are not here concerned.

It was urged by Mr. Beaulieu that the respondent, as the incumbent of an office of state, so long as he was proceeding in "good faith," was free to act in a matter of this kind virtually as he pleased. The office of Attorney-General traditionally and by statute carries duties that relate to advising the Executive, including here, administrative bodies, enforcing the public law and directing the administration of justice. In any decision of the statutory body in this case, he had no part to play beyond giving advice on legal questions arising. In that role his action should have been limited to advice on the validity of a revocation for such a reason or purpose and what that advice should have been does not seem to me to admit of any doubt. To pass from this limited scope of action to that of bringing about a step by the Commission beyond the bounds prescribed by the legislature for its exclusive action converted what was done into his personal act.

"Good faith" in this context, applicable both to the respondent and the general manager, means carrying out the statute according to its intent and for its purpose; it means good faith in acting with a rational appreciation of that intent and purpose and not with an improper intent and for an alien purpose; it does not mean for the purposes of punishing a person for exercising an unchallengeable right; it does not mean arbitrarily and illegally attempting to divest a citizen of an incident of his civil status. ...

The damages suffered involved the vocation of the appellant within the province. Any attempt at a precise computation or estimate must assume probabilities in an area of uncertainty and risk. The situation is one which the Court should approach as a jury would, in a view of its broad features; and in the best consideration I can give to them, the damages should be fixed at the sum of $25,000 plus that allowed by the trial court.

I would therefore allow the appeals, set aside the judgment of the Court of Queen's Bench and restore the judgment at trial modified by increasing the damages to the sum of $33,123.53. The appellant should have his costs in the Court of Queen's Bench and in this Court.

CARTWRIGHT J. (dissenting): ... The evidence of the respondent is ... that the suggestion of cancelling the permit was made by M. Archambault, and there is no evidence to the contrary.

There has been a difference of opinion in the Courts below as to whether what was said by the respondent to M. Archambault amounted to an order to cancel or merely to an "approbation énergique" of a decision already made. I do not find it necessary to choose between these conflicting views as I propose to assume for the purposes of this appeal that what was said by the respondent was so far a determining factor in the cancellation of the permit as to render him liable for the damages caused thereby to the appellant if the cancellation was an actionable wrong giving rise to a right of action for damages.

All of the Judges in the Courts below who have dealt with that aspect of the matter have concluded that the respondent acted throughout in the honest belief that he was fulfilling his duty to the Province, and this conclusion is supported by the evidence.

The opinion of M. Archambault and of the respondent appears to have been that a permit to sell liquor under the Act is a privilege in the gift of the Province which ought not to be given to, or allowed to continue to be enjoyed by, one who was actively supporting members of a group of persons who were engaged in a concerted campaign to vilify the Province and were persistently acting in contravention of existing by-laws. Once it is found, as I think it must be on the evidence, that this opinion was honestly entertained, I have reached the conclusion, for reasons that will appear, that the Court cannot inquire as to whether there was sufficient evidence to warrant its formation or as to whether it constituted a reasonable ground for cancellation of the permit.

[Cartwright examines the provisions of the *Act Respecting Alcoholic Liquors.*]

On a consideration of these sections and of the remainder of the Act I am unable to find that the Legislature has, either expressly or by necessary implication, laid down any rules to guide the commission as to the circumstances under which it may refuse to grant a permit or may cancel a permit already granted. In my opinion the intention of the legislature, to be gathered from the whole Act, was to enumerate (i) certain cases in which the granting of a permit is forbidden, and (ii) certain cases in which the cancellation of a permit is mandatory, and, in all other cases to commit the decision as to whether a permit should be granted, refused or cancelled to the unfettered discretion of the commission. I conclude that the function of the commission in making that decision is administrative and not judicial or quasi-judicial. The submission of counsel for the respondent, made in the following words, appears to me to be well founded:

> Under the Statute, no one has a pre-existing right to obtain a permit, and the permit being granted under the condition that it may be cancelled at any time, and no cause of cancellation being mentioned and no form of procedure being indicated, the cancellation is a discretionary decision of a purely administrative character.

[Cartwright endorses the view that administrative bodies like the liquor commission base their orders, "not on legal rights and liabilities, but on policy and expediency."]

... I should perhaps mention that there is, in the record, no room for any suggestion that the respondent coerced an unwilling Commission into making a decision contrary to the view of the latter as to what that decision should be. ...

ABBOTT J.: ... The proposition that in Canada a member of the executive branch of government does not make the law but merely carries it out or administers it requires no citation of authority to support it. Similarly, I do not find it necessary to cite from the wealth of authority supporting the principle that a public officer is responsible for acts done by him without legal justification. I content myself with quoting the well known passage from Dicey's "Law of the Constitution," 9th ed., p. 193, where he says

> ... every official, from the Prime Minister down to a constable or a collector of taxes, is under the [same]

responsibility for every act done without legal justification as any other citizen. The Reports abound with cases in which officials have been brought before the courts, and made, in their personal capacity, liable to punishment, or to the payment of damages, for acts done in their official character but in excess of their lawful authority. A colonial governor, a secretary of state, a military officer, and all subordinates, though carrying out the commands of their official superiors, are as responsible for any act which the law does not authorize as is any private and unofficial person.

In the instant case, the respondent was given no statutory power to interfere in the administration or direction of the Quebec Liquor Commission although as Attorney-General of the Province the Commission and its officers could of course consult him for legal opinions and legal advice. The Commission is not a department of government in the accepted sense of that term. Under the *Alcoholic Liquor Act* the Commission is an independent body with corporate status and with the powers and responsibilities conferred upon it by the Legislature. The Attorney-General is given no power under the said Act to intervene in the administration of the affairs of the Commission nor does the *Attorney-General's Department Act*, R.S.Q. 1941, c. 46, confer any such authority upon him.

I have no doubt that in taking the action which he did, the respondent was convinced that he was acting in what he conceived to be the best interests of the people of his province but this, of course, has no relevance to the issue of his responsibility in damages for any acts done in excess of his legal authority. I have no doubt also that respondent knew and was bound to know as Attorney-General that neither as Premier of the province nor as Attorney-General was he authorized in law to interfere with the administration of the Quebec Liquor Commission or to give an order or an authorization to any officer of that body to exercise a discretionary authority entrusted to such officer by the statute.

It follows, therefore, that in purporting to authorize and instruct the manager of the Quebec Liquor Commission to cancel appellant's licence, the respondent was acting without any legal authority whatsoever. Moreover, as I have said, I think respondent was bound to know that he was acting without such authority.

The respondent is therefore liable under art. 1053 of the *Civil Code* for the damages sustained by the appellant, by reason of the acts done by respondent in excess of his legal authority.

3   Attorney General of Canada v. Lavell and Bédard, 1974

A new chapter in Canadian civil liberties was inaugurated in 1960 with the enactment of the *Canadian Bill of Rights*. Technically, the new *Bill of Rights* was not an addition to Canada's formal Constitution. It was passed as an ordinary *Act* of the federal Parliament. As such it did not apply to the provinces and could be set aside by subsequent federal legislation. The Act had two main clauses. Section 1 declared that in Canada certain fundamental rights and freedoms "have existed and shall continue to exist without discrimination by reason of race, national origin, colour, religion or sex." It listed such fundamental rights as the right to life, liberty, security of the person, and enjoyment of property and the right not to be deprived thereof except by due process of law; the individual's right to equality before the law and protection of the law; and freedom of religion, speech, assembly, association, and the press. Section 2 provided that unless the *Bill of Rights* was explicitly set aside, every federal law shall "be so construed and applied as not to abrogate, abridge or infringe" the rights and freedoms set out in the Bill. It added to the rights listed in section 1 a list of procedural rights, including the right of arrested persons to legal counsel, *habeas corpus*, the presumption of innocence, the right to an interpreter, and the right to a fair hearing when a person's rights or duties are being determined. The final section of the Bill provided that the *Bill of Rights* would not apply to anything done under the *War Measures Act*.

The first real test of the Supreme Court's treatment of the *Bill of Rights* came in 1963 in the *Robertson and Rosetanni* case.[1] Robertson and Rosetanni had been charged with an offence under the federal *Lord's Day Act*, namely, operating a bowling alley on Sunday. On appeal their main defence was that the *Lord's Day Act* conflicted with the *Canadian Bill of Rights* and was therefore inoperative. Justice Ritchie (supported by the three Quebec justices, Taschereau, Fauteux, and Abbott) wrote the majority's opinion, dismissing the appeal. His approach to the *Bill of Rights* was basically conservative. He interpreted it not as a charter designed to enlarge the fundamental rights and freedoms of Canadians, but as a means of conserving these rights in their 1960 form. The *Canadian Bill of Rights*, he argued, "is not concerned with 'human rights and fundamental freedoms' in any abstract sense, but rather with such 'rights and freedoms' as they existed in Canada immediately before the statute was enacted." His review of Canadian history and jurisprudence revealed that the concept of religious freedom was well enshrined in Canadian law as was Lord's Day observance legislation long before 1960. Thus he concluded that the freedom of religion guaranteed by the *Bill of Rights* was not infringed by the *Lord's Day Act*. Justice Cartwright, the sole dissenter, rejected the implication in the majority's position that the *Bill of Rights* could have no effect on laws enacted before the *Bill of Rights*. In his view, section 5 made it clear that the Bill was "to apply to all laws of Canada already in existence at the time it came into force as well as those thereafter enacted."

---

1   [1963] S.C.R. 651.

If Canadian civil libertarians were dismayed by the court's decision in *Robertson and Rosetanni*, they found new ground for hope in the court's next major decision on the *Bill of Rights*. This did not occur until 1970 in the *Drybones* decision, which concerned the compatibility of provisions in the *Indian Act* restricting the drinking rights of Indians with the egalitarian provisions of the *Bill of Rights*. Ironically, on this occasion, the positions of Cartwright and Ritchie were completely reversed. Justice Ritchie still spoke for the majority, but this time it was an "activist" majority willing to use the *Bill of Rights* to invalidate a long-established piece of federal legislation. Cartwright, now Chief Justice, along with Justices Abbott and Pigeon, refused to give the Bill such a wide-reaching effect.

The Supreme Court's decision in the *Lavell and Bédard* case indicated that a majority of the judges felt that the court had gone too far in an "activist" direction in *Drybones*. The majority opinion did not retreat from the position established in *Drybones* that the *Bill of Rights* can render inoperative legislation that clearly violates rights enshrined in the Bill, but it did considerably water down the significance of the right to equality before the law.

The decision dealt with appeals in two cases involving indigenous women who claimed that the *Indian Act* infringed their right to equality before the law under the *Bill of Rights*. The *Indian Act*, enacted under the federal power over "Indians, and Lands reserved to Indians," covers only those indigenous peoples historically designated as "Indians." It does not apply to the Inuit or the Métis, who were added as "Aboriginal Peoples" with constitutional status in 1982. Indeed, not even all those who count as "Indians" in the constitutional sense have registered "status" under the Act, which explains the historically common distinction between status and non-status Indians. *Lavell and Bédard* turned on this distinction.

Section 12(1)(*b*) of the *Indian Act* deprived women of their status under the Act, including their right to hold property and live on a reserve if they married someone without Indian status. In contrast, a man with Indian status who married a non-status woman could retain his status. Thus, Mrs. Lavell and Mrs. Bédard argued that section 12(1)(*b*) constituted discrimination by reason of sex in violation of the *Bill of Rights*. While they were supported by the Native Council of Canada representing non-status Indians and by several non-indigenous women's organizations, most of the organizations representing status Indians, including eight provincial and two territorial organizations and the National Indian Brotherhood, intervened to oppose Mrs. Lavell and Mrs. Bédard.

The Supreme Court decided, 5 to 4, that section 12(1)(*b*) did not constitute a violation of equality before the law. Again, Justice Ritchie wrote the majority opinion. Just as it is difficult to reconcile his opinion in *Drybones* with the position he had taken earlier in *Robertson and Rosetanni*, it is a daunting task to trace a thread of consistency between his approach to equality before the law in *Lavell and Bédard* and his treatment of that concept in *Drybones*. Citing A.V. Dicey, the 19th-century English constitutional writer, as his authority, Justice Ritchie now defined equality before the law not as a substantive requirement of the law itself, but as a requirement of the way in which laws are administered. The *Indian Act* might well discriminate against women, but so long as it was applied equally to all whom it affected there would be no violation of equality before the law. To this argument Justice Ritchie added the concern expressed by Justice Pigeon in his dissenting opinion in *Drybones*: it would be unreasonable to extend the *Bill of Rights* so far as to make it impossible for Parliament to enact special legislation concerning the property and civil rights of Indians.

Justice Laskin, as was so often the case in civil liberties cases, wrote a vigorous dissent. He could not reconcile the majority's interpretation of equality before the law with the court's decision in *Drybones*. The opening paragraph of section 1 of the *Canadian Bill of Rights*, in his view, amounted to a prohibition of legal classifications based on race, national origin, colour, religion, or sex. In this sense, the *Canadian Bill of Rights* was more specific and categorical than the equal protection of laws clause in the American Constitution, which did not prohibit any specific form of discrimination, leaving it to the judiciary to distinguish reasonable and unreasonable forms of discrimination. Laskin could not see why laws based on Parliament's power under section 91(24) of the *B.N.A. Act* to legislate in relation to Indians should enjoy any special immunity from the *Bill of Rights*. To decide otherwise in this case would, in his view, compound racial inequality with sexual inequality. Justice Laskin's dissent was supported by Justices Spence, Hall, and Abbott. Justice Abbott had dissented in *Drybones*, but regarded that decision as now requiring him to support Justice Laskin's dissent. Justice Pigeon, on the other hand, who also dissented in *Drybones*, this time joined the majority and appeared to regard the results of this case as supportive of the position that he had taken in *Drybones*.

The most promising explanation for the logical difficulties posed by the majority opinion is political, not jurisprudential. The judges had been made aware that ruling section 12(1)(*b*) inoperative would cause political and policy difficulties not posed by the *Drybones* decision, and they drew back in an attempt to avoid the political thicket Justice Cartwright had warned them about in *Drybones*.

The central question was whether a broad interpretation of the *Bill of Rights* equality guarantee would undermine the entire *Indian Act*. This concern had been expressed by Justice Pigeon in his dissenting opinion in *Drybones*. By the time of the *Lavell and Bédard* case, the Indian community had become alerted to the threat posed to the *Indian Act* by this jurisprudence and had mobilized to oppose it. Although Indians were not happy with all aspects of the Act and its administration, they were not prepared to abandon the idea of special status as such. Not long before, they had successfully resisted the Trudeau government's 1969 proposal to dismantle the *Indian Act* in favour of an individualized concept of equal Canadian citizenship, and they worried that their political victory might now be judicially undone.

In addition to the implicit challenge to the idea of special status, serious political problems were raised by the possible invalidation of section 12(1)(*b*) itself. The liquor provisions of the *Indian Act* struck down in *Drybones* were relatively unimportant parts of the Act, with few implications for the system of special status established there. Their invalidation did not really change anything. To the contrary, in most of the country they had already been repealed under local option provisions of the *Indian Act* and they were nowhere actively supported. Thus, in *Drybones*, the "Supreme Court was invited to strike down the feeble remnants of 19th century Indian liquor laws."[2] To do so, moreover, would create no legal gap and pose no policy dilemmas; the relevant laws for the rest of the population would now simply apply to Indians as well.

The same could not be said of the status-defining provisions of section 12(1)(*b*). Some way of determining status was required, and if these rules were invalidated what would replace them? The court, which could invalidate them, could not itself fill the legal gap that

---

2 Douglas Sanders, "The Bill of Rights and the Indian Act" in Anne Bayefsky and Mary Eberts, eds., *Equality Rights and the Charter* (Toronto: Carswell, 1985) 539.

would ensue. Furthermore, what would be the practical, particularly the financial, implications of returning status to women who had lost it? Through the minister of Indian Affairs, the National Indian Brotherhood expressed strong opposition "to the principles contained in the *Lavell* decision [in the Federal Court] and, in particular, to the effects which they fear it will have on their already overcrowded reserves and their already overcrowded schools." For example, the minister estimated that it would cost $1 million to reimburse women like Lavell for the share of band funds they did not receive following their marriages to non-Indians, "even if the principle of the *Lavell* case only applies to marriages which have taken place since the *Canadian Bill of Rights* was enacted."[3]

The existence of major political problems and the extent of the opposition to the invalidation of section 12(1)(*b*) was underlined for the Supreme Court by the number of aspiring interveners clamouring at its door. Whereas in *Drybones* the judges were faced with an antiquated and insignificant section of the Act that nobody was willing to defend, in *Lavell and Bédard* they saw the federal government and all the status Indian organizations lining up in vigorous support of the status quo. Indeed, "the provincial Indian Associations, along with the National Indian Brotherhood, joined together in support of a single submission to the Court in support of section 12(1)(*b*), a rare show of unity and organization."[4] In this context, the concerns Justice Cartwright expressed in *Drybones* about the dangers of the political thicket must have loomed much larger for the court as a whole.

After *Lavell and Bédard* the Supreme Court rejected a series of attacks on discriminatory provisions in federal legislation. In *Burnshine*,[5] the court dismissed an attack on provisions of the *Prisons and Reformatories Act* under which young offenders in British Columbia and Ontario may serve longer periods of detention than adults or youths in other provinces. In the *Canard* case,[6] the court held that provisions of the *Indian Act* giving a federal minister the power to administer the estates of Indians did not infringe their right to equality before the law. Justice Laskin (who between these two cases had been elevated to the chief justiceship) wrote dissents in both cases.

The *Bliss* case[7] concerned amendments to the *Unemployment Insurance Act* that created a special pregnancy benefit, but made it conditional on serving a much longer employment period than required for other benefits and denied a woman who left the workforce because of pregnancy access to the ordinary benefits. The court unanimously (Chief Justice Laskin did not participate in this decision) held that these provisions involved no denial of equality before the law. Justice Ritchie, who authored the court's opinion, contended that they were "an integral part of a legislative scheme enacted for valid federal objectives and they are concerned with conditions from which men are excluded. Any inequality between the sexes in this area is not created by legislation but by nature." The idea that so long as legislation serves "a valid federal objective" it is a justifiable discrimination was enunciated three years

---

3 *Ibid.* at 543.

4 Carl Baar, "Using Process Theory to Explain Judicial Decision Making" (1986) 1 *Canadian Journal of Law and Society* 86.

5 *R. v. Burnshine*, [1975] 1 S.C.R. 693.

6 *Attorney General of Canada v. Canard*, [1976] 1 S.C.R. 170.

7 *Bliss v. Attorney General of Canada*, [1979] 1 S.C.R. 183.

earlier in the *Prata* case,[8] in which the court unanimously rejected the contention that provisions of the *Immigration Act* restricting the rights of persons deemed to be security risks constituted a denial of equality before the law.

However, there was still no clear consensus among the members of the Supreme Court as to whether the test of "serving a valid federal objective" means more than that legislation should be in relation to a matter constitutionally within the federal Parliament's jurisdiction. The *MacKay* case, decided in 1980, provided a good test of the justices' position on this question. The case concerned provisions of the *National Defence Act,* under which a member of the armed forces had been convicted by a court martial for a number of drug offences committed at a military base. While the court decided, 7 to 2, that in these circumstances there was no denial of equality before the law, two of the judges who supported the majority (Justices McIntyre and Dickson) took the position that equality before the law would be violated by the broad provisions of the Act that subjected members of the armed forces to military trials for *all* criminal offences, even those having no relationship to a military context. In reaching this conclusion, Justice McIntyre held that, in determining whether a discriminatory classification in federal legislation served a valid federal objective and therefore did not violate equality before the law, the court must decide whether the inequality "has been created rationally in the sense that it is not arbitrary or capricious and not based upon any ulterior motive ... and whether it is a necessary departure from the general principle of universal application of the law for the attainment of some necessary and desirable social objective."[9] The two dissenting judges, Chief Justice Laskin and Justice Estey, also appeared to accept the view that discriminatory laws must be based on reasonable classifications. Still, this test of the rationality of legislative classifications, borrowed from American constitutional law, was endorsed by a majority of Supreme Court judges.

The equality clause of the *Charter of Rights,* section 15, was certainly meant to have a more significant effect than the equality provisions in the *Canadian Bill of Rights.* Indeed, the section contains wording explicitly intended to counteract the *Lavell and Bédard* and *Bliss* cases. In addition to equality before the law and the equal protection of the law, section 15 protects equality under the law (to overrule *Lavell and Bédard*) and equal benefit of the law (to overrule *Bliss*). The section stipulates that these rights are to be enjoyed "without discrimination and, in particular, without discrimination based on race, national or ethnic origin, colour, religion, sex, age or mental or physical disability." An interpretation imposed on the equal protection of laws by the U.S. Supreme Court is explicitly overcome by providing that affirmative action laws that discriminate in order to improve the condition of disadvantaged individuals or groups shall not be regarded as violating the equality rights.

Indigenous women did not have to wait for the Charter to overcome the *Indian Act*'s discrimination against them. In 1977, Sandra Lovelace took her case to a hearing before the United Nation's Human Rights Committee. The committee ruled that the section of Canada's *Indian Act* that had been upheld in *Lavell and Bédard* violated the United Nations Convention on Civil and Political Rights.[10] Although this decision was not legally binding

---

8   *Prata v. Minister of Manpower & Immigration,* [1976] 1 S.C.R. 376.

9   *MacKay v. The Queen,* [1980] 2 S.C.R. 370 at 407.

10   *Lovelace v. Canada,* No. 24/1977. Selected Decisions of the Human Rights Committee Under the Optional Protocol, U.N. Doc. CCPR/OP/1 (1988), 86-90.

on Canada, it was a key factor in putting political pressure on the federal government to amend the Act. In 1985, section 12(1)(*b*) was removed from the Act, restoring the status of an estimated 22,000 Indian women who had lost it under that provision. The status of the children of these women was left to be determined by Indian bands, which were given power to determine their own membership systems.

The *Charter of Rights and Freedoms* has clear constitutional status and is much more comprehensive in its rights coverage than the *Canadian Bill of Rights*. It has eclipsed the Bill as an instrument for litigating civil rights in Canada. The Supreme Court's sterile and inconsistent jurisprudence interpreting the *Bill of Rights* stands as a marker of where Charter jurisprudence will not go. However, the *Canadian Bill of Rights* remains on the statute book. The one point where it might have practical significance is its recognition of a right to property and the right not to be deprived thereof except by due process of law. The Charter contains no right of property. ∼

Discussion Questions

1. Can *Drybones* be distinguished from *Lavell and Bédard*?

2. How appropriate was it for Justice Pigeon to side with the majority in *Lavell and Bédard* if, as he concedes for the sake of argument, *Drybones* cannot be distinguished?

3. Justice Ritchie concludes that the principle of "equality in the administration and application of the law" was not infringed. How could it have been infringed in the application of section 12(1)(*b*) of the *Indian Act*? Assess the pros and cons of this equality principle.

ATTORNEY GENERAL OF CANADA
v. LAVELL AND BÉDARD
[1974] S.C.R. 1349

Judgment: August 27, 1973.

Present: Fauteux C.J. and Abbott, Martland, Judson, Ritchie, Hall, Spence, Pigeon, and Laskin JJ.

Interveners: Six Nations Band of Indians of the County of Brant; Native Council of Canada; Rose Wilhelm, Alberta Committee on Indian Rights for Indian Women Inc., Viola Shannacaffo, University Women's Club of Toronto, University Women Graduates Ltd., North Toronto Business and Professional Women's Club Inc., and Monica Agnes Turner; Treaty Voice of Alberta, Anishnarvbekwek of Ontario Inc.; Indian Association of Alberta, the Union of British Columbia Indian Chiefs, the Manitoba Indian Brotherhood Inc., the Union of New Brunswick Indians, the Indian Brotherhood of the Northwest Territories, the Union of Nova Scotia Indians, the Union of Ontario Indians, the Federation of Saskatchewan Indians, the Indian Association of Quebec, the Yukon Native Brotherhood, and the National Indian Brotherhood.

The judgment of Fauteux C.J. and Martland, Judson, and Ritchie JJ. was delivered by

RICHIE J.: … These appeals, which were heard together, are from two judgments holding that the provisions of s. 12(1) (*b*) of the *Indian Act*, R.S.C. 1970, c. I-6, are rendered inoperative by s. 1(*b*) of the *Canadian Bill of Rights*, 1960 (Can.), c. 44, as denying equality before the law to the two respondents.

Both respondents were registered Indians and "Band" members within the meaning of s. 11(*b*) of the *Indian Act* when they elected to marry non-Indians and thereby relinquished their status as Indians in conformity with the said s. 12(1)(*b*) which reads as follows:

> 12.(1) The following persons are not entitled to be registered, namely,
>   (*b*) a woman who married a person who is not an Indian, unless that woman is subsequently the wife or widow of a person described in section 11.

It is contended on behalf of both respondents that s. 12(1)(*b*) of the *Act* should be held to be inoperative as discriminating between Indian men and women and as being in conflict with the provisions of the *Canadian Bill of Rights* and particularly s. 1 thereof which provides:

> 1. It is hereby recognized and declared that in Canada there have existed and shall continue to exist without discrimination by reason of race, national origin, colour, religion or sex, the following human rights and fundamental freedoms, namely, ...
>> (*b*) the right of the individual to equality before the law and the protection of the law; ...

... The contention which formed the basis of the argument submitted by both respondents was that they had been denied equality before the law by reason of sex, and I propose to deal with the matter on this basis. ...

In my opinion the exclusive legislative authority vested in Parliament under s. 91(24) could not have been effectively exercised without enacting laws establishing the qualifications required to entitle persons to status as Indians and to the use and benefit of Crown "lands reserved for Indians." The legislation enacted to this end was, in my view, necessary for the implementation of the authority so vested in Parliament under the constitution.

To suggest that the provisions of the *Bill of Rights* have the effect of making the whole *Indian Act* inoperative as discriminatory is to assert that the Bill has rendered Parliament powerless to exercise the authority entrusted to it under the constitution of enacting legislation which treats Indians living on Reserves differently from other Canadians in relation to their property and civil rights. The proposition that such a wide effect is to be given to the *Bill of Rights* was expressly reserved by the majority of this Court in the case of *The Queen v. Drybones* [[1970] S.C.R. 282], at 298, to which reference will hereafter be made, and I do not think that it can be sustained.

What is at issue here is whether the *Bill of Rights* is to be construed as rendering inoperative one of the conditions imposed by Parliament for the use and occupation of Crown lands reserved for Indians. These conditions were imposed as a necessary part of the structure created by Parliament for the internal administration of the life of Indians on reserves and their entitlement to the use and benefit of Crown lands situate thereon, they were thus imposed, in discharge of Parliament's constitutional function under s. 91(24) and in my view can only be changed by plain statutory language expressly enacted for the purpose. It does not appear to me that Parliament can be taken to have made or intended to make such a change by the use of broad general language directed at the statutory proclamation of the fundamental rights and freedoms enjoyed by all Canadians, and I am therefore of opinion that the *Bill of Rights* had no such effect. ...

The contention that the *Bill of Rights* is to be construed as overriding all of the special legislation imposed by Parliament under the *Indian Act* is, in my view, fully answered by Pigeon J. in his dissenting opinion in the *Drybones* case where he said, at p. 304:

> If one of the effects of the *Canadian Bill of Rights* is to render inoperative all legal provisions whereby Indians as such are not dealt with in the same way as the general public, the conclusion is inescapable that Parliament, by the enactment of the Bill, has not only fundamentally altered the status of the Indians in that indirect fashion but has also made any future use of federal legislative authority over them subject to the requirement of expressly declaring every time "that the law shall operate notwithstanding the *Canadian Bill of Rights.*" I find it very difficult to believe that Parliament so intended when enacting the Bill. If a virtual suppression of federal legislation over Indians as such was meant, one would have expected this important change to be made explicitly not surreptitiously so to speak. ...

In considering the meaning to be given to section 1(*b*) of the *Bill of Rights*, regard must of course be had to what was said by Mr. Justice Laskin, speaking in this regard for the whole of the Court in *Curr v. The Queen* [[1972] S.C.R. 889, at pp. 896 and 897], where he interpreted sections 1(*a*) and 1(*b*) of the Bill in the following passage:

> In considering the reach of s. 1(*a*) and s. 1(*b*), and, indeed, of s. 1 as a whole, I would observe, first, that the section is given its controlling force over federal law by its referential incorporation into s. 2; and, second, that I do not read it as making the existence of any of the forms of prohibited discrimination, a *sine qua non* of its operation. Rather, the prohibited discrimination is an additional lever to which federal legislation must respond. Putting the matter another way, federal legislation which does not offend s. 1 in respect of any of the prohibited kinds of discrimination may nonetheless be offensive to s. 1 if it is violative of what is specified in any of the clauses (*a*) to (*f*) of s. 1. It is, *a fortiori*, offensive if there is discrimination by reason of race so as to deny equality before the law. That is what this Court decided in *Regina v. Drybones* and I need say no more on this point.
>
> It is, therefore, not an answer to reliance by the appellant on s. 1(*a*) and s. 1(*b*) of the *Canadian Bill of Rights* that s. 223 does not discriminate against any person by reason of race, national origin, colour, religion or sex. The absence of such discrimination still leaves open the question whether s. 223 can be construed and applied without abrogating, abridging or infringing the rights of the individual listed in s. 1(*a*) and s. 1(*b*).

My understanding of this passage is that the effect of s. 1 of the *Bill of Rights* is to guarantee to all Canadians the rights specified in paragraphs (*a*) to (*f*) of that section, irrespective of race, national origin, colour or sex. This interpretation appears to me to be borne out by the French version which reads:

> 1. *Il est par les présentes reconnu et déclaré que les droits de l'homme et les libertés fondamentales ci-après énoncés ont existé et continueront à exister pour tout individu au Canada quels que soient sa race, son origine nationale, sa couleur, sa religion ou son sexe:*

It was stressed on behalf of the respondents that the provisions of s. 12(1)(*b*) of the *Indian Act* constituted "discrimination by reason of sex" and that the section could be declared inoperative on this ground alone even if such discrimination did not result in the infringement of any of the rights and freedoms specifically guaranteed by s. 1 of the Bill.

I can find no support for such a contention in the *Curr* case in which, in any event, no question of any kind of discrimination was either directly or indirectly involved. My own understanding of the passage which I have quoted from that case was that it recognized the fact that the primary concern evidenced by the first two sections of the *Bill of Rights* is to ensure that the rights and freedoms thereby recognized and declared shall continue to exist for all Canadians, and it follows, in my view, that those sections cannot be invoked unless one of the enumerated rights and freedoms has been denied to an individual Canadian or group of Canadians. Section 2 of the *Bill of Rights* provides for the manner in which the rights and freedoms which are recognized and declared by s. 1 are to be enforced and the effect of this section is that every law of Canada shall "be so construed and applied as not to abrogate, abridge or infringe or authorize the abrogation, abridgment or infringement of any of the rights and freedoms herein recognized and declared ... ," (*i.e.* by s. 1). There is no language anywhere in the *Bill of Rights* stipulating that the laws of Canada are to be construed without discrimination unless that discrimination involves the denial of one of the guaranteed rights and freedoms, but when, as in the case of *The Queen v. Drybones, supra*, denial of one of the enumerated rights is occasioned by reason of discrimination, then, as Mr. Justice Laskin has said, the discrimination affords an "additional lever to which federal legislation must respond."

The opening words of s. 2 of the *Bill of Rights* are, in my view, determinative of the test to be applied in deciding whether the section here impugned is to be declared inoperative. The words to which I refer are:

> 2. Every law of Canada shall, unless it is expressly declared by an act of the Parliament of Canada that it

shall operate notwithstanding the *Canadian Bill of Rights*, be so construed and applied as not to abrogate, abridge or infringe or authorize the abrogation, abridgement or infringement of the freedoms herein recognized and declared ...

In the course of the reasons for judgment rendered on behalf of the majority of this Court in *The Queen v. Drybones, supra*, this language was interpreted in the following passage at p. 294:

> It seems to me that a more realistic meaning must be given to the words in question and they afford, in my view, the clearest indication that s. 2 is intended to mean and does mean that if a law of Canada cannot be "sensibly construed and applied" so that it does not abrogate, abridge or infringe one of the rights and freedoms, recognized and declared by the *Bill*, then such law is inoperative "unless it is expressly declared by an Act of the Parliament of Canada that it shall operate notwithstanding the *Canadian Bill of Rights*."

Accordingly, in my opinion, the question to be determined in these appeals is confined to deciding whether the Parliament of Canada in defining the prerequisites of Indian status so as not to include women of Indian birth who have chosen to marry non-Indians, enacted a law which cannot be sensibly construed and applied without abrogating, abridging or infringing the rights of such women to equality before the law.

In my view the meaning to be given to the language employed in the *Bill of Rights* is the meaning which it bore in Canada at the time when the *Bill* was enacted, and it follows that the phrase "equality before the law" is to be construed in light of the law existing in Canada at that time.

In considering the meaning to be attached to "equality before the law" as those words occur in section 1(*b*) of the *Bill*, I think it important to point out that in my opinion this phrase is not effective to invoke the egalitarian concept exemplified by the 14th Amendment of the U.S. Constitution as interpreted by the courts of that country. (See *Smythe v. The Queen* [[1971] S.C.R. 680 *per* Fauteux C.J. at pp. 683 and 686]). I think rather that, having regard to the language employed in the second paragraph of the preamble to the *Bill of Rights*, the phrase "equality before the law" as used in s. 1 is to be read in its context as a part of "the rule of law" to which overriding authority is accorded by the terms of that paragraph.

In this connection I refer to Stephens *Commentaries on the Laws of England*, 21st Ed. 1950, where it is said in Vol. III at p. 337:

> Now the great constitutional lawyer Dicey writing in 1885 was so deeply impressed by the absence of arbitrary

governments present and past, that he coined the phrase "the rule of law" to express the regime under which Englishmen lived; and he tried to give precision to it in the following words which have exercised a profound influence on all subsequent thought and conduct.

> That the "rule of law" which forms a fundamental principle of the constitution has three meanings or may be regarded from three different points of view. ...

The second meaning proposed by Dicey is the one with which we are here concerned and it was stated in the following terms:

> It means again equality before the law or the equal subjection of all classes to the ordinary law of the land administered by the ordinary courts; the "rule of law" in this sense excludes the idea of any exemption of officials or others from the duty of obedience to the law which governs other citizens or from the jurisdiction of the ordinary courts.

"Equality before the law" in this sense is frequently invoked to demonstrate that the same law applies to the highest official of government as to any other ordinary citizen, and in this regard Professor F.R. Scott, in delivering the Plaunt Memorial Lectures on Civil Liberties and Canadian Federalism in 1959, speaking of the case of *Roncarelli v. Duplessis* [[1959] S.C.R. 121], had occasion to say:

> It is always a triumph for the law to show that it is applied equally to all without fear or favour. This is what we mean when we say that all are equal before the law.

The relevance of these quotations to the present circumstances is that "equality before the law" as recognized by Dicey as a segment of the rule of law, carries the meaning of equal subjection of all classes to the ordinary law of the land *as administered by the ordinary courts*, and in my opinion the phrase "equality before the law" as employed in section 1(*b*) of the *Bill of Rights* is to be treated as meaning equality in the administration or application of the law by the law enforcement authorities and the ordinary courts of the land. This construction is, in my view, supported by the provisions of subsections (*a*) to (*g*) of s. 2 of the *Bill* which clearly indicate to me that it was equality in the administration and enforcement of the law with which Parliament was concerned when it guaranteed the continued existence of "equality before the law."

Turning to the *Indian Act* itself, it should first be observed that by far the greater part of that *Act* is concerned with the internal regulation of the lives of Indians on Reserves and that the exceptional provisions dealing with the conduct of Indians off Reserves and their contacts with other Canadian citizens fall into an entirely different category. ...

A careful reading of the *Act* discloses that section 95 (formerly 94) is the only provision therein made which creates an offence for any behaviour of an Indian *off* a Reserve and it will be plain that there is a wide difference between legislation such as s. 12(1)(*b*) governing the civil rights of designated persons living on Indian Reserves to the use and benefit of Crown lands, and criminal legislation such as s. 95 which creates an offence punishable at law for Indians to act in a certain fashion when *off* a Reserve. The former legislation is enacted as a part of the plan devised by Parliament, under s. 91(24) for the regulation of the internal domestic life of Indians on Reserves. The latter is criminal legislation exclusively concerned with behaviour of Indians off a Reserve. ...

The *Drybones* case can, in my opinion, have no application to the present appeals as it was in no way concerned with the internal regulation of the lives of Indians *on* Reserves or their right to the use and benefit of Crown lands thereon, but rather deals exclusively with the effect of the *Bill of Rights* on a section of the *Indian Act* creating a crime with attendant penalties for the conduct by Indians *off* a Reserve in an area where non-Indians, who were also governed by federal law, were not subject to any such restriction.

The fundamental distinction between the present case and that of *Drybones*, however, appears to me to be that the impugned section in the latter case could not be enforced without denying equality of treatment in the administration and enforcement of the law before the ordinary courts of the land to a racial group, whereas no such inequality of treatment between Indian men and women flows as a necessary result of the application of s. 12(1)(*b*) of the *Indian Act*.

To summarize the above, I am of opinion:

1. That the *Bill of Rights* is not effective to render inoperative legislation, such as s. 12(1)(*b*) of the *Indian Act*, passed by the Parliament of Canada in discharge of its constitutional function under s. 91(24) of the *B.N.A. Act*, to specify how and by whom Crown lands reserved for Indians are to be used;

2. that the *Bill of Rights* does not require federal legislation to be declared inoperative unless it offends against one of the rights specifically guaranteed by section 1, but where legislation is found to be discriminatory, this affords an added reason for rendering it ineffective;

3. that equality before the law under the *Bill of Rights* means equality of treatment in the enforcement and application of the laws of Canada before the law enforcement authorities and the ordinary courts of the land, and no such inequality is necessarily entailed in the construction and application of s. 12(1)(*b*). ...

ABBOTT J. (dissenting): The facts which are not in dispute are set out in the reasons of Ritchie and Laskin JJ. which I have had the advantage of reading. I am in agreement with the reasons of Laskin J. and wish to add only a few observations.

I share his view that the decision of this Court in *The Queen v. Drybones* [[1970] S.C.R. 282] cannot be distinguished from the two cases under appeal although in these two appeals the consequences of the discrimination by reason of sex under s. 12(1)(*b*) of the *Indian Act* are more serious than the relatively minor penalty for the drinking offence under s. 94 of the *Act* which was in issue in *Drybones*.

In that case, this Court rejected the contention that s. 1 of the *Canadian Bill of Rights* provided merely a canon of construction for the interpretation of legislation existing when the *Bill* was passed. With respect I cannot interpret "equality before the law" as used in s. 1(*b*) of the *Bill* as meaning simply "the equal subjection of all classes to the ordinary law of the land as administered by the ordinary courts" to use the language of Dicey which is quoted in the reasons of Ritchie J.

Unless the words "without discrimination by reason of race, national origin, colour, religion or sex" used in s. 1 are to be treated as mere rhetorical window dressing, effect must be given to them in interpreting the section. I agree with Laskin J. that s. 1(*b*) must be read as if those words were recited therein.

In my view the *Canadian Bill of Rights* has substantially affected the doctrine of the supremacy of Parliament. Like any other statute it can of course be repealed or amended, or a particular law declared to be applicable notwithstanding the provisions of the *Bill.* In form the supremacy of Parliament is maintained but in practice I think that it has been substantially curtailed. In my opinion that result is undesirable, but that is a matter for consideration by Parliament not the courts.

Ritchie J. said in his reasons for judgment in *Drybones* that the implementation of the *Bill of Rights* by the courts can give rise to great difficulties and that statement has been borne out in subsequent litigation. Of one thing I am certain, the *Bill* will continue to supply ample grist to the judicial mills for some time to come. ...

The judgment of Hall, Spence, and Laskin JJ. was delivered by

LASKIN J. (dissenting): ... In my opinion, unless we are to depart from what was said in *Drybones*, both appeals now before us must be dismissed. I have no disposition to reject what was decided in *Drybones*; and on the central issue of prohibited discrimination as catalogued in s. 1 of the *Canadian Bill of Rights*, it is, in my opinion, impossible to distinguish *Drybones* from the two cases in appeal. If, as in *Drybones*, discrimination by reason of race makes certain statutory provisions inoperative, the same result must follow as to statutory provisions which exhibit discrimination by reason of sex. ...

In both cases, which were argued together, leave was given to various bodies and organizations and to a number of individuals to intervene by representation and by submissions to this Court. The position of the Attorney General of Canada in the *Lavell* case was supported by counsel appearing on behalf of The Indian Association of Alberta, The Union of British Columbia Indian Chiefs, The Manitoba Indian Brotherhood Inc., The Union of New Brunswick Indians, The Indian Brotherhood of the Northwest Territories, The Union of Nova Scotia Indians, The Union of Ontario Indians, The Federation of Saskatchewan Indians, The Indian Association of Quebec, The Yukon Native Brotherhood and The National Indian Brotherhood, by counsel appearing on behalf of the Six Nations Band and by counsel appearing on behalf of the Treaty Voice of Alberta Association. The position of the respondent was supported by counsel appearing for the Native Council of Canada, by counsel appearing for Rose Wilhelm, Alberta Committee on Indian Rights for Indian Women Inc., Viola Shannacappo, University Women's Club of Toronto and University Women Graduates Limited, The North Toronto Business and Professional Women's Club Inc. and Monica Agnes Turner, and by counsel for Anishnawbekwek of Ontario Incorporated. There was the same division of support for the appellants and the respondent in the *Bédard* case, in which the Attorney General of Canada also intervened to support the position of the appellants. ...

The contentions of the appellants in both cases in appeal, stripped of their detail, amount to a submission that the *Canadian Bill of Rights* does not apply to Indians on a Reserve, nor to Indians in their relations to one another whether or not on a Reserve. This submission does not deny that the effect of s. 12(1)(*b*) of the *Indian Act* is to prescribe substantive discrimination by reason of sex, a differentiation in the treatment of Indian men and Indian women when they marry non-Indians, this differentiation being exhibited in the loss by the women of their status as Indians under the *Act.* It does, however, involve the assertion that the particular discrimination upon which the two appeals are focused is not offensive to the relevant provisions of the *Canadian Bill of Rights*; and it also involves the assertion that the *Drybones* case is distinguishable or, if not, that it has been overcome by the re-enactment of the *Indian Act* in the Revised Statutes of Canada, 1970, including the then s. 94 (now s. 95) which was in issue in that case. I regard this last-mentioned assertion, which is posited on the fact that the *Canadian Bill of Rights* was not so re-enacted, as simply an oblique appeal for the overruling of the *Drybones* case.

The *Drybones* case decided two things. It decided first— and this decision was a necessary basis for the second point in it—that the *Canadian Bill of Rights* was more than a mere interpretation statute whose terms would yield to a contrary intention; it had paramount force when a federal enactment conflicted with its terms, and it was the incompatible federal enactment which had to give way. This was the issue upon which the then Chief Justice of this Court, Chief Justice Cartwright, and Justices Abbott and Pigeon, dissented. Pigeon J. fortified his view on this main point by additional observations, bringing into consideration, *inter alia*, s. 91(24) of the *British North America Act*. The second thing decided by *Drybones* was that the accused in that case, an Indian under the *Indian Act*, was denied equality before the law, under s. 1(*b*) of the *Canadian Bill of Rights*, when it was made a punishable offence for him, on account of his race, to do something which his fellow Canadians were free to do without being liable to punishment for an offence. Ritchie J., who delivered the majority opinion of the Court, reiterated this basis of decision by concluding his reasons as follows:

> It appears to me to be desirable to make it plain that these reasons for judgment are limited to a situation in which, under the laws of Canada, it is made an offence punishable at law on account of race, for a person to do something which all Canadians who are not members of that race may do with impunity.

It would be unsupportable in principle to view the *Drybones* case as turning on the fact that the challenged s. 94 of the *Indian Act* created an offence visited by punishment. The gist of the judgment lay in the legal disability imposed upon a person by reason of his race when other persons were under no similar restraint. If for the words "on account of race" there are substituted the words "on account of sex" the result must surely be the same where a federal enactment imposes disabilities or prescribes disqualifications for members of the female sex which are not imposed upon members of the male sex in the same circumstances.

It is said, however, that although this may be so as between males and females in general, it does not follow where the distinction on the basis of sex is limited as here to members of the Indian race. This, it is said further, does not offend the guarantee of "equality before the law" upon which the *Drybones* case proceeded. I wish to deal with these two points in turn and to review, in connection with the first point, the legal consequences for an Indian woman under the *Indian Act* when she marries a non-Indian.

It appears to me that the contention that a differentiation on the basis of sex is not offensive to the *Canadian Bill of Rights* where that differentiation operates only among Indians under the *Indian Act* is one that compounds racial inequality even beyond the point that the *Drybones* case found

unacceptable. In any event, taking the *Indian Act* as it stands, as a law of Canada whose various provisions fall to be assessed under the *Canadian Bill of Rights*, I am unable to appreciate upon what basis the command of the *Canadian Bill of Rights*, that laws of Canada shall operate without discrimination by reason of sex, can be ignored in the operation of the *Indian Act*.

The *Indian Act* defines an Indian as a person who is registered as an Indian pursuant to the *Act* or is entitled to be so registered. It is registration or registrability upon a Band list or upon a general list that is the key to the scheme and application of the *Act*. The Registrar, charged with keeping the membership records, is the person to whom protests may be made by a Band Council or by an affected person respecting the inclusion or deletion of a name from the Indian Register. By s. 9(2) his decision on a protest is final subject to a reference to a judge under s. 9(3). The *Lavell* case arose in this way. Section 11 of the *Act* enumerates the persons entitled to be registered, and it is common ground that both Mrs. Lavell and Mrs. Bédard were so entitled prior to their respective marriages. Section 12 lists the classes of persons not entitled to be registered, and the only clause thereof relevant here is subsection 1(*b*) which I have already quoted. Section 14 has a peripheral relevance to the present case in its provision that a woman member of a Band who marries a person outside that Band ceases to be a member thereof but becomes a member of the Band of which her husband is a member. There is no absolute disqualification of an Indian woman from registrability on the Indian Register (that is, as a member on the general list) by marrying outside a Band unless the marriage is to a non-Indian.

Registration or registrability entitles an Indian as a member of a Band (and that was the status of both Mrs. Lavell and Mrs. Bédard prior to their respective marriages) to the use and benefit of the Reserve set aside for the Band. This may take the form of possession or occupation of particular land in the Reserve under an allotment by the Council of the Band with the approval of the responsible Minister, and it may be evidenced by a certificate of possession or a certificate of occupation, the latter representing possession for a limited period only. Indians may make wills disposing of their property, and it may also pass on intestacy, in either case subject to approval or control of the Minister or of a competent court; and in the case of a devise or descent of land in a Reserve the claimant's possession must be approved by the Minister under s. 49. Section 50 has only a remote bearing on the *Bédard* case in providing that a person who is not entitled to reside on a Reserve does not by devise or descent acquire a right to possession or occupation of land in that Reserve. It begs the question in that the issue here is whether or not Mrs. Bédard became disentitled to reside on the land in the Reserve which was left to her by her mother upon the latter's death in 1969. The fact that the respondent's brother now holds a certificate of possession of all the land formerly possessed by the mother, that certificate having been issued after the respondent transferred her interest to her brother in February, 1971, does not affect the overriding question of the respondent's right to reside on the land, having her brother's consent to residence thereon.

Indians entitled to be registered and to live on a Reserve are members of a society in which, through Band Councils, they share in the administration of the Reserve subject to overriding governmental authority. There is provision for election of councillors by Band members residing on a Reserve, and I note that there is no statutory discrimination between Indian men and women either as qualified electors or as qualified candidates for election as councillors. Other advantages that come from membership in the social unit relate to farm operations and to eligibility for governmental loans for various enumerated purposes.

Section 12(1)(*b*) effects a statutory excommunication of Indian women from this society but not of Indian men. Indeed, as was pointed out by counsel for the Native Council of Canada, the effect of ss. 11 and 12(1)(*b*) is to excommunicate the children of a union of an Indian woman with a non-Indian. There is also the invidious distinction, invidious at least in the light of the *Canadian Bill of Rights*, that the *Indian Act* creates between brothers and sisters who are Indians and who respectively marry non-Indians. The statutory banishment directed by s. 12(1)(*b*) is not qualified by the provision in s. 109(2) for a governmental order declaring an Indian woman who has married a non-Indian to be enfranchised. Such an order is not automatic and no such order was made in relation to Mrs. Bédard; but when made the woman affected is, by s. 110, deemed not to be an Indian within the *Indian Act* or any other statute or law. It is, if anything, an additional legal instrument of separation of an Indian woman from her native society and from her kin, a separation to which no Indian man who marries a non-Indian is exposed.

It was urged, in reliance in part on history, that the discrimination embodied in the *Indian Act* under s. 12(1)(*b*) is based upon a reasonable classification of Indians as a race, that the *Indian Act* reflects this classification and that the paramount purpose of the *Act* to preserve and protect the members of the race is promoted by the statutory preference for Indian men. Reference was made in this connection to various judgments of the Supreme Court of the United States to illustrate the adoption by that Court of reasonable classifications to square with the due process clause of the Fifth Amendment and with due process and equal protection under the

Fourteenth Amendment. Those cases have at best a marginal relevance because the *Canadian Bill of Rights* itself enumerates prohibited classifications which the judiciary is bound to respect; and, moreover, I doubt whether discrimination on account of sex, where as here it has no biological or physiological rationale, could be sustained as a reasonable classification even if the direction against it was not as explicit as it is in the *Canadian Bill of Rights*.

I do not think it is possible to leap over the telling words of s. 1, "without discrimination by reason of race, national origin, colour, religion or sex," in order to explain away any such discrimination by invoking the words "equality before the law" in clause (*b*) and attempting to make them alone the touchstone of reasonable classification. That was not done in the *Drybones* case; and this Court made it clear in *Curr v. The Queen*, that federal legislation, which might be compatible with the command of "equality before the law" taken alone, may nonetheless be inoperative if it manifests any of the prohibited forms of discrimination. In short, the proscribed discriminations in s. 1 have a force either independent of the subsequently enumerated clauses (*a*) to (*f*) or, if they are found in any federal legislation, they offend those clauses because each must be read as if the prohibited forms of discrimination were recited therein as a part thereof.

This seems to me an obvious construction of s. 1 of the *Canadian Bill of Rights*. When that provision states that the enumerated human rights and fundamental freedoms shall continue to exist "without discrimination by reason of race, national origin, colour, religion or sex," it is expressly adding these words to clauses (*a*) to (*f*). Section 1(*b*) must read therefore as "the right of the individual to equality before the law and the protection of the law without discrimination by reason of race, national origin, colour, religion or sex." It is worth repeating that this is what emerges from the *Drybones* case and what is found in the *Curr* case.

There is no clear historical basis for the position taken by the appellants, certainly not in relation to Indians in Canada as a whole, and this was in effect conceded during the hearing in this Court. In any event, history cannot avail against the clear words of ss. 1 and 2 of the *Canadian Bill of Rights*. It is s. 2 that gives this enactment its effective voice, because without it s. 1 would remain a purely declaratory provision. Section 2 brings the terms of s. 1 into its orbit, and its reference to "every law of Canada" is a reference, as set out in s. 5(2), to any Act of the Parliament of Canada enacted before or after the effective date of the *Canadian Bill of Rights*. Pre-existing Canadian legislation as well as subsequent Canadian legislation is expressly made subject to the commands of the *Canadian Bill of Rights*, and those commands, where they are as clear as the one which is relevant here, cannot be diluted by appeals to history. Ritchie J. in his reasons in the *Drybones* case touched on this very point when he rejected the contention that the terms of s. 1 of the *Canadian Bill of Rights* must be circumscribed by the provisions of Canadian statutes in force at the date of the enactment of the *Canadian Bill of Rights*: see [1970] S.C.R. 282, at pp. 295-296. I subscribe fully to the rejection of that contention. Clarity here is emphasized by looking at the French version of the *Canadian Bill of Rights* which speaks in s. 1 of the enumerated human rights and fundamental freedoms "*pour tout individu au Canada quels que soient sa race, son origine nationale, sa couleur, sa religion ou son sexe.*"

In my opinion, the appellants' contentions gain no additional force because the *Indian Act*, including the challenged s. 12(1)(*b*) thereof, is a fruit of the exercise of Parliament's exclusive legislative power in relation to "Indians, and Lands reserved for the Indians" under s. 91(24) of the *British North America Act*. Discriminatory treatment on the basis of race or colour or sex does not inhere in that grant of legislative power. The fact that its exercise may be attended by forms of discrimination prohibited by the *Canadian Bill of Rights* is no more a justification for a breach of the *Canadian Bill of Rights* than there would be in the case of the exercise of any other head of federal legislative power involving provisions offensive to the *Canadian Bill of Rights*. The majority opinion in the *Drybones* case dispels any attempt to rely on the grant of legislative power as a ground for escaping from the force of the *Canadian Bill of Rights*. The latter does not differentiate among the various heads of legislative power; it embraces all exercises under whatever head or heads they arise. Section 3 which directs the Minister of Justice to scrutinize every Bill to ascertain whether any of its provisions are inconsistent with ss. 1 and 2 is simply an affirmation of this fact which is evident enough from ss. 1 and 2.

There was an intimation during the argument of these appeals that the *Canadian Bill of Rights* is properly invoked only to resolve a clash under its terms between two federal statutes, and the *Drybones* case was relied on in that connection. It is a spurious contention, if seriously advanced, because the *Canadian Bill of Rights* is itself the indicator to which any Canadian statute or any provision thereof must yield unless Parliament has declared that the statute or the particular provision is to operate notwithstanding the *Canadian Bill of Rights*. A statute may in itself be offensive to the *Canadian Bill of Rights*, or it may be by relation to another statute that it is so offensive.

I would dismiss both appeals with costs.

PIGEON J.: I agree in the result with Ritchie J. I certainly cannot disagree with the view I did express in *The Queen v. Drybones* [at p. 304] that the enactment of the *Canadian Bill of Rights* was not intended to effect a virtual suppression of federal legislation over Indians. My difficulty is Laskin J.'s strongly reasoned opinion that, unless we are to depart from what was said by the majority in *Drybones*, these appeals should be dismissed because, if discrimination by reason of race makes certain statutory provisions inoperative, the same result must follow as to statutory provisions which exhibit discrimination by reason of sex. In the end, it appears to me, that, in the circumstances, I need not reach a firm conclusion on that point. Assuming the situation is such as Laskin J. says, it cannot be improper for me to adhere to what was my dissenting view, when a majority of those who did not agree with it in respect of a particular section of the *Indian Act*, now adopt it for the main body of this important statute.

I would observe that this result does not conflict with any of our decisions subsequent to *Drybones*. In no case was the *Canadian Bill of Rights* given an invalidating effect over prior legislation.

In *Lowry and Lepper v. The Queen* [(1972), 26 D.L.R. (3d) 224] and in *Brownridge v. The Queen* [[1972] S.C.R. 926], the application of criminal legislation, past and subsequent, was held to be subject to provisions respecting a "fair hearing" and "the right to retain and instruct counsel." These decisions are important illustrations of the effectiveness of the *Bill* without any invalidating effect.

In *Smythe v. The Queen* [[1971] S.C.R. 680] it was held that provisions for stiffer penalties depending on the method of prosecution were not rendered inoperative by the *Canadian Bill of Rights* as infringing equality before the law, although the choice of the method of prosecution always depends on executive discretion.

In *Curr v. The Queen* [[1972] S.C.R. 889] recent *Criminal Code* provisions for compulsory breath analysis were held not to infringe the right to the "protection of the law" any more than the right to the "protection against self-crimination."

Finally, in *Duke v. The Queen* [[1972] S.C.R. 917] these same provisions were said not to deprive the accused of a "fair trial" although proclaimed without some paragraphs contemplating a specimen being offered and given on request to the suspect.

B. FUNDAMENTAL FREEDOMS

4   The Queen v. Big M Drug Mart Ltd., 1985

*B*ig *M Drug Mart* was among the first Charter cases to be decided by the Supreme Court. It clearly demonstrates the contrast between the Supreme Court's treatment of the *Charter of Rights and Freedoms* and its treatment two decades earlier of the *Canadian Bill of Rights*. In 1963 in *Robertson and Rosetanni*[1] the court, with only one dissent, found that the federal *Lord's Day Act* did not contravene the right to freedom of religion in the *Canadian Bill of Rights*. Twenty-two years later, in *Big M*, the court struck down the federal *Lord's Day Act* on the ground that it violated the right to freedom of conscience and religion in section 2 of the Charter.

In its initial approach to the *Bill of Rights*, the court had adopted the view that the rights and freedoms in that document must be no wider than what was provided for under Canadian law at the time the Bill was adopted. There was no trace of that "frozen rights" thesis in the court's early treatment of the Charter. The fact that the *Lord's Day Act* had been on the statute book since 1906 had no bearing on whether it violated the Charter's guarantee of religious freedom. In *Robertson and Rosetanni*, the majority considered the effect, not the purpose, of the legislation, and held that because compulsory Sunday closing did not actually force anyone to worship in a Christian manner it did not affect freedom of religion. In *Big M*, for all of the justices except Justice Wilson, analysis of the challenged legislation began with the purpose behind the legislation at the time of its enactment. In the court's view, that purpose in 1906 was clearly religious—to secure the observance by all of the Christian Sabbath. Legislation passed for such a purpose, in the court's view, clearly violated the right to freedom of religion.

The majority and Justice Wilson differed on whether the assessment of challenged legislation should begin with its purpose or effect, while agreeing that if either the purpose or effect of legislation violates the Charter the legislation must be considered unconstitutional. Perhaps the majority's preference for beginning with the purpose of legislation was to avoid, if possible, the extensive examination of the practical consequences of legislation. Justice Wilson was less diffident about the judiciary's capacity for this kind of policy analysis.

Central to the court's "purposive" approach to Charter interpretation was Chief Justice Dickson's inquiry into the meaning of "freedom of religion." The purpose he looks for here is not the stated intent of the Charter's drafters, but the broad historical reasons for this freedom becoming a cherished ideal in western civilization. While this "purposive" approach

---

1   [1963] S.C.R. 651. For a discussion of this case, see case 3.

may yield a fairly generous interpretation of Charter rights and freedoms, the chief justice was careful to point out that it must not be pushed so far as to "overshoot the actual purpose of the right or freedom in question." The chief justice was laying the groundwork for a moderate activism.

The court's decision in *Big M* by no means settled the Sunday-closing issue in Canada. By ruling out a religious or moral rationale for Sunday-closing legislation, it eliminated the criminal law power, the only basis for federal legislation, thereby leaving this controversial policy issue to the provinces. All the provinces had developed more contemporary and secular legislation regulating commercial activities on Sundays. The following year, in *Edwards Books*,[2] the court upheld Ontario's *Retail Business Holiday Act*, which prohibited most retailing on Sundays, but exempted the owners of small businesses whose religion required them to close their stores on Saturdays.

The Supreme Court's decision in *Big M Drug Mart* recognizes that a major transformation has taken place in Canadian society. Canada was no longer to be considered, in any official or legal sense, a Christian society. Chief Justice Dickson's opinion brought into play, for the first time, section 27 of the Charter, directing the courts to interpret the Charter "in a manner consistent with the preservation and enhancement of the multicultural heritage of Canadians." The chief justice cited this section as a further reason for interpreting the right to freedom of religion as excluding laws enacted for the purpose of enforcing the precepts of the Christian religion. Religious pluralism is to be an essential ingredient of the cultural pluralism of the modern Canadian state. ⁓

Discussion Questions

1. Justice Wilson differs with Chief Justice Dickson on the "appropriate analytic approach to a Charter case." What is the disagreement? Does it matter?

2. For Chief Justice Dickson, what is the difference between characterizing the purpose of a statute and the purpose of a Charter provision?

3. In the light of *Big M*, what is the constitutional status of Christmas and Easter holidays?

---

2   [1986] 2 S.C.R. 713.

HER MAJESTY THE QUEEN v.
BIG M DRUG MART LTD.
[1985] 1 S.C.R. 295

Hearing: March 6, 7, 1984; Judgment: April 24, 1985.

Present: Dickson C.J. and Ritchie,* Beetz, McIntyre, Chouinard, Lamer, and Wilson JJ.

Interveners: The Attorney General of Canada, the Attorney General of New Brunswick, and the Attorney General of Saskatchewan.

* Ritchie J. took no part in the judgment.

The judgment of Dickson C.J. and Beetz, McIntyre, Chouinard, and Lamer JJ. was delivered by

[1] **DICKSON C.J.:** Big M Drug Mart Ltd. was charged with unlawfully carrying on the sale of goods, on Sunday, May 30, 1982 in the City of Calgary, Alberta, contrary to the *Lord's Day Act*, R.S.C. 1970, c. L-13.

[2] Big M has challenged the constitutionality of the *Lord's Day Act*, both in terms of the division of powers and the *Canadian Charter of Rights and Freedoms*. Such challenge places in issue before this Court, for the first time, one of the fundamental freedoms protected by the *Charter*, the guarantee of "freedom of conscience and religion" entrenched in s. 2.

[3] The constitutional validity of Sunday observance legislation has in the past been tested largely through the division of powers provided in ss. 91 and 92 of the *Constitution Act, 1867*. Freedom of religion has been seen to be a matter falling within federal legislative competence. Today, following the advent of the *Constitution Act, 1982*, we must address squarely the fundamental issues raised by individual rights and freedoms enshrined in the *Charter*, as well as those concerned with legislative powers. ...

V. The Characterization of the Lord's Day Act

... [48] There are obviously two possible ways to characterize the purpose of Lord's Day legislation, the one religious, namely securing public observance of the Christian institution of the Sabbath and the other secular, namely providing a uniform day of rest from labour. It is undoubtedly true that both elements may be present in any given enactment, indeed it is almost inevitable that they will be, considering that such laws combine a prohibition of ordinary employment for one day out of seven with a specification that this day of rest shall be the Christian Sabbath—Sunday. In the Anglo-Canadian tradition this intertwining is to be seen as far back as early Saxon times in such laws as that promulgated by Ine, King of Wessex from 688–725. ...

[51] Historically, there seems little doubt that it was religious purpose which underlay the enactment of English Lord's Day legislation. From early times the moral exhortation found in the Fourth Commandment (Exodus 20: 8-11) "Remember the Sabbath day, to keep it holy" increasingly became a legislative imperative. The first major piece of legislation, *The Sunday Fairs Act*, 27 Hen. 6, c. 5, prefaced its prohibition of fairs and markets on Sunday with a recital of "abomenable injuries and offences done to Almighty God and to his Saints" because of bodily labour, deceitful bargaining, drunkenness and religious non-observance associated with fairs. Following the Reformation under Henry VIII, religious observance acquired an added political significance and a number of statutes aimed at securing religious conformity were promulgated. ...

[52] Under Charles I the first modern Sunday observance statutes were enacted and their religious purpose is reflected in their titles, *An Act for punishing divers Abuses committed on the Lord's Day, called Sunday*, 1 Car. 1, c. 1 and *An Act for the further Reformation of sundry Abuses committed on the Lord's Day, commonly called Sunday*, 3 Car. 1, c. 2. During the Commonwealth or Interregnum period, the Puritan Parliament passed strict laws prohibiting the profanation of the Lord's Day by any form of marketing, travel, worldly labour, sports or recourse to taverns, tobacco shops or restaurants. With the Restoration came *An Act for the better Observation of the Lord's Day commonly called Sunday*, 29 Car. 2, c. 7, also known as the *Sunday Observance Act*. As its full title indicates, the primary object of this legislation, like that of its predecessors, was clearly religious rather than secular. ...

[53] The *Sunday Observance Act* of 1677 served as a model for Canadian pre-Confederation legislation, especially *An Act to prevent the Profanation of the Lord's Day, commonly called Sunday, in Upper Canada*, 1845 (Can.), c. 45, which substantially re-enacted the English law with only minor alterations designed to suit it to the specific conditions and activities of Upper Canada. It was this statute, as re-enacted by the post-Confederation legislature of Ontario (R.S.O. 1897, c. 246), that the Privy Council found to be beyond the competence of the province to enact in *Attorney-General for Ontario v. Hamilton Street Railway Co.*, [1903] A.C. 524, a decision which lay behind the passage in 1906 of the federal *Lord's Day Act*. Like the Ontario *Act*, the federal *Act* embodied the basic framework and much of the language of the English *Sunday Observance Act* of 1677. After four consolidations, it still exhibits these same essential characteristics in its present form. ...

[54] From the time of Confederation until the Privy Council decision in 1903 in *Hamilton Street Railway, supra*, it was the widely-held view that Sunday observance legislation fell within provincial purview under the *Constitution Act, 1867* as being a matter falling under either s. 92(13), property and civil rights within the province, or s. 92(16), a matter of merely local or private nature in the Province. Several of the provinces passed laws prohibiting Sunday activities. In the *Hamilton Street Railway* case the Ontario statute fell to be considered. Aylesworth K.C. argued before the Privy Council that the primary object of the *Act* under consideration was the promotion of public order, safety and morals, and not the regulation of civil rights as between subject and subject. That view would seem to have prevailed, as their Lordships held that the *Act* as a whole was beyond the competence of the Ontario Legislature to enact. ...

[55] ... The Parliament of Canada passed the federal *Lord's Day Act*, 1906 (Can.), c. 27, with what would appear to have been some degree of reluctance because, firstly, s. 14 provided that nothing in the *Act* should be construed to repeal or in any way affect "any provisions of any Act or law relating in any way to the observance of the Lord's Day in force in any province of Canada when this *Act* comes into force." Sunday observance legislation in force in a province at the time it entered Confederation was expressly preserved. Secondly, while the *Act* prohibited a very few activities unconditionally, such as shooting in such a manner as to disturb public worship or observance of the day, or selling foreign newspapers, the most important sections of the *Act* made other activities

unlawful only to the extent that provincial legislation did not provide otherwise.

[56] Acting under the authority of the federal *Lord's Day Act*, the provinces have enacted legislation such as the *Lord's Day (Ontario) Act*, R.S.O. 1980, c. 253, and *The Lord's Day (Saskatchewan) Act*, R.S.S. 1978, c. L-34. Provincial legislation of this nature was upheld by the Judicial Committee of the Privy Council in *Lord's Day Alliance of Canada v. Attorney-General for Manitoba*, [1925] A.C. 384, and more recently by this Court in *Lord's Day Alliance of Canada v. Attorney General of British Columbia*, [1959] S.C.R. 497. ...

[65] We come now to the case of *Robertson and Rosetanni* [(1963) S.C.R. 651], *supra*, to which much attention was directed during argument. The appellants were convicted on a charge of operating a bowling alley on a Sunday, contrary to the *Lord's Day Act*. They contended that the *Canadian Bill of Rights*, R.S.C. 1970, App. III, had in effect repealed s. 4 of the *Lord's Day Act* or, in any event, rendered it inoperative. The Court, Cartwright J. dissenting, rejected the contention and dismissed the appeal. ...

[73] The United States Supreme Court has sustained the constitutionality of Sunday observance legislation against First Amendment challenges: *McGowan v. Maryland*, 366 U.S. 420 (1961); *Braunfeld v. Brown*, 366 U.S. 599 (1961), *Gallagher v. Crown Kosher Super Market of Massachusetts, Inc.*, 366 U.S. 617 (1961), and *Two Guys from Harrison-Allentown, Inc. v. McGinley*, 366 U.S. 582 (1961). Despite the undoubted religious motivation of the state laws in question at the time of their passage and their clear origin in the religiously coercive statutes of Stuart England, Chief Justice Warren, writing for the majority, found that those statutes had evolved to become purely secular labour regulation. In his view, none of the impugned state statutes violated the First Amendment guarantee of freedom of religion. Whatever religious terminology still appeared in the legislation (such as the use of the term "Lord's Day" in the Maryland statute) was to be seen simply as a historical curiosity. ...

[77] It is somewhat ironic that the United States courts upheld the validity of Sunday observance laws, characterizing them as secular in order not to run afoul of the religion clauses of the First Amendment, while in contrast, in *Robertson v. Rosetanni*, *supra*, the Court found in the same type of legislation, a religious purpose in order to sustain its *vires* as criminal law. At the same time it accorded to the legislation a secular effect in order not to bring it into conflict with the religious freedom recognized and declared in the *Canadian Bill of Rights*. ...

VI. Purpose and Effect of Legislation

[78] A finding that the *Lord's Day Act* has a secular purpose is, on the authorities, simply not possible. Its religious purpose, in compelling sabbatical observance, has been long-established and consistently maintained by the courts of this country.

[79] The Attorney General for Alberta concedes that the *Act* is characterized by this religious purpose. He contends, however, that it is not the purpose but the effects of the *Act* which are relevant. In his submission, *Robertson and Rosetanni*, *supra*, is support for the proposition that it is effects alone which must be assessed in determining whether legislation violates a constitutional guarantee of freedom of religion.

[80] I cannot agree. In my view, both purpose and effect are relevant in determining constitutionality; either an unconstitutional purpose or an unconstitutional effect can invalidate legislation. All legislation is animated by an object the legislature intends to achieve. This object is realized through the impact produced by the operation and application of the legislation. Purpose and effect respectively, in the sense of the legislation's object and its ultimate impact, are clearly linked, if not indivisible. Intended and actual effects have often been looked to for guidance in assessing the legislation's object and thus, its validity.

[81] Moreover, consideration of the object of legislation is vital if rights are to be fully protected. The assessment by the courts of legislative purpose focuses scrutiny upon the aims and objectives of the legislature and ensures they are consonant with the guarantees enshrined in the *Charter*. The declaration that certain objects lie outside the legislature's power checks governmental action at the first stage of unconstitutional conduct. Further, it will provide more ready and more vigorous protection of constitutional rights by obviating the individual litigant's need to prove effects violative of *Charter* rights. It will also allow courts to dispose of cases where the object is clearly improper, without inquiring into the legislation's actual impact. ...

[88] In short, I agree with the respondent that the legislation's purpose is the initial test of constitutional validity and its effects are to be considered when the law under review has passed or, at least, has purportedly passed the purpose test. If the legislation fails the purpose test, there is no need to consider further its effects, since it has already been demonstrated to be invalid. Thus, if a law with a valid purpose interferes by its impact, with rights or freedoms, a litigant could still argue the effects of the legislation as a means to defeat its applicability and possibly its validity. In short, the effects test will only be necessary to defeat legislation with a valid purpose; effects can never be relied upon to save legislation with an invalid purpose.

[89] A second related submission is made by the Attorney General of Saskatchewan with respect to the characterization of the *Lord's Day Act*. Both Stevenson, Prov. Ct. J., at trial, and

the American Supreme Court, in its quartet on Sunday observance legislation, suggest that the purpose of legislation may shift, or be transformed over time by changing social conditions. ... A number of objections can be advanced to this "shifting purpose" argument.

[90] First, there are the practical difficulties. No legislation would be safe from a revised judicial assessment of purpose. Laws assumed valid on the basis of persuasive and powerful authority could, at any time, be struck down as invalid. Not only would this create uncertainty in the law, but it would encourage re-litigation of the same issues and, it could be argued, provide the courts with a means by which to arrive at a result dictated by other than legal considerations. ...

[91] Furthermore, the theory of a shifting purpose stands in stark contrast to fundamental notions developed in our law concerning the nature of "Parliamentary intention." Purpose is a function of the intent of those who drafted and enacted the legislation at the time, and not of any shifting variable. ...

[93] While the effect of such legislation as the *Lord's Day Act* may be more secular today than it was in 1677 or in 1906, such a finding cannot justify a conclusion that its purpose has similarly changed. In result, therefore, the *Lord's Day Act* must be characterized as it has always been, a law the primary purpose of which is the compulsion of sabbatical observance.

VII. Freedom of Religion

[94] A truly free society is one which can accommodate a wide variety of beliefs, diversity of tastes and pursuits, customs and codes of conduct. A free society is one which aims at equality with respect to the enjoyment of fundamental freedoms and I say this without any reliance upon s. 15 of the *Charter*. Freedom must surely be founded in respect for the inherent dignity and the inviolable rights of the human person. The essence of the concept of freedom of religion is the right to entertain such religious beliefs as a person chooses, the right to declare religious beliefs openly and without fear of hindrance or reprisal, and the right to manifest religious belief by worship and practice or by teaching and dissemination. But the concept means more than that.

[95] Freedom can primarily be characterized by the absence of coercion or constraint. If a person is compelled by the state or the will of another to a course of action or inaction which he would not otherwise have chosen, he is not acting of his own volition and he cannot be said to be truly free. One of the major purposes of the *Charter* is to protect, within reason, from compulsion or restraint. Coercion includes not only such blatant forms of compulsion as direct commands to act or refrain from acting on pain of sanction, coercion includes indirect forms of control which determine or limit alternative courses of conduct available to others. Freedom in

a broad sense embraces both the absence of coercion and constraint, and the right to manifest beliefs and practices. Freedom means that, subject to such limitations as are necessary to protect public safety, order, health, or morals or the fundamental rights and freedoms of others, no one is to be forced to act in a way contrary to his beliefs or his conscience.

[96] What may appear good and true to a majoritarian religious group, or to the state acting at their behest, may not, for religious reasons, be imposed upon citizens who take a contrary view. The *Charter* safeguards religious minorities from the threat of "the tyranny of the majority."

[97] To the extent that it binds all to a sectarian Christian ideal, the *Lord's Day Act* works a form of coercion inimical to the spirit of the *Charter* and the dignity of all non-Christians. In proclaiming the standards of the Christian faith, the *Act* creates a climate hostile to, and gives the appearance of discrimination against, non-Christian Canadians. It takes religious values rooted in Christian morality and, using the force of the state, translates them into a positive law binding on believers and non-believers alike. The theological content of the legislation remains as a subtle and constant reminder to religious minorities within the country of their differences with, and alienation from, the dominant religious culture.

[98] Non-Christians are prohibited for religious reasons from carrying out activities which are otherwise lawful, moral and normal. The arm of the state requires all to remember the Lord's day of the Christians and to keep it holy. The protection of one religion and the concomitant non-protection of others imports disparate impact destructive of the religious freedom of the collectivity.

[99] I agree with the submission of the respondent that to accept that Parliament retains the right to compel universal observance of the day of rest preferred by one religion is not consistent with the preservation and enhancement of the multicultural heritage of Canadians. To do so is contrary to the expressed provisions of s. 27. ...

[100] If I am a Jew or a Sabbatarian or a Muslim, the practice of my religion at least implies my right to work on a Sunday if I wish. It seems to me that any law purely religious in purpose, which denies me that right, must surely infringe my religious freedom. ...

[103] Much of the argument before this Court on the issue of the meaning of freedom of conscience and religion was in terms of "free exercise" and "establishment." These categories derive from the guarantee of freedom of religion in the First Amendment to the Constitution of the United States. The relevant part of the First Amendment reads:

> Congress shall make no law respecting an establishment of religion, or prohibiting the free exercise thereof; ...

[104] It is the appellant's argument that unlike the American *Bill of Rights*, the *Canadian Charter of Rights and Freedoms* does not include an "establishment clause." He urged therefore that the protection of freedom of conscience and religion extends only to the "free exercise" of religion. ...

[105] In my view this recourse to categories from the American jurisprudence is not particulary helpful in defining the meaning of freedom of conscience and religion under the *Charter*. The adoption in the United States of the categories "establishment" and "free exercise" is perhaps an inevitable consequence of the wording of the First Amendment. The cases illustrate, however, that these are not two totally separate and distinct categories, but rather, as the Supreme Court of the United States has frequently recognized, in specific instances "the two clauses may overlap." ...

[106] Thus while it is true that in its four Sunday closing cases the United States Supreme Court does categorize compulsory religious observance as a potential violation of the "anti-establishment" principle, more frequently and more typically these same words signify the very different principle of the prohibition of preferential treatment of, or state financial support to, particular religions or religious institutions.

[107] In further support for this line of argument the appellant cites s. 29 of the *Charter* quoted earlier, and s. 93 of the *Constitution Act, 1867*. These provisions were cited as proof of the non-existence of an anti-establishment principle because they guarantee existing rights to financial support from the state for denominational schools. The respondent replies that these express provisions constitute specific and limited exceptions to the general principle of religious freedom which would otherwise prohibit any support or preference to denominational schools. Subsequent cases will decide the extent to which the *Charter* allows for state financial support for, or preferential treatment of, particular religions or religious institutions. That issue is not before us in the present case. ...

[115] It is not necessary to reopen the issue of the meaning of freedom of religion under the *Canadian Bill of Rights*, because whatever the situation under that document, it is certain that the *Canadian Charter of Rights and Freedoms* does not simply "recognize and declare" existing rights as they were circumscribed by legislation current at the time of the *Charter's* entrenchment. The language of the *Charter* is imperative. It avoids any reference to existing or continuing rights but rather proclaims in the ringing terms of s. 2 that:

> Everyone has the following fundamental freedoms:
> (*a*) Freedom of conscience and religion.

I agree with the submission of the respondent that the *Charter* is intended to set a standard upon which *present as well as future* legislation is to be tested. ...

[116] This Court has already, in some measure, set out the basic approach to be taken in interpreting the *Charter*. In *Hunter v. Southam Inc.*, [1984] 2 S.C.R. 145, this Court expressed the view that the proper approach to the definition of the rights and freedoms guaranteed by the *Charter* was a purposive one. The meaning of a right or freedom guaranteed by the *Charter* was to be ascertained by an analysis of the *purpose* of such a guarantee; it was to be understood, in other words, in the light of the interests it was meant to protect.

[117] In my view this analysis is to be undertaken, and the purpose of the right or freedom in question is to be sought by reference to the character and the larger objects of the *Charter* itself, to the language chosen to articulate the specific right or freedom, to the historical origins of the concepts enshrined, and where applicable, to the meaning and purpose of the other specific rights and freedoms with which it is associated within the text of the *Charter*. The interpretation should be, as the judgment in *Southam* emphasizes, a generous rather than a legalistic one, aimed at fulfilling the purpose of the guarantee and securing for individuals the full benefit of the *Charter's* protection. At the same time it is important not to overshoot the actual purpose of the right or freedom in question, but to recall that the *Charter* was not enacted in a vacuum, and must therefore, as this Court's decision in *Law Society of Upper Canada v. Skapinker*, [1984] 1 S.C.R. 357, illustrates, be placed in its proper linguistic, philosophic and historical contexts.

[118] With regard to freedom of conscience and religion, the historical context is clear. As they are relevant to the *Charter*, the origins of the demand for such freedom are to be found in the religious struggles in post-Reformation Europe. The spread of new beliefs, the changing religious allegiance of kings and princes, the shifting military fortunes of their armies and the consequent repeated redrawing of national and imperial frontiers led to situations in which large numbers of people—sometimes even the majority in a given territory—found themselves living under rulers who professed faiths different from, and often hostile to, their own and subject to laws aimed at enforcing conformity to religious beliefs and practices they did not share.

[119] English examples of such laws, passed during the Tudor and Stuart periods have been alluded to in the discussion above of the criminal law character of Sunday observance legislation. Opposition to such laws was confined at first to those who upheld the prohibited faiths and practices, and was designed primarily to avoid the disabilities and penalties to which these specific adherents were subject. As a consequence, when history or geography put power into the hands of these erstwhile victims of religious oppression the persecuted all too often became the persecutors.

[120] Beginning, however, with the Independent faction within the Parliamentary party during the Commonwealth or Interregnum, many, even among those who shared the basic beliefs of the ascendent religion, came to voice opposition to the use of the State's coercive power to secure obedience to religious precepts and to extirpate non-conforming beliefs. The basis of this opposition was no longer simply a conviction that the State was enforcing the wrong set of beliefs and practices but rather the perception that belief itself was not amenable to compulsion. Attempts to compel belief or practice denied the reality of individual conscience and dishonoured the God that had planted it in His creatures. It is from these antecedents that the concepts of freedom of religion and freedom of conscience became associated, to form, as they do in s. 2(*a*) of our *Charter*, the single integrated concept of "freedom of conscience and religion."

[121] What unites enunciated freedoms in the American First Amendment, s. 2(*a*) of the *Charter* and in the provisions of other human rights documents in which they are associated is the notion of the centrality of individual conscience and the inappropriateness of governmental intervention to compel or to constrain its manifestation. In *Hunter v. Southam Inc., supra,* the purpose of the *Charter* was identified, at p. 155, as "the unremitting protection of individual rights and liberties." It is easy to see the relationship between respect for individual conscience and the valuation of human dignity that motivates such unremitting protection.

[122] It should also be noted, however, that an emphasis on individual conscience and individual judgment also lies at the heart of our democratic political tradition. The ability of each citizen to make free and informed decisions is the absolute prerequisite for the legitimacy, acceptability, and efficacy of our system of self-government. It is because of the centrality of the rights associated with freedom of individual conscience both to basic beliefs about human worth and dignity and to a free and democractic political system that American jurisprudence has emphasized the primacy or "firstness" of the First Amendment. It is this same centrality that in my view underlies their designation in the *Canadian Charter of Rights and Freedoms* as "fundamental." They are the *sine qua non* of the political tradition underlying the *Charter*.

[123] Viewed in this context, the purpose of freedom of conscience and religion becomes clear. The values that underlie our political and philosophic traditions demand that every individual be free to hold and to manifest whatever beliefs and opinions his or her conscience dictates, provided *inter alia* only that such manifestations do not injure his or her neighbours or their parallel rights to hold and manifest beliefs and opinions of their own. Religious belief and practice are historically prototypical and, in many ways, paradigmatic of conscientiously-held beliefs and manifestations and are therefore protected by the *Charter*. Equally protected, and for the same reasons, are expressions and manifestations of religious non-belief and refusals to participate in religious practice. It may perhaps be that freedom of conscience and religion extends beyond these principles to prohibit other sorts of governmental involvement in matters having to do with religion. For the present case it is sufficient in my opinion to say that whatever else freedom of conscience and religion may mean, it must at the very least mean this: government may not coerce individuals to affirm a specific religious belief or to manifest a specific religious practice for a sectarian purpose. ...

[133] In my view, the guarantee of freedom of conscience and religion prevents the government from compelling individuals to perform or abstain from performing otherwise harmless acts because of the religious significance of those acts to others. The element of religious compulsion is perhaps somewhat more difficult to perceive (especially for those whose beliefs are being enforced) when, as here, it is non-action rather than action that is being decreed, but in my view compulsion is nevertheless what it amounts to.

[134] I would like to stress that nothing in these reasons should be read as suggesting any opposition to Sunday being spent as a religious day; quite the contrary. It is recognized that for a great number of Canadians, Sunday is the day when their souls rest in God, when the spiritual takes priority over the material, a day which, to them, gives security and meaning because it is linked to Creation and the Creator. It is a day which brings a balanced perspective to life, an opportunity for man to be in communion with man and with God. In my view, however, as I read the *Charter*, it mandates that the legislative preservation of a Sunday day of rest should be secular, the diversity of belief and non-belief, the diverse socio-cultural backgrounds of Canadians make it constitutionally incompetent for the federal Parliament to provide legislative preference for any one religion at the expense of those of another religious persuasion.

[135] In an earlier time, when people believed in the collective responsibility of the community toward some deity, the enforcement of religious conformity may have been a legitimate object of government, but since the *Charter*, it is no longer legitimate. With the *Charter*, it has become the right of every Canadian to work out for himself or herself what his or her religious obligations, if any, should be and it is not for the state to dictate otherwise. The state shall not use the criminal sanctions at its disposal to achieve a religious purpose, namely, the uniform observance of the day chosen by the Christian religion as its day of rest.

[136] On the authorities and for the reasons outlined, the true purpose of the *Lord's Day Act* is to compel the observance

of the Christian Sabbath and I find the *Act*, and especially s. 4 thereof, infringes upon the freedom conscience and religion guaranteed in s. 2(*a*) of the *Charter*. ...

VIII. Section 1 of the Charter

... [138] The appellant submits that even if the *Lord's Day Act* does involve a violation of freedom of conscience and religion as guaranteed by s. 2(*a*) of the *Charter*, the provisions of the *Act* constitute a reasonable limit, demonstrably justifiable in a free and democratic society on that right and that therefore the *Act* can be saved pursuant to s. 1 of the *Charter*. ...

[140] Two reasons have been advanced to justify the legislation here in issue as a reasonable limit. It can be urged that the choice of the day of rest adhered to by the Christian majority is the most practical. This submission is really no more than an argument of convenience and expediency and is fundamentally repugnant because it would justify the law upon the very basis upon which it is attacked for violating s. 2(*a*).

[141] The other more plausible argument is that everyone accepts the need and value of a universal day of rest from all work, business and labour and it may as well be the day traditionally observed in our society. I accept the secular justification for a day of rest in a Canadian context and the reasonableness of a day of rest has been clearly enunciated by the courts in the United States of America. The first and fatal difficulty with this argument is, as I have said, that it asserts an objective which has never been found by this Court to be the motivation for the legislation. It seems disingenuous to say that the legislation is valid criminal law and offends s. 2(*a*) because it compels the observance of a Christian religious duty, yet is still a reasonable limit demonstrably justifiable because it achieves the secular objective the legislators did not primarily intend. The appellant can no more assert under s. 1 a secular objective to validate legislation which in pith and substance involves a religious matter than it could assert a secular objective as the basis for the argument that the legislation does not offend s. 2(*a*). While there is no authority on this point, it seems clear that Parliament cannot rely upon an *ultra vires* purpose under s. 1 of the *Charter*. This use of s. 1 would invite colourability, allowing Parliament to do indirectly what it could not do directly. ...

IX. Classification

[144] The third question put in issue by this Court is this:

Is the *Lord's Day Act*, R.S.C. 1970, c. L-13, and especially s. 4 thereof enacted pursuant to the criminal law power under s. 91(27) of the *Constitution Act, 1867*?

[145] All members of the Alberta Court of Appeal agreed that settled authority compelled the conclusion that the *Lord's*

Day Act was competent to Parliament pursuant to its power to legislate in relation to criminal law under s. 91(27). The appellant and his supporting interveners submit that the Court of Appeal was correct in their conclusion and the respondent concedes the point. ...

[149] It should be noted, however, that this conclusion as to the federal Parliament's legislative competence to enact the *Lord's Day Act* depends on the identification of the purpose of the *Act* as compelling observance of Sunday by virtue of its religious significance. Were its purpose not religious but rather the secular goal of enforcing a uniform day of rest from labour, the *Act* would come under s. 92(13), property and civil rights in the province and, hence, fall under provincial rather than federal competence. ...

WILSON J.: ...

[153] In his reasons for judgment Dickson J. (Chief Justice at the date of the judgment) has canvassed in a most thorough fashion all the substantive questions entailed in the analysis of constitutionality and has come to the conclusion that the *Lord's Day Act* is validly enacted pursuant to the federal criminal law power under s. 91(27) of the *Constitution Act, 1867*. He has concluded, however, that it infringes upon the right to freedom of religion in s. 2(*a*) of the *Charter* and that such infringement cannot be justified under s. 1 of the *Charter*. I agree with those conclusions and the only issue I wish to address in these reasons is the appropriate analytic approach to a *Charter* case, in a word, the distinction between the analysis demanded by the *Charter* and the analysis traditionally pursued in resolving division of powers litigation under ss. 91 and 92 of the *Constitution Act, 1867*.

[154] It is, of course, trite law that the analytic starting point in a division of powers case is the determination of the "pith and substance" of the challenged enactment. In the words of Professor Bora Laskin (as he then was) the court endeavours to achieve a "distillation of the 'constitutional value' represented by the challenged legislation ... and its attribution to a head of power." ...

[156] The division of powers jurisprudence is repleat with instances where the analytic focal point in determining whether a given piece of legislation is *ultra vires* the enacting legislature is the purpose or primary function of the legislation. Only when the effects of the legislation so directly impinge on some other subject matter as to reflect some alternative or ulterior purpose do the effects themselves take on analytic significance. ...

[158] In my view, the constitutional entrenchment of civil liberties in the *Canadian Charter of Rights and Freedoms* necessarily changes the analytic approach the courts must adopt in such cases. As Chief Justice Burger indicated in the

celebrated anti-discrimination case of *Griggs v. Duke Power Co.*, 401 U.S. 424 (1970), at p. 432, the starting point for any analysis of a civil rights violation is "the *consequences* of [discriminatory] employment practices, not simply the motivation." Speaking in the context of equality rights as they pertain to employment, Burger C.J. stated at p. 432:

> ... good intent or absence of discriminatory intent does not redeem employment procedures or testing mechanisms that operate as "built-in headwinds" for minority groups. ...

While it remains perfectly valid to evaluate the purpose underlying a particular enactment in order to determine whether the legislature has acted within its constitutional authority in division of powers terms, the *Charter* demands an evaluation of the impingement of even *intra vires* legislation on the fundamental rights and freedoms of the individual. It asks not whether the legislature has acted for a purpose that is within the scope of the authority of that tier of government, but rather whether in so acting it has had the effect of violating an entrenched individual right. It is, in other words, first and foremost an effects-oriented document. ...

[161] Applying such reasoning to the case at bar, one can agree with Dickson J. at p. 337, that in enacting the *Lord's Day Act* "[t]he arm of the state requires all to remember the Lord's day of the Christians and to keep it holy," and that "[t]he protection of one religion and the concomitant non-protection of others imports disparate impact destructive of the religious freedom of the collectivity." Accordingly, the *Act* infringes upon the freedom of conscience and religion guaranteed in s. 2(*a*) of the *Charter*. This is not, however, because the statute was enacted for this *purpose* but because it has this *effect*. In my view, so long as a statute has such an actual or potential effect on an entrenched right, it does not matter what the purpose behind the enactment was. ...

[164] Accordingly, I agree with Dickson J. that the appeal in this case must be dismissed. The *Lord's Day Act* is in pith and substance legislation with a criminal law purpose and is therefore enacted by Parliament pursuant to the federal criminal law power in s. 91(27) of the *Constitution Act, 1867*. In so far as the *Charter of Rights* is concerned, however, I believe that the appropriate analytic starting point is the effect rather than the purpose of the enactment. ...

5 Ford v. Quebec (Attorney General), 1988

The decision that the Supreme Court of Canada rendered on December 15, 1988 striking down Quebec's French-only sign law is one of the court's most important Charter decisions. The decision moved constitutional jurisprudence in two different directions simultaneously: while it embraced a wide interpretation of "freedom of expression" as a constitutional right, it also established a broad basis for legislatures to use the power they have under section 33 of the Charter to override constitutional rights and freedoms. In addition to these important developments in the interpretation of the Charter, the decision had a major impact on constitutional politics in Canada.

This was by no means the first Supreme Court decision overturning sections of Bill 101, the *Charter of the French Language*, introduced by the Parti Québécois (PC) government in 1977. In 1979, the court struck down provisions of Bill 101 making French the official language of the province's legislature and courts. Another decision in 1984 forced Quebec to open its English schools to Canadians moving to Quebec from other provinces.[1] Both decisions were based on entrenched constitutional language rights to which the legislative override in the Charter did not apply. But the attack on sections of Bill 101 making French the exclusive language for commercial signs and firm names was based not on specific language rights but on the right to freedom of expression—a right found in section 2(*b*) of the *Canadian Charter* (a section to which the override does apply) as well as in Quebec's *Charter of Human Rights and Freedoms.*

In June 1982, just two months after the Charter was proclaimed, Quebec's National Assembly, in a defiant gesture against the constitutional settlement of 1982 to which Quebec had not consented, passed a law re-enacting all laws passed prior to the Charter, but adding to each a section invoking the override.[2] After five years, in 1987, this omnibus use of the override lapsed and was not renewed. However, Quebec had used the override a second time: in February 1984, a law came into force applying the override just to the French-only sign provision of Bill 101. This override, if valid, was still in force when the Supreme Court was deciding the sign case. But the section of Bill 101 requiring French-only firm names had not been protected from judicial review by the override clause. Also, the Quebec *Charter of Human Rights* contained a right to freedom of expression, and it had not been overridden. Thus, whether or not an override was still in force, the Supreme Court had to consider the compatibility of French-only commercial regulations with the right to freedom of expression.

---

1 These cases are discussed in the introduction to case 31.

2 For a discussion of the "notwithstanding clause," or "override," as it is often called, see the Introduction to this book.

In the 1985 election campaign in which the Liberals, led by Robert Bourassa, threw the PQ out of office, the Liberals indicated that they would lift restrictions on the use of bilingual commercial signs. This promise was important in attracting some outstanding representatives of Quebec's English-speaking minority to the Liberal team. On the other hand, it threatened to alienate many Quebec Francophones who regarded the French-only sign policy as essential for ensuring that the public face of Quebec would be French.

After the election, Premier Bourassa decided not to act on this controversial issue until the constitutional litigation under way had run its course. A number of firms had challenged provisions of Bill 101 requiring French-only commercial signs and firm names.[3] A challenge had also been brought by Alan Singer, the owner of a stationery shop in an English-speaking district of Montreal, against provisions of Bill 101 that, for some commercial activities—for instance, the publication of catalogues and the signs of firms employing less than four persons or specializing in foreign products—required the use of French, but also permitted the use of another language.[4] Like other politicians, Bourassa hoped that the court might take a deeply divisive issue off his hands.

The litigation may have given the premier a temporary reprieve, but when the court's decision finally came down it did not make his political burden any lighter. On the contrary, the Supreme Court's finding that laws prohibiting the use of any language other than French violated the right to freedom of expression in both the Canadian Charter and the Quebec Charter deepened the resentment of the English-speaking community. The right to advertise in the language of one's choice could now be referred to as "a fundamental right." On the other hand, the court's argument that a French-only policy was not necessary to preserve the French face of Quebec failed to make much impression on the Francophone majority.

The court took a remarkably liberal approach to the concept of "freedom of expression." It built into this freedom a new, universal language right—a right to communicate in one's own language, a right, it argued, that is essential to personal identity. The court rejected arguments that commercial speech should be excluded from freedom of expression. It recognized that when consumer-protection regulations of advertising are under review consideration would have to be given to competing policy interests. But the court took the position that this kind of balancing was to be done not by narrowly defining freedom of expression but by considering the justification for limits on the right under section 1 of the Charter. Applying section 1 to the cases at hand, the court felt that the objective of maintaining the predominantly French character of Quebec could justify requiring the use of French on a joint-use basis and even a law requiring the "marked predominance" of the French language. However, it saw no evidence justifying the exclusive use of French. Hence it struck down the French-only provisions attacked in *Ford*, but upheld bilingual requirements attacked by Singer.

While the court's expansive interpretation of freedom of expression expanded the basis for judicial review, the court in *Ford* made it easier for legislatures to use section 33 of the

---

3 Only one of the five businesses raising the challenge—Valerie Ford's wool shop—was not incorporated. Her name appears to have been used for the citation in this case because equality rights arguments were also made in the case and the Supreme Court had not yet decided whether equality rights extend to corporations.

4 The citation for the Supreme Court decision in this case is *Devine v. Quebec (Attorney General)*, [1988] 2 S.C.R. 790.

Charter, the override clause, to immunize their laws from judicial review. Quebec's Court of Appeal had found Quebec's broad-brush use of the override to be unconstitutional, insisting that to fulfill its democratic purpose the override must be used in an accountable way with the legislature indicating precisely which rights and freedoms it was overriding. But here in *Ford* the Supreme Court rejected this argument: it would come too close to requiring "a *prima facie* justification of the decision to exercise the override." The Supreme Court made it clear that it wished to minimize judicial review of the use of the override.

And use the override is exactly what Premier Bourassa did in response to the court's decision. After agonizing for 48 hours, Bourassa announced his decision to bring in legislation permitting bilingual signs indoors but requiring French-only signs outside. To fend off a court challenge, the override clause was applied to this legislation. The new law, Bill 178, cost Bourassa the services of three of his Anglophone ministers and aroused the ire of English-speaking Quebecers. From the other side it was attacked by the opposition PQ party and by many Quebec Francophones who resented compromising the French-only program of Bill 101.

In the arena of constitutional politics Bourassa's action was a bombshell. By December 1988, there remained only two provinces, Manitoba and New Brunswick, whose legislatures had not approved the Meech Lake package of constitutional amendments. On the day after the Supreme Court decision, the premier of Manitoba, Gary Filmon, introduced the Meech Lake Accord in the Manitoba legislature. But a few days later, following Premier Bourassa's decision to use the override and restore a unilingual French policy for outdoor signs, Filmon announced that he was suspending legislative consideration of the Meech Lake Accord. Legislative hearings, he said, "may invite a very negative anti-Quebec backlash."[5]

So at this stage the Meech Lake Accord, with its controversial clause recognizing Quebec as a "distinct society," was stalled if not dead. Although this meant that the prospects of a constitutional reconciliation with Quebec were dimmed, the French majority in Quebec learned through these events that the 1982 constitutional changes had left them with considerable power to protect their distinctive culture. For all Canadians the really ominous implication of these events was that they pointed to a deep gulf between the French majority in Quebec and the non-French majority in Canada over what should be regarded as fundamental in Canadian constitutionalism. ∼

Discussion Questions

1. In what way is the court's treatment of section 1 in this case exceptional?

2. In what sense does the underlying issue in this case involve two conflicting visions of Canada?

3. What light does this case shed on the use of the override clause in the Charter?

---

5   *The Globe and Mail* (20 December 1988).

FORD v. QUEBEC (ATTORNEY GENERAL)
[1988] 2 S.C.R. 712

Hearing: November 16, 17, 18, 1987; Judgment: December 15, 1988.

Present: Dickson C.J. and Beetz, Estey,* McIntyre, Lamer, Wilson, and Le Dain* JJ.

Interveners: The Attorney General of Canada, the Attorney General for Ontario, and the Attorney General for New Brunswick. 1987: November 16, 17, 18; 1988: December 15.

* Estey and Le Dain JJ. took no part in the judgment.

[1] **THE COURT:** The principal issue in this appeal is whether ss. 58 and 69 of the Quebec *Charter of the French Language*, R.S.Q., c. C-11, which require that public signs and posters and commercial advertising shall be in the French language only and that only the French version of a firm name may be used, infringe the freedom of expression guaranteed by s. 2(*b*) of the *Canadian Charter of Rights and Freedoms* and s. 3 of the Quebec *Charter of Human Rights and Freedoms*, R.S.Q., c. C-12. There is also an issue as to whether ss. 58 and 69 of the *Charter of the French Language* infringe the guarantee against discrimination based on language in s. 10 of the Quebec *Charter of Human Rights and Freedoms*. The application of the *Canadian Charter of Rights and Freedoms* turns initially on whether there is a valid and applicable override provision, enacted pursuant to s. 33 of the Canadian *Charter*, that ss. 58 and 69 of the *Charter of the French Language* shall operate notwithstanding s. 2(*b*) of the Canadian *Charter*.

[2] The appeal is by leave of this Court from the judgment of the Quebec Court of Appeal on December 22, 1986, [1987] R.J.Q. 80, 5 Q.A.C. 119, 36 D.L.R. (4th) 374, dismissing the appeal of the Attorney General of Quebec from the judgment of Boudreault J. in the Superior Court for the District of Montreal on December 28, 1984, [1985] C.S. 147, 18 D.L.R. (4th) 711, which, on an application for a declaratory judgment, declared s. 58 of the *Charter of the French Language* to be inoperative to the extent that it prescribes that public signs and posters and commercial advertising shall be solely in the French language. The appeal is also from the judgment of the Court of Appeal in so far as it allowed the incidental appeal of the respondents from the judgment of Boudreault J. and declared s. 69 of the *Charter of the French Language* to be inoperative to the extent that it prescribes that only the French version of a firm name may be used. In allowing the incidental appeal the Court of Appeal also declared ss. 205 to 208 of the *Charter of the French Language* respecting offences, penalties and other sanctions for a contravention of any of its provisions to be inoperative in so far as they apply to ss. 58 and 69.

I. The Respondents' Application for a Declaratory Judgment

[3] On February 15, 1984 the respondents brought a motion for a declaratory judgment pursuant to art. 454 of the Quebec *Code of Civil Procedure* and s. 24(1) of the *Canadian Charter of Rights and Freedoms*. The commercial advertising and signs displayed by the five respondents are described in paragraphs 1 to 5 of their petition as follows:

1. La Chaussure Brown's Inc. ("Brown's") operates a business of retail shoe stores throughout the Province of Quebec, and since at least September 1, 1981, it has used and displayed within and on its premises of its store situated in the Fairview Shopping Centre, 6801 Trans-Canada Highway, Pointe-Claire, commercial advertising containing the following words:

BRAVO	BRAVO
"Brown's quality Bravo's price"	"la qualité a tout prix."

2. Valerie Ford, carrying on business under the firm name and style of Les Lainages du Petit Mouton Enr. ("Ford"), operates a retail store selling, *inter alia*, wool, and since at least September 1, 1981, she has used and displayed on her premises at 311 St. Johns Boulevard, Pointe-Claire, an exterior sign containing the following words:

"laine   wool"

3. Nettoyeur et Tailleur Masson Inc. ("Nettoyeur Masson") carries on the business of a tailor and dry cleaner, and since at least September 1, 1981, it has used and displayed on its premises at 3259 Masson Street, Montreal an exterior sign containing the following words:

NETTOYEURS	Masson inc.	CLEANERS
TAILLEUR	TAILOR	
SERVICE	ALTERATIONS	
	REPAIRS	
1 HEURE	1 HOUR	

4. McKenna Inc. ("McKenna") carries on business as a florist in the City of Montreal and since at least September 1, 1981, it has used and displayed on its premises at 4509 Côte Des Neiges Road, Montreal, an exterior sign containing the following words:

"Fleurs   McKENNA   Flowers"

5. La Compagnie de Fromage Nationale Ltée ("Fromage Nationale") carries on the business of a cheese distributor and since at least September 1, 1981, it has used and displayed on its premises at 9001 Salley Street, Ville LaSalle, exterior signs containing the following words:

"NATIONAL CHEESE Co Ltd.
La Cie de FROMAGE NATIONALE Ltée"

[4] The petition further alleges that the respondents La Chaussure Brown's Inc., Valerie Ford and La Compagnie de Fromage Nationale Ltée received a *mise en demeure* from the Commission de surveillance de la langue française advising them that their signs were not in conformity with the provisions of the *Charter of the French Language* and calling on them to conform to such provisions and that the respondents McKenna Inc. and Nettoyeur et Tailleur Masson Inc. were charged with violation of the *Charter of the French Language*.

[5] The respondents conclude in their petition for a declaration that they have the right, notwithstanding ss. 58, 69 and 205 to 208 of the *Charter of the French Language*, to use the signs, posters and commercial advertising described in their petition and a declaration that ss. 58 and 69 and ss. 205 to 208, as they apply to ss. 58 and 69 of the *Charter of the French Language*, are inoperative and of no force or effect.

II. The Relevant Legislative and Constitutional Provisions

[6] To facilitate an understanding of the issues in the appeal, as they are reflected in the reasons for judgment of the Superior Court and the Court of Appeal and in the constitutional questions and submissions of the parties in this Court, it is desirable at this point to set out the relevant legislative and constitutional provisions.

A. The Charter of the French Language

[7] Sections 1, 58, 69, 89, 205, 206 ... of the *Charter of the French Language*, R.S.Q., c. C-11, provide:

1. French is the official language of Québec.

58. Public signs and posters and commercial advertising shall be solely in the official language.

Notwithstanding the foregoing, in the cases and under the conditions or circumstances prescribed by regulation of the Office de la langue française, public signs and posters and commercial advertising may be both in French and in another language or solely in another language.

69. Subject to section 68, only the French version of a firm name may be used in Québec.

89. Where this act does not require the use of the official language exclusively, the official language and another language may be used together.

205. Every person who contravenes a provision of this act other than section 136 or of a regulation made under this act by the Gouvernement or by the Office de

la langue française is guilty of an offence and liable, in addition to costs,

 (a) for each offence, to a fine of $30 to $575 in the case of a natural person, and of $60 to $1150 in the case of an artificial person.

 (b) for any subsequent offence within two years of a first offence, to a fine of $60 to $1150 in the case of a natural person, and of $575 to $5750 in the case of an artificial person.

206. A business firm guilty of an offence contemplated in section 136 is liable, in addition to costs, to a fine of $125 to $2300 for each day during which it carries on its business without a certificate.

B. The Quebec Charter of Human Rights and Freedoms

[8] Sections 3, 9.1 and 10 of the *Quebec Charter of Human Rights and Freedoms*, R.S.Q., c. C-12, provide:

3. Every person is the possessor of the fundamental freedoms, including freedom of conscience, freedom of religion, freedom of opinion, freedom of expression, freedom of peaceful assembly and freedom of association.

9.1 In exercising his fundamental freedoms and rights, a person shall maintain a proper regard for democratic values, public order and the general well-being of the citizens of Québec.

In this respect, the scope of the freedoms and rights, and limits to their exercise, may be fixed by law.

10. Every person has a right to full and equal recognition and exercise of his human rights and freedoms, without distinction, exclusion or preference based on race, colour, sex, pregnancy, sexual orientation, civil status, age except as provided by law, religion, political convictions, language, ethnic or national origin, social condition, a handicap or the use of any means to palliate a handicap.

Discrimination exists where such a distinction, exclusion or preference has the effect of nullifying or impairing such right.

[9] Sections 51 and 52 of the *Quebec Charter of Human Rights and Freedoms*, R.S.Q., c. C-12, provide:

51. The Charter shall not be so interpreted as to extend, limit or amend the scope of a provision of law except to the extent provided in section 52.

52. No provision of any Act, even subsequent to the Charter, may derogate from sections 1 to 38, except so far as provided by those sections, unless such Act expressly states that it applies despite the Charter.

[10] Prior to its amendment by s. 16 of *An Act to amend the Charter of Human Rights and Freedoms*, S.Q. 1982, c. 61, s. 52 of the Quebec *Charter* read as follows:

52. Sections 9 to 38 prevail over any provision of any subsequent act which may be inconsistent therewith unless such act expressly states that it applies despite the Charter. ...

IV. The Constitutional Questions and the Issues in the Appeal

[20] On the appeal to this Court the following constitutional questions were stated by Lamer J. in his order of May 11, 1987:

1. Are section 214 of the *Charter of the French Language*, R.S.Q. 1977, c. C-11, as enacted by S.Q. 1982, c. 21, s. 1, and s. 52 of *An Act to amend the Charter of the French Language*, S.Q. 1983, c. 56, inconsistent with s. 33(1) of the *Constitution Act, 1982* and therefore inoperative and of no force or effect under s. 52(1) of the latter Act?

2. If the answer to question 1 is affirmative, to the extent that they require the exclusive use of the French language, are ss. 58 and 69, and ss. 205 to 208 to the extent they apply thereto, of the *Charter of the French Language*, R.S.Q. 1977, c. C-11, as amended by S.Q. 1983, c. 56, inconsistent with the guarantee of freedom of expression under s. 2(b) of the *Canadian Charter of Rights and Freedoms*?

3. If the answer to question 2 is affirmative in whole or in part, are ss. 58 and 69, and ss. 205 to 208 to the extent they apply thereto, of the *Charter of the French Language*, R.S.Q. 1977, c. C-11, as amended by S.Q. 1983, c. 56, justified by the application of s. 1 of the *Canadian Charter of Rights and Freedoms* and therefore not inconsistent with the *Constitution Act, 1982*?

[21] The issues in the appeal, as reflected in the above constitutional questions, the reasons for judgment of the Superior Court and the Court of Appeal and the submissions in this Court, may be summarized as follows:

1. Is section 58 or s. 69 of the *Charter of the French Language* protected from the application of s. 2(b) of the *Canadian Charter of Rights and Freedoms* by a valid and applicable override provision enacted in conformity with s. 33 of the Canadian *Charter*?

2. What are the dates from which s. 3 of the Quebec *Charter of Human Rights and Freedoms* took precedence, in case of conflict, over ss. 58 and 69 of the *Charter of the French Language*?

3. Does the freedom of expression guaranteed by s. 2(b) of the Canadian *Charter* and by s. 3 of the Quebec *Charter* include the freedom to express oneself in the language of one's choice?

4. Does the freedom of expression guaranteed by s. 2(b) of the Canadian *Charter* and s. 3 of the Quebec *Charter* extend to commercial expression?

5. If the requirement of the exclusive use of French by ss. 58 and 69 of the *Charter of the French Language* infringes the freedom of expression guaranteed by s. 2(b) of the Canadian *Charter* and s. 3 of the Quebec *Charter*, is the limit on freedom of expression imposed by ss. 58 and 69 justified under s. 1 of the Canadian *Charter* and s. 9.1 of the Quebec *Charter*?

6. Do sections 58 and 69 of the *Charter of the French Language* infringe the guarantee against discrimination based on language in s. 10 of the Quebec *Charter of Human Rights and Freedoms*?

[22] Submissions with respect to the validity and application of the override provisions in issue, as well as the content of freedom of expression and the effect of s. 1 of the Canadian *Charter* and s. 9.1 of the Quebec *Charter*, were also made in the appeals in *Devine v. Quebec (Attorney General)*, [1988] 2 S.C.R. 790, and *Irwin Toy Ltd. v. Quebec (Attorney General)*, S.C.C., No. 20074, which were heard at the same time as this appeal. They will necessarily be taken into consideration in disposing of the issues in this appeal.

V. Is Section 58 or Section 69 of the Charter of the French Language Protected from the Application of Section 2(b) of the Canadian Charter of Rights and Freedoms by a Valid and Applicable Override Provision Enacted in Conformity with Section 33 of the Canadian Charter?

[23] ... [T]here are two override provisions in issue: (a) s. 214 of the *Charter of the French Language*, which was enacted by s. 1 of *An Act respecting the Constitution Act, 1982*, S.Q. 1982, c. 21; and (b) s. 52 of *An Act to amend the Charter of the French Language*, S.Q. 1983, c. 56. The two override provisions are in identical terms, reading as follows: "This Act shall operate notwithstanding the provisions of sections 2 and 7 to 15 of the *Constitution Act, 1982* (Schedule B of the *Canada Act*, chapter 11 in the 1982 volume of *Acts of Parliament of the United Kingdom*)." The issue of validity that is common to both s. 214 and s. 52 is whether a declaration in this form is one that is made in conformity with the override authority conferred by s. 33 of the *Canadian Charter of Rights and Freedoms*. There are additional issues of validity applicable to s. 214 of the *Charter of the French Language* arising from the

manner of its enactment, that is, the "omnibus" character of the Act which enacted it, and from the retrospective effect given to s. 214 by s. 7 of the Act, which has been quoted above.

[24] Section 214 of the *Charter of the French Language* ceased to have effect by operation of s. 33(3) of the *Canadian Charter of Rights and Freedoms* five years after it came into force, and it was not re-enacted pursuant to s. 33(4) of the *Charter*. If the retrospective effect to April 17, 1982 given to s. 214 by s. 7 of *An Act respecting the Constitution Act, 1982*, was valid, s. 214 ceased to have effect on April 17, 1987. If not, it ceased to have effect on June 23, 1987, which was five years after the enacting Act came into force on the day of its sanction. In either case the question of the validity of s. 214 is moot, on the assumption, which was the one on which the appeal was argued, that on an application for a declaratory judgment in a case of this kind the Court should declare the law as it exists at the time of its judgment. We were, nevertheless, invited by the parties in this appeal and the appeals that were heard at the same time to rule on the validity of the standard override provision as enacted by *An Act respecting the Constitution Act, 1982*, because of the possible significance of that issue in cases pending before other tribunals. Before considering how the Court should respond to that invitation we propose to consider the other override provision in issue which, as we have said, raises a common question of validity.

[25] Section 52 of *An Act to amend the Charter of the French Language*, which was proclaimed in force on February 1, 1984, will not cease to have effect by operation of s. 33(3) of the *Canadian Charter of Rights and Freedoms* until February 1, 1989. It is therefore necessary to consider its validity since the Attorney General of Quebec contends that it protects s. 58 of the *Charter of the French Language* from the application of s. 2(*b*) of the *Canadian Charter of Rights and Freedoms*. ...

[27] Those who challenged the constitutionality of the override provisions in s. 214 of the *Charter of the French Language* and s. 52 of *An Act to amend the Charter of the French Language* placed particular reliance on the judgment of the Quebec Court of Appeal in *Alliance des professeurs de Montréal v. Procureur général du Québec, supra*, in which the Court of Appeal held that the standard override provision was *ultra vires* and null as not being in conformity with the authority conferred by s. 33 of the *Canadian Charter of Rights and Freedoms*. ...

[28] In that case the petitioners, Alliance des professeurs de Montréal, sought declarations that s. 1 and other provisions of *An Act respecting the Constitution Act, 1982*, which purported to add the standard override provision to all provincial legislation enacted up to June 23, 1982, and the standard override provisions enacted in some forty-nine statutes after

that date were *ultra vires* and null as not being in conformity with s. 33 of the *Canadian Charter of Rights and Freedoms*. Thus the petitioners put in issue not only the validity of the standard override provision as enacted by the "omnibus" *Act respecting the Constitution Act, 1982*, but also its validity as separately enacted in particular statutes. ...

[29] The essential contention in *Alliance des professeurs*, as in the present appeals, against the validity of the standard override provision, which was rejected by the Superior Court but upheld by the Court of Appeal, was that the provision did not sufficiently specify the guaranteed rights or freedoms which the legislation intended to override. In support of this contention reliance was placed not only on the wording of s. 33(1) and (2) of the *Charter* but on general considerations concerning the effectiveness of the democratic process. For convenience the standard override provision that is in issue, as well as s. 33(1) and (2) of the *Charter*, are quoted again:

> This Act shall operate notwithstanding the provisions of sections 2 and 7 to 15 of the *Constitution Act, 1982* (Schedule B of the *Canada Act*, chapter 11 in the 1982 volume of the *Acts of the Parliament of the United Kingdom*).
>
> **33.**(1) Parliament or the legislature of a province may expressly declare in an Act of Parliament or of the legislature, as the case may be, that the Act or a provision thereof shall operate notwithstanding a provision included in section 2 or sections 7 to 15 of this *Charter*.
>
> (2) An Act or a provision of an Act in respect of which a declaration made under this section is in effect shall have such operation as it would have but for the provision of this *Charter* referred to in the declaration.

[30] It was contended that the words "a provision included in section 2 or sections 7 to 15 of this *Charter*" in s. 33(1) and the words "but for the provision of this *Charter* referred to in the declaration" in s. 33(2) indicate that in order to be valid, a declaration pursuant to s. 33 must specify the particular provision within a section of the *Charter* which Parliament or the legislature of a province intends to override. That is, the specific guaranteed right or freedom to be overridden must be referred to in the words of the *Charter* and not merely by the number of the section or paragraph in which it appears. The rationale underlying this contention is that the nature of the guaranteed right or freedom must be sufficiently drawn to the attention of the members of the legislature and of the public so that the relative seriousness of what is proposed may be perceived and reacted to through the democratic process. As the Attorney General for Ontario, who argued against the constitutionality of the standard

override provision, put it, there must be a "political cost" for overriding a guaranteed right or freedom. ...

[33] In the course of argument different views were expressed as to the constitutional perspective from which the meaning and application of s. 33 of the *Canadian Charter of Rights and Freedoms* should be approached: the one suggesting that it reflects the continuing importance of legislative supremacy, the other suggesting the seriousness of a legislative decision to override guaranteed rights and freedoms and the importance that such a decision be taken only as a result of a fully informed democratic process. These two perspectives are not, however, particularly relevant or helpful in construing the requirements of s. 33. Section 33 lays down requirements of form only, and there is no warrant for importing into it grounds for substantive review of the legislative policy in exercising the override authority in a particular case. The requirement of an apparent link or relationship between the overriding Act and the guaranteed rights or freedoms to be overridden seems to be a substantive ground of review. It appears to require that the legislature identify the provisions of the Act in question which might otherwise infringe speci-fied guaranteed rights or freedoms. That would seem to require a *prima facie* justification of the decision to exercise the override authority rather than merely a certain formal expression of it. There is, however, no warrant in the terms of s. 33 for such a requirement. A legislature may not be in a position to judge with any degree of certainty what provisions of the *Canadian Charter of Rights and Freedoms* might be successfully invoked against various aspects of the Act in ques-tion. For this reason it must be permitted in a particular case to override more than one provision of the *Charter* and indeed all of the provisions which it is permitted to override by the terms of s. 33. The standard override provision in issue in this appeal is, therefore, a valid exercise of the authority conferred by s. 33 in so far as it purports to override all of the provisions in s. 2 and ss. 7 to 15 of the *Charter*. The essential requirement of form laid down by s. 33 is that the override declaration must be an express declaration that an Act or a provision of an Act shall operate notwithstanding a provision included in s. 2 or ss. 7 to 15 of the *Charter*. With great respect for the contrary view, this Court is of the opinion that a s. 33 declaration is sufficiently express if it refers to the number of the section, subsection or paragraph of the *Charter* which contains the provision or provisions to be overridden. Of course, if it is intended to override only a part of the provision or provisions contained in a section, subsection or paragraph then there would have to be a sufficient reference in words to the part to be overridden. ...

[34] Therefore, s. 52 of *An Act to amend the Charter of the French Language* is a valid and subsisting exercise of the override authority conferred by s. 33 of the *Canadian Charter of Rights and Freedoms* that protects s. 58 of the *Charter of the French Language* from the application of s. 2(*b*) of the Cana-dian *Charter*. Section 69 of the *Charter of the French Language* is not so protected since it was not affected by *An Act to amend the Charter of the French Language*. In the result, as indicated in the following Part VI of these reasons, s. 58 is subject to s. 3 of the Quebec *Charter of Human Rights and Freedoms* while s. 69 is subject to both s. 2(*b*) of the Canadian *Charter* and s. 3 of the Quebec *Charter*.

[35] Before leaving Part V of these reasons, it remains to be considered whether the Court should exercise its discretion to rule on the other aspects of the validity of the standard over-ride provision as enacted by *An Act respecting the Constitution Act, 1982*: the "omnibus" character of the enactment; and the retrospective effect given to the override provision. These issues affect both s. 214 of the *Charter of the French Language*, which is in issue in this appeal and in the *Devine* appeal and s. 364 of the *Consumer Protection Act*, R.S.Q., c. P-40.1, in the *Irwin Toy* appeal. The Court has concluded that although both of these provisions have ceased to have effect it is better that all questions concerning their validity should be settled in these appeals because of their possible continuing importance in other cases. Given the conclusion that the enactment of the standard override provision in the form indicated above is a valid exercise of the authority conferred by s. 33 of the *Cana-dian Charter of Rights and Freedoms*, this Court is of the opin-ion that the validity of its enactment is not affected by the fact that it was introduced into all Quebec statutes enacted prior to a certain date by a single enactment. That was an effective exercise of legislative authority that did not prevent the over-ride declaration so enacted in each statute from being an express declaration within the meaning of s. 33 of the Cana-dian *Charter*. Counsel referred to this form of enactment as reflecting an impermissibly "routine" exercise of the override authority or even a "perversion" of it. It was even suggested that it amounted to an attempted amendment of the *Charter*. These are once again essentially submissions concerning per-missible legislative policy in the exercise of the override authority rather than what constitutes a sufficiently express declaration of override. As has been stated, there is no warrant in s. 33 for such considerations as a basis of judicial review of a particular exercise of the authority conferred by s. 33. The Court is of a different view, however, concerning the retro-spective effect given to the standard override provision by s. 7 of *An Act respecting the Constitution Act, 1982*. ... In providing that s. 1, which re-enacted all of the Quebec statutes adopted before April 17, 1982 with the addition in each of the standard override provision, should have effect from that date, s. 7 pur-ported to give retrospective effect to the override provision. ...

[36] ... In *Gustavson Drilling (1964) Ltd. v. Minister of National Revenue*, [1977] 1 S.C.R. 271, Dickson J. (as he then was) wrote, for the majority (at p. 279):

> The general rule is that statutes are not to be construed as having retrospective operation unless such a construction is expressly or by necessary implication required by the language of the Act.

Where, as here, an enabling provision is ambiguous as to whether it allows for retroactive legislation, the same rule of construction applies. In this case, s. 33(1) admits of two interpretations; one that allows Parliament or a legislature to enact retroactive override provisions, the other that permits prospective derogation only. We conclude that the latter and narrower interpretation is the proper one, and that s. 7 cannot give retrospective effect to the override provision. Section 7 of *An Act respecting the Constitution Act, 1982*, is to the extent of this inconsistency with s. 33 of the Canadian *Charter*, of no force or effect, with the result that the standard override provisions enacted by s. 1 of that *Act* came into force on June 23, 1982 in accordance with the first paragraph of s. 7. ...

VII. Whether the Freedom of Expression Guaranteed by Section 2(b) of the Canadian Charter of Rights and Freedoms and by Section 3 of the Quebec Charter of Human Rights and Freedoms Includes the Freedom to Express Oneself in the Language of One's Choice

[39] In so far as this issue is concerned, the words "freedom of expression" in s. 2(*b*) of the Canadian *Charter* and s. 3 of the Quebec *Charter* should be given the same meaning. As indicated above, both the Superior Court and the Court of Appeal held that freedom of expression includes the freedom to express oneself in the language of one's choice. After indicating the essential relationship between expression and language by reference to dictionary definitions of both, Boudreault J. in the Superior Court said that in the ordinary or general form of expression there cannot be expression without language. Bisson J.A. in the Court of Appeal said that he agreed with the reasons of Boudreault J. on this issue and expressed his own view in the form of the following question: "Is there a purer form of freedom of expression than the spoken language and written language?" He supported his conclusion by quotation of the following statement of this Court in *Reference re Manitoba Language Rights*, [1985] 1 S.C.R. 721, at p. 744: "The importance of language rights is grounded in the essential role that language plays in human existence, development and dignity. It is through language that we are able to form concepts; to structure and order the world around us. Language bridges the gap between isolation and community, allowing humans to delineate the rights and duties they hold in respect of one another, and thus to live in society."

[40] The conclusion of the Superior Court and the Court of Appeal on this issue is correct. Language is so intimately related to the form and content of expression that there cannot be true freedom of expression by means of language if one is prohibited from using the language of one's choice. Language is not merely a means or medium of expression; it colours the content and meaning of expression. It is, as the preamble of the *Charter of the French Language* itself indicates, a means by which a people may express its cultural identity. It is also the means by which the individual expresses his or her personal identity and sense of individuality. That the concept of "expression" in s. 2(*b*) of the Canadian *Charter* and s. 3 of the Quebec *Charter* goes beyond mere content is indicated by the specific protection accorded to "freedom of thought, belief [and] opinion" in s. 2 and to "freedom of conscience" and "freedom of opinion" in s. 3. That suggests that "freedom of expression" is intended to extend to more than the content of expression in its narrow sense.

[41] The Attorney General of Quebec made several submissions against the conclusion reached by the Superior Court and the Court of Appeal on this issue, the most important of which may be summarized as follows: (a) in determining the meaning of freedom of expression the Court should apply the distinction between the message and the medium which must have been known to the framers of the Canadian and Quebec *Charters*; (b) the express provision for the guarantee of language rights in ss. 16 to 23 of the Canadian *Charter* indicate that it was not intended that a language freedom should result incidentally from the guarantee of freedom of expression in s. 2(*b*); (c) the recognition of a freedom to express oneself in the language of one's choice under s. 2(*b*) of the Canadian *Charter* and s. 3 of the Quebec *Charter* would undermine the special and limited constitutional position of the specific guarantees of language rights in s. 133 of the *Constitution Act, 1867* and ss. 16 to 23 of the Canadian *Charter* that was emphasized by the Court in *MacDonald v. City of Montreal*, [1986] 1 S.C.R. 460, and *Société des Acadiens du Nouveau-Brunswick Inc. v. Association of Parents for Fairness in Education*, [1986] 1 S.C.R. 549; and (d) the recognition that freedom of expression includes the freedom to express oneself in the language of one's choice would be contrary to the views expressed on this issue by the European Commission of Human Rights and the European Court of Human Rights.

[42] The distinction between the message and the medium was applied by Dugas J. of the Superior Court in *Devine v. Procureur général du Québec, supra*, in holding that freedom of expression does not include freedom to express oneself in

the language of one's choice. It has already been indicated why that distinction is inappropriate as applied to language as a means of expression because of the intimate relationship between language and meaning. As one of the authorities on language quoted by the appellant Singer in the *Devine* appeal, J. Fishman, *The Sociology of Language* (1972), at p. 4, puts it: "... language is not merely a *means* of interpersonal communication and influence. It is not merely a *carrier* of content, whether latent or manifest. Language itself *is* content, a reference for loyalties and animosities, an indicator of social statuses and personal relationships, a marker of situations and topics as well as of the societal goals and the large-scale value-laden arenas of interaction that typify every speech community." ...

[43] The second and third of the submissions of the Attorney General of Quebec which have been summarized above, with reference to the implications for this issue of the express or specific guarantees of language rights in s. 133 of the *Constitution Act, 1867*, and ss. 16 to 23 of the *Canadian Charter of Rights and Freedoms*, are closely related and may be addressed together. These special guarantees of language rights do not, by implication, preclude a construction of freedom of expression that includes the freedom to express oneself in the language of one's choice. ... The central unifying feature of all of the language rights given explicit recognition in the Constitution of Canada is that they pertain to governmental institutions and for the most part they oblige the government to provide for, or at least tolerate, the use of both official languages. In this sense they are more akin to rights, properly understood, than freedoms. They grant entitlement to a specific benefit from the government or in relation to one's dealing with the government. Correspondingly, the government is obliged to provide certain services or benefits in both languages or at least permit use of either language by persons conducting certain affairs with the government. ... In contrast, what the respondents seek in this case is a freedom as that term was explained by Dickson J. (as he then was) in *R. v. Big M Drug Mart Ltd.*, [1985] 1 S.C.R. 295, at p. 336: "Freedom can primarily be characterized by the absence of coercion or constraint. If a person is compelled by the state or the will of another to a course of action or inaction which he would not otherwise have chosen, he is not acting of his own volition and he cannot be said to be truly free. One of the major purposes of the *Charter* is to protect, within reason, from compulsion or restraint." The respondents seek to be free of the state imposed requirement that their commercial signs and advertising be in French only, and seek the freedom, in the entirely private or non-governmental realm of commercial activity, to display signs and advertising in the language of their choice as well as that of French. Manifestly the respondents are not seeking to use the language of their choice in any form of direct relations with any branch of government and are not seeking to oblige government to provide them any services or other benefits in the language of their choice. In this sense the respondents are asserting a freedom, the freedom to express oneself in the language of one's choice in an area of non-governmental activity, as opposed to a language right of the kind guaranteed in the Constitution. The recognition that freedom of expression includes the freedom to express oneself in the language of one's choice does not undermine or run counter to the special guarantees of official language rights in areas of governmental jurisdiction or responsibility. ...

[44] The decisions of the European Commission of Human Rights and the European Court of Human Rights on which the Attorney General of Quebec relied are all distinguishable on the same basis, apart from the fact that, as Bisson J.A. observed in the Court of Appeal, they arose in an entirely different constitutional context. They all involved claims to language rights in relations with government that would have imposed some obligation on government. ...

VIII. Whether the Guarantee of Freedom of Expression Extends to Commercial Expression

[45] In argument there arose a question whether the above issue is an issue in this appeal. The Attorney General of Quebec contended that if the guarantee of freedom of expression included the freedom to express oneself in the language of one's choice the respondents must still show that the guarantee extends to commercial expression. The respondents disputed this on the ground that the challenged provisions are directed to the language used and not to regulation of the substantive content of the expression. At the same time they made alternative submissions that the guarantee extended to commercial expression. The Attorney General of Quebec is correct on this issue: there cannot be a guaranteed freedom to express oneself in the language of one's choice in respect of a form or kind of expression that is not covered by the guarantee of freedom of expression. The question whether the guarantee of freedom of expression in s. 2(*b*) of the Canadian *Charter* and s. 3 of the Quebec *Charter* extends to the kind of expression contemplated by ss. 58 and 69 of the *Charter of the French Language*, which for convenience is referred to as commercial expression, is therefore an issue in this appeal. The submissions that were made on the question of commercial expression in the *Devine* and *Irwin Toy* appeals will be considered in determining that issue in this appeal.

[46] It was not disputed that the public signs and posters, the commercial advertising, and the firm name referred to in ss. 58 and 69 of the *Charter of the French Language* are forms of expression, and it was also assumed or accepted in

argument that the expression contemplated by these provisions may be conveniently characterized or referred to as commercial expression. Sections 58 and 69 appear in Chapter VII of the *Charter of the French Language*, entitled "The Language of Commerce and Business." It must be kept in mind, however, that while the words "commercial expression" are a convenient reference to the kind of expression contemplated by the provisions in issue, they do not have any particular meaning or significance in Canadian constitutional law, unlike the corresponding expression "commercial speech," which in the United States has been recognized as a particular category of speech entitled to First Amendment protection of a more limited character than that enjoyed by other kinds of speech. The issue in the appeal is not whether the guarantee of freedom of expression in s. 2(*b*) of the Canadian *Charter* and s. 3 of the Quebec *Charter* should be construed as extending to particular categories of expression, giving rise to difficult definitional problems, but whether there is any reason why the guarantee should not extend to a particular kind of expression, in this case the expression contemplated by ss. 58 and 69 of the *Charter of the French Language*. Because, however, the American experience with the First Amendment protection of "commercial speech" was invoked in argument, as it has been in other cases, both for and against the recognition in Canada that the guarantee of freedom of expression extends to the kinds of expression that may be described as commercial expression, it is convenient to make brief reference to it at this point.

[47] In *Valentine v. Chrestensen*, 316 U.S. 52 (1942), the Supreme Court of the United States declined to afford First Amendment protection to speech which did no more than propose a commercial transaction. Some thirty-four years later, in *Virginia State Board of Pharmacy v. Virginia Citizens Consumer Council Inc.*, 425 U.S. 748 (1976), the Supreme Court affirmed a repudiation of the notion that commercial speech constituted an unprotected exception to the First Amendment guarantee. *Virginia Pharmacy* concerned a Virginia statute which prohibited pharmacists from advertising prices for prescription drugs. The statute was challenged by customers who asserted a First Amendment right to receive drug price information that the pharmacist wished to communicate. The speech at issue was purely commercial in that it simply proposed a commercial transaction. By holding that price advertising was not outside the First Amendment, the Court rejected the central premise of the commercial speech doctrine—that is, that business advertising which merely solicits a commercial transaction is susceptible to government regulation on the same terms as any other aspect of the market place. The reasons of Blackmun J., writing for the Court, focus on the informative function of the speech from the point of

view of the listener whose interest, it was said, "may be as keen, if not keener by far, than his interest in the day's most urgent political debate" (p. 763). The rationale stated by the Court for a First Amendment protection of commercial speech was the interest of the individual consumer and the society generally in the free flow of commercial information as indispensable to informed economic choice. The reasons are careful to note, however, that although commercial speech is protected it is entitled to a lesser degree of protection than that afforded to other forms of speech. ...

[48] By 1980, when the Court decided *Central Hudson Gas & Electric Corp. v. Public Service Commission of New York*, 447 U.S. 557 (1980), it was apparent that some control of truthful advertising was legitimate as long as the regulation directly advanced a substantial state interest. Powell J., writing for the Court, formulated a four-part analysis for determining whether a particular regulation of commercial speech is consistent with the First Amendment, which he summed up as follows at p. 566:

> In commercial speech cases, then, a four-part analysis has developed. At the outset, we must determine whether the expression is protected by the First Amendment. For commercial speech to come within that provision, it at least must concern lawful activity and not be misleading. Next, we ask whether the asserted governmental interest is substantial. If both inquiries yield positive answers, we must determine whether the regulation directly advances the governmental interest asserted, and whether it is not more extensive than is necessary to serve that interest.

... It has been observed that this test is very similar to the test that was adopted by this Court in *R. v. Oakes*, [1986] 1 S.C.R. 103, for justification under s. 1 of the *Charter*. The *Central Hudson* test has been described as "an uneasy compromise" between competing strains of commercial speech theory. It is an attempt to balance the legitimacy of government regulations intended to protect consumers from harmful commercial speech with the belief that a free market in ideas and information is necessary to an informed and autonomous consumer.

[49] In *Posadas de Puerto Rico Associates v. Tourism Co. of Puerto Rico*, 106 S.Ct. 2968 (1986), the Court applied the *Central Hudson* test in a manner that attracted much criticism as reflecting, in the opinion of some commentators, an excessively deferential attitude to government regulation in the face of little or no demonstration by the state that the legislative means it had adopted either directly advanced the asserted substantial interest or minimally restricted first amendment interests. See, for example, Philip B. Kurland, "*Posadas de Puerto Rico v. Tourism Company*: 'Twas Strange, 'Twas Passing

Strange; 'Twas Pitiful, 'Twas Wondrous Pitiful," [1986] *Sup. Ct. Rev.* 1; and "The Supreme Court—Leading Cases" (1986), 100 *Harv. L. Rev.* 100, at p. 172. *Posadas* reflects how differences of view or emphasis in the application of the *Central Hudson* test can determine the effective extent of the protection of commercial speech from legislative limitation or restriction. It reveals the tension between two values: the value of the free circulation of commercial information and the value of consumer protection against harmful commercial speech. The American experience with the constitutional protection of commercial speech further indicates the difficulties inherent in its application, in particular the degree to which the courts are involved in the evaluation of regulatory policy in the field of consumer protection. The American jurisprudence with respect to commercial speech has been the subject of much scholarly analysis and criticism. Among the leading articles are the following: Jackson and Jeffries, "Commercial Speech: Economic Due Process and the First Amendment" (1979), 65 *Va. L. Rev.* 1; Weinberg, "Constitutional Protection of Commercial Speech" (1982), 82 *Colum. L. Rev.* 720; and Lively, "The Supreme Court and Commercial Speech: New Words with an Old Message" (1987), 72 *Minn. L. Rev.* 289. There is also an analysis of the American jurisprudence in the very helpful article on commercial expression by Professor Robert J. Sharpe, "Commercial Expression and the Charter" (1987), 37 *U. of T.L.J.* 229.

[50] In the case at bar Boudreault J. in the Superior Court held that the guarantee of freedom of expression in s. 3 of the Quebec *Charter* extended to commercial expression. He relied particularly on the reasoning in the American decisions, quoting at length from the judgment of Blackmun J. in *Virginia Pharmacy* for the rationale underlying the protection of commercial speech in the United States. He emphasized, as does that case, that it is not only the speaker but the listener who has an interest in freedom of expression. In the Court of Appeal, Bisson J.A. applied the judgment of the majority of the Court on this issue in *Irwin Toy Ltd. v. Procureur général du Québec*, [1986] R.J.Q. 2441, and quoted from the opinions of Jacques J.A. and Vallerand J.A. in that case. In *Irwin Toy*, Jacques J.A. held that there was no basis on the face of s. 2(*b*) of the Canadian *Charter* for distinguishing, in respect of the guarantee of freedom of expression, between different kinds of expression, whether they be of a political, artistic, cultural or other nature. He held that commercial expression was as much entitled to protection as other kinds of expression because of the important role played by it in assisting persons to make informed economic choices. He added, however, that commercial expression might be subject to reasonable limits under s. 1 of the Canadian *Charter* of a kind that would not be reasonable in the case of political expression. ...

[51] In the course of argument reference was made to two other Canadian decisions which reflect the contrasting positions on the question whether freedom of expression should extend to commercial expression: the majority decision of the Ontario Divisional Court in *Re Klein and Law Society of Upper Canada* (1985), 16 D.L.R. (4th) 489, and the unanimous decision of the Alberta Court of Appeal in *Re Grier and Alberta Optometric Association* (1987), 42 D.L.R. (4th) 327. In *Klein*, on which the Attorney General of Quebec and those who supported his contention that freedom of expression should not extend to commercial expression placed particular reliance, the relevant issue was whether the Rules of Professional Conduct of the Law Society of Upper Canada prohibiting fee advertising by solicitors infringed the guarantee of freedom of expression in s. 2(*b*) of the *Charter*. After referring to the pre-*Charter* decisions on freedom of speech and the American jurisprudence on commercial speech, Callaghan J., with whom Eberle J. concurred, concluded that the guarantee of freedom of expression in s. 2(*b*) should not extend to commercial expression. He held that commercial expression was unrelated to political expression, which in his view was the principal if not exclusive object of the protection afforded by s. 2(*b*). He said at p. 532: "The *Charter* reflects a concern with the political rights of the individual and does not, in my view, reflect a similar concern with the economic sphere nor with its incidents such as commercial speech" and "*Prima facie* then, the freedom of expression guaranteed by s. 2(*b*) of the *Charter* would appear to apply to the expression of ideas relating to the political and governmental domains of the country. (I leave aside the question of whether or not artistic expression falls within s. 2(*b*))." After a very full discussion of American jurisprudence and experience with respect to the First Amendment protection of commercial speech Callaghan J. expressed the view that there were good reasons for not following it, among them the extent to which such protection involved the courts in a difficult case-by-case review of regulatory policy. He concluded as follows at p. 539: "I would conclude that there is no reason to expand the meaning of the word 'expression' in s. 2(*b*) of the *Charter* to cover pure commercial speech. Commercial speech contributes nothing to democratic government because it says nothing about how people are governed or how they should govern themselves. It does not relate to government policies or matters of public concern essential to a democratic process. It pertains to the economic realm and is a matter appropriate to regulation by the Legislature." ...

[52] In *Grier*, the Alberta Court of Appeal (Lieberman, Kerans and Irving JJ.A.) held that a brochure mailed by a licensed optometrist to patients and others quoting prices for various services was protected expression within the meaning

of s. 2(*b*) of the *Charter*. It declined to follow *Klein* on the question of commercial expression and expressed agreement with the decision of the Quebec Court of Appeal in *Irwin Toy* on that question. ...

[53] The submissions of the Attorney General of Quebec and those who supported him on this issue may be summarized as follows. The scope of a guaranteed freedom must be determined, as required by *R. v. Big M Drug Mart Ltd.*, *supra*, in the light of the character and larger objects of the Canadian *Charter* and the linguistic, philosophic and historical context of the particular freedom. There is no historical basis for a guarantee of freedom of commercial expression in pre-*Charter* jurisprudence, in which recognition was given, on the basis of the division of powers and the "implied bill of rights," to freedom of political expression. Freedom of expression appears in both the Canadian *Charter* and the Quebec *Charter* under the heading of "Fundamental Freedoms"; there is nothing fundamental about commercial expression. A guarantee of freedom of expression which embraces commercial advertising would be the protection of an economic right, when both the Canadian *Charter* and the Quebec *Charter* clearly indicate that they are not concerned with the protection of such rights. The American decisions recognizing a limited First Amendment protection for commercial speech must be seen in the context of a constitution that protects the right of property, whereas that right was deliberately omitted from the protection afforded by s. 7 of the Canadian *Charter*. This Court, in refusing to constitutionalize the right to strike, has recognized that the Canadian *Charter* does not extend to economic rights or freedoms. To extend freedom of expression beyond political expression, and possibly artistic and cultural expression, would trivialize that freedom and lead inevitably to the adoption of different justificatory standards under s. 1 according to the kind of expression involved. The terms of s. 1, as interpreted and applied by the courts, do not permit of such differential application. Freedom of commercial expression, and in particular commercial advertising, does not serve any of the values that would justify its constitutional protection. Commercial advertising is manipulative and seeks to condition or control economic choice rather than to provide the basis of a truly informed choice. As the American experience shows, the recognition of a limited protection for commercial expression involves an evaluation of regulatory policy that is better left to the legislature. Academic criticism of the American approach to commercial speech and judicial expression of misgivings concerning it provide sufficient reason for declining to follow it.

[54] It is apparent to this Court that the guarantee of freedom of expression in s. 2(*b*) of the Canadian *Charter* and s. 3 of the Quebec *Charter* cannot be confined to political expression, important as that form of expression is in a free and democratic society. The pre-*Charter* jurisprudence emphasized the importance of political expression because it was a challenge to that form of expression that most often arose under the division of powers and the "implied bill of rights," where freedom of political expression could be related to the maintenance and operation of the institutions of democratic government. But political expression is only one form of the great range of expression that is deserving of constitutional protection because it serves individual and societal values in a free and democratic society.

[55] The post-*Charter* jurisprudence of this Court has indicated that the guarantee of freedom of expression in s. 2(*b*) of the *Charter* is not to be confined to political expression. In holding, in *RWDSU v. Dolphin Delivery Ltd.*, [1986] 2 S.C.R. 573, that secondary picketing was a form of expression within the meaning of s. 2(*b*) the Court recognized that the constitutional guarantee of freedom of expression extended to expression that could not be characterized as political expression in the traditional sense but, if anything, was in the nature of expression having an economic purpose. ...

[56] Various attempts have been made to identify and formulate the values which justify the constitutional protection of freedom of expression. Probably the best known is that of Professor Thomas I. Emerson in his article, "Toward a General Theory of the First Amendment" (1963), 72 *Yale L.J.* 877, where he sums up these values as follows at p. 878:

> The values sought by society in protecting the right to freedom of expression may be grouped into four broad categories. Maintenance of a system of free expression is necessary (1) as assuring individual self-fulfillment, (2) as a means of attaining the truth, (3) as a method of securing participation by the members of the society in social, including political, decision-making, and (4) as maintaining the balance between stability and change in society.

The third and fourth of these values would appear to be closely related if not overlapping. Generally the values said to justify the constitutional protection of freedom of expression are stated as three-fold in nature, as appears from the article by Professor Sharpe referred to above on "Commercial Expression and the Charter," where he speaks of the three "rationales" for such protection as follows at p. 232:

> The first is that freedom of expression is essential to intelligent and democratic self-government. ... The second theory is that freedom of expression protects an open exchange of views, thereby creating a competitive market-place of ideas which will enhance the search for the truth. ...

The third theory values expression for its own sake. On this view, expression is seen as an aspect of individual autonomy. Expression is to be protected because it is essential to personal growth and self-realization.

[57] While these attempts to identify and define the values which justify the constitutional protection of freedom of expression are helpful in emphasizing the most important of them, they tend to be formulated in a philosophical context which fuses the separate questions of whether a particular form or act of expression is within the ambit of the interests protected by the value of freedom of expression and the question whether that form or act of expression, in the final analysis, deserves protection from interference under the structure of the Canadian *Charter* and the Quebec *Charter*. These are two distinct questions and call for two distinct analytical processes. The first, at least for the Canadian *Charter*, is to be determined by the purposive approach to interpretation set out by this Court in *Hunter v. Southam Inc.*, [1984] 2 S.C.R. 145, and *Big M Drug Mart Ltd.*, *supra*. The second, the question of the limitation on the protected values, is to be determined under s. 1 of the *Charter* as interpreted in *Oakes*, *supra*, and *R. v. Edwards Books and Art Ltd.*, [1986] 2 S.C.R. 713. The division between the two analytical processes has been established by this Court in the above decisions. First, consideration will be given to the interests and purposes that are meant to be protected by the particular right or freedom in order to determine whether the right or freedom has been infringed in the context presented to the court. If the particular right or freedom is found to have been infringed, the second step is to determine whether the infringement can be justified by the state within the constraints of s. 1. It is within the perimeters of s. 1 that courts will in most instances weigh competing values in order to determine which should prevail.

[58] In order to address the issues presented by this case it is not necessary for the Court to delineate the boundaries of the broad range of expression deserving of protection under s. 2(*b*) of the Canadian *Charter* or s. 3 of the Quebec *Charter*. It is necessary only to decide if the respondents have a constitutionally protected right to use the English language in the signs they display, or more precisely, whether the fact that such signs have a commercial purpose removes the expression contained therein from the scope of protected freedom.

[59] In our view, the commercial element does not have this effect. Given the earlier pronouncements of this Court to the effect that the rights and freedoms guaranteed in the Canadian *Charter* should be given a large and liberal interpretation, there is no sound basis on which commercial expression can be excluded from the protection of s. 2(*b*) of the *Charter*. It is worth noting that the courts below applied

a similar generous and broad interpretation to include commercial expression within the protection of freedom of expression contained in s. 3 of the Quebec *Charter*. Over and above its intrinsic value as expression, commercial expression which, as has been pointed out, protects listeners as well as speakers plays a significant role in enabling individuals to make informed economic choices, an important aspect of individual self-fulfillment and personal autonomy. The Court accordingly rejects the view that commercial expression serves no individual or societal value in a free and democratic society and for this reason is undeserving of any constitutional protection.

[60] Rather, the expression contemplated by ss. 58 and 69 of the *Charter of the French Language* is expression within the meaning of both s. 2(*b*) of the Canadian *Charter* and s. 3 of the Quebec *Charter*. This leads to the conclusion that s. 58 infringes the freedom of expression guaranteed by s. 3 of the Quebec *Charter* and s. 69 infringes the guaranteed freedom of expression under both s. 2(*b*) of the Canadian *Charter* and s. 3 of the Quebec *Charter*. Although the expression in this case has a commercial element, it should be noted that the focus here is on choice of language and on a law which prohibits the use of a language. We are not asked in this case to deal with the distinct issue of the permissible scope of regulation of advertising (for example to protect consumers) where different governmental interests come into play, particularly when assessing the reasonableness of limits on such commercial expression pursuant to s. 1 of the Canadian *Charter* or to s. 9.1 of the Quebec *Charter*. It remains to be considered whether the limit imposed on freedom of expression by ss. 58 and 69 is justified under either s. 1 of the Canadian *Charter* or s. 9.1 of the Quebec *Charter*, as the case may be.

IX. Whether the Limit Imposed on Freedom of Expression by Sections 58 and 69 of the Charter of the French Language Is Justified Under Section 9.1 of the Quebec Charter of Human Rights and Freedoms and Section 1 of the Canadian Charter of Rights and Freedoms

[61] The issues raised in this part are as follows: (a) the meaning of s. 9.1 of the Quebec *Charter* and whether its role and effect are essentially different from that of s. 1 of the Canadian *Charter*; (b) whether the requirement of the exclusive use of French by ss. 58 and 69 of the *Charter of the French Language* is a limit within the meaning of s. 9.1 and s. 1; (c) whether the material (hereinafter referred to as the s. 1 and s. 9.1 materials) relied on by the Attorney General of Quebec in justification of the limit is properly before the Court; and (d) whether the material justifies the prohibition of the use of any language other than French.

A. The Meaning of Section 9.1 of the Quebec Charter of Human Rights and Freedoms

[62] The issue here is whether s. 9.1 is a justificatory provision similar in its purpose and effect to s. 1 of the Canadian *Charter* and if so what is the test to be applied under it. Section 9.1 is worded differently from s. 1, and it is convenient to set out the two provisions again for comparison, as well as the test under s. 1. Section 9.1 of the Quebec *Charter of Human Rights and Freedoms*, which was added to the *Charter* by *An Act to amend the Charter of Human Rights and Freedoms*, S.Q. 1982, c. 61, s. 2 and entered into force by proclamation on October 1, 1983, reads as follows:

> 9.1. In exercising his fundamental freedoms and rights, a person shall maintain a proper regard for democratic values, public order and the general well-being of the citizens of Québec.
>
> In this respect, the scope of the freedoms and rights, and limits to their exercise, may be fixed by law.

Section 1 of the Canadian *Charter* provides:

> 1. The *Canadian Charter of Rights and Freedoms* guarantees the rights and freedoms set out in it subject only to such reasonable limits prescribed by law as can be demonstrably justified in a free and democratic society.

The test under s. 1 of the Canadian *Charter* was laid down by this Court in *R. v. Oakes, supra*, and restated by the Chief Justice in *R. v. Edwards Books and Art Ltd., supra*, as follows at pp. 768-69:

> Two requirements must be satisfied to establish that a limit is reasonable and demonstrably justified in a free and democratic society. First, the legislative objective which the limitation is designed to promote must be of sufficient importance to warrant overriding a constitutional right. It must bear on a "pressing and substantial concern." Second, the means chosen to attain those objectives must be proportional or appropriate to the ends. The proportionality requirement, in turn, normally has three aspects: the limiting measures must be carefully designed, or rationally connected, to the objective; they must impair the right as little as possible; and their effects must not so severely trench on individual or group rights that the legislative objective, albeit important, is nevertheless outweighed by the abridgment of rights. The Court stated that the nature of the proportionality test would vary depending on the circumstances. Both in articulating the standard of proof and in describing the criteria comprising the proportionality requirement the Court has been careful to avoid rigid and inflexible standards.

[63] It was suggested in argument that because of its quite different wording s. 9.1 was not a justificatory provision similar to s. 1 but merely a provision indicating that the fundamental freedoms and rights guaranteed by the Quebec *Charter* are not absolute but relative and must be construed and exercised in a manner consistent with the values, interests and considerations indicated in s. 9.1—"democratic values, public order and the general well-being of the citizens of Québec." In the case at bar the Superior Court and the Court of Appeal held that s. 9.1 was a justificatory provision corresponding to s. 1 of the Canadian *Charter* and that it was subject, in its application, to a similar test of rational connection and proportionality. This Court agrees with that conclusion. ...

B. Whether the Prohibition of the Use of Any Language Other than French by Sections 58 and 69 of the Charter of the French Language Is a "Limit" on Freedom of Expression Within the Meaning of Section 1 of the Canadian Charter and Section 9.1 of the Quebec Charter

[64] The respondents contended that ss. 58 and 69 of the *Charter of the French Language* were not subject to justification under s. 1 of the *Canadian Charter of Rights and Freedoms* because they prescribe a denial or negation of freedom of expression rather than a limit on it within the meaning of that provision. In support of this contention they referred to the opinion to this effect of Deschênes C.J. in the Superior Court and of a majority of the Court of Appeal in *Quebec Association of Protestant School Boards v. Procureur général du Québec*, [1982] C.S. 673, at pp. 689-93; [1983] C.A. 77, at p. 78. They submitted that while this Court did not rule on the general question whether a denial or negation of a guaranteed right or freedom could be a limit within s. 1, it did not expressly or implicitly disavow the opinion expressed by the Superior Court and the Court of Appeal (*Attorney General of Quebec v. Quebec Association of Protestant School Boards*, [1984] 2 S.C.R. 66, at p. 78). ...

[65] In the *Quebec Association of Protestant School Boards* case, the minority language educational rights created by s. 23 of the Canadian *Charter* were, as the Court observed, of a very specific, special and limited nature, unlike the fundamental rights and freedoms guaranteed by other provisions. They were well defined rights for specific classes of persons. In the opinion of the Court, the effect of ss. 72 and 73 of Bill 101 was to create an exception to s. 23 for Quebec, that is, to make it inapplicable as a whole in Quebec. There was thus what amounted to a complete denial in Quebec of the rights created by s. 23. The extent of the denial was co-extensive with the potential exercise of the very specific and limited rights created

by s. 23. Such an exception to s. 23, as the Court characterized it, was tantamount to an impermissible attempt to override or amend s. 23. An exception of such effect could not be a limit within the meaning of s. 1 of the *Charter*. Thus in so far as the distinction between a complete denial of a right or freedom and a limitation of it is concerned, the *Quebec Association of Protestant School Boards* is a rather unique example of a truly complete denial of guaranteed rights—a denial that is co-extensive with the complete scope of the potential exercise of the rights. The decision is thus not authority for the proposition that where the effect of a legislative provision is to deny or prohibit the exercise of a guaranteed right or freedom in a limited area of its potential exercise that provision cannot be a limit on the right or freedom subject to justification under s. 1.

[66] In the opinion of this Court, apart from the rare case of a truly complete denial of a guaranteed right or freedom in the sense indicated above, the distinction between the negation of a right or freedom and the limitation of it is not a sound basis for denying the application of s. 1 of the *Charter*. Many, if not most, legislative qualifications of a right or freedom in a particular area of its potential exercise will amount to a denial of the right or freedom to that limited extent. If this effect were to mean that s. 1 could have no application in such a case, the section could have little application in practice. ...

C. The Admissibility of the Section 1 and Section 9.1 Materials Submitted in Justification of the Limit Imposed on Freedom of Expression by Sections 58 and 69 of the Charter of the French Language

[68] In the Court of Appeal the Attorney General of Quebec attached to his factum certain material of a justificatory nature which Bisson J.A. referred to as linguistic and sociological studies from Quebec and elsewhere and which the respondents describe in their factum in this Court as "numerous sociological, demographic and linguistic studies." The respondents moved to have this material struck from the record as not being in conformity with art. 507 of the *Code of Civil Procedure* and art. 10 of the Rules of Practice of the Court of Appeal respecting the parts of the record that must be attached to or form part of a factum. The ground of attack was presumably that the material did not form part of the record before the trial judge. ...

[71] In view of the fact that the parties did not appear to be taken by surprise or placed at an unfair disadvantage by the submission of the s. 1 and s. 9.1 materials in this Court, but showed themselves fully prepared to argue the merits of the material, which they did, this Court is of the opinion that the material should be considered as properly before the Court and should be considered by it. The material is of the kind that has been invited and considered by the Court in other cases involving the application of s. 1 of the *Charter*, without having been subjected to the evidentiary testing of the adversary process. It is material that is treated similarly to treatises and articles in other judicial contexts. Due regard should be given, however, to the submissions of the appellant Singer in *Devine* concerning some of the statistical material.

D. Whether the Section 1 and Section 9.1 Materials Justify the Prohibition of the Use of Any Language Other than French

[72] The section 1 and s. 9.1 materials consist of some fourteen items ranging in nature from the general theory of language policy and planning to statistical analysis of the position of the French language in Quebec and Canada. The material deals with two matters of particular relevance to the issue in the appeal: (a) the vulnerable position of the French language in Quebec and Canada, which is the reason for the language policy reflected in the *Charter of the French Language*; and (b) the importance attached by language planning theory to the role of language in the public domain, including the communication or expression by language contemplated by the challenged provisions of the *Charter of the French Language*. As to the first, the material amply establishes the importance of the legislative purpose reflected in the *Charter of the French Language* and that it is a response to a substantial and pressing need. Indeed, this was conceded by the respondents both in the Court of Appeal and in this Court. The vulnerable position of the French language in Quebec and Canada was described in a series of reports by commissions of inquiry beginning with the Report of the Royal Commission on Bilingualism and Biculturalism in 1969 and continuing with the Parent Commission and the Gendron Commission. It is reflected in statistics referred to in these reports and in later studies forming part of the materials, with due adjustment made in the light of the submissions of the appellant Singer in *Devine* with respect to some of the later statistical material. The causal factors for the threatened position of the French language that have generally been identified are: (a) the declining birth rate of Quebec francophones resulting in a decline in the Quebec francophone proportion of the Canadian population as a whole; (b) the decline of the francophone population outside Quebec as a result of assimilation; (c) the greater rate of assimilation of immigrants to Quebec by the anglophone community of Quebec; and (d) the continuing dominance of English at the higher levels of the economic sector. These factors have favoured the use of the

English language despite the predominance in Quebec of a francophone population. Thus, in the period prior to the enactment of the legislation at issue, the "*visage linguistique*" of Quebec often gave the impression that English had become as significant as French. This "*visage linguistique*" reinforced the concern among francophones that English was gaining in importance, that the French language was threatened and that it would ultimately disappear. It strongly suggested to young and ambitious francophones that the language of success was almost exclusively English. It confirmed to anglophones that there was no great need to learn the majority language. And it suggested to immigrants that the prudent course lay in joining the anglophone community. The aim of such provisions as ss. 58 and 69 of the *Charter of the French Language* was, in the words of its preamble, "to see the quality and influence of the French language assured." The threat to the French language demonstrated to the government that it should, in particular, take steps to assure that the "*visage linguistique*" of Quebec would reflect the predominance of the French language.

[73] The section 1 and s. 9.1 materials establish that the aim of the language policy underlying the *Charter of the French Language* was a serious and legitimate one. They indicate the concern about the survival of the French language and the perceived need for an adequate legislative response to the problem. Moreover, they indicate a rational connection between protecting the French language and assuring that the reality of Quebec society is communicated through the "*visage linguistique*." The section 1 and s. 9.1 materials do not, however, demonstrate that the requirement of the use of French only is either necessary for the achievement of the legislative objective or proportionate to it. That specific question is simply not addressed by the materials. Indeed, in his factum and oral argument the Attorney General of Quebec did not attempt to justify the requirement of the exclusive use of French. He concentrated on the reasons for the adoption of the *Charter of the French Language* and the earlier language legislation, which, as was noted above, were conceded by the respondents. The Attorney General of Quebec relied on what he referred to as the general democratic legitimacy of Quebec language policy without referring explicitly to the requirement of the exclusive use of French. In so far as proportionality is concerned, the Attorney General of Quebec referred to the American jurisprudence with respect to commercial speech, presumably as indicating the judicial deference that should be paid to the legislative choice of means to serve an admittedly legitimate legislative purpose, at least in the area of commercial expression. He did, however, refer in justification of the requirement of the exclusive use of French to the attenuation of this requirement reflected in ss. 59 to 62 of the *Charter of the French Language* and the regulations. He submitted that these exceptions to the requirement of the exclusive use of French indicate the concern for carefully designed measures and for interfering as little as possible with commercial expression. The qualifications of the requirement of the exclusive use of French in other provisions of the *Charter of the French Language* and the regulations do not make ss. 58 and 69 any less prohibitions of the use of any language other than French as applied to the respondents. The issue is whether any such prohibition is justified. In the opinion of this Court it has not been demonstrated that the prohibition of the use of any language other than French in ss. 58 and 69 of the *Charter of the French Language* is necessary to the defence and enhancement of the status of the French language in Quebec or that it is proportionate to that legislative purpose. Since the evidence put to us by the government showed that the predominance of the French language was not reflected in the "*visage linguistique*" of Quebec, the governmental response could well have been tailored to meet that specific problem and to impair freedom of expression minimally. Thus, whereas requiring the predominant display of the French language, even its marked predominance, would be proportional to the goal of promoting and maintaining a French "*visage linguistique*" in Quebec and therefore justified under the Quebec *Charter* and the Canadian *Charter*, requiring the exclusive use of French has not been so justified. French could be required in addition to any other language or it could be required to have greater visibility than that accorded to other languages. Such measures would ensure that the "*visage linguistique*" reflected the demography of Quebec: the predominant language is French. This reality should be communicated to all citizens and non-citizens alike, irrespective of their mother tongue. But exclusivity for the French language has not survived the scrutiny of a proportionality test and does not reflect the reality of Quebec society. Accordingly, we are of the view that the limit imposed on freedom of expression by s. 58 of the *Charter of the French Language* respecting the exclusive use of French on public signs and posters and in commercial advertising is not justified under s. 9.1 of the Quebec *Charter*. In like measure, the limit imposed on freedom of expression by s. 69 of the *Charter of the French Language* respecting the exclusive use of the French version of a firm name is not justified under either s. 9.1 of the Quebec *Charter* or s. 1 of the Canadian *Charter*. ...

X. Do Sections 58 and 69 of the Charter of the French Language Infringe the Guarantee Against Discrimination Based on Language in Section 10 of the Quebec Charter of Human Rights and Freedoms?

[74] In view of the above conclusion it is not necessary to the disposition of the appeal that the Court should pronounce

on the contention of the respondents that ss. 58 and 69 of the *Charter of the French Language* are inoperative as infringing the guarantee against discrimination based on language in s. 10 of the Quebec *Charter of Human Rights and Freedoms*. In view, however, of the fact that this issue is also raised in the *Devine* appeal and the Superior Court and the Court of Appeal addressed it in both cases it is probably desirable that this Court should do so as well because of the general importance of the question.

[75] For convenience s. 10 of the Quebec *Charter* is quoted again:

> 10. Every person has a right to full and equal recognition and exercise of his human rights and freedoms, without distinction, exclusion or preference based on race, colour, sex, pregnancy, sexual orientation, civil status, age except as provided by law, religion, political convictions, language, ethnic or national origin, social condition, a handicap or the use of any means to palliate a handicap.
>
> Discrimination exists where such a distinction, exclusion or preference has the effect of nullifying or impairing such right. ...

[82] Thus in addressing the question whether s. 58 of the *Charter of the French Language* infringes the guarantee against discrimination based on language in s. 10 of the Quebec *Charter of Human Rights and Freedoms* we are obliged to consider the effect of s. 58, in so far as that may be ascertained. The second observation to be made here is that in order for a distinction based on a prohibited ground to constitute discrimination within the meaning of s. 10 it must have the effect of nullifying or impairing the right to full and equal recognition and exercise of a human right or freedom, which must mean a human right or freedom recognized by the Quebec *Charter of Human Rights and Freedoms*. With these observations in mind we turn to the question whether s. 58 infringes s. 10. It purports, as was said by the Superior Court and the Court of Appeal, to apply to everyone, regardless of their language of use, the requirement of the exclusive use of French. It has the effect, however, of impinging differentially on different classes of persons according to their language of use. Francophones are permitted to use their language of use while anglophones and other non-francophones are prohibited from doing so. Does this differential effect constitute a distinction based on language within the meaning of s. 10 of the Quebec *Charter?* In this Court's opinion it does. Section 58 of the *Charter of the French Language*, because of its differential effect or impact on persons according to their language of use, creates a distinction between such persons based on language of use. It is then necessary to consider whether this

distinction has the effect of nullifying or impairing the right to full and equal recognition and exercise of a human right or freedom recognized by the Quebec *Charter*. The human right or freedom in issue in this case is the freedom to express oneself in the language of one's choice, which has been held to be recognized by s. 3 of the Quebec *Charter*. In this case, the limit imposed on that right was not a justifiable one under s. 9.1 of the Quebec *Charter*. The distinction based on language of use created by s. 58 of the *Charter of the French Language* thus has the effect of nullifying the right to full and equal recognition and exercise of this freedom. Section 58 is therefore also of no force or effect as infringing s. 10 of the Quebec *Charter*. The same conclusion must apply to s. 69 of the *Charter of the French Language*. We note that since one of the respondents, Valerie Ford, is an individual and not a corporation, it is unnecessary in this case to decide whether corporations are entitled to claim the benefit of equality guarantees and we do not do so.

[83] For these reasons the appeal is dismissed with costs and the constitutional questions are answered as follows:

1. Are section 214 of the *Charter of the French Language*, R.S.Q. 1977, c. C-11, as enacted by S.Q. 1982, c. 21, s. 1, and s. 52 of *An Act to amend the Charter of the French Language*, S.Q. 1983, c. 56, inconsistent with s. 33(1) of the *Constitution Act, 1982* and therefore inoperative and of no force or effect under s. 52(1) of the latter *Act?*

Answer: No, except in so far as s. 214 is given retrospective effect by s. 7 of *An Act respecting the Constitution Act, 1982*, S.Q. 1982, c. 21.

2. If the answer to question 1 is affirmative, to the extent that they require the exclusive use of the French language, are ss. 58 and 69, and ss. 205 to 208 to the extent they apply thereto, of the *Charter of the French Language*, R.S.Q. 1977, c. C-11, as amended by S.Q. 1983, c. 56, inconsistent with the guarantee of freedom of expression under s. 2(b) of the *Canadian Charter of Rights and Freedoms?*

Answer: In so far as s. 214 of the *Charter of the French Language* has ceased to have effect but s. 52 of *An Act to amend the Charter of the French Language* remains in effect, s. 58 of the *Charter of the French Language* is protected from the application of the *Canadian Charter of Rights and Freedoms* but it is inoperative as infringing the guarantee of freedom of expression in s. 3 of the Quebec *Charter of Human Rights and Freedoms* and the guarantee against discrimination based on language in s. 10 of the Quebec *Charter*. In so far as s. 214 of the *Charter of the French Language* has ceased to have effect,

s. 69 thereof is inconsistent with the guarantee of freedom of expression under s. 2(b) of the *Canadian Charter of Rights and Freedoms.* Sections 205 to 208 of the *Charter of the French Language* to the extent they apply to s. 69 thereof are inconsistent with the guarantee of freedom of expression under s. 2(b) of the *Canadian Charter of Rights and Freedoms.* Section 69 of the *Charter of the French Language,* and ss. 205 to 208 thereof, to the extent they apply to ss. 58 and 69, are also inconsistent with the guarantee of freedom of expression under s. 3 of the Quebec *Charter of Human Rights and Freedoms.*

3. If the answer to question 2 is affirmative in whole or in part, are ss. 58 and 69, and ss. 205 to 208 to the extent they apply thereto, of the *Charter of the French Language,* R.S.Q. 1977, c. C-11, as amended by S.Q.

1983, c. 56, justified by the application of s. 1 of the *Canadian Charter of Rights and Freedoms* and therefore not inconsistent with the *Constitution Act, 1982?*

Answer: Section 58 of the *Charter of the French Language* is not justified under s. 9.1 of the Quebec *Charter of Human Rights and Freedoms.* Section 69 of the *Charter of the French Language,* and ss. 205 to 208 thereof, to the extent they apply to s. 69, are not justified under s. 1 of the *Canadian Charter of Rights and Freedoms* and are therefore inconsistent with the *Constitution Act, 1982.* Nor is s. 69 of the *Charter of the French Language,* or ss. 205 to 208 thereof, to the extent they apply to ss. 58 and 69, justified under s. 9.1 of the Quebec *Charter of Human Rights and Freedoms.*

6 R. v. Butler, 1992

All nine Supreme Court judges (via two opinions) voted to uphold the censorship of obscenity in *Butler*. At issue was section 163(8) of the *Criminal Code*, which defined prohibited obscenity as "any publication a dominant characteristic of which is the undue exploitation of sex, or of sex and any one or more of the following subjects, namely, crime, horror, cruelty and violence." As in the case of hate speech, obscenity was expression protected by section 2(*b*) of the Charter, meaning that the censorship provision could be sustained only as a section 1 "reasonable limit" on freedom of expression. At the same time, and again like hate speech, obscenity was judged to fall some distance from the core freedom-of-expression values—"the search for truth, participation in the political process, and individual self-fulfilment"—making its restriction "easier to justify [under section 1] than other infringements."

Did the censorship law have the kind of "pressing and substantial" purpose required of a "reasonable limit" under the *Oakes* test? Not if the law's purpose was simply to protect moral sensibilities from the public display of any kind of explicit sexuality. That was indeed the purpose of censorship laws in the past, but "the prevention of 'dirt for dirt's sake,'" wrote Justice Sopinka, "is not a legitimate objective which would justify the violation of one of the most fundamental freedoms enshrined in the *Charter*." A valid objective must emphasize "not moral disapproval but the avoidance of harm to society." Justice Sopinka was careful to reject a strict separation of law and morality. Indeed, he considered "moral corruption and harm to society [not as] distinct, but [as] inextricably linked [because it] is moral corruption of a certain kind which leads to the detrimental effect on society." His point was that while immorality may indeed cause the kind of harm needed for section 1 justification, not everything traditionally considered immoral causes such harm. Whether a depiction of sexuality was harmful was to be determined by "community standards," which had changed over time. No doubt, those who previously prohibited "dirt for dirt's sake" thought they were preventing "harm to society," but "our understanding of the harms caused by these materials has developed considerably."

For Justice Sopinka, this meant that in the Charter era a censorship law could not fully cover three common categories of pornography: (1) explicit sex with violence; (2) explicit sex without violence, but which subjects people to treatment that is degrading or dehumanizing; and (3) explicit sex without violence that is neither degrading nor dehumanizing. The first two categories were clearly harmful according to modern "community standards"; the third, with the crucial exception of child pornography, was not. As long as it depicts adults, the third kind of pornography is "good pornography" (or "erotica") that celebrates consensual sexuality based on equality between the participants. Bad pornography, the kind that could legitimately be censored, especially involved harm to women and children. Finding that section 163(8) was indeed targeted at the "harmful" categories of pornography and not at the legitimate "erotica," Justice Sopinka concluded that it met the "pressing and substantial purpose" part of the *Oakes* test.

Justice Sopinka had clearly responded to the request by the Women's Legal Education and Action Fund (LEAF) "to redefine the rationale for the *Criminal Code* obscenity provisions by focusing on its equality implications for women and children."[1] This feminist reading of section 163(8) attracted international attention as a pathbreaking innovation. *The New York Times* reported that the decision made "Canada the first place in the world that says what is obscene is what harms women."[2] The prominent American feminist Catherine MacKinnon, who had helped write LEAF's factum, devoted significant portions of her 1993 book *Only Words* to praising the innovation wrought by *Butler*.[3] Kathleen Mahoney, another co-author of LEAF's factum, called the ruling "world historic."[4]

Had this "world historic" innovation been in the minds of the legislators who enacted section 163 in 1959? It seems unlikely, and that posed a difficulty for Justice Sopinka. In *Big M Drug Mart* (case 4), the court, rejecting the idea that a "shifting purpose" had transformed the obviously religious *Lord's Day Act* into secular day-of-rest legislation, insisted that the legislative purpose subjected to Charter scrutiny had to be what was in the minds of the legislature at the time of enactment. If he wished to respect the *Big M* precedent, as he clearly did, Justice Sopinka had to show that his innovative reading of section 163(8) did not amount to a "shifting purpose." He did so by distinguishing a "permissible shift in emphasis" from a complete shift in purpose. Preventing harm had always been the purpose of section 163; there had simply been a "shift in emphasis" in how we understand harm.[5] LEAF had considered asking the court "to strike down the *Criminal Code* provisions and [invite] Parliament to introduce new legislation,"[6] but decided to press instead for a significant reinterpretation of the existing law. The former strategy would have required no "shifting purpose"; the latter required at least a "shift in emphasis."

Justice Gonthier (joined by Justice L'Heureux-Dubé) concurred in the result and supported much of the majority's reasoning, but thought that the modern understanding of harm might still reach adult "erotica" in some cases. Gonthier emphasized the distinction between private activity and its public representation in various media. A sexual activity that is good and meaningful in private can be stripped of its human significance when it is represented to the public in ways that do not "reflect the richness of human sexuality, but rather turn it into pure animality." Such misrepresentations of human sexuality can be more or less problematic depending on the kind of media and publicity involved. Thus, a portrayal of explicit "erotica" that would be of little concern in the pages of a book might, "[i]f found

---

1   Karen Busby, "LEAF and Pornography: Litigating on Equality and Sexual Representations" (1994) 9 *Canadian Journal of Law and Society* 169.

2   (28 February 1992).

3   Catherine MacKinnon, *Only Words* (Boston: Harvard University Press, 1993).

4   Stephen Bindman, "Top court upholds anti-pornography law," *Montreal Gazette* (28 February 1992) B1.

5   Not everyone finds the distinction persuasive. See Jonathon Daniels, "Valid Despite Vagueness: The Relationship Between Vagueness and Shifting Objective" (1994) *Saskatchewan Law Review* 58.

6   Busby, *supra* note 1.

on a billboard sign, ... be an undue exploitation of sex, because the community does not tolerate it, on the basis of its harmfulness." Gonthier worried that Justice Sopinka's liberation of "erotica" might extend too far.

In *R. v. Keegstra* (1990),[7] an earlier hate-speech case (see the introduction to *Whatcott*, case 10), Justice Sopinka (along with Justice La Forest) had joined in Justice McLachlin's opinion that the hate-speech provision of the *Criminal Code* was not rationally connected to its objective because, instead of promoting egalitarian sentiments, censorship was more likely to strengthen racist expression. In *Butler*, Sopinka (with the support of McLachlin and La Forest) came to the opposite conclusion about the censorship of obscenity: "In contrast to the hate-monger who may succeed, by the sudden media attention, in gaining an audience, the prohibition of obscene materials does nothing to promote the pornographer's cause." Censorship of obscenity, in other words, does not irrationally produce the opposite of what it intends. But does it actually produce what it intends? What if obscenity is a reflection or symptom of bad attitudes rather than their cause? What if it actually provides a safety valve for the safe release of attitudes that might otherwise be acted out in truly harmful ways? Would censorship not then be irrational? Perhaps, but the social science evidence on whether obscenity is harmful is contradictory and inconclusive. Here, Sopinka reaffirmed the holding of earlier decisions that "in the face of inconclusive social science evidence" legislatures need only a "reasonable basis" for their ameliorative initiatives, a criterion fulfilled in the case of the obscenity provision. Similarly, on the basis of precedents holding that a law need not be perfectly tailored in order to satisfy the "minimal impairment" part of the *Oakes* test, Sopinka found that section 163 met that test and that its "restriction on freedom of expression [did] not outweigh the importance of the legislative objective."

The judicial agreement in *Butler* stands in stark contrast not only to the earlier disagreement in *Keegstra* but also to the subsequent disagreement in *R. v. Zundel*, which was heard and decided at roughly the same time as *Butler*.[8] Ernst Zundel, a Holocaust denier, had been charged under section 181 of the *Criminal Code*, which made it an indictable offence for anyone to "wilfully" publish "a statement, tale or news that he knows is false and that causes or is likely to cause injury or mischief to a public interest." As in *Keegstra*, a 7-judge panel split 4 to 3, but this time Justice McLachlin wrote the majority opinion invalidating the law. She was joined by Justices La Forest and Sopinka, who had supported her *Keegstra* dissent, and by Justice L'Heureux-Dubé, who had been part of the *Keegstra* majority. For McLachlin, the "false news" provision was an unreasonable limit on freedom of expression because its original purpose—dating back to 1275—was to protect the King and the nobles against slander that might undermine their legitimacy and destabilize the state. This could not be the kind of "pressing and substantial purpose" needed to override freedom of expression in the Charter era. The dissenting judgment, written by Justice Gonthier, argued that this original purpose had evolved in the same way that the purpose of the obscenity provision at stake in *Butler* had evolved. While the original purpose of the false-news provision may have been to protect the interest of the nobles, it was now targeted at "the dissemination of

---

7   The case report for *R. v. Keegstra*, [1990] 3 S.C.R. 697 is available in the instructor's supplements package.

8   *Butler* was heard on June 6, 1991 and decided on February 27, 1992; *Zundel* was heard on December 10, 1991 and decided on August 27, 1992.

false information which strikes at important interests of *society as a whole*" (emphasis added). This, for Justice Gonthier, was a "permissible shift in emphasis" rather than the kind of "shifting purpose" rejected in *Big M*. Justice McLachlin's majority, all of whom had agreed in *Butler* to introduce the distinction Gonthier was using, vigorously disagreed. It is by no means uncommon to see a concept unanimously introduced to resolve one case fuelling disagreement in others down the road.

While LEAF and pro-censorship feminists exulted in their victory in *Butler*, others, including libertarian feminists and gay and lesbian activists, opposed the decision. It was argued, for example, that *Butler*'s criminalizing of violent, degrading, and dehumanizing sex would disproportionately affect gay and lesbian pornography, where sado-masochistic portrayals do not involve structured inequality between the sexes and may be strongly related to sexual identity. In this view, the *Butler* definition of illegal pornography was fundamentally "heterosexist" and did not leave enough room for sexual diversity. This issue arrived at the Supreme Court in 2000 in *Little Sisters Book and Art Emporium v. Canada*.[9] Little Sisters is a gay and lesbian bookstore whose imports had indeed been disproportionately targeted at the border by Canada Customs. The Supreme Court agreed that Customs had been applying the law in a discriminatory manner, but rejected the position, supported by LEAF, "that sado-masochism performs an emancipatory role in gay and lesbian culture and should therefore be judged by a different standard from that applicable to heterosexual culture." The *Butler* standard of harm, as determined by "community standards," would apply equally to heterosexual and homosexual pornography.

The court revisited the issue of obscenity again in 2001 in *R. v. Sharpe*.[10] In the immediate aftermath of *Butler*, the federal government added a new, explicit child-pornography dimension to the *Criminal Code*. Among other things, the new section 163.1 criminalizes not just the "possession" of child pornography for purposes of distribution or sale but also purely private possession of such material. John Robin Sharpe was charged on both counts for possessing such material as "Sam Paloc's Boyabuse—Flogging, Fun and Fortitude: A Collection of Kiddiekink Classics." He did not constitutionally challenge the charge of possession for distribution and sale, but argued that prohibiting mere private possession could not be justified as a reasonable limit on freedom of expression. The trial court and a majority of the Court of Appeal agreed with him, striking down the simple possession provision and bringing its enforcement temporarily to a halt in British Columbia. As soon as the trial court handed down its decision in January 1999 there was an immense public outcry. All parties in the House of Commons severely criticized the decision, though they disagreed about the appropriate response, with the Reform Party opposition advocating the use of section 33 of the Charter to immediately restore the provision and the Liberal government expressing its confidence that higher courts, including ultimately the Supreme Court, would overrule the trial court.[11] The Liberals were wrong about the Court of Appeal, but right about the Supreme Court.

---

9   2000 SCC 69, [2000] 2 S.C.R. 1120.

10   2000 SCC 2, [2001] 1 S.C.R. 45.

11   See Rainer Knopff, "A Delicate Dance: The Courts and the Chrétien Government, 1993-2000" in Leslie A. Pal, ed., *How Ottawa Spends 2001-2002: Power in Transition* (Toronto: Oxford University Press, 2001).

The court heard *Sharpe* on January 18 and 19, 2000, but did not hand down its decision until January 26, 2001. This was two to three times the normal gestation period, leading to speculation that the court dragged out its ruling until after the 2000 election.[12] In the event, the court unanimously upheld the prohibition of simple possession of child pornography. Three of the judges—L'Heureux-Dubé, Gonthier, and Bastarache—would have upheld the law without reservation. Writing for the other six, Justice McLachlin read two exceptions into the provision. First, the prohibition of simple possession would not extend to "any written material or visual representation created by the accused alone, and held by the accused alone, exclusively for his or her own personal use." To illustrate, Justice McLachlin used the example of a teenager's confidential diary. Second, the provision would not reach "any visual recording, created by or depicting the accused, provided it does not depict unlawful sexual activity and is held by the accused exclusively for private use." Here the example was "a teenage couple [who created and kept] sexually explicit pictures featuring each other alone, or together engaged in lawful sexual activity, provided these pictures were created together and shared only with one another."

In *Sharpe*, as elsewhere, Justice McLachlin was on the more libertarian side of a freedom-of-expression issue, though this was much more moderate libertarianism than had been exhibited by the lower courts. McLachlin's *Sharpe* decision, in writing new meaning into the legislation, represented important legal innovation in the context of overall deference to a government policy. The same, of course, was true of Justice Sopinka's *Butler* opinion, which, while not activist in the sense of striking down a law, was widely recognized as a dramatic—even "world historic"—interpretive innovation. ⁓

Discussion Questions

1. What would Justice Gonthier be prepared to censor that Justice Sopinka would not? How significant is this disagreement?

2. Justices Sopinka and McLachlin vote to strike down the censorship of hate speech in *Keegstra* and to uphold the censorship of obscenity in *Butler*. Are you persuaded by Justice Sopinka's explanation of this difference?

---

12 "Analysts speculate judges may be holding back pornography ruling for political reasons," *The National Post* (15 November 2000).

R. v. BUTLER
[1992] 1 S.C.R. 452

Hearing: June 6, 1991; Judgment: February 27, 1992.

Present: Lamer C.J. and La Forest, L'Heureux-Dubé, Sopinka, Gonthier, Cory, McLachlin, Stevenson, and Iacobucci JJ.

Interveners: The Attorney General of Canada, the Attorney General for Ontario, the Attorney General of Quebec, the Attorney General of British Columbia, the Attorney General for Alberta, Canadian Civil Liberties Association, Manitoba Association for Rights and Liberties, British Columbia Civil Liberties Association, Women's Legal Education and Action Fund, and G.A.P. (Group Against Pornography) Inc.

The judgment of Lamer C.J. and La Forest, Sopinka, Cory, McLachlin, Stevenson, and Iacobucci JJ. was delivered by

SOPINKA J.: This appeal calls into question the constitutionality of the obscenity provisions of the *Criminal Code*, R.S.C., 1985, c. C-46, s. 163. They are attacked on the ground that they contravene s. 2(*b*) of the *Canadian Charter of Rights and Freedoms*. ...

... [T]his appeal should be confined to the examination of the constitutional validity of s. 163(8) only. ...

(8) For the purposes of this Act, any publication a dominant characteristic of which is the undue exploitation of sex, or of sex and any one or more of the following subjects, namely, crime, horror, cruelty and violence, shall be deemed to be obscene.

... Pornography can be usefully divided into three categories: (1) explicit sex with violence, (2) explicit sex without violence but which subjects people to treatment that is degrading or dehumanizing, and (3) explicit sex without violence that is neither degrading nor dehumanizing. Violence in this context includes both actual physical violence and threats of physical violence. Relating these three categories to the terms of s. 163(8) of the *Code*, the first, explicit sex coupled with violence, is expressly mentioned. Sex coupled with crime, horror or cruelty will sometimes involve violence. Cruelty, for instance, will usually do so. But, even in the absence of violence, sex coupled with crime, horror or cruelty may fall within the second category. As for category (3), subject to the exception referred to below, it is not covered.

Some segments of society would consider that all three categories of pornography cause harm to society because they tend to undermine its moral fibre. Others would contend that none of the categories cause harm. Furthermore there is a range of opinion as to what is degrading or dehumanizing. See *Pornography and Prostitution in Canada: Report of the Special Committee on Pornography and Prostitution* (1985) (the Fraser Report), vol. 1, at p. 51. Because this is not a matter that is susceptible of proof in the traditional way and because we do not wish to leave it to the individual tastes of judges, we must have a norm that will serve as an arbiter in determining what amounts to an undue exploitation of sex. That arbiter is the community as a whole.

The courts must determine as best they can what the community would tolerate others being exposed to on the basis of the degree of harm that may flow from such exposure. Harm in this context means that it predisposes persons to act in an anti-social manner as, for example, the physical or mental mistreatment of women by men, or, what is perhaps debatable, the reverse. Anti-social conduct for this purpose is conduct which society formally recognizes as incompatible with its proper functioning. The stronger the inference of a risk of harm the lesser the likelihood of tolerance. The inference may be drawn from the material itself or from the material and other evidence. Similarly evidence as to the community standards is desirable but not essential.

In making this determination with respect to the three categories of pornography referred to above, the portrayal of

sex coupled with violence will almost always constitute the undue exploitation of sex. Explicit sex which is degrading or dehumanizing may be undue if the risk of harm is substantial. Finally, explicit sex that is not violent and neither degrading nor dehumanizing is generally tolerated in our society and will not qualify as the undue exploitation of sex unless it employs children in its production.

If material is not obscene under this framework, it does not become so by reason of the person to whom it is or may be shown or exposed nor by reason of the place or manner in which it is shown. The availability of sexually explicit materials in theatres and other public places is subject to regulation by competent provincial legislation. Typically such legislation imposes restrictions on the material available to children. See *Nova Scotia Board of Censors v. McNeil*, [1978] 2 S.C.R. 662.

[It is also necessary to determine whether the] undue exploitation of sex [is] the main object of the work or [whether] this portrayal of sex [is] essential to a wider artistic, literary, or other similar purpose? Since the threshold determination must be made on the basis of community standards, that is, whether the sexually explicit aspect is undue, its impact when considered in context must be determined on the same basis. The court must determine whether the sexually explicit material when viewed in the context of the whole work would be tolerated by the community as a whole. Artistic expression rests at the heart of freedom of expression values and any doubt in this regard must be resolved in favour of freedom of expression. ...

In light of our recent decision in *R. v. Keegstra*, [1990] 3 S.C.R. 697, the respondent, and most of the parties intervening in support of the respondent, do not take issue with the proposition that s. 163 of the *Criminal Code* violates s. 2(*b*) of the *Charter*. In *Keegstra*, we were unanimous in advocating a generous approach to the protection afforded by s. 2(*b*) of the *Charter*. Our Court confirmed the view expressed in *Reference re ss. 193 and 195.1(1)(c) of the Criminal Code (Man.)*, [1990] 1 S.C.R. 1123 (the *"Prostitution Reference"*), that activities cannot be excluded from the scope of the guaranteed freedom on the basis of the content or meaning being conveyed. ...

Meaning sought to be expressed need not be "redeeming" in the eyes of the court to merit the protection of s. 2(*b*), whose purpose is to ensure that thoughts and feelings may be conveyed freely in non-violent ways without fear of censure.

In this case, both the purpose and effect of s. 163 are specifically to restrict the communication of certain types of materials based on their content. In my view, there is no doubt that s. 163 seeks to prohibit certain types of expressive activity and thereby infringes s. 2(*b*) of the *Charter*.

Before turning to consider whether this infringement is justified under s. 1 of the *Charter*, I wish to address the argument advanced by the Attorney General of B.C. that in applying s. 2(*b*), a distinction should be made between films and written works. It is argued that by its very nature, the medium of the written word is such that it is, when used, inherently an attempt to convey meaning. In contrast, British Columbia argues that the medium of film can be used for a purpose "not significantly communicative." In its factum, British Columbia maintains that if the activity captured in hard core pornographic magazines and videotapes is itself not expression, the fact that they are reproduced by the technology of a camera does not magically transform them into "expression": the appellant cannot hide behind the label "film" to claim protection for the reproduction of activity the sole purpose of which is to arouse or shock.

In my view, this submission cannot be maintained. This position is not far from that taken by the majority of the Court of Appeal, that the depiction of purely physical activity does not convey meaning. First, I cannot agree with the premise that purely physical activity, such as sexual activity, cannot be expression. Second, in creating a film, regardless of its content, the maker of the film is consciously choosing the particular images which together constitute the film. In choosing his or her images, the creator of the film is attempting to convey some meaning. The meaning to be ascribed to the work cannot be measured by the reaction of the audience, which, in some cases, may amount to no more than physical arousal or shock. Rather, the meaning of the work derives from the fact that it has been intentionally created by its author. To use an example, it may very well be said that a blank wall in itself conveys no meaning. However, if one deliberately chooses to capture that image by the medium of film, the work necessarily has some meaning for its author and thereby constitutes expression. The same would apply to the depiction of persons engaged in purely sexual activity.

D. Is Section 163 Justified Under Section 1 of the Charter?

The appellant argues that the provision is so vague that … it does not qualify as "a limit prescribed by law"; … so imprecise that it is not a reasonable limit. …

Standards which escape precise technical definition, such as "undue," are an inevitable part of the law. … It is within the role of the judiciary to attempt to interpret these terms. If such interpretation yields an intelligible standard, the threshold test for the application of s. 1 is met. In my opinion, the interpretation of s. 163(8) in prior judgments which I have reviewed, as supplemented by these reasons, provides an intelligible standard. …

The respondent argues that there are several pressing and substantial objectives which justify overriding the freedom to distribute obscene materials. Essentially, these objectives are the avoidance of harm resulting from antisocial attitudinal changes that exposure to obscene material causes and the public interest in maintaining a "decent society." On the other hand, the appellant argues that the objective of s. 163 is to have the state act as "moral custodian" in sexual matters and to impose subjective standards of morality.

The obscenity legislation and jurisprudence prior to the enactment of s. 163 were evidently concerned with prohibiting the "immoral influences" of obscene publications and safeguarding the morals of individuals into whose hands such works could fall. …

I agree with Twaddle J.A. of the Court of Appeal that this particular objective is no longer defensible in view of the *Charter*. To impose a certain standard of public and sexual morality, solely because it reflects the conventions of a given community, is inimical to the exercise and enjoyment of individual freedoms, which form the basis of our social contract. … The prevention of "dirt for dirt's sake" is not a legitimate objective which would justify the violation of one of the most fundamental freedoms enshrined in the *Charter*.

On the other hand, I cannot agree with the suggestion of the appellant that Parliament does not have the right to legislate on the basis of some fundamental conception of morality for the purposes of safeguarding the values which are integral to a free and democratic society. As Dyzenhaus ["Obscenity and the Charter: Autonomy and Equality" (1991), 1 C.R. (4th) 367], at p. 376, writes:

> Moral disapprobation is recognized as an appropriate response when it has its basis in *Charter* values.

As the respondent and many of the interveners have pointed out, much of the criminal law is based on moral conceptions of right and wrong and the mere fact that a law is grounded in morality does not automatically render it illegitimate. In this regard, criminalizing the proliferation of materials which undermine another basic *Charter* right may indeed be a legitimate objective.

In my view, however, the overriding objective of s. 163 is not moral disapprobation but the avoidance of harm to society. …

The harm was described in the following way in the Report on Pornography by the Standing Committee on Justice and Legal Affairs (MacGuigan Report) (1978), at p. 18:4:

> The clear and unquestionable danger of this type of material is that it reinforces some unhealthy tendencies in Canadian society. The effect of this type of material is to reinforce male–female stereotypes to the detriment of both sexes. It attempts to make degradation, humiliation,

victimization, and violence in human relationships appear normal and acceptable. A society which holds that egalitarianism, non-violence, consensualism, and mutuality are basic to any human interaction, whether sexual or other, is clearly justified in controlling and prohibiting any medium of depiction, description or advocacy which violates these principles.

The appellant argues that to accept the objective of the provision as being related to the harm associated with obscenity would be to adopt the "shifting purpose" doctrine explicitly rejected in *R. v. Big M Drug Mart Ltd.*, [1985] 1 S.C.R. 295. This Court concluded in that case that a finding that the *Lord's Day Act* has a secular purpose was not possible given that its religious purpose, in compelling sabbatical observance, has been long-established and consistently maintained by the courts. ...

I do not agree that to identify the objective of the impugned legislation as the prevention of harm to society, one must resort to the "shifting purpose" doctrine. First, the notions of moral corruption and harm to society are not distinct, as the appellant suggests, but are inextricably linked. It is moral corruption of a certain kind which leads to the detrimental effect on society. Second, and more importantly, I am of the view that with the enactment of s. 163, Parliament explicitly sought to address the harms which are linked to certain types of obscene materials. The prohibition of such materials was based on a belief that they had a detrimental impact on individuals exposed to them and consequently on society as a whole. Our understanding of the harms caused by these materials has developed considerably since that time; however this does not detract from the fact that the purpose of this legislation remains, as it was in 1959, the protection of society from harms caused by the exposure to obscene materials. ...

A permissible shift in emphasis was built into the legislation when, as interpreted by the courts, it adopted the community standards test. Community standards as to what is harmful have changed since 1959.

This being the objective, is it pressing and substantial? Does the prevention of the harm associated with the dissemination of certain obscene materials constitute a sufficiently pressing and substantial concern to warrant a restriction on the freedom of expression? In this regard, it should be recalled that in *Keegstra, supra*, this Court unanimously accepted that the prevention of the influence of hate propaganda on society at large was a legitimate objective. ...

This Court has thus recognized that the harm caused by the proliferation of materials which seriously offend the values fundamental to our society is a substantial concern which justifies restricting the otherwise full exercise of the freedom of expression. In my view, the harm sought to be avoided in the case of the dissemination of obscene materials is similar. ...

In reaching the conclusion that legislation proscribing obscenity is a valid objective which justifies some encroachment on the right to freedom of expression, I am persuaded in part that such legislation may be found in most free and democratic societies. As Nemetz C.J.B.C. aptly pointed out in *R. v. Red Hot Video*, [(1985), 45 C.R. (3d) 36 (B.C.C.A.)], for centuries democratic societies have set certain limits to freedom of expression. He cited (at p. 40) the following passage of Dickson J.A. (as he then was) in *R. v. Great West News Ltd.*, *supra*, at p. 309:

> ... [A]ll organized societies have sought in one manner or another to suppress obscenity. The right of the state to legislate to protect its moral fibre and well-being has long been recognized, with roots deep in history. It is within this frame that the Courts and Judges must work.

The advent of the *Charter* did not have the effect of dramatically depriving Parliament of a power which it has historically enjoyed. It is also noteworthy that the criminalization of obscenity was considered to be compatible with the *Canadian Bill of Rights*. ...

The enactment of the impugned provision is also consistent with Canada's international obligations (Agreement for the Suppression of the Circulation of Obscene Publications and the Convention for the Suppression of the Circulation of and Traffic in Obscene Publications).

Finally, it should be noted that the burgeoning pornography industry renders the concern even more pressing and substantial than when the impugned provisions were first enacted. I would therefore conclude that the objective of avoiding the harm associated with the dissemination of pornography in this case is sufficiently pressing and substantial to warrant some restriction on full exercise of the right to freedom of expression. The analysis of whether the measure is proportional to the objective must, in my view, be undertaken in light of the conclusion that the objective of the impugned section is valid only in so far as it relates to the harm to society associated with obscene materials. Indeed, the section as interpreted in previous decisions and in these reasons is fully consistent with that objective. The objective of maintaining conventional standards of propriety, independently of any harm to society, is no longer justified in light of the values of individual liberty which underlie the *Charter*. ...

In assessing whether the proportionality test is met, it is important to keep in mind the nature of expression which has been infringed. In the *Prostitution Reference, supra*, Dickson C.J. wrote, at p. 1136:

When a *Charter* freedom has been infringed by state action that takes the form of criminalization, the Crown bears the heavy burden of justifying that infringement. Yet, the expressive activity, as with any infringed *Charter* right, should also be analysed in the particular context of the case. Here, the activity to which the impugned legislation is directed is expression with an economic purpose. It can hardly be said that communications regarding an economic transaction of sex for money lie at, or even near, the core of the guarantee of freedom of expression.

The values which underlie the protection of freedom of expression relate to the search for truth, participation in the political process, and individual self-fulfilment. The Attorney General for Ontario argues that of these, only "individual self-fulfilment," and only in its most base aspect, that of physical arousal, is engaged by pornography. On the other hand, the civil liberties groups argue that pornography forces us to question conventional notions of sexuality and thereby launches us into an inherently political discourse. In their factum, the B.C. Civil Liberties Association adopts a passage from R. West, "The Feminist-Conservative Anti-Pornography Alliance and the 1986 Attorney General's Commission on Pornography Report" (1987), 4 *Am. Bar Found. Res. Jo.* 681, at p. 696:

> Good pornography has value because it validates women's will to pleasure. It celebrates female nature. It validates a range of female sexuality that is wider and truer than that legitimated by the non-pornographic culture. Pornography (when it is good) celebrates both female pleasure and male rationality.

A proper application of the test should not suppress what West refers to as "good pornography." The objective of the impugned provision is not to inhibit the celebration of human sexuality. However, it cannot be ignored that the realities of the pornography industry are far from the picture which the B.C. Civil Liberties Association would have us paint. Shannon J., in *R. v. Wagner*, [(1985), 43 C.R. (3d) 318 (Alta. Q.B.)], described the materials more accurately when he observed, at p. 331:

> Women, particularly, are deprived of unique human character or identity and are depicted as sexual playthings, hysterically and instantly responsive to male sexual demands. They worship male genitals and their own value depends upon the quality of their genitals and breasts.

In my view, the kind of expression which is sought to be advanced does not stand on an equal footing with other kinds of expression which directly engage the "core" of the freedom of expression values.

This conclusion is further buttressed by the fact that the targeted material is expression which is motivated, in the overwhelming majority of cases, by economic profit. This Court held in *Rocket v. Royal College of Dental Surgeons of Ontario*, [1990] 2 S.C.R. 232, at p. 247, that an economic motive for expression means that restrictions on the expression might "be easier to justify than other infringements."

I will now turn to an examination of the three basic aspects of the proportionality test.

… [T]he rational link between s. 163 and the objective of Parliament relates to the actual causal relationship between obscenity and the risk of harm to society at large. On this point, it is clear that the literature of the social sciences remains subject to controversy. …

In the face of inconclusive social science evidence, the approach adopted by our Court in *Irwin Toy* is instructive. In that case, the basis for the legislation was that television advertising directed at young children is *per se* manipulative. The Court made it clear, at p. 994, that in choosing its mode of intervention, it is sufficient that Parliament had a *reasonable basis*:

> In the instant case, the Court is called upon to assess competing social science evidence respecting the appropriate means for addressing the problem of children's advertising. The question is whether the government had a reasonable basis, on the evidence tendered, for concluding that the ban on all advertising directed at children impaired freedom of expression as little as possible given the government's pressing and substantial objective.

And at p. 990:

> … [T]he Court also recognized that the government was afforded a margin of appreciation to form legitimate objectives based on somewhat inconclusive social science evidence.

Similarly, in *Keegstra, supra*, the absence of proof of a causative link between hate propaganda and hatred of an identifiable group was discounted as a determinative factor in assessing the constitutionality of the hate literature provisions of the *Criminal Code*. Dickson C.J. stated, at p. 776:

> First, to predicate the limitation of free expression upon proof of actual hatred gives insufficient attention to the severe psychological trauma suffered by members of those identifiable groups targeted by hate propaganda. Second, it is clearly difficult to prove a causative link between a specific statement and hatred of an identifiable group.

McLachlin J. (dissenting) expressed it as follows, at p. 857:

> To view hate propaganda as "victimless" in the absence of any proof that it moved its listeners to hatred is to discount the wrenching impact that it may have on members of the target group themselves. ... Moreover, it is simply not possible to assess with any precision the effects that expression of a particular message will have on all those who are ultimately exposed to it.

... Accordingly, I am of the view that there is a sufficiently rational link between the criminal sanction, which demonstrates our community's disapproval of the dissemination of materials which potentially victimize women and which restricts the negative influence which such materials have on changes in attitudes and behaviour, and the objective.

Finally, I wish to distinguish this case from *Keegstra*, in which the minority adopted the view that there was no rational connection between the criminalization of hate propaganda and its suppression. As McLachlin J. noted, prosecutions under the *Criminal Code* for racist expression have attracted extensive media coverage. The criminal process confers on the accused publicity for his or her causes and succeeds even in generating sympathy. The same cannot be said of the kinds of expression sought to be suppressed in the present case. The general availability of the subject materials and the rampant pornography industry are such that, in the words of Dickson C.J. in *Keegstra*, "pornography is not dignified by its suppression." In contrast to the hate-monger who may succeed, by the sudden media attention, in gaining an audience, the prohibition of obscene materials does nothing to promote the pornographer's cause. ...

In determining whether less intrusive legislation may be imagined, this Court stressed in the *Prostitution Reference, supra,* that it is not necessary that the legislative scheme be the "perfect" scheme, but that it be appropriately tailored *in the context of the infringed right* (at p. 1138). Furthermore, in *Irwin Toy, supra,* Dickson C.J., Lamer and Wilson JJ. stated, at p. 999:

> While evidence exists that other less intrusive options reflecting more modest objectives were available to the government, there is evidence establishing the necessity of a ban to meet the objectives the government had reasonably set. This Court will not, in the name of minimal impairment, take a restrictive approach to social science evidence and require legislatures to choose the least ambitious means to protect vulnerable groups.

There are several factors which contribute to the finding that the provision minimally impairs the freedom which is infringed.

First, the impugned provision does not proscribe sexually explicit erotica without violence that is not degrading or dehumanizing. It is designed to catch material that creates a risk of harm to society. ...

Second, materials which have scientific, artistic or literary merit are not captured by the provision. As discussed above, the court must be generous in its application of the "artistic defence." For example, in certain cases, materials such as photographs, prints, books and films which may undoubtedly be produced with some motive for economic profit, may nonetheless claim the protection of the *Charter* in so far as their defining characteristic is that of aesthetic expression, and thus represent the artist's attempt at individual fulfilment. The existence of an accompanying economic motive does not, of itself, deprive a work of significance as an example of individual artistic or self-fulfilment.

Third, in considering whether the provision minimally impairs the freedom in question, it is legitimate for the court to take into account Parliament's past abortive attempts to replace the definition with one that is more explicit. In *Irwin Toy*, our Court recognized that it is legitimate to take into account the fact that earlier laws and proposed alternatives were thought to be less effective than the legislation that is presently being challenged. The attempt to provide exhaustive instances of obscenity has been shown to be destined to fail (Bill C-54, 2nd Sess., 33rd Parl.). It seems that the only practicable alternative is to strive towards a more abstract definition of obscenity which is contextually sensitive and responsive to progress in the knowledge and understanding of the phenomenon to which the legislation is directed. In my view, the standard of "undue exploitation" is therefore appropriate. The intractable nature of the problem and the impossibility of precisely defining a notion which is inherently elusive makes the possibility of a more explicit provision remote. In this light, it is appropriate to question whether, and at what cost, greater legislative precision can be demanded.

Fourth, while the discussion in this appeal has been limited to the definition portion of s. 163, I would note that the impugned section, with the possible exception of subs. 1, which is not in issue here, has been held by this Court not to extend its reach to the private use or viewing of obscene materials. ...

Accordingly, it is only the public distribution and exhibition of obscene materials which is in issue here.

Finally, I wish to address the arguments of the interveners, the Canadian Civil Liberties Association and Manitoba Association for Rights and Liberties, that the objectives of this kind of legislation may be met by alternative, less intrusive measures. First, it is submitted that reasonable time, manner and place restrictions would be preferable to outright prohibition.

I am of the view that this argument should be rejected. Once it has been established that the objective is the avoidance of harm caused by the degradation which many women feel as "victims" of the message of obscenity, and of the negative impact exposure to such material has on perceptions and attitudes towards women, it is untenable to argue that these harms could be avoided by placing restrictions on access to such material. Making the materials more difficult to obtain by increasing their cost and reducing their availability does not achieve the same objective. Once Parliament has reasonably concluded that certain acts are harmful to certain groups in society and to society in general, it would be inconsistent, if not hypocritical, to argue that such acts could be committed in more restrictive conditions. The harm sought to be avoided would remain the same in either case.

It is also submitted that there are more effective techniques to promote the objectives of Parliament. For example, if pornography is seen as encouraging violence against women, there are certain activities which discourage it—counselling rape victims to charge their assailants, provision of shelter and assistance for battered women, campaigns for laws against discrimination on the grounds of sex, education to increase the sensitivity of law enforcement agencies and other governmental authorities. In addition, it is submitted that education is an under-used response.

It is noteworthy that many of the above suggested alternatives are in the form of *responses* to the harm engendered by negative attitudes against women. The role of the impugned provision is to control the dissemination of the very images that contribute to such attitudes. Moreover, it is true that there are additional measures which could alleviate the problem of violence against women. However, given the gravity of the harm, and the threat to the values at stake, I do not believe that the measure chosen by Parliament is equalled by the alternatives which have been suggested. Education, too, may offer a means of combating negative attitudes to women, just as it is currently used as a means of addressing other problems dealt with in the *Code*. However, there is no reason to rely on education alone. It should be emphasized that this is in no way intended to deny the value of other educational and counselling measures to deal with the roots and effects of negative attitudes. Rather, it is only to stress the arbitrariness and unacceptability of the claim that such measures represent the sole legitimate means of addressing the phenomenon. Serious social problems such as violence against women require multi-pronged approaches by government. Education and legislation are not alternatives but complements in addressing such problems. There is nothing in the *Charter* which requires Parliament to choose between such complementary measures.

The final question to be answered in the proportionality test is whether the effects of the law so severely trench on a protected right that the legislative objective is outweighed by the infringement. The infringement on freedom of expression is confined to a measure designed to prohibit the distribution of sexually explicit materials accompanied by violence, and those without violence that are degrading or dehumanizing. As I have already concluded, this kind of expression lies far from the core of the guarantee of freedom of expression. It appeals only to the most base aspect of individual fulfilment, and it is primarily economically motivated.

The objective of the legislation, on the other hand, is of fundamental importance in a free and democratic society. It is aimed at avoiding harm, which Parliament has reasonably concluded will be caused directly or indirectly, to individuals, groups such as women and children, and consequently to society as a whole, by the distribution of these materials. It thus seeks to enhance respect for all members of society, and non-violence and equality in their relations with each other.

I therefore conclude that the restriction on freedom of expression does not outweigh the importance of the legislative objective.

I conclude that while s. 163(8) infringes s. 2(*b*) of the *Charter*, freedom of expression, it constitutes a reasonable limit and is saved by virtue of the provisions of s. 1. ...

The reasons of L'Heureux-Dubé and Gonthier JJ. were delivered by

GONTHIER J.: I have had the benefit of the reasons of Justice Sopinka and, while I agree both with his disposition of the case and with his reasons generally, I wish to add to them with respect to the judicial interpretation of s. 163 of the *Criminal Code*, R.S.C., 1985, c. C-46, and to its constitutional validity.

Section 163 of the *Code* offers a peculiar structure. Its subject matter, obscene materials, comprises the dual elements of representation and content. Representation here is understood in the sense of public suggestion. A representation is a portrayal, a description meant to evoke something to the mind and senses. ... By "content" I mean of course the content of the representation.

It is the combination of the two, the representation and its content, that attracts criminal liability. A representation as such is not enough, of course, to create the subject matter of s. 163, but neither is an act included in the content of s. 163 of the *Code*, without an element of representation. ...

... The type of scenes vividly described in *R. v. Wagner* (1985), 43 C.R. (3d) 318 (Alta. Q.B.), *R. v. Doug Rankine Co.* (1983), 9 C.C.C. (3d) 53 (Ont. Co. Ct.) or *R. v. Ramsingh* (1984), 14 C.C.C. (3d) 230 (Man. Q.B.), might perhaps be legal if done between consenting adults, but they become obscene when they are represented.

Without launching into a lengthy debate on the reasons why Parliament may have enacted s. 163 of the *Code* ... it can be seen that the combination of representation and content that constitutes obscenity leads to many ills. ... Obscene materials ... convey a distorted image of human sexuality, by making public and open elements of the human nature which are usually hidden behind a veil of modesty and privacy. D. A. Downs, *The New Politics of Pornography* (1989), aptly describes how these materials do not reflect the richness of human sexuality, but rather turn it into pure animality, at p. 183:

> ... the deeper objection to sheer pornography or obscenity ... is that it represents a retreat from the human dilemma and the responsibility of acknowledging the tensions in our nature. Sheer pornography also reduces us to the lower aspects of our natures by stripping away the modesty that arises from our encounter with our animality. ...

To summarize ... the particular combination of a representation and its content that forms the subject matter of s. 163 of the *Code* was seen by Parliament as putting forward a distorted image of human sexuality, which in turn can induce harmful behavioural changes. This must be kept in mind when interpreting s. 163 of the *Code*. ...

... Sopinka J. essentially aligns the definition of obscenity in s. 163(8) of the *Code* with the definition of pornography nowadays. He introduces a three-part categorization that has surfaced in contemporary theory, and that had been adopted in some Canadian cases throughout the 80s:

(a) Explicit sex with violence, which generally constitutes "undue exploitation of sex" within the meaning of s. 163(8) of the *Code*, on the basis of demonstrable harm;

(b) Explicit sex that is degrading or dehumanizing, which will be "undue exploitation of sex" if it creates a substantial risk of harm; the risk of harm can be assessed with reference to the tolerance of the community, under the "community standard of tolerance" test; and

(c) Explicit sex that is neither violent nor degrading or dehumanizing, which will not generally fall under s. 163(8) of the *Code*, according to Sopinka J.

I must say at the outset that I differ only with respect to the third category of materials. I am not prepared to affirm as boldly as my colleague Sopinka J. does that it escapes the application of s. 163(8). ...

The dual nature, as representation and content, of the subject matter of s. 163 comes into play here. Yet the classification proposed by my colleague Sopinka J. focuses only on content. The content of the first two categories of materials is so likely to harm that the characteristics of the representation do not really matter: if there is violence or degradation or dehumanization, as long as the element of representation is present, harm will probably ensue.

The content of the third category of materials is generally perceived as unlikely to cause harm, as Sopinka J. rightly points out. He mentions as an exception child pornography, i.e. materials in the production of which children were employed. This exception is important, since it obviously flows from the high likelihood of harm ensuing from the production and dissemination of child pornography.

In addition to this exception, it is quite conceivable that the representation may cause harm, even if its content as such may not be seen as harmful. ...

... After all, it is the element of representation that gives this material its power of suggestion, and it seems quite conceivable that this power may cause harm despite the apparent neutrality of the content. A host of factors could intervene in the manner of representation to affect the characterization of the material, among which are the medium, the type or the use.

The medium provides a good example. Indeed the differences between the various media are not acknowledged often enough in opinions dealing with s. 163 of the *Code*. ...

Nevertheless it seems natural to me that the likelihood of harm, and the tolerance of the community, may vary according to the medium of representation, even if the content stays the same. Let me take, as an example, an explicit portrayal of "plain" sexual intercourse, where two individuals are making love. This falls within the third category of Sopinka J. If found in words in a book, it is unlikely to be of much concern (if found in a children's book, though, this may be different). If found depicted in a magazine or in a movie, the likelihood of harm increases but remains low. If found on a poster, it is already more troublesome. If found on a billboard sign, then I would venture that it may well be an undue exploitation of sex, because the community does not tolerate it, on the basis of its harmfulness.

The harmfulness, in the billboard sign example, would come from the immediacy of the representation, inasmuch as the sign stands all by itself (as opposed to a passage in a book, a film or a magazine). Its message is at once crude and inescapable. It distorts human sexuality by taking it out of any context whatsoever and projecting it to the public. This example goes to the extreme, of course, but it is meant to show that the element of representation may create a likelihood of harm that may lead to the application of s. 163 of the *Code*, even if the content of the representation as such is not objectionable.

As I mentioned, the medium of representation is but one variable pertaining to representation that may trigger the application of s. 163 to third-category materials. The overall type or use of the representation, be it education, art, advertising, sexual arousal or other, may also be relevant, among other factors. These factors tie in to the "internal necessities" test to some extent. This test, if it is to find a place within the interpretive framework of Sopinka J., must intervene at the representational level, to change the characterization that would ensue from a mere look at the content of the materials.

For these reasons, therefore, I would hold that materials falling within Sopinka J.'s third category (explicit sex with neither violence nor degradation or dehumanization), while generally less likely to cause harm than those of the first two categories, may nevertheless come within the definition of obscene at s. 163(8) of the *Code*, if their content (child pornography) or their representational element (the manner of representation) is found conducive of harm. ...

The assessment of the risk of harm here depends on the tolerance of the community, as is the case with the second category of materials. This brings me to outline a certain shift in the meaning of "tolerance." In *Towne Cinema*, [[1985] 1 S.C.R. 494], Dickson C.J. formulated the community standard test as follows at p. 508:

> ... it is a standard of *tolerance*, not taste, that is relevant. What matters is not what Canadians think is right for themselves to see. What matters is what Canadians would not abide other Canadians seeing because it would be beyond the contemporary Canadian standard of tolerance to allow them to see it. [Emphasis in original.]

It is unclear from this excerpt what the basis of tolerance is. It seems that tolerance is for taste the conceptual equivalent of the reasonable person to the actual plaintiff: an abstraction, an average perhaps. Tolerance would be some form of enlightened, altruistic taste, which would factor in and sum up the tastes of the whole population.

In the mind of Dickson C.J., there exists no necessary relationship between tolerance and harm, as he mentions at p. 505:

> However, as I have noted above, there is no *necessary* coincidence between the undueness of publications which degrade people by linking violence, cruelty or other forms of dehumanizing treatment with sex, and the community standard of tolerance. Even if certain sex related materials were found to be within the standard of tolerance of the

community, it would still be necessary to ensure that they were not "undue" in some other sense, for example in the sense that they portray persons in a degrading manner as objects of violence, cruelty, or other forms of dehumanizing treatment. [Emphasis in original.]

Sopinka J. uses the community standard of tolerance to gauge the risk of harm. In this context, tolerance must be related to the harm. It must mean not only tolerance of the materials, but also tolerance of the harm which they may bring about. It is a more complicated and more reflective form of tolerance than what was considered by Dickson C.J. in *Towne Cinema, supra*. Such a development is fully in accordance with the emphasis put by this Court on harm as the central element in the interpretation of s. 163(8).

In the context of the third category, the harm sought to be avoided is the same as in the first two categories, that is attitudinal changes. While this type of harm was clear in the case of the first category and was probable in the case of the second, it is perhaps more remote here, and will likely occur only in a limited number of cases. The main difference between the second and third categories lies in the presumed likelihood of harm: while degrading or dehumanizing materials are likely to cause harm regardless of whether the community may be ready to tolerate such harm, materials which show no violence, no degradation or dehumanization are less likely to cause harm, and the evidence with respect to the lack of tolerance of the community will be central. Still the risk of harm flowing from the content or the representational element of third-category materials is not always so slight as my colleague Sopinka J. pictures it. If the community cannot tolerate this risk of harm, then in my opinion these materials, even though they may offer a non-violent, non-degrading, non-dehumanizing content, will constitute undue exploitation of sex and will fall under the definition of obscenity at s. 163(8) of the *Code*. ...

With respect to the constitutional aspects of this case, I am in agreement with Sopinka J., and I wish only to complement his reasons on the objective of s. 163 of the *Code*.

In his reasons, Sopinka J. rules out the possibility that "public morality" can be a legitimate objective for s. 163 of the *Code* and, while admitting that Parliament may legislate to protect "fundamental conceptions of morality," he goes on to conclude that the true objective of s. 163 is the avoidance of harm to society.

In my opinion, the distinction between the two orders of morality advanced by my colleague is correct, and the avoidance of harm to society is but one instance of a fundamental conception of morality.

First of all, I cannot conceive that the State could not legitimately act on the basis of morality. Since its earliest

Charter pronouncements, this Court has acknowledged this possibility. In *R. v. Big M Drug Mart Ltd.*, [1985] 1 S.C.R. 295, Dickson J. (as he then was) wrote for the Court at p. 337:

> Freedom means that, subject to such limitations as are necessary to protect public safety, order, health, or morals or the fundamental rights and freedoms of others, no one is to be forced to act in a way contrary to his beliefs or his conscience.

Morality is also listed as one of the grounds for which freedom of expression can be restricted in the *European Convention on Human Rights* at article 10:

> 1. Everyone has the right to freedom of expression.…
> 2. The exercise of these freedoms, since it carries with it duties and responsibilities, may be subject to such formalities, conditions, restrictions or penalties as are prescribed by law and are necessary in a democratic society, in the interests of national security, territorial integrity or public safety, for the prevention of disorder or crime, for the protection of health or morals, for the protection of the reputation or rights of others, for preventing the disclosure of information received in confidence, or for maintaining the authority and impartiality of the judiciary.

The European Court of Human Rights has recognized the validity of prohibitions of obscene materials in English and Swiss law, respectively, on the basis that they concern morals, in the *Handyside Case*, judgment of 7 December 1976, Series A No. 24 and in the *Case of Müller and Others*, judgment of 24 May 1988, Series A No. 133.

Indeed the problem is not so much to assess whether morality is a valid objective under the *Charter* as to determine under which conditions it is a pressing and substantial objective. Not all moral claims will be sufficient to warrant an override of *Charter* rights. As R. Dworkin wrote in the chapter of *Taking Rights Seriously* (1977) entitled "Liberty and Moralism" at p. 255:

> The claim that a moral consensus exists is not itself based on a poll. It is based on an appeal to the legislator's sense of how his community reacts to some disfavored practice. But this same sense includes an awareness of the grounds on which that reaction is generally supported. If there has been a public debate involving the editorial columns, speeches of his colleagues, the testimony of interested groups, and his own correspondence, these will sharpen his awareness of what arguments and positions are in the field. He must sift these arguments and positions, suppose general principles or theories vast parts of the population could not be supposed to accept, and so on.

This task that Dworkin assigns to Parliament is also entrusted to this Court in *Charter* review. Two dimensions are important here, which allow one to distinguish between morality in the general sense and "fundamental conceptions of morality."

First of all, the moral claims must be grounded. They must involve concrete problems such as life, harm, well-being, to name a few, and not merely differences of opinion or of taste. Parliament cannot restrict *Charter* rights simply on the basis of dislike; this is what is meant by the expression "substantial and pressing" concern.

Secondly, a consensus must exist among the population on these claims. They must attract the support of more than a simple majority of people. In a pluralistic society like ours, many different conceptions of the good are held by various segments of the population. The guarantees of s. 2 of the *Charter* protect this pluralistic diversity. However, if the holders of these different conceptions agree that some conduct is not good, then the respect for pluralism that underlies s. 2 of the *Charter* becomes less insurmountable an objection to State action (this argument has recently been rejuvenated and reformulated in S. Gardbaum, "Why the Liberal State Can Promote Moral Ideals After All" (1991), 104 *Harv. L. Rev.* 1350). In this sense a wide consensus among holders of different conceptions of the good is necessary before the State can intervene in the name of morality. This is also comprised in the phrase "pressing and substantial."

The avoidance of harm caused to society through attitudinal changes certainly qualifies as a "fundamental conception of morality." After all, one of the chief aspirations of morality is the avoidance of harm. It is well grounded, since the harm takes the form of violations of the principles of human equality and dignity. Obscene materials debase sexuality. They lead to the humiliation of women, and sometimes to violence against them. This is more than just a matter of taste. Without entering into the examination of the rational connection, some empirical evidence even elucidates the link between these materials and actual violence. Even then, as was said by this Court in *Irwin Toy Ltd. v. Quebec (Attorney General)*, [1989] 1 S.C.R. 927, in *R. v. Keegstra*, [1990] 3 S.C.R. 697, and as is reiterated by my colleague in his reasons, scientific proof is not required, and reason and common experience will often suffice.

Furthermore, taking into account that people hold different conceptions about good taste and the acceptable level of sexual explicitness, most would agree that these attitudinal changes are serious and warrant State intervention (civil liberty groups who advocated that this Court strike down s. 163 of the *Code* concede that harm can justify State intervention, but they deny that any harm flows from obscene materials; that is a different question).

I agree with Sopinka J. that s. 163 of the *Code* aims at preventing harm to society and I fully endorse his analysis, and as I tried to demonstrate I would not hesitate to affirm that the prevention of harm is a moral objective that is valid under s. 1 of the *Charter*.

I also agree with Sopinka J.'s analysis of the proportionality between the restriction effected by s. 163 of the *Code* and its objectives. I would add a remark, however, on the first factor listed by Sopinka J. under the minimal impairment branch of the proportionality test, that is the exception for materials of the third category. Contrary to Sopinka J., I consider that the third category may sometimes attract criminal liability. The requirement that the impugned materials exceed the community standard of tolerance of harm provides sufficient precision and protection for those whose activities are at stake.

This is so as, on the one hand, the field of sexual exploitation is one of first apprehension, directly related to one of the primary aspects of human personality, and well known to all, including particularly those engaged in it. On the other hand, the criterion of tolerance of harm by the community as a whole is one that, by definition, reflects the general level of tolerance throughout all sectors of the community, hence generally of all its members. It is therefore a very demanding criterion to meet as it must be by definition generally known or apprehended. It is indeed not far removed from the domain of public notoriety and, inasmuch as it falls within it, may be the subject of judicial notice not requiring specific proof.

Subject to the foregoing comments, I otherwise concur both with the reasons and the disposition of the case of my colleague Sopinka J.

RJR-MacDonald Inc. v. Canada (Attorney General), 1995

In this case, major tobacco companies claimed that a federal ban on tobacco advertising fell beyond Ottawa's criminal law power and constituted an unreasonable infringement of the Charter's freedom-of-expression guarantee. Speaking through seven separate opinions (most of them short), a substantial majority (7 to 2) of the court found that the ban was valid criminal law while a narrow majority (5 to 4) voted to strike it down on freedom-of-expression grounds. We reproduce below only the primary majority and dissenting opinions on the Charter issue.

The law at issue prohibited the advertising and promotion of tobacco products and required the packaging for those products to display non-attributed warnings about the toxic ingredients and negative health effects of tobacco. As in other freedom-of-expression cases, a Charter violation was (mostly) conceded, and the analysis turned mainly on determining whether the law could be justified as a "reasonable limit" under section 1.

The court has established two ways of determining how much deference is owed to Parliament in the section 1 stage of analysis. First, as we have seen,[1] the farther the infringed expression falls from the "core" freedom-of-expression values—"the search for political, artistic and scientific truth, the protection of individual autonomy and self-development, and the *promotion of public participation in the democratic process*"—the lower the standard justification. Second, because courts have well-established expertise in matters of criminal law, where the state acts as the "singular antagonist of the individual," they can apply higher levels of scrutiny than when legislation is aimed at "mediating between different groups" or social interests, which requires policy judgments that lie outside traditional judicial expertise.

While both the main opinions in the case—Justice McLachlin's for the majority and Justice La Forest's for the minority—agreed with these distinctions in principle, they applied them very differently. Thus, while La Forest saw the kind of expression at stake in this case—commercial advertising aimed at increasing profits—as falling far from the core of expression values, McLachlin rejected his reliance on the profit motive, pointing out that booksellers and newspaper owners—surely close to the core—were also profit-oriented enterprises. And while La Forest saw the legislation as compromising "among the competing interests of smokers, non-smokers and manufacturers, with an eye to protecting vulnerable groups in society," and thus as "the very type of legislation to which this Court has generally accorded a high degree of deference," McLachlin observed that it was also a criminal law that "pits the state against the offender." In any case, said McLachlin, "[t]o carry judicial

---

1 See *R. v. Keegstra*, [1990] 3 S.C.R. 697, available in the instructor's supplements package, and *R. v. Butler* (case 6).

deference to the point of accepting Parliament's view simply on the basis that the problem is serious and the solution difficult"—as she clearly thought La Forest had done—"would be to diminish the role of the courts in the constitutional process and to weaken the structure of rights upon which our constitution and our nation is founded."

One of the reasons La Forest considered the problem serious and the solution difficult is that the law was 20 years in the making and that similarly protracted policy processes had led at least 20 other liberal democracies to enact similar laws. Moreover, in countries such as France and the United States, such laws had been upheld as constitutional. Justice McLachlin was unimpressed.

Given their different orientations to the question of deference, the contrasting conclusions of McLachlin and La Forest on the components of the *Oakes* test come as no surprise. While La Forest found the law to pass all parts of the test, McLachlin saw it as failing all parts of the critical proportionality component.

True, both sides conceded that the law had a "pressing and substantial purpose," but McLachlin defined that purpose more narrowly than did La Forest. For La Forest, the compelling purpose of the law was "protecting Canadians from the health risks associated with tobacco use, and informing them about these risks." For McLachlin, this overly broad purpose made it too easy to find the means proportional. Her narrower purpose was to "prevent people in Canada from being persuaded by advertising and promotion to use tobacco products [and] to discourage people who see the package from tobacco use."

Did a total advertising ban actually prevent people from being persuaded to use tobacco products? In addressing this question, McLachlin distinguished between "informational" and "lifestyle" advertising. Informational advertising simply identifies brands and may even provide useful information about different levels of toxins in various brands. Lifestyle advertising, by contrast, associates smoking with attractive people and activities. While McLachlin thought that "lifestyle advertising may, as a matter of common sense, be seen as having a tendency to discourage those who might otherwise cease tobacco use from doing so," she could find no solid connection, either in empirical scientific evidence or in "reason and logic," between a ban on informational advertising and its intended effect. It was "hard to imagine," she wrote, "how the presence of a tobacco logo on a cigarette lighter, for example, would increase consumption; yet, such use is banned." She concluded that a total ban—one that encompassed purely informational advertising—was not rationally connected to its purpose. Similarly, although a limited prohibition of only lifestyle advertising might pass the minimal impairment part of proportionality analysis, a total ban clearly infringed that criterion.

For Justice La Forest it was not nearly as clear that a ban of informational advertising was irrational, even in the light of Justice McLachlin's more narrowly defined purpose. As a "powerful common sense observation," he found it "difficult to believe that Canadian tobacco companies would spend over 75 million dollars every year on advertising if they did not know that advertising increases the consumption of their product." The government, he maintained, was entitled to come to a similar common-sense conclusion. For Justice McLachlin, such "common sense" did not satisfy the section 1 criterion for evidence or logic sufficient to "demonstrate" the need for a total ban. But note that when McLachlin justified her preferred option of a ban limited to "lifestyle" advertising, she did so "as a matter of [her own] common sense." The tension between the standard McLachlin applied to government policy preferences and the standard she applied to her own has not gone unremarked in the literature.[2]

RJR-MacDonald attracted considerable attention and controversy. Perhaps most dramatically, it led Ed Broadbent, former national leader of the New Democratic Party, to change his mind about the Charter's section 33 notwithstanding clause. When the Charter was being drafted and enacted, Broadbent had opposed section 33. At a 20th-anniversary Charter conference in Ottawa in 2002, he expressed his outrage that the *RJR* court had given the economic freedom of corporations priority over public health. He now understood, he announced, why section 33 was a useful Charter provision. *RJR* was for him a prime example of a case that deserved a "notwithstanding" response.

In response to the *RJR* decision—subscribing to the then fashionable notion of interinstitutional "dialogue"—the government enacted a new advertising ban, one that carefully followed Justice McLachlin's recommended limitation to "lifestyle" advertising. That law, too, was challenged by tobacco companies in a subsequent case, *JTI-Macdonald*.[3] This time, a unanimous court, speaking through now Chief Justice McLachlin, upheld the law as a "reasonable limit" on freedom of expression. ~

Discussion Questions

1. How and why did Justices McLachlin and La Forest disagree on the minimal impairment component of the *Oakes* test? Which of their arguments do you find most persuasive?

2. Justices McLachlin and La Forest disagree about whether an advertising ban limited to "lifestyle advertising" can be effective. What do you think about the evidence and arguments they use to support their contrary views?

3. Should Parliament have resorted to the section 33 notwithstanding clause to override the majority ruling in *RJR-MacDonald*?

---

2   Janet Hiebert, *Charter Conflicts* (Montreal and Kingston: McGill-Queen's University Press, 2002) at 77-78.

3   *Canada (Attorney General) v. JTI-Macdonald Corp.*, 2007 SCC 30, [2007] 2 S.C.R. 610.

RJR-MACDONALD INC. v. THE ATTORNEY GENERAL OF CANADA
[1995] 3 S.C.R. 199

Hearing: November 29, 30, 1994; Judgment: September 21, 1995.

Present: Lamer C.J. and La Forest, L'Heureux-Dubé, Sopinka, Gonthier, Cory, McLachlin, Iacobucci, and Major JJ.

Interveners: The Attorney General for Ontario, the Heart and Stroke Foundation of Canada, the Canadian Cancer Society, the Canadian Council on Smoking and Health, the Canadian Medical Association, and the Canadian Lung Association.

The reasons of La Forest, L'Heureux-Dubé, and Gonthier JJ. were delivered by

[2] **LA FOREST J.** (dissenting): The issues in these appeals are whether the *Tobacco Products Control Act*, S.C. 1988, c. 20 (the "Act"), falls within the legislative competence of the Parliament of Canada under s. 91 of the *Constitution Act, 1867*, either as criminal law or under the peace, order and good government clause, and if so whether it constitutes an infringement of freedom of expression under s. 2(*b*) of the *Canadian Charter of Rights and Freedoms* which is not justified under s. 1 of the *Charter*. In broad terms, the Act prohibits, subject to specified exceptions, all advertising and promotion of tobacco products, and prohibits the sale of a tobacco product unless the package containing it sets forth prescribed health warnings and a list of the toxic constituents of the product and of the smoke produced from its combustion. ...

[58] The Attorney General conceded that the prohibition on advertising and promotion under the Act constitutes an infringement of the appellants' right to freedom of expression under s. 2(*b*) of the *Charter*, and directed his submissions solely to justifying the infringement under s. 1 of the *Charter*. In my view, the Attorney General was correct in making this concession. ...

[59] [H]owever, it is appropriate to draw attention to the fact that the Attorney General did not concede that s. 9 of the Act, which requires tobacco manufacturers to place an unattributed health warning on packages of these products, constitutes an infringement of the appellants' right to freedom of expression. In my view, the Attorney General was correct in not making this concession. However, since there is considerable overlap between my discussion of this issue and my discussion of s. 1, I shall for convenience address this distinct issue separately at the conclusion of my general s. 1 analysis. ...

[61] The appellants have conceded that the objective of protecting Canadians from the health risks associated with tobacco use, and informing them about these risks, is pressing and substantial. Rather than focusing upon the objective, the appellants submit that the measures employed under the Act are not proportional to the objective. ...

[63] This Court has on many occasions affirmed that the *Oakes* requirements must be applied flexibly, having regard to the specific factual and social context of each case. The word "reasonable" in s. 1 necessarily imports flexibility. ... This Court has on many occasions stated that the evidentiary requirements under s. 1 will vary substantially depending upon both the nature of the legislation and the nature of the right infringed. ...

[67] It appears ... that there is a significant gap between our understanding of the health *effects* of tobacco consumption and of the root *causes* of tobacco consumption. In my view, this gap raises a fundamental institutional problem that must be taken into account in undertaking the s. 1 balancing. Simply put, a strict application of the proportionality analysis in cases of this nature would place an impossible onus on Parliament by requiring it to produce definitive social scientific evidence respecting the root causes of a pressing area of social concern every time it wishes to address its effects. This could have the effect of virtually paralyzing the operation of government in the socio-economic sphere. As I noted in *McKinney* [*v. University of Guelph*, [1990] 3 S.C.R. 229], at pp. 304-5, predictions respecting the ramifications of legal rules upon the social and economic order are not matters capable of precise measurement, and are often "the product of a mix of conjecture, fragmentary knowledge, general experience and knowledge of the needs, aspirations and resources of society, and other components." To require

Parliament to wait for definitive social science conclusions every time it wishes to make social policy would impose an unjustifiable limit on legislative power by attributing a degree of scientific accuracy to the art of government which, in my view, is simply not consonant with reality. ...

[68] In several recent cases, this Court has recognized the need to attenuate the *Oakes* standard of justification when institutional constraints analogous to those in the present cases arise. ... [For example, i]n drawing a distinction between legislation aimed at "mediating between different groups," where a lower standard of s. 1 justification may be appropriate, and legislation where the state acts as the "singular antagonist of the individual," where a higher standard of justification is necessary, the Court in *Irwin Toy* was drawing upon the more fundamental institutional distinction between the legislative and judicial functions that lies at the very heart of our political and constitutional system. Courts are specialists in the protection of liberty and the interpretation of legislation and are, accordingly, well placed to subject criminal justice legislation to careful scrutiny. However, courts are not specialists in the realm of policy-making, nor should they be. This is a role properly assigned to the elected representatives of the people, who have at their disposal the necessary institutional resources to enable them to compile and assess social science evidence, to mediate between competing social interests and to reach out and protect vulnerable groups. In according a greater degree of deference to social legislation than to legislation in the criminal justice context, this Court has recognized these important institutional differences between legislatures and the judiciary.

[69] ... In enacting this legislation, Parliament was facing a difficult policy dilemma. On the one hand, Parliament is aware of the detrimental health effects of tobacco use, and has a legitimate interest in protecting Canadians from, and in informing them about, the dangers of tobacco use. Health underlies many of our most cherished rights and values, and the protection of public health is one of the fundamental responsibilities of Parliament. On the other hand, however, it is clear that a prohibition on the manufacture, sale or use of tobacco products is unrealistic. Nearly seven million Canadians use tobacco products, which are highly addictive. Undoubtedly, a prohibition of this nature would lead to an increase in illegal activity, smuggling and, quite possibly, civil disobedience. Well aware of these difficulties, Parliament chose a less drastic, and more incremental, response to the tobacco health problem. In prohibiting the advertising and promotion of tobacco products, as opposed to their manufacture or sale, Parliament has sought to achieve a compromise among the competing interests of smokers, non-smokers and manufacturers, with an eye to protecting vulnerable groups in society.

Given the fact that advertising, by its very nature, is intended to influence consumers and create demand, this was a reasonable policy decision. Moreover, ... the Act is the product of a legislative process dating back to 1969, when the first report recommending a full prohibition on tobacco advertising was published; see *Report of the Standing Committee on Health, Welfare and Social Affairs on Tobacco and Cigarette Smoking* [(1969)], *supra*. In drafting this legislation, Parliament took into account the views of Canadians from many different sectors of society, representing many different interests. Indeed, the legislative committee responsible for drafting Bill C-51, which was subsequently adopted by Parliament as the Act, heard from 104 organizations during hearings in 1988 representing a variety of interests, including medicine, transport, advertising, smokers' rights, non-smokers' rights, and tobacco production.

[70] Seen in this way, it is clear that the Act is the very type of legislation to which this Court has generally accorded a high degree of deference. In drafting this legislation, which is directed toward a laudable social goal and is designed to protect vulnerable groups, Parliament was required to compile and assess complex social science evidence and to mediate between competing social interests. Decisions such as these are properly assigned to our elected representatives, who have at their disposal the necessary resources to undertake them, and who are ultimately accountable to the electorate. ...

[71] Turning now to the nature of the right infringed under the Act, it is once again necessary to place the appellants' claim in context. This Court has recognized, in a line of freedom of expression cases dating back to *Edmonton Journal, supra*, that, depending on its nature, expression will be entitled to varying levels of constitutional protection. ...

[72] ... In *Keegstra* ... , Dickson C.J. identified these fundamental or "core" values as including the search for political, artistic and scientific truth, the protection of individual autonomy and self-development, and the promotion of public participation in the democratic process. When state action places such values in jeopardy, this Court has been careful to subject it to a searching degree of scrutiny. ...

[73] In cases where the expression in question is farther from the "core" of freedom of expression values, this Court has applied a lower standard of justification. For example, in *Keegstra*, where a majority of this Court ruled that a prohibition on hate speech under s. 319(2) of the *Criminal Code*, R.S.C., 1985, c. C-46, was a justifiable limitation on freedom of expression, Dickson C.J. found that this limited infringement was justified because hate propaganda was a form of expression that was only remotely related to "core" free expression values. ...

[74] This Court adopted a similar approach in *R. v. Butler*, [1992] 1 S.C.R. 452, where it found a prohibition upon publications whose dominant characteristic was the "undue exploitation of sex" under s. 163(8) of the *Criminal Code*, R.S.C., 1985, c. C-46, to be a justifiable infringement upon freedom of expression. In so ruling, this Court found it significant, at p. 500, that "the kind of expression which is sought to be advanced does not stand on an equal footing with other kinds of expression which directly engage the 'core' of the freedom of expression values." ... The Court has adopted a similar approach with respect to prostitution, which was also accorded a lower level of protection in the *Prostitution Reference*. ...

[75] In my view, the harm engendered by tobacco, and the profit motive underlying its promotion, place this form of expression as far from the "core" of freedom of expression values as prostitution, hate mongering, or pornography, and thus entitle it to a very low degree of protection under s. 1. It must be kept in mind that tobacco advertising serves no political, scientific or artistic ends; nor does it promote participation in the political process. Rather, its sole purpose is to inform consumers about, and promote the use of, a product that is harmful, and often fatal, to the consumers who use it. The main, if not sole, motivation for this advertising is, of course, profit. ...

[76] The appellants, both of whom are large multinational corporations, spend millions of dollars every year to promote their products (in 1987 alone, RJR and Imperial spent over $75 million dollars on advertising and promotion). ... The sophistication of the advertising campaigns employed by these corporations, in my view, undermines their claim to freedom of expression protection because it creates an enormous power differential between these companies and tobacco consumers in the "marketplace of ideas." ... The power differential between advertiser and consumer is even more pronounced with respect to children who, as this Court observed in *Irwin Toy*, at p. 987, are "particularly vulnerable to the techniques of seduction and manipulation abundant in advertising." ... In this respect, it is critical to keep in mind Dickson C.J.'s reminder in *Edwards Books* [[1986] 2 S.C.R. 713], at p. 779:

> In interpreting and applying the *Charter* I believe that the courts must be cautious to ensure that it does not simply become an instrument of better situated individuals to roll back legislation which has as its object the improvement of the condition of less advantaged persons.

[77] I conclude, therefore, that an attenuated level of s. 1 justification is appropriate in these cases. ... With these observations firmly in mind, I now proceed to an application of the proportionality test. ...

[83] ... The appellants ... base their argument principally upon the claim that there is no rational connection between the prohibition on advertising and promotion of tobacco products under ss. 4, 5, 6, and 8 and the objective of reducing tobacco consumption. In my view, the appellants' argument fails. ...

[84] I begin with what I consider to be a powerful common sense observation. Simply put, it is difficult to believe that Canadian tobacco companies would spend over 75 million dollars every year on advertising if they did not know that advertising increases the consumption of their product. In response to this observation, the appellants insist that their advertising is directed solely toward preserving and expanding brand loyalty among smokers, and not toward expanding the tobacco market by inducing non-smokers to start. In my view, the appellants' claim is untenable for two principal reasons. First, brand loyalty alone will not, and logically cannot, maintain the profit levels of these companies if the overall number of smokers declines. A proportionate piece of a smaller pie is still a smaller piece. ... Second, even if this Court were to accept the appellants' brand loyalty argument, the appellants have not adequately addressed the further problem that even commercials targeted solely at brand loyalty may also serve as inducements for smokers not to quit. ...

[86] ... [T]he power of the common-sense connection between advertising and consumption is sufficient to satisfy the rational connection requirement.

[87] However, it is not necessary to rely solely upon common sense to reach this conclusion. ...

[92] [A] number of reports introduced at trial ... attest to the causal connection between tobacco advertising and consumption. ...

[93] The views expressed in these reports are not, of course, definitive or conclusive. Indeed, there is currently a lively debate in the social sciences respecting the connection between advertising and consumption, a debate that has been carried on for years and will no doubt persist well into the near future. However, these reports attest, at the very least, to the existence of what LeBel J.A. called a "body of opinion" supporting the existence of a causal connection between advertising and consumption. ...

[94] ... I conclude that there is a rational connection between the prohibition on advertising and consumption under ss. 4, 5, 6 and 8 of the Act and the reduction of tobacco consumption. ...

[95] The next step in the proportionality analysis is to determine whether the legislative means chosen impair the right or freedom in question as little as possible. The appellants submit that Parliament has unjustifiably imposed a complete prohibition on tobacco advertising and promotion when it

could have imposed a partial prohibition with equal effectiveness. They suggest that Parliament could have instituted a partial prohibition by forbidding "lifestyle" advertising (which seeks to promote an image by associating the consumption of the product with a particular lifestyle) or advertising directed at children, without at the same time prohibiting "brand preference" advertising (which seeks to promote one brand over another based on the colour and design of the package) or "informational" advertising (which seeks to inform the consumer about product content, taste and strength and the availability of different or new brands). According to the appellants, there is no need to prohibit brand preference or informational advertising because both are targeted solely at smokers, and serve a beneficial function by promoting consumer choice.

[96] In my view, the appellants' argument fails. ... [T]he minimal impairment requirement does not impose an obligation on the government to employ the least intrusive measures available. Rather, it only requires it to demonstrate that the measures employed were the least intrusive, *in light of both the legislative objective and the infringed right.* ...

[97] ... It must be kept in mind that the infringed right at issue in these cases is the right of tobacco corporations to advertise the only legal product sold in Canada which, when used precisely as directed, harms and often kills those who use it. As I discussed above, I have no doubt that Parliament could validly have employed the criminal law power to prohibit the manufacture and sale of tobacco products, and that such a prohibition would have been fully justifiable under the *Charter.* There is no right to sell harmful products in Canada, nor should there be. Thus, in choosing to prohibit solely the advertisement of tobacco products, it is clear that Parliament in fact adopted a relatively *unintrusive* legislative approach to the control of tobacco products. ... Under the Act, tobacco companies continue to enjoy the right to manufacture and sell their products, to engage in public or private debate concerning the health effects of their products, and to publish consumer information on their product packages pertaining to the content of the products. The prohibition under this Act serves only to prevent these companies from employing sophisticated marketing and social psychology techniques to induce consumers to purchase their products. This type of expression, which is directed solely toward the pursuit of profit, is neither political nor artistic in nature, and therefore falls very far from the "core" of freedom of expression values discussed by this Court in *Keegstra.* ...

[98] Furthermore, ... the measures adopted under the Act were the product of an intensive 20-year public policy process, which involved extensive consultation with an array of national and international health groups and numerous

studies, and educational and legislative programs. Over the course of this 20-year period, the government adopted an incremental legislative approach by experimenting with a variety of less intrusive measures before determining that a full prohibition on advertising was necessary. ...

[99] ... It is of great significance, in my view, that over 20 democratic nations have, in recent years, adopted complete prohibitions on tobacco advertising similar to those adopted under the Act, including Australia, New Zealand, Norway, Finland and France. It is also of significance that the constitutionality of full advertising prohibitions have been upheld by the French Conseil constitutionnel (Décision No. 90-283 DC (Jan. 8, 1991) declaring the *Loi n° 91-32 relative à la lutte contre le tabagisme et l'alcoolisme*, which prohibits all direct and indirect tobacco advertising), to be constitutionally valid and by American courts (upholding full prohibitions on alcohol advertising and gambling advertising as a reasonable limitation on freedom of expression under the United States Constitution in *Central Hudson* [*Gas & Electric Corp. v. Public Service Commission of New York*, 447 U.S. 557 (1980)]; *Oklahoma Telecasters* [699 F.2d 490 (1983)]; *Metromedia* [453 U.S. 490 (1981)]; *Posadas* [*de Puerto Rico Associates v. Tourism Co. of Puerto Rico*, 478 U.S. 328 (1986)]; *Dunagin* [*v. City of Oxford, Mississippi*, 718 F.2d 738 (1983)]). The decisions of the American courts, which have traditionally been jealous guardians of the right to freedom of expression, are particularly instructive in this context because they demonstrate that the adoption of a full prohibition upon tobacco advertising is perceived as neither novel nor radical in other democratic nations. Given the background of the legislation and the overwhelming acceptance by other democratic countries of this type of prohibition as a reasonable means for combating the serious evils flowing from the sale and distribution of tobacco products, it seems difficult to argue that the impugned legislation is not a reasonable limit on the appellants' rights demonstrably justified in a free and democratic society under s. 1 of the *Charter*. ...

[103] Moreover, in considering the comparative advantages of partial and full advertising prohibitions, it is also significant that, in countries where governments have instituted partial prohibitions upon tobacco advertising such as those suggested by the appellants, the tobacco companies have developed ingenious tactics to circumvent the restrictions. For example, when France attempted to institute a partial prohibition on tobacco advertising in the 1980s (by prohibiting "lifestyle" tobacco advertising but not informational or brand preference advertising), the tobacco companies devised techniques for associating their product with "lifestyle" images which included placing pictures on the brand name and

reproducing those pictures when an advertisement showed the package, and taking out a full-page magazine advertisement and subcontracting three-quarters of the advertisement to Club Med, whose lifestyle advertisements contributed to a lifestyle association for the brand; see Luc Joossens, "Strategy of the Tobacco Industry Concerning Legislation on Tobacco Advertising in some Western European Countries" in *Proceedings of the 5th World Conference on Smoking and Health* (1983).

[104] Thus, it appears that Parliament had compelling reasons for rejecting a partial prohibition on advertising and instituting a full prohibition. In this light, it would be highly artificial for this Court to decide, on a purely abstract basis, that a partial prohibition on advertising would be as effective as a full prohibition. In my view, this is precisely the type of "line drawing" that this Court has identified as being within the institutional competence of legislatures and not courts. ...

[107] In reaching the conclusion that the Act satisfies the *Oakes* minimal impairment criterion, I am well aware of the statements of this Court in *Ford* [*v. Quebec (Attorney General)*, [1988] 2 S.C.R. 712], and *Rocket* [*v. Royal College of Dental Surgeons of Ontario*, [1990] 2 S.C.R. 232], to the effect that a complete prohibition on a type of expression will be more difficult to justify than a partial prohibition. In my view, however, these decisions are fully distinguishable from the present cases. Once again, I emphasize the importance of context in the minimal impairment analysis. In *Rocket*, this Court found that a prohibition on advertising by dentists under s. 37(39) and (40) of *Regulation 447 of the Health Disciplines Act*, R.R.O. 1980, was an infringement of s. 2(*b*) and could not be justified under s. 1. ...

[108] ... [T]he contrast with *Rocket* could not be more striking. Making an informed choice about dentists serves to promote health by allowing patients to seek out the best care; making an informed choice about tobacco simply permits consumers to choose between equally dangerous products. ...

[109] A similar contrast can be drawn between the present cases and *Ford, supra*. ... While, in these cases, the Act prohibits only tobacco advertising, in *Ford*, the law prohibited all non-French commercial expression in Quebec. It was therefore much broader in scope than the prohibition under the Act. Moreover, while the Act prohibits expression that has little or no connection with "core" freedom of expression values, the commercial expression in *Ford* was intimately connected with such core values. The impugned law in that case represented an attempt by the government of Quebec to eradicate the commercial use in public of any language other than French. Given the close historical relationship between language, culture and politics in Canada, it cannot seriously be denied that the implications of this prohibition extended well

beyond the commercial sphere and impacted upon the dignity of all minority language groups in Quebec. ...

[112] The third part of the proportionality analysis requires a proportionality between the deleterious and the salutary effects of the measures. ... For the reasons I have given with respect to both the nature of the legislation and the nature of the right infringed in these cases, it is my view that the deleterious effects of this limitation, a restriction on the rights of tobacco companies to advertise products for profit that are inherently dangerous and harmful, do not outweigh the legislative objective of reducing the number of direct inducements for Canadians to consume these products.

[113] I now turn to the appellants' final argument, namely, that s. 9 of the Act constitutes an unjustifiable infringement of their freedom of expression by compelling them to place on tobacco packages an unattributed health message. I agree, to use Wilson J.'s phrase, that if the effect of this provision is "to put a particular message into the mouth of the plaintiff, as is metaphorically alleged to be the case here," the section runs afoul of s. 2(*b*) of the *Charter*; see *Lavigne* [*v. Ontario Public Service Employees Union*, [1991] 2 S.C.R. 211], at p. 267. ... [However] it must be remembered that this statement is *unattributed* and I have some difficulty in seeing, in the context in which it was made, that it can in any real sense be considered to be attributed to the appellants. Simply because tobacco manufacturers are required to place unattributed warnings on their products does not mean that they must endorse these messages, or that they are perceived by consumers to endorse them. In a modern state, labelling of products, and especially products for human consumption, are subject to state regulation as a matter of course. It is common knowledge amongst the public at large that such statements emanate from the government, not the tobacco manufacturers. In this respect, there is an important distinction between messages directly *attributed* to tobacco manufacturers, which would create the impression that the message emanates from the appellants and would violate their right to silence, and the *unattributed* messages at issue in these cases, which emanate from the government and create no such impression. Seen in this way, the mandatory health warnings under s. 9 are no different from unattributed labelling requirements under the *Hazardous Products Act*, under which manufacturers of hazardous products are required to place unattributed warnings, such as "DANGER" or "POISON," and hazard symbols, such as skull and crossbones on their products; see *Consumer Chemicals and Containers Regulations*, SOR/88-556. I should add that the issue has ramifications for many other spheres of activity where individuals may in certain prescribed circumstances be required to place danger signs on facilities used by the public or on construction sites, and so on. This is not really an expression of opinion by the person in control of the facility or the construction site. It is rather a requirement imposed by the government as a condition of participating in a regulated activity.

[116] Even if I were of the view that there was an infringement, I am firmly convinced that it is fully justifiable under s. 1. Once again, I stress the importance of context in the s. 1 analysis. The appellants are large corporations selling a product for profit which, on the basis of overwhelming evidence, is dangerous, yet maintain the right to engage in "counterspeech" against warnings which do nothing more than bring the dangerous nature of these products to the attention of consumers. Given that the objective of the unattributed health message requirement is simply to increase the likelihood that every literate consumer of tobacco products will be made aware of the risks entailed by the use of that product, and that these warnings have no political, social or religious content, it is clear that we are a long way in this context from cases where the state seeks to coerce a lone individual to make political, social or religious statements without a right to respond. I believe a lower level of constitutional scrutiny is justified in this context. These cases seem to me to be a far more compelling situation than *Slaight* [*Communications Inc. v. Davidson*, [1989] 1 S.C.R. 1038], where a majority of the Court held the infringement there was justified under s. 1. The *Charter* was essentially enacted to protect individuals, not corporations. It may, at times it is true, be necessary to protect the rights of corporations so as to protect the rights of the individual. But I do not think this is such a case, and I again draw inspiration from the statement of Dickson C.J. in *Edwards Books, supra,* at p. 779, that the courts must ensure that the *Charter* not become simply an instrument "of better situated individuals to roll back legislation which has as its object the improvement of the condition of less advantaged persons."

[117] In my view, the requirement that health warnings must be unattributed is also proportional to the objective of informing consumers about the risks of tobacco use. Unattributed warnings are rationally connected to this objective because they increase the visual impact of the warning. It is not difficult to see that bold unattributed messages on a tobacco package (such as, for example, "SMOKING CAN KILL YOU") are more striking to the eye than messages cluttered by subtitles and attributions. Moreover, the attribution of the warnings also tends to dilute the factual impact of the messages. As Brossard J.A. observed, at p. 383:

> ... [I]t seems to me to leap to the eye that an "attributed" message can quickly become meaningless, or even ridiculous.

As an example, the message that is supposed to come from the "Surgeon-General" remains a message imputed to an abstract entity or a political body which obviously cannot by simple decree make something hazardous that otherwise would not be. This, it seems to me, rationally weakens and attenuates the message.

These considerations are particularly relevant with respect to Parliament's goal of protecting children, who constitute the largest single group of new smokers every year in this country. In a report submitted at trial ("A Report on the Special Vulnerabilities of Children and Adolescents" [(1989)]), Dr. Michael J. Chandler observed that adolescents are apt to disregard or disobey messages from perceived authority figures. On this basis, he concluded that attributed warnings would be less effective in deterring adolescents from smoking. He stated, at p. 19:

> Adolescents are predisposed, as a function of their persistent cognitive immaturity, to view public disagreements between "experts" as evidence that everything is simply a matter of subjective opinion, and a licence to "do their own thing." A warning by Health and Welfare Canada on a publicly advertised product would provide them with just the sort of evidence they feel is required to justify doing whatever impulsive thing occurs to them at the moment.

[118] Thus, although the unattributed health warning requirement precludes large corporations from disseminating on their product packages the view that tobacco products are not harmful, I believe that any concern arising from this technical infringement of their rights is easily outweighed by the pressing health concerns raised by tobacco consumption. As noted by Dickson C.J. in *Edwards Books, supra*, at p. 759, the *Charter* does not require the elimination of "minuscule" constitutional burdens, and legislative action that increases the costs of exercising a right need not be prohibited if the burden is "trivial" or "insubstantial." In these cases, the only cost associated with the unattributed warning requirement is a potential reduction in profits. In my view, this is a cost that manufacturers of dangerous products can reasonably be expected to bear, given the health benefits of effective health warnings. As I stated in *Thomson Newspapers Ltd. v. Canada (Director of Investigation and Research, Restrictive Trade Practices Commission)*, [1990] 1 S.C.R. 425, at pp. 506-7:

> In a modern industrial society, it is generally accepted that many activities in which individuals can engage must nevertheless to a greater or lesser extent be regulated by the state to ensure that the individual's pursuit of his or her self-interest is compatible with the community's interest in the realization of collective goals and aspirations. ...

The following is the judgment delivered by

[122] **McLACHLIN J.:** ...

[124] ... I agree with La Forest J. that the prohibition on advertising and promotion of tobacco products constitutes a violation of the right to free expression as the Attorney General conceded. Unlike La Forest J., I take the view that s. 9 of the Act, which requires tobacco manufacturers to place an unattributed health warning on tobacco packages, also infringes the right of free expression. As La Forest J. notes in para. 113, this Court has previously held that "freedom of expression necessarily entails the right to say nothing or the right not to say certain things": *Slaight Communications Inc. v. Davidson*, [1989] 1 S.C.R. 1038, at p. 1080, *per* Lamer J. (as he then was). Under s. 9(2), tobacco manufacturers are prohibited from displaying on their packages any writing other than the name, brand name, trade mark, and other information required by legislation. The combination of the unattributed health warnings and the prohibition against displaying any other information which would allow tobacco manufacturers to express their own views, constitutes an infringement of the right to free expression guaranteed by s. 2(*b*) of the *Charter*.

[125] The only remaining question is whether these infringements of the right of free expression are saved under s. 1 of the *Charter*, as being reasonable and "demonstrably justified in a free and democratic society." Acknowledging that the evidence of justification is problematic, La Forest J. concludes that it nevertheless suffices to justify the infringement of the right of free expression, given the importance of the legislative goal, the context of the law and the need to defer to Parliament on such an important and difficult issue. With respect, I cannot agree. ...

[135] ... It is established that the deference accorded to Parliament or the legislatures may vary with the social context in which the limitation on rights is imposed. For example, it has been suggested that greater deference to Parliament or the Legislature may be appropriate if the law is concerned with the competing rights between different sectors of society than if it is a contest between the individual and the state: *Irwin Toy* [*Ltd. v. Quebec (Attorney General)*, [1989] 1 S.C.R. 927], at pp. 993-94; *Stoffman v. Vancouver General Hospital*, [1990] 3 S.C.R. 483, at p. 521. However, such distinctions may not always be easy to apply. For example, the criminal law is generally seen as involving a contest between the state and the accused, but it also involves an allocation of priorities between the accused and the victim, actual or potential. The cases at bar provide a cogent example. We are concerned with a criminal law, which pits the state against the offender. But the social values reflected in this criminal law lead La Forest J. to conclude that "the Act

is the very type of legislation to which this Court has generally accorded a high degree of deference" (para. 70). ...

[136] [H]owever, care must be taken not to extend the notion of deference too far. Deference must not be carried to the point of relieving the government of the burden which the *Charter* places upon it of demonstrating that the limits it has imposed on guaranteed rights are reasonable and justifiable. ... To carry judicial deference to the point of accepting Parliament's view simply on the basis that the problem is serious and the solution difficult, would be to diminish the role of the courts in the constitutional process and to weaken the structure of rights upon which our constitution and our nation is founded. ...

[138] [W]hile I agree with La Forest J. that context, deference and a flexible and realistic standard of proof are essential aspects of the s. 1 analysis, these concepts ... must not be attenuated to the point that they relieve the state of the burden the *Charter* imposes of demonstrating that the limits imposed on our constitutional rights and freedoms are reasonable and justifiable in a free and democratic society. ...

[142] Against this background, I return to the cases at bar and the factors for s. 1 justification discussed in *Oakes*.

[143] The question at this stage is whether the objective of the infringing measure is sufficiently important to be capable in principle of justifying a limitation on the rights and freedoms guaranteed by the constitution. Given the importance of the *Charter* guarantees, this is not easily done. To meet the test, the objective must be one of pressing and substantial importance.

[144] Care must be taken not to overstate the objective. The objective relevant to the s. 1 analysis is *the objective of the infringing measure*, since it is the infringing measure and nothing else which is sought to be justified. If the objective is stated too broadly, its importance may be exaggerated and the analysis compromised. As my colleague has noted, the *Tobacco Products Control Act* is but one facet of a complex legislative and policy scheme to protect Canadians from the health risks of tobacco use. However, the objective of the impugned measures themselves is somewhat narrower than this. The objective of the advertising ban and trade mark usage restrictions must be to prevent people in Canada from being persuaded by advertising and promotion to use tobacco products. The objective of the mandatory package warning must be to discourage people who see the package from tobacco use. Both constitute important objectives, although the significance of the targeted decrease in consumption is reduced by the government's estimate that despite the ban, 65 percent of the Canadian magazine market will contain tobacco advertisements, given that the ban applies only to Canadian media and not to imported publications. ...

[146] While the limited objective of reducing tobacco-associated health risks by reducing advertising-related consumption and providing warnings of dangers is less significant than the broad objective of protecting Canadians generally from the risks associated with tobacco use, it nevertheless constitutes an objective of sufficient importance to justify overriding the right of free expression guaranteed by the *Charter*. Even a small reduction in tobacco use may work a significant benefit to the health of Canadians and justify a properly proportioned limitation of right of free expression. ...

[153] As a first step in the proportionality analysis, the government must demonstrate that the infringements of the right of free expression worked by the law are rationally connected to the legislative goal of reducing tobacco consumption. It must show a causal connection between the infringement and the benefit sought on the basis of reason or logic. To put it another way, the government must show that the restriction on rights serves the intended purpose. This must be demonstrated on a balance of probabilities.

[154] The causal relationship between the infringement of rights and the benefit sought may sometimes be proved by scientific evidence showing that as a matter of repeated observation, one affects the other. Where, however, legislation is directed at changing human behaviour, as in the case of the *Tobacco Products Control Act*, the causal relationship may not be scientifically measurable. In such cases, this Court has been prepared to find a causal connection between the infringement and benefit sought on the basis of reason or logic, without insisting on direct proof of a relationship between the infringing measure and the legislative objective. ...

[155] ... [In fact,] there was no direct evidence of a scientific nature showing a causal link between advertising bans and decrease in tobacco consumption.

[156] This leaves the question of whether there is less direct evidence that suggests as a matter of "reason" or "logic" that advertising bans and package warnings lead to a reduction in tobacco use. The evidence relied upon by La Forest J. in support of rational connection falls into this category. ...

[157] The question is whether this evidence establishes that it is reasonable or logical to conclude that there is a causal link between tobacco advertising and unattributed health warnings and tobacco use. To use the words of the Meese Commission on Pornography relied on in *Butler*, at p. 502, "would [it] be surprising ... to find otherwise"? The government argues that it would be "surprising ... to find otherwise." Why would tobacco companies spend great sums on advertising if not to increase the consumption of tobacco, it asks?

[158] To this the tobacco companies reply that their advertising is directed not at increasing the size of the total market but at obtaining a larger share of the existing market.

The evidence indicates that one of the thrusts of the advertising programs of tobacco companies is securing a larger market share, but there is also evidence suggesting that advertising is used to increase the total market. For example, the Court was referred to an Imperial Tobacco Ltd. ("Imperial") document, *Project Viking*, vol. I: *A Behavioural Model of Smoking*, a market research study carried out to determine an advertising strategy for the company. The report suggests that advertising should be directed to "expanding the market, or at the very least, forestalling its decline" by proactively recruiting new smokers and reassuring present smokers who might otherwise quit in response to vigorous anti-smoking publicity. Moreover, while purely informational advertising may not increase the total market, lifestyle advertising may, as a matter of common sense, be seen as having a tendency to discourage those who might otherwise cease tobacco use from doing so. Conversely, package warnings, attributed or not, may be seen as encouraging people to reduce or cease using tobacco. All this taken together with the admittedly inconclusive scientific evidence is sufficient to establish on a balance of probabilities a link based on reason between certain forms of advertising, warnings and tobacco consumption.

[159] On the other hand, there does not appear to be any causal connection between the objective of decreasing tobacco consumption and the absolute prohibition on the use of a tobacco trade mark on articles other than tobacco products which is mandated by s. 8 of the Act. There is no causal connection based on direct evidence, nor is there, in my view, a causal connection based in logic or reason. It is hard to imagine how the presence of a tobacco logo on a cigarette lighter, for example, would increase consumption; yet, such use is banned. I find that s. 8 of the Act fails the rational connection test. ...

[160] As the second step in the proportionality analysis, the government must show that the measures at issue impair the right of free expression as little as reasonably possible in order to achieve the legislative objective. The impairment must be "minimal," that is, the law must be carefully tailored so that rights are impaired no more than necessary. The tailoring process seldom admits of perfection and the courts must accord some leeway to the legislator. If the law falls within a range of reasonable alternatives, the courts will not find it overbroad merely because they can conceive of an alternative which might better tailor objective to infringement: see *Reference re ss. 193 and 195.1(1)(c) of the Criminal Code (Man.)*, [1990] 1 S.C.R. 1123, at pp. 1196-97; *R. v. Chaulk*, [1990] 3 S.C.R. 1303, at pp. 1340-41; *Ramsden v. Peterborough (City)*, [1993] 2 S.C.R. 1084, at pp. 1105-06. On the other hand, if the government fails to explain why a significantly less intrusive and equally effective measure was not chosen, the law may fail. ...

[162] I turn first to the prohibition on advertising contained in s. 4 of the Act. It is, as has been observed, complete. It bans all forms of advertising of Canadian tobacco products while explicitly exempting all foreign advertising of non-Canadian products which are sold in Canada. It extends to advertising which arguably produces benefits to the consumer while having little or no conceivable impact on consumption. Purely informational advertising, simple reminders of package appearance, advertising for new brands and advertising showing relative tar content of different brands—all these are included in the ban. Smoking is a legal activity yet consumers are deprived of an important means of learning about product availability to suit their preferences and to compare brand content with an aim to reducing the risk to their health.

[163] As this Court has observed before, it will be more difficult to justify a complete ban on a form of expression than a partial ban: *Ramsden v. Peterborough (City)*, *supra*, at pp. 1105-06; *Ford v. Quebec (Attorney General)*, *supra*, at pp. 772-73. The distinction between a total ban on expression, as in *Ford* where the legislation at issue required commercial signs to be exclusively in French, and a partial ban such as that at issue in *Irwin Toy*, *supra*, is relevant to the margin of appreciation which may be allowed the government under the minimal impairment step of the analysis. In *Rocket*, *supra*, the law imposed a complete advertising ban on professionals seeking to advertise their services. I concluded that while the government had a pressing and substantial objective, and while that objective was rationally connected to the means chosen, the minimal impairment requirement was not met since the government had exceeded a reasonable margin of appreciation given the need for consumers to obtain useful information about the services provided. A full prohibition will only be constitutionally acceptable under the minimal impairment stage of the analysis where the government can show that only a full prohibition will enable it to achieve its objective. Where, as here, no evidence is adduced to show that a partial ban would be less effective than a total ban, the justification required by s. 1 to save the violation of free speech is not established.

[164] As noted in my analysis of rational connection, while one may conclude as a matter of reason and logic that lifestyle advertising is designed to increase consumption, there is no indication that purely informational or brand preference advertising would have this effect. The government had before it a variety of less intrusive measures when it enacted the total ban on advertising, including: a partial ban which would allow information and brand preference advertising; a ban on lifestyle advertising only; measures such as those in Quebec's *Consumer Protection Act*, R.S.Q., c. P-40.1, to prohibit advertising aimed at children and adolescents; and labelling requirements only (which Health and Welfare believed would

be preferable to an advertising ban: A.J. Liston's testimony). In my view, any of these alternatives would be a reasonable impairment of the right to free expression, given the important objective and the legislative context. ...

[169] La Forest J. supports his conclusion that Parliament should be permitted to choose such measures as it sees fit by contrasting the importance of Parliament's objective with the low value of the expression at issue. This way of answering the minimal impairment requirement raises a number of concerns. First, to argue that the importance of the legislative objective justifies more deference to the government at the stage of evaluating minimal impairment, is to engage in the balancing between objective and deleterious effect contemplated by the third stage of the proportionality analysis in *Oakes*. While it may not be of great significance where this balancing takes place, care must be taken not to devalue the need for demonstration of minimum impairment by arguing the legislation is important and the infringement of no great moment.

[170] Second, just as care must be taken not to overvalue the legislative objective beyond its actual parameters, so care must be taken not to undervalue the expression at issue. Commercial speech, while arguably less important than some forms of speech, nevertheless should not be lightly dismissed. For example, in *Rocket, supra*, this Court struck down restrictions on dental advertising on the ground that the minimal impairment requirement had not been met. The *Health Disciplines Act*, R.S.O. 1980, c. 196, prohibited forms of advertising which far from being unprofessional, might have benefited consumers and contributed to their health. The same may be said here. Tobacco consumption has not been banned in Canada. Yet the advertising ban deprives those who lawfully choose to smoke of information relating to price, quality and even health risks associated with different brands. It is no answer to suggest, as does my colleague, (para. 108) that the tobacco companies have failed to establish the true benefits of such information. Under s. 1 of the *Charter*, the onus rests on the government to show why restrictions on these forms of advertising are required.

[171] Third, in finding that the commercial speech here at issue is entitled "to a very low degree of protection under s. 1" (para. 75) and that "an attenuated level of s. 1 justification is appropriate in these cases" (para. 77), La Forest J. places a great deal of reliance on the fact that the appellants are motivated by profit. I note that the same may be said for many business persons or corporations that challenge a law as contrary to freedom of expression. While this Court has stated that restrictions on commercial speech may be easier to justify than other infringements, no link between the claimant's motivation and the degree of protection has been recognized. Book sellers, newspaper owners, toy sellers—all are linked by their shareholders' desire

to profit from the corporation's business activity, whether the expression sought to be protected is closely linked to the core values of freedom of expression or not. In my view, motivation to profit is irrelevant to the determination of whether the government has established that the law is reasonable or justified as an infringement of freedom of expression.

[172] It remains to consider whether the requirement that the warning be unattributed pursuant to s. 9 of the Act fails to meet the minimum impairment requirement of proportionality. The appellant corporations contend that a warning similar to that used in the United States, which identifies the author as the Surgeon General, would be equally effective while avoiding the inference some may draw that it is the corporations themselves who are warning of the danger. They object not only to being forced to say what they do not wish to say, but also to being required to do so in a way that associates them with the opinion in question. This impairs their freedom of expression, they contend, more than required to achieve the legislative goal.

[173] The government is clearly justified in requiring the appellants to place warnings on tobacco packaging. The question is whether it was necessary to prohibit the appellants from attributing the message to the government and whether it was necessary to prevent the appellants from placing on their packaging any information other than that allowed by the regulations.

[174] As with the advertising ban, it was for the government to show that the unattributed warning, as opposed to an attributed warning, was required to achieve its objective of reducing tobacco consumption among those who might read the warning. Similarly, it was for the government to show why permitting tobacco companies to place additional information on tobacco packaging, such as a statement announcing lower tar levels, would defeat the government's objective. This it has failed to do. ...

[175] Having found the requirement of minimum impairment is not satisfied for ss. 4 and 9 of the Act, it is unnecessary to proceed to the final stage of the proportionality analysis under s. 1—balancing the negative effects of the infringement of rights against the positive benefits associated with the legislative goal. A finding that the law impairs the right more than required contradicts the assertion that the infringement is proportionate. Neither the fact that commercial expression may be entitled to a lesser degree of protection than certain other forms of expression, nor the importance of reducing tobacco consumption, even to a small extent, negate this proposition. Freedom of expression, even commercial expression, is an important and fundamental tenet of a free and democratic society. If Parliament wishes to infringe this freedom, it must be prepared to offer good and sufficient justification for the infringement and its ambit. This it has not done.

8   Syndicat Northcrest v. Amselem, 2004

Is it appropriate for the Supreme Court to assess religious doctrine to determine whether a religious claim has a legitimate foundation? And under what circumstances should an individual's religious belief prevail over an otherwise valid legal obligation? These questions were at the heart of this case and generated divergent opinions among the justices.

The appellants were Orthodox Jews whose condominium association refused to authorize the temporary construction of a succah on an individual's balcony (a small enclosed hut that is erected and in which Jews are commanded to "dwell" temporarily during the festival of Succot). As a compromise the association proposed a communal succah, but the appellants rejected this and instead erected a succcah on each of their balconies, after which the association applied for a judicial order for removal. However, according to the evidence available to the court, only one of the appellants believed he had a religious obligation to reside in his own succah. For the others, the argument for a personal rather than communal succah was best characterized as an argument of convenience.

The case was argued under the Quebec *Charter of Human Rights and Freedoms*, but the Supreme Court made clear that its approach to freedom of religion was equally applicable to the Canadian Charter. The court differed significantly on how it interpreted the scope of this protected right. The 5-to-4 majority ruled that freedom of religion protects practices even if they are not part of an established religious belief and are not necessarily regarded as obligatory by the individual claimant. In so doing, the majority emphasized that were the court to require an individual to prove that his or her religious practices are supported by a mandatory doctrine of faith, this would constitute judicial interference and place the court in the inappropriate role of being the arbiter of religious dogma. Although the majority indicated that it is valid for judges to inquire into the sincerity of a claimant's belief, they must recognize that religious beliefs are fluid, rarely static, and therefore courts should emphasize a person's belief at the time of the alleged interference. The majority concluded that freedom of religion had been infringed in a significant manner and considered the impact of accommodation for other condominium owners and the association as sufficiently minimal to justify permitting the appellants to set up succoth on their individual balconies for the duration of Succot.

In contrast, the dissenting judgment of Justice Bastarache adopted a much more narrow approach to freedom of religion that requires an individual to demonstrate the nexus between personal beliefs and the precepts of his or her religion. The dissenting judgment emphasized the importance of demonstrating that a belief is genuinely religious and not secular-based.

The majority endorsement of an understanding of freedom of religion that is not necessarily based on established religious beliefs expands the potential for conflicts to arise between individual practices that are defended as necessary for an individual's religious beliefs but that contravene bylaws or broader public laws. This interpretation of freedom of religion also raises the question of whether a valid reason or justification exists for courts to reject claims of accommodation for other moral choices that do not necessarily stem from religious convictions.[1] ～

Discussion Questions

1. Do you agree with the majority's view that religious practices should be protected even if they are not mandated by religious precepts (in this case, individual rather than communal succoth)? What are some of the implications of this broad view of freedom of religion?

2. Are you persuaded or not by Justice Binnie's dissenting view, that the appellants had in effect undermined the force of their claim that their religious rights should be accommodated because of their prior act of purchasing a condominium where the association's rules clearly preclude the use of a balcony to establish a succah?

---

1   Richard Moon, "Religious Commitment and Identity: *Syndicat Northcrest v. Amselem*" (2005) 29 *Supreme Court Law Review* 29 SCLR (2d) 216.

SYNDICAT NORTHCREST v. AMSELEM
2004 SCC 47, [2004] 2 S.C.R. 47

Hearing: January 19 2004; Judgment: June 30 2004

Present: McLachlin C.J. and Iacobucci, Major, Bastarache, Binnie, Arbour, LeBel, Deschamps, and Fish JJ.

Interveners: Evangelical Fellowship of Canada, Seventh-day Adventist Church in Canada, World Sikh Organization of Canada and Ontario Human Rights Commission.

The judgment of McLachlin C.J. and Iacobucci, Major, Arbour, and Fish JJ. was delivered by

IACOBUCCI J.:

I. Introduction

[1] An important feature of our constitutional democracy is respect for minorities, which includes, of course, religious minorities … . Indeed, respect for and tolerance of the rights and practices of religious minorities is one of the hallmarks of an enlightened democracy. But respect for religious minorities is not a stand-alone absolute right; like other rights, freedom of religion exists in a matrix of other correspondingly important rights that attach to individuals. Respect for minority rights must also coexist alongside societal values that are central to the make-up and functioning of a free and democratic society. This appeal requires the Court to deal with the interrelationship between fundamental rights both at a conceptual level and for a practical outcome.

[2] More specifically, the cases which are the subject of this appeal involve a religious claim by the appellants for the setting up of a "succah" for nine days a year in the pursuit of their religious beliefs on their co-owned property under the Quebec *Charter of Human Rights and Freedoms* … . The Quebec courts denied the claim. With respect, I disagree and would allow the appeal.

[3] … I find that the appellants' religious freedom under the Quebec *Charter* has been infringed … . While the respondent has raised rights to enjoy property and personal security as justification for its refusal to allow a succah to be set up, I find that the impairment of the appellants' religious freedom is serious whereas I conclude that the intrusion on the respondent's rights is minimal. As such, I hold that the appellants must be permitted to set up succahs on their balconies, provided that the succahs remain only for the limited time necessary—in this case nine days—, allow for an emergency access route, and conform, as much as possible, with the general aesthetics of the property. …

II. Background

[4] The appellants, all Orthodox Jews, are divided co-owners of residential units in "Place Northcrest," two luxury buildings forming part of "Le Sanctuaire du Mont-Royal" (the "Sanctuaire"), a larger complex in Montréal … .

[5] In late September 1996, Mr. Amselem, at the time a new resident of the Sanctuaire, set up a "succah" on his balcony for the purposes of fulfilling a biblically mandated obligation during the Jewish religious festival of Succot. A succah is a small enclosed temporary hut or booth, traditionally made of wood or other materials such as fastened canvas, and open to the heavens, in which, it has been acknowledged, Jews are commanded to "dwell" temporarily during the festival of Succot, which commences annually with nightfall on the fifteenth day of the Jewish month of Tishrei. This nine-day festival, which begins in late September or early- to mid-October, commemorates the 40-year period during which, according to Jewish tradition, the Children of Israel wandered in the desert, living in temporary shelters.

[6] Under the Jewish faith, in commemoration of the festival's historical connection and as a symbolic demonstration of their faith in the divine, Jews are obligated to dwell in these succahs, as their ancestors did in the desert. Orthodox Jews observe this biblically mandated commandment of "dwelling" in a succah by transforming the succah into the practitioner's primary residence for the entire holiday period. They are required to take all their meals in the succah; they customarily conduct certain religious ceremonies in the succah; they are required, weather permitting, to sleep in the succah; and they are otherwise required to generally make the succah their primary abode for the entirety of the festival period, health and weather permitting.

[7] Technically, a succah must minimally consist of a three-walled, open-roofed structure which must meet certain size specifications in order to fulfill the biblical commandment of dwelling in it properly according to the requirements of the Jewish faith. While a succah is usually festively decorated interiorly, there are no aesthetic requirements as to its exterior appearance.

[8] During the first two and last two days of the Succot holiday, as well as during any intermittent Saturday, Orthodox Jews are normally forbidden from *inter alia* turning electricity on or off and riding in cars or elevators. Similarly, during the Saturday(s) falling within the nine-day festival, Orthodox Jews are forbidden from carrying objects outside of their private domiciles in the absence of a symbolic enclosure, or *eruv*.

[9] After Mr. Amselem put up his succah in September 1996, the syndicate of co-ownership, Syndicat Northcrest (the "respondent" or "Syndicat"), requested its removal, claiming the succah was in violation of the Sanctuaire's by-laws as stated in the declaration of co-ownership, which *inter alia* prohibited decorations, alterations and constructions on the Sanctuaire's balconies: ... . None of the appellants had read the declaration of co-ownership prior to purchasing or occupying their individual units.

[10] Mr. Fonfeder similarly placed a succah on his balcony in September 1996, but received no notice or complaint.

[11] A year later, on October 6, 1997, and pursuant to the regulations in the declaration of co-ownership, Mr. Amselem requested permission from the Syndicat to set up a succah on, and thus enclose part of, his balcony to celebrate the same holiday of Succot. The Syndicat refused, invoking the restrictions in the declaration of co-ownership. ...

[13] In a letter dated October 10, 1997, the Syndicat proposed to allow Mr. Amselem, in conjunction with the other Orthodox Jewish residents of the building, including the appellants Mr. Fonfeder and Mr. Klein, to set up a communal succah in the Sanctuaire's gardens.

[14] In their October 14, 1997 letter to the Syndicat, the appellants expressed their dissatisfaction with the respondent's proposed accommodation. They explained why a communal succah would not only cause extreme hardship with their religious observance, but would also be contrary to their personal religious beliefs which, they claimed, called for "their own succah, each on his own balcony."

[15] In their letter, the appellants implored the Syndicat to accede to their request and permit their own individual succahs, which they undertook to set up "in such a way that they would not block any doors, would not obstruct fire lanes, [and] would pose no threat to safety or security in any way." The Syndicat refused their request.

[16] Each of the appellants nonetheless proceeded to set up a succah on his or her balcony. Apart from Mr. Amselem and Mr. Fonfeder in September 1996, the appellants in this appeal had not set up succahs on their balconies at the Sanctuaire in prior years; in those years they had celebrated the holiday as guests with family and friends, using their hosts' succahs.

[17] In response, the respondent Syndicat filed an application for permanent injunction prohibiting the appellants from setting up succahs and, if necessary, permitting their demolition. The application was granted by the Superior Court on June 5, 1998. ...

V. Issues

[35] In my view, the key issues before us are: (1) whether the clauses in the by-laws of the declaration of co-ownership, which contained a general prohibition against decorations or constructions on one's balcony, infringe the appellants' freedom of religion protected under the Quebec *Charter*; (2) if so, whether the refusal by the respondent to permit the setting up of a succah is justified by its reliance on the co-owners' rights to enjoy property under s. 6 of the Quebec *Charter* and their rights to personal security under s. 1 thereof; and

(3) whether the appellants waived their rights to freedom of religion by signing the declaration of co-ownership.

VI. Analysis

[36] In my view, apart from the content and scope of freedom of religion, the interplay of the rights in the Quebec *Charter* is governed by its unique content and structure. In the reasons that follow, I begin with an analysis of freedom of religion. I then briefly go on to discuss the respondent's justification in limiting the exercise of religious freedom in this case.

A. Freedom of Religion

[37] The analysis that follows sets out the principles that are applicable in cases where an individual alleges that his or her freedom of religion is infringed under the Quebec *Charter* or under the *Canadian Charter of Rights and Freedoms*. In my view, the trial judge and the majority of the Court of Appeal took, with respect, an unduly restrictive view of freedom of religion.

(1) Definition of Religious Freedom

...

[39] In order to define religious freedom, we must first ask ourselves what we mean by "religion." While it is perhaps not possible to define religion precisely, some outer definition is useful since only beliefs, convictions and practices rooted in religion, as opposed to those that are secular, socially based or conscientiously held, are protected by the guarantee of freedom of religion. Defined broadly, religion typically involves a particular and comprehensive system of faith and worship. Religion also tends to involve the belief in a divine, superhuman or controlling power. In essence, religion is about freely and deeply held personal convictions or beliefs connected to an individual's spiritual faith and integrally linked to one's self-definition and spiritual fulfilment, the practices of which allow individuals to foster a connection with the divine or with the subject or object of that spiritual faith.

[40] What then is the definition and content of an individual's protected right to religious freedom under the Quebec (or the Canadian) *Charter*? This Court has long articulated an expansive definition of freedom of religion, which revolves around the notion of personal choice and individual autonomy and freedom. ...

[43] The emphasis then is on personal choice of religious beliefs. ... [C]laimants seeking to invoke freedom of religion should not need to prove the objective validity of their beliefs in that their beliefs are objectively recognized as valid by other members of the same religion, nor is such an inquiry appropriate for courts to make ... .

[46] ... [O]ur Court's past decisions and the basic principles underlying freedom of religion support the view that freedom of religion consists of the freedom to undertake practices and harbour beliefs, having a nexus with religion, in which an individual demonstrates he or she sincerely believes or is sincerely undertaking in order to connect with the divine or as a function of his or her spiritual faith, irrespective of whether a particular practice or belief is required by official religious dogma or is in conformity with the position of religious officials.

[47] But, at the same time, this freedom encompasses objective as well as personal notions of religious belief, "obligation," precept, "commandment," custom or ritual. Consequently, both obligatory as well as voluntary expressions of faith should be protected under the Quebec (and the Canadian) *Charter*. It is the religious or spiritual essence of an action, not any mandatory or perceived-as-mandatory nature of its observance, that attracts protection. An inquiry into the mandatory nature of an alleged religious practice is not only inappropriate, it is plagued with difficulties. ...

[49] To require a person to prove that his or her religious practices are supported by a mandatory doctrine of faith, leaving it for judges to determine what those mandatory doctrines of faith are, would require courts to interfere with profoundly personal beliefs. ...

[50] In my view, the State is in no position to be, nor should it become, the arbiter of religious dogma. Accordingly, courts should avoid judicially interpreting and thus determining, either explicitly or implicitly, the content of a subjective understanding of religious requirement, "obligation," precept, "commandment," custom or ritual. Secular judicial determinations of theological or religious disputes, or of contentious matters of religious doctrine, unjustifiably entangle the court in the affairs of religion.

[51] That said, while a court is not qualified to rule on the validity or veracity of any given religious practice or belief, or to choose among various interpretations of belief, it is qualified to inquire into the sincerity of a claimant's belief, where sincerity is in fact at issue. ...

[53] Assessment of sincerity is a question of fact that can be based on several non-exhaustive criteria, including the credibility of a claimant's testimony ... as well as an analysis of whether the alleged belief is consistent with his or her other current religious practices. It is important to underscore, however, that it is inappropriate for courts rigorously to study and focus on the past practices of claimants in order to determine whether their current beliefs are sincerely held. Over the course of a lifetime, individuals change and so can their beliefs. Religious beliefs, by their very nature, are fluid and rarely static. Because of the vacillating nature of religious

belief, a court's inquiry into sincerity, if anything, should focus not on past practice or past belief but on a person's belief at the time of the alleged interference with his or her religious freedom. ...

[56] [A]t the first stage of a religious freedom analysis, an individual advancing an issue premised upon a freedom of religion claim must show the court that (1) he or she has a practice or belief, having a nexus with religion, which calls for a particular line of conduct, either by being objectively or subjectively obligatory or customary, or by, in general, subjectively engendering a personal connection with the divine or with the subject or object of an individual's spiritual faith, irrespective of whether a particular practice or belief is required by official religious dogma or is in conformity with the position of religious officials; and (2) he or she is sincere in his or her belief. Only then will freedom of religion be triggered.

(2) Infringement of Religious Freedom

[57] Once an individual has shown that his or her religious freedom is triggered, as outlined above, a court must then ascertain whether there has been enough of an interference with the exercise of the implicated right so as to constitute an infringement of freedom of religion under the Quebec (or the Canadian) *Charter*.

[58] ... Section 2(*a*) of the Canadian *Charter* prohibits only burdens or impositions on religious practice that are non-trivial. ...

[59] It consequently suffices that a claimant show that the impugned contractual or legislative provision (or conduct) interferes with his or her ability to act in accordance with his or her religious beliefs *in a manner that is more than trivial or insubstantial*. The question then becomes: what does this mean?

[60] At this stage, as a general matter, one can do no more than say that the context of each case must be examined to ascertain whether the interference is more than trivial or insubstantial. But it is important to observe what examining that context involves.

[61] In this respect, it should be emphasized that not every action will become summarily unassailable and receive automatic protection under the banner of freedom of religion. No right, including freedom of religion, is absolute. ... This is so because we live in a society of individuals in which we must always take the rights of others into account. ...

[62] [O]ur jurisprudence does not allow individuals to do absolutely anything in the name of that freedom. Even if individuals demonstrate that they sincerely believe in the religious essence of an action, for example, that a particular practice will subjectively engender a genuine connection with the divine or with the subject or object of their faith, and even if

they successfully demonstrate non-trivial or non-insubstantial interference with that practice, they will still have to consider how the exercise of their right impacts upon the rights of others in the context of the competing rights of private individuals. Conduct which would potentially cause harm to or interference with the rights of others would not automatically be protected. The ultimate protection of any particular *Charter* right must be measured in relation to other rights and with a view to the underlying context in which the apparent conflict arises.

[63] Indeed, freedom of religion, like all other rights, applicable either as against the State or, under the Quebec *Charter*, in its private dimension as against another individual, may be made subject to overriding societal concerns. As with other rights, not every interference with religious freedom would be actionable, in accordance with the limitations on the exercise of fundamental rights recognized by the Quebec *Charter*.

(3) Alleged Justification for the Limit on the Exercise of Freedom of Religion

[64] The respondent in the instant appeal has argued that the rights of the co-owners to peacefully enjoy property and to personal security limit the exercise of the appellants' religious freedom under the circumstances. ... [W]hereas I find the appellants' rights to freedom of religion significantly impaired, on the facts of this case the impact on the respondent's rights at issue is, at best, minimal and thus cannot be construed as validly limiting the exercise of the appellants' religious freedom.

B. Application to the Facts

(1) Freedom of Religion and Infringement

(a) As Pertaining to Setting Up One's Own Succah

[65] As outlined above, the first step in successfully advancing a claim that an individual's freedom of religion has been infringed is for a claimant to demonstrate that he or she sincerely believes in a practice or belief that has a nexus with religion. The second step is to then demonstrate that the impugned conduct of a third party interferes with the individual's ability to act in accordance with that practice or belief in a manner that is non-trivial. At trial, Rochon J., relying primarily on the testimony of Rabbi Levy, whose testimony he found more compelling than that of Rabbi Ohana, found that the impugned clauses in the declaration of co-ownership did not infringe the appellants' rights to freedom of religion since, according to him, Judaism does not require its adherents to build their own succah. ... With respect, I believe their approach was mistaken.

[66] ... First, the trial judge's methodology was faulty in that he chose between two competing rabbinical authorities on a question of Jewish law. Second, he seems to have based his findings with respect to freedom of religion solely on what he perceived to be the objective obligatory requirements of Judaism. He thus failed to recognize that freedom of religion under the Quebec (and the Canadian) *Charter* does not require a person to prove that his or her religious practices are supported by any mandatory doctrine of faith.

[67] Furthermore, in my opinion, any incorporation of distinctions between "obligation" and "custom" or ... between "objective obligation" and "subjective obligation or belief" within the framework of a religious freedom analysis is dubious, unwarranted and unduly restrictive. In my view, when courts undertake the task of analysing religious doctrine in order to determine the truth or falsity of a contentious matter of religious law, or when courts attempt to define the very concept of religious "obligation," as has been suggested in the courts below, they enter forbidden domain. It is not within the expertise and purview of secular courts to adjudicate questions of religious doctrine.

[68] Similarly, to frame the right either in terms of objective religious "obligation" or even as the sincere subjective belief that an obligation exists and that the practice is *required* would lead to arbitrary and hierarchical determinations of religious "obligation," would exclude religious custom from protection, and would disregard the value of non-obligatory religious experiences by excluding those experiences from protection. ...

[69] Rather, as I have stated above, regardless of the position taken by religious officials and in religious texts, provided that an individual demonstrates that he or she sincerely believes that a certain practice or belief is experientially religious in nature in that it is either objectively required by the religion, *or* that he or she subjectively believes that it is required by the religion, *or* that he or she sincerely believes that the practice engenders a personal, subjective connection to the divine or to the subject or object of his or her spiritual faith, and as long as that practice has a nexus with religion, it should trigger the protection of s. 3 of the Quebec *Charter* or that of s. 2(*a*) of the Canadian *Charter*, or both, depending on the context. ...

[72] [I]f freedom of religion encompasses not only what adherents feel sincerely obliged to do, but also includes what an individual demonstrates he or she sincerely believes or is sincerely undertaking in order to engender a connection with the divine or with the subject or object of his or her spiritual faith, then the proper test would be whether the appellants sincerely believe that dwelling in or setting up their *own* individual succah is of religious significance to them, irrespective of whether they subjectively believe that their religion *requires* them to build their own succah. This is because it is hard to qualify the value of religious experience. Religious fulfilment is by its very nature subjective and personal. To some, the religious and spiritual significance of building and eating in one's own succah could vastly outweigh the significance of a strict fulfilment of the biblical commandment of "dwelling" in a succah, and that, in and of itself, would suffice in grounding a claim of freedom of religion.

[73] [A]ll of the appellants have, in my opinion, successfully implicated freedom of religion.

[74] According to the governing principles, however, in order for a triggered right of religious freedom to have been infringed, the interference with the right needs to be more than trivial or insubstantial. ... It is evident that in respect of Mr. Amselem the impugned clauses of the declaration of co-ownership interfere with his right in a substantial way. ... A communal succah is simply not an option. Thus, his right is definitely infringed.

[75] In respect of Mr. Klein and Mr. Fonfeder, a finding of infringement depends upon what the substance of their belief was. If they sincerely believed that they must build their own succah because doing so engenders a greater connection with the divine or with their faith, then their rights to freedom of religion will be infringed by the declaration of co-ownership to the same extent as Mr. Amselem's. ...

[76] In my opinion, this has been successfully proven. At trial, the appellants testified as to the substantially distressing nature of the burden imposed upon them by the prohibition and the available alternatives. The appellants believe that they must eat every meal in the succah throughout the nine-day holiday. Imposing on others for the entire holiday amounts to a severe burden, especially when dealing with children, as testified to by Mr. Klein.

[77] Similarly, a communal succah, as the respondent proposes, would force the appellants to carry food and utensils from their units on elevated floors to the succah, and traverse the expanse of the property to the Sanctuaire's gardens for every course at every meal throughout the holiday. Since Orthodox Jews are precluded from using elevators on the Sabbath and on the first two and last two days of the Succot holiday, this would amount to forcing Orthodox Jewish residents, including the elderly among them, to climb up and down numerous flights of stairs throughout each meal for much of the nine-day holiday period. Furthermore, by being forced to share all meals with the other Jewish residents of the complex, a communal succah would also preclude the intimate celebration of the holiday with immediate family. Those who choose to sleep in the succah, weather permitting, would have to do so communally and in the open, far from

the proximity and safety of their individual units. Such distress is even objectively substantial and would undoubtedly, as the appellants assert, detract from the joyous celebration of the holiday and thus constitute a non-trivial interference with and an infringement of their rights to religious freedom.

...

[78] [T]there is no doubt whatsoever from the record that all of the appellants sincerely believe that they must fulfill the biblically mandated obligation, perhaps not necessarily of having one's own succah, but of "dwelling" in *a* succah for the entire nine-day festival of Succot. This thus triggers freedom of religion. The question then becomes, once again, whether the appellants' rights have been infringed. ...

[79] The burdens placed upon the appellants as a result of the operation of the impugned clauses, either by requiring them to celebrate the holiday by imposing on others or by forcing them, as suggested by the respondent, to celebrate in a communal succah, are evidently substantial. Preventing the appellants from building their own succah therefore constitutes a non-trivial interference with their protected rights to dwell in *a* succah during the festival of Succot, which all acknowledge they sincerely regard as a religious requirement. The result is that the impugned stipulations in the declaration of co-ownership infringe upon the appellants' freedom of religion under s. 3 of the Quebec *Charter*. ...

(2) The Alleged Justification for the Limit on the Exercise of Freedom of Religion in this Case

[82] Against the appellants' rights, the respondent Syndicat claims that the potential setting up of succahs on the appellants' balconies for the nine-day holiday of Succot would interfere with the co-owners' rights to the peaceful enjoyment of their property and to personal security, protected under ss. 6 and 1 of the Quebec *Charter*, respectively, thus justifying the total blanket prohibition against setting up succahs.

[83] ... In essence, the Syndicat is requesting in the name of the co-ownership that the appellants cease and desist from setting up these succahs, claiming that their presence negatively affects the co-owners' aesthetic, economic, and security interests in the property.

[84] In the final analysis, however, I am of the view that the alleged intrusions or deleterious effects on the respondent's rights or interests under the circumstances are, at best, minimal and thus cannot be reasonably considered as imposing valid limits on the exercise of the appellants' religious freedom. ...

[87] In a multiethnic and multicultural country such as ours, which accentuates and advertises its modern record of respecting cultural diversity and human rights and of promoting tolerance of religious and ethnic minorities—and is in many ways an example thereof for other societies—the argument of the respondent that nominal, minimally intruded-upon aesthetic interests should outweigh the exercise of the appellants' religious freedom is unacceptable. Indeed, mutual tolerance is one of the cornerstones of all democratic societies. ...

VII. Conclusions and Disposition

[103] Based on the foregoing analysis, I find that the impugned provisions in the declaration of co-ownership prohibiting constructions on the appellants' balconies infringe the appellants' freedom of religion under the Quebec *Charter*. ... The appellants are thus legally entitled to set up succahs on their balconies for a period lasting no longer than the holiday of Succot, so long as the succahs allow room for a passageway in case of emergency as well as conform, as much as possible, with the general aesthetics of the property. ...

English version of the reasons of Bastarache, LeBel, and Deschamps JJ. delivered by **BASTARACHE J.** (dissenting): ...

[135] [T]his Court has interpreted freedom of religion as protecting both religious beliefs, which are considered to be highly personal and private in nature, and consequent religious practices. However, a religion is a system of beliefs and practices based on certain religious precepts. A nexus between personal beliefs and the religion's precepts must therefore be established. ... The approach I have adopted here requires not only a personal belief or the adoption of a religious practice that is supported by a personal belief, but also a genuine connection between the belief and the person's religion. In my view, the only way the trial judge can establish that a person has a sincere belief, or has sincerely adopted a religious practice that is genuinely connected with the religion he or she claims to follow, is by applying an objective test. It is one thing to assert that a practice is protected even though certain followers of the religion do not think that the practice is included among the religion's precepts and quite another to assert that a practice must be protected when none of the followers think it is included among those precepts. If, pursuant to s. 3, a practice must be connected with the religion, the connection must be objectively identifiable.

[136] This Court has also noted on a number of occasions that freedom of religion, like any other freedom, is not absolute. ...

[137] In light of the foregoing, a method must be established for determining the scope of the protection that freedom of religion affords a claimant. ... [T]here are in fact two elements to consider in analysing freedom of religion. First, there is the freedom to believe and to profess one's beliefs;

second, there is the right to manifest one's beliefs, primarily by observing rites, and by sharing one's faith by establishing places of worship and frequenting them. Thus, although private beliefs have a purely personal aspect, the other dimension of the right has genuine social significance and involves a relationship with others. It would be an error to reduce freedom of religion to a single dimension. ...

[139] The first step of the analysis therefore consists in examining the belief of a claimant who adopts a particular religious practice in accordance with the rites prescribed by his or her religion. To this end, evidence must be introduced to establish the nature of the belief or conviction, that is, to determine upon what religious precept the belief or conviction is based. ... The onus is on the person seeking to be excused from obeying a law, a rule of internal management or another legal obligation to show that the precept in question is genuinely religious and not secular. ...

[140] ... The test is reasonable belief in the existence of a religious precept. In the absence of such proof, the court cannot assess the effects of the provisions or standards that, according to the claimant, infringe the rights of one or more members of a religious group. ... To this end, expert testimony will be useful, as it can serve to establish the fundamental practices and precepts of a religion the individual claims to practise.

[141] In the second step, the judge considers the sincerity of the claimant's religious beliefs. ... [T]he claimant must establish that he or she has a sincere belief and that this belief is objectively connected to a religious precept that follows from a text or another article of faith. It is not necessary to prove that the precept objectively creates an obligation, but it must be established that the claimant sincerely believes he or she is under an obligation that follows from the precept. ...

[143] ... Although consistency in religious practice may be indicative of the sincerity of a claimant's beliefs, it is the claimant's overall personal credibility and evidence of his or her current religious practices that matter. The essential test must be the claimant's intention and serious desire to obey the fundamental precepts of his or her religion. Previous practice is but one among a number of means of demonstrating this intention. ...

[146] [E]ven if religious conduct, practices or expression that could infringe or affect the rights of others in a private law context are protected *a priori* by the *purpose* of freedom of religion, they are not necessarily protected under the *right* to freedom of religion. While the purpose of freedom of religion is defined broadly, the right to freedom of religion is restricted. ...

[152] [Section] 9.1 of the Quebec *Charter* is a tool for interpreting rights and freedoms that is similar to, but

different in a number of ways from, s. 1 of the Canadian *Charter*. ... The important difference, however, is that the first paragraph of s. 9.1, insofar as it does not require that the infringement of a right or freedom result from the application of the law, applies only to private law relationships, that is, to infringements of the rights and freedoms of private individuals by other private individuals. ...

[154] ... To reconcile all the rights and values at issue in light of the wording of the first paragraph of s. 9.1 of the Quebec *Charter* involves finding a balance and a compromise consistent with the public interest in the specific context of the case. ...

[155] A court engaged in a reconciliation exercise must ask itself two questions: (1) Has the purpose of the fundamental right been infringed? (2) If so, is this infringement legitimate, taking into account democratic values, public order, and the general well-being? A negative answer to the second question would indicate that a fundamental right has been violated. ...

C. Application to the Facts

...

[162] ... Based on the evidence that was adduced and accepted by the trial judge, I accept that the appellants sincerely believe that, whenever possible, it would be preferable for them to erect their own succahs; however, it would not be a divergence from their religious precept to accept another solution, so long as the fundamental obligation of eating their meals in a succah was discharged. I therefore cannot accept that the appellants sincerely believe, based on the precepts of their religion that they are relying on, that they are under an obligation to erect their *own* succahs on their balconies, patios or porches. Rather, it is their practice of eating or celebrating Succot in *a* succah that is protected by the guarantee of freedom of religion set out in s. 3 of the Quebec *Charter*. The declaration of co-ownership does not hinder this practice, as it does not bar the appellants from celebrating Succot in a succah, whether at the homes of friends or family or even in a communal succah, as proposed by the respondent. Consequently, the prohibition against erecting their own succahs does not infringe the purpose of the appellants' right to freedom of religion. Any inconvenience resulting from the prohibition against erecting individual succahs is not sufficient to elevate the preference to the status of a mandatory religious practice.

[163] In the case of the appellant Amselem, however, the trial judge concluded that he was [TRANSLATION] "the only one who saw the obligation to erect a succah on his own property in terms of a divine command" (p. 1909). Assuming that his belief is sincere, which the trial judge accepted, and that it

is based on a precept of his religion, in accordance with the interpretation of the Book of Nechemiah, Chapter 8, verses 13 to 18, ... it is necessary to turn to the second step and to interpret the prohibitions imposed by the declaration of co-ownership in light of s. 9.1 of the Quebec *Charter* to determine whether they violate Mr. Amselem's right to freedom of religion. ...

[165] ... Mr. Amselem's freedom of religion is in conflict with the right of each of the other co-owners to the peaceful enjoyment and free disposition of their property under s. 6 of the Quebec *Charter* and their right to life and to personal security under s. 1 thereof. These rights must be reconciled. The reconciliation must also take into account the other circumstances of this case, such as the contractual rights arising out of the declaration of co-ownership which is binding on the parties, the application of the *Civil Code of Québec*, the negotiations that took place and the offers made by the parties in an attempt to find an acceptable solution. The exercise of rights with a regard for public order and the general well-being of citizens makes this necessary.

[166] In the case at bar, the right to the peaceful enjoyment and free disposition of one's property is included in the purpose of the restrictions provided for in the declaration of co-ownership. The restrictions are aimed first and foremost at preserving the market value of the dwelling units held in co-ownership. They also protect the co-owners' right to enjoy the common portions reserved for exclusive use while preserving the building's style and its aesthetic appearance of a luxury building, not to mention the use of the balconies to evacuate the building in a dangerous situation. The total ban on erecting anything whatsoever, including succahs, on the balconies is necessary to attain this goal, since without it, harmony cannot be maintained and emergency routes will be compromised. In this situation, freedom of religion imposes limits on the exercise of the rights of all the co-owners. ...

[176] In the case at bar, not only is there a conflict between the right to freedom of religion and property rights, but the right to freedom of religion is also in conflict with the right to life and personal security, and with contractual rights. ...

[177] In the end, the appellants rejected the Syndicat's offer, citing a multitude of problems and details, but they never proposed anything other than the erection of succahs

on their balconies. It is clear that the communal succah would be a source of inconvenience for Mr. Amselem, but the individual succah, too, was a source of genuine inconvenience for the other co-owners: in particular, it obstructed an emergency route, and the elevators were blocked during the construction while being used to transport the materials. ...

[178] [I]t must not be forgotten that the declaration of co-ownership was drafted in an effort to preserve the rights of all the co-owners, without distinction. It must also be borne in mind that the compromise proposed by the respondent, namely the erection, at the expense of all the co-owners, of a communal succah on land belonging to all the co-owners located next to the building, would have had the desired result of upholding the parties' rights under ss. 6, 1 and 3 of the Quebec *Charter*. Such a solution ... does not amount to repudiating freedom of religion, but rather to facilitating the exercise thereof in a way that takes the rights of others and the general well-being into account.

[179] With respect to s. 1 of the Quebec *Charter*, it is difficult to imagine how granting a right of way in emergency situations, which is essential to the safety of all the occupants of the co-owned property, could fail to justify the prohibition against setting up succahs, especially in light of the compromise proposed by the respondent. I see no need to revisit the trial judge's findings of fact on this subject.

[180] This leads me to conclude that, since Mr. Amselem's right to freedom of religion cannot be exercised in harmony with the rights and freedoms of others or with the general well-being, the infringement of Mr. Amselem's right is legitimate. Even though the declaration of co-ownership's prohibition against building prevents the appellants from erecting succahs on their balconies, porches or patios, it does not violate their freedom of religion. ...

[Justice Binnie offered separate dissenting reasons. He argued that the appellants were in the best position to determine their religious requirements and cannot afterward reasonably insist on accommodations at the expense of the competing legal rights of other owners. He also argued that there is a vast difference between invoking freedom of religion to resist interference by the state and invoking this claim to shield oneself against co-owners in a private building.]

Multani v. Commission scolaire Marguerite-Bourgeoys, 2006

Like *Amselem* (see case 8), *Multani* concerns the extent to which otherwise prohibited conduct becomes permissible if it is linked to or based on religious belief.

Multani, a young Sikh boy, accidently dropped a kirpan he was wearing while playing in a Quebec schoolyard. A kirpan is a ceremonial dagger that carries religious significance for Sikhs. But weapons of all sorts are banned from school property. School officials suggested that Multani seal the kirpan in his clothing so that it could neither fall out nor be easily removed. Multani's father was amenable to this "reasonable accommodation" of his son's religious beliefs, but higher school authorities rejected the compromise, insisting that kirpans are dangerous weapons. On appeal from the school commission's decision, the Quebec Superior Court restored the initial arrangement, but this decision was reversed by the Quebec Court of Appeal.

Amselem and *Multani* feature in a simmering drama in Quebec that surrounds the limits of multiculturalism. Dependent on immigration to maintain its share of the Canadian population, Quebec has had to reconcile its commitment to cultural distinctness with the realities of an increasingly multicultural population. Quebec nationalism has largely been shorn of its ethnic character and has focused on maintaining the integrity of the French language. But tensions between the cultural practices of Sikh, Muslim, and Orthodox Jewish groups and the norms of the Quebec way of life flare up frequently in both local and provincial politics. For example, in January 2007, the Quebec municipality of Hérouxville published an inflammatory "*code de vie*" that contained xenophobic overtones. Subsequently, the Quebec government appointed a commission of inquiry into the accommodation of cultural minorities. And the issue has arisen with some regularity in electoral politics. As *Amselem* and *Multani* show, the Supreme Court of Canada has generally been solicitous of the rights of Quebec minorities and cannot be discounted as a contributing factor in these controversies.

In *Multani*, a unanimous eight-judge panel of the Supreme Court reversed the Quebec Court of Appeal and declared null the decision banning the kirpan. (Multani had long since moved on from the school where the dispute arose.) In a judgment written by Justice Louise Charron, five members of the panel applied the Charter directly to the decision of the school's governing board, finding a violation of section 2(a) and concluding that the commission failed to justify the limitation of religious freedom under the terms of section 1. Charron's judgment incorporated the well-established law of reasonable accommodation into Charter section 1 analysis. That judgment is excerpted here.

Two other justices concurred in the result, but quarrelled with the direct application of the Charter to administrative bodies like the school commission. Writing for Justice Abella, Justice Marie Deschamps preferred to dispose of the case on the basis of administrative law principles according to which courts shall disturb decisions of administrative boards, agencies, and commissions only when those decisions are unreasonable on the facts. In other words, because administrative agencies were created precisely to relieve courts of the burden of adjudicating myriad claims of right, courts should generally defer to administrative decisions reasonably arrived at. In Deschamps's opinion, the Quebec Superior Court applied the administrative law principle properly and should not have been reversed on appeal.

For his part, Justice LeBel reopened an issue of Charter interpretation that many Supreme Court watchers might have thought was closed. Early in the Charter era, Supreme Court justices toyed with a "definitional" approach to Charter rights according to which Charter claims would have to conform to strictly defined Charter rights in order to force governments to justify rights violations under section 1 analysis. A definitional approach would place a greater persuasive burden on Charter claimants and relieve governments of some of the work in justifying the constitutionality of laws.[1] The court later repudiated this approach, arguing that rights should be broadly defined, making a violation easier to demonstrate and placing on the state the burden of justifying rights infringements.[2]

Not so fast, wrote LeBel in this case. "Case law developed over 20 years or more can no doubt be used to support any opinion or position. A variety of quotations can be taken from this Court's successive decisions. Attempts can be made to distinguish those decisions or to reconcile them. Doing this would probably not lead to the conclusion that the Court intended to create a straitjacket in which it would be confined when trying to resolve issues relating to the application of the *Canadian Charter* fairly and efficiently. The Court has not ruled out the possibility of reconciling or delimiting rights before applying s. 1."[3] With this claim he sought to apply a definitional limit on freedom of religion. But he did so with a candour surprising all but the legal realist.

The Supreme Court addressed the issue of religious accommodation again three years later in *Alberta v. Hutterian Brethren of Wilson Colony.*[4] The Wilson Colony Hutterites object, on religious grounds, to being photographed. From 1974 to 2003, Alberta allowed an exemption from the general requirement of personal photos on driver's licences. When that exemption was rescinded in 2003, Wilson Colony went to court, claiming the right to religious accommodation. The *Multani* precedent seemed to weigh heavily in their favour. If Sikh students could bring kirpans into the classroom, why couldn't Hutterites drive without photos on their licences? Both the trial court and the Alberta Court of Appeal agreed with the Hutterites. So did three of the seven judges on the Supreme Court panel. But those three were in dissent. The four-judge majority saw no need for a *Multani*-style accommodation of the Hutterites' religious claims. The tension between *Hutterian Brethren* and such earlier decisions as *Amselem* and *Multani* has not only attracted the attention of observers,[5] but

---

1   For an example of the definitional approach, see Justice Bertha Wilson's dissenting reasons in *R. v. Jones*, [1986] 2 S.C.R. 284.

2   *R. v. Oakes* (case 14).

3   *Multani* at para. 149, per LeBel J.

4   *Alberta v. Hutterian Brethren of Wilson Colony*, 2009 SCC 37, [2009] 2 S.C.R. 567.

5   See, for example, Janet Epp Buckingham, "Drivers Needed: Tough Choices from *Alberta v. Wilson Colony of Hutterian Brethren*" (2010) 18 *Constitutional Forum* 3; Christopher Bird, "The Globe Gets it Wrong in *Hutterian Brethren* (But Only Partially)" *The Court* (31 July 2009); Moin Yahya, "Driver's Licence Photos: Security Concerns Shouldn't Trump Religious Freedom," *The Lawyers Weekly* (28 August 2009).

also played an interesting role in the reference case concerning the constitutionality of the *Criminal Code* prohibition of polygamy launched by British Columbia in 2010. In that case, polygamy's defenders emphasized the accommodationist approach of *Multani*, while their opponents underlined *Hutterian Brethren*.[6] Justice Bauman's judgment upholding the prohibition of polygamy clearly benefitted from *Hutterian Brethren*.[7] ∿

Discussion Questions

1. How does a Charter claimant establish that his or her religious freedom has been infringed?

2. The Supreme Court distinguished public school property from courtrooms and aircraft for the purposes of the lawful exercise of the right to wear a kirpan. How does context affect the exercise of this freedom? Is the court's distinction persuasive?

3. Multani sought exemption from a rule of general application. "Reasonable accommodation" is the principle commonly used to describe this remedy for the adverse effect of a general rule or law. What limits should apply to such accommodations? How shall a court determine such limits?

---

6   For a full account of this litigation, see Tyson Dean Kennedy, "Methinks the Amicus Doth Protest Too Much: Adjudicating Canada's Polygamy Policy," MA thesis, University of Calgary, 2012.

7   *Reference re: Section 293 of the Criminal Code of Canada*, 2011 BCSC 1588.

MULTANI v. COMMISSION SCOLAIRE MARGUERITE-BOURGEOYS
2006 SCC 6, [2006] 1 S.C.R. 256

Hearing: April 12, 2005; Judgment: March 2, 2006.

Present: McLachlin C.J. and Major,* Bastarache, Binnie, LeBel, Deschamps, Fish, Abella, and Charron JJ.

Interveners: World Sikh Organization of Canada, Canadian Civil Liberties Association, Canadian Human Rights Commission, and Ontario Human Rights Commission.

* Major J. took no part in the judgment.

English version of the judgment of McLachlin C.J. and Bastarache, Binnie, Fish, and Charron JJ. delivered by

CHARRON J.:

1. Introduction

[1] This appeal requires us to determine whether the decision of a school board's council of commissioners prohibiting one of the students under its jurisdiction from wearing a kirpan to school as required by his religion infringes the student's freedom of religion. If we find that it does, we must determine whether that infringement is a reasonable limit that can be justified by the need to maintain a safe environment at the school. ...

4. Issues

...

[22] There is no question that the *Canadian Charter* applies to the decision of the council of commissioners, despite the decision's individual nature. The council is a creature of statute and derives all its powers from statute. Since the legislature cannot pass a statute that infringes the *Canadian Charter*, it cannot, through enabling legislation, do the same thing by delegating a power to act to an administrative decision maker: see *Slaight Communications [Inc. v. Davidson*, [1989] 1 S.C.R. 1038], at pp. 1077-78. As was explained in *Eldridge v. British Columbia (Attorney General)*, [1997] 3 S.C.R. 624, at para. 20, the *Canadian Charter* can apply in two ways:

> First, legislation may be found to be unconstitutional on its face because it violates a *Charter* right and is not saved by s. 1. In such cases, the legislation will be invalid and

the Court compelled to declare it of no force or effect pursuant to s. 52(1) of the *Constitution Act, 1982.* Secondly, the *Charter* may be infringed, not by the legislation itself, but by the actions of a delegated decision-maker in applying it. In such cases, the legislation remains valid, but a remedy for the unconstitutional action may be sought pursuant to s. 24(1) of the *Charter.*

Deschamps and Abella JJ. take the view that the Court must apply s. 1 of the *Canadian Charter* only in the first case. I myself believe that the same analysis is necessary in the second case, where the decision maker has acted pursuant to an enabling statute, since any infringement of a guaranteed right that results from the decision maker's actions is also a limit "prescribed by law" within the meaning of s. 1. On the other hand ... when the delegated power is not exercised in accordance with the enabling legislation, a decision not authorized by statute is not a limit "prescribed by law" and therefore cannot be justified under s. 1.

[23] In the case at bar, no one is suggesting that the council of commissioners failed to act in accordance with its enabling legislation. It is thus necessary to determine ... whether the council of commissioners' decision infringes, as alleged, Gurbaj Singh's freedom of religion. ... [W]here the legislation pursuant to which an administrative body has made a contested decision confers a discretion (in the instant case, the choice of means to keep schools safe) and does not confer, either expressly or by implication, the power to limit the rights and freedoms guaranteed by the *Canadian Charter*, the decision should, if there is an infringement, be subjected to the test set out in s. 1 of the *Canadian Charter* to ascertain whether it constitutes a reasonable limit that can be demonstrably justified in a free and democratic society. If it is not justified, the administrative body has exceeded its authority in making the contested decision.

5.2 Internal Limits of Freedom of Religion, or Justification Within the Meaning of Section 1?

[24] The parties have been unable to agree on the most appropriate analytical approach. The appellant considers it clear that the council of commissioners' decision infringes his son's freedom of religion protected by s. 2(*a*) of the *Canadian Charter*. In response to the respondents' submissions, he maintains that only a limit that meets the test for the application of s. 1 of the *Canadian Charter* can be justified. The Attorney General of Quebec concedes that the prohibition against the appellant's son wearing his kirpan to school infringes the son's freedom of religion, but submits that, regardless of the conditions ordered by the Superior Court, the prohibition is a fair limit on freedom of religion, which is not an absolute right.

[25] According to the CSMB, freedom of religion has not been infringed, because it has internal limits. The CSMB considers that, in the instant case, the freedom of religion guaranteed by s. 2(*a*) must be limited by imperatives of public order, safety, and health, as well as by the rights and freedoms of others. In support of this contention, it relies primarily on *Trinity Western University v. British Columbia College of Teachers*, [2001] 1 S.C.R. 772, 2001 SCC 31, in which the Court defined the scope of the rights in issue (freedom of religion and the right to equality) in order to resolve any potential conflict. The CSMB is of the view that, in the case at bar, delineating the rights in issue in this way would preserve Gurbaj Singh's freedom of religion while, as in *Trinity Western University*, circumscribing his freedom to act in accordance with his beliefs. According to this line of reasoning, the outcome of this appeal would be decided at the stage of determining whether freedom of religion has been infringed rather than at the stage of reconciling the rights of the parties under s. 1 of the *Canadian Charter.*

[26] This Court has clearly recognized that freedom of religion can be limited when a person's freedom to act in accordance with his or her beliefs may cause harm to or interfere with the rights of others. ... However, the Court has on numerous occasions stressed the advantages of reconciling competing rights by means of a s. 1 analysis. For example, in *B. (R.) v. Children's Aid Society of Metropolitan Toronto*, [1995] 1 S.C.R. 315, the claimants, who were Jehovah's Witnesses, contested an order that authorized the administration of a blood transfusion to their daughter. While acknowledging that freedom of religion could be limited in the best interests of the child, La Forest J., writing for the majority of the Court, stated the following, at paras. 109-10:

> This Court has consistently refrained from formulating internal limits to the scope of freedom of religion in cases where the constitutionality of a legislative scheme was raised; it rather opted to balance the competing rights under s. 1 of the *Charter* ... .
>
> In my view, it appears sounder to leave to the state the burden of justifying the restrictions it has chosen. Any ambiguity or hesitation should be resolved in favour of individual rights. Not only is this consistent with the broad and liberal interpretation of rights favoured by this Court, but s. 1 is a much more flexible tool with which to balance competing rights than s. 2(*a*). ...

> ...

[28] It is important to distinguish these decisions from the ones in which the Court did not conduct a s. 1 analysis because there was no conflict of fundamental rights. For example, in *Trinity Western University*, the Court, asked to

resolve a potential conflict between religious freedoms and equality rights, concluded that a proper delineation of the rights involved would make it possible to avoid any conflict in that case. Likewise, in *Amselem*, a case concerning the *Quebec Charter*, the Court refused to pit freedom of religion against the right to peaceful enjoyment and free disposition of property, because the impact on the latter was considered "at best, minimal" (para. 64). Logically, where there is not an apparent infringement of more than one fundamental right, no reconciliation is necessary at the initial stage.

[29] In the case at bar, the Court does not at the outset have to reconcile two constitutional rights, as only freedom of religion is in issue here. Furthermore, since the decision genuinely affects both parties and was made by an administrative body exercising statutory powers, a contextual analysis under s. 1 will enable us to balance the relevant competing values in a more comprehensive manner.

[30] This Court has frequently stated, and rightly so, that freedom of religion is not absolute and that it can conflict with other constitutional rights. However, since the test governing limits on rights was developed in *Oakes*, the Court has never called into question the principle that rights are reconciled through the constitutional justification required by s. 1 of the *Canadian Charter*. ...

[31] Thus, the central issue in the instant case is best suited to a s. 1 analysis. But before proceeding with this analysis, I will explain why the contested decision clearly infringes freedom of religion.

6. Infringement of Freedom of Religion

[32] This Court has on numerous occasions stressed the importance of freedom of religion. ...

[34] In *Amselem*, the Court ruled that, in order to establish that his or her freedom of religion has been infringed, the claimant must demonstrate (1) that he or she sincerely believes in a practice or belief that has a nexus with religion, and (2) that the impugned conduct of a third party interferes, in a manner that is non-trivial or not insubstantial, with his or her ability to act in accordance with that practice or belief.

[35] The fact that different people practise the same religion in different ways does not affect the validity of the case of a person alleging that his or her freedom of religion has been infringed. What an individual must do is show that he or she sincerely believes that a certain belief or practice is required by his or her religion. The religious belief must be asserted in good faith and must not be fictitious, capricious or an artifice (*Amselem*, at para. 52). In assessing the sincerity of the belief, a court must take into account, *inter alia*, the credibility of the testimony of the person asserting the

particular belief and the consistency of the belief with his or her other current religious practices (*Amselem*, at para. 53).

[36] In the case at bar, Gurbaj Singh must therefore show that he sincerely believes that his faith requires him at all times to wear a kirpan made of metal. Evidence to this effect was introduced and was not contradicted. No one contests the fact that the orthodox Sikh religion requires its adherents to wear a kirpan at all times. The affidavits of chaplain Manjit Singh and of Gurbaj Singh explain that orthodox Sikhs must comply with a strict dress code requiring them to wear religious symbols commonly known as the Five Ks: (1) the kesh (uncut hair); (2) the kangha (a wooden comb); (3) the kara (a steel bracelet worn on the wrist); (4) the kaccha (a special undergarment); and (5) the kirpan (a metal dagger or sword). Furthermore, Manjit Singh explains in his affidavit that the Sikh religion teaches pacifism and encourages respect for other religions, that the kirpan must be worn at all times, even in bed, that it must not be used as a weapon to hurt anyone, and that Gurbaj Singh's refusal to wear a symbolic kirpan made of a material other than metal is based on a reasonable religiously motivated interpretation.

[37] Much of the CSMB's argument is based on its submission that [TRANSLATION] "the kirpan is essentially a dagger, a weapon designed to kill, intimidate or threaten others." With respect, while the kirpan undeniably has characteristics of a bladed weapon capable of wounding or killing a person, this submission disregards the fact that, for orthodox Sikhs, the kirpan is above all a religious symbol. Chaplain Manjit Singh mentions in his affidavit that the word "kirpan" comes from "kirpa," meaning "mercy" and "kindness," and "aan," meaning "honour." There is no denying that this religious object could be used wrongly to wound or even kill someone, but the question at this stage of the analysis cannot be answered definitively by considering only the physical characteristics of the kirpan. Since the question of the physical makeup of the kirpan and the risks the kirpan could pose to the school board's students involves the reconciliation of conflicting values, I will return to it when I address justification under s. 1 of the *Canadian Charter*. In order to demonstrate an infringement of his freedom of religion, Gurbaj Singh does not have to establish that the kirpan is not a weapon. He need only show that his personal and subjective belief in the religious significance of the kirpan is sincere.

[38] Gurbaj Singh says that he sincerely believes he must adhere to this practice in order to comply with the requirements of his religion. ...

[39] Furthermore, Gurbaj Singh's refusal to wear a replica made of a material other than metal is not capricious. He genuinely believes that he would not be complying with the requirements of his religion were he to wear a plastic or

wooden kirpan. The fact that other Sikhs accept such a compromise is not relevant. ...

[40] Finally, the interference with Gurbaj Singh's freedom of religion is neither trivial nor insignificant. Forced to choose between leaving his kirpan at home and leaving the public school system, Gurbaj Singh decided to follow his religious convictions and is now attending a private school. The prohibition against wearing his kirpan to school has therefore deprived him of his right to attend a public school.

[41] Thus, there can be no doubt that the council of commissioners' decision prohibiting Gurbaj Singh from wearing his kirpan to Sainte-Catherine-Labouré school infringes his freedom of religion. This limit must therefore be justified under s. 1 of the *Canadian Charter*.

7. Section 1 of the Canadian Charter

...

7.1 Importance of the Objective

[44] As stated by the Court of Appeal, the council of commissioners' decision [TRANSLATION] "was motivated by [a pressing and substantial] objective, namely, to ensure an environment conducive to the development and learning of the students. This requires [the CSMB] to ensure the safety of the students and the staff. This duty is at the core of the mandate entrusted to educational institutions" (para. 77). The appellant concedes that this objective is laudable and that it passes the first stage of the test. The respondents also submitted fairly detailed evidence consisting of affidavits from various stakeholders in the educational community explaining the importance of safety in schools and the upsurge in problems relating to weapons and violence in schools.

[45] Clearly, the objective of ensuring safety in schools is sufficiently important to warrant overriding a constitutionally protected right or freedom. It remains to be determined what level of safety the governing board was seeking to achieve by prohibiting the carrying of weapons and dangerous objects, and what degree of risk would accordingly be tolerated. ... [T]he possibilities range from a desire to ensure absolute safety to a total lack of concern for safety. Between these two extremes lies a concern to ensure a reasonable level of safety.

[46] Although the parties did not present argument on the level of safety sought by the governing board, the issue was addressed by the intervener Canadian Human Rights Commission, which correctly stated that the standard that seems to be applied in schools is reasonable safety, not absolute safety. The application of a standard of absolute safety could result in the installation of metal detectors in schools, the prohibition of all potentially dangerous objects (such as scissors, compasses, baseball bats and table knives in the

cafeteria) and permanent expulsion from the public school system of any student exhibiting violent behaviour. Apart from the fact that such a standard would be impossible to attain, it would compromise the objective of providing universal access to the public school system.

[47] On the other hand, when the governing board approved the article in question of the *Code de vie*, it was not seeking to establish a minimum standard of safety. As can be seen from the affidavits of certain stakeholders from the educational community, violence and weapons are not tolerated in schools, and students exhibiting violent or dangerous behaviour are punished. Such measures show that the objective is to attain a certain level of safety beyond a minimum threshold.

[48] I therefore conclude that the level of safety chosen by the governing council and confirmed by the council of commissioners was reasonable safety. The objective of ensuring a reasonable level of safety in schools is without question a pressing and substantial one.

7.2 Proportionality

7.2.1 Rational Connection

[Justice Charron holds that the commission's decision to ban the kirpan is rationally connected to its policy against the carrying of weapons.]

7.2.2 Minimal Impairment

[50] The second stage of the proportionality analysis is often central to the debate as to whether the infringement of a right protected by the *Canadian Charter* can be justified. The limit, which must minimally impair the right or freedom that has been infringed, need not necessarily be the least intrusive solution. In *RJR-MacDonald Inc. v. Canada (Attorney General)*, [1995] 3 S.C.R. 199, at para. 160, this Court defined the test as follows:

> The impairment must be "minimal," that is, the law must be carefully tailored so that rights are impaired no more than necessary. The tailoring process seldom admits of perfection and the courts must accord some leeway to the legislator. If the law falls within a range of reasonable alternatives, the courts will not find it overbroad merely because they can conceive of an alternative which might better tailor objective to infringement. ...

[51] The approach to the question must be the same where what is in issue is not legislation, but a decision rendered pursuant to a statutory discretion. Thus, it must be determined whether the decision to establish an absolute prohibition against wearing a kirpan "falls within a range of reasonable alternatives."

[52] In considering this aspect of the proportionality analysis, Lemelin J. expressed the view that [TRANSLATION] "[t]he duty to accommodate this student is a corollary of the minimal impairment [test]" (para. 92). In other words, she could not conceive of the possibility of a justification being sufficient for the purposes of s. 1 if reasonable accommodation is possible (para. 75). This correspondence of the concept of reasonable accommodation with the proportionality analysis is not without precedent. In *Eldridge*, at para. 79, this Court stated that, in cases concerning s. 15(1) of the *Canadian Charter*, "reasonable accommodation" was equivalent to the concept of "reasonable limits" provided for in s. 1 of the *Canadian Charter*.

[53] In my view, this correspondence between the legal principles is logical. In relation to discrimination, the courts have held that there is a duty to make reasonable accommodation for individuals who are adversely affected by a policy or rule that is neutral on its face, and that this duty extends only to the point at which it causes undue hardship to the party who must perform it. Although it is not necessary to review all the cases on the subject, the analogy with the duty of reasonable accommodation seems to me to be helpful to explain the burden resulting from the minimal impairment test with respect to a particular individual, as in the case at bar. In my view, Professor José Woehrling correctly explained the relationship between the duty to accommodate or adapt and the *Oakes* analysis in the following passage:

[TRANSLATION] Anyone seeking to disregard the duty to accommodate must show that it is necessary, in order to achieve a legitimate and important legislative objective, to apply the standard in its entirety, without the exceptions sought by the claimant. More specifically, in the context of s. 1 of the *Canadian Charter*, it is necessary, in applying the test from *R. v. Oakes*, to show, in succession, that applying the standard in its entirety constitutes a rational means of achieving the legislative objective, that no other means are available that would be less intrusive in relation to the rights in question (minimal impairment test), and that there is proportionality between the measure's salutary and limiting effects. At a conceptual level, the minimal impairment test, which is central to the section 1 analysis, corresponds in large part with the undue hardship defence against the duty of reasonable accommodation in the context of human rights legislation. This is clear from the Supreme Court's judgment in *Edwards Books*, in which the application of the minimal impairment test led the Court to ask whether the Ontario legislature, in prohibiting stores from opening on Sundays and allowing certain exceptions for stores that were closed on Saturdays, had done enough to accommodate merchants who, for religious reasons, had to observe a day of rest on a day other than Sunday.

(J. Woehrling, "L'obligation d'accommodement raisonnable et l'adaptation de la société à la diversité religieuse" (1998), 43 *McGill L.J.* 325, at p. 360)

[54] The council of commissioners' decision establishes an absolute prohibition against Gurbaj Singh wearing his kirpan to school. The respondents contend that this prohibition is necessary, because the presence of the kirpan at the school poses numerous risks for the school's pupils and staff. It is important to note that Gurbaj Singh has never claimed a right to wear his kirpan to school without restrictions. Rather, he says that he is prepared to wear his kirpan under the above-mentioned conditions imposed by Grenier J. of the Superior Court. Thus, the issue is whether the respondents have succeeded in demonstrating that an absolute prohibition is justified.

[55] According to the CSMB, to allow the kirpan to be worn to school entails the risks that it could be used for violent purposes by the person wearing it or by another student who takes it away from him, that it could lead to a proliferation of weapons at the school, and that its presence could have a negative impact on the school environment. In support of this last point, the CSMB submits that the kirpan is a symbol of violence and that it sends the message that the use of force is the way to assert rights and resolve conflicts, in addition to undermining the perception of safety and compromising the spirit of fairness that should prevail in schools, in that its presence suggests the existence of a double standard. Let us look at those arguments.

7.2.2.1 Safety in Schools

[56] According to the respondents, the presence of kirpans in schools, even under certain conditions, creates a risk that they will be used for violent purposes, either by those who wear them or by other students who might take hold of them by force.

[57] The evidence shows that Gurbaj Singh does not have behavioural problems and has never resorted to violence at school. The risk that this particular student would use his kirpan for violent purposes seems highly unlikely to me. In fact, the CSMB has never argued that there was a risk of his doing so.

[58] As for the risk of another student taking his kirpan away from him, it also seems to me to be quite low, especially if the kirpan is worn under conditions such as were imposed by Grenier J. of the Superior Court. In the instant case, if the kirpan were worn in accordance with those conditions, any student wanting to take it away from Gurbaj Singh would first

have to physically restrain him, then search through his clothes, remove the sheath from his guthra, and try to unstitch or tear open the cloth enclosing the sheath in order to get to the kirpan. There is no question that a student who wanted to commit an act of violence could find another way to obtain a weapon, such as bringing one in from outside the school. Furthermore, there are many objects in schools that could be used to commit violent acts and that are much more easily obtained by students, such as scissors, pencils and baseball bats.

[59] In her brief reasons, Grenier J. explained that her decision was based in part on the fact that [TRANSLATION] "the evidence revealed no instances of violent incidents involving kirpans in schools in Quebec" and on "the state of Canadian and American law on this matter" (para. 6). In fact, the evidence in the record suggests that, over the 100 years since Sikhs have been attending schools in Canada, not a single violent incident related to the presence of kirpans in schools has been reported. ...

[60] ...

> Sikhs may wear kirpans in schools in Surrey, British Columbia. Although no other Ontario school board has expressly addressed the issue with the same depth as the Peel board, students may wear kirpans in the North York Board of Education and the Etobicoke Board of Education (which has a limit of six inches in size). No school boards in the Metropolitan Toronto area have a policy prohibiting or restricting kirpans. There is no evidence that kirpans have sparked a violent incident in any school, no evidence that any other school board in Canada bans kirpans, and no evidence of a student anywhere in Canada using a kirpan as a weapon. [*Peel Board of Education v. Ontario Human Rights Commission* (1991), 3 O.R. (3d) 531 at 533]...

[62] The respondents maintain that freedom of religion can be limited even in the absence of evidence of a real risk of significant harm, since it is not necessary to wait for the harm to occur before correcting the situation. They submit that the same line of reasoning that was followed in *Hothi v. R.*, [1985] 3 W.W.R. 256 (Man. Q.B.) (aff'd [1986] 3 W.W.R. 671 (Man. C.A.)), and *Nijjar v. Canada 3000 Airlines Ltd.* (1999), 36 C.H.R.R. D/76 (Can. Trib.), in which the wearing of kirpans was prohibited in courts and on airplanes, should apply in this case. As was mentioned above, Lemelin J. of the Court of Appeal pointed out that safety concerns are no less serious in schools.

[63] There can be no doubt that safety is just as important in schools as it is on airplanes and in courts. However, it is important to remember that the specific context must always

be borne in mind in resolving the issue. In *Nijjar*, Mr. Nijjar's complaint that he had been denied the right to wear his kirpan aboard a Canada 3000 Airlines aircraft was dismissed because, *inter alia*, he had failed to demonstrate that wearing a kirpan in a manner consistent with Canada 3000's policies would be contrary to his religious beliefs. It was apparent from Mr. Nijjar's testimony that wearing one particular type of kirpan rather than another was a matter of personal preference, not of religious belief. While it concluded that Mr. Nijjar had not been discriminated against on the basis of his religion, the Canadian Human Rights Tribunal did nevertheless consider the issue of reasonable accommodation. It made the following comment at para. 123 of its decision:

> In assessing whether or not the respondent's weapons policy can be modified so as to accommodate Sikhs detrimentally affected, consideration must be given to the environment in which the rule must be applied. In this regard, we are satisfied that aircraft present a unique environment. Groups of strangers are brought together and are required to stay together, in confined spaces, for prolonged periods of time. Emergency medical and police assistance are not readily accessible.

Then, at para. 125, the Tribunal distinguished the case before it from *Pandori* [*v. Peel Bd. of Education* (1990), 12 C.H.R.R. D/364, aff'd (1991), 3 O.R. (3d) 531 (*sub nom. Peel Board of Education v. Ontario Human Rights Commission*)]:

> Unlike the school environment in issue in the *Pandori* case, where there is an ongoing relationship between the student and the school and with that a meaningful opportunity to assess the circumstances of the individual seeking the accommodation, air travel involves a transitory population. Significant numbers of people are processed each day, with minimal opportunity for assessment. It will be recalled that Mr. Kinnear testified that Canada 3000 check-in personnel have between forty-five and ninety seconds of contact with each passenger.

[64] *Hothi* also involved special circumstances. The judge who prohibited the wearing of a kirpan in the courtroom was hearing the case of an accused charged with assault under s. 245 of the *Criminal Code*, R.S.C. 1970, c. C-34. Dewar C.J. of the Manitoba Court of Queen's Bench considered (at p. 259) the special nature of courts and stated the following about the prohibition against wearing kirpans in courtrooms:

> [It] serves a transcending public interest that justice be administered in an environment free from any influence which may tend to thwart the process. Possession in the courtroom of weapons, or articles capable of use as such, by parties or others is one such influence.

[65] The facts in the case at bar are more similar to the facts in *Pandori* than to those in *Nijjar* and *Hothi*. The school environment is a unique one that permits relationships to develop among students and staff. These relationships make it possible to better control the different types of situations that arise in schools. The Ontario board of inquiry commented on the special nature of the school environment in *Pandori*, at para. 197:

> Courts and schools are not comparable institutions. One is a tightly circumscribed environment in which contending elements, adversarially aligned, strive to obtain justice as they see it, with judge and/or jury determining the final outcome. Schools on the other hand are living communities which, while subject to some controls, engage in the enterprise of education in which both teachers and students are partners. Also, a court appearance is temporary (a Khalsa Sikh could conceivably deal with the prohibition of the kirpan as he/she would on an airplane ride) and is therefore not comparable to the years a student spends in the school system.

[66] Although there is no need in the instant case for this Court to compare the desirable level of safety in a given environment with the desirable level in a school environment, these decisions show that each environment is a special case with its own unique characteristics that justify a different level of safety, depending on the circumstances.

[67] Returning to the respondents' argument, I agree that it is not necessary to wait for harm to be done before acting, but the existence of concerns relating to safety must be unequivocally established for the infringement of a constitutional right to be justified. Given the evidence in the record, it is my opinion that the respondents' argument in support of an absolute prohibition—namely that kirpans are inherently dangerous—must fail.

7.2.2.2 Proliferation of Weapons in Schools

[68] The respondents also contend that allowing Gurbaj Singh to wear his kirpan to school could have a ripple effect. They submit that other students who learn that orthodox Sikhs may wear their kirpans will feel the need to arm themselves so that they can defend themselves if attacked by a student wearing a kirpan.

[69] This argument is essentially based on the one discussed above, namely that kirpans in school pose a safety risk to other students, forcing them to arm themselves in turn in order to defend themselves. For the reasons given above, I am of the view that the evidence does not support this argument. It is purely speculative and cannot be accepted in the instant case: see *Eldridge*, at para. 89. Moreover, this argument merges

with the next one, which relates more specifically to the risk of poisoning the school environment. I will therefore continue with the analysis.

7.2.2.3 Negative Impact on the School Environment

[70] The respondents submit that the presence of kirpans in schools will contribute to a poisoning of the school environment. They maintain that the kirpan is a symbol of violence and that it sends the message that using force is the way to assert rights and resolve conflict, compromises the perception of safety in schools and establishes a double standard.

[71] The argument that the wearing of kirpans should be prohibited because the kirpan is a symbol of violence and because it sends the message that using force is necessary to assert rights and resolve conflict must fail. Not only is this assertion contradicted by the evidence regarding the symbolic nature of the kirpan, it is also disrespectful to believers in the Sikh religion and does not take into account Canadian values based on multiculturalism.

[72] As for the submissions based on the other students' perception regarding safety and on feelings of unfairness that they might experience, these appear to stem from the affidavit of psychoeducator Denis Leclerc, who gave his opinion concerning a study in which he took part that involved, *inter alia*, questioning students and staff from 14 high schools belonging to the CSMB about the socio-educational environment in schools. The results of the study seem to show that there is a mixed or negative perception regarding safety in schools. It should be noted that this study did not directly address kirpans, but was instead a general examination of the situation in schools in terms of safety. Mr. Leclerc is of the opinion that the presence of kirpans in schools would heighten this impression that the schools are unsafe. He also believes that allowing Gurbaj Singh to wear a kirpan would engender a feeling of unfairness among the students, who would perceive this permission as special treatment. He mentions, for example, that some students still consider the right of Muslim women to wear the chador to be unfair, because they themselves are not allowed to wear caps or scarves.

[73] It should be noted that, in a letter submitted to counsel for the appellants, psychologist Mathieu Gattuso indicated that, in light of the generally accepted principles concerning expert evidence, Denis Leclerc's affidavit does not constitute an expert opinion. It is clear from the examination of Mr. Leclerc that he did not study the situation in schools that authorize the wearing of kirpans and that, in his affidavit, he was merely giving a personal opinion.

[74] With respect for the view of the Court of Appeal, I cannot accept Denis Leclerc's position. Among other

concerns, the example he presents concerning the chador is particularly revealing. To equate a religious obligation such as wearing the chador with the desire of certain students to wear caps is indicative of a simplistic view of freedom of religion that is incompatible with the *Canadian Charter*. Moreover, his opinion seems to be based on the firm belief that the kirpan is, by its true nature, a weapon. The CSMB itself vigorously defends this same position. For example, it states the following in its factum (at paras. 37-38):

> [TRANSLATION] Although kirpans were presented to the trial judge at the hearing, she failed to rule on the true nature of the kirpan. On the contrary, she seemed, in light of her comments, to accept the appellants' argument that in today's world, the kirpan has only symbolic value for Sikhs.
>
> Yet whatever it may symbolize, the kirpan is still essentially a dagger, *a weapon designed to kill, intimidate or threaten others.* [Emphasis added.]

These assertions strip the kirpan of any religious significance and leave no room for accommodation. The CSMB also makes the following statement (at para. 51):

> [TRANSLATION] It is thus a paralogism ... to liken a weapon to all objects whose purpose is not to kill or wound but that could potentially be used as weapons, such as compasses, paper cutters, baseball bats, sporting equipment, or cars. Does this mean that we should stop studying geometry or playing baseball?

[75] The appellants are perhaps right to state that the only possible explanation for the acceptance of these other potentially dangerous objects in schools is that the respondents consider the activities in which those objects are used to be important, while accommodating the religious beliefs of the appellant's son is not.

[76] Religious tolerance is a very important value of Canadian society. If some students consider it unfair that Gurbaj Singh may wear his kirpan to school while they are not allowed to have knives in their possession, it is incumbent on the schools to discharge their obligation to instil in their students this value that is, as I will explain in the next section, at the very foundation of our democracy.

[77] In my opinion, the respondents have failed to demonstrate that it would be reasonable to conclude that an absolute prohibition against wearing a kirpan minimally impairs Gurbaj Singh's rights.

7.2.3 *Effects of the Measure*

[78] Since we have found that the council of commissioners' decision is not a reasonable limit on religious freedom, it is not strictly necessary to weigh the deleterious effects of this measure against its salutary effects. I do believe, however, like the intervener Canadian Civil Liberties Association, that it is important to consider some effects that could result from an absolute prohibition. An absolute prohibition would stifle the promotion of values such as multiculturalism, diversity, and the development of an educational culture respectful of the rights of others. This Court has on numerous occasions reiterated the importance of these values. For example, in *Ross*, the Court stated the following, at para. 42:

> A school is a communication centre for a whole range of values and aspirations of a society. In large part, it defines the values that transcend society through the educational medium. The school is an arena for the exchange of ideas and must, therefore, be premised upon principles of tolerance and impartiality so that all persons within the school environment feel equally free to participate.

In *R. v. M. (M.R.)*, [1998] 3 S.C.R. 393, at para. 3, the Court made the following observation:

> [S]chools ... have a duty to foster the respect of their students for the constitutional rights of all members of society. Learning respect for those rights is essential to our democratic society and should be part of the education of all students. These values are best taught by example and may be undermined if the students' rights are ignored by those in authority.

Then, in *Trinity Western University*, the Court stated the following, at para. 13:

> Our Court [has] accepted ... that teachers are a medium for the transmission of values. ... Schools are meant to develop civic virtue and responsible citizenship, to educate in an environment free of bias, prejudice and intolerance.

[79] A total prohibition against wearing a kirpan to school undermines the value of this religious symbol and sends students the message that some religious practices do not merit the same protection as others. On the other hand, accommodating Gurbaj Singh and allowing him to wear his kirpan under certain conditions demonstrates the importance that our society attaches to protecting freedom of religion and to showing respect for its minorities. The deleterious effects of a total prohibition thus outweigh its salutary effects. ...

9. Remedy

[81] Section 24(1) of the *Canadian Charter* reads as follows:

Anyone whose rights or freedoms, as guaranteed by this Charter, have been infringed or denied may apply to a court of competent jurisdiction to obtain such remedy as the court considers appropriate and just in the circumstances.

[82] Given that Gurbaj Singh no longer attends Sainte-Catherine-Labouré school, it would not be appropriate to restore the judgment of the Superior Court, as requested by the appellants. The Court accordingly considers that the appropriate and just remedy is to declare the decision prohibiting Gurbaj Singh from wearing his kirpan to be null.

10. Disposition

[83] I would allow the appeal, set aside the decision of the Court of Appeal, and declare the decision of the council of commissioners to be null, with costs throughout.

10 Saskatchewan (Human Rights Commission) v. Whatcott, 2013

Free speech is among the most precious of civil liberties and is sometimes called the "queen of rights" because free speech is required to vindicate all the other rights a constitution guarantees. The Supreme Court has been precise about the value of free speech and expression. We prize free speech, declared the court in *Keegstra* in 1990,[1] because it advances one or more of the following values: the scientific search for truth; the fostering of political and democratic participation; and the individual pursuit of self-fulfillment through artistic, literary, and other endeavours.[2]

On the one hand, the Supreme Court has been generous in its treatment of expression. Taking "expression" to be a broader category than "speech," the court interprets s. 2(b) of the Charter to protect any activity that conveys meaning, except violence. On the other hand, the court has set limits to free expression. Essentially, expression enjoys protection to the degree that its content advances one or more of the three values of free speech. Not all expression is constitutionally equal. Unlike American courts, the Canadian Supreme Court is prepared to evaluate the substance of what one says in order to judge its constitutional merits. Some types of expression advance free speech values to a high degree and thus are invulnerable to state regulation, while other types advance these values to a lesser degree or not at all and thus can be legitimately restricted by the state. For example, advertising conveys meaning but economic expression is somewhat removed from the core of free speech values.[3] Pornography has been held to advance only base human desires for self-fulfillment and thus rests at a point more peripheral to the core.[4]

In 1971, Parliament added to the *Criminal Code* a provision prohibiting the wilful promotion of hatred against an identifiable group in other than a private conversation. When Eckville, Alberta high school teacher Jim Keegstra was discovered to have taught his students that the Holocaust was a fabrication to curry international support for the state of Israel, he was prosecuted under this provision and ultimately found guilty. He challenged the constitutionality of the law, arguing that it was an excessive, unmanageable restriction on free speech that would catch much legitimate, high-value speech and otherwise frighten

---

1   *R. v. Keegstra*, [1990] 3 S.C.R. 697.

2   See *Keegstra, ibid.* In that decision the Supreme Court of Canada relies on free speech values because these have been developed in American scholarship and jurisprudence. See Thomas I. Emerson, "Toward a General Theory of the First Amendment" (1963) 72 *Yale Law Journal* 877.

3   *Ford v. Quebec (Attorney General)*, [1988] 2 S.C.R. 712; *Irwin Toy Ltd. v. Quebec (Attorney General)*, [1989] 1 S.C.R. 927. See, for a somewhat more salutary account of commercial expression, *RJR-MacDonald Inc. v. Canada (Attorney General)*, [1995] 3 S.C.R. 199.

4   *R. v. Butler*, [1992] 1 S.C.R. 452; but see also *Little Sisters Book and Art Emporium v. Canada (Minister of Justice)*, 2000 SCC 69, [2000] 2 S.C.R. 1120.

many into remaining silent rather than risk prosecution. By a 4-to-3 vote, the Supreme Court in *Keegstra* upheld the law against attack, arguing that it was narrowly tailored to catch only the most vehement expressions of hatred, and that it in fact *advances* free speech values by creating public space for free expression by members of groups targeted by hate-mongers. For the majority, much rested on the relationship between hate speech and the core values of free speech. Properly defined, hate speech is far from the core of free speech values and thus can be reasonably limited by the state if it wishes to do so.

Whatcott concerns not criminal law but Saskatchewan's human rights code, which at the time contained a provision prohibiting the publication, display, or distribution of material "that exposes or tends to expose to hatred, ridicules, belittles or otherwise affronts the dignity of any person or class of persons on the basis of a prohibited ground [of discrimination]." Bill Whatcott distributed flyers sharply criticizing homosexuality, and thereby became the subject of a complaint.

Three issues were paramount in the Supreme Court appeal. First, what is hatred and can it be defined in a manner that leaves free from regulation speech that is merely offensive, intemperate, or unpopular? Second, if hatred can be stably defined, is the legislation nonetheless in violation of the Charter's protection of freedom of expression? Third, if the provision survives constitutional scrutiny, are Whatcott's flyers to be caught in its net?

Justice Rothstein (occupying at the time one of the Western Canadian seats on the court), wrote a unanimous judgment for six other colleagues, holding that hatred is capable of stable, objective definition; that the provision largely survives Charter review; and that some of Whatcott's flyers meet the definition of hatred that he laid out. Chief Justice McLachlin, the only justice in this case who heard Keegstra's appeal in 1990, seems to have had a change of heart. She wrote a trenchant, persuasive dissent in *Keegstra*, voting to strike down the *Criminal Code* ban on the wilful promotion of hatred; but here she votes with the panel to uphold Saskatchewan's ban on hate speech, even though human rights tribunals lack the procedural safeguards of a criminal court and despite the absence of defences in Saskatchewan's law. ~

Discussion Questions

1. Section 1 of the Charter requires all reasonable limits on rights to be "demonstrably justified." In other words, the defender of a law must provide evidence that it is a reasonable limit on a right. What is the role of evidence in *Whatcott*? What consequences must a publication produce in order for it to contravene hate bans? How can we know when these consequences occur? For the Supreme Court in this case, how important is evidence?

2. Decisions vindicating the status of minorities (here, sexual minorities) are generally thought to be what Charter review is all about: applying a Charter right to protect a minority group from majoritarian prejudices. In this case, however, the Saskatchewan legislature passed a law protecting members of several groups, including gays and lesbians, from hateful communications that affront the dignity of individuals. Put another way, in 2013 the Supreme Court affirmed majoritarian sentiment by upholding a law against Charter attack. Can one imagine a similar decision having been rendered in 1986, long before public opinion supported the insertion of sexual orientation as a prohibited ground of discrimination in human rights laws? Must a court, in the end, rely on majoritarian public support for its decisions?

SASKATCHEWAN (HUMAN RIGHTS COMMISSION) v. WHATCOTT
2013 SCC 11, [2013] 1 S.C.R. 467

Hearing: October 12, 2011; Judgment: February 27, 2013.

Present: McLachlin C.J. and LeBel, Deschamps,* Fish, Abella, Rothstein, and Cromwell JJ.

* Deschamps J. took no part in the judgment.

The judgment of the Court was delivered by   .

ROTHSTEIN J.:

I. Introduction

...

[2] The Saskatchewan legislature included a provision in its human rights legislation prohibiting hate publications. While emphasizing the importance of freedom of expression in a subsection of the provision, the intent of the statute is to suppress a certain type of expression which represents a potential cause of the discriminatory practices the human rights legislation seeks to eliminate. Our task is to determine whether the legislature's approach is constitutional.

[3] Four complaints were filed with the Saskatchewan Human Rights Commission ("Commission") concerning four flyers published and distributed by the respondent, William Whatcott. The flyers were distributed to the public and targeted homosexuals and were challenged by the complainants on the basis that they promoted hatred against individuals because of their sexual orientation. The Saskatchewan Human Rights Tribunal ("Tribunal") held that the flyers constituted publications that contravened s. 14 of *The Saskatchewan Human Rights Code*, S.S. 1979, c. S-24.1 ("*Code*") as they exposed persons to hatred and ridicule on the basis of their sexual orientation: (2005), 52 C.H.R.R. D/264. Section 14(1)(b) of the *Code* prohibits the publication or display of any representation "that exposes or tends to expose to hatred, ridicules, belittles or otherwise affronts the dignity of any person or class of persons on the basis of a prohibited ground." The *Code* lists "sexual orientation" as a prohibited ground (s. 2(1)(m.01)(vi)). ...

III. Relevant Statutory Provisions

[12] At issue is s. 14 of the *Code*. It provides:

14.(1) *No person shall publish or display*, or cause or permit to be published or displayed, on any lands or premises or in a newspaper, through a television or radio broadcasting station or any other broadcasting device, or in any printed matter or publication or by means of any other medium that the person owns, controls, distributes or sells, *any representation*, including any notice, sign, symbol, emblem, article, statement or other representation:

(a) tending or likely to tend to deprive, abridge or otherwise restrict the enjoyment by any person or class of persons, on the basis of a prohibited ground, of any right to which that person or class of persons is entitled under law; or

(b) *that exposes or tends to expose to hatred, ridicules, belittles or otherwise affronts the dignity of any person or class of persons on the basis of a prohibited ground.*

(2) *Nothing in subsection (1) restricts the right to freedom of expression under the law upon any subject.* ...

V. Issues

[19] The issues on appeal are whether s. 14(1)(b) of the *Code* infringes s. 2(*a*) and/or s. 2(*b*) of the *Charter* and, if so, whether the infringement is demonstrably justified under s. 1 of the Charter. If s. 14(1)(b) is found to survive the constitutional challenge, the issue will be whether the Tribunal's decision should have been upheld on appeal under s. 32(1) of the *Code*.

VI. The Definition of "Hatred"

[Rothstein discusses the 1990 trilogy of cases concerning the constitutionality of hate speech. The leading case is *Canada (Human Rights Commission) v. Taylor*, [1990] 3 S.C.R. 892. That case examined s. 13 (since repealed) of the *Canadian Human Rights Act*, which proscribed communication by telephonic means of "any matter that is likely to expose a person or persons to hatred or contempt by reason of the fact that that person or those persons are identifiable on the basis of a prohibited ground of discrimination."]

[24] In assessing whether s. 13(1) minimally impairs freedom of expression, Dickson C.J. rejected the submission that it was overbroad and excessively vague. In his view, there was no conflict between providing a meaningful interpretation of s. 13(1) and protecting freedom of expression "so long as the interpretation of the words 'hatred' and 'contempt' is fully informed by an awareness that Parliament's objective is to protect the equality and dignity of all individuals by reducing the incidence of harm-causing expression" (p. 927). Dickson C.J. concluded that s. 13(1) "*refers to unusually strong and deep-felt emotions of detestation, calumny and vilification*" (p. 928 (emphasis added)). In his view, as long as tribunals required the ardent and extreme nature of feeling described by "hatred or contempt," there was "little danger that subjective opinion as to offensiveness will supplant the proper meaning of the section" (p. 929). ...

B. Criticisms of the Taylor Definition of Hatred

[26] The conclusion in *Taylor* about legislation similar to what is at issue in this case is not, however, determinative. Mr. Whatcott challenges the constitutionality of a different legislative provision, interpreted and applied over 20 years later, and in the context of a different prohibited ground.

[27] Mr. Whatcott and some interveners argue that there are a number of problems with the *Taylor* interpretation of "hatred" and with prohibiting hate speech generally. The criticisms tend to fall within two general categories, relating to either subjectivity or overbreadth. Criticisms concerning subjectivity are that the definition

1. leads to arbitrary and inconsistent results because it captures expression that an arbitrator or judge subjectively finds offensive or repugnant;
2. is a vague, emotive concept that is inherently subjective and unworkable; and
3. infringes freedom of expression in irrational ways not tied to the legislative objectives.

[28] Criticisms relating to overbreadth are that the definition or a particular legislative prohibition

1. is overreaching and captures more expression than is intended or necessary;
2. has a chilling effect on public debate, religious expression and media coverage of issues about moral conduct and social policy;
3. does not give legislative priority to freedom of expression;
4. restricts private communications;
5. should require intention;
6. should require proof of actual harm or discrimination; and
7. should provide for defences, such as a defence of truth.

[29] Some of these criticisms are directed to the manner in which a specific legislative prohibition is formulated. To the extent that they apply to s. 14(1)(b) of the *Code*, they will be addressed in the course of analyzing the constitutionality of that provision.

[30] However, I will first consider whether, in light of the criticisms, the definition of "hatred" established in *Taylor* remains valid, or should be modified or rejected.

C. Subjectivity

[31] In my view, the criticisms point to two conceptual challenges to achieving a consistent application of a prohibition against hate speech. One is how to deal with the inherent subjectivity of the concept of "hatred." Another is a mistaken propensity to focus on the ideas being expressed, rather than on the *effect* of the expression.

[32] Criticisms about the inherent subjectivity of "hatred" can be broken into two separate concerns. The first is that the prohibition will lead to arbitrary and inconsistent results, depending on the subjective views of judges and arbitrators. The second is that a prohibition predicated on "hatred" is too vague and inherently subjective to ever be applied objectively. The resulting uncertainty about its application will have a chilling effect on expression. I will deal with each of these concerns in turn.

(1) The Reasonable Person

[Rothstein considers the problem of subjectivity—that hatred to one is disapproval to another. If the proscription of hate speech is subjective, the legal standard is unstable and all sorts of speech may be caught in its net. He arrives at a three-fold standard for determining what is hateful.]

(a) The Meaning of "Hatred or Contempt"

[39] In order to adhere to the legislative choice of the words "hatred or contempt," Dickson C.J. emphasized [in *Taylor*] the importance of interpreting them in a manner that did not include emotions of lesser intensities. In his view, prohibitions of hate speech should not be triggered by lesser gradations of disapprobation, so as to capture offensive comments or expressions of dislike. Interpreting "hatred or contempt" to include feelings of dislike would expand their meaning beyond what was contemplated by the legislature and could capture expression which, while derogatory, does not cause the type of harm that human rights legislation seeks to eliminate. As long as a tribunal is aware of the purpose behind s. 13(1) of the [*Canadian Human Rights Act*] and "pays heed to the ardent and extreme nature of feeling described in the phrase 'hatred or contempt,'" Dickson C.J. reasoned that "there is little danger that subjective opinion as to offensiveness will supplant the proper meaning of the section": *Taylor*, at p. 929.

[40] ... Dickson C.J. found that, according to the tribunal, s. 13(1) refers to "unusually strong and deep-felt emotions of detestation, calumny and vilification": *Taylor*, at p. 928. The legislative prohibition should therefore only apply to expression of an unusual and extreme nature.

[41] In my view, "detestation" and "vilification" aptly describe the harmful effect that the *Code* seeks to eliminate. Representations that expose a target group to detestation tend to inspire enmity and extreme ill-will against them, which goes beyond mere disdain or dislike. Representations vilifying a person or group will seek to abuse, denigrate or delegitimize

them, to render them lawless, dangerous, unworthy or unacceptable in the eyes of the audience. Expression exposing vulnerable groups to detestation and vilification goes far beyond merely discrediting, humiliating or offending the victims. ...

[43] Not all prohibitions of hate speech include the word "contempt," and s. 14(1)(b) of the *Code* does not. The tribunal in *Nealy* noted that the concept of "hatred" does not mandate a particular motive for the emotion, and that the word "contempt" added an element of looking down on or treating the object as inferior. While I agree with the tribunal that it is possible to hate someone one considers "superior," in my view the term "hatred" in the context of human rights legislation includes a component of looking down on or denying the worth of another. The act of vilifying a person or group connotes accusing them of disgusting characteristics, inherent deficiencies or immoral propensities which are too vile in nature to be shared by the person who vilifies. Even without the word "contempt" in the legislative prohibition, delegitimizing a group as unworthy, useless or inferior can be a component of exposing them to hatred. Such delegitimization reduces the target group's credibility, social standing and acceptance within society and is a key aspect of the social harm caused by hate speech. ...

[46] [C]ourts have been guided by the *Taylor* definition of hatred and have generally identified only extreme and egregious examples of delegitimizing expression as hate speech. This approach excludes merely offensive or hurtful expression from the ambit of the provision and respects the legislature's choice of a prohibition predicated on "hatred." ...

D. Focusing on the Effects of Hate Speech

...

[51] The distinction between the expression of repugnant ideas and expression which exposes groups to hatred is crucial to understanding the proper application of hate speech prohibitions. Hate speech legislation is not aimed at discouraging repugnant or offensive ideas. It does not, for example, prohibit expression which debates the merits of reducing the rights of vulnerable groups in society. It only restricts the use of expression exposing them to hatred as a part of that debate. It does not target the ideas, but their mode of expression in public and the effect that this mode of expression may have. ...

E. Confirming a Modified Definition of "Hatred"

[55] As will be apparent from the preceding discussion, in my view the *Taylor* definition of "hatred," with some modifications, provides a workable approach to interpreting the word "hatred" as it is used in prohibitions of hate speech. The guidance provided by *Taylor* should reduce the risk of subjective applications of such legislative restrictions, provided that three main prescriptions are followed.

[56] First, courts are directed to apply the hate speech prohibitions *objectively*. In my view, the reference in *Taylor* to "unusually strong and deep-felt emotions" (at p. 928) should not be interpreted as imposing a subjective test or limiting the analysis to the intensity with which the author of the expression feels the emotion. The question courts must ask is whether a reasonable person, aware of the context and circumstances surrounding the expression, would view it as exposing the protected group to hatred.

[57] Second, the legislative term "hatred" or "hatred or contempt" is to be interpreted as being restricted to those extreme manifestations of the emotion described by the words "detestation" and "vilification." This filters out expression which, while repugnant and offensive, does not incite the level of abhorrence, delegitimization and rejection that risks causing discrimination or other harmful effects.

[58] Third, tribunals must focus their analysis on the effect of the expression at issue. Is the expression likely to expose the targeted person or group to hatred by others? The repugnancy of the ideas being expressed is not, in itself, sufficient to justify restricting the expression. The prohibition of hate speech is not designed to censor ideas or to compel anyone to think "correctly." Similarly, it is irrelevant whether the author of the expression intended to incite hatred or discriminatory treatment or other harmful conduct towards the protected group. The key is to determine the likely effect of the expression on its audience, keeping in mind the legislative objectives to reduce or eliminate discrimination. ...

VII. Standard of Review in Constitutional Questions

[61] The standard of review on the constitutionality of s. 14(1)(b) of the *Code* is correctness: see *Dunsmuir v. New Brunswick*, 2008 SCC 9, [2008] 1 S.C.R. 190, at para. 58.

VIII. Constitutional Analysis

[The court easily finds that the legislative provision violates s. 2(b) of the Charter.]

B. Section 1—Whether the Infringement Is Demonstrably Justified in a Free and Democratic Society

...

(1) The Approach to Freedom of Expression Under Section 1

...

[65] ... McLachlin C.J., writing for the majority in *Sharpe*, explained succinctly the values underlying freedom of expression first recognized in *Irwin Toy*, being "individual

self-fulfilment, finding the truth through the open exchange of ideas, and the political discourse fundamental to democracy" (para. 23).

[66] We are ... required to balance the fundamental values underlying freedom of expression (and, later, freedom of religion) in the context in which they are invoked, with competing Charter rights and other values essential to a free and democratic society, in this case, a commitment to equality and respect for group identity and the inherent dignity owed to all human beings ... .

(2) Is the Objective for Which the Limit Is Imposed Pressing and Substantial?

...

[70] The objective of s. 14(1)(b) may be ascertained directly from the *Code* in which it is found. Section 3 states that the objectives of the *Code* are

(a) to promote recognition of the inherent dignity and the equal inalienable rights of all members of the human family; and
(b) to further public policy in Saskatchewan that every person is free and equal in dignity and rights and to discourage and eliminate discrimination.

[71] Hate speech is, at its core, an effort to marginalize individuals based on their membership in a group. Using expression that exposes the group to hatred, hate speech seeks to delegitimize group members in the eyes of the majority, reducing their social standing and acceptance within society. When people are vilified as blameworthy or undeserving, it is easier to justify discriminatory treatment. The objective of s. 14(1)(b) may be understood as reducing the harmful effects and social costs of discrimination by tackling certain causes of discriminatory activity. ...

[73] In *Keegstra*, [[1990] 3 S.C.R. 697] at pp. 746-47, Dickson C.J. found that two types of harm were of a pressing and substantial concern. First, he referred to the grave psychological and social consequences to individual members of the targeted group from the humiliation and degradation caused by hate propaganda. Second, he noted the harmful effects on society at large by increasing discord and by affecting a subtle and unconscious alteration of views concerning the inferiority of the targeted group.

[74] Hate speech, therefore, rises beyond causing emotional distress to individual group members. It can have a societal impact. If a group of people are considered inferior, subhuman, or lawless, it is easier to justify denying the group and its members equal rights or status. ... As the majority becomes desensitized by the effects of hate speech, the concern is that some members of society will demonstrate their rejection of the vulnerable group through conduct. Hate speech lays the groundwork for later, broad attacks on vulnerable groups. These attacks can range from discrimination, to ostracism, segregation, deportation, violence and, in the most extreme cases, to genocide: see *Taylor* and *Keegstra*.

[75] Hate speech is not only used to justify restrictions or attacks on the rights of protected groups on prohibited grounds. As noted by Dickson C.J., at p. 763 of *Keegstra*, hate propaganda opposes the targeted group's ability to find self-fulfillment by articulating their thoughts and ideas. It impacts on that group's ability to respond to the substantive ideas under debate, thereby placing a serious barrier to their full participation in our democracy. Indeed, a particularly insidious aspect of hate speech is that it acts to cut off any path of reply by the group under attack. It does this not only by attempting to marginalize the group so that their reply will be ignored: it also forces the group to argue for their basic humanity or social standing, as a precondition to participating in the deliberative aspects of our democracy.

[76] To use an example related to the present case, the suggestion that homosexual conduct should not be discussed in schools because homosexuals are pedophiles requires the protected group to first defeat the absolutist position that all homosexuals are pedophiles in order to justify a level of societal standing that would then permit participation in the larger debate of whether homosexual conduct should be discussed in schools. In this way, the expression inhibits the protected group from interacting and participating in free expression and public debate. ...

(3) Proportionality

[78] It is next necessary to consider whether s. 14(1)(b) of the *Code* is proportionate to its objective. Here perfection is not required. Rather the legislature's chosen approach must be accorded considerable deference. As McLachlin C.J. explained in *Canada (Attorney General) v. JTI-Macdonald Corp.*, 2007 SCC 30, [2007] 2 S.C.R. 610 ("*JTI*"), at para. 41, "[e]ffective answers to complex social problems ... may not be simple or evident. There may be room for debate about what will work and what will not, and the outcome may not be scientifically measurable." We must ask whether Parliament has chosen one of several reasonable alternatives ... .

(a) Is the Limit Rationally Connected to the Objective?

(i) Societal Versus Individual Harm

...

[80] ... Hate speech seeks to marginalize individuals based on their group characteristics. As such, in order to satisfy the rational connection requirement, the expression captured under legislation restricting hate speech must rise to a level

beyond merely impugning individuals: it must seek to marginalize the group by affecting its social status and acceptance in the eyes of the majority.

[81] This is not to diminish the harm that might occur to individuals through attacks on their group. ... However, in the context of hate speech, this harm is derivative of the larger harm inflicted on the group, rather than purely individual.

[82] Societal harm flowing from hate speech must be assessed as objectively as possible. The feelings of the publisher or victim are not the test ... . While the emotional damage from hate speech is indeed troubling, protecting the emotions of an individual group member is not rationally connected to the overall purpose of reducing discrimination. While it would certainly be expected that hate speech would prompt emotional reactions from members of the targeted group, in the context of hate speech legislation, these reactions are only relevant as a derivative effect of the attack on the group. As a derivative effect, these are not sufficient to justify an infringement of s. 2(*b*). Instead, the focus must be on the likely effect of the hate speech on how individuals external to the group might reconsider the social standing of the group. Ultimately, it is the need to protect the societal standing of vulnerable groups that is the objective of legislation restricting hate speech.

[83] Section 14(1)(b) of the *Code* reflects this approach. The prohibition only limits the display or publication of representations, such as through newspapers or other printed matter, or through television or radio broadcasting. In other words, it only prohibits *public* communications of hate speech. ...

(ii) Wording of Section 14(1)(b) of the Code

...

[88] Although the expansive words "ridicules, belittles or otherwise affronts the dignity of" have essentially been ignored when applying s. 14(1)(b), it is a matter of concern to some interveners that "the legislation has never been amended, and no declaration has ever been made to read down the impugned law" (Christian Legal Fellowship factum, at para. 22), and that the express wording of the provision contributes to its chilling effect: Canadian Journalists for Free Expression factum, at para. 5.

[89] In my view, expression that "ridicules, belittles or otherwise affronts the dignity of" does not rise to the level of ardent and extreme feelings that were found essential to the constitutionality of s. 13(1) of the [*Canadian Human Rights Act*] in *Taylor*. Those words are not synonymous with "hatred" or "contempt." Rather, they refer to expression which is derogatory and insensitive, such as representations criticizing or making fun of protected groups on the basis of their commonly shared characteristics and practices, or on stereotypes. ...

[91] There may be circumstances where expression that "ridicules" members of a protected group goes beyond humour or satire and risks exposing the person to detestation and vilification on the basis of a prohibited ground of discrimination. In such circumstances, however, the risk results from the intensity of the ridicule reaching a level where the target becomes exposed to hatred. While ridicule, taken to the extreme, can conceivably lead to exposure to hatred, in my view, "ridicule" in its ordinary sense would not typically have the potential to lead to the discrimination that the legislature seeks to address.

[92] Thus, in order to be rationally connected to the legislative objective of eliminating discrimination and the other societal harms of hate speech, s. 14(1)(b) must only prohibit expression that is likely to cause those effects through exposure to hatred. I find that the words "ridicules, belittles or otherwise affronts the dignity of" in s. 14(1)(b) are not rationally connected to the legislative purpose of addressing systemic discrimination of protected groups. The manner in which they infringe freedom of expression cannot be justified under s. 1 of the Charter and, consequently, they are constitutionally invalid.

[93] It remains to determine whether the words "ridicules, belittles or otherwise affronts the dignity of" can be severed from s. 14(1)(b) of the *Code*, or whether their removal would transform the provision into something which was clearly outside the intention of the legislature. It is significant that in the course of oral argument before this Court, the Attorney General for Saskatchewan endorsed the manner in which the words "ridicules, belittles or otherwise affronts the dignity of" were read out in [*Human Rights Commission (Sask.) v.*] *Bell* [(1994), 120 Sask. R. 122 (C.A.)]. I accept his view that the offending words can be severed without contravening the legislative intent.

[94] Given my determination that these words are unconstitutional, it is time to formally strike out those words from s. 14(1)(b) of the *Code*. The provision would therefore read:

> (b) that exposes or tends to expose to hatred any person or class of persons on the basis of a prohibited ground.

...

(iii) Effectiveness

[96] Mr. Whatcott contends that s. 14(1)(b) is not rationally connected to its objective because its effect runs counter to that objective. While the legislative objective is to stop hate speech, he submits that the effect of the prohibition has been

to (a) allow the Commission to discriminate against religious speech on sexual behaviour; (b) grant those found in contravention of s. 14(1)(b) an audience before which to promote their martyrdom; (c) increase hate crimes, as acknowledged by the Commission; and (d) increase hatred against Christian people due to their demonization by the Commission. ...

[98] As to effectiveness, Dickson C.J. indicated, at pp. 923-24 of *Taylor*, that one should not be quick to assume that prohibitions against hate speech are ineffectual. In his view, the process of hearing a complaint and, if necessary, of issuing a cease and desist order, "reminds Canadians of our fundamental commitment to equality of opportunity" and the eradication of intolerance. The failure of the prohibition to render hate speech extinct or stop hate crimes is not fatal. As McLachlin C.J. noted for the majority in *Alberta v. Hutterian Brethren of Wilson Colony*, 2009 SCC 37, [2009] 2 S.C.R. 567, "[t]he government must show that it is reasonable to suppose that the limit may further the goal, not that it will do so" (para. 48). ...

(b) Minimal Impairment

...

(i) Alternative Methods of Furthering the Legislature's Objectives

[102] Two alternatives have been suggested that would better serve the goal of eradicating hate speech than the provisions of the *Code*. One is that trust should be placed in the "marketplace of ideas" to arrive at the appropriate balancing of competing rights and conflicting views. The other is that the prosecution of hate speech ought to be left to the criminal law.

[103] The notion of leaving the regulation of hate speech to the "marketplace of ideas" has long been advocated by critics of the regulation of hate speech ... . Under this theory, unfettered debate is the most effective way for rational beings to attain the truth, thus accomplishing one of the three purposes of freedom of expression.

[104] I do not say that the marketplace of ideas may not be a reasonable alternative, and where a legislature is so minded, it will not enact hate speech legislation. However, in *Keegstra*, Dickson C.J. set out a compelling rationale for why Parliament's preference to regulate hate speech through legislation rather than to trust it to the hands of the marketplace was also reasonable. He noted that "the state should not be the sole arbiter of truth, but neither should we overplay the view that rationality will overcome all falsehoods in the unregulated marketplace of ideas" (p. 763). In his view, paradoxically, hate speech undermines the principles upon which freedom of expression is based and "contributes little to the ...

quest for truth, the promotion of individual self-development or the protection and fostering of a vibrant democracy where the participation of all individuals is accepted and encouraged" (p. 766). That is because a common effect of hate speech is to discourage the contributions of the minority. While hate speech may achieve the self-fulfillment of the publisher, it does so by reducing the participation and self-fulfillment of individuals within the vulnerable group. These drawbacks suggest that this alternative is not without its concerns.

[105] Others suggest that to minimally impair expression, hate speech should be dealt with through criminal law prohibitions or other prohibitions restricting only speech which threatens, advocates or justifies violence ... . Still, others suggest that when legislators seek to limit freedom of expression, the justificatory threshold should be raised to require actual evidence of harm as opposed to mere reasonable belief in the risk of harm ... . On the other side, the Attorney General for Saskatchewan argues that the imposition of remedial measures rather than punitive sanctions is far less intrusive on the constitutional values protected by s. 2, and therefore more acceptable under s. 1 of the Charter: factum, at para. 58. The Commission argues that the Criminal Code provisions regulate only the most extreme forms of hate speech, advocating genocide or inciting a "breach of the peace": A.F., at para. 85. In contrast, human rights legislation "provides accessible and inexpensive access to justice" for disadvantaged victims to assert their right to dignity and equality: A.F., at para. 83. Aboriginal interveners say that only a civil remedy that is not dependent on state prosecution will provide an effective mechanism to address discriminatory speech. As noted by Sopinka J. in *Zurich Insurance Co. v. Ontario (Human Rights Commission)*, [1992] 2 S.C.R. 321, at p. 339, human rights legislation is "often the final refuge of the disadvantaged and the disenfranchised." Therefore, this alternative may reduce impairment at the cost of effectiveness.

[106] Having canvassed the proposed alternatives to the civil law remedy, I cannot say that any one represents such a superior approach as to render the others unreasonable. Section 14(1)(b) of the *Code* is within the range of reasonable alternatives that was available to the legislature.

(ii) Overbreadth

[107] Section 14(1)(b) is alleged to be overreaching, so that it captures more expression than is necessary to satisfy the legislative objectives, and thereby fails to minimally impair the right to freedom of expression. It is also criticized for having a chilling effect on expression (including religious expression), public debate and media coverage on issues about moral conduct and social policy.

1. Wording of Section 14 of the Code

...

[110] ... The objective behind s. 14(1)(b) is not to censor ideas or to legislate morality. The legislative objective of the entire provision is to address harm from hate speech while limiting freedom of expression as little as possible.

[111] In my view, once the additional words are severed from s. 14(1)(b), the remaining prohibition is not overbroad. A limitation predicated on expression which exposes groups to hatred tries to distinguish between healthy and heated debate on controversial topics of political and social reform, and impassioned rhetoric which seeks to incite hatred as a means to effect reform. The boundary will not capture all harmful expression, but it is intended to capture expression which, by inspiring hatred, has the potential to cause the type of harm that the legislation is trying to prevent. In that way, the limitation is not overbroad, but rather tailored to impair freedom of expression as little as possible.

2. Nature of the Expression

[112] Violent expression and expression that threatens violence does not fall within the protected sphere of s. 2(*b*) of the Charter: *R. v. Khawaja*, 2012 SCC 69, [2012] 3 S.C.R. 555, at para. 70. However, apart from that, not all expression will be treated equally in determining an appropriate balancing of competing values under a s. 1 analysis. That is because different types of expression will be relatively closer to or further from the core values behind the freedom, depending on the nature of the expression. This will, in turn, affect its value relative to other Charter rights, the exercise or protection of which may infringe freedom of expression. ...

[114] Hate speech is at some distance from the spirit of s. 2(*b*) because it does little to promote, and can in fact impede, the values underlying freedom of expression. As noted by Dickson C.J. in *Keegstra*, expression can be used to the detriment of the search for truth (p. 763). As earlier discussed, hate speech can also distort or limit the robust and free exchange of ideas by its tendency to silence the voice of its target group. It can achieve the self-fulfillment of the publisher, but often at the expense of that of the victim. These are important considerations in balancing hate speech with competing Charter rights and in assessing the constitutionality of the prohibition in s. 14(1)(b) of the *Code*.

3. Political Discourse

...

[116] The purpose of hate speech legislation is to restrict the use of representations likely to expose protected groups to hatred and its harmful effects. The expression captured under hate speech laws is of an extreme nature. Framing that speech as arising in a "moral" context or "within a public policy debate" does not cleanse it of its harmful effect. Indeed, if one understands an effect of hate speech as curtailing the ability of the affected group to participate in the debate, relaxing the standard in the context of political debate is arguably more rather than less damaging to freedom of expression. ...

[117] Finding that certain expression falls within political speech does not close off an enquiry into whether the expression constitutes hate speech. Hate speech may often arise as a part of a larger public discourse but, as discussed in *Keegstra* and *Taylor*, it is speech of a restrictive and exclusionary kind. Political expression contributes to our democracy by encouraging the exchange of opposing views. Hate speech is antithetical to this objective in that it shuts down dialogue by making it difficult or impossible for members of the vulnerable group to respond, thereby stifling discourse. Speech that has the effect of shutting down public debate cannot dodge prohibition on the basis that it promotes debate. ...

[119] The polemicist may still participate on controversial topics that may be characterized as "moral" or "political." However, words matter. In the context of this case, Mr. Whatcott can express disapproval of homosexual conduct and advocate that it should not be discussed in public schools or at university conferences. Section 14(1)(b) only prohibits his use of hate-inspiring representations against homosexuals in the course of expressing those views. ...

4. Sexual Orientation Versus Sexual Behaviour

[121] Mr. Whatcott argues that the publications at issue in this case were critical of same-sex behaviour, as distinct from sexual orientation, and therefore did not contravene s. 14(1)(b) of the *Code*. If s. 14(1)(b) restricts criticisms of the behaviour of others, it is overbroad and unconstitutional. Mr. Whatcott also submits that comment on the sexual behaviour of others has always been allowed as part of free speech, and part of freedom of conscience and religion. He argues that the law must allow diversity of viewpoints on whether sexual matters are moral or immoral.

[122] I agree that sexual orientation and sexual behaviour can be differentiated for certain purposes. However, in instances where hate speech is directed toward behaviour in an effort to mask the true target, the vulnerable group, this distinction should not serve to avoid s. 14(1)(b). One such instance is where the expression does not denigrate certain sexual conduct in and of itself, but only when it is carried out by same-sex partners. Another is when hate speech is directed at behaviour that is integral to and inseparable from the identity of the group. ...

[124] Courts have ... recognized that there is a strong connection between sexual orientation and sexual conduct.

Where the conduct that is the target of speech is a crucial aspect of the identity of the vulnerable group, attacks on this conduct stand as a proxy for attacks on the group itself. If expression targeting certain sexual behaviour is framed in such a way as to expose persons of an identifiable sexual orientation to what is objectively viewed as detestation and vilification, it cannot be said that such speech only targets the behaviour. It quite clearly targets the vulnerable group. Therefore, a prohibition is not overbroad for capturing expression of this nature.

(iii) Intent, Proof, and Defences

[125] Critics of s. 14(1)(b) of the *Code* claim that it is also overbroad because (i) it does not require intent by the publisher; (ii) it does not require proof of harm; and (iii) it does not provide for any defences.

1. INTENT

[126] In *Taylor*, Dickson C.J. justified the lack of a legislative requirement to prove intent by emphasizing that systemic discrimination is more widespread than intentional discrimination and that the focus of the legislation should be on effects and not intent … .

[127] The preventive measures found in human rights legislation reasonably centre on effects, rather than intent. I see no reason to depart from this approach.

2. PROOF OF HARM

…

[129] In answer to the specific criticism that a prohibition against hate speech lacked a requirement to prove actual harm, Dickson C.J. argued in *Keegstra* (at p. 776) that both the difficulty of establishing a causal link between an expressive statement and the resulting hatred, and the seriousness of the harm to which vulnerable groups are exposed by hate speech, justifies the imposition of preventive measures that do not require proof of actual harm.

[130] Critics argue that the deference to the legislature shown by this Court in *Keegstra*, *Taylor*, *Butler* and *Sharpe* is an abdication of its duty to require that limitations on Charter rights be "demonstrably justified" under the s. 1 analysis … . The basic nature of the criticism is that it is an unacceptable impairment of freedom of expression to allow its restriction to be justified by the mere likelihood or risk of harm, rather than a clear causal link between hate speech and harmful or discriminatory acts against the vulnerable group.

[131] Such an approach, however, ignores the particularly insidious nature of hate speech. The end goal of hate speech is to shift the environment from one where harm against vulnerable groups is not tolerated to one where hate speech has created a place where this is either accepted or a blind eye is turned.

[132] This Court has addressed such criticism in a number of situations involving the applicability of s. 1 and has adopted a "reasonable apprehension of harm" approach. This approach recognizes that a precise causal link for certain societal harms ought not to be required. A court is entitled to use common sense and experience in recognizing that certain activities, hate speech among them, inflict societal harms. …

[135] [T]he discriminatory effects of hate speech are part of the everyday knowledge and experience of Canadians. I am of the opinion that the Saskatchewan legislature is entitled to a reasonable apprehension of societal harm as a result of hate speech.

3. LACK OF DEFENCES

[136] In the context of civil liability for contravening a limitation on a certain type of expression such as defamation, the types of defences that are generally raised relate to the truth of the factual statements made. The legislature of Saskatchewan has not provided a defence of truth or any other defence as a basis upon which to avoid being found in contravention of s. 14(1)(b) of the *Code* (other than that private communications are not included in the prohibition). …

[139] Critics find the absence of a defence of truth of particular concern, given that seeking truth is one of the strongest justifications for freedom of expression. They argue that the right to speak the truth should not be lightly restricted, and that any restriction should be seen as a serious infringement.

[140] I agree with the argument that the quest for truth is an essential component of the "marketplace of ideas" which is, itself, central to a strong democracy. The search for truth is also an important part of self-fulfilment. However, I do not think it is inconsistent with these views to find that not all truthful statements must be free from restriction. Truthful statements can be interlaced with harmful ones or otherwise presented in a manner that would meet the definition of hate speech.

[141] As Dickson C.J. stated in *Keegstra*, at p. 763, there is "very little chance that statements intended to promote hatred against an identifiable group are true, or that their vision of society will lead to a better world." To the extent that truthful statements are used in a manner or context that exposes a vulnerable group to hatred, their use risks the same potential harmful effects on the vulnerable groups that false statements can provoke. The vulnerable group is no less worthy of protection because the publisher has succeeded in turning true statements into a hateful message. In not providing for a defence of truth, the legislature has said that even

truthful statements may be expressed in language or context that exposes a vulnerable group to hatred.

[142] Some interveners argued that there should be a defence of sincerely held belief. In their view, speech that is made in good faith and on the basis of the speaker's religious beliefs should be given greater protection, or constitute an absolute defence to any prohibition. These arguments anticipate the question still to be considered of whether an infringement of s. 2(*a*) of the Charter by s. 14(1)(b) would be justified under a s. 1 analysis. It is sufficient here to say that if the sincerity of a religious belief would automatically preclude the finding of a contravention of s. 14(1)(b), the s. 1 analysis would be derailed with no balancing of the competing rights.

[143] Apart from that concern, the fact that a person circulates a hate publication in the furtherance of a sincere religious belief goes to the question of the subjective view of the publisher, which is irrelevant to the objective application of the definition of hatred. Allowing the dissemination of hate speech to be excused by a sincerely held belief would, in effect, provide an absolute defence and would gut the prohibition of effectiveness.

[144] Mr. Whatcott makes the argument that human rights commissions should not over-analyze speech to the point "where less sophisticated citizens are unable to participate in debates about morality and public education without fear of prosecution": R.F., at para. 57. He submits that freedom of expression "does not restrict public debate to articulate elites" (para. 58). With respect, the definition does not require that the expression be scholarly, rational, objective or inoffensive. The definition of "hatred" does not differentiate between the literate and illiterate, eloquent or inarticulate. Whether or not a publisher of hateful expression is sincere in his or her beliefs, or lacks the sophistication to realize that prohibitions such as s. 14(1)(b) of the *Code* exist, the aim of the prohibition remains the protection of vulnerable groups. Where, objectively, the definition of hatred is met, s. 14(1)(b) is engaged. However, with mediation available, it should be possible for inadvertent violations to be rectified so that publications that do not include hate speech can continue. ...

(c) Whether the Benefits Outweigh the Deleterious Effects

...

[148] As is apparent from the above analysis, in my opinion, the benefits of the suppression of hate speech and its harmful effects outweigh the detrimental effect of restricting expression which, by its nature, does little to promote the values underlying freedom of expression. Section 14(1)(b) of the *Code* represents a choice by the legislature to discourage hate speech and its harmful effects on both the vulnerable

group and on society as a whole, in a manner that is conciliatory and remedial. In cases such as the present, the process under the legislation can provide guidance to individuals like Mr. Whatcott, so that they can continue expressing their views in a way that avoids falling within the narrow scope of expression captured by the statutory prohibition. The protection of vulnerable groups from the harmful effects emanating from hate speech is of such importance as to justify the minimal infringement of expression that results from the restriction of materials of this kind.

[149] It was argued before this Court that the imposition of fines or the requirement to pay compensation to the victims of hate speech has a detrimental, chilling effect on expression that outweighs the benefits of reducing "potential harm." As in tort law, an award of damages made pursuant to the *Code* is characterized as compensatory, not punitive, and is directed at compensating the victim. However, the circumstances in which a compensation award will be merited should be rare and will often involve repeat litigants who refuse to participate in a conciliatory approach. ...

C. Section 2(a) of the Charter

[152] I now turn to a consideration of whether s. 14(1)(b) infringes the Charter guarantee of freedom of conscience and religion under s. 2(*a*). Mr. Whatcott argues that, to the extent that s. 14(1)(b) of the *Code* precludes criticism of same-sex conduct or activity, it infringes freedom of religion under s. 2(*a*). He submits that sexual conduct has long been a topic of religious discussion and debate, and that "[o]bjection to same-sex sexual activity is common among religious people. They object because they believe this conduct is harmful; and many religious people also believe that they are obligated to do good and warn others of the danger": R.F., at para. 78. Mr. Whatcott contends that s. 2(*a*) protects his right to proclaim this aspect of his religion. ...

[155] An infringement of s. 2(*a*) of the Charter will be established where: (1) the claimant sincerely holds a belief or practice that has a nexus with religion; and (2) the provision at issue interferes with the claimant's ability to act in accordance with his or her religious beliefs .... The interference must be more than trivial or insubstantial, so that it threatens actual religious beliefs or conduct.

[156] It was not in dispute that Mr. Whatcott sincerely believes that his religion requires him to proselytize homosexuals. To this end, he appears to employ expression of an extreme and graphic nature to make his point more compelling. To the extent that his choice of expression is caught by the hatred definition in s. 14(1)(b), the prohibition will substantially interfere with Mr. Whatcott's ability to disseminate his belief by display or publication of those representations.

Section 14(1)(b) of the *Code* infringes freedom of conscience and religion as guaranteed under s. 2(*a*) of the Charter. ...

D. Section 1 Analysis

...

[163] For the purposes of the application of s. 14(1)(b) of the *Code*, it does not matter whether the expression at issue is religiously motivated or not. If, viewed objectively, the publication involves representations that expose or are likely to expose the vulnerable group to detestation and vilification, then the religious expression is captured by the legislative prohibition. In other words, Mr. Whatcott and others are free to preach against same-sex activities, to urge its censorship from the public school curriculum and to seek to convert others to their point of view. Their freedom to express those views is unlimited, except by the narrow requirement that they not be conveyed through hate speech.

[164] For the same reasons set out earlier in the s. 1 analysis in the case of freedom of expression, in my view, the words "ridicules, belittles or otherwise affronts the dignity of" are not rationally connected to the legislative purpose of addressing systemic discrimination of protected groups, nor tailored to minimally impair freedom of religion. I find the remaining prohibition of any representation "that exposes or tends to expose to hatred" any person or class of persons on the basis of a prohibited ground to be a reasonable limit on freedom of religion and demonstrably justified in a free and democratic society.

IX. Application of Section 14(1)(b) to Mr. Whatcott's Flyers

[Mr. Whatcott distributed four flyers in Regina and Saskatoon, and some were delivered to people's homes. They are all highly critical of homosexuality. One claims that Saskatchewan schools should not promote the same-sex lifestyle and equates homosexuality with filth and disease. Others condemn ads in magazines seeking boys for the sexual satisfaction of older men. These flyers can be viewed in Appendix B of the Supreme Court's full decision in *Whatcott*, available at http://canlii.ca/t/fw8x4.

In his assessment of the human rights tribunal's decision as to the hateful character of the flyers, Justice Rothstein notes at paragraph 175 that "it was not unreasonable for the Tribunal in this case to isolate the phrases it considered to be in issue. If, despite the context of the entire publication, even one phrase or sentence is found to bring the publication, as a whole, in contravention of the *Code*, this precludes publication of the flyer in its current form." He remarks at paragraph 190 that "[w]hether or not Mr. Whatcott intended his expression to incite hatred against homosexuals, in my view it was reasonable for the Tribunal to hold that, by equating homosexuals with carriers of disease, sex addicts, pedophiles and predators who would proselytize vulnerable children and cause their premature death," two of the impugned flyers "would objectively be seen as exposing homosexuals to detestation and vilification." He also notes that two flyers promoted discriminatory treatment of homosexuals. He generally affirms the tribunal's decision condemning the flyers.

However, at paragraph 196, Rothstein held that the contents of two flyers, while offensive, did not expose homosexuals to detestation and vilification. He was also unwilling to cite biblical passages in the flyers as evidence of hateful expression.]

11 Saskatchewan Federation of Labour v. Saskatchewan, 2015

In 1984, during the Charter's infancy, Saskatchewan enacted legislation that temporarily prevented strikes and lockouts in the dairy industry. When the Saskatchewan Court of Appeal invalidated this law for unreasonably infringing the Charter's section 2(d) guarantee of "freedom of association," the province appealed to the Supreme Court. This appeal became part of the "labour trilogy" that was decided by the court in 1987.[1] In the meantime, Saskatchewan used a section 33 notwithstanding clause to protect another back-to-work law from Charter challenge. The Supreme Court rendered this notwithstanding clause unnecessary, however, when its judgments in the labour trilogy found that the Charter protected neither collective bargaining nor the right to strike.

Twenty years later, in *Health Services*,[2] the Supreme Court explicitly overruled half of the labour-trilogy doctrine, declaring that its earlier grounds "for the exclusion of collective bargaining from the *Charter*'s protection of freedom of association do not withstand principled scrutiny and should be rejected."[3] A series of subsequent cases then specified some of the requirements of meaningful collective bargaining.[4] However, neither *Health Services* nor its progeny clearly rejected the exclusion of a right to strike from Charter protection. That final stake in the heart of the 1987 trilogy was left to the 2015 case excerpted here.

Saskatchewan Federation of Labour concerned two statutes enacted by the province in 2008, about a year after *Health Services* was decided. The *Trade Union Amendment Act*, which made it more difficult to certify and easier to decertify labour unions, was upheld by all seven judges on the Supreme Court panel. *The Public Service Essential Services Act* (PSESA), which prohibited strikes by public sector "essential services employees," aroused serious disagreement among the judges.

For Justice Abella, who wrote the five-judge majority opinion, the right to strike was "an indispensable component" of the right to meaningful collective bargaining, and it was time for the court "to give this conclusion constitutional benediction." Without a right to strike, she insisted, "a constitutionalized right to bargain collectively is meaningless." Her majority struck down the PSESA as an unreasonable limit on the right to strike.

Why, one might wonder, did the court wait until 2015 to give authoritative benediction to such a critically important implication of collective bargaining as the right to strike?

---

1 *Reference Re Public Service Employee Relations Act (Alta.)*, [1987] 1 S.C.R. 313; *PSAC v. Canada*, [1987] 1 S.C.R. 424; *RWDSU v. Saskatchewan*, [1987] 1 S.C.R. 460.

2 *Health Services and Support—Facilities Subsector Bargaining Assn. v. British Columbia*, 2007 SCC 27, [2007] 2 S.C.R. 391.

3 *Ibid.* at para. 22.

4 *Ontario (Attorney General) v. Fraser*, 2011 SCC 20, [2011] 2 S.C.R. 3; *Mounted Police Association of Ontario v. Canada (Attorney General)*, 2015 SCC 1, [2015] 1 S.C.R. 3; *Meredith v. Canada (Attorney General)*, 2015 SCC 2, [2015] 1 S.C.R. 125.

Because, answered Justices Rothstein and Wagner in their jointly authored dissent, no such implication had ever existed. In their view, the court had stopped short of declaring a right to strike for good reasons, not because it failed to appreciate the true outcome of its jurisprudential logic. Those reasons had been unanimously recognized by the court in 2002, when it described "the appropriate balance between employers and unions [as] a delicate and essentially political matter ... better dealt with by legislatures than courts."[5] For Rothstein and Wagner, the majority had wrongly ignored "this sage warning ... despite the fact that this balance is not any less delicate or political today than it was in 2002." The dissenters saw no warrant for a newly constitutionalized right to strike.

In response to the majority's decision, Saskatchewan's premier, Brad Wall, indicated that if his government could not adjust the legislation to meet the Supreme Court's criteria, it would use the Charter's notwithstanding clause to achieve its objectives.[6] Ironically, the "notwithstanding" solution that proved unnecessary in the mid-1980s was back in play three decades later. ~

Discussion Questions

1. Does the distinction between public-sector and private-sector unions affect your thinking about the issues in this case?

2. Why do Justices Rothstein and Wagner agree to the reversal of precedent in *Bedford* (case 25) and *Carter* (case 26) but not in *Saskatchewan Federation of Labour*?

3. Legal scholar Dwight Newman argues that after *Saskatchewan Federation of Labour*, "[i]t would not be surprising—and might be legally prudent—for governments to make proactive use of the notwithstanding clause in the special circumstances of various pieces of back-to-work legislation, simply to avoid unnecessary constitutional litigation."[7] Do you agree?

---

5 *R.W.D.S.U., Local 558 v. Pepsi-Cola Canada Beverages (West) Ltd.*, 2002 SCC 8, [2002] 1 S.C.R. 156 at para. 85.

6 "Brad Wall Open to Using 'Notwithstanding Clause' Over Labour Ruling," CBC News (4 February 2015).

7 Dwight Newman, "A Court Gone Astray on the Right to Strike," *National Post* (26 February 2015).

SASKATCHEWAN FEDERATION OF LABOUR v. SASKATCHEWAN
2015 SCC 4, [2015] 1 S.C.R. 245

Hearing: November 7, 2014; Judgment: April 14, 2015.

Present: McLachlin C.J. and LeBel, Abella, Rothstein, Cromwell, Karakatsanis, and Wagner JJ.

Interveners: Attorney General of Canada, Attorney General of Ontario, Attorney General of Quebec, Attorney General of British Columbia, Attorney General of Alberta, Attorney General of Newfoundland and Labrador, Saskatchewan Union of Nurses, SEIU-West, United Nurses of Alberta, Alberta Federation of Labour, Professional Institute of the Public Service of Canada, Canadian Constitution Foundation, Air Canada Pilots' Association, British Columbia Civil Liberties Association, Conseil du patronat du Québec, Canadian Employers Council, Canadian Union of Postal Workers, International Association of Machinists and Aerospace Workers, British Columbia Teachers' Federation, Hospital

Employees' Union, Canadian Labour Congress, Public Service Alliance of Canada, Alberta Union of Provincial Employees, Confédération des syndicats nationaux, Regina Qu'Appelle Regional Health Authority, Cypress Regional Health Authority, Five Hills Regional Health Authority, Heartland Regional Health Authority, Sunrise Regional Health Authority, Prince Albert Parkland Regional Health Authority, Saskatoon Regional Health Authority, National Union of Public and General Employees, Canada Post Corporation and Air Canada

The judgment of McLachlin C.J. and LeBel, Abella, Cromwell, and Karakatsanis was delivered by

ABELLA J.:

[1] In the *Alberta Reference* (*Reference re Public Service Employee Relations Act (Alta.)*, [1987] 1 S.C.R. 313), this Court held that the freedom of association guaranteed under s. 2(*d*) of the *Canadian Charter of Rights and Freedoms* did not protect the right to collective bargaining or to strike. Twenty years later, in *Health Services and Support—Facilities Subsector Bargaining Assn. v. British Columbia*, [2007] 2 S.C.R. 391, this Court held that s. 2(*d*) protects the right of employees to engage in a meaningful process of collective bargaining. The rights were further enlarged in *Ontario (Attorney General) v. Fraser*, [2011] 2 S.C.R. 3, where the Court accepted that a meaningful process includes employees' rights to join together to pursue workplace goals, to make collective representations to the employer, and to have those representations considered in good faith, including having a means of recourse should the employer not bargain in good faith. And, most recently, in *Mounted Police Association of Ontario v. Canada (Attorney General)*, [2015] 1 S.C.R. 3, the Court recognized that a process of collective bargaining could not be meaningful if employees lacked the independence and choice to determine and pursue their collective interests. Clearly the arc bends increasingly towards workplace justice.

[2] The question in this appeal is whether a prohibition on designated employees participating in strike action for the purpose of negotiating the terms and conditions of their employment amounts to a substantial interference with their right to a meaningful process of collective bargaining and, as a result, violates s. 2(*d*) of the *Charter*. ...

[3] The conclusion that the right to strike is an essential part of a meaningful collective bargaining process in our system of labour relations is supported by history, by jurisprudence, and by Canada's international obligations. ... The right to strike is not merely derivative of collective bargaining, it is an indispensable component of that right. It seems to me to be the time to give this conclusion constitutional benediction. ...

[24] ... Along with their right to associate, speak through a bargaining representative of their choice, and bargain collectively with their employer through that representative, the right of employees to strike is vital to protecting the meaningful process of collective bargaining within s. 2(*d*). ... [W]ithout the right to strike, "a constitutionalized right to bargain collectively is meaningless."

[25] Where strike action is limited in a way that substantially interferes with a meaningful process of collective bargaining, it must be replaced by one of the meaningful dispute resolution mechanisms commonly used in labour relations. Where essential services legislation provides such an alternative mechanism, it would more likely be justified under s. 1 of the *Charter*. In my view, the failure of any such mechanism in the *PSESA* is what ultimately renders its limitations constitutionally impermissible. ...

[30] The evolution in the Court's approach to s. 2(*d*) was most recently summarized by McLachlin C.J. and LeBel J. in *Mounted Police*, where they said:

> The jurisprudence on freedom of association under s. 2(*d*) of the *Charter* ... falls into two broad periods. The first period is marked by a restrictive approach to freedom of association. The second period gradually adopts a generous and purposive approach to the guarantee.
>
> ...
>
> ... after an initial period of reluctance to embrace the full import of the freedom of association guarantee in the field of labour relations, the jurisprudence has evolved to affirm a generous approach to that guarantee. This approach is centred on the purpose of encouraging the individual's self-fulfillment and the collective realization of human goals, consistent with democratic values, as informed by "the historical origins of the concepts enshrined" in s. 2(*d*) .... [paras. 30 and 46]

[31] They confirmed that freedom of association under s. 2(*d*) seeks to preserve "employee autonomy against the superior power of management" in order to allow for a meaningful process of collective bargaining (para. 82).

[32] Given the fundamental shift in the scope of s. 2(*d*) since the *Alberta Reference* was decided, the trial judge was entitled to depart from precedent and consider the issue in accordance with this Court's revitalized interpretation of s. 2(*d*): *Canada (Attorney General) v. Bedford*, [2013] 3 S.C.R. 1101, at para. 42.

[33] Dickson C.J.'s dissenting reasons in the *Alberta Reference* were influential in the development of the more "generous approach" in the recent jurisprudence. Recognizing that association "has always been vital as a means of protecting the essential needs and interests of working people" (at p. 368),

and that Canada's international human rights obligations required protection for both the formation and essential activities of labour unions, including collective bargaining and the freedom to strike, Dickson C.J. concluded that "effective constitutional protection of the associational interests of employees in the collective bargaining process requires concomitant protection of their freedom to withdraw ... their services [collectively], subject to s. 1 of the *Charter*" (at p. 371). ...

[34] His views are supported by the history of strike activity in Canada and globally. ...

[51] [That history] reveals that while strike action has variously been the subject of legal protections and prohibitions, the ability of employees to withdraw their labour in concert has long been essential to meaningful collective bargaining. Protection under s. 2(*d*), however, does not depend solely or primarily on the historical/legal pedigree of the right to strike. Rather, the right to strike is constitutionally protected because of its crucial role in a meaningful process of collective bargaining. ...

[53] In *Health Services*, this Court recognized that the *Charter* values of "[h]uman dignity, equality, liberty, respect for the autonomy of the person and the enhancement of democracy" supported protecting the right to a meaningful process of collective bargaining within the scope of s. 2(*d*) (para. 81). And, most recently, drawing on these same values, in *Mounted Police* it confirmed that protection for a meaningful process of collective bargaining requires that employees have the ability to pursue their goals and that, at its core, s. 2(*d*) aims

> to protect the individual from "state-enforced isolation in the pursuit of his or her ends." ... The guarantee functions to protect individuals against more powerful entities. By banding together in the pursuit of common goals, individuals are able to prevent more powerful entities from thwarting their legitimate goals and desires. In this way, the guarantee of freedom of association empowers vulnerable groups and helps them work to right imbalances in society. It protects marginalized groups and makes possible a more equal society. [para. 58]

[54] The right to strike is essential to realizing these values and objectives through a collective bargaining process because it permits workers to withdraw their labour in concert when collective bargaining reaches an impasse. Through a strike, workers come together to participate directly in the process of determining their wages, working conditions and the rules that will govern their working lives ([Judy] Fudge and [Eric] Tucker, ["The Freedom to Strike in Canada: A Brief Legal History" (2009-2010), 15 C.L.E.L.J. 333] at p. 334). ...

This collective action at the moment of impasse is an affirmation of the dignity and autonomy of employees in their working lives.

[55] Striking—the "powerhouse" of collective bargaining—also promotes equality in the bargaining process: England, at p. 188. This Court has long recognized the deep inequalities that structure the relationship between employers and employees, and the vulnerability of employees in this context. In the *Alberta Reference*, Dickson C.J. observed that

> [t]he role of association has always been vital as a means of protecting the essential needs and interests of working people. Throughout history, workers have associated to overcome their vulnerability as individuals to the strength of their employers. [p. 368]

And this Court affirmed in *Mounted Police* that

> ... s. 2(*d*) functions to prevent individuals, who alone may be powerless, from being overwhelmed by more powerful entities, while also enhancing their strength through the exercise of collective power. Nowhere are these dual functions of s. 2(*d*) more pertinent than in labour relations. Individual employees typically lack the power to bargain and pursue workplace goals with their more powerful employers. Only by banding together in collective bargaining associations, thus strengthening their bargaining power with their employer, can they meaningfully pursue their workplace goals.
>
> The right to a meaningful process of collective bargaining is therefore a necessary element of the right to collectively pursue workplace goals in a meaningful way ... . [The] process of collective bargaining will not be meaningful if it denies employees the power to pursue their goals. [paras. 70-71] ...

[56] In their dissent, my colleagues suggest that s. 2(*d*) should not protect strike activity as part of a right to a meaningful process of collective bargaining because "true workplace justice looks at the interests of all implicated parties" (para. 125), including employers. In essentially attributing equivalence between the power of employees and employers, this reasoning, with respect, turns labour relations on its head, and ignores the fundamental power imbalance which the entire history of modern labour legislation has been scrupulously devoted to rectifying. It drives us inevitably to Anatole France's aphoristic fallacy: "The law, in its majestic equality, forbids the rich as well as the poor to sleep under bridges, to beg in the streets, and to steal bread."

[57] Strike activity itself does not guarantee that a labour dispute will be resolved in any particular manner, or that it will be resolved at all. And, as the trial judge recognized, strike

action has the potential to place pressure on *both* sides of a dispute to engage in good faith negotiations. But what it does permit is the employees' ability to engage in negotiations with an employer on a more equal footing (see *Williams v. Aristocratic Restaurants (1947) Ltd.*, [1951] S.C.R. 762, at p. 780; *Mounted Police*, at paras. 70-71). ...

[62] Canada's international human rights obligations also mandate protecting the right to strike as part of a meaningful process of collective bargaining. These obligations led Dickson C.J. to observe that

> there is a clear consensus amongst the [International Labour Organization] adjudicative bodies that [*Convention (No. 87) concerning freedom of association and protection of the right to organize*, 68 U.N.T.S. 17 (1948)] goes beyond merely protecting the formation of labour unions and provides protection of their essential activities—that is of collective bargaining and the freedom to strike. [*Alberta Reference*, at p. 359]

[63] At the time of the *Alberta Reference*, Dickson C.J.'s reliance on Canada's commitments under international law did not attract sufficient collegial support to lift his views out of their dissenting status, but his approach has more recently proven to be a magnetic guide. ...

[75] This historical, international, and jurisprudential landscape suggests compellingly to me that s. 2(*d*) has arrived at the destination sought by Dickson C.J. in the *Alberta Reference*, namely, the conclusion that a meaningful process of collective bargaining requires the ability of employees to participate in the collective withdrawal of services for the purpose of pursuing the terms and conditions of their employment through a collective agreement. Where good faith negotiations break down, the ability to engage in the collective withdrawal of services is a necessary component of the process through which workers can continue to participate meaningfully in the pursuit of their collective workplace goals. In this case, the suppression of the right to strike amounts to a substantial interference with the right to a meaningful process of collective bargaining.

[76] In their dissenting reasons, however, my colleagues urge deference to the legislature in interpreting the scope of s. 2(*d*). This Court has repeatedly held that the rights enumerated in the *Charter* should be interpreted generously: *Hunter v. Southam Inc.*, [1984] 2 S.C.R. 145, at p. 156; *R. v. Big M Drug Mart Ltd.*, [1985] 1 S.C.R. 295, at p. 344. It is not clear to me why s. 2(*d*) should be interpreted differently: *Health Services*, at para. 26; *R. v. Advance Cutting & Coring Ltd.*, [2001] 3 S.C.R. 209, at para. 162; *Mounted Police*, at para. 47. In the context of constitutional adjudication, deference is a conclusion, not an analysis. It certainly plays a role in s. 1,

where, if a law is justified as proportionate, the legislative choice is maintained. But the whole purpose of *Charter* review is to assess a law for constitutional compliance. If the touchstone of *Charter* compliance is deference, what is the point of judicial scrutiny?

[77] This brings us to the test for an infringement of s. 2(*d*). The right to strike is protected by virtue of its unique role in the collective bargaining process. In *Health Services*, this Court established that s. 2(*d*) prevents the state from substantially interfering with the ability of workers, acting collectively through their union, to exert meaningful influence over their working conditions through a process of collective bargaining (para. 90). And in *Mounted Police*, McLachlin C.J. and LeBel J. confirmed that

> [t]he balance necessary to ensure the meaningful pursuit of workplace goals can be disrupted in many ways. Laws and regulations may restrict the subjects that can be discussed, or impose arbitrary outcomes. They may ban recourse to collective action by employees without adequate countervailing protections, thus undermining their bargaining power. ... Whatever the nature of the restriction, *the ultimate question to be determined is whether the measures disrupt the balance between employees and employer that s. 2(d) seeks to achieve, so as to substantially interfere with meaningful collective bargaining.* ... [Emphasis added; para. 72.]

[78] The test, then, is whether the legislative interference with the right to strike in a particular case amounts to a substantial interference with collective bargaining. The *PSESA* demonstrably meets this threshold because it prevents designated employees from engaging in *any* work stoppage as part of the bargaining process. It must therefore be justified under s. 1 of the *Charter*.

[79] The maintenance of essential public services is self-evidently a pressing and substantial objective, as the Unions acknowledge. The Unions also accept the trial judge's further conclusion that the government's objective—ensuring the continued delivery of essential services—is rationally connected to the "basic structure of the legislation, including the sanctions imposed on employees and their unions to ensure compliance with its provisions."

[80] The determinative issue here, in my view, is whether the means chosen by the government are minimally impairing, that is, "carefully tailored so that rights are impaired no more than necessary" (*RJR-MacDonald Inc. v. Canada (Attorney General)*, [1995] 3 S.C.R. 199, at para. 160).

[81] ... The *unilateral* authority of public employers to determine whether and how essential services are to be maintained during a work stoppage with no adequate review

mechanism, and the absence of a meaningful dispute resolution mechanism to resolve bargaining impasses, justify the trial judge's conclusion that the *PSESA* impairs the s. 2(*d*) rights more than is necessary. ...

[85] [T]he fact that a service is provided exclusively through the public sector does not inevitably lead to the conclusion that it is properly considered "essential." In some circumstances, the public may well be deprived of a service as a result of strike action without being deprived of any essential service at all that would justifiably limit the ability to strike during negotiations. ...

[87] Under the *PSESA*, ... the categories of workers whose right to strike may be abrogated because they provide essential services is subject to the employer's unilateral discretion. The scheme requires a public employer and a trade union to first attempt to negotiate the terms of an essential services agreement. Section 6(2) of the *Act* contemplates that the employer must "advise the trade union" of the services it considers to be essential within the meaning of the *Act*. And where the employer is the Government of Saskatchewan, the prescribed essential services have been identified by regulation, without any room for further discussion about what constitutes an essential service. It is, as a result, not even clear that the scheme necessarily contemplates that the designation of certain services as essential will be the subject of negotiation under an agreement.

[88] Moreover, s. 7(2) of the *PSESA* states that under an essential services agreement, the number of employees within each classification "is to be determined without regard to the availability of other persons to provide essential services." As the trial judge found:

> The apparent purpose of s. 7(2) is to enable managers and non-union administrators to avoid the inconvenience and pressure that would ordinarily be brought to bear by a work stoppage. Yet if qualified personnel are available to deliver requisite services, it should not matter if they are managers or administrators. If anything s. 7(2) works at cross purposes to ensuring the uninterrupted delivery of essential services during a work stoppage. [para. 192]

[89] And in the event that an agreement cannot be reached, s. 9(2) gives a public employer the unilateral authority to dictate whether and how essential services will be maintained, including the authority to determine the classifications of employees who must continue to work during the work stoppage, the number and names of employees within each classification, and, for public employers other than the Government of Saskatchewan, the essential services that are to be maintained. As the trial judge found, "[o]f the unilateral designations made by public employers under s. 9(2) only one, that

of the number of employees required to work, is subject to review by the [Saskatchewan Labour Relations Board]." There is no jurisdiction for the Board to even *consider* significant dimensions of an employer's unilateral designation with regard to the maintenance of essential services, such as whether any particular service is essential, or which job classifications involve the delivery of genuinely essential services.

[90] There is no evidence to support Saskatchewan's position that the objective of ensuring the continued delivery of essential services requires unilateral rather than collaborative decision-making authority. And its view that public employers can be relied upon to make fair decisions has the potential to sacrifice the right to a meaningful process of collective bargaining on the altar of aspirations. The history of barriers to collective bargaining over the past century represents a compelling reality check to such optimism.

[91] And even where an employee has been prohibited from participating in strike activity, the *PSESA* does not tailor his or her responsibilities to the performance of essential services alone. Section 18(1)(a) of the *PSESA* requires that in the event of a work stoppage, all essential services employees must continue "the duties of [their] employment with the public employer in accordance with the terms and conditions of the last collective bargaining agreement" and must not fail to continue those duties "without lawful excuse" (s. 18(2)). Requiring those affected employees to perform both essential *and* non-essential work during a strike action undercuts their ability to participate meaningfully in and influence the process of pursuing collective workplace goals.

[92] All this is in addition to the absence of an impartial and effective dispute resolution process to challenge public employer designations under s. 9(2) of the legislation, a particular concern in light of the significant definitional latitude given to public employers. ... The definition of "essential services" under the *PSESA* requires basic judgments to be made about when life, health, safety, or environmental concerns, among others, justify essential services designation. These are fundamental questions, yet all are permitted to be answered unilaterally by the employer under the *Act* with no access to an effective dispute resolution mechanism for reviewing disputed employer designations.

[93] Nor is there any access to a meaningful alternative mechanism for resolving bargaining impasses, such as arbitration. Paul Weiler persuasively explained why such an alternative is crucial for essential services employees:

> If we pull all the teeth of a union by requiring provision of imperative public safety services, such that any remaining strike option does not afford the union significant bargaining leverage, then I believe the union should have

access to arbitration at its option. [Emphasis deleted; p. 237.] ...

[96] Given the breadth of essential services that the employer is entitled to designate unilaterally without an independent review process, and the absence of an adequate, impartial and effective alternative mechanism for resolving collective bargaining impasses, there can be little doubt that the trial judge was right to conclude that the scheme was not minimally impairing. Quite simply, it impairs the s. 2(*d*) rights of designated employees much more widely and deeply than is necessary to achieve its objective of ensuring the continued delivery of essential services.

[97] *The Public Service Essential Services Act* is therefore unconstitutional. ...

The reasons of Rothstein and Wagner JJ. were delivered by

ROTHSTEIN AND WAGNER JJ. (dissenting in part):

...

[105] McLachlin C.J. and LeBel J., writing for a unanimous Court in *R.W.D.S.U., Local 558 v. Pepsi-Cola Canada Beverages (West) Ltd.*, 2002 SCC 8, [2002] 1 S.C.R. 156, cautioned that

[j]udging the appropriate balance between employers and unions is a delicate and essentially political matter. Where the balance is struck may vary with the labour climates from region to region. This is the sort of question better dealt with by legislatures than courts. Labour relations is a complex and changing field, and courts should be reluctant to put forward simplistic dictums. [para. 85]

Thirteen years later, the majority in this case ignores this sage warning in reaching its conclusion. Our colleagues have taken it upon themselves to determine "the appropriate balance between employers and unions," despite the fact that this balance is not any less delicate or political today than it was in 2002. In our respectful view, the majority is wrong to intrude into the policy development role of elected legislators by constitutionalizing the right to strike. ...

[117] The majority's justification for disturbing the government's policy choices fails to acknowledge the constitutional guarantees that already exist to protect employees. ... This Court has asserted on numerous occasions that s. 2(*d*) guarantees *meaningful* collective bargaining (see *Health Services, Fraser* and *Mounted Police*). Therefore, a right to collective bargaining without a right to strike cannot possibly be "meaningless," as the majority states (para. 24). ... What the majority is constitutionalizing is a particular policy, which cuts directly against this Court's approach to s. 2(*d*) most recently stated in *Mounted Police*: "... th[e] right is one that

guarantees a process rather than an outcome or access to a particular model of labour relations" (para. 67). ...

[123] ... The majority's reasons will make all statutory limits on the right to strike presumptively unconstitutional, a significant concern since all labour relations statutes contain extensive limits on the conditions under which workers may strike. Will governments be forced to defend all of these limits under s. 1 of the *Charter*, no matter how ingrained they may be in Canadian labour relations? What is the true scope of this new, constitutionalized right to strike? Despite our general understanding of *Charter* rights applying broadly to all Canadians, has the majority now created a fundamental freedom that can only be exercised by government employees and the 17 percent of the private sector workforce that is unionized?: R. J. Adams, *Labour Left Out: Canada's Failure to Protect and Promote Collective Bargaining as a Human Right* (2006), at p. 19. Are workers without collective agreements able to exercise this new right? The majority sidesteps these fundamental questions. ...

[125] Under the rubric of "workplace justice," our colleagues, relying on a 19th century conception of the relationship between employers and workers, enshrine a political understanding of this concept that favours the interests of employees over those of employers and even over those of the public. While employees are granted constitutional rights, constitutional obligations are imposed on employers. Employers and the public are equally as entitled to justice as employees—true workplace justice looks at the interests of all implicated parties. ...

[127] In the private sector, strikes operate as an economic weapon, a stand-off as to whether employers can forgo or limit carrying on business for longer than employees can forgo wages. In the public sector, strikes are a political tool. The public expects that public services, and especially essential services, will be delivered. Thus unions attempt to pressure the government to agree to certain demands in order that these services be reinstated. Public sector labour disputes are also unique in that the government as employer must take into account that any additional expenditures incurred to meet employee demands will come from public funds. To hold that s. 2(*d*) of the *Charter* protects a particular economic or political weapon of employees, the right to strike together with employer obligations and demands on public resources, plainly tips the balance of power against employers and the public and fails to respect the important role played by democratically elected legislators in balancing the complex competing interests at stake in labour relations. Under a statutory scheme, the legislature is able to make adjustments in appropriate circumstances (e.g. back-to-work legislation or restrictions on strikes by essential service workers). When the right

to strike is constitutionalized, elected legislators are faced with an unwarranted hurdle that interferes with their ability to achieve this balance. ...

[131] ... The trial judge in this case held, and the majority agrees, that without the right to strike "a constitutionalized right to bargain collectively is meaningless" (2012 SKQB 62, 390 Sask. R. 196, at para. 92; majority reasons, at para. 24). With respect, this is plainly incorrect—it is not the threat of work stoppage that motivates good faith bargaining. Before *Health Services*, there was a legal duty on employers to bargain in good faith under various labour relations statutes. ... After *Health Services*, this duty was constitutionalized. It is the statutory duty, and is now this *constitutional duty*, not the possibility of job action, that compels employers to bargain in good faith. To say that this constitutional right is meaningless without a concomitant constitutionalized dispute resolution process would be to say that individuals can never vindicate their rights through the courts or other public institutions. ...

[134] The majority asserts that employees must have some "means of recourse should the employer not bargain in good faith" (para. 29). In the event that bargaining does not occur in good faith, workers *have* recourse: they can bring a claim under the relevant statutory provision or, in some cases, directly under s. 2(*d*) of the *Charter*, which is precisely what was done in *Health Services*. ...

[141] In *Bedford*, this Court explained that a lower court may deviate from binding appellate jurisprudence where there is a new legal issue or a significant change in the circumstances or evidence:

> ... a trial judge can consider and decide arguments based on *Charter* provisions that were not raised in the earlier case; this constitutes a new legal issue. Similarly, the matter may be revisited if new legal issues are raised as a consequence of significant developments in the law, or if there is a change in the circumstances or evidence that fundamentally shifts the parameters of the debate. [para. 42]

In this case, neither developments in the s. 2(*d*) jurisprudence, nor any change in the circumstances of Canadian labour relations justifies the trial judge's departure from Supreme Court precedent.

[142] ... With respect, the sources relied on by the majority to demonstrate [a] change in circumstances do not provide a basis to overturn the many relevant precedents of this Court.

[143] Many of the sources identified by the majority existed at the time this Court rendered its decisions in the Labour Trilogy. For instance, the history of strike activity in Canada and abroad canvassed by the majority at paras. 36 to 55 was information available to this Court when it considered the Labour Trilogy appeals. It cannot now form the basis for an entirely different result than that reached by this Court in 1987. The criterion that, in order for a precedent to be overruled, there must be "a change in the circumstances or evidence that fundamentally shifts the parameters of the debate" (*Bedford*, at para. 42) is manifestly unsatisfied.

[144] While there has been an evolution in the s. 2(*d*) jurisprudence sufficient to be termed a "significant developmen[t] in the law" (*Bedford*, at para. 42), that evolution does not support departing from the Labour Trilogy's conclusion that there is no constitutional right to strike. If anything, developments in the law since 1987 support a finding that the right to freedom of association *does not* require constitutionalization of the right to strike. This is because recent s. 2(*d*) jurisprudence has already established a right to collective bargaining that protects the ability of workers in associations "to exert meaningful influence over working conditions through a process of collective bargaining conducted in accordance with the duty to bargain in good faith" and mandates "both employer and employees to meet and to bargain in good faith, in the pursuit of a common goal of peaceful and productive accommodation" (*Health Services*, at para. 90). ...

[146] The majority in this appeal states that the supposed absence of any dispute resolution mechanism in the *PSESA* "is what ultimately renders its limitations [on the right to strike] constitutionally impermissible" (para. 25).

[147] However, a finding that there is a constitutional right to strike (or to an alternative statutory dispute resolution process), is an express contradiction of this Court's ruling in *Fraser* that s. 2(*d*) of the *Charter* does not require a statutory dispute resolution process (para. 41). While s. 2(*d*) jurisprudence has evolved since 1987, such changes cannot be used to justify contradicting the decisions that brought about these very same changes.

[148] Even more puzzling, the majority claims that the Court affirmed in *Fraser* that a meaningful process under s. 2(*d*) of the *Charter* must include some "means of recourse should the employer not bargain in good faith" (para. 29). They do so despite explicit language to the contrary in that case (see *Fraser*, at para. 41). In misinterpreting the content of *Fraser*, our colleagues overrule that decision without acknowledging that they are doing so.

[149] The more "generous approach" to s. 2(*d*) of the *Charter*, referred to by the majority at para. 33, does not license this Court to indeterminately expand the scope of freedom of association. In imposing constitutional limitations on the legislature in this case, the majority disregards *stare decisis* and the certainty and predictability it is intended to foster.

[Justice Rothstein then explains at length why he thinks that "[i]nternational law is of no help to this Court in determining whether freedom of association in s. 2(*d*) of the *Charter* includes a right to strike." Among other things, he argues, contrary to the majority, that there exists "no clear consensus under international law that the right to strike is an essential element of freedom of association."]

[161] For the reasons above, s. 2(*d*) does not confer a *Charter* right to strike. The question remains whether the *PSESA* nevertheless violates the right to a process of meaningful collective bargaining protected under s. 2(*d*). In our respectful view, it does not. ...

[164] First, the *PSESA* facilitates consultation between employers and unions regarding the designation of essential services. Although the right to collective bargaining under s. 2(*d*) does not protect a particular outcome (*Fraser*, at para. 45), the fact that essential services agreements have been achieved in the provincial public sector during the currency of the *PSESA* indicates that there has been no substantial interference with the right to meaningful collective bargaining. The first collective agreement to be signed after the *PSESA* came into force—the 2009-2012 agreement between the Public Service Commission ("PSC") and the Saskatchewan Government and General Employees' Union ("SGEU")—was signed only eight months after the preceding agreement ended, over three months faster than the average time to reach a collective agreement. Essential services agreements were also signed between the PSC and the SGEU, and between the PSC and the Canadian Union of Public Employees, Local 600. Tentative collective agreements were reached between the Saskatchewan Association of Health Organizations and each of the Canadian Union of Public Employees, the Service Employees International Union, and the SGEU in August 2010; these were later ratified.

[165] Moreover, s. 6 of the *PSESA* requires public employers to negotiate with trade unions with a view to concluding an essential services agreement. The evidence demonstrates that such good faith collective bargaining took place. For instance, the trial judge held that urban municipalities, the University of Regina, and the University of Saskatchewan all engaged in meaningful consultations with unions (para. 189). In fact, the Government of Saskatchewan *exceeded* the requirements of s. 6(3) of the *PSESA*: the PSC consulted the SGEU regarding which services (other than those relating to health and safety) would be designated as essential in *The Public Service Essential Services Regulations*, R.R.S., c. P-42.2, Reg. 1. As a result of these consultations, a number of changes were made to the *Regulations*.

[166] Second, this Court determined in both *Health Services* and *Fraser* that s. 2(*d*) does not entail a right to a dispute resolution mechanism. A violation of s. 2(*d*) cannot be found here simply on allegations that the legislation does not provide an adequate dispute resolution process. ...

[167] Finally, the appellants argue that this Court must defer to the trial judge's finding that, in absence of the ability of workers to strike, there can be no assurance that collective bargaining will occur in good faith. ... [T]his mischaracterizes the primary purpose of the strike, which is to exert political and economic pressure, not to ensure good faith collective bargaining, which is protected by statute and, since *Health Services*, by s. 2(*d*) of the *Charter*. ...

[170] ... A right to strike is not required to ensure the s. 2(*d*) guarantee of freedom of association. ...

[173] Because the *PSESA* does not violate s. 2(*d*) of the *Charter*, it is unnecessary to engage in an analysis under s. 1.

C. DEMOCRATIC RIGHTS

12 Sauvé v. Canada (Chief Electoral Officer), 2002

Section 3 of the Charter gives every Canadian citizen the right to vote. At the same time, section 1 permits such "reasonable limits" on this right as "can be demonstrably justified in a free and democratic society." A variety of historical disqualifications based on such criteria as sex, race, and wealth had already been found to be "unreasonable limits" on the franchise well before the Charter came into effect. Others—for example, the traditional disqualification of judges and the mentally disabled—have been abandoned since, and partly because of, the Charter's advent.[1] We know that some reasonable limits remain, however, because age restrictions continue to enjoy almost universal support. Could the traditional disqualification of imprisoned criminals—another persistent holdout against the trend of franchise expansion—be similarly maintained? In *Sauvé* (2002),[2] a narrowly (and intensely) divided court decided that it could not. The case also raised section 15 equality-rights issues,[3] but these occupied little of the court's attention[4] and did not affect the outcome.

Several years earlier, the same litigant, Richard Sauvé, had already brought the issue to the Supreme Court. *Sauvé* (1993)[5] considered what was then a blanket prisoner disqualification, under which a petty offender who elected brief imprisonment in lieu of a fine might find himself disenfranchised on voting day while his accomplice paid the fine and voted. By the time *Sauvé* (1993) reached the Supreme Court, the law had been altered to disqualify only criminals imprisoned for terms of two years or more, but the judges preferred not to comment on this change, choosing instead to invalidate only the previous blanket disqualification. For Richard Sauvé this was a pyrrhic victory. As a convicted murderer he was

---

1 See *Muldoon v. Canada*, [1988] 3 F.C. 628 (T.D.) and *Canadian Disability Rights Council v. Canada*, [1988] 3 F.C. 622 (T.D.).

2 *Sauvé v. Canada (Chief Electoral Officer)*, 2002 SCC 68, [2002] 3 S.C.R. 519.

3 This was either because prisoners deserved the status of an "analogous group" under section 15 or because the impact of the disqualification fell more heavily on Aboriginals, who are disproportionately represented in the prison population.

4 The majority, having found the disqualification unconstitutional under section 3, did not think it necessary to address section 15. In brief reasons, the minority denied that the disqualification infringed section 15.

5 *Sauvé v. Canada (Attorney General)*, [1993] 2 S.C.R. 438.

imprisoned for more than two years and thus continued to be disenfranchised by the new law. Undaunted, Sauvé launched a new case.

Writing for the five-judge majority in *Sauvé* (2002), Justice McLachlin doubted that the prisoner disqualification met even the "pressing and substantial purpose" requirement of the *Oakes* test,[6] but she was likely prevented from deciding the case on this basis by the precedent of *Sauvé* (1993). In that earlier case, the nine judges of the Supreme Court, including Justice McLachlin, unanimously invalidated the blanket disqualification in an unusually terse, one-paragraph opinion, the substance of which is contained in a single sentence:

> In our view, [the blanket disqualification] is drawn too broadly and fails to meet the proportionality test, particularly the minimal impairment component of the test, as expressed in the s. 1 jurisprudence of the Court.

In focusing entirely on the proportionality test, *Sauvé* (1993) clearly assumed that even a blanket disqualification of prisoners has the kind of compelling purpose required by the first part of the *Oakes* test. Having agreed to this in the earlier case, Justice McLachlin could not easily find that the less draconian disqualification at issue in *Sauvé* (2002) lacked a compelling purpose. However, grudgingly, she thus conceded a compelling purpose and moved on to the question of proportional means.

Writing for *Sauvé* (2002)'s four-judge minority, Justice Gonthier, who had also participated in *Sauvé* (1993), was happy to focus on proportional means. If the blanket disqualification in *Sauvé* (1993) "particularly" failed "the minimal impairment component" of the *Oakes* test, the government's task was to find more finely tuned means to its end. For Gonthier, this is precisely what the much vaunted concept of "dialogue" between courts and legislatures is all about. In his view, the appropriate legislative response in this particular dialogue was to disqualify only more serious criminals, as defined by the length of their incarceration. But what length, exactly? Just as those who agree in principle on an age-based voting restriction often disagree on what the cut-off age should be, so those who agree on a length-of-sentence criterion for prisoner disqualification can disagree on what the sentence cut-off should be. For example, while the government had chosen two years as the cut-off, the Royal Commission on Electoral Reform and Party Financing (the Lortie Commission) had previously suggested a 10-year sentence as the appropriate threshold for disqualification.[7] Gonthier was not inclined to micromanage this issue. The government's two-year threshold was good enough to meet the minimal impairment standard.

The two-year threshold wasn't good enough for Justice McLachlin. But neither would she agree to a longer sentence as more appropriate. In fact, she made it abundantly clear that no disqualification, no matter how finely tailored, would pass constitutional muster in her view. How is this possible, given that she had agreed to ground her conclusions on the issue of proportional means, as *Sauvé* (1993) requires? Had the cryptic judgment in *Sauvé* (1993) read simply that the disqualification "fails to meet the minimal impairment component" of

---

6   This is usually the easiest hurdle to clear in the *Oakes* test. See the introduction to *Oakes*, case 14.

7   Royal Commission on Electoral Reform and Party Financing, *Final Report* (Ottawa: Minister of Supply and Services, 1991) vol. I at 45.

the *Oakes* test, McLachlin would indeed have been reduced to debating the right length of sentence to use as a threshold for disqualification. But *Sauvé* (1993) speaks of the proportionality test as a whole; indeed, by "particularly" emphasizing its minimal impairment component, it implicitly holds the door open to the possible involvement of the proportionality test's other components.[8]

Justice McLachlin walked through this door, especially with respect to the rational-connection component of proportionality. Rational connection requires that the challenged legislative means must actually achieve the compelling purpose to which they are directed. Only if they do, does it make sense to proceed to issues of minimal impairment. The judges unanimously agree that conclusive scientific proof is not required to establish such a rational connection between means and ends; the logic and common sense of a "reasonable person" will do. Because McLachlin's "reasonable person" could imagine no prisoner disqualification that achieves any plausible compelling purpose, none could meet the rational-connection test. Nor could there be any room for "dialogue" about "irrational" legislative means. Disagreeing with Gonthier's view that there had been appropriate dialogue about how best to achieve minimal impairment of the right to vote, McLachlin insisted that to apply the concept in this instance would debase it to a rule of "if at first you don't succeed, try, try again." It is not healthy dialogue to keep attempting what is fundamentally irrational.

Wherever McLachlin saw irrationality, Gonthier discerned plausible and defensible positions. Social contract theory, for example, which McLachlin saw as utterly hostile to a prisoner disqualification, was for Gonthier an important justification of the disqualification. In grounding the legitimacy of government on the foundational consent of its citizens (as institutionalized in democracies through public elections), contract theory establishes a "vital symbolic, theoretical and practical connection between having a voice in making the law and being obliged to obey it." Part of consenting to government, in other words, is agreeing to abide by its laws. For McLachlin, this meant that one cannot—as the government claimed to be doing—teach people to be law abiding by depriving them of the pedagogical tool best suited to teaching this lesson—the vote. In support of this position, she quoted John Stuart Mill's claim that "the possession and the exercise of political, and among others of electoral, rights, is one of the chief instruments both of moral and of intellectual training for the popular mind."[9]

---

8 Given the judicial preferences on display in *Sauvé* (2002), it is difficult to escape the conclusion that the key sentence of *Sauvé* (1993) was, in fact, the carefully crafted outcome of a strategic compromise between the contending factions. On the strategic dimensions of *Sauvé* and many other Canadian cases, see Rainer Knopff, Dennis Baker, and Sylvia LeRoy, "Courting Controversy: Strategic Judicial Decision Making" in James Kelly and Christopher Manfredi, eds., *Contested Constitutionalsim: Reflections on the Canadian Charter of Rights and Freedoms* (Vancouver: UBC Press, 2009).

9 This quotation does not, of course, directly address the issue of prisoner voting. When he explicitly considers that question elsewhere, Mill admits that "[a]s far as the direct influence of [prisoners'] votes went, it would scarcely be worthwhile to exclude them," but that "[a]s an aid to the great object of giving a moral character to the exercise of the suffrage, it might be expedient that in the case of crimes evincing a high degree of insensibility to social obligation, the deprivation of this and other civic rights should form part of the sentence." *The Collected Works of John Stuart Mill* (Toronto: University of Toronto Press, 1977) 322n. Mill, moreover, was not a social contract theorist.

For Gonthier, by contrast, nothing could be more appropriate from the standpoint of the social contract than to temporarily deprive those who break the law of their law-making role. How else can one effectively teach the "connection between having a voice in making the law and being obliged to obey it"? To do otherwise is symbolically to demean the dignity of the vote. Just as McLachlin found support for her position in J.S. Mill, Gonthier could easily have invoked such contract theorists as Kant in support of his. "In my role as colegislator making the penal law," wrote Kant, "I cannot be the same person who, as a subject, is punished by the law; for, as a subject who is also a criminal, I cannot have a voice in legislation."[10]

This kind of vigorous point and counterpoint characterizes the extensive debate between the majority and dissenting opinions in Sauvé (2002); that debate repays careful investigation. ∼

Discussion Questions

1. Are all prisoner-voting disqualifications unjustified for the same reasons as previous racial and sexual disqualifications, or are some justified by relevant differences from these historical disqualifications?

2. The section 33 notwithstanding clause cannot be used to override judicial decisions based on section 3 of the Charter. What effect should this have on how activist or deferential judges should be in applying section 3?

3. The day the Supreme Court issued its judgment in *Sauvé* (2002) has been described as "the day the dialogue died"?[11] Do you agree?

---

10   Immanuel Kant, *The Metaphysical Elements of Justice*, Part 1 of *The Metaphysics of Morals*, trans. John Ladd (Indianapolis: Bobbs-Merrill, 1978) at 105. For a review of how the thought of many other philosophers bears on the question of prisoner voting, see Zdravko Planinc, "Should Imprisoned Criminals Have a Constitutional Right to Vote?" (1987) *Canadian Journal of Law and Society* 2.

11   Christopher Manfredi, "The Day the Dialogue Died: A Comment on Sauvé v. Canada" (2007) 45 *Osgoode Hall Law Journal* 105.

SAUVÉ v. CANADA (CHIEF ELECTORAL OFFICER)
2002 SCC 68, [2002] 3 S.C.R. 519

Hearing: December 10, 2001; Judgment: October 31, 2002.

Present: McLachlin C.J. and L'Heureux-Dubé, Gonthier, Iacobucci, Major, Bastarache, Binnie, Arbour, and LeBel JJ.

Interveners: The Attorney General for Alberta, the Attorney General of Manitoba, the Canadian Association of Elizabeth Fry Societies, the John Howard Society of Canada, the British Columbia Civil Liberties Association, the Aboriginal Legal Services of Toronto Inc., and the Canadian Bar Association.

The judgment of McLachlin C.J. and Iacobucci, Binnie, Arbour, and LeBel JJ. was delivered by

THE CHIEF JUSTICE:

[1] The right of every citizen to vote, guaranteed by s. 3 of the *Canadian Charter of Rights and Freedoms*, lies at the heart of Canadian democracy. The law at stake in this appeal denies the right to vote to a certain class of people—those serving sentences of two years or more in a correctional institution. The question is whether the government has established that this denial of the right to vote is allowed under s. 1 of the *Charter* as a "reasonable limit ... demonstrably justified in a

free and democratic society." I conclude that it is not. The right to vote, which lies at the heart of Canadian democracy, can only be trammeled for good reason. Here, the reasons offered do not suffice. ...

[6] The respondents concede that the voting restriction at issue violates s. 3 of the *Charter*. The restriction is thus invalid unless demonstrably justified under s. 1. I shall therefore proceed directly to the s. 1 analysis. ...

[8] My colleague Justice Gonthier ... argues that in justifying limits on the right to vote under s. 1, we owe deference to Parliament because we are dealing with "philosophical, political and social considerations," because of the abstract and symbolic nature of the government's stated goals, and because the law at issue represents a step in a dialogue between Parliament and the courts.

[9] I must, with respect, demur. The right to vote is fundamental to our democracy and the rule of law and cannot be lightly set aside. Limits on it require not deference, but careful examination. This is not a matter of substituting the Court's philosophical preference for that of the legislature, but of ensuring that the legislature's proffered justification is supported by logic and common sense. ...

[13] The core democratic rights of Canadians do not fall within a "range of acceptable alternatives" among which Parliament may pick and choose at its discretion. Deference may be appropriate on a decision involving competing social and political policies. It is not appropriate, however, on a decision to limit fundamental rights. This case is not merely a competition between competing social philosophies. It represents a conflict between the right of citizens to vote—one of the most fundamental rights guaranteed by the *Charter*—and Parliament's denial of that right. Public debate on an issue does not transform it into a matter of "social philosophy," shielding it from full judicial scrutiny. It is for the courts, unaffected by the shifting winds of public opinion and electoral interests, to safeguard the right to vote guaranteed by s. 3 of the *Charter*.

[14] *Charter* rights are not a matter of privilege or merit, but a function of membership in the Canadian polity that cannot lightly be cast aside. This is manifestly true of the right to vote, the cornerstone of democracy, exempt from the incursion permitted on other rights through s. 33 override.

[15] The *Charter* charges courts with upholding and maintaining an inclusive, participatory democratic framework within which citizens can explore and pursue different conceptions of the good. While a posture of judicial deference to legislative decisions about social policy may be appropriate in some cases, the legislation at issue does not fall into this category. To the contrary, it is precisely when legislative choices threaten to undermine the foundations of the participatory democracy guaranteed by the *Charter* that courts

must be vigilant in fulfilling their constitutional duty to protect the integrity of this system.

[16] Nor can I concur in the argument that the philosophically-based or symbolic nature of the government's objectives in itself commands deference. ... Parliament cannot use lofty objectives to shield legislation from *Charter* scrutiny. Section 1 requires valid objectives *and* proportionality.

[17] Finally, the fact that the challenged denial of the right to vote followed judicial rejection of an even more comprehensive denial, does not mean that the Court should defer to Parliament as part of a "dialogue." Parliament must ensure that whatever law it passes, at whatever stage of the process, conforms to the Constitution. The healthy and important promotion of a dialogue between the legislature and the courts should not be debased to a rule of "if at first you don't succeed, try, try again."

[18] While deference to the legislature is not appropriate in this case, legislative justification does not require empirical proof in a scientific sense. While some matters can be proved with empirical or mathematical precision, others, involving philosophical, political and social considerations, cannot. In this case, it is enough that the justification be convincing, in the sense that it is sufficient to satisfy the reasonable person looking at all the evidence and relevant considerations, that the state is justified in infringing the right at stake to the degree it has: see *RJR-MacDonald* [*Inc. v. The Attorney General of Canada*, [1995] 3 S.C.R. 199], at para. 154, *per* McLachlin J.; *R. v. Butler*, [1992] 1 S.C.R. 452, at pp. 502-3, *per* Sopinka J. What is required is "rational, reasoned defensibility": *RJR-MacDonald*, at para. 127. Common sense and inferential reasoning may supplement the evidence: *R. v. Sharpe*, [2001] 1 S.C.R. 45, 2001 SCC 2, at para. 78, *per* McLachlin C.J. However, one must be wary of stereotypes cloaked as common sense, and of substituting deference for the reasoned demonstration required by s. 1.

[19] Keeping in mind these basic principles of *Charter* review, I approach the familiar stages of the *Oakes* test. I conclude that the government's stated objectives of promoting civic responsibility and respect for the law and imposing appropriate punishment, while problematically vague, are capable in principle of justifying limitations on *Charter* rights. However, the government fails to establish proportionality, principally for want of a rational connection between denying the vote to penitentiary inmates and its stated goals. ...

[21] ... [T]he government asserts two broad objectives as the reason for this denial of the right to vote: (1) to enhance civic responsibility and respect for the rule of law; and (2) to provide additional punishment, or "enhance the general purposes of the criminal sanction." The record leaves in doubt how much these goals actually motivated Parliament; the

Parliamentary debates offer more fulmination than illumination. However, on the basis of "some glimmer of light," the trial judge at p. 878 concluded that they could be advanced as objectives of the denial. I am content to proceed on this basis. ...

[22] ... Vague and symbolic objectives such as these almost guarantee a positive answer to this question. Who can argue that respect for the law is not pressing? Who can argue that proper sentences are not important? Who can argue that either of these goals, taken at face value, contradict democratic principles? However, precisely because they leave so little room for argument, vague and symbolic objectives make the justification analysis more difficult. Their terms carry many meanings, yet tell us little about why the limitation on the right is necessary, and what it is expected to achieve in concrete terms. ...

[23] ... If Parliament can infringe a crucial right such as the right to vote simply by offering symbolic and abstract reasons, judicial review either becomes vacuously constrained or reduces to a contest of "our symbols are better than your symbols." Neither outcome is compatible with the vigorous justification analysis required by the *Charter*. ...

[26] Quite simply, the government has failed to identify particular problems that require denying the right to vote, making it hard to say that the denial is directed at a pressing and substantial purpose. Nevertheless, despite the abstract nature of the government's objectives and the rather thin basis upon which they rest, prudence suggests that we proceed to the proportionality analysis, rather than dismissing the government's objectives outright. ...

[27] At this stage the government must show that the denial of the right to vote will promote the asserted objectives (the rational connection test); that the denial does not go further than reasonably necessary to achieve its objectives (the minimal impairment test); and that the overall benefits of the measure outweigh its negative impact (the proportionate effect test). ...

[28] Will denying the right to vote to penitentiary inmates enhance respect for the law and impose legitimate punishment? The government must show that this is likely, either by evidence or in reason and logic: *RJR-MacDonald*, *supra*, at para. 153.

[29] The government advances three theories to demonstrate rational connection between its limitation and the objective of enhancing respect for law. First, it submits that depriving penitentiary inmates of the vote sends an "educative message" about the importance of respect for the law to inmates and to the citizenry at large. Second, it asserts that allowing penitentiary inmates to vote "demeans" the political system. Finally, it takes the position that disenfranchisement

is a legitimate form of punishment, regardless of the specific nature of the offence or the circumstances of the individual offender. In my respectful view, none of these claims succeed.

[30] The first asserted connector with enhancing respect for the law is the "educative message" or "moral statement" theory. The problem here, quite simply, is that denying penitentiary inmates the right to vote is bad pedagogy. It misrepresents the nature of our rights and obligations under the law, and it communicates a message more likely to harm than to help respect for the law.

[31] Denying penitentiary inmates the right to vote misrepresents the nature of our rights and obligations under the law and consequently undermines them. In a democracy such as ours, the power of lawmakers flows from the voting citizens, and lawmakers act as the citizens' proxies. This delegation from voters to legislators gives the law its legitimacy or force. Correlatively, the obligation to obey the law flows from the fact that the law is made by and on behalf of the citizens. In sum, the legitimacy of the law and the obligation to obey the law flow directly from the right of every citizen to vote. As a practical matter, we require all within our country's boundaries to obey its laws, whether or not they vote. But this does not negate the vital symbolic, theoretical and practical connection between having a voice in making the law and being obliged to obey it. This connection, inherited from social contract theory and enshrined in the *Charter*, stands at the heart of our system of constitutional democracy.

[32] The government gets this connection exactly backwards when it attempts to argue that depriving people of a voice in government teaches them to obey the law. ... [I]f we accept that governmental power in a democracy flows from the citizens, it is difficult to see how that power can legitimately be used to disenfranchise the very citizens from whom the government's power flows.

[33] Reflecting this truth, the history of democracy is the history of progressive enfranchisement. The universal franchise has become, at this point in time, an essential part of democracy. From the notion that only a few meritorious people could vote (expressed in terms like class, property and gender), there gradually evolved the modern precept that all citizens are entitled to vote as members of a self-governing citizenry. ... Under s. 3 of the *Charter*, the final vestiges of the old policy of selective voting have fallen, including the exclusion of persons with a "mental disease" and federally appointed judges: see *Canadian Disability Rights Council v. Canada*, [1988] 3 F.C. 622 (T.D.); and *Muldoon v. Canada*, [1988] 3 F.C. 628 (T.D.). The disenfranchisement of inmates takes us backwards in time and retrenches our democratic entitlements. ...

[35] More broadly, denying citizens the right to vote runs counter to our constitutional commitment to the inherent

worth and dignity of every individual. As the South African Constitutional Court said in *August v. Electoral Commission*, 1999 (3) SALR 1, at para. 17, "[t]he vote of each and every citizen is a badge of dignity and of personhood. Quite literally, it says that everybody counts." ...

[36] In recognition of the seminal importance of the right to vote in the constellation of rights, the framers of the *Charter* accorded it special protections. Unlike other rights, the right of every citizen to vote cannot be suspended under the "notwithstanding clause." ...

[37] The government's vague appeal to "civic responsibility" is unhelpful, as is the attempt to lump inmate disenfranchisement together with legitimate voting regulations in support of the government's position. The analogy between youth voting restrictions and inmate disenfranchisement breaks down because the type of judgment Parliament is making in the two scenarios is very different. In the first case, Parliament is making a decision based on the experiential situation of all citizens when they are young. It is not saying that the excluded class is unworthy to vote, but regulating a modality of the universal franchise. In the second case, the government is making a decision that some people, whatever their abilities, are not morally worthy to vote—that they do not "deserve" to be considered members of the community and hence may be deprived of the most basic of their constitutional rights. But this is not the lawmakers' decision to make. The *Charter* makes this decision for us by guaranteeing the right of "every citizen" to vote and by expressly placing prisoners under the protective umbrella of the *Charter* through constitutional limits on punishment. The *Charter* emphatically says that prisoners are protected citizens, and short of a constitutional amendment, lawmakers cannot change this.

[38] The theoretical and constitutional links between the right to vote and respect for the rule of law are reflected in the practical realities of the prison population and the need to bolster, rather than to undermine, the feeling of connection between prisoners and society as a whole. The government argues that disenfranchisement will "educate" and rehabilitate inmates. However, disenfranchisement is more likely to become a self-fulfilling prophecy than a spur to reintegration. Depriving at-risk individuals of their sense of collective identity and membership in the community is unlikely to instill a sense of responsibility and community identity, while the right to participate in voting helps teach democratic values and social responsibility (testimony of Professor Jackson, appellant's record at pp. 2001-2). As J. S. Mill wrote:

> To take an active interest in politics is, in modern times, the first thing which elevates the mind to large interests and contemplations; the first step out of the narrow bounds of

individual and family selfishness, the first opening in the contracted round of daily occupations. ... The possession and the exercise of political, and among others of electoral, rights, is one of the chief instruments both of moral and of intellectual training for the popular mind. ...

(J. S. Mill, "Thoughts on Parliamentary Reform" (1859), in J.M. Robson, ed., *Essays on Politics and Society*, Vol. XIX (1977), at pp. 322-23)

To deny prisoners the right to vote is to lose an important means of teaching them democratic values and social responsibility. ...

[42] The government also argues that denying penitentiary inmates the vote will enhance respect for law because allowing people who flaunt the law to vote demeans the political system. ... But ... the argument that only those who respect the law should participate in the political process is a variant on the age-old unworthiness rationale for denying the vote. ...

[43] ... Until recently, large classes of people, prisoners among them, were excluded from the franchise [on] the assumption that they were not fit or "worthy" of voting—whether by reason of class, race, gender or conduct. ... We should reject the retrograde notion that "worthiness" qualifications for voters may be logically viewed as enhancing the political process and respect for the rule of law. ...

[45] This brings us to the government's final argument for rational connection—that disenfranchisement is a legitimate weapon in the state's punitive arsenal against the individual lawbreaker. ...

[46] The argument, stripped of rhetoric, proposes that it is open to Parliament to add a new tool to its arsenal of punitive implements—denial of constitutional rights. I find this notion problematic. I do not doubt that Parliament may limit constitutional rights in the name of punishment, provided that it can justify the limitation. But it is another thing to say that a particular class of people for a particular period of time will completely lose a particular constitutional right. This is tantamount to saying that the affected class is outside the full protection of the *Charter*. It is doubtful that such an unmodulated deprivation, particularly of a right as basic as the right to vote, is capable of justification under s. 1. Could Parliament justifiably pass a law removing the right of all penitentiary prisoners to be protected from cruel and unusual punishment? I think not. What of freedom of expression or religion? Why, one asks, is the right to vote different?

[47] The social compact requires the citizen to obey the laws created by the democratic process. But it does not follow that failure to do so nullifies the citizen's continued membership in the self-governing polity. Indeed, the remedy of

imprisonment for a term rather than permanent exile implies our acceptance of continued membership in the social order. Certain rights are justifiably limited for penal reasons, including aspects of the right to liberty, security of the person, mobility, and security against search and seizure. But whether a right is justifiably limited cannot be determined by observing that an offender has, by his or her actions, withdrawn from the social compact. Indeed, the right of the state to punish and the obligation of the criminal to accept punishment is tied to society's acceptance of the criminal as a person with rights and responsibilities. Other *Charter* provisions make this clear. Thus s. 11 protects convicted offenders from unfair trials, and s. 12 from "cruel and unusual treatment or punishment."

[48] The second flaw in the argument that s. 51(*e*) furthers legitimate punishment is that it does not meet the dual requirements that punishment must not be arbitrary and must serve a valid criminal law purpose. Absence of arbitrariness requires that punishment be tailored to the acts and circumstances of the individual offender: *R. v. Smith*, [1987] 1 S.C.R. 1045, at p. 1073. In the immortal words of Gilbert and Sullivan, the punishment should fit the crime. Section 51(*e*) *qua* punishment bears little relation to the offender's particular crime. It makes no attempt to differentiate among inmates serving sentences of two years and those serving sentences of twenty. It is true that those serving shorter sentences will be deprived of the right to vote for a shorter time. Yet the correlation of the denial with the crime remains weak. It is not only the violent felon who is told he is an unworthy outcast; a person imprisoned for a non-violent or negligent act, or an Aboriginal person suffering from social displacement receives the same message. They are not targeted, but they are caught all the same. For them the message is doubly invidious—not that they are cast out for their apparently voluntary rejection of society's norms, but that they are cast out arbitrarily, in ways that bear no necessary relation to their actual situation or attitude towards state authority.

[49] Punishment must also fulfill a legitimate penal purpose. ... These include deterrence, rehabilitation, retribution, and denunciation. ... Neither the record nor common sense supports the claim that disenfranchisement deters crime or rehabilitates criminals. On the contrary, as Mill recognized long ago, participation in the political process offers a valuable means of teaching democratic values and civic responsibility.

[50] This leaves retribution and denunciation. Parliament may denounce unlawful conduct. But it must do so in a way that closely reflects the moral culpability of the offender and his or her circumstances. ... Denunciation as a symbolic expression of community values must be individually tailored in order to fulfill the legitimate penal purpose of condemning a *particular* offender's conduct (see *M. (C.A.)* [*R. v.*, [1996] 1 S.C.R. 500], at para. 81) and to send an appropriate "educative message" about the importance of law-abiding behavior.

[51] Section 51(*e*) imposes blanket punishment on all penitentiary inmates regardless of the particular crimes they committed, the harm they caused, or the normative character of their conduct. It is not individually tailored to the particular offender's act. It does not, in short, meet the requirements of denunciatory, retributive punishment. It follows that it is not rationally connected to the goal of imposing legitimate punishment. ...

[53] I conclude that the government has failed to establish a rational connection between s. 51(*e*)'s denial of the right to vote and the objectives of enhancing respect for the law and ensuring appropriate punishment.

[54] If the denial of a right is not rationally connected to the government's objectives, it makes little sense to go on to ask whether the law goes further than is necessary to achieve the objective. I simply observe that if it were established that denying the right to vote sends an educative message that society will not tolerate serious crime, the class denied the vote—all those serving sentences of two years or more—is too broad, catching many whose crimes are relatively minor and who cannot be said to have broken their ties to society. Similarly, if it were established that this denial somehow furthers legitimate sentencing goals, it is plain that the marker of a sentence of two years or more catches many people who, on the government's own theory, should not be caught. ...

[57] If a connection could be shown between the denial of the right to vote and the government's objectives, the negative effects of denying citizens the right to vote would greatly outweigh the tenuous benefits that might ensue. ...

[60] The negative effects of s. 51(*e*) upon prisoners have a disproportionate impact on Canada's already disadvantaged Aboriginal population, whose over-representation in prisons reflects "a crisis in the Canadian criminal justice system": *R. v. Gladue*, [1999] 1 S.C.R. 688, at para. 64, *per* Cory and Iacobucci JJ. To the extent that the disproportionate number of Aboriginal people in penitentiaries reflects factors such as higher rates of poverty and institutionalized alienation from mainstream society, penitentiary imprisonment may not be a fair or appropriate marker of the degree of individual culpability. ...

The reasons of L'Heureux-Dubé, Gonthier, Major, and Bastarache JJ. were delivered by

GONTHIER J. (dissenting):

[68] ... The Chief Justice and I are in agreement that the right to vote is profoundly important, and ought not to be demeaned. Our differences lie principally in the fact that she subscribes to a philosophy whereby the temporary

disenfranchising of criminals does injury to the rule of law, democracy and the right to vote, while I prefer deference to Parliament's reasonable view that it strengthens these same features of Canadian society.

[69] The reasons of the Chief Justice refer to the historical evolution of the franchise in Canada. This evolution has generally involved the weeding out of discriminatory exclusions. It is undeniable and, obviously, to be applauded, that, over time, Canada has been evolving towards the universalization of the franchise in such a manner. The provision in question in the case at bar, however, is strikingly and qualitatively different from these past discriminatory exclusions. It is a temporary suspension from voting based exclusively on the serious criminal *activity* of the offender. It is the length of the sentence, reflecting the nature of the offence and the criminal activity committed, that results in the temporary disenfranchisement during incarceration. ...

[70] ... While there is little logical correlation between maintaining a "decent and responsible citizenry" and any of the past discriminatory exclusions (such as land-ownership, religion, gender, ethnic background), there clearly is such a logical connection in the case of distinguishing persons who have committed serious criminal offences. "*Responsible* citizenship" does not relate to what gender, race, or religion a person belongs to, but is logically related to whether or not a person engages in serious criminal activity. ...

[73] The reasons of the Chief Justice express the view that the temporary disenfranchisement of serious criminal offenders necessarily undermines their inherent "worth" or "dignity." I disagree. In fact, it could be said that the notion of punishment is predicated on the dignity of the individual: it recognizes serious criminals as rational, autonomous individuals who have made choices. When these citizens exercise their freedom in a criminal manner, society imposes a concomitant responsibility for that choice. ...

[74] If there is any negative connotation associated with this temporary disenfranchisement, it arises from the fact that a criminal act was perpetrated, an act for which the criminal offender is consequently being punished. This is not stereotyping. Criminal acts are rightly condemned by society. Serious criminals being punished and temporarily disenfranchised are not in any way of less "worth" or "dignity" because social condemnation is of the criminal acts and its purpose is not to diminish the individual prisoner as a person. ...

[92] ... [T]here seem generally to be two options available for dealing with the issue at hand. The first, that chosen by the Chief Justice, is to prefer an inclusive approach to democratic participation for serious criminal offenders incarcerated for two years or more. This view locates democratic participation as a central dimension of rehabilitation, insofar as the

incarcerated offenders remain citizens with the fullest exercise of their democratic rights. By the same token, the unrestricted franchise enhances democratic legitimacy of government, and confirms or enhances the citizenship or standing of prisoners in society. To do otherwise, it is suggested, undermines the "dignity" or "worth" of prisoners. The alternative view, adopted by Parliament, considers that the temporary suspension of the prisoner's right to vote, in fact, enhances the general purposes of the criminal sanction, including rehabilitation. It does so by underlining the importance of civic responsibility and the rule of law. This approach sees the temporary removal of the vote as a deterrent to offending or re-offending and the return of the vote as an inducement to reject further criminal conduct. In withdrawing for a time one expression of political participation concurrently with personal freedom, the significance of both are enhanced. Rather than undermine the dignity or worth of prisoners, the removal of their vote takes seriously the notion that they are free actors and attaches consequences to actions that violate certain core values as expressed in the *Criminal Code*.

[93] Both of these approaches, however, entail accepting logically prior political or social philosophies about the nature and content of the right to vote. The former approach, that accepted by the reasons of the Chief Justice, entails accepting a philosophy that preventing criminals from voting does damage to both society and the individual, and undermines prisoners' inherent worth and dignity. The latter approach also entails accepting a philosophy, that not permitting serious incarcerated criminals to vote is a social rejection of serious crime which reflects a moral line which safeguards the social contract and the rule of law and bolsters the importance of the nexus between individuals and the community. Both of these social or political philosophies, however, are *aimed at the same goal*: that of supporting the fundamental importance of the right to vote itself. Further, both of these social or political philosophies are supported by the practices of the various Canadian provinces, the practices of other liberal democracies, and academic writings. Finally, neither position can be proven empirically—rather, the selection of one over the other is largely a matter of philosophical preference. What is *key* to my approach is that the acceptance of one or the other of these social or political philosophies dictates much of the constitutional analysis which ensues, since the reasonableness of any limitation upon the right to vote and the appropriateness of particular penal theories and their relation to the right to vote will logically be related to whether or not the justification for that limitation is based upon an "acceptable" social or political philosophy.

[94] The reasons of the Chief Justice hold ... that the challenge of the Government is to present a justification that

is "convincing, in the sense that it is sufficient to satisfy the reasonable person looking at all the evidence and relevant considerations, that the state is justified in infringing the right at stake to the degree it has." ...

[95] The reasons of the Chief Justice apply something seemingly more onerous than the "justification" standard referred to just above. She describes the right to vote as a "core democratic right" and suggests that its exemption from the s. 33 override somehow raises the bar for the government in attempting to justify its restriction (paras. 13 and 14). This altering of the justification standard is problematic in that it seems to be based upon the view that there is only one plausible social or political philosophy upon which to ground a justification for or against the limitation of the right. This approach, however, is incorrect on a basic reading of s. 1 of the *Charter*, which clearly does not constrain Parliament or authorize this Court to prioritize one reasonable social or political philosophy over reasonable others, but only empowers this Court to strike down those limitations which are not reasonable and which cannot be justified in a free and democratic society.

[96] ... It does not follow from the fact that Parliament is denied the authority to remove or qualify the right to vote in its sole discretion under s. 33 that limitations on that right may not be justified under s. 1, or that a more onerous s. 1 analysis must necessarily apply .... It does not behoove the Court to read s. 33 into s. 3 by finding in s. 3, when divorced from s. 1, the statement of a political philosophy which pre-empts another political philosophy which is reasonable and justified under the latter section. The *Charter* was not intended to monopolize the ideological space. ...

[100] In her reasons, the Chief Justice claims ... that Parliament is relying on "lofty objectives," and suggests at para. 23 that the presence of "symbolic and abstract" objectives is problematic. However, the reasons of the Chief Justice have the very same objective—to protect the value of the right to vote and the rule of law—and rely on equally vague concepts. Breaking down the meaning and value of the right to vote, one is unavoidably led to abstract and symbolic concepts such as the rule of law, the legitimacy of law and government, and the meaning of democracy. The Chief Justice discusses these concepts at length, along with theories of individual motivation. For instance, relying on the philosopher J.S. Mill, she suggests at para. 38 that "[t]o deny prisoners the right to vote is to lose an important means of teaching them democratic values and social responsibility." This type of statement is as symbolic, abstract and philosophical as the government's claim that denying serious incarcerated criminals the right to vote will strengthen democratic values and social responsibility. ...

[104] Linden J.A., in the Federal Court of Appeal below, stressed the importance of deference to Parliament. In para. 56 of his reasons, he stated:

> This case is another episode in the continuing dialogue between courts and legislatures on the issue of prisoner voting. In 1992 and 1993, two appeal courts and the Supreme Court of Canada held that a blanket disqualification of prisoners from voting, contained in earlier legislation which was challenged, violated section 3 of the Charter and could not be saved by section 1 of the Charter. Parliament responded to this judicial advice by enacting legislation aimed at accomplishing part of its objectives while complying with the Charter. That legislation, which is being challenged in this case, disqualifies from voting only prisoners who are serving sentences of two years or more. [Footnotes omitted.]

This Court has stressed the importance of "dialogue" in *Vriend v. Alberta*, [1998] 1 S.C.R. 493, at paras. 138-39 and in *Mills* [*R. v.*, [1999] 3 S.C.R. 668], at paras. 20, 57 and 125. (See also P.W. Hogg and A.A. Bushell, "The Charter Dialogue Between Courts and Legislatures" (1997), 35 *Osgoode Hall L.J.* 75.) I am of the view that since this case is about evaluating choices regarding social or political philosophies and about shaping, giving expression, and giving practical application to values, especially values that may lie outside the *Charter* but are of fundamental importance to Canadians, "dialogue" is of particular importance. In my view, especially in the context of the case at bar, the heart of the dialogue metaphor is that neither the courts nor Parliament hold a monopoly on the determination of values. Importantly, the dialogue metaphor *does not signal a lowering of the s. 1 justification standard*. It simply suggests that when, after a full and rigorous s. 1 analysis, Parliament has satisfied the court that it has established a reasonable limit to a right that is demonstrably justified in a free and democratic society, the dialogue ends; the court lets Parliament have the last word and does not substitute Parliament's reasonable choices with its own. ...

[109] What social or political philosophy has motivated Parliament to insist on the temporary disenfranchisement of prisoners? Is it reasonable and rational? I suggest that, in enacting s. 51(*e*) of the Act and in providing a justification of that provision before the courts, Parliament has indicated that it has drawn a line. This line reflects a moral statement about serious crime, and about its significance to and within the community. The core of this moral statement is the denunciation of serious crime, serious antisocial acts. Parliament has indicated that criminal conduct of such severity that it warrants imprisonment for a sentence of two years or more also carries with it the disenfranchisement of the offender for the duration of his or her incarceration. ...

[115] The denunciation of crime and its effects on society is often explained by reference to the notion of the social contract. The social contract is the theoretical basis upon which the exercise of rights and participation in the democratic process rests. In my view, the social contract necessarily relies upon the acceptance of the rule of law and civic responsibility and on society's need to promote the same. The preamble to the *Charter* establishes that "… Canada is founded upon principles that recognize the supremacy of God and the rule of law. …" In *Reference re Manitoba Language Rights*, [1985] 1 S.C.R. 721, at p. 750, this Court cited with approval a passage from *The Authority of Law* (1979) by Professor Raz, wherein he states that " 'The rule of law' means literally what it says. … It has two aspects: (1) that people should be ruled by the law and obey it, and (2) that the law should be such that people will be able to be guided by it." The important point arising from that passage is the corollary that promoting law-abiding behaviour can be thought to be a dimension of the rule of law as well. Further, the rule of law, as was said in the *Reference re Secession of Quebec*, [1998] 2 S.C.R. 217, at p. 257, "vouchsafes to the citizens and residents of the country a stable, predictable and ordered society in which to conduct their affairs." Given its fundamental importance in our society, it is not surprising that Parliament occasionally insists to take some action to promote it, to safeguard it. As was stated by Wilson J. in *Operation Dismantle v. The Queen*, [1985] 1 S.C.R. 441, at p. 489: "There is no liberty without law and there is no law without some restriction of liberty: see Dworkin, *Taking Rights Seriously* (1977), p. 267."

[116] Permitting the exercise of the franchise by offenders incarcerated for serious offences undermines the rule of law and civic responsibility because such persons have demonstrated a great disrespect for the community in their committing serious crimes: such persons have attacked the stability and order within our community. Society therefore may choose to curtail temporarily the availability of the vote to serious criminals both to punish those criminals and to insist that civic responsibility and respect for the rule of law, as goals worthy of pursuit, are prerequisites to democratic participation. I say "goals worthy of pursuit" because it is clear that not all those who are otherwise eligible to vote are guaranteed to exercise civic responsibility, since, for example, there may be serious criminal offenders who may have avoided being apprehended and therefore still vote. This does not, however, detract from the laudability of the goal.

[117] Related to the notion of the social contract is the importance of reinforcing the significance of the relationship between individuals and their community when it comes to voting. This special relationship is inherent in the fact that it is only "citizens" who are guaranteed the right to vote within s. 3 of the *Charter*. This limitation of the scope of s. 3 of the *Charter* stands in stark contrast to the protections offered by the fundamental freedoms, legal rights, and equality rights in the *Charter*, which are available to "everyone" or to "every individual." I am of the view that this limitation reflects the special relationship, characterized by entitlements and responsibilities, between citizens and their community. It is this special relationship and its responsibilities which serious criminal offenders have assaulted. …

[120] From the perspective of the person whose criminal activity has resulted in their temporary disenfranchisement, their benefiting from society brought with it the responsibility to be subjected to the sanctions which the state decides will be attached to serious criminal activity such as they have chosen to undertake. This understanding is complemented by the rehabilitative view that those who are in jail will hope and expect to regain the exercise of the vote on their release from incarceration, just like they hope and expect to regain the exercise of the fullest expressions of their liberty. Once released from prison, they are on the road to reintegration into the community. Obtaining the vote once released or paroled is a recognition of regaining the nexus with the community that was temporarily suspended during the incarceration. …

[135] I now turn to the application of the *Oakes* test. …

[139] Parliament's two principal objectives in s. 51(*e*) of the Act, accepted by both the trial judge and the Federal Court of Appeal below, are: the enhancement of civic responsibility and respect for the rule of law, and the enhancement of the general purposes of the criminal sanction. Above, I developed the view that these objectives are based upon a reasonable and rational social or political philosophy. Thus, I am of the view that any provision which seeks to advance such objectives clearly has a pressing and substantial purpose. …

[150] This Court has unanimously agreed that "[r]ational connection is to be established, upon a civil standard, through reason, logic or simply common sense": *RJR-MacDonald, supra, per* La Forest J., at para. 86, McLachlin J., at paras. 156-58, and Iacobucci J., at para. 184; referred to in *Thomson Newspapers* [*Co. v. Canada (Attorney General)*, [1998] 1 S.C.R. 877], at para. 39. The existence of scientific proof is simply of probative value in supporting this reason, logic or common sense. In the case at bar, as discussed above, a causal relationship between disenfranchising prisoners and the objectives approved of above is not empirically demonstrable. However, this Court has clearly stated that Parliament must be afforded a margin of appreciation in regard to legitimate objectives which may, nonetheless, be based upon somewhat inconclusive social science evidence: Sopinka J. in *Butler, supra*, at pp. 502-3. … Thus, it is clear that this Court's approach to this dimension of the test demands not the strongest

connection, the most convincing rational connection, but a logical or rational connection.

[157] ... [R]eason, logic and common sense, as well as extensive expert evidence support a conclusion that there is a rational connection between disenfranchising offenders incarcerated for serious crimes and the objectives of promoting civic responsibility and the rule of law and the enhancement of the general objectives of the penal sanction. The rational connection between the disenfranchisement and the first objective is explained above, in my discussion of dignity and the fact that removing the right to vote from serious incarcerated criminals does no injury to, but rather recognizes their dignity. It is also explained ... below in my discussion of the salutary effects of the measure [where] I discuss the legislation's expression of societal values and its signalling effect. The Chief Justice prefers a different line of reasoning. Citing J.S. Mill as her authority, she states that "denying penitentiary inmates the right to vote is more likely to send messages that undermine respect for the law and democracy than messages that enhance those values" (para. 41). However, apart from one philosopher, she provides no support for this contention; she simply replaces one reasonable position with another, dismissing the government's position as "unhelpful" (para. 37 of the Chief Justice's reasons).

[158] The rational connection between the legislation and the enhancement of the criminal sanction is also elaborated on elsewhere. Below, ... on minimal impairment, I explain at length that the disenfranchisement is carefully tailored to apply to perpetrators of serious crimes. I therefore disagree with the Chief Justice's statement that denial of the right to vote is insufficiently tailored and therefore not rationally connected to legitimate punishment. ...

[160] The Crown must demonstrate that the impairment of rights is minimal, i.e. that the law was carefully tailored so that *Charter* rights are impaired no more than is necessary to meet the legislative provision's objectives. ... This analysis does not, notably, require the Crown to have adopted the absolutely least intrusive means for promoting the purpose, although it does require that the Crown prefer a significantly less intrusive means if it is of *equal effectiveness*. ...

[161] I emphasize that it was "particularly" on the ground of minimal impairment that this Court, in the first *Sauvé* case, established that the previous s. 51(*e*) of the Act, which disenfranchised all prisoners regardless of the duration of their incarceration, was contrary to the *Charter* and incapable of being justified under s. 1. Our decision was, at pp. 439-40:

> We are all of the view that these appeals should be dismissed.
>
> The Attorney General of Canada has properly conceded that s. 51(*e*) of the *Canada Elections Act*, R.S.C.,

1985, c. E-2, contravenes s. 3 of the *Canadian Charter of Rights and Freedoms* but submits that s. 51(*e*) is saved under s. 1 of the *Charter*. We do not agree. In our view, s. 51(*e*) is drawn too broadly and fails to meet the proportionality test, particularly the minimal impairment component of the test, as expressed in the s. 1 jurisprudence of the Court.

The language of Iacobucci J.'s reasons seem to imply that, while Parliament's complete ban of prisoner voting in the old provision was unconstitutional, Parliament was free to investigate where an appropriate line could be drawn. This is exactly what it was in the process of doing at the time the first *Sauvé* case was heard. It has drawn a line in the form of s. 51(*e*) of the Act.

[162] The appellants and their experts have argued that there are less intrusive means for the Crown to pursue its objectives: disenfranchisement could be left to the discretion of the sentencing judge; as *per* the Lortie Commission, only those convicted of the most serious offences (those punishable by a maximum of life) and the most serious sentences (those punishable by 10 years in jail or more) could lose the vote; an offence-oriented approach could define specific types of crimes which could be seen as bearing a rational connection to the franchise; or the measure could allow for the vote to be restored if the offender demonstrated good behaviour while incarcerated. To these I add that it is obvious that any higher cutoff line, i.e. 5, 10, or 25 years of incarceration, would also, technically, be less intrusive.

[163] I am of the view that no less intrusive measure would be equally effective. Since Parliament has drawn a line which identifies which incarcerated offenders have committed serious enough crimes to warrant being deprived of the vote, any alternative line will not be of equal effectiveness. Equal effectiveness is a dimension of the analysis that should not be underemphasized, as it relates directly to Parliament's ability to pursue its legitimate objectives effectively. Any other line insisted upon amounts to *second-guessing* Parliament as to what amounts to "serious" crime. ...

[174] In my view, it is particularly inappropriate, in the case at bar, to find the justification of the limitation of the right to be unconvincing at this phase of the *Oakes* test. First, as was noted above, there is a need for deference to Parliament in its drawing of a line, especially since this Court gave the impression that it was up to Parliament to do exactly that after the first *Sauvé* case was heard in 1993. Second, also as developed above, the analysis of social and political philosophies and the accommodation of values in the context of the *Charter* must be sensitive to the fact that there may be many possible reasonable and rational balances. Developing this point, it is important to note that, given the theoretical nature

of the arguments raised by both parties in the case at bar, they do not gain proportionally in strength as the bar is moved higher. Symbolic and theoretical justifications such as employed in this case do not get stronger as the line changes. The fundamental premises underlying the line chosen would be the same if the cutoff was 10 years, or even 25 years. See, for example, *Driskell* [*v. Manitoba (Attorney General)*, [1999] 11 W.W.R. 615], in which similar analytical problems to those in the case at bar arose and resulted in a line of five years being held unconstitutional. Line drawing, amongst a range of acceptable alternatives, is for Parliament. ...

[175] The final prong of the *Oakes* test demands that the effects of the limiting measure (the impugned provision) must not so severely trench on *Charter* rights that the legislative objective, albeit important, is outweighed by the infringement of the rights. ...

[178] It is my view that the arguments in this dimension of the analysis are basically either persuasive or not. If the objectives are taken to reflect a moral choice by Parliament which has great symbolic importance and effect and which are based on a reasonable social or political philosophy, then their resulting weight is great indeed. Over all, while the temporary disenfranchisement is clear, the salutary effects and objectives are, in my view, of greater countervailing weight. Generally, I agree with the analysis of Linden J.A. at the Federal Court of Appeal below to this effect. ...

[181] Linden J.A. found that the primary salutary effect was that the legislation, *intrinsically*, expresses societal values in relation to serious criminal behaviour and the right to vote in our society. He thus concluded ... that it has more than symbolic effect:

> This legislation sends a message signalling Canadian values, to the effect that those people who are found guilty of the most serious crimes will, while separated from society, lose access to one of the levers of electoral power. This is an extremely important message, one which is not sent by incarceration alone. Incarceration is essentially separation from the community. Incarceration alone signals a denunciation of the offender's anti-societal behaviour and indicates society's hope for rehabilitation through separation from the community. Incarceration by itself, however, leaves those convicted of serious crimes free to exercise all the levers of electoral power open to all law-abiding citizens. This maintains a political parity between those convicted of society's worst crimes and their victims. Disqualification from voting, however, signals a denunciation of the criminal's anti-societal behaviour *and* sends the message that those people convicted of causing the worst forms of indignity to others will be deprived of one aspect of the political equality of

citizens—the right to vote. It can be said that, in this context, "kindness toward the criminal can be an act of cruelty toward his victims, and the larger community." [Footnotes omitted; emphasis in original.]

Linden J.A. suggested that value emerges from the signal or message that those who commit serious crimes will temporarily lose one aspect of the political equality of citizens. Therefore, "the enactment of the measure is itself a salutary effect." I agree. ...

[188] When the objectives and the salutary effects are viewed in the totality of the context, they outweigh the temporary disenfranchisement of the serious criminal offender which mirrors the fact of his or her incarceration. In my view, Parliament has enacted a law which is reasonable, and which is justified in a free and democratic society. ...

[204] The reasons of the Chief Justice, at para. 60, refer to the fact that this Court, in *R. v. Gladue*, [1999] 1 S.C.R. 688, noted that the over-representation of Aboriginal persons in the criminal justice system and the prison population reflects a "crisis in the Canadian criminal justice system." I agree that a sad and pressing social problem exists, but suggest that it is quite a leap to then say that Parliament is incapable of enacting a provision which disenfranchises serious criminal offenders who have been sentenced to two or more years of incarceration. As noted above, it is not plausible to say that the temporary disenfranchisement is in some way targeted at Aboriginal people: it hinges only upon the commission of serious criminal offences. If there is a problem with the over-representation of Aboriginal people in our criminal justice system and prisons, then that issue must continue to be addressed, by not only continuing to pay attention to the sentencing considerations pursuant to s. 718.2(*e*) of the *Criminal Code*, which are specifically aimed at such a reduction, but also by addressing some of the root causes of the over-representation identified by this Court in *Gladue*, *supra*, including poverty, substance abuse, lack of education, lack of employment opportunities, and bias against Aboriginal people. The continuing need to address these factors does not, however, preclude the ability of Parliament to address other pressing social problems, including denouncing serious crime, enhancing the meaning of the criminal sanction and promoting civic responsibility and the rule of law, which s. 51(*e*) of the Act is directed to. Also in *Gladue*, at para. 78, this Court stated that it is unreasonable to assume that Aboriginal people do not believe in goals of punishment such as denunciation, deterrence and separation, to which I add, obviously, the principle of rehabilitation. These goals of punishment, as discussed above, are related to the temporary disenfranchisement of serious criminal offenders and are ultimately aimed at the reintegration of offenders, Aboriginal or otherwise, back into the community.

Harper v. Canada
(Attorney General), 2004

Before he became prime minister of Canada, Stephen Harper served for a time as president of the National Citizens Coalition (NCC), a conservative public interest group. Harper enthusiastically continued the NCC's lengthy campaign, begun under his predecessor, against legal restrictions on "third party" spending in election campaigns. The case below, bearing Harper's name, culminates the litigation component of the NCC campaign.

"Third parties," as the term is used in this context, are political interests other than the registered parties and candidates who officially compete for electoral office. They include individuals and interest groups such as the NCC. Laws that impose election spending limits on political parties, as Canada's have since 1974, can be circumvented if non-electoral interests may spend freely in ways that might benefit or harm official candidates and parties. Thus election spending limits typically target both official and third parties. At the same time, the high value of freedom of expression in liberal democracies weighs against restricting all election spending to official parties; citizens, both individually and in groups, are typically left some freedom to make their political views known outside political parties. How much money can they spend in exercising this freedom, and in what ways can they spend it, without making a mockery of the very idea of election spending limits? That question divided the Supreme Court in *Harper*.

The NCC began its litigation campaign against what it called "gag laws" in the 1980s. Between 1984 and 2003, it successfully persuaded an unbroken succession of trial and appeal courts in Alberta and Ontario to strike down the third-party spending limits.[1] Until *Harper*, these judgments were not appealed to the Supreme Court and thus technically prevailed only in the jurisdiction of the court deciding them. Nevertheless, the difficulty and confusion of applying third-party spending limits differentially across the country meant that they were not applied anywhere in the federal elections of 1984, 1988, 1993, and 2000.

In the meantime, a slightly different political spending issue had come out of Quebec and was making its way to the Supreme Court. Seeking to equalize the two sides in a referendum campaign, Quebec's referendum law allowed only those affiliated with the official "Oui" and "Non" committees to make significant campaign expenditures. During the 1992 referendum on the Charlottetown Accord, Quebec's Equality Party, led by Robert Libman, encouraged abstention from the vote. Because his party could not reasonably promote this position in affiliation with either official committee, Libman challenged the spending restrictions in

---

1 *National Citizens' Coalition v. Canada (Attorney General)*, [1984] 5 W.W.R. 436 (Alta. Q.B.); *Somerville v. Canada (Attorney General)* (25 June 1993), Calgary, oral judgment (Alta. Q.B.) (unreported); *Somerville v. Canada (Attorney General)* (1996), 39 Alta. L.R. (3d) 326 (Alta. C.A.); *Harper v. Canada (Attorney General)* (2001), 93 Alta. L.R. (3d) 281 (Q.B.); *Harper v. Canada (Attorney General)* (2002), 14 Alta. L.R. (4th) 4 (C.A.); and *Canada (Commissioner of Canada Elections) v. National Citizens' Coalition*, 2003 CarswellOnt 3947 (Ct. J.).

court. Although *Libman*[2] concerned referenda rather than elections, it raised essentially the same freedom-of-expression issues that the NCC had so successfully pursued.

Reaching the Supreme Court in 1997, *Libman* (and by implication the NCC) met with mixed results. On the one hand, the court's unanimous, unsigned opinion struck down Quebec's third-party spending rules as infringing freedom of expression in a manner too restrictive to meet the "minimal impairment" requirement of the *Oakes* test.[3] On the other hand, and more important, the court enthusiastically embraced the principle of spending limits on third parties. The purpose of such limits—to ensure democratic fairness by equalizing the persuasive power and resources of the political contenders—was "pressing and substantial" and third-party spending limits were a "rational" way of achieving this purpose. Quebec simply had to tailor its restrictions more carefully in order to satisfy the minimal-impairment requirement. Strikingly, the court suggested that Quebec would find a laudable example in the $1,000 federal third-party spending limit struck down by the Alberta Court of Appeal in 1996. In doing so, the judges tipped their hand on how they were likely to treat the NCC's litigation campaign when it reached them. The NCC, under Stephen Harper's leadership, would soon give them the opportunity.

Harper launched his challenge before an Alberta court in 2000 in response to revised federal third-party spending limits of $150,000, not more than $3,000 of which could be spent to promote or oppose particular candidates within any electoral district. Included within the spending limits was the promotion of any position "associated" with a registered party or candidate. Harper argued that the law violated both the Charter's section 2 right to freedom of expression and its section 3 right to vote. In its 2004 judgment, the Supreme Court unanimously rejected the section 3 challenge, but disagreed on section 2. We reproduce only the section 2 disagreement below.

Given how praiseworthy the *Libman* judgment had found the previous, less liberal, federal third-party spending limits, it comes as no surprise to find the court upholding the revised law. What may seem surprising is Chief Justice McLachlin's dissenting judgment (joined by Justices Major and Binnie), which found the new limits too "draconian" to pass constitutional muster. After all, Justices McLachlin and Major had both been part of the unanimous *Libman* court. The preferences they make evident in *Harper* are certainly consistent with the bottom-line outcome of *Libman*, which struck down even more "draconian" provincial spending limits, but they sit uneasily with *Libman*'s praise of the existing $1,000 federal limit on third-party spending, which must have appeared equally unjustifiable to Justices McLachlin and Major. A plausible speculation is that they considered *Libman*'s support of the earlier federal limits as non-binding *obiter dictum*, and thus something they could live with in order to gain the advantages of unsigned unanimity when undertaking something as controversial as striking down Quebec's referendum law. The sensitivity of Quebec to Charter-based intrusions of the Supreme Court is well known and likely to be particularly acute regarding matters as entangled with autonomist sentiments as referendum laws. When turning to federal legislation, Justices McLachlin and Major obviously felt freer to express their disagreement.

Chief Justice McLachlin's dissent emphasized that "[p]olitical speech, the type of speech here at issue, is the single most important and protected type of expression. It lies at the

---

2   *Libman v. Quebec (Attorney General)*, [1997] 3 S.C.R. 569.

3   According to the court, the limits were "so restrictive that they come close to being a total ban."

core of the guarantee of free expression." This meant that a higher or more searching degree of scrutiny should be applied at the stage of section 1 analysis than when the expression fell further from the core. In fact, Justice McLachlin is often inclined to apply a high standard of justification even in cases involving expression much more distant from the "core" of free expression, such as the commercial advertising at stake in *RJR-MacDonald* (case 7). Indeed, Justice McLachlin arguably applied an even higher degree of scrutiny to the restrictions on tobacco advertising in *RJR-MacDonald* than she did to the political expression at issue in *Harper*. In *RJR-MacDonald*, she found the advertising ban to fail both the rational connection and minimal impairment components of proportionality analysis, while in *Harper* she found a "rational connection"[4] and focused on the law's failure to meet the "minimal impairment" criterion. In short, she saw the tobacco advertising ban as more problematic from a section 1 perspective than the limit on third-party political expression.

Chief Justice McLachlin, of course, was at least consistently libertarian in voting to strike down both the *RJR-MacDonald* advertising ban and the *Harper* political spending limits. But although her view prevailed in *RJR-MacDonald*, it lost in *Harper*. This poses another anomaly—namely, that "the political speech at issue in *Harper* fared no better than obscene pornography [*Butler*, case 6] ... and rather worse than tobacco advertising."[5] ∽

Discussion Questions

1. Why does each side in this judicial dispute think it is supported by the *Libman* precedent?

2. The "minimal impairment" criterion of the *Oakes* test is central to the disagreement between the majority and dissenting opinions. Why do the judges disagree on this issue and who do you think gets the better of the debate?

3. Can the law at issue in *Harper* be seen as part of the interinstitutional "dialogue" between courts and legislatures? If so, is it legitimate dialogue?

---

4 She appeared to do so because of the *Libman* precedent, which had also found a rational connection. This part of the *Libman* judgment could not as easily be treated as *obiter dictum* as the praise of the federal $1,000 spending limit on third parties.

5 Robert E. Charney and S. Zachary Green, "It's My Party and I'll Run If I Want To: Figueroa, Harper, and the Animal Alliance Environment Voters Party" (2006) 21 *National Journal of Constitutional Law* 257 at 268.

HARPER v. CANADA (ATTORNEY GENERAL)
2004 SCC 33; [2004] 1 S.C.R. 827

Hearing: February 10, 2004; Judgment: May 18, 2004.

Present: McLachlin C.J. and Iacobucci, Major, Bastarache, Binnie, Arbour, LeBel, Deschamps, and Fish JJ.

Interveners: Attorney General of Ontario, Attorney General of Quebec, Attorney General of Manitoba, Democracy Watch and National Anti-Poverty Organization, Environment Voters, a division of Animal Alliance of Canada, and John Herbert Bryden.

The reasons of McLachlin C.J. and Major and Binnie JJ. were delivered by

[1] **THE CHIEF JUSTICE AND MAJOR J.** (dissenting in part): This Court has repeatedly held that liberal democracy demands the free expression of political opinion, and affirmed that political speech lies at the core of the *Canadian Charter of Rights and Freedoms'* guarantee of free expression. It has held that the freedom of expression includes the right to attempt to persuade through peaceful interchange. And it has observed that the electoral process is the primary means by which the average citizen participates in the public discourse

that shapes our polity. The question now before us is whether these high aspirations are fulfilled by a law that effectively denies the right of an ordinary citizen to give meaningful and effective expression to her political views during a federal election campaign.

[2] The law at issue sets advertising spending limits for citizens—called third parties—at such low levels that they cannot effectively communicate with their fellow citizens on election issues during an election campaign. The practical effect is that effective communication during the writ period is confined to registered political parties and their candidates. Both enjoy much higher spending limits. This denial of effective communication to citizens violates free expression where it warrants the greatest protection—the sphere of political discourse. As in *Libman v. Quebec (Attorney General)*, [1997] 3 S.C.R. 569, the incursion essentially denies effective free expression and far surpasses what is required to meet the perceived threat that citizen speech will drown out other political discourse. It follows that the law is inconsistent with the guarantees of the *Charter* and, hence, invalid. ...

[3] The *Canada Elections Act*, S.C. 2000, c. 9, sets limits for spending on advertising for individuals and groups. It limits citizens to spending a maximum of $3,000 in each electoral district up to a total of $150,000 nationally. Section 350 provides:

> **350.** (1) A third party shall not incur election advertising expenses of a total amount of more than $150,000 during an election period in relation to a general election.
>
> (2) Not more than $3,000 of the total amount referred to in subsection (1) shall be incurred to promote or oppose the election of one or more candidates in a given electoral district, including by
>
> > (*a*) naming them;
> >
> > (*b*) showing their likenesses;
> >
> > (*c*) identifying them by their respective political affiliations; or
> >
> > (*d*) taking a position on an issue with which they are particularly associated.

Section 350(2)(*d*) is particularly restrictive. It prohibits individuals from spending more than the allowed amounts on any issue with which a candidate is "particularly associated." The candidates in an election are typically associated with a wide range of views on a wide range of issues. The evidence shows that the effect of the limits is to prevent citizens from effectively communicating their views on issues during an election campaign.

[4] The limits do not permit citizens to effectively communicate through the national media. The Chief Electoral Officer testified that it costs approximately $425,000 for a one-time full-page advertisement in major Canadian newspapers. The Chief Electoral Officer knows from personal experience that this is the cost of such communication with Canadians, because he used this very method to inform Canadians of the changes to the *Canada Elections Act* prior to the last federal election. It is telling that the Chief Electoral Officer would have been unable to communicate this important change in the law to Canadians were he subject—as are other Canadians—to the national expenditure limit of $150,000 imposed by the law.

[5] Nor do the limits permit citizens to communicate through the mail. The Canada Post bulk mailing rate for some ridings amounts to more than $7,500, effectively prohibiting citizens from launching a mail campaign in these ridings without exceeding the $3,000 limit.

[6] The $3,000 riding limits are further reduced by the national limit of $150,000, which precludes citizens from spending the maximum amount in each of the 308 ridings in Canada. This effectively diminishes the $3,000 riding maximum. Quite simply, it puts effective radio and television communication within constituencies or throughout the country beyond the reach of "third party" citizens.

[7] Under the limits, a citizen may place advertisements in a local paper within her constituency. She may print some flyers and distribute them by hand or post them in conspicuous places. She may write letters to the editor of regional and national newspapers and hope they will be published. In these and other ways, she may be able to reach a limited number of people on the local level. But she cannot effectively communicate her position to her fellow citizens throughout the country in the ways those intent on communicating such messages typically do—through mail-outs and advertising in the regional and national media. The citizen's message is thus confined to minor local dissemination with the result that effective local, regional and national expression of ideas becomes the exclusive right of registered political parties and their candidates.

[8] Comparative statistics underline the meagerness of the limits. The national advertising spending limits for citizens represent 1.3 percent of the national advertising limits for political parties. In Britain, a much more geographically compact country, the comparable ratio is about 5 percent. It is argued that the British limits apply to different categories of advertising over a greater period, but the discrepancy nevertheless remains significant.

[9] It is therefore clear that the *Canada Elections Act*'s advertising limits prevent citizens from effectively communicating their views on election issues to their fellow citizens, restricting them instead to minor local communication.

As such, they represent a serious incursion on free expression in the political realm. The Attorney General raises three reasons why this restriction is justified as a reasonable limit in a free and democratic society under s. 1 of the *Charter*: to ensure the equality of each citizen in elections; to prevent the voices of the wealthy from drowning out those of others; and to preserve confidence in the electoral system. Whether that is so is the question in this appeal. ...

[10] One cannot determine whether an infringement of a right is justified without examining the seriousness of the infringement. Our jurisprudence on the guarantee of the freedom of expression establishes that some types of expression are more important and hence more deserving of protection than others. To put it another way, some restrictions on freedom of expression are easier to justify than others.

[11] Political speech, the type of speech here at issue, is the single most important and protected type of expression. It lies at the core of the guarantee of free expression. ...

[16] The ability to engage in effective speech in the public square means nothing if it does not include the ability to attempt to persuade one's fellow citizens through debate and discussion. This is the kernel from which reasoned political discourse emerges. Freedom of expression must allow a citizen to give voice to her vision for her community and nation, to advocate change through the art of persuasion in the hope of improving her life and indeed the larger social, political and economic landscape. ...

[17] Freedom of expression protects not only the individual who speaks the message, but also the recipient. Members of the public—as viewers, listeners and readers—have a right to information on public governance, absent which they cannot cast an informed vote; see *Edmonton Journal* [*v. Alberta (Attorney General)*, [1989] 2 S.C.R. 1326], at pp. 1339-40. Thus the *Charter* protects listeners as well as speakers; see *Ford v. Quebec (Attorney General)*, [1988] 2 S.C.R. 712 , at pp. 766-67. ...

[19] The *Canada Elections Act* undercuts the right to listen by withholding from voters an ingredient that is critical to their individual and collective deliberation: substantive analysis and commentary on political issues of the day. The spending limits impede the ability of citizens to communicate with one another through public fora and media during elections and curtail the diversity of perspectives heard and assessed by the electorate. Because citizens cannot mount effective national television, radio and print campaigns, the only sustained messages voters see and hear during the course of an election campaign are from political parties.

[20] It is clear that the right here at issue is of vital importance to Canadian democracy. In the democracy of ancient Athens, all citizens were able to meet and discuss the issues of the day in person. In our modern democracy, we cannot speak personally with each of our fellow citizens. We can convey our message only through methods of mass communication. Advertising through mail-outs and the media is one of the most effective means of communication on a large scale. We need only look at the reliance of political parties on advertising to realize how important it is to actually reaching citizens—in a word, to effective participation. The ability to speak in one's own home or on a remote street corner does not fulfill the objective of the guarantee of freedom of expression, which is that each citizen be afforded the opportunity to present her views for public consumption and attempt to persuade her fellow citizens. Pell J.'s observation could not be more apt: "[s]peech without effective communication is not speech but an idle monologue in the wilderness"; see *United States v. Dellinger*, 472 F.2d 340 (7th Cir. 1972), at p. 415.

[21] This is the perspective from which we must approach the question whether the limitation on citizen spending is justified. It is no answer to say that the citizen can speak through a registered political party. The citizen may hold views not espoused by a registered party. The citizen has a right to communicate those views. The right to do so is essential to the effective debate upon which our democracy rests, and lies at the core of the free expression guarantee. That does not mean that the right cannot be limited. But it does mean that limits on it must be supported by a clear and convincing demonstration that they are necessary, do not go too far, and enhance more than harm the democratic process. ...

[22] ... The Attorney General states that the objective of the legislation is to promote fair elections.

[23] In more concrete terms, the limits are purported to further three objectives: first, to favour equality, by preventing those with greater means from dominating electoral debate; second, to foster informed citizenship, by ensuring that some positions are not drowned out by others (this is related to the right to participate in the political process by casting an informed vote); third, to enhance public confidence by ensuring equality, a better informed citizenship and fostering the appearance and reality of fairness in the democratic process.

[24] These are worthy social purposes, endorsed as pressing and substantial by this Court in *Libman*. ...

[29] The Attorney General has offered no evidence to support a connection between the limits on citizen spending and electoral fairness. However, reason or logic may establish the requisite causal link; see *Sharpe* [*R. v.*, [2001] 1 S.C.R. 45, 2001 SCC 2]; *R. v. Butler*, [1992] 1 S.C.R. 452 . In *Thomson Newspapers* [*Co. v. Canada (Attorney General)*, [1998] 1 S.C.R. 877], the Court accepted as reasonable the conclusion that polls exert significant influence on the electoral process and individual electoral choice. More to the point, in *Libman*,

supra, the Court concluded that electoral spending limits are rationally connected to the objective of fair elections. While some of the evidence on which this conclusion was based has since been discredited, the conclusion that limits may in theory further electoral fairness is difficult to gainsay.

[30] Nevertheless, the supposition that uncontrolled spending could favour the messages of wealthier citizens or adversely affect the ability of less wealthy citizens to become informed on electoral issues is not irrational, particularly in a regime where party spending is limited. It follows that spending limits may, at least in principle, promote electoral fairness. ...

[32] ... "The impairment must be 'minimal,' that is, the law must be carefully tailored so that rights are impaired no more than necessary": *RJR-MacDonald Inc. v. Canada (Attorney General)*, [1995] 3 S.C.R. 199, at para. 160. ...

[34] ... The Attorney General presented no evidence that wealthier Canadians—alone or in concert—will dominate political debate during the electoral period absent limits. It offered only the hypothetical possibility that, without limits on citizen spending, problems could arise. ... This minimizes the Attorney General's assertions of necessity and lends credence to the argument that the legislation is an overreaction to a non-existent problem.

[35] On the other side of the equation, the infringement on the right is severe. We earlier reviewed the stringency of the limits. They prevent citizens from effectively communicating with their fellow citizens on election issues during a campaign. Any communication beyond the local level is effectively rendered impossible, and even at that level is seriously curtailed. The spending limits do not allow citizens to express themselves through mail-outs within certain ridings, radio and television media, nor the national press. Citizens are limited to 1.3 percent of the expenditures of registered political parties. This is significantly lower than other countries that have also imposed citizen spending limits. It is not an exaggeration to say that the limits imposed on citizens amount to a virtual ban on their participation in political debate during the election period. In actuality, the only space left in the marketplace of ideas is for political parties and their candidates. The right of each citizen to have her voice heard, so vaunted in *Figueroa* [*v. Canada (Attorney General)*, [2003] 1 S.C.R. 912, 2003 SCC 37], is effectively negated unless the citizen is able or willing to speak through a political party.

[36] On this point, this case is indistinguishable from *Libman, supra,* where the Court held that the spending limits imposed on citizens in the course of a referendum campaign did not satisfy the requirement of minimal impairment. ...

[37] In *Libman, supra,* at para. 63, the Court stated that "[i]t can be seen from the evidence that the legislature went

to considerable lengths, in good faith, in order to adopt means that would be as non-intrusive as possible while at the same time respecting the objective it had set." Here, too, Parliament's good faith is advanced, said to be evidenced by the ongoing *dialogue* with the courts as to where the limits should be set. But as in *Libman,* good faith cannot remedy an impairment of the right to freedom of expression.

[38] There is no demonstration that limits this draconian are required to meet the perceived dangers of inequality, an uninformed electorate and the public perception that the system is unfair. On the contrary, the measures may themselves exacerbate these dangers. Citizens who cannot effectively communicate with others on electoral issues may feel they are being treated unequally compared to citizens who speak through political parties. The absence of their messages may result in the public being less well informed than it would otherwise be. And a process that bans citizens from effective participation in the electoral debate during an election campaign may well be perceived as unfair. These fears may be hypothetical, but no more so than the fears conjured by the Attorney General in support of the infringement.

[39] This is not to suggest that election spending limits are never permissible. On the contrary, this Court in *Libman* has recognized that they are an acceptable, even desirable, tool to ensure fairness and faith in the electoral process. Limits that permit citizens to conduct effective and persuasive communication with their fellow citizens might well meet the minimum impairment test. The problem here is that the draconian nature of the infringement—to effectively deprive all those who do not or cannot speak through political parties of their voice during an election period—overshoots the perceived danger. Even recognizing that "[t]he tailoring process seldom admits of perfection" (*RJR-MacDonald, supra,* at para. 160), and according Parliament a healthy measure of deference, we are left with the fact that nothing in the evidence suggests that a virtual ban on citizen communication through effective advertising is required to avoid the hypothetical evils of inequality, a misinformed public and loss of public confidence in the system. ...

[40] The same logic that leads to the conclusion that the Attorney General has not established that the infringement minimally impairs the citizen's right of free speech applies equally to the final stage of the proportionality analysis, which asks us to weigh the benefits conferred by the infringement against the harm it may occasion.

[41] Given the unproven and speculative nature of the danger the limits are said to address, the possible benefits conferred by the law are illusory. ...

[42] Having had the advantage of reviewing the reasons of Bastarache J., we believe it is important to make three

observations. First, whether or not citizens dispose of sufficient funds to meet or exceed the existing spending limits is irrelevant. What is important is that citizens have the capacity, should they so choose, to exercise their right to free political speech. The spending limits as they currently stand do not allow this. Instead, they have a chilling effect on political speech, forcing citizens into a Hobson's choice between not expressing themselves at all or having their voice reduced to a mere whisper. Faced with such options, citizens could not be faulted for choosing the former.

[43] Second, it is important to recognize that the spending limits do not constrain the right of only a few citizens to speak. They constrain the political speech of all Canadians, be they of superior or modest means. Whether it is a citizen incurring expenditures of $3001 for leafleting in her riding or a group of citizens pooling 1501 individual contributions of $100 to run a national advertising campaign, the *Charter* protects the right to free political speech.

[44] Finally, even it *were* true that spending limits constrained the political speech rights of only a few citizens, it would be no answer to say, as suggests Bastarache J., at para. 112, that few citizens can afford to spend more than the limits anyway. This amounts to saying that even if the breach of s. 2(*b*) is not justified, it does not matter because it affects only a few people. *Charter* breaches cannot be justified on this basis. Moreover, one may question the premise that only a few people are affected by the spending limits. Indeed, if so few can afford to spend more than the existing limits, why, one may ask, are they needed? ...

The judgment of Iacobucci, Bastarache, Arbour, LeBel, Deschamps, and Fish JJ. was delivered by

BASTARACHE J.: ...

[75] The central issue at this stage of the analysis is the nature and sufficiency of the evidence required for the Attorney General to demonstrate that the limits imposed on freedom of expression are reasonable and justifiable in a free and democratic society. The Attorney General of Canada alleges that the lower courts erred in requiring scientific proof that harm had actually occurred and, specifically, by requiring conclusive proof that third party advertising influences voters and election outcomes, rendering them unfair. ...

[77] The legislature is not required to provide scientific proof based on concrete evidence of the problem it seeks to address in every case. Where the court is faced with inconclusive or competing social science evidence relating the harm to the legislature's measures, the court may rely on a reasoned apprehension of that harm. ...

[86] The Attorney General of Canada argues that although the impugned provisions limit the political expression of some, the provisions enhance the political expression of others. This Court explored this dichotomy in *Libman, supra*, at para. 61:

> ... the legislature's objective, namely to enhance the exercise of the right to vote, must be borne in mind. Thus, while the impugned provisions do in a way restrict one of the most basic forms of expression, namely political expression, *the legislature must be accorded a certain deference to enable it to arbitrate between the democratic values of freedom of expression and referendum fairness.* The latter is related to the very values the Canadian *Charter* seeks to protect, in particular the political equality of citizens that is at the heart of a free and democratic society. *The impugned provisions impose a balance between the financial resources available to the proponents of each option* in order to ensure that the vote by the people will be free and informed and that the discourse of each option can be heard. *To attain this objective, the legislature had to try to strike a balance between absolute freedom of individual expression and equality among the different expressions for the benefit of all. From this point of view, the impugned provisions are therefore not purely restrictive of freedom of expression. Their primary purpose is to promote political expression by ensuring an equal dissemination of points of view and thereby truly respecting democratic traditions.* [Emphasis added.]

Further, by limiting political expression, the spending limits bring greater balance to the political discourse and allow for more meaningful participation in the electoral process. Thus, the provisions also enhance a second *Charter* right, the right to vote.

[87] Under the egalitarian model of elections, Parliament must balance the rights and privileges of the participants in the electoral process: candidates, political parties, third parties and voters. Advertising expense limits may restrict free expression to ensure that participants are able to meaningfully participate in the electoral process. For candidates, political parties and third parties, meaningful participation means the ability to inform voters of their position. For voters, meaningful participation means the ability to hear and weigh many points of view. The difficulties of striking this balance are evident. Given the right of Parliament to choose Canada's electoral model and the nuances inherent in implementing this model, the Court must approach the justification analysis with deference. The lower courts erred in failing to do so (Paperny J.A., at para. 135). In the end, the electoral system, which regulates many aspects of an election, including its duration and the control and reimbursement of expenses, reflects a political choice, the details of which are better left to Parliament.

[88] On balance, the contextual factors favour a deferential approach to Parliament in determining whether the third party advertising expense limits are demonstrably justified in a free and democratic society. Given the difficulties in measuring this harm, a reasoned apprehension that the absence of third party election advertising limits will lead to electoral unfairness is sufficient. ...

[91] The overarching objective of the third party election advertising limits is electoral fairness. Equality in the political discourse promotes electoral fairness and is achieved, in part, by restricting the participation of those who have access to significant financial resources. The more voices that have access to the political discourse, the more voters will be empowered to exercise their right in a meaningful and informed manner. Canadians understandably have greater confidence in an electoral system which ultimately encourages increased participation.

[92] For the purpose of the s. 1 analysis, however, "it is desirable to state the purpose of the limiting provision as precisely and specifically as possible so as to provide a clear framework for evaluating its importance, and the precision with which the means have been crafted to fulfil that objective"; see *Thomson Newspapers*, at para. 98. More narrowly characterized, the objectives of the third party election advertising scheme are threefold: first, to promote equality in the political discourse; second, to protect the integrity of the financing regime applicable to candidates and parties; and third, to ensure that voters have confidence in the electoral process. ...

[Keeping in mind that it is not necessary "to provide evidence of actual harm to demonstrate that each objective is pressing and substantial," Justice Bastarache concluded that all three objectives do indeed fulfill this requirement.]

[104] At this stage of the analysis, the Attorney General "must show a causal connection between the infringement and the benefit sought on the basis of reason or logic"; see *RJR-MacDonald, supra*, at para. 153. The lower courts erred by demanding too stringent a level of proof, in essence, by requiring the Attorney General to establish an empirical connection between third party spending limits and the objectives of s. 350. There is sufficient evidence establishing a rational connection between third party advertising expense limits and promoting equality in the political discourse, protecting the integrity of the financing regime applicable to candidates and parties, and maintaining confidence in the electoral process.

[105] To establish that third party advertising expense limits promote equality in the political discourse, the Attorney General must establish, first, that political advertising influences voters, and second, that in the absence of regulation some voices could dominate and, in effect, drown others out. ...

[106] ... That political advertising influences voters accords with logic and reason. Surely, political parties, candidates, interest groups and corporations for that matter would not spend a significant amount of money on advertising if it was ineffective. Indeed, advertising is the primary expenditure of candidates and political parties.

[107] Where advertising influences the electorate, and those who have access to significant financial resources are able to purchase an unlimited amount of advertising, it follows that they will be able to dominate the electoral discourse to the detriment of others, both speakers and listeners. An upper limit on the amount that third parties can dedicate to political advertising curtails their ability to dominate the electoral debate. Thus, third party advertising expense limits are rationally connected to promoting equality in the political discourse. ...

[108] Third party advertising can directly support a particular candidate or political party. Third party advertising can also indirectly support a candidate or political party by taking a position on an issue associated with that candidate or political party. In effect, third party advertising can create an imbalance between the financial resources of each candidate or political party; see *Libman, supra*, at para. 44. For candidate and political party spending limits to be truly effective, the advertising expenses of third parties must also be limited. Indeed, the Lortie Commission concluded that the electoral financing regime would be destroyed if third party advertising was not limited concomitantly with candidate and political party spending (Berger J.A., dissenting, at para. 261). The Commission explained, at p. 327 of the Lortie Report:

> If individuals or groups were permitted to run parallel campaigns augmenting the spending of certain candidates or parties, those candidates or parties would have an unfair advantage over others not similarly supported. At the same time, candidates or parties who were the target of spending by individuals or groups opposed to their election would be put at a disadvantage compared with those who were not targeted. Should such activity become widespread, the purpose of the legislation would be destroyed, the reasonably equal opportunity the legislation seeks to establish would vanish, and the overall goal of restricting the role of money in unfairly influencing election outcomes would be defeated.

Thus, limiting third party advertising expenses is rationally connected with preserving the integrity of the financing regime set for candidates and parties.

[109] Limits on third party advertising expenses foster confidence in the electoral process in three ways. The limits

address the perception that candidates and political parties can circumvent their spending limits through the creation of *special interest groups*. The limits also prevent the possibility that the wealthy can dominate the electoral discourse and dictate the outcome of elections. Finally, the limits assist in preventing overall advertising expenses from escalating. Thus, third party advertising expense limits advance the perception that access to the electoral discourse does not require wealth to be competitive with other electoral participants. Canadians, in turn, perceive the electoral process as substantively fair as it provides for a reasonable degree of equality between citizens who wish to participate in that process. ...

[110] To be reasonable and demonstrably justified, the impugned measures must impair the infringed right or freedom as little as possible. The oft-cited quote from *RJR-MacDonald*, *supra*, at para. 160, sets out the appropriate standard:

> The impairment must be "minimal," that is, the law must be carefully tailored so that rights are impaired no more than necessary. The tailoring process seldom admits of perfection and the courts must accord some leeway to the legislator. If the law falls within a range of reasonable alternatives, the courts will not find it overbroad merely because they can conceive of an alternative which might better tailor objective to infringement.

Thus, the impugned measures need not be the least impairing option. ...

[112] The Chief Justice and Major J. assert that short of spending well over $150,000 nationally and $3,000 in a given electoral district, citizens cannot effectively communicate their views on election issues to their fellow citizens (para. 9). Respectfully, this ignores the fact that third party advertising is not restricted prior to the commencement of the election period. Outside this time, the limits on third party intervention in political life do not exist. Any group or individual may freely spend money or advertise to make its views known or to persuade others. In fact, many of these groups are not formed for the purpose of an election but are already organized and have a continued presence, mandate and political view which they promote. Many groups and individuals will reinforce their message during an electoral campaign.

[113] The nature of Canada's political system must be considered when deciding whether individuals and groups who engage in election advertising will be affected unduly by the limits set out in s. 350. First, as the Court discussed in *Figueroa*, there are few obstacles for individuals to join existing political parties or to create their own parties to facilitate individual participation in elections. Still, some will participate outside the party affiliations; this explains why the

existence of multiple organizations and parties of varying sizes requires Parliament to balance their participation during the election period. Further, the reality in Canada is that regardless of the spending limits in the Act, the vast majority of Canadian citizens simply cannot spend $150,000 nationally or $3,000 in a given electoral district. What prevents most citizens from effectively exercising their right of political free speech as defined by the Chief Justice and Major J. is a lack of means, not legislative restrictions. Contrary to what the Chief Justice and Major J. say at para. 44, I do not suggest that since the breach of s. 2(*b*) only affects a few people, it is therefore justifiable. As discussed, the objective is to ensure the political discourse is not dominated by those who have greater resources. The proper focus is on protecting the right to meaningful participation of the entire electorate. Let me now examine in more detail how this is achieved.

[114] Section 350 minimally impairs the right to free expression. The definition of "election advertising" in s. 319 only applies to advertising that is associated with a candidate or party. Where an issue is not associated with a candidate or political party, third parties may partake in an unlimited advertising campaign.

[115] The $3,000 limit per electoral district and $150,000 national limit allow for meaningful participation in the electoral process while respecting the right to free expression. Why? First, because the limits established in s. 350 allow third parties to advertise in a limited way in some expensive forms of media such as television, newspaper and radio. But, more importantly, the limits are high enough to allow third parties to engage in a significant amount of low cost forms of advertising such as computer generated posters or leaflets or the creation of a 1-800 number. In addition, the definition of "election advertising" in s. 319 does not apply to many forms of communication such as editorials, debates, speeches, interviews, columns, letters, commentary, the news and the Internet which constitute highly effective means of conveying information. Thus, as the trial judge concluded, at para. 78, the limits allow for "modest, national, informational campaigns and reasonable electoral district informational campaigns."

[116] Second, the limits set out in s. 350 are justifiably lower than the candidate and political party advertising limits, as recommended by the Lortie Commission. As this Court explained in *Libman*, *supra*, at paras. 49-50, the third party limit must be low enough to ensure that a particular candidate who is targeted by a third party has sufficient resources to respond. It cannot be forgotten that small political parties, who play an equally important role in the electoral process, may be easily overwhelmed by a third party having access to significant financial resources. The limits must also account for the fact that third parties generally have lower overall

expenses than candidates and political parties. The limits must also appreciate that third parties tend to focus on one issue and may therefore achieve their objective less expensively. Thus, the limits seek to preserve a balance between the resources available to candidates and parties taking part in an election and those resources that might be available to third parties during this period. Professor Fletcher confirmed (in evidence) that the limits set out in s. 350 achieve this goal.

[117] The Chief Justice and Major J. rely on the higher ratio of advertising spending limits for citizens to political parties in Britain as compared to Canada as evidence that the Canadian spending limits are too low (para. 8). In my view, this comparison is inappropriate. The British provisions apply to different categories of advertising and apply over different time periods.

[118] Certainly, one can conceive of less impairing limits. Indeed, any limit greater than $150,000 would be less impairing. Nevertheless, s. 350 satisfies this stage of the *Oakes* analysis. The limits allow third parties to inform the electorate of their message in a manner that will not overwhelm candidates, political parties or other third parties. The limits preclude the voices of the wealthy from dominating the political discourse, thereby allowing more voices to be heard. The limits allow for meaningful participation in the electoral process and encourage informed voting. The limits promote a free and democratic society. ...

[119] The final stage of the *Oakes* analysis requires the Court to weigh the deleterious effects against the salutary effects.

[120] Section 350 has several salutary effects. It enhances equality in the political discourse. By ensuring that affluent

groups or individuals do not dominate the political discourse, s. 350 promotes the political expression of those who are less affluent or less capable of obtaining access to significant financial resources and ensures that candidates and political parties who are subject to spending limits are not overwhelmed by third party advertising. Section 350 also protects the integrity of the candidate and political party spending limits by ensuring that these limits are not circumvented through the creation of phony third parties. Finally, s. 350 promotes fairness and accessibility in the electoral system and consequently increases Canadians' confidence in it. The deleterious effect of s. 350 is that the spending limits do not allow third parties to engage in unlimited political expression. That is, third parties are permitted to engage in informational but not necessarily persuasive campaigns, especially when acting alone. When weighed against the salutary effects of the legislation, the limits must be upheld. As the Court explained in *Libman, supra*, at para. 84:

> [P]rotecting the fairness of referendum campaigns is a laudable objective that will *necessarily* involve certain restrictions on freedom of expression. *Freedom of political expression, so dear to our democratic tradition, would lose much value if it could only be exercised in a context in which the economic power of the most affluent members of society constituted the ultimate guidepost of our political choices.* Nor would it be much better served by a system that undermined the confidence of citizens in the referendum process. [First emphasis in original; second emphasis added.]

Accordingly, s. 350 should be upheld as a demonstrably justified limit in a free and democratic society.

D. LEGAL RIGHTS

 **R v. Oakes, 1986**

The Charter has "judicialized politics and politicized the judiciary" in part because interpretive controversies over the meaning of vaguely formulated rights are political as well as legal controversies, with policy consequences extending well beyond the confines of the particular case. Giving concrete meaning to broad constitutional standards, however, does not exhaust the political aspects of the judicial task. If a right, having been defined, is found to be violated, the court must ask whether the violation is saved by section 1 of the Charter, which permits such "reasonable limits prescribed by law as are demonstrably justified in a free and democratic society." This question makes the political nature of Charter jurisprudence even more transparent; it is clearly not a traditionally legal question, as the Supreme Court has itself admitted. Despite the ritual judicial denial of the claim that constitutional review involves second-guessing the wisdom of legislative choices, many observers think that this is precisely what section 1 requires.

In the *Oakes* case, the Supreme Court attempted a comprehensive articulation of the standards it would use in addressing the section 1 question. The case involved a "reverse onus" provision in the *Narcotic Control Act*, under which someone found guilty of "possession" was deemed also to be guilty of "trafficking" unless he could prove otherwise. Having been found guilty of the first charge, Oakes claimed that the reverse onus violated his section 11(*d*) right to be presumed innocent (of trafficking) until proven guilty. The court agreed, and thereby set aside the established interpretation of a similar guarantee of the presumption of innocence in the *Canadian Bill of Rights*. The fact that there might be a "rational connection" between the "basic fact" (possession) and the "presumed fact" (trafficking) was considered irrelevant to establishing the violation because "a basic fact may rationally tend to prove a presumed fact, but not prove its existence beyond a reasonable doubt," as required in criminal cases. Justice Dickson was careful to add, however, that such a rational connection could be used as part of a section 1 defence.

To establish a section 1 defence, the onus is on the state to demonstrate to a "very high degree of probability" that the Charter violation is justified by a "pressing and substantial" objective, and that the means used are "proportional" to that objective. Proportional means have three characteristics: (1) they are not arbitrary and thus actually achieve the objective—that is, they are "rationally connected" to the objective; (2) they impair the right as little as possible; and (3) their costs are proportional to their benefits—that is, "the more severe the deleterious effects, the more [pressing and substantial] the objective must be."

The court readily conceded that controlling drug trafficking was a sufficiently compelling purpose to justify a violation of Charter rights. The means, however, were not proportional to this end because the reverse onus applied to all cases of possession and there was no "rational connection" between trafficking and possession of small quantities of illegal drugs.

The court's deference regarding the objective of the policy characterizes most, though not all, forays by the court into section 1 analysis. This is perhaps not surprising. Challenging the very purpose of a policy would most obviously place the court in a naked political confrontation with the legislature. On the other hand, if the court accepts the purpose of the law, and limits its scrutiny to the means chosen to achieve that purpose, it might be easier to sustain the claim that it is not second-guessing the wisdom of legislative policy.[1] In *Oakes*, for example, the court's judgment may be read as saying no more than that the legislature had been somewhat insensitive or careless in determining how to achieve its legitimate end. Indeed, having conceded the legitimacy of some violation of Charter rights to control trafficking, the court implied that more carefully tailored and hence less intrusive means were possible—perhaps a reverse onus that applied only to possession of sufficiently "large" quantities.

As subsequent cases show,[2] however, the court cannot consistently hide the political nature of section 1 jurisprudence by concentrating on the question of means. To reject legislative means, the court must compare them, more or less explicitly, to "better" alternatives. But political controversy is as often about means as it is about ends, and the legislative choice of means may be carefully, rather than carelessly, deliberated. In such cases, some will consider the judicial evaluation of alternative means to be no less a matter of second-guessing policy wisdom than is the evaluation of objectives. ∼

Discussion Questions

1. Why did the court decide the same issue differently under the Bill of Rights? Why did it overrule the Bill of Rights precedent?

2. Suppose section 11(*d*) of the Charter simply protected the right of an accused to be tried "according to law in a fair and public hearing by an independent and impartial tribunal," without any explicit reference to the presumption of innocence. What difference, if any, would (should) this have made to the court's ruling?

3. Assess Chief Justice Dickson's reasons for concluding that the purpose of the challenged law was sufficiently pressing and substantial "to warrant overriding a constitutionally protected right or freedom in certain cases."

---

1 See Patrick Monahan, *Politics and the Constitution: The Charter, Federalism, and the Supreme Court of Canada* (Toronto: Carswell/Methuen, 1987) 67-68.

2 See, for example, the discussion of *R. v. Edwards Books and Art Ltd.*, [1986] 2 S.C.R. 713.

THE QUEEN v. DAVID EDWIN OAKES
[1986] 1 S.C.R. 103

Hearing: March 12, 1985; Judgment: February 28, 1986.

Present: Dickson C.J. and Estey, McIntyre, Chouinard, Lamer, Wilson, and Le Dain JJ.

The judgment of Dickson C.J., Chouinard, Lamer, Wilson, and Le Dain JJ. was delivered by

[1] **DICKSON C.J.:** This appeal concerns the constitutionality of s. 8 of the *Narcotic Control Act*, R.S.C. 1970, c. N-1. The section provides, in brief, that if the Court finds the accused in possession of a narcotic, he is presumed to be in possession for the purpose of trafficking. Unless the accused can establish the contrary, he must be convicted of trafficking. The Ontario Court of Appeal held that this provision constitutes a "reverse onus" clause and is unconstitutional because it violates one of the core values of our criminal justice system, the presumption of innocence, now entrenched in s. 11(*d*) of the *Canadian Charter of Rights and Freedoms*. The Crown has appealed. ...

[3] The respondent, David Edwin Oakes, was charged with unlawful possession of a narcotic for the purpose of trafficking, contrary to s. 4(2) of the *Narcotic Control Act*. He elected trial by magistrate without a jury. At trial, the Crown adduced evidence to establish that Mr. Oakes was found in possession of eight one gram vials of *cannabis* resin in the form of hashish oil. Upon a further search conducted at the police station, $619.45 was located. Mr. Oakes told the police that he had bought ten vials of hashish oil for $150 for his own use, and that the $619.45 was from a workers' compensation cheque. He elected not to call evidence as to possession of the narcotic. Pursuant to the procedural provisions of s. 8 of the *Narcotic Control Act*, the trial judge proceeded to make a finding that it was beyond a reasonable doubt that Mr. Oakes was in possession of the narcotic.

[4] Following this finding, Mr. Oakes brought a motion to challenge the constitutional validity of s. 8 of the *Narcotic Control Act*, which he maintained imposes a burden on an accused to prove that he or she was not in possession for the purpose of trafficking. He argued that s. 8 violates the presumption of innocence contained in s. 11(*d*) of the *Charter*. ...

[15] Before examining the presumption of innocence contained in s. 11(*d*) of the *Charter*, it is necessary to clarify the meaning of s. 8 of the *Narcotic Control Act*. The procedural steps contemplated by s. 8 were clearly outlined by Branca J.A. in *R. v. Babcock and Auld*.

[Justice Branca observed that the trial of an accused charged with trafficking was divided into two parts. First, the trial

"proceeds as if it was a prosecution ... on a simple charge of possession," with the burden of proof resting on the Crown. Second, if simple possession is proven, the onus shifts to the accused to prove that he was not in possession for the purposes of trafficking.]

[26] I conclude that s. 8 of the *Narcotic Control Act* contains a reverse onus provision imposing a legal burden on an accused to prove on a balance of probabilities that he or she was not in possession of a narcotic for the purpose of trafficking. It is therefore necessary to determine whether s. 8 of the *Narcotic Control Act* offends the right to be "presumed innocent until proven guilty" as guaranteed by s. 11(*d*) of the *Charter*. ...

[28] To interpret the meaning of s. 11(*d*), it is important to adopt a purposive approach. ... To identify the underlying purpose of the *Charter* right in question ... it is important to begin by understanding the cardinal values it embodies.

[29] The presumption of innocence is a hallowed principle lying at the very heart of criminal law. Although protected expressly in s. 11(*d*) of the *Charter*, the presumption of innocence is referable and integral to the general protection of life, liberty and security of the person contained in s. 7 of the *Charter* (see *Re B.C. Motor Vehicle Act* ...). The presumption of innocence protects the fundamental liberty and human dignity of any and every person accused by the State of criminal conduct. An individual charged with a criminal offence faces grave social and personal consequences, including potential loss of physical liberty, subjection to social stigma and ostracism from the community, as well as other social, psychological and economic harms. In light of the gravity of these consequences, the presumption of innocence is crucial. It ensures that until the State proves an accused's guilt beyond all reasonable doubt, he or she is innocent. This is essential in a society committed to fairness and social justice. The presumption of innocence confirms our faith in humankind; it reflects our belief that individuals are decent and law-abiding members of the community until proven otherwise.

[30] The presumption of innocence has enjoyed long-standing recognition at common law. In the leading case, *Woolmington v. Director of Public Prosecutions*, [1935] A.C. 462 (H.L.), Viscount Sankey wrote at pp. 481-82:

Throughout the web of the English Criminal Law one golden thread is always to be seen, that it is the duty of the prosecution to prove the prisoner's guilt subject to what I have already said as to the defence of insanity and subject also to any statutory exception. If, at the end of and on the whole of the case, there is a reasonable doubt, created by the evidence given by either the prosecution or the prisoner, as to whether the prisoner killed the deceased with a malicious intention, the prosecution has not made out the case and the prisoner is entitled to an acquittal. No matter what the charge or where the trial, the principle that the prosecution must prove the guilt of the prisoner is part of the common law of England and no attempt to whittle it down can be entertained. ...

[32] In light of the above, the right to be presumed innocent until proven guilty requires that s. 11(*d*) have, at a minimum, the following content. First, an individual must be proven guilty beyond a reasonable doubt. Second, it is the State which must bear the burden of proof. ... Third, criminal prosecutions must be carried out in accordance with lawful procedures and fairness. The latter part of s. 11(*d*), which requires the proof of guilt "according to law in a fair and public hearing by an independent and impartial tribunal," underlines the importance of this procedural requirement. ...

[33] Having considered the general meaning of the presumption of innocence, it is now, I think, desirable to review briefly the authorities on reverse onus clauses in Canada and other jurisdictions. ...

[34] Section 2(*f*) of the *Canadian Bill of Rights*, which safeguards the presumption of innocence, provides:

> ... no law of Canada shall be construed or applied so as to ...
>
> (f) deprive a person charged with a criminal offence of the right to be presumed innocent until proved guilty according to law in a fair and public hearing by an independent and impartial tribunal. ...

The wording of this section closely parallels that of s. 11(*d*). For this reason, one of the Crown's primary contentions is that the *Canadian Bill of Rights* jurisprudence should be determinative of the outcome of the present appeal.

[35] The leading case decided under s. 2(*f*) of the *Canadian Bill of Rights* and relied on by the Crown, is *R. v. Appleby* [[1972] S.C.R. 303], *supra*. In that case, the accused had challenged s. 224A(1)(*d*) (now s. 237(1)(*a*)) of the *Criminal Code*, R.S.C. 1970, c. C-34, which imposes a burden upon an accused to prove that he or she, though occupying the driver's seat, did not enter the vehicle for the purpose of setting it in motion and did not, therefore, have care and control. This Court rejected the arguments of the accused that s. 2(*f*) had been violated; it relied on the *Woolmington* case which held that the presumption of innocence was subject to "statutory exceptions." As Ritchie J. stated in his judgment for the majority at pp. 315-16:

> It seems to me, therefore, that if Woolmington's case is to be accepted, the words "presumed innocent until proved guilty according to law ..." as they appear in s. 2(*f*) of the

Bill of Rights, must be taken to envisage a law which recognizes the existence of statutory exceptions reversing the onus of proof with respect to one or more ingredients of an offence in cases where certain specific facts have been proved by the Crown in relation to such ingredients. ...

[38] Although there are important lessons to be learned from the *Canadian Bill of Rights* jurisprudence, it does not constitute binding authority in relation to the constitutional interpretation of the *Charter*. As this Court held in *R. v. Big M Drug Mart Ltd.* [[1985] 1 S.C.R. 295], *supra*, the *Charter*, as a constitutional document, is fundamentally different from the statutory *Canadian Bill of Rights*, which was interpreted as simply recognizing and declaring existing rights. (See also *Singh v. Minister of Employment and Immigration*, [1985] 1 S.C.R. 177 *per* Wilson J.; *R. v. Therens*, [1985] 1 S.C.R. 613, *per* Le Dain J.). ...

[39] With this in mind, one cannot but question the appropriateness of reading into the phrase "according to law" in s. 11(*d*) of the *Charter* the statutory exceptions acknowledged in *Woolmington* and in *Appleby*. The *Woolmington* case was decided in the context of a legal system with no constitutionally entrenched human rights document. In Canada, we have tempered parliamentary supremacy by entrenching important rights and freedoms in the Constitution. Viscount Sankey's statutory exception proviso is clearly not applicable in this context and would subvert the very purpose of the entrenchment of the presumption of innocence in the *Charter*. I do not, therefore, feel constrained in this case by the interpretation of s. 2(*f*) of the *Canadian Bill of Rights* presented in the majority judgment in *Appleby*. Section 8 of the *Narcotic Control Act* is not rendered constitutionally valid simply by virtue of the fact that it is a statutory provision. ...

[59] As we have seen, the potential for a rational connection between the basic fact and the presumed fact to justify a reverse onus provision has been elaborated in some of the cases discussed above and is now known as the "rational connection test." In the context of s. 11(*d*), however, the following question arises: if we apply the rational connection test to the consideration of whether s. 11(*d*) has been violated, are we adequately protecting the constitutional principle of the presumption of innocence? ... A basic fact may rationally tend to prove a presumed fact, but not prove its existence beyond a reasonable doubt. An accused person could thereby be convicted despite the presence of a reasonable doubt. This would violate the presumption of innocence.

[60] I should add that this questioning of the constitutionality of the "rational connection test" as a guide to interpreting s. 11(*d*) does not minimize its importance. The appropriate stage for invoking the rational connection test, however, is

under s. 1 of the *Charter*. This consideration did not arise under the *Canadian Bill of Rights* because of the absence of an equivalent to s. 1. At the Court of Appeal level in the present case, Martin J.A. sought to combine the analysis of s. 11(*d*) and s. 1 to overcome the limitations of the *Canadian Bill of Rights* jurisprudence. To my mind, it is highly desirable to keep s. 1 and s. 11(*d*) analytically distinct. Separating the analysis into two components is consistent with the approach this Court has taken to the *Charter* to date. ...

[61] To return to s. 8 of the *Narcotic Control Act*, I am in no doubt whatsoever that it violates s. 11(*d*) of the *Charter* by requiring the accused to prove on a balance of probabilities that he was not in possession of the narcotic for the purpose of trafficking. Mr. Oakes is compelled by s. 8 to prove he is *not* guilty of the offence of trafficking. He is thus denied his right to be presumed innocent and subjected to the potential penalty of life imprisonment unless he can rebut the presumption. This is radically and fundamentally inconsistent with the societal values of human dignity and liberty which we espouse, and is directly contrary to the presumption of innocence enshrined in s. 11(*d*). Let us turn now to s. 1 of the *Charter*. ...

[63] It is important to observe at the outset that s. 1 has two functions: first, it constitutionally guarantees the rights and freedoms set out in the provisions which follow; and, second, it states explicitly the exclusive justificatory criteria (outside of s. 33 of the *Constitution Act, 1982*) against which limitations on those rights and freedoms must be measured. Accordingly, any s. 1 inquiry must be premised on an understanding that the impugned limit violates constitutional rights and freedoms—rights and freedoms which are part of the supreme law of Canada. ...

[64] A second contextual element of interpretation of s. 1 is provided by the words "free and democratic society." Inclusion of these words as the final standard of justification for limits on rights and freedoms refers the Court to the very purpose for which the *Charter* was originally entrenched in the Constitution: Canadian society is to be free and democratic. The Court must be guided by the values and principles essential to a free and democratic society which I believe embody, to name but a few, respect for the inherent dignity of the human person, commitment to social justice and equality, accommodation of a wide variety of beliefs, respect for cultural and group identity, and faith in social and political institutions which enhance the participation of individuals and groups in society. The underlying values and principles of a free and democratic society are the genesis of the rights and freedoms guaranteed by the *Charter* and the ultimate standard against which a limit on a right or freedom must be shown, despite its effect, to be reasonable and demonstrably justified.

[65] The rights and freedoms guaranteed by the *Charter* are not, however, absolute. It may become necessary to limit rights and freedoms in circumstances where their exercise would be inimical to the realization of collective goals of fundamental importance. For this reason, s. 1 provides criteria of justification for limits on the rights and freedoms guaranteed by the *Charter*. These criteria impose a stringent standard of justification, especially when understood in terms of the two contextual considerations discussed above, namely, the violation of a constitutionally guaranteed right or freedom and the fundamental principles of a free and democratic society.

[66] The onus of proving that a limit on a right or freedom guaranteed by the *Charter* is reasonable and demonstrably justified in a free and democratic society rests upon the party seeking to uphold the limitation. It is clear from the text of s. 1 that limits on the rights and freedoms enumerated in the *Charter* are exceptions to their general guarantee. The presumption is that the rights and freedoms are guaranteed unless the party invoking s. 1 can bring itself within the exceptional criteria which justify their being limited. This is further substantiated by the use of the word "demonstrably" which clearly indicates that the onus of justification is on the party seeking to limit. ...

[67] The standard of proof under s. 1 is the civil standard, namely, proof by a preponderance of probability. The alternative criminal standard, proof beyond a reasonable doubt, would, in my view, be unduly onerous on the party seeking to limit. Concepts such as "reasonableness," "justifiability" and "free and democratic society" are simply not amenable to such a standard. Nevertheless, the preponderance of probability test must be applied rigorously. Indeed, the phrase "demonstrably justified" in s. 1 of the *Charter* supports this conclusion. Within the broad category of the civil standard, there exist different degrees of probability depending on the nature of the case. ...

[68] Having regard to the fact that s. 1 is being invoked for the purpose of justifying a violation of the constitutional rights and freedoms the *Charter* was designed to protect, a very high degree of probability will be, in the words of Lord Denning, "commensurate with the occasion." Where evidence is required in order to prove the constituent elements of a s. 1 inquiry, and this will generally be the case, it should be cogent and persuasive and make clear to the Court the consequences of imposing or not imposing the limit. ... A court will also need to know what alternative measures for implementing the objective were available to the legislators when they made their decisions. I should add, however, that there may be cases where certain elements of the s. 1 analysis are obvious or self-evident.

[69] To establish that a limit is reasonable and demonstrably justified in a free and democratic society, two central

criteria must be satisfied. First, the objective, which the measures responsible for a limit on a *Charter* right or freedom are designed to serve, must be "of sufficient importance to warrant overriding a constitutionally protected right or freedom": *R. v. Big M Drug Mart Ltd., supra*, at p. 352. The standard must be high in order to ensure that objectives which are trivial or discordant with the principles integral to a free and democratic society do not gain s. 1 protection. It is necessary, at a minimum, that an objective relate to concerns which are pressing and substantial in a free and democratic society before it can be characterized as sufficiently important.

[70] Second, once a sufficiently significant objective is recognized, then the party invoking s. 1 must show that the means chosen are reasonable and demonstrably justified. This involves "a form of proportionality test": *R. v. Big M Drug Mart Ltd., supra*, at p. 352. Although the nature of the proportionality test will vary depending on the circumstances, in each case courts will be required to balance the interests of society with those of individuals and groups. There are, in my view, three important components of a proportionality test. First, the measures adopted must be carefully designed to achieve the objective in question. They must not be arbitrary, unfair or based on irrational considerations. In short, they must be rationally connected to the objective. Second, the means, even if rationally connected to the objective in this first sense, should impair "as little as possible" the right or freedom in question: *R. v. Big M Drug Mart Ltd., supra*, at p. 352. Third, there must be a proportionality between the *effects* of the measures which are responsible for limiting the *Charter* right or freedom, and the objective which has been identified as of "sufficient importance."

[71] With respect to the third component, it is clear that the general effect of any measure impugned under s. 1 will be the infringement of a right or freedom guaranteed by the *Charter*; this is the reason why resort to s. 1 is necessary. The inquiry into effects must, however, go further. A wide range of rights and freedoms are guaranteed by the *Charter*, and an almost infinite number of factual situations may arise in respect of these. Some limits on rights and freedoms protected by the *Charter* will be more serious than others in terms of the nature of the right or freedom violated, the extent of the violation, and the degree to which the measures which impose the limit trench upon the integral principles of a free and democratic society. Even if an objective is of sufficient importance, and the first two elements of the proportionality test are satisfied, it is still possible that, because of the severity of the deleterious effects of a measure on individuals or groups, the measure will not be justified by the purposes it is intended to serve. The more severe the deleterious effects of a measure, the more important the objective must be if the measure is to

be reasonable and demonstrably justified in a free and democratic society.

[72] Having outlined the general principles of a s. 1 inquiry, we must apply them to s. 8 of the *Narcotic Control Act*. Is the reverse onus provision in s. 8 a reasonable limit on the right to be presumed innocent until proven guilty beyond a reasonable doubt as can be demonstrably justified in a free and democratic society?

[73] The starting point for formulating a response to this question is, as stated above, the nature of Parliament's interest or objective which accounts for the passage of s. 8 of the *Narcotic Control Act*. According to the Crown, s. 8 of the *Narcotic Control Act* is aimed at curbing drug trafficking by facilitating the conviction of drug traffickers. In my opinion, Parliament's concern that drug trafficking be decreased can be characterized as substantial and pressing. The problem of drug trafficking has been increasing since the 1950s at which time there was already considerable concern. ... Throughout this period, numerous measures were adopted by free and democratic societies, at both the international and national levels. ...

[76] The objective of protecting our society from the grave ills associated with drug trafficking, is, in my view, one of sufficient importance to warrant overriding a constitutionally protected right or freedom in certain cases. Moreover, the degree of seriousness of drug trafficking makes its acknowledgement as a sufficiently important objective for the purposes of s. 1, to a large extent, self-evident. The first criterion of a s. 1 inquiry, therefore, has been satisfied by the Crown.

[77] The next stage of inquiry is a consideration of the means chosen by Parliament to achieve its objective. The means must be reasonable and demonstrably justified in a free and democratic society. As outlined above, this proportionality test should begin with a consideration of the rationality of the provision: is the reverse onus clause in s. 8 rationally related to the objective of curbing drug trafficking? At a minimum, this requires that s. 8 be internally rational; there must be a rational connection between the basic fact of possession and the presumed fact of possession for the purpose of trafficking. Otherwise, the reverse onus clause could give rise to unjustified and erroneous convictions for drug trafficking of persons guilty only of possession of narcotics.

[78] In my view, s. 8 does not survive this rational connection test. As Martin J.A. of the Ontario Court of Appeal concluded, possession of a small or negligible quantity of narcotics does not support the inference of trafficking. In other words, it would be irrational to infer that a person had an intent to traffic on the basis of his or her possession of a very small quantity of narcotics. The presumption required under s. 8 of the *Narcotic Control Act* is overinclusive and could lead to results in certain cases which would defy both

rationality and fairness. In light of the seriousness of the offence in question, which carries with it the possibility of imprisonment for life, I am further convinced that the first component of the proportionality test has not been satisfied by the Crown.

[79] Having concluded that s. 8 does not satisfy this first component of proportionality, it is unnecessary to consider the other two components. ...

[Justices Estey and McIntyre concurred in the reasons of Chief Justice Dickson with respect to the relationship of section 11(*d*) and section 1 of the *Charter*, but adopted the reasons of Justice Martin in the court below for the disposition of all other issues.]

R. v. Mills, 1999

Few Supreme Court rulings have provoked more conversation about the significant role that gender plays in legal rulings than Charter decisions dealing with rules of evidence in sexual assault trials, as is evident in *R. v. Mills* and *R. v Seaboyer.*[1]

In 1991 in *R. v. Seaboyer*, a majority of the court disagreed with how Parliament had reformed the rules of evidence in sexual assault trials. Before legislative reforms were introduced in 1982, the common law had permitted questioning about the prior sexual conduct of a complainant without proof of how this information was relevant to a specific issue in the trial. This form of questioning would often undermine the credibility of the woman who alleged that she had been sexually assaulted, by allowing inferences to be drawn that she was not to be believed and had likely consented to the alleged sexual assault. This legal tactic also had the effect of discouraging many women from pressing or pursuing claims that they had been sexually assaulted. The reform legislation prevented defence lawyers from cross-examining and leading evidence about a complainant's sexual conduct, with three exceptions: rebuttal evidence, evidence going to identity, and evidence relating to consent to sexual activity on the same occasion as the trial incident. The court was seriously divided about whether the excluded information undermines the Charter right to make a full answer and defence to the charge of sexual assault. However, the majority concluded that the impugned legislation had the potential to exclude otherwise admissible evidence that might be highly relevant to the defence.

The Supreme Court's ruling provoked widespread criticism from women's groups who worried that the ruling would preserve inappropriate stereotypes about women and sexual assault and that it would also discourage the reporting of sexual assault. The decision also generated broad public discussion about when, if ever, a woman's sexual history is relevant in the context of sexual assault trials. Initially, the federal government indicated that it would try to address the majority's concerns about the exclusionary rule. But after extensive lobbying by and consultation with women's groups, Kim Campbell, then minister of justice, interpreted the situation as an opportunity to fundamentally change the way the law deals with sexual assault, by addressing and defining consent in sexual relations.[2]

However, within a few years of this legislative response to *Seaboyer*, women's groups and those working with rape crisis centres became concerned about a new trend in sexual assault cases, where defence counsel tried to access a wide range of women's private medical and therapeutic records. Many interpreted these efforts as a way to undermine a sexual assault

---

1 [1991] 2 S.C.R. 577 (the case report for *Seaboyer* can be found in the instructor's supplements package).

2 For discussion about Parliament's response to both cases, see Janet L. Hiebert, *Charter Conflicts: What is Parliament's Role?*, ch. 5.

complainant's credibility and/or discourage sexual assault victims from pursuing criminal charges. No legislation was in place to govern whether or how this access should be granted. When the issue reached the Supreme Court, the justices divided 5-to-4 on the rules for governing the release of these records.[3] The majority established a relatively low standard for gaining access to these records, whereas the minority thought far more consideration should be given for what it characterized as the "pernicious role" that past evidential rules in the *Criminal Code* and the common law have played in the legal system. The government responded to the ruling by introducing legislation to clarify when and under what circumstances these private materials could be accessed. What was unusual about this legislative response was that rather than revise the legislation to correspond to the majority's ruling, the legislation instead reflected the minority's perspective on this issue. The legislation also included a preamble that emphasized the importance of equality and privacy as appropriate judicial considerations when determining whether access to therapeutic and private records can be obtained, and sought to remind judges that in the past courts have not given due regard to these rights.[4]

Parliament's legislative response was challenged and upheld in *R. v. Mills*. Despite the fact that Parliament had ignored the majority's approach to the issue in *R. v. O'Connor*, the Supreme Court backed down in *Mills*. The court ruled that despite Parliament's determination to legislate an approach that differs from the majority ruling, Parliament, nevertheless, was "scrupulously respectful of the requirements of the Charter." The court characterized this as an example of dialogue and stated that "the mere fact" that the legislation does not "mirror" the court's earlier ruling "does not render it unconstitutional." ～

Discussion Questions

1. Is the use of a legislative preamble an appropriate way for Parliament to clarify its position on how Charter considerations appropriately guide legislation?

2. Is the metaphor of dialogue a useful way to assess the legislative response to this ruling?

---

3   *R. v. O'Connor*, [1995] 4 S.C.R. 411.

4   Hiebert, *supra* note 2.

R. v. MILLS
[1999] 3 S.C.R. 668

Hearing: January 19, 1999; Judgment: November 25, 1999.

Present: Lamer C.J. and L'Heureux-Dubé, Gonthier, Cory,* McLachlin, Iacobucci, Major, Bastarache, and Binnie JJ.

Interveners: The Attorney General of Canada, the Attorney General for Ontario, the Attorney General of Quebec, the Attorney General of Nova Scotia, the Attorney General of Manitoba, the Attorney General of British Columbia, the Attorney General of Prince Edward Island, the Attorney General for Saskatchewan, the Canadian Mental Health Association, the Canadian Psychiatric Association, the Child and Adolescent Services Association, the Criminal Lawyers' Association (Ontario), the Association québécoise des avocats et avocates de la défense, the Women's Legal Education and Action Fund, the Canadian Civil Liberties Association, the Canadian Council of Criminal Defence Lawyers, the Alberta Association of Sexual Assault Centres, and the Sexual Assault Centre of Edmonton.

* Cory J. took no part in the judgment.

[1] **THE CHIEF JUSTICE** (dissenting in part): The issue in this appeal is whether Bill C-46 (now S.C. 1997, c. 30) strikes the appropriate constitutional balance between protecting the accused's right to a fair trial and the privacy and equality rights of complainants and witnesses when an accused seeks access to their confidential records in sexual assault proceedings. While I agree with McLachlin and Iacobucci JJ.'s finding that Bill C-46 complies with ss. 7 and 11(*d*) of the *Canadian Charter of Rights and Freedoms* as it applies to the production of records in the possession of third parties, I take a different view of the legislative regime's approach to records in the hands of the Crown. In my opinion, Bill C-46's treatment of records that form part of the case to meet tips the balance too heavily in favour of privacy to the detriment of the accused's right to make full answer and defence.

[2] As my colleagues have explained, s. 278.2(2) of the *Criminal Code*, R.S.C., 1985, c. C-46, extends the application of the legislative scheme for the production of therapeutic records to documents in the Crown's possession or control. If the complainant or witness expressly waives the protection of the legislation, then the records may be produced to the accused as at common law according to the principles in *R. v. Stinchcombe*, [1991] 3 S.C.R. 326.

[3] Absent waiver, however, Bill C-46 requires the accused to submit to the same two-stage procedure for production applicable to records held by third parties: disclosure to the trial judge and production to the accused. The first stage obliges the accused to establish that the record in the Crown's possession is "likely relevant to an issue at trial or to the competence of a witness to testify" (ss. 278.3(3)(*b*) and 278.5(1)(*b*)). The trial judge must also decide whether disclosure to the court is "necessary in the interests of justice" and consider the salutary and deleterious effects of production on the accused's right to make full answer and defence, and on the complainant's or witness's right to privacy and equality (s. 278.5(1)(*c*) and 278.5(2)). If the first step is satisfied, the second stage involves judicial inspection of the documents to determine whether and to what extent they should be produced to the accused (ss. 278.6 to 278.91).

[4] My colleagues observe that the majority in *R. v. O'Connor*, [1995] 4 S.C.R. 411, did not comment on the procedure applicable to the production of records which the Crown possesses in the absence of an express waiver. Parliament was unquestionably free to fashion a legislative scheme to address this issue. I agree … that the courts' creation of a common law procedure for production does not curtail Parliament's jurisdiction to modify that scheme, particularly after having the benefit of evaluating its impact. However, I cannot agree with my colleagues that the legislative means chosen are impeccably consistent with ss. 7 and 11(*d*) of the *Charter*.

[5] As this Court maintained in *Stinchcombe, supra*, at p. 336, the right of an accused to make full answer and defence is a pillar of criminal justice on which we rely heavily to prevent the conviction of the innocent. It is a principle of fundamental justice protected by ss. 7 and 11(*d*) of the *Charter*. Flowing from the right to make full answer and defence is the Crown's constitutional and ethical duty to disclose all information in its possession reasonably capable of affecting the accused's ability to raise a reasonable doubt concerning his innocence: *R. v. Egger*, [1993] 2 S.C.R. 451, at p. 466. This obligation is subject only to the Crown's discretion to withhold disclosure on the basis that the material is irrelevant or privileged.

[6] The duty of disclosure is premised on the presumption that material in the Crown's possession has probative value. The *O'Connor* majority endorsed this presumption at para. 12, where we surmised that "[g]enerally speaking, the Crown would not obtain possession or control of therapeutic records unless the information the records contained was somehow relevant to the case against the accused." This reasoning applies with even greater force, in my view, when the Crown seeks access to documents without the complainant's cooperation, such as by way of a search warrant.

[7] McLachlin and Iacobucci JJ. emphasize in their reasons that the Crown's duty of disclosure is not absolute. The *Charter* entrenches the right to a fair trial, they maintain, not the best trial. The principles of fundamental justice do not guarantee the most favourable procedures conceivable. All of this is true. However, in my respectful view my colleagues understate the importance of Crown disclosure to trial fairness. Disclosure of records in the Crown's hands furthers the search for truth as it enables the defence to challenge the accuracy and cogency of the prosecution's case. The accused's ability to access relevant information that may ultimately deprive him of his liberty strikes at the very core of the principles of fundamental justice.

[8] The requirement in Bill C-46 that the accused must prove the relevance of records that form part of the case to meet is a serious incursion on the meaningful exercise of the right to make full answer and defence. Not only does the legislative scheme supplant the presumption of relevance, but it also raises the relevance bar. The standard of relevance which the accused must satisfy according to ss. 278.3(3)(*b*) and 278.5(1)(*b*)—likely relevance to an issue at trial or to the competence of a witness to testify—is higher than that required for disclosure under a *Stinchcombe* application, which is whether the information "may be useful to the defence": *O'Connor, supra*, at para. 22, and *Stinchcombe, supra*, at p. 345.

[9] Moreover, I do not agree with McLachlin and Iacobucci JJ.'s assertion that the notification requirement in

s. 278.2(3) provides the accused with much assistance in establishing the likely relevance of a document in the Crown's possession. I reiterate the concerns which the majority expressed in *O'Connor, supra*, at paras. 25-26, about placing an accused in the position of having to persuade the trial judge that documents are relevant without any knowledge of their contents. It will be difficult indeed for an accused to establish the likely relevance of a record which he knows to exist, but which he has never seen. By displacing the presumption of relevance and increasing the relevance threshold, ss. 278.3(3)(*b*) and 278.5(1)(*b*) give the Crown a distinct advantage over the defence, as it holds information that the accused must surmount a significant obstacle to obtain. These provisions therefore infringe the accused's right to a fair trial.

[10] Having found that ss. 278.3(3)(*b*) and 278.5(1)(*b*) violate ss. 7 and 11(*d*) of the *Charter* as they apply to records in the Crown's possession, I must consider whether the infringement is a reasonable limit prescribed by law that is demonstrably justified in a free and democratic society. I am mindful that violations of s. 7 are rarely saved by s. 1: *New Brunswick (Minister of Health and Community Services) v. G. (J.)*, [1999] 3 S.C.R. 46, at para. 99. ... Iacobucci J. summarized the analytical framework applicable to s. 1 as follows in *Egan v. Canada*, [1995] 2 S.C.R. 513, at para. 182:

> A limitation to a constitutional guarantee will be sustained once two conditions are met. First, the objective of the legislation must be pressing and substantial. Second, the means chosen to attain this legislative end must be reasonable and demonstrably justifiable in a free and democratic society. In order to satisfy the second requirement, three criteria must be satisfied: (1) the rights violation must be rationally connected to the aim of the legislation; (2) the impugned provision must minimally impair the *Charter* guarantee; and (3) there must be a proportionality between the effect of the measure and its objective so that the attainment of the legislative goal is not outweighed by the abridgement of the right.

[11] Without a doubt, Bill C-46 was adopted to address a pressing and substantial objective, which is the protection of the privacy and equality rights of complainants and witnesses in the context of sexual assault trials. The legislative scheme also rationally advances this important aim. In my opinion, however, ss. 278.3(3)(*b*) and 278.5(1)(*b*) fail to protect those rights in a manner that minimally impairs the right of an accused to make full answer and defence. The requirement that the accused must demonstrate the likely relevance of records held by the Crown is more intrusive than reasonably necessary to achieve the legislative goals: see *M. v. H.*, [1999] 2 S.C.R. 3, at para. 118. In addition, the risk of

suppressing relevant evidence and of convicting an innocent person outweighs the salutary effects of the impugned provisions on privacy and equality rights. I accordingly conclude that the violations are not justified by s. 1.

[12] While in my view ss. 278.3(3)(*b*) and 278.5(1)(*b*) are unconstitutional as they apply to records in the Crown's hands, I remain sensitive that the production of therapeutic records to the defence is injurious to a complainant's privacy rights. Indeed, disclosure may be all the more invasive to a complainant's dignity and psychological integrity when they are obtained by the Crown without her consent.

[13] In this regard, I emphasize that records which the Crown procures absent waiver would still be subject to the principles in *Stinchcombe*. The prosecution would be free to rebut the presumption that the documents are relevant. I remark in passing that this may be difficult for the Crown to accomplish in respect of documents obtained pursuant to a search warrant, as in most cases the evidentiary basis upon which the warrant was secured will itself be disclosed. As with any *Stinchcombe* application, the Crown may likewise attempt to resist disclosure by demonstrating that the records are privileged.

[14] If the Crown is unable to discharge this burden, then the records should be disclosed to the trial judge rather than the accused (as they normally would under a *Stinchcombe* application), because of the privacy rights at stake, if the trial judge is satisfied that the other requirements in s. 278.5(1) and (2) are met. The second stage of the legislative regime— judicial examination of the documents to determine whether and to what extent they should be produced to the accused— would then proceed according to the criteria in ss. 278.6 to 278.91, as explained by my colleagues. In my view, relieving the accused of the burden of showing relevance strikes a more appropriate balance between the various rights at stake. It removes a significant barrier to the accused's ability to raise a reasonable doubt concerning his innocence while preserving a large measure of protection for the privacy and equality rights of complainants and witnesses.

[15] I turn last to a consideration of the appropriate remedy under s. 52(1) of the *Constitution Act, 1982*. My finding of unconstitutionality is limited to two provisions of an otherwise complex legislative scheme. I believe that a combination of reading down the sections and reading in new language is the most appropriate way to vindicate the *Charter* rights at play "while refraining from intrusion into the legislative sphere beyond what is necessary": *R. v. Laba*, [1994] 3 S.C.R. 965, at p. 1012, *per* Sopinka J. Sections 278.3(3)(*b*) and 278.5(1)(*b*) of the *Criminal Code* should therefore be interpreted such that they no longer apply to an application for the production of records in the Crown's possession.

Language along the following lines should be read into both ss. 278.3(3)(*b*) and 278.5(1)(*b*): "unless the record is in the possession or control of the prosecutor in the proceedings, in which case this paragraph does not apply." The principles for Crown disclosure enunciated in *Stinchcombe* and *O'Connor* would partially apply instead of those paragraphs, such that the Crown would have the opportunity to show the trial judge that the documents are irrelevant or privileged. ...

The judgment of L'Heureux-Dubé, Gonthier, McLachlin, Iacobucci, Major, Bastarache, and Binnie JJ. was delivered by

McLACHLIN AND IACOBUCCI JJ.:

I. Introduction

[17] The question of when accused persons should have access to private records of complainants and witnesses in sexual assault trials is a vexed one. This Court addressed this issue in *R. v. O'Connor*, [1995] 4 S.C.R. 411. Following this decision, and a lengthy consultation process, Parliament reviewed the issue and drafted Bill C-46, (now S.C. 1997, c. 30) which came into force on May 12, 1997 and amended the *Criminal Code*, R.S.C., 1985, c. C-46. The issue in the present appeal is whether Bill C-46 is constitutional. The resolution of this appeal requires understanding how to define competing rights, avoiding the hierarchical approach rejected by this Court in *Dagenais v. Canadian Broadcasting Corp.*, [1994] 3 S.C.R. 835, at p. 877. On the one hand stands the accused's right to make full answer and defence. On the other hand stands the complainant's and witness's right to privacy. Neither right may be defined in such a way as to negate the other and both sets of rights are informed by the equality rights at play in this context. Underlying this question is the relationship between the courts and Parliament when Parliament alters a judicially created common law procedure that already embodies *Charter* standards.

II. Summary

[18] This appeal presents an apparent conflict among the rights to full answer and defence, privacy, and equality, all of which are protected by the *Canadian Charter of Rights and Freedoms* (ss. 7 and 11(*d*), s. 8, and s. 15, respectively). The underlying issue is what is required by the "principles of fundamental justice" protected by s. 7. Bill C-46 reflects Parliament's effort at balancing these rights. Our task is to decide whether Parliament's balance is a constitutional one. ...

[20] As noted above, this Court has previously addressed the issue of disclosure of third party records in sexual assault proceedings: see *O'Connor, supra*. However, it is important to keep in mind that the decision in *O'Connor* is not necessarily the last word on the subject. The law develops through

dialogue between courts and legislatures: see *Vriend v. Alberta*, [1998] 1 S.C.R. 493. Against the backdrop of *O'Connor*, Parliament was free to craft its own solution to the problem consistent with the *Charter*.

[21] As this Court's decision in *Dagenais, supra*, makes clear, *Charter* rights must be examined in a contextual manner to resolve conflicts between them. Therefore, unlike s. 1 balancing, where societal interests are sometimes allowed to override *Charter* rights, under s. 7 rights must be defined so that they do not conflict with each other. The rights of full answer and defence, and privacy, must be defined in light of each other, and both must be defined in light of the equality provisions of s. 15.

[22] Turning to the legislation at issue in this appeal, we find it constitutional. It is undisputed that there are several important respects in which Bill C-46 differs from the regime set out in *O'Connor*. However, these differences are not fatal because Bill C-46 provides sufficient protection for all relevant *Charter* rights. There are, admittedly, several provisions in the Bill that are subject to differing interpretations. However, in such situations we will interpret the legislation in a constitutional manner where possible: see *Slaight Communications Inc. v. Davidson*, [1989] 1 S.C.R. 1038, at p. 1078. By so doing, we conclude that Bill C-46 is a constitutional response to the problem of production of records of complainants or witnesses in sexual assault proceedings. ...

(1) The O'Connor Regime and Bill C-46

[43] The respondent in this appeal and several interveners argued that the provisions of Bill C-46 are unconstitutional to the extent that they are inconsistent with the reasons of the majority of this Court in *O'Connor, supra*. ...

[44] This Court's decision in *O'Connor* concerned the common law procedure to be followed by an accused seeking production of therapeutic records in the hands of third parties. As a preliminary matter, Lamer C.J. and Sopinka J., for the majority on the issue of production, also discussed the issue of disclosure of therapeutic records in the hands of the Crown. In their opinion, the Crown's obligation to disclose records in its possession or control, as established in *Stinchcombe, supra*, is unaltered by the confidential nature of therapeutic records where the records have been shared with the Crown or "confidentiality has been waived for the purpose of proceeding against the accused" (para. 9). Even if privileged, these records must be disclosed to the accused where "clearly relevant and important to the ability of the accused to raise a defence" (para. 11).

[45] In the context of ordering production of records that are in the hands of third parties, Lamer C.J. and Sopinka J. outlined a two-stage process. At the first stage, the issue is

whether the document sought by the accused ought to be produced to the judge; at the second stage, the trial judge must balance the competing interests to decide whether to order production to the accused. At the first stage, the onus is on the accused to establish that the information in question is "*likely to be relevant*" (para. 19 (emphasis in original)). Unlike in the Crown disclosure context, where relevance is understood to mean "may be useful to the defence," the threshold of *likely relevance* in this context requires that the presiding judge be satisfied "that there is a reasonable possibility that the information is logically probative to *an issue at trial or the competence of a witness to testify*" (para. 22 (emphasis in original)). This shift in onus and the higher threshold, as compared to when records are in the possession of the Crown, was necessitated by the fact that the information in question is not part of the state's "case to meet," the state has not been given access to it, and third parties are under no obligation to assist the defence.

[46] Lamer C.J. and Sopinka J. held that the threshold of likely relevance at this first stage is not a significant or onerous burden. It is meant to prevent requests for production that are "speculative, fanciful, disruptive, unmeritorious, obstructive and time-consuming" (para. 24). Although Lamer C.J. and Sopinka J. disagreed with L'Heureux-Dubé J. that therapeutic records are rarely relevant to the accused, they declined to set out "categories of relevance" (para. 27).

[47] If the first stage is passed, the record is disclosed to the court and the application for production moves onto the second stage where the judge determines whether the record should be produced to the accused. At this second stage, Lamer C.J. and Sopinka J. require the trial judge to balance the competing interests in order to determine whether a non-production order would be a reasonable limit on the accused's ability to make full answer and defence. They list a series of factors that trial judges should consider in making this determination (at para. 31):

> (1) [T]he extent to which the record is necessary for the accused to make full answer and defence; (2) the probative value of the record in question; (3) the nature and extent of the reasonable expectation of privacy vested in that record; (4) whether production of the record would be premised upon any discriminatory belief or bias; and (5) the potential prejudice to the complainant's dignity, privacy or security of the person that would be occasioned by production of the record in question.

Although L'Heureux-Dubé J., for the minority on this issue, outlined the same five factors as the majority, she also included two additional factors: the integrity of the trial process and the societal interest in reporting sexual crimes. Lamer C.J. and Sopinka J. held that the former is better dealt with when determining admissibility of the evidence and that the latter, while a relevant factor, was "not a paramount consideration" as there are many other avenues open to the trial judge to protect this interest than declining production (at paras. 32 and 33).

(b) Bill C-46

[48] On May 12, 1997, approximately 17 months after this Court released its decision in *O'Connor*, Bill C-46 came into force. Bill C-46 sets out a process to govern the production of the private records of complainants and witnesses in sexual assault trials in place of the common law regime this Court established in *O'Connor*. The preamble to the Bill indicates that Parliament was concerned about the incidence of sexual violence and abuse in Canadian society, its prevalence against women and children, and its "particularly disadvantageous impact on the equal participation of women and children in society and on the rights of women and children to security of the person, privacy and equal benefit of the law as guaranteed by sections 7, 8, 15 and 28 of the [*Charter*]." The preamble expressly declares that Parliament seeks to provide a framework of laws that are fair to and protect the rights of both accused persons and complainants.

[49] While the Bill retains the two-stage structure set out in *O'Connor*, there are significant differences between the two regimes. ...

[50] Bill C-46 begins by defining the records to which it applies: "any form of record that contains personal information for which there is a reasonable expectation of privacy," excluding investigatory or prosecutorial records: s. 278.1. It goes on to define the types of offences that will trigger its application: s. 278.2(1). Generally, these are sexual assault and similar sexual offences. Section 278.2(1) states that an accused person charged with these offences cannot obtain the records relating to complainants or witnesses covered by s. 278.1, except in accordance with the process set out by the Bill.

[51] A third preliminary section, s. 278.2(2), states that the Bill applies to records in the possession or control of any person, including the Crown prosecutor, unless the complainant or witness "has expressly waived the application of [the Bill]." Absent waiver, documents in the possession of the prosecution are treated in the same manner as documents in the hands of a private individual or organization and therefore are subject to disclosure pursuant to the Bill's procedures.

[52] Yet another preliminary provision sets out "assertions" that are "not sufficient on their own" on an application for production to establish that a record is "likely relevant to an issue at trial or to the competence of a witness to testify": s. 278.3(4).

[53] This brings us to the heart of the Bill—the process established to govern the production of private records to an accused person in sexual offence proceedings. Like *O'Connor*, Parliament has set up a two-stage process: (1) disclosure to the judge; and (2) production to the accused. At the first stage, the accused must establish that the record sought is "likely relevant to an issue at trial or to the competence of a witness to testify" and that "the production of the record is necessary in the interests of justice" (s. 278.5(1)). Bill C-46 diverges from *O'Connor* by directing the trial judge to consider the salutary and deleterious effects of production to the court on the accused's right to full answer and defence and the complainant's or witness's right to privacy and equality. A series of factors is listed that the trial judge is directed to take into account in deciding whether the document should be produced to the court (s. 278.5(2)):

(a) the extent to which the record is necessary for the accused to make a full answer and defence;
(b) the probative value of the record;
(c) the nature and extent of the reasonable expectation of privacy with respect to the record;
(d) whether production of the record is based on a discriminatory belief or bias;
(e) the potential prejudice to the personal dignity and right to privacy of any person to whom the record relates;
(f) society's interest in encouraging the reporting of sexual offences;
(g) society's interest in encouraging the obtaining of treatment by complainants of sexual offences; and
(h) the effect of the determination on the integrity of the trial process.

[54] If the requirements of this first stage are met, the record will be ordered produced to the trial judge. At the second stage, the judge looks at the record in the absence of the parties (s. 278.6(1)), holds a hearing if necessary (s. 278.6(2)), and determines whether the record should be produced on the basis that it is "likely relevant to an issue at trial or to the competence of a witness to testify" and that its production is "necessary in the interests of justice" (s. 278.7). Again at this stage, the judge must consider the salutary and deleterious effects on the accused's right to make full answer and defence and on the right to privacy and equality of the complainant or witness, and is directed to "take into account" the factors set out at s. 278.5(2): s. 278.7(2). When ordering production, the judge may impose conditions on production: s. 278.7(3).

[55] The respondent and several supporting interveners argue that Bill C-46 is unconstitutional to the extent that it establishes a regime for production that differs from or is inconsistent with that established by the majority in *O'Connor*. However, it does not follow from the fact that a law passed by Parliament differs from a regime envisaged by the Court in the absence of a statutory scheme, that Parliament's law is unconstitutional. Parliament may build on the Court's decision, and develop a different scheme as long as it remains constitutional. Just as Parliament must respect the Court's rulings, so the Court must respect Parliament's determination that the judicial scheme can be improved. To insist on slavish conformity would belie the mutual respect that underpins the relationship between the courts and legislature that is so essential to our constitutional democracy: *Vriend, supra*. We turn now to a brief discussion of that relationship.

(2) Relationship Between the Courts and the Legislature Generally

[56] A posture of respect towards Parliament was endorsed by this Court in *Slaight Communications, supra*, at p. 1078, where we held that if legislation is amenable to two interpretations, a court should choose the interpretation that upholds the legislation as constitutional. Thus courts must presume that Parliament intended to enact constitutional legislation and strive, where possible, to give effect to this intention.

[57] This Court has also discussed the relationship between the courts and the legislature in terms of a dialogue, and emphasized its importance to the democratic process. In *Vriend, supra*, at para. 139, Iacobucci J. stated:

> To my mind, a great value of judicial review and this dialogue among the branches is that each of the branches is made somewhat accountable to the other. The work of the legislature is reviewed by the courts and the work of the court in its decisions can be reacted to by the legislature in the passing of new legislation (or even overarching laws under s. 33 of the *Charter*). This dialogue between and accountability of each of the branches have the effect of enhancing the democratic process, not denying it.

… If the common law were to be taken as establishing the only possible constitutional regime, then we could not speak of a dialogue with the legislature. Such a situation could only undermine rather than enhance democracy. Legislative change and the development of the common law are different. As this Court noted in *R. v. Salituro*, [1991] 3 S.C.R. 654, at p. 666, the common law changes incrementally, "while complex changes to the law with uncertain ramifications should be left to the legislature." While this dialogue obviously is of a somewhat different nature when the common law rule involves interpretation of the *Charter*, as in *O'Connor*, it remains a dialogue nonetheless.

[58] Moreover, in this Court's recent decision *Reference re Secession of Quebec*, [1998] 2 S.C.R. 217, we affirmed the proposition that constitutionalism can facilitate democracy rather than undermine it, and that one way in which it does this is by ensuring that fundamental human rights and individual freedoms are given due regard and protection (at paras. 74-78). Courts do not hold a monopoly on the protection and promotion of rights and freedoms; Parliament also plays a role in this regard and is often able to act as a significant ally for vulnerable groups. This is especially important to recognize in the context of sexual violence. The history of the treatment of sexual assault complainants by our society and our legal system is an unfortunate one. Important change has occurred through legislation aimed at both recognizing the rights and interests of complainants in criminal proceedings, and debunking the stereotypes that have been so damaging to women and children, but the treatment of sexual assault complainants remains an ongoing problem. If constitutional democracy is meant to ensure that due regard is given to the voices of those vulnerable to being overlooked by the majority, then this court has an obligation to consider respectfully Parliament's attempt to respond to such voices.

[59] Parliament has enacted this legislation after a long consultation process that included a consideration of the constitutional standards outlined by this Court in *O'Connor*. While it is the role of the courts to specify such standards, there may be a range of permissible regimes that can meet these standards. It goes without saying that this range is not confined to the specific rule adopted by the Court pursuant to its competence in the common law. In the present case, Parliament decided that legislation was necessary in order to address the issue of third party records more comprehensively. As is evident from the language of the preamble to Bill C-46, Parliament also sought to recognize the prevalence of sexual violence against women and children and its disadvantageous impact on their rights, to encourage the reporting of incidents of sexual violence, to recognize the impact of the production of personal information on the efficacy of treatment, and to reconcile fairness to complainants with the rights of the accused. Many of these concerns involve policy decisions regarding criminal procedure and its relationship to the community at large. Parliament may also be understood to be recognizing "horizontal" equality concerns, where women's inequality results from the acts of other individuals and groups rather than the state, but which nonetheless may have many consequences for the criminal justice system. It is perfectly reasonable that these many concerns may lead to a procedure that is different from the common law position but that nonetheless meets the required constitutional standards.

[60] We cannot presume that the legislation is unconstitutional simply because it is different from the common law position. The question before us is not whether Parliament can amend the common law; it clearly can. The question before us is whether in doing so Parliament has nonetheless outlined a constitutionally acceptable procedure for the production of private records of complainants in sexual assault trials. This question is considered at length below, following the discussion of the constitutional rights at stake in this appeal. …

[The majority discussed tensions between the requirements for a full answer and defence, privacy, and equality, and why no single principle should be considered to trump another, but instead should be defined in light of competing principles.]

[94] In summary, the following broad considerations apply to the definition of the rights at stake in this appeal. The right of the accused to make full answer and defence is a core principle of fundamental justice, but it does not automatically entitle the accused to gain access to information contained in the private records of complainants and witnesses. Rather, the scope of the right to make full answer and defence must be determined in light of privacy and equality rights of complainants and witnesses. It is clear that the right to full answer and defence is not engaged where the accused seeks information that will only serve to distort the truth-seeking purpose of a trial, and in such a situation, privacy and equality rights are paramount. On the other hand, where the information contained in a record directly bears on the right to make full answer and defence, privacy rights must yield to the need to avoid convicting the innocent. Most cases, however, will not be so clear, and in assessing applications for production, courts must determine the weight to be granted to the interests protected by privacy and full answer and defence in the particular circumstances of each case. Full answer and defence will be more centrally implicated where the information contained in a record is part of the case to meet or where its potential probative value is high. A complainant's privacy interest is very high where the confidential information contained in a record concerns the complainant's personal identity or where the confidentiality of the record is vital to protect a therapeutic relationship. …

D. Analysis of Sections 278.1 to 278.91 of Bill C-46

[96] In enacting Bill C-46, Parliament was concerned with preserving an accused's access to private records that may be relevant to an issue on trial, while protecting the right to privacy of complainants and witnesses to the greatest extent possible. Notwithstanding Parliament's good intentions, the respondent suggests that Bill C-46 violates the constitutional

right of the accused to a fair trial and full defence on a number of grounds. We will consider each in turn.

(1) The Definition of Documents Subject to the Legislation: Sections 278.1 and 278.2(1)

[97] ... [T]he Bill applies to all records of complainants and witnesses in sexual offence proceedings containing "personal information for which there is a reasonable expectation of privacy," including "medical, psychiatric, therapeutic, counselling, education, employment, child welfare, adoption and social services records, personal journals and diaries, and records containing personal information the production or disclosure of which is protected by any other Act of Parliament or a provincial legislature." ...

[99] [T]he legislation applies only to records "for which there is a *reasonable* expectation of privacy" (s. 278.1 (emphasis added)). Only documents that truly raise a legally recognized privacy interest are caught and protected: see *R. v. Regan* (1998), 174 N.S.R. (2d) 230 (S.C.). The Bill is therefore carefully tailored to reflect the problem Parliament was addressing—how to preserve an accused's access to private records that may be relevant to an issue on trial while protecting, to the greatest extent possible, the privacy rights of the subjects of such records, including both complainants and witnesses. By limiting its coverage to records in which there is a reasonable expectation of privacy, the Bill is consistent with the definition of s. 8 privacy rights discussed above. Moreover, as will be discussed below, the mere fact that records are within the ambit of Bill C-46 will not, in itself, prevent the accused from obtaining access to them. Applied in this way, ss. 278.1 and 278.2(1) will not catch more records than they should, and are not overly broad.

[100] It must also be remembered that the definition of records in ss. 278.1 and 278.2(1) simply establishes the starting point for the analysis proposed by the Bill. Documents falling within the ambit of these provisions, after being subject to the legislative regime, may or may not be ordered to be disclosed to the accused. It is therefore the procedures established by the Bill and not the spectrum of records subject to these procedures that will determine the fairness or constitutionality of the legislation. If the legislative regime fairly provides access to all constitutionally required documents, then the spectrum of records brought under the Bill, if in keeping with the Bill's objectives, cannot be challenged.

[101] The broad scope of Bill C-46 has also been challenged as imposing an excessive burden on judicial resources. However, the Bill safeguards the efficiency and resources of the judicial system while furthering its objective of protecting, to the greatest extent possible, the rights of all those involved in sexual offence proceedings, by mandating that judges can

only review the records in question once these records have been established as likely relevant and their production to the court has been established as necessary in the interests of justice. The balancing process required at the first stage ensures that records are not needlessly or casually produced to the court for review: see *O'Connor*, *supra*, at para. 152, *per* L'Heureux-Dubé J. Moreover, as many interveners have pointed out, production of records to the court had become almost routine in sexual assault cases. It is unlikely that Bill C-46's procedures will be substantially more onerous on judicial resources. Finally, Parliament, with the benefit of a full legislative inquiry, has ruled on such questions of administrative convenience. We see no reason to disturb its conclusion. If the system proves unworkable in practice, then Parliament, not this Court, is better positioned to fix it.

(2) Third Party Records in the Possession of the Crown: Sections 278.2(2) and (3)

[102] The next provision at issue extends the application of the legislative regime for the production of private records to records "in the possession or control of any person," including the Crown: s. 278.2(2). ...

[104] The respondent objects to the fact that this provision prevents the automatic disclosure of all relevant and non-privileged information in the possession of the Crown. He submits that this is contrary to the constitutional obligation upon the Crown set out in *Stinchcombe*, and is inconsistent with this Court's conclusion in *O'Connor* that "the Crown's disclosure obligations established in the *Stinchcombe* decision are unaffected by the confidential nature of therapeutic records" (para. 13, *per* Lamer C.J. and Sopinka J.). The respondent also argues that s. 278.2(2) gives the Crown an unfair advantage in that only the accused is subject to the legislative regime. The Crown can obtain private records through the complainant directly or through the power of a search warrant. The Bill not only exempts the Crown from the obligation to comply with the legislation regime when seeking private records, but also allows the Crown to possess information that the defence does not have.

[105] The first response to the respondent's argument is that it is premature. Section 278.2 simply defines the scope of the legislation. It does not by itself deny access to documents to which the defence is constitutionally entitled. If the procedures set out in the sections that follow fairly provide access to all constitutionally required documents, then the accused has no constitutional complaint.

[106] Second, the argument that this provision contradicts *Stinchcombe* and *O'Connor* rests on an overstatement of the Crown obligation to disclose that was affirmed in those

cases. It is true that *Stinchcombe* spoke of a duty on the Crown to disclose to the defence all relevant documents in the Crown's possession, subject to privilege. Privacy interests, however, were not at issue in *Stinchcombe*. In *O'Connor*, the Court considered the Crown's obligation to disclose private records in the context of sexual offence proceedings where the complainant has made an informed waiver of her privacy rights. The majority in *O'Connor* concluded that "the Crown's well-established duty to disclose all information in its possession is not affected by the confidential nature of therapeutic records": *O'Connor*, *supra*, at para. 7. This conclusion, however, was premised upon the assumption that the records in the Crown's possession have been freely and voluntarily surrendered by the complainant or witness: "where the documents in question have been shared with an agent of the state (namely, the Crown), it is apparent that the complainant's privacy interest in those records has disappeared" (*O'Connor*, *supra*, at para. 8). Lamer C.J. and Sopinka J. further found that "fairness must require that if the complainant is *willing to release* this information in order to further the criminal prosecution, then the accused should be entitled to use the information in the preparation of his or her defence" (*O'Connor*, *supra*, at para. 9 (emphasis added)). Bill C-46 imposes the same waiver rule. Where a fully informed complainant expressly waives the protection of the legislation, by declaration or by voluntarily providing her records to the Crown, the Bill C-46 procedure does not apply and the records are producible as at common law: s. 278.2(2). Bill C-46 thus conforms to the constitutional standard of *O'Connor*.

[107] The respondent argues, however, that *O'Connor* should not be read as requiring the disclosure of confidential records pursuant to *Stinchcombe only* in cases of an express waiver and that s. 278.2(2) is unconstitutional. He asserts that any reasonable expectation of privacy is lost once the records are in the possession of the Crown, regardless of how the records came into the Crown's possession. Once in the Crown's hands, the records become "the property of the public" to be used to ensure that justice is done and must be disclosed pursuant to the common law.

[108] This argument erroneously equates Crown possession or control with a total loss of any reasonable expectation of privacy. Privacy is not an all or nothing right. It does not follow from the fact that the Crown has possession of the records that any reasonable expectation of privacy disappears. Privacy interests in modern society include the reasonable expectation that private information will remain confidential to the persons to whom and restricted to the purposes for which it was divulged, *Dyment* [*R. v.*, [1988] 2 S.C.R. 417], at p. 429. Where private information is disclosed to individuals outside of those to whom, or for purposes other than for which,

it was originally divulged, the person to whom the information pertains may still hold a reasonable expectation of privacy in this information, *R. v. Boudreau*, [1998] O.J. No. 3526 (QL) (Gen. Div.), at para. 18. Third party records may fall into the possession of the Crown without the knowledge, consent, or assistance of the complainant or witness. Where the complainant or witness has not expressly waived her privacy right, Parliament can legitimately take steps to protect those privacy rights. Such protection is to be found in the procedures for production set out in ss. 278.5 and 278.7 of the Bill.

[109] The *O'Connor* majority did not address what procedure was to be followed where third party records were in the possession of the Crown without the existence of an express waiver. It was therefore open to Parliament to fill this void legislatively. Viewed in this context, s. 278.2(2) ensures that the range of interests triggered by production will be balanced pursuant to the procedure set out in ss. 278.5 and 278.7. The mere fact that this procedure differs from that set out in *Stinchcombe* does not, without more, establish a constitutional violation. As noted, *Stinchcombe* and *O'Connor* did not address the situation at issue here, namely, records in the Crown's possession in which a complainant or witness has a reasonable, and non-waived, expectation of privacy. We are thus returned to our starting point—that s. 278.2 in itself violates no rights and any violation can be determined only by examining its impact in conjunction with ss. 278.5 through 278.8.

[110] When the arguments that s. 278.2 is inconsistent with *Stinchcombe* and *O'Connor* are cleared away, the respondent's fundamental objection to the section emerges—it unfairly favours the Crown. The Crown can obtain the complainant's private records through a search warrant or subpoena. Where the complainant or witness does not expressly waive the protection of the legislation, the accused can get these documents only by applying under the Bill C-46 regime. If the accused does not succeed, the Crown may possess documents that the accused does not have. This, it is argued, puts the Crown at an advantage.

[111] All this is true. But it begs the real question—is the Crown's advantage unconstitutional? In other words, does it deprive the accused of his right to make full answer and defence? That will be so only if the legislation prevents the accused from getting access to all constitutionally required documents. There is no principle of fundamental justice that the Crown and defence must enjoy precisely the same privileges and procedures. ... The real question is whether the procedures that Parliament has enacted prevent the accused from making full answer and defence. This is the true meaning of the passage from *O'Connor*, *supra*, at para. 34, which states that "[f]airness requires that the accused be treated on an equal footing" with the Crown, which has access to search warrants.

Obviously, the search warrant procedure involves a different array of factors from those that are relevant to production of third party records to the accused. All that was meant by this passage is that the accused must have a procedure for obtaining evidence that respects all the relevant constitutional rights at stake, just as the prosecution does through the warrant process. As we will explain below, Bill C-46 is just such a procedure.

[112] In *Stinchcombe*, this Court acknowledged that the Crown, by virtue of its unique role as agent of the state, has greater access to certain types of information than the accused. The Court therefore imposed a duty on the Crown to disclose all relevant information to the defence. The goal behind imposing this duty upon the Crown was not, however, to ensure equivalency of treatment between the accused and the Crown. Rather, the duty to disclose was imposed to advance the overall fairness, justice, efficacy, and truth finding elements of criminal proceedings. Since the right to full answer and defence must be defined in light of other principles of fundamental justice, that right is not an absolute one. Thus, while acknowledging the disparity in access to certain types of information, Sopinka J. conditioned the Crown's duty to disclose by investing in the Crown a discretion to withhold information where necessary to respect the rules of privilege, to protect persons from harassment or injury, or where this information is clearly irrelevant, at pp. 336 and 339. Similarly, in *O'Connor*, *supra*, at para. 16, Lamer C.J. and Sopinka J. held:

> ... *Stinchcombe* recognized that, even in the context of disclosure, there are limits on the right of an accused to access information. For example, when the Crown asserts that the information is privileged, the trial judge must then balance the competing claims at issue. In such cases, the information will only be disclosed where the trial judge concludes that the asserted privilege "does not constitute a reasonable limit on the constitutional right to make full answer and defence" (*Stinchcombe*, at p. 340).

Stinchcombe and *O'Connor* accept that it is constitutionally permissible for the Crown to be subject to different treatment, to different procedures, or even to end up with documents that the accused has not seen, as long as the accused can make full answer and defence and the trial is fundamentally fair.

[113] ... [W]hen addressing the disparity of treatment between defence counsel and the Crown, we must remember the specific problem Bill C-46 was enacted to address. Through Bill C-46, Parliament sought to preserve an accused's access to private records that may be relevant to the defence in a sexual offence proceeding while protecting, to the greatest extent possible, the privacy rights of complainants and witnesses. The context of the Bill is one in which defence counsel were routinely seeking access to the private records of complainants or witnesses in sexual offence proceedings. ... The greater procedural burden placed on the accused under Bill C-46 reflects the fact that unlike the Crown, the accused bears no responsibility to protect the rights of others. To protect such rights, when they are threatened by the acts of the accused, greater procedural protections are required. ...

[116] We conclude that the fact that s. 278.2 may result in the Crown holding documents that the accused does not possess does not of itself deprive the accused of the right to make full answer and defence. Parliament has balanced the inevitably advantageous documentary position the prosecution enjoys with safeguards to protect the accused's interest in getting those documents that may be relevant to the defence. Provided the remainder of Bill C-46 permits the accused to obtain the documents to which the defence is entitled, the fact that the Crown may possess documents that the accused does not, does not vitiate the process. Section 278.2 is constitutional in that it does not violate ss. 7 or 11(*d*) of the *Charter*.

(3) The "Insufficient Grounds" Section: Section 278.3(4)

[117] Section 278.3(4) lists a series of "assertions" that cannot "on their own" establish that a record is likely relevant. The respondent submits that on a plain reading, this provision prevents the accused from relying on the listed factors when attempting to establish the likely relevance of the records. This, he argues, interferes with the right to make full answer and defence by restricting what the judge can consider in determining whether the records must be produced to the defence. The legislation raises the bar for production, he asserts, making it difficult if not impossible for the accused to meet the likely relevance test of ss. 278.5 and 278.7. The Respondent contends that it is unconstitutional to exclude the assertions listed in s. 278.3(4) as irrelevant.

[118] This submission forgets that when legislation is susceptible to more than one interpretation, we must always choose the constitutional reading. See *Slaight*, *supra*, at p. 1078. This mistake leads the respondent to overstate the purpose and effect of s. 278.3(4). ... It does not entirely prevent an accused from relying on the factors listed, but simply prevents reliance on bare "*assertions*" of the listed matters, where there is no other evidence and they stand "on their own."

[119] As has frequently been noted, speculative myths, stereotypes, and generalized assumptions about sexual assault victims and classes of records have too often in the past hindered the search for truth and imposed harsh and irrelevant burdens on complainants in prosecutions of sexual offences. See *Seaboyer* [*R. v.*, [1991] 2 S.C.R. 577], at p. 634. The myths that a woman's testimony is unreliable unless she made a complaint shortly after the event (recent complaint), or if she

has had previous sexual relations, are but two of the more notorious examples of the speculation that in the past has passed for truth in this difficult area of human behaviour and the law. The notion that consultation with a psychiatrist is, by itself, an indication of untrustworthiness is a more recent, but equally invidious, example of such a myth. The purpose of s. 278.3(4) is to prevent these and other myths from forming the entire basis of an otherwise unsubstantiated order for production of private records. ...

[121] We conclude that s. 278.3(4) does not violate ss. 7 or 11(*d*) of the *Charter*.

(4) The First Stage: Production to the Judge—Sections 278.4 and 278.5

[122] Bill C-46, as noted, contemplates a two-stage procedure for gaining access to documents. At the first stage, the issue is whether the document should be produced to the judge. If that stage is passed, the judge looks at the document to determine whether it should be produced to the accused. Section 278.5 establishes the procedure for production to the judge at the first stage. ...

[125] Parliament, after studying the issue, concluded that the rights of both the complainant and the accused should be considered when deciding whether to order production to the judge. In coming to this conclusion, Parliament must be taken to have determined, as a result of lengthy consultations, and years of Parliamentary study and debate, that trial judges have sufficient evidence to engage in an informed balancing process at this stage. Parliament began consultations on the production of complainants' private records in sexual assault cases in June 1994. The *O'Connor* decision became a part of that discussion when it was released December 14, 1995, and was subsequently addressed in the consultations which continued until March 1997. In developing the Bill C-46 production regime, we must therefore remember that Parliament had the benefit of information not available to the Court when it penned *O'Connor*. Specifically, Parliament had the advantage of being able to assess how the *O'Connor* regime was operating. The record indicates that Parliament received many submissions that under the *O'Connor* regime, private records were routinely being produced to the court at the first stage, leading to the recurring violation of the privacy interests of complainants and witnesses. While it is true that little statistical data existed at the time of the drafting of Bill C-46 on the application of *O'Connor*, it was open to Parliament to give what weight it saw fit to the evidence presented at the consultations. As a result of the consultation process, Parliament decided to supplement the "likely relevant" standard for production to the judge proposed in *O'Connor* with the further requirement that production be "necessary in the interests of

justice." The result was s. 278.5. This process is a notable example of the dialogue between the judicial and legislative branches discussed above. This Court acted in *O'Connor*, and the legislature responded with Bill C-46. As already mentioned, the mere fact that Bill C-46 does not mirror *O'Connor* does not render it unconstitutional.

[126] Section 278.5(1) requires the accused at the stage of production to a judge to demonstrate not only that the information is "likely relevant" but, in addition, that the production of the record "is necessary in the interests of justice." The first requirement takes up the unanimous view in *O'Connor* that the accused, to get production to the judge, must show that the record is "likely relevant." The additional requirement that production to the judge be "necessary in the interests of justice" encompasses (but is not confined to) the concern of the minority in *O'Connor* that even where likely relevance is shown, there should be room for the court to consider the rights and interests of all those affected by disclosure before documents are ordered disclosed to the court.

[127] Section 278.5(1) is followed by s. 278.5(2) which gives substance to the requirement that trial judges consider the broad range of rights and interests affected before ordering disclosure to the court. Under this section, a trial judge is required to consider the salutary and deleterious effects of production to the court on the accused's right to make full answer and defence and on the rights to privacy and equality of the complainant or witness and any other person to whom the record relates. The section directs the trial judge to "take into account" a series of factors in deciding whether the document should be produced to the court: (a) the extent to which the record is necessary for the accused to make full answer and defence; (b) the probative value of the record; (c) the nature and extent of the reasonable expectation of privacy with respect to the record; (d) whether production of the record is based on a discriminatory belief or bias; (e) the potential prejudice to the personal dignity and right to privacy of any person to whom the record relates; (f) society's interest in encouraging the reporting of sexual offences; (g) society's interest in encouraging the obtaining of treatment by complainants of sexual offences; and (h) the effect of the determination on the integrity of the trial process.

[128] ... [The respondent's] objection is that the accused must ... show that disclosure to the judge is "necessary in the interests of justice." He argues that this requires a weighing and balancing of interests that cannot properly be done without reviewing the documents in question. To this end, s. 278.5 calls upon the trial judge to do the impossible—to weigh competing rights in a vacuum. The respondent contends that likely relevance should be the only requirement at the stage of deciding whether the judge can see the document. In

imposing the additional requirement that production be established as "necessary in the interests of justice," s. 278.5 risks depriving the accused of documents relevant to his defence and hence is unconstitutional.

[129] The question comes down to this: once likely relevance is established, is it necessarily unconstitutional that a consideration of the rights and interests of those affected by production to the court might result in production not being ordered? The answer to this question depends on whether a consideration of the range of rights and interests affected, in addition to a finding of likely relevance, will ultimately prevent the accused from seeing documents that are necessary to enable him to defend himself—to raise all the defences that might be open to him at trial. The non-disclosure of third party records with a high privacy interest that may contain relevant evidence will not compromise trial fairness where such non-disclosure would not prejudice the accused's right to full answer and defence. ...

[133] The criterion in s. 278.5 that production must be "necessary in the interests of justice" invests trial judges with the discretion to consider the full range of rights and interests at issue before ordering production, in a manner scrupulously respectful of the requirements of the *Charter*; see: *Baron* [*v. Canada*, [1993] 1 S.C.R. 416], at p. 442, *per* Sopinka J. The fact that the approach set out in s. 278.5 does not accord with *O'Connor*'s pronouncement, at para. 24, that at the stage of production to the Court, "considerations of privacy should not enter into the analysis," does not render it unconstitutional. In *O'Connor*, the Court was operating in a legislative vacuum, and fashioned what it considered to be the preferred common law rule. While the rule from that case was of course informed by the *Charter*, it should not be read as a rigid constitutional template. As discussed above, the relationship between the courts and legislatures allows a range of constitutional options. While this Court may have considered it preferable not to consider privacy rights at the production stage, that does not preclude Parliament from coming to a different conclusion, so long as its conclusion is consistent with the *Charter* in its own right. As we have explained, the Bill's directive to consider what is "necessary in the interests of justice," read correctly, does include appropriate respect for the right to full answer and defence.

[134] This leaves the argument that the judge cannot consider the factors listed in s. 278.5(2) without looking at the documents. However, s. 278.5(2) does not require that the judge engage in a conclusive and in-depth evaluation of each of the factors. It rather requires the judge to "take them into account"—to the extent possible at this early stage of proceedings—in deciding whether to order a particular record produced to himself or herself for inspection. Section 278.5(2)

serves as a check-list of the various factors that may come into play in making the decision regarding production to the judge. Therefore, while the s. 278.5(2) factors are relevant, in the final analysis the judge is free to make whatever order is "necessary in the interests of justice"—a mandate that includes all of the applicable "principles of fundamental justice" at stake. ...

[138] We conclude that s. 278.5 is constitutional. The respondent's argument depends on reading the requirement in s. 278.5(1)(*c*), that production can only be ordered where "necessary in the interests of justice," as capable of blocking production even where the accused might constitutionally require access to the documents in question. A finding of unconstitutionality also hinges on reading s. 278.5(2) as consisting of a check-list of factors and rights to be conclusively assessed and weighed-off against one other. Such readings, however, cannot stand. It can never be in the interests of justice for an accused to be denied the right to make full answer and defence and, pursuant to s. 278.5(2) the trial judge is merely directed to "consider" and "take into account" the factors and rights listed. Where the record sought can be established as "likely relevant," the judge must consider the rights and interests of all those affected by production and decide whether it is necessary in the interests of justice that he or she take the next step of viewing the documents. If in doubt, the interests of justice require that the judge take that step.

(5) Stage Two: Production to the Accused, Section 278.7—The Consideration of Societal Interests, Sections 278.5(2)(f) and (g), and the Integrity of the Trial Process, Section 278.5(2)(h)

[139] Once the first hurdle is passed and the records are produced to the judge, the judge must determine whether it is in the interests of justice that they be produced to the defence. Again the judge must be satisfied that the records are "likely relevant" and that production, this time to the accused, is necessary in the interests of justice. In making this decision, the judge must once again consider the factors set out in s. 278.5(2).

[140] The respondent accepts that weighing competing interests is appropriate at this second stage of the analysis. However, the respondent contends that the requirement under s. 278.7(2), that the trial judge take the factors specified in s. 278.5(2)(*a*) to (*h*) into account, inappropriately alters the constitutional balance established in *O'Connor*. Specifically, the respondent contends that ss. 278.5(2)(*f*) and (*g*) elevate the societal interest in encouraging the reporting of sexual offences and encouraging of treatment of complainants of sexual offences, to a status equal to the accused's right to make full answer and defence. This, he suggests, alters the constitutional balance established in *O'Connor*, where the majority specifically determined these factors to be of secondary

importance to defence interests in any balancing of competing interests and better taken into account through other avenues. The respondent also contends that s. 278.5(2)(*h*) unfairly requires trial judges to consider the effect of disclosure on the integrity of the trial process. The respondent submits that this is a question going to admissibility.

[141] ... Trial judges are not required to rule conclusively on each of the factors nor are they required to determine whether factors relating to the privacy and equality of the complainant or witness "outweigh" factors relating to the accused's right to full answer and defence. To repeat, trial judges are only asked to "take into account" the factors listed in s. 278.5(2) when determining whether production of part or all of the impugned record to the accused is necessary in the interest of justice (s. 278.7(1)). ...

[143] This leaves the argument that s. 278.5(2)(*h*) goes to admissibility and that any consideration of it at the stage of production distorts the fairness of the trial. While the *O'Connor* majority held that this factor was "more appropriately dealt with at the admissibility stage," this conclusion does not amount to a finding that a consideration of this factor at the stage of production would result in unfairness to the accused: see *O'Connor*, at para. 32. As noted above, when preparing Bill C-46 Parliament had the advantage of being able to assess how the *O'Connor* regime was operating. From the information available to Parliament and the submissions it received during the consultation process, Parliament concluded that the effect of production on the integrity of the trial was a factor that should be included in the list of factors for trial judges to "take into account" at both stages of an application for production. Several interveners have interpreted this factor as requiring courts to consider, along with the other enumerated factors, whether the search for truth would be advanced by the production of the records in question; that is, the question is whether the material in question would introduce discriminatory biases and beliefs into the fact-finding process. We agree with this interpretation of the inquiry required by s. 278.5(2) (*h*) and believe it to be in keeping with the purposes set out in the preamble of the legislation.

[144] By giving judges wide discretion to consider a variety of factors and requiring them to make whatever order is necessary in the interest of justice at both stages of an application for production, Parliament has created a scheme that permits judges not only to preserve the complainant's privacy and equality rights to the maximum extent possible, but also to ensure that the accused has access to the documents required to make full answer and defence. ...

VII. Conclusion and Disposition

[146] ... We answer the constitutional questions as follows:

1. Do ss. 278.1 to 278.91 of the *Criminal Code*, R.S.C., 1985, c. C-46, infringe s. 7 of the *Canadian Charter of Rights and Freedoms*?

   Answer: No.

2. If so, is the infringement demonstrably justified in a free and democratic society?

   Answer: Given the answer to question 1, it is not necessary to answer this question.

3. Do ss. 278.1 to 278.91 of the *Criminal Code*, R.S.C., 1985, c. C-46, infringe s. 11(*d*) of the *Canadian Charter of Rights and Freedoms*?

   Answer: No.

4. If so, is the infringement demonstrably justified in a free and democratic society?

   Answer: Given the answer to question 3, it is not necessary to answer this question.

16   Charkaoui v. Canada (Citizenship and Immigration), 2007

Like other Western countries, Canada responded to the 9/11 terrorist attacks with sympathy for the United States and concern about its own security against terrorism. In addition, concerns circulated about Canada's large immigrant population serving as a base from which incursions into the United States could be launched and as a fund-raising network for financing terrorism abroad. For liberal democracies, responding to terrorism is bedevilling. On the one hand, liberal democracies are founded on individual rights whose importance only increases when pressure mounts for their abridgment. Clamping down on rights in the face of threats to national security seems like razing a village in order to save it. On the other hand, as Michael Ignatieff argues, liberal democracies are not suicide pacts. They are vulnerable to attack because of their very openness and are entitled to protect themselves from those who exploit liberal freedoms for terrorist causes.[1]

This difficult balance between security and rights is directly engaged in the following decision. Adil Charkaoui and two others, Hassan Almrei and Mohamed Harkat, were subjects of "security certificates" issued by the minister of Citizenship and Immigration and the minister of Public Safety and Emergency Preparedness. Such certificates are issued in respect to persons considered by the government to be threats to Canada's national security. Under the *Immigration and Refugee Protection Act* (IRPA) (proclaimed in November 2001, but debated in the House of Commons before 9/11), permanent residents and foreign nationals in Canada named in security certificates are rendered "inadmissible" in Canada—and subject to deportation—if the government considers that there is sufficient evidence that their presence constitutes a threat to national security, and if a Federal Court judge confirms the reasonableness of the certificate. The judicial hearing is mandatory, but the government can request that the hearing be held *in camera*, without the named person present.

Information on the basis of which a judicial determination is made may be considered harmful to national security if disclosed to the named individual and to the public, more generally. Accordingly, the Act provided that in such cases the relevant information could be kept from the named individual, his or her counsel, and from the public. In reviewing the reasonableness of the security certificate's issue, the judge would have access only to the government's information, not to the named individual's reaction to it or to the named person's evidence raised in reaction to the government's information.

In *Charkaoui*, the court examined whether the security certificate process ran afoul of principles of procedural fairness guaranteed by the Charter. In a unanimous decision written by Chief Justice Beverley McLachlin, the court found two Charter breaches in the security certificate system. First, the court held that the rules limiting the appellants' access to the information forming the basis for the government's position intruded too onerously on

---

1 Michael Ignatieff, *The Lesser Evil: Political Ethics in an Age of Terror* (Toronto: Penguin, 2004).

their right to a fair hearing protected by section 7 of the Charter. Someone in jeopardy at the hands of the state has a right to know the case against him or her and to be able to respond to that case. "Here the principle has not merely been limited; it has been effectively gutted," McLachlin wrote. "How can one meet a case one does not know?" Second, the Act made a distinction between permanent residents and foreign nationals in Canada. Permanent residents, if detained, were entitled to a mandatory review within 48 hours of their detention. Foreign nationals were subject to mandatory detention and their detention could not be reviewed until 120 days had elapsed from the judicial determination of the reasonableness of the certificate. The court considered the more onerous treatment of foreign nationals to be arbitrary and thus contrary to the section 9 protection against arbitrary detention and against the section 10(*c*) right to have the validity of one's detention confirmed by way of *habeas corpus*.

Both breaches were found to be unjustifiable under section 1 analysis. While section 1, as a matter of course, applies to breaches of sections 9 and 10(*c*), it has been somewhat more controversial in respect to section 7 violations. In a sense, section 7 contains its own limiting clause. The provision guarantees the right to life, liberty, and security of the person and these can only be limited in accordance with the principles of fundamental justice. Can a limit on a section 7 right be contrary to the principles of fundamental justice as set out in section 7 and yet justified as a reasonable limitation under the terms of section 1? In *Re B.C. Motor Vehicle Act* (case 20), the court was divided on the question. Justice Wilson, writing on her own behalf, suggested that if a limit on a section 7 right has been effected "through a violation of the principles of fundamental justice, the enquiry, in my opinion, ends there and the limit cannot be sustained under s. 1." Writing for the majority, Justice Lamer averred that section 1 "may, for reasons of administrative expediency, successfully come to the rescue of an otherwise violation of section 7, but only in cases arising out of exceptional conditions, such as natural disasters, the outbreak of war, epidemics, and the like." While the court routinely undertakes a section 1 analysis following a finding that government action has violated section 7, a majority has not yet used section 1 to save such a violation.[2]

So it was here. In its application of the minimal-impairment branch of the *Oakes* test to the judicial hearing provisions of the *Immigration and Refugee Protection Act*, the court referred to several other examples, both domestic and foreign, of procedures that have combined the safeguarding of national security with fair-hearing rights of persons alleged to have threatened it. The harsh IRPA regime was found not to constitute a minimal impairment of Charter rights. While the court gave the government one year to devise a more Charter-friendly security certificate process, its section 1 analysis substantially set out the terms of such a process. The government, in October 2007, introduced legislation in Parliament that adopts the special advocate system used in the United Kingdom and suggested in this case by the chief justice as a possible way of meeting the minimal impairment requirement.

The court was mindful of a public inquiry unfolding as the appellants' cases were winding through the judicial system. In 2002, while changing planes in the United States en route to Canada, Canadian citizen Maher Arar was detained and deported to Syria by American authorities, on the strength of RCMP information linking him to terrorist groups. Arar was tortured while in Syria and gave a false confession. Upon Arar's return to Canada in 2003,

---

2   Peter Hogg, *Constitutional Law of Canada*, 5th ed., vol. 2 (Toronto: Carswell, 2007) 156.

a commission of inquiry was created, which later found that RCMP information shared with American authorities, and likely forming the basis for Arar's deportation to Syria, was erroneous. In January 2007, Arar was offered an apology and compensation of over $10 million by the Canadian government.

Arar's ordeal garnered special attention by the court in *Charkaoui*. It appeared to influence the court's decision. Would the court have decided this case differently if timing and political events were different? For example, what if a terrorist incident occurred in Canada a short time before the hearing or the decision itself? The court's authority depends on continuing public confidence in its processes and its decision-making. Decisions wildly out of step with the public temper may reduce public confidence in the institution. That having been said, the judicial function is premised on its insulation from intemperate public opinion. It is instructive in this regard that in the wake of the 9/11 attacks, the court was deliberating on a case it heard earlier in 2001 concerning the constitutionality of the impending deportation of an alleged Tamil Tiger fundraiser and member. The appellant argued that he was going to be deported to torture in Sri Lanka and that he had no access to the information on the basis of which the government claimed the contrary. In circumstances similar to those of the appellants in *Charkaoui*, he did not have the opportunity to respond to the government's case. The court, in January 2002, ordered a new deportation hearing, giving little hint of sensitivity to heightened public concern about terrorism and national security.[3] ∿

Discussion Questions

1. What influence does the experience of other countries in implementing national security policy exert on the Supreme Court of Canada in *Charkaoui*?

2. In *Re B.C. Motor Vehicle Act* (1985), the court considered the relationship between section 7 and section 1. How does that treatment compare to the court's consideration of the same issue in this case?

3. Heightened national security concerns are either legitimate or not. Should the legitimacy of such concerns influence the courts' assessment of the constitutionality of policies limiting the rights of persons suspected of threatening national security?

---

3   *Suresh v. Canada (Minister of Citizenship and Immigration)*, 2002 SCC 1, [2002] 1 S.C.R. 3.

CHARKAOUI v. CANADA (CITIZENSHIP AND IMMIGRATION)
2007 SCC 9, [2007] 1 S.C.R. 350

Hearing: June 13, 14, 15, 2006; Judgment: February 23, 2007.

Present: McLachlin C.J. and Bastarache, Binnie, LeBel, Deschamps, Fish, Abella, Charron, and Rothstein JJ.

Interveners: Attorney General of Ontario, Amnesty International, British Columbia Civil Liberties Association, Canadian Bar Association, Canadian Civil Liberties Association, Canadian Council for Refugees, African Canadian Legal Clinic, International Civil Liberties Monitoring Group, National Anti-Racism Council of Canada, Canadian Arab Federation, Canadian Council on American-Islamic Relations, Canadian Muslim Civil Liberties Association, Criminal Lawyers' Association (Ontario), Federation of Law Societies of Canada, University of Toronto, Faculty of Law—International Human Rights Clinic, Human Rights Watch.

The judgment of the Court was delivered by

THE CHIEF JUSTICE:

I. Introduction

[1] One of the most fundamental responsibilities of a government is to ensure the security of its citizens. This may

require it to act on information that it cannot disclose and to detain people who threaten national security. Yet in a constitutional democracy, governments must act accountably and in conformity with the Constitution and the rights and liberties it guarantees. These two propositions describe a tension that lies at the heart of modern democratic governance. It is a tension that must be resolved in a way that respects the imperatives both of security and of accountable constitutional governance.

[2] In this case, we are confronted with a statute, the *Immigration and Refugee Protection Act*, S.C. 2001, c. 27 ("*IRPA*"), that attempts to resolve this tension in the immigration context by allowing the Minister of Citizenship and Immigration (the "Minister"), and the Minister of Public Safety and Emergency Preparedness (collectively "the ministers") to issue a certificate of inadmissibility leading to the detention of a permanent resident or foreign national deemed to be a threat to national security. The certificate and the detention are both subject to review by a judge, in a process that may deprive the person named in the certificate of some or all of the information on the basis of which the certificate was issued or the detention ordered. The question is whether the solution that Parliament has enacted conforms to the Constitution, and in particular the guarantees in the *Canadian Charter of Rights and Freedoms* that protect against unjustifiable intrusions on liberty, equality and the freedom from arbitrary detention and from cruel and unusual treatment.

[3] I conclude that the *IRPA* unjustifiably violates s. 7 of the *Charter* by allowing the issuance of a certificate of inadmissibility based on secret material without providing for an independent agent at the stage of judicial review to better protect the named person's interests. I also conclude that some of the time limits in the provisions for continuing detention of a foreign national violate ss. 9 and 10(*c*) because they are arbitrary. I find that s. 12 has not been shown to be violated since a meaningful detention review process offers relief against the possibility of indefinite detention. Finally, I find that there is no breach of the s. 15 equality right.

II. Background

[4] The provisions of the *IRPA* at issue in this case, reproduced in the Appendix, are part of Canada's immigration law. Their purpose is to permit the removal of non-citizens living in Canada—permanent residents and foreign nationals—on various grounds, including connection with terrorist activities. The scheme permits deportation on the basis of confidential information that is not to be disclosed to the person named in the certificate or anyone acting on the person's behalf or in his or her interest. The scheme was meant to "facilitat[e] the early removal of persons who are inadmissible on serious grounds, including persons posing a threat to the security of Canada" (*Clause by Clause Analysis* (2001), at p. 72). In reality, however, it may also lead to long periods of incarceration.

[5] The *IRPA* requires the ministers to sign a certificate declaring that a foreign national or permanent resident is inadmissible to enter or remain in Canada on grounds of security, among others: s. 77. A judge of the Federal Court then reviews the certificate to determine whether it is reasonable: s. 80. If the state so requests, the review is conducted *in camera* and *ex parte*. The person named in the certificate has no right to see the material on the basis of which the certificate was issued. Non-sensitive material may be disclosed; sensitive or confidential material must not be disclosed if the government objects. The named person and his or her lawyer cannot see undisclosed material, although the ministers and the reviewing judge may rely on it. At the end of the day, the judge must provide the person with a summary of the case against him or her—a summary that does not disclose material that might compromise national security. If the judge determines that the certificate is reasonable, there is no appeal and no way to have the decision judicially reviewed: s. 80(3).

[6] The consequences of the issuance and confirmation of a certificate of inadmissibility vary, depending on whether the person is a permanent resident of Canada or a foreign national whose right to remain in Canada has not yet been confirmed. Permanent residents who the ministers have reasonable grounds to believe are a danger to national security *may* be held in detention. In order to detain them, the ministers must issue a warrant stating that the person is a threat to national security or to another person, or is unlikely to appear at a proceeding or for removal. Foreign nationals, meanwhile, *must* be detained once a certificate is issued: under s. 82(2), the detention is automatic. While the detention of a permanent resident must be reviewed within 48 hours, a foreign national, on the other hand, must apply for review, but may not do so until 120 days after a judge of the Federal Court determines the certificate to be reasonable. In both cases, if the judge finds the certificate to be reasonable, it becomes a removal order. Such an order deprives permanent residents of their status; their detention is then subject to review on the same basis as that of other foreign nationals.

[7] The removal order cannot be appealed and may be immediately enforced, thus eliminating the requirement of holding or continuing an examination or an admissibility hearing: s. 81(*b*). The detainee, whether a permanent resident or a foreign national, may no longer apply for protection: s. 81(*c*). Additionally, a refugee or a protected person determined to be inadmissible on any of the grounds for a certificate loses the protection of the principle of non-refoulement

under s. 115(1) if, in the opinion of the Minister, the person should not be allowed to remain in Canada on the basis of the nature and severity of acts committed or of danger to the security of Canada: s. 115(2). This means that he or she may, at least in theory, be deported to torture.

[8] A permanent resident detained under a certificate is entitled to a review of his or her detention every six months. Under s. 83(3), a judge must order the detention of a permanent resident to be continued if the judge is satisfied that the person continues to pose a danger to security or to the safety of another, or is unlikely to appear at a proceeding or for removal.

[9] The detention of foreign nationals, on the other hand, is mandatory. If a foreign national has not been removed within 120 days of the certificate being found reasonable by a judge, however, the judge may order the person released on appropriate conditions if "satisfied that the foreign national will not be removed from Canada within a reasonable time and that the release will not pose a danger to national security or to the safety of any person": s. 84(2). Even if released, the foreign national may be deported.

[10] Mr. Charkaoui is a permanent resident, while Messrs. Harkat and Almrei are foreign nationals who had been recognized as Convention refugees. All were living in Canada when they were arrested and detained. At the time of the decisions on appeal, all had been detained for some time— since 2003, 2002 and 2001 respectively. In 2001, a judge of the Federal Court determined Mr. Almrei's certificate to be reasonable; another determined Mr. Harkat's certificate to be reasonable in 2005. The reasonableness of Mr. Charkaoui's certificate has yet to be determined. Messrs. Charkaoui and Harkat were released on conditions in 2005 and 2006 respectively, but Mr. Harkat has been advised that he will be deported to Algeria, which he is contesting in other proceedings. Mr. Almrei remains in detention. In all these cases, the detentions were based on allegations that the individuals constituted a threat to the security of Canada by reason of involvement in terrorist activities. In the course of their detentions, all three appellants challenged, unsuccessfully, the constitutionality of the *IRPA*'s certificate scheme and detention review process.

III. Issues

[11] The appellants argue that the *IRPA*'s certificate scheme under which their detentions were ordered is unconstitutional. They argue that it violates five provisions of the *Charter*: the s. 7 guarantee of life, liberty and security of the person; the s. 9 guarantee against arbitrary detention; the s. 10(c) guarantee of a prompt review of detention; the s. 12 guarantee against cruel and unusual treatment; and the s. 15 guarantee of equal protection and equal benefit of the law. ...

A. Does the Procedure Under the IRPA for Determining the Reasonableness of the Certificate Infringe Section 7 of the Charter, and If So, Is the Infringement Justified Under Section 1 of the Charter?

1. Is Section 7 of the Charter Engaged?

... [18] In determining whether s. 7 applies, we must look at the interests at stake rather than the legal label attached to the impugned legislation. As Professor Hamish Stewart writes:

> Many of the principles of fundamental justice were developed in criminal cases, but their application is not restricted to criminal cases: they apply whenever one of the three protected interests is engaged. Put another way, the principles of fundamental justice apply in *criminal* proceedings, not because they are criminal proceedings, but because the liberty interest is always engaged in criminal proceedings. [Emphasis in original.]

> ("Is Indefinite Detention of Terrorist Suspects Really Constitutional?" (2005), 54 *U.N.B.L.J.* 235, at p. 242)

I conclude that the appellants' challenges to the fairness of the process leading to possible deportation and the loss of liberty associated with detention raise important issues of liberty and security, and that s. 7 of the *Charter* is engaged.

2. How Do Security Considerations Affect the Section 7 Analysis?

[19] Section 7 of the *Charter* requires that laws that interfere with life, liberty and security of the person conform to the principles of fundamental justice—the basic principles that underlie our notions of justice and fair process. These principles include a guarantee of procedural fairness, having regard to the circumstances and consequences of the intrusion on life, liberty or security. ...

[22] The question at the s. 7 stage is whether the principles of fundamental justice relevant to the case have been observed in substance, having regard to the context and the seriousness of the violation. The issue is whether the process is fundamentally unfair to the affected person. If so, the deprivation of life, liberty or security of the person simply does not conform to the requirements of s. 7. The inquiry then shifts to s. 1 of the *Charter*, at which point the government has an opportunity to establish that the flawed process is nevertheless justified having regard, notably, to the public interest.

[23] It follows that while administrative constraints associated with the context of national security may inform the analysis on whether a particular process is fundamentally unfair, security concerns cannot be used to excuse procedures that do not conform to fundamental justice at the s. 7 stage of the analysis. If the context makes it impossible to adhere to the

principles of fundamental justice in their usual form, adequate substitutes may be found. But the principles must be respected to pass the hurdle of s. 7. That is the bottom line.

[24] In the instant case, the context is the detention, incidental to their removal or an attempt to remove them from the country, of permanent residents and foreign nationals who the ministers conclude pose a threat to national security. This context may impose certain administrative constraints that may be properly considered at the s. 7 stage. Full disclosure of the information relied on may not be possible. The executive branch of government may be required to act quickly, without recourse, at least in the first instance, to the judicial procedures normally required for the deprivation of liberty or security of the person.

[25] At the same time, it is a context that may have important, indeed chilling, consequences for the detainee. The seriousness of the individual interests at stake forms part of the contextual analysis. As this Court stated in *Suresh*, "[t]he greater the effect on the life of the individual by the decision, the greater the need for procedural protections to meet the common law duty of fairness and the requirements of fundamental justice under s. 7 of the *Charter*" (para. 118). Thus, "factual situations which are closer or analogous to criminal proceedings will merit greater vigilance by the courts": *Dehghani v. Canada (Minister of Employment and Immigration)*, [1993] 1 S.C.R. 1053, at p. 1077, *per* Iacobucci J.

[26] The potential consequences of deportation combined with allegations of terrorism have been under a harsh spotlight due to the recent report of the Commission of Inquiry into the Actions of Canadian Officials in Relation to Maher Arar. Mr. Arar, a Canadian citizen born in Syria, was detained by American officials and deported to Syria. The report concludes that it is "very likely that, in making the decisions to detain and remove Mr. Arar to Syria, the U.S. authorities relied on information about Mr. Arar provided by the RCMP," including unfounded suspicions linking Mr. Arar to terrorist groups: *Report of the Events Relating to Maher Arar: Analysis and Recommendations* (2006) ("Arar Inquiry"), at p. 30. In Syria, Mr. Arar was tortured and detained under inhumane conditions for over 11 months. In his report, Commissioner O'Connor recommends enhanced review and accountability mechanisms for agencies dealing with national security, including not only the Royal Canadian Mounted Police, but also Citizenship and Immigration Canada and the Canada Border Services Agency. He notes that these immigration-related institutions can have an important impact on individual rights but that there is a lack of transparency surrounding their activities because their activities often involve sensitive national security information that cannot be disclosed to the public: *A New Review Mechanism for*

the RCMP's National Security Activities (2006), at pp. 562-65. Moreover, the sensitive nature of security information means that investigations lead to fewer prosecutions. This, in turn, restricts the ability of courts to guarantee individual rights: "Unless charges are laid, ... the choice of investigative targets, methods of information collection and exchange, and means of investigation generally will not be subject to judicial scrutiny, media coverage or public debate" (p. 439).

[27] The procedures required to conform to the principles of fundamental justice must reflect the exigencies of the security context. Yet they cannot be permitted to erode the essence of s. 7. The principles of fundamental justice cannot be reduced to the point where they cease to provide the protection of due process that lies at the heart of s. 7 of the *Charter*. The protection may not be as complete as in a case where national security constraints do not operate. But to satisfy s. 7, meaningful and substantial protection there must be.

3. Relevant Principles of Fundamental Justice

[28] The overarching principle of fundamental justice that applies here is this: before the state can detain people for significant periods of time, it must accord them a fair judicial process. ...

[29] This basic principle has a number of facets. It comprises the right to a *hearing*. It requires that the hearing be *before an independent and impartial magistrate*. It demands a *decision by the magistrate on the facts and the law*. And it entails the *right to know the case put against one*, and the *right to answer that case*. Precisely how these requirements are met will vary with the context. But for s. 7 to be satisfied, each of them must be met in substance.

[30] The *IRPA* process includes a hearing. The process consists of two phases, one executive and one judicial. There is no hearing at the executive phase that results in issuance of the certificate. However, this is followed by a review before a judge, where the named person is afforded a hearing. Thus, the first requirement, that of a hearing, is met.

[31] Questions arise, however, on the other requirements, namely: that the judge be independent and impartial; that the judge make a judicial decision based on the facts and the law; and finally, that the named person be afforded an opportunity to meet the case put against him or her by being informed of that case and being allowed to question or counter it. I conclude that the *IRPA* scheme meets the first requirement of independence and impartiality, but fails to satisfy the second and third requirements, which are interrelated here.

4. Is the Judge Independent and Impartial?

[32] Although the scope of the required hearing can vary according to context (*Baker v. Canada (Minister of Citizenship*

and Immigration), [1999] 2 S.C.R. 817), a hearing must include "[a]n independent judicial phase and an impartial judge" (*Ferras*, at para. 25). This requirement is also consistent with the unwritten constitutional principle of judicial independence: *Reference re Remuneration of Judges of the Provincial Court of Prince Edward Island*, [1997] 3 S.C.R. 3. It has also been called "the cornerstone of the common law duty of procedural fairness" (*Application under s. 83.28 of the Criminal Code (Re)*, [2004] 2 S.C.R. 248, 2004 SCC 42 ("*Re Bagri*"), at para. 81), and is necessary in order to ensure judicial impartiality: *R. v. Lippé*, [1991] 2 S.C.R. 114, at p. 139. It is not enough that the judge in fact be independent and impartial; fundamental justice requires that the judge also appear to be independent and impartial. This flows from the fact that judicial independence has two facets: actual independence and perceived independence (*Valente v. The Queen*, [1985] 2 S.C.R. 673, at p. 689).

[33] The *IRPA* scheme provides for the certificate issued by the ministers to be reviewed by a "designated judge," a judge of the Federal Court of Canada. The question here is whether, from an institutional perspective, the role assigned to designated judges under the *IRPA* leads to a perception that independence and impartiality are compromised.

[34] The designated judge has been aptly described as the "cornerstone of the procedure established by Parliament" in the *IRPA* (*Charkaoui (Re)*, [2004] 3 F.C.R. 32, 2003 FC 1419, at para. 120, *per* Noël J.). The judge is the sole avenue of review for the named person and the only person capable of providing the essential judicial component of the process.

[35] When reviewing the certificate, the judge sees all the material relied on by the government. But if the government claims confidentiality for certain material, the judge cannot share this material with the named person. The judge must make his or her decision without hearing any objections the named person might be able to make, were he or she granted access to the whole of the record. Part of the hearing may be held *in camera*, with only the judge and the government lawyers in the room. The named person is not there. His or her lawyer is not there. There is no one to speak for the person or to test the evidence put against him or her.

[36] These circumstances may give rise to a perception that the designated judge under the *IRPA* may not be entirely independent and impartial as between the state and the person named in the certificate. ...

[37] Three related concerns arise with respect to independence and impartiality. First is the concern that the *IRPA* may be perceived to deprive the judge of his or her independent judicial role and co-opt the judge as an agent of the executive branch of government. Second is the concern that the designated judge functions as an investigative

officer rather than a judge. Third is the concern that the judge, whose role includes compensating for the fact that the named person may not have access to material and may not be present at the hearing, will become associated with this person's case.

[38] The first concern is linked to the degree of deference that the judge accords to the ministers' conclusion that the facts supported the issuance of a certificate and the detention of the named person. Judges working under the process have eschewed an overly deferential approach, insisting instead on a searching examination of the reasonableness of the certificate on the material placed before them. ...

[42] I conclude that a non-deferential role for the designated judge goes some distance toward alleviating the first concern, that the judge will be perceived to be in the camp of the government.

[43] The second concern is that the judge may be seen to function more as an investigator than as an independent and impartial adjudicator. The law is clear that the principles of fundamental justice are breached if a judge is reduced to an executive, investigative function. At the same time, the mere fact that a judge is required to assist in an investigative activity does not deprive the judge of the requisite independence. ...

[44] The *IRPA* provisions before the Court ... preserve the essential elements of the judicial role. ...

[45] The third concern is that the judge's role as sole protector of the named person's interest may associate the judge, in fact or perception, with that interest. A judge who is obliged to take on a "defence" role in the absence of counsel may unconsciously become associated with that camp: *R. v. Taubler* (1987), 20 O.A.C. 64, at p. 71; *R. v. Turlon* (1989), 49 C.C.C. (3d) 186 (Ont. C.A.), at p. 191. This concern must be balanced against the opposite concern that the judge may appear to be part of the government scheme and hence in the government's camp. The critical consideration, however, is that the *IRPA* permits—indeed requires—the judge to conduct the review in an independent and judicial fashion. Provided the judge does so, the scheme cannot be condemned on the ground that he or she is, in fact or perception, in the named person's camp.

[46] I conclude that, on its face, the *IRPA* process is designed to preserve the independence and impartiality of the designated judge, as required by s. 7. Properly followed by judges committed to a searching review, it cannot be said to compromise the perceived independence and impartiality of the designated judge.

[47] I note that this conclusion conclusively rebuts the appellant Charkaoui's contention that the *IRPA* breaches the unwritten constitutional principle of judicial independence affirmed in *Provincial Court Judges' Assn. of New Brunswick v.*

New Brunswick (Minister of Justice), [2005] 2 S.C.R. 286, 2005 SCC 44.

5. Is the Decision Based on the Facts and the Law?

[48] To comply with s. 7 of the *Charter*, the magistrate must make a decision based on the facts and the law. In the extradition context, the principles of fundamental justice have been held to require, "at a minimum, a meaningful judicial assessment of the case on the basis of the evidence and the law. A judge considers the respective rights of the litigants or parties and makes findings of fact on the basis of evidence and applies the law to those findings. Both facts and law must be considered for a true adjudication. Since *Bonham's Case* [(1610), 8 Co. Rep. 113b, 77 E.R. 646], the essence of a judicial hearing has been the treatment of facts revealed by the evidence in consideration of the substantive rights of the parties as set down by law" (*Ferras*, at para. 25). The individual and societal interests at stake in the certificate of inadmissibility context suggest similar requirements.

[49] The *IRPA* process at issue seeks to meet this requirement by placing material before the judge for evaluation. As a practical matter, most if not all of the material that the judge considers is produced by the government and can be vetted for reliability and sufficiency only by the judge. The normal standards used to ensure the reliability of evidence in court do not apply: s. 78(*j*). The named person may be shown little or none of the material relied on by the ministers and the judge, and may thus not be in a position to know or challenge the case against him or her. It follows that the judge's decision, while based on the evidence before him or her, may not be based on all of the evidence available.

[50] There are two types of judicial systems, and they ensure that the full case is placed before the judge in two different ways. In inquisitorial systems, as in Continental Europe, the judge takes charge of the gathering of evidence in an independent and impartial way. By contrast, an adversarial system, which is the norm in Canada, relies on the parties— who are entitled to disclosure of the case to meet, and to full participation in open proceedings—to produce the relevant evidence. The designated judge under the *IRPA* does not possess the full and independent powers to gather evidence that exist in the inquisitorial process. At the same time, the named person is not given the disclosure and the right to participate in the proceedings that characterize the adversarial process. The result is a concern that the designated judge, despite his or her best efforts to get all the relevant evidence, may be obliged—perhaps unknowingly—to make the required decision based on only part of the relevant evidence. ...

[51] Judges of the Federal Court have worked assiduously to overcome the difficulties inherent in the role the *IRPA* has assigned to them. To their credit, they have adopted a pseudo-inquisitorial role and sought to seriously test the protected documentation and information. But the role remains *pseudo-*inquisitorial. The judge is not afforded the power to independently investigate all relevant facts that true inquisitorial judges enjoy. At the same time, since the named person is not given a full picture of the case to meet, the judge cannot rely on the parties to present missing evidence. The result is that, at the end of the day, one cannot be sure that the judge has been exposed to the whole factual picture.

[52] Similar concerns arise with respect to the requirement that the decision be based on the law. Without knowledge of the information put against him or her, the named person may not be in a position to raise legal objections relating to the evidence, or to develop legal arguments based on the evidence. The named person is, to be sure, permitted to make legal representations. But without disclosure and full participation throughout the process, he or she may not be in a position to put forward a full legal argument.

6. Is the "Case to Meet" Principle Satisfied?

[53] Last but not least, a fair hearing requires that the affected person be informed of the case against him or her, and be permitted to respond to that case. This right is well established in immigration law. ...

[54] Under the *IRPA*'s certificate scheme, the named person may be deprived of access to some or all of the information put against him or her, which would deny the person the ability to know the case to meet. Without this information, the named person may not be in a position to contradict errors, identify omissions, challenge the credibility of informants or refute false allegations. This problem is serious in itself. It also underlies the concerns, discussed above, about the independence and impartiality of the designated judge, and the ability of the judge to make a decision based on the facts and law.

[55] Confidentiality is a constant preoccupation of the certificate scheme. The judge "shall ensure" the confidentiality of the information on which the certificate is based and of any other evidence if, in the opinion of the judge, disclosure would be injurious to national security or to the safety of any person: s. 78(*b*). At the request of either minister "at any time during the proceedings," the judge "shall hear" information or evidence in the absence of the named person and his or her counsel if, in the opinion of the judge, its disclosure would be injurious to national security or to the safety of any person: s. 78(*e*). The judge "shall provide" the named person with a summary of information that enables him or her to be reasonably informed of the circumstances giving rise to the

certificate, but the summary cannot include anything that would, in the opinion of the judge, be injurious to national security or to the safety of any person: s. 78(*h*). Ultimately, the judge may have to consider information that is not included in the summary: s. 78(*g*). In the result, the judge may be required to decide the case, wholly or in part, on the basis of information that the named person and his or her counsel never see. The named person may know nothing of the case to meet, and although technically afforded an opportunity to be heard, may be left in a position of having no idea as to what needs to be said.

[56] The same concerns arise with respect to the detention review process under ss. 83 and 84 of the *IRPA*. Section 78 applies to detention reviews under s. 83, and it has been found to apply to detention reviews under s. 84(2): *Almrei v. Canada (Minister of Citizenship and Immigration)*, [2005] 3 F.C.R. 142, 2005 FCA 54, at paras. 71-72.

[57] The right to know the case to be met is not absolute. Canadian statutes sometimes provide for *ex parte* or *in camera* hearings, in which judges must decide important issues after hearing from only one side. In *Rodgers*, the majority of this Court declined to recognize notice and participation as invariable constitutional norms, emphasizing a context-sensitive approach to procedural fairness. ...

[58] More particularly, the Court has repeatedly recognized that national security considerations can limit the extent of disclosure of information to the affected individual. In *Chiarelli*, this Court found that the Security Intelligence Review Committee could, in investigating certificates under the former *Immigration Act, 1976*, S.C. 1976-77, c. 52 (later R.S.C. 1985, c. I-2), refuse to disclose details of investigation techniques and police sources. The context for elucidating the principles of fundamental justice in that case included the state's "interest in effectively conducting national security and criminal intelligence investigations and in protecting police sources" (p. 744). In *Suresh*, this Court held that a refugee facing the possibility of deportation to torture was entitled to disclosure of all the information on which the Minister was basing his or her decision, "[s]ubject to privilege or similar valid reasons for reduced disclosure, such as safeguarding confidential public security documents" (para. 122). And, in *Ruby v. Canada (Solicitor General)*, [2002] 4 S.C.R. 3, 2002 SCC 75, the Court upheld the section of the *Privacy Act*, R.S.C. 1985, c. P-21, that mandates *in camera* and *ex parte* proceedings where the government claims an exemption from disclosure on grounds of national security or maintenance of foreign confidences. The Court made clear that these societal concerns formed part of the relevant context for determining the scope of the applicable principles of fundamental justice (paras. 38-44). ...

[61] In the context of national security, non-disclosure, which may be extensive, coupled with the grave intrusions on liberty imposed on a detainee, makes it difficult, if not impossible, to find substitute procedures that will satisfy s. 7. Fundamental justice requires substantial compliance with the venerated principle that a person whose liberty is in jeopardy must be given an opportunity to know the case to meet, and an opportunity to meet the case. Yet the imperative of the protection of society may preclude this. Information may be obtained from other countries or from informers on condition that it not be disclosed. Or it may simply be so critical that it cannot be disclosed without risking public security. This is a reality of our modern world. If s. 7 is to be satisfied, either the person must be given the necessary information, or a substantial substitute for that information must be found. Neither is the case here.

[62] The only protection the *IRPA* accords the named person is a review by a designated judge to determine whether the certificate is reasonable. The ministers argue that this is adequate in that it maintains a "delicate balance" between the right to a fair hearing and the need to protect confidential security intelligence information. The appellants, on the other hand, argue that the judge's efforts, however conscientious, cannot provide an effective substitute for informed participation.

[63] I agree with the appellants. The issue at the s. 7 stage, as discussed above, is not whether the government has struck the right balance between the need for security and individual liberties; that is the issue at the stage of s. 1 justification of an established limitation on a *Charter* right. The question at the s. 7 stage is whether the basic requirements of procedural justice have been met, either in the usual way or in an alternative fashion appropriate to the context, having regard to the government's objective and the interests of the person affected. The fairness of the *IRPA* procedure rests entirely on the shoulders of the designated judge. Those shoulders cannot by themselves bear the heavy burden of assuring, in fact and appearance, that the decision on the reasonableness of the certificate is impartial, is based on a full view of the facts and law, and reflects the named person's knowledge of the case to meet. The judge, working under the constraints imposed by the *IRPA*, simply cannot fill the vacuum left by the removal of the traditional guarantees of a fair hearing. The judge sees only what the ministers put before him or her. The judge, knowing nothing else about the case, is not in a position to identify errors, find omissions or assess the credibility and truthfulness of the information in the way the named person would be. Although the judge may ask questions of the named person when the hearing is reopened, the judge is prevented from asking questions that might disclose the protected

information. Likewise, since the named person does not know what has been put against him or her, he or she does not know what the designated judge needs to hear. If the judge cannot provide the named person with a summary of the information that is sufficient to enable the person to know the case to meet, then the judge cannot be satisfied that the information before him or her is sufficient or reliable. Despite the judge's best efforts to question the government's witnesses and scrutinize the documentary evidence, he or she is placed in the situation of asking questions and ultimately deciding the issues on the basis of incomplete and potentially unreliable information.

[64] The judge is not helpless; he or she can note contradictions between documents, insist that there be at least some evidence on the critical points, and make limited inferences on the value and credibility of the information from its source. Nevertheless, the judge's activity on behalf of the named person is confined to what is presented by the ministers. The judge is therefore not in a position to compensate for the lack of informed scrutiny, challenge and counter-evidence that a person familiar with the case could bring. Such scrutiny is the whole point of the principle that a person whose liberty is in jeopardy must know the case to meet. Here that principle has not merely been limited; it has been effectively gutted. How can one meet a case one does not know? ...

8. Is the Limit Justified Under Section 1 of the Charter?

... [68] The protection of Canada's national security and related intelligence sources undoubtedly constitutes a pressing and substantial objective. Moreover, the *IRPA*'s provisions regarding the non-disclosure of evidence at certificate hearings are rationally connected to this objective. ...

[69] The realities that confront modern governments faced with the challenge of terrorism are stark. In the interest of security, it may be necessary to detain persons deemed to pose a threat. At the same time, security concerns may preclude disclosure of the evidence on which the detention is based. But these tensions are not new. As we shall see, Canada has already devised processes that go further in preserving s. 7 rights while protecting sensitive information; until recently, one of these solutions was applicable in the security certificate context. Nor are these tensions unique to Canada: in the specific context of anti-terrorism legislation, the United Kingdom uses special counsel to provide a measure of protection to the detained person's interests, while preserving the confidentiality of information that must be kept secret. These alternatives suggest that the *IRPA* regime, which places on the judge the entire burden of protecting the person's interest, does not minimally impair the rights of non-citizens, and hence cannot be saved under s. 1 of the *Charter*.

(a) Less Intrusive Alternatives

[70] This is not the first time Canada has had to reconcile the demands of national security with the procedural rights guaranteed by the *Charter*. In a number of legal contexts, Canadian government institutions have found ways to protect sensitive information while treating individuals fairly. In some situations, the solution has involved the use of special counsel, in a manner closely approximating an adversarial process.

[71] The Security Intelligence Review Committee ("SIRC") is an independent review body that monitors the activities of the Canadian Security Intelligence Service ("CSIS"). Established in 1984 under the *Canadian Security Intelligence Service Act*, S.C. 1984, c. 21 (now R.S.C. 1985, c. C-23), SIRC is composed of three to five members of the Privy Council who are not currently serving in Parliament. Under the former *Immigration Act*, SIRC had the power to vet findings of inadmissibility based on alleged threats to national security; a ministerial certificate could not be issued without a SIRC investigation. If the Minister of Employment and Immigration and the Solicitor General were of the opinion that a non-citizen was inadmissible due to involvement in organized crime, espionage, subversion, acts of violence, etc., they were first obliged to make a report to SIRC: *Immigration Act*, s. 39(2). SIRC would then investigate the grounds for the report, providing the affected person with "a statement summarizing such information available to it as will enable the person to be as fully informed as possible of the circumstances giving rise to the report": s. 39(6). After completing its investigation, SIRC would send a report to the Governor in Council containing its recommendation as to whether a security certificate should be issued: s. 39(9). A copy of the same report would be provided to the non-citizen: s. 39(10). If the Governor in Council was satisfied that the non-citizen was inadmissible on appropriate grounds, he or she could then direct the Minister of Employment and Immigration to issue a security certificate: s. 40(1).

[72] Empowered to develop its own investigative procedures, SIRC established a formal adversarial process, with "a court-like hearing room" and "procedures that mirrored judicial proceedings as much as possible." The process also included an independent panel of lawyers with security clearances to act as counsel to SIRC (M. Rankin, "The Security Intelligence Review Committee: Reconciling National Security with Procedural Fairness" (1990), 3 *C.J.A.L.P.* 173, at p. 179).

[73] A SIRC member presiding at a hearing had the discretion to balance national security against procedural fairness in determining how much information could be disclosed to the affected person. The non-citizen and his or her counsel would normally be present in the hearing room, except when

sensitive national security evidence was tendered. (The presiding SIRC member would decide whether to exclude the non-citizen during certain testimony.) At such a juncture, independent, security-cleared SIRC counsel would act on behalf of the non-citizen. The SIRC counsel were instructed to cross-examine witnesses for CSIS "with as much vigour as one would expect from the complainant's counsel" (Rankin, at p. 184; SIRC *Annual Report 1988-1989* (1989) ("SIRC *Annual Report*"), at p. 64). At the end of this *ex parte* portion of the hearing, the excluded person would be brought back into the room and provided with a summary, which would include "the gist of the evidence, without disclosing the national security information" (SIRC *Annual Report*, at p. 64). The SIRC counsel would negotiate the contents of the summary with CSIS, under the supervision of the presiding SIRC member (*ibid.*). The affected person and his or her counsel would then be allowed to ask their own questions, and to cross-examine on the basis of the summary (Rankin, at p. 184).

[74] In the words of Professor Rankin, SIRC's procedures represented "an attempt to preserve the best features of the adversarial process with its insistence on vigorous cross-examination, but not to run afoul of the requirements of national security" (p. 185). These procedures illustrate how special counsel can provide not only an effective substitute for informed participation, but can also help bolster actual informed participation by the affected person. Since the special counsel had a role in determining how much information would be included in the summary, disclosure was presumably more complete than would otherwise have been the case. Sensitive national security information was still protected, but the executive was required to justify the breadth of this protection.

[75] In 1988 Parliament added s. 40.1 to the *Immigration Act* to empower the Minister and the Solicitor General to issue security certificates in respect of foreign nationals. Section 40.1 effectively bypassed the SIRC investigation process where foreign nationals were concerned, instead referring the certificate to a designated judge of the Federal Court for subsequent review. Security certificates in respect of permanent residents remained subject to SIRC scrutiny until 2002, when Parliament repealed the *Immigration Act* and replaced it with the *IRPA*.

[76] Certain elements of SIRC process may be inappropriate to the context of terrorism. Where there is a risk of catastrophic acts of violence, it would be foolhardy to require a lengthy review process *before* a certificate could be issued. But it was not suggested before this Court that SIRC's special counsel system had not functioned well in connection with the review of certificates under the *Immigration Act*, nor was

any explanation given for why, under the new system for vetting certificates and reviewing detentions, a special counsel process had not been retained.

[77] The SIRC process is not the only example of the Canadian legal system striking a better balance between the protection of sensitive information and the procedural rights of individuals. A current example is found in the *Canada Evidence Act*, R.S.C. 1985, c. C-5 ("*CEA*"), which permits the government to object to the disclosure of information on grounds of public interest, in proceedings to which the Act applies: ss. 37 to 39. Under the recent amendments to the *CEA* set out in the *Anti-terrorism Act*, S.C. 2001, c. 41, a participant in a proceeding who is required to disclose or expects to disclose potentially injurious or sensitive information, or who believes that such information might be disclosed, must notify the Attorney General about the potential disclosure, and the Attorney General may then apply to the Federal Court for an order prohibiting the disclosure of the information: ss. 38.01, 38.02, 38.04. The judge enjoys considerable discretion in deciding whether the information should be disclosed. If the judge concludes that disclosure of the information would be injurious to international relations, national defence or national security, but that the public interest in disclosure outweighs in importance the public interest in non-disclosure, the judge may order the disclosure of all or part of the information, on such conditions as he or she sees fit. No similar residual discretion exists under the *IRPA*, which requires judges not to disclose information the disclosure of which would be injurious to national security or to the safety of any person. Moreover, the *CEA* makes no provision for the use of information that has not been disclosed. While the *CEA* does not address the same problems as the *IRPA*, and hence is of limited assistance here, it illustrates Parliament's concern under other legislation for striking a sensitive balance between the need for protection of confidential information and the rights of the individual.

[78] Crown and defence counsel in the recent Air India trial (*R. v. Malik*, [2005] B.C.J. No. 521 (QL), 2005 BCSC 350) were faced with the task of managing security and intelligence information and attempting to protect procedural fairness. The Crown was in possession of the fruits of a 17-year-long investigation into the terrorist bombing of a passenger aircraft and a related explosion in Narita, Japan. It withheld material on the basis of relevance, national security privilege and litigation privilege. Crown and defence counsel came to an agreement under which defence counsel obtained consents from their clients to conduct a preliminary review of the withheld material, on written undertakings not to disclose the material to anyone, including the client. Disclosure in a specific trial, to a select group of counsel on undertakings, may

not provide a working model for general deportation legislation that must deal with a wide variety of counsel in a host of cases. Nevertheless, the procedures adopted in the Air India trial suggest that a search should be made for a less intrusive solution than the one found in the *IRPA*.

[79] The Arar Inquiry provides another example of the use of special counsel in Canada. The Commission had to examine confidential information related to the investigation of terrorism plots while preserving Mr. Arar's and the public's interest in disclosure. The Commission was governed by the *CEA*. To help assess claims for confidentiality, the Commissioner was assisted by independent security-cleared legal counsel with a background in security and intelligence, whose role was to act as *amicus curiae* on confidentiality applications. The scheme's aim was to ensure that only information that was rightly subject to national security confidentiality was kept from public view. There is no indication that these procedures increased the risk of disclosure of protected information.

[80] Finally, I note the special advocate system employed by the Special Immigration Appeals Commission ("SIAC") in the United Kingdom. SIAC and the special advocate system were created in response to *Chahal v. United Kingdom*, 15 November 1996, *Reports of Judgments and Decisions* 1996-V, p. 1831, in which the European Court of Human Rights had held that the procedure then in place was inadequate. The court in *Chahal* commented favourably on the idea of security-cleared counsel instructed by the court, identifying it as being Canadian in origin (perhaps referring to the procedure developed by SIRC).

[81] The U.K.'s special advocate system resembles the Canadian SIRC model. Section 6(1) of the *Special Immigration Appeals Commission Act 1997* (U.K.), 1997, c. 68, states that the special advocate is appointed to "represent the interests of an appellant" in any proceedings before SIAC from which the appellant and his or her legal representatives are excluded. Section 6(4), however, specifies that the special advocate "shall not be responsible to the person whose interests he is appointed to represent." Rule 35 of the *Special Immigration Appeals Commission (Procedure) Rules 2003*, S.I. 2003/1034, sets out the special advocate's three main functions: (1) to make submissions to the Commission at any hearings from which the appellant and the appellant's representatives are excluded; (2) to cross-examine witnesses at any such hearings; and (3) to make written submissions to the Commission. After seeing the protected information, the special advocate may not communicate with the appellant or the appellant's representative without authorization from the Commission: rule 36. If the special advocate requests such authorization, the Commission gives the Secretary of State an opportunity to object to the proposed communication before deciding whether to authorize it: rule 38.

[82] The use of special advocates has received widespread support in Canadian academic commentary. Professor Roach, for example, criticizes the Court of Appeal's conclusion in *Charkaoui (Re)*, 2004 FCA 421, that such a measure is not constitutionally required:

> In my view, this approach was in error because *in camera* and *ex parte* hearings offend basic notions of a fair hearing and *special advocates constitute one example of an approach that is a more proportionate response to reconciling the need to keep some information secret and the need to ensure as much fairness and adversarial challenge as possible.* [Emphasis added.]
>
> (K. Roach, "Ten Ways to Improve Canadian Anti-Terrorism Law" (2006), 51 *Crim. L.Q.* 102, at p. 120)

[83] This said, the U.K.'s special advocate system has also been criticized for not going far enough. In April 2005, the House of Commons Constitutional Affairs Committee published a report on the operation of SIAC and the use of special advocates (*The operation of the Special Immigration Appeals Commission (SIAC) and the use of Special Advocates*). The Committee listed three important disadvantages faced by special advocates: (1) once they have seen the confidential material, they cannot, subject to narrow exceptions, take instructions from the appellant or the appellant's counsel; (2) they lack the resources of an ordinary legal team, for the purpose of conducting in secret a full defence; and (3) they have no power to call witnesses (para. 52).

[84] Despite these difficulties, SIAC itself has commented favourably on the assistance provided by special advocates, stating that as a result of the "rigorous cross-examination" of the government's evidence by the special advocate, it was satisfied that the government's assertions were unsupported by the evidence (*M. v. Secretary of State for the Home Department*, [2004] UKSIAC 17/2002 (BAILII), March 8, 2004, at para. 10). The England and Wales Court of Appeal upheld SIAC's decision: [2004] 2 All E.R. 863, [2004] EWCA Civ 324.

(b) The IRPA Scheme Does Not Minimally Impair the Named Person's Rights

[85] Parliament is not required to use the *perfect*, or least restrictive, alternative to achieve its objective: *R. v. Chaulk*, [1990] 3 S.C.R. 1303. However, bearing in mind the deference that is owed to Parliament in its legislative choices, the alternatives discussed demonstrate that the *IRPA* does not minimally impair the named person's rights.

[86] Under the *IRPA*, the government effectively decides what can be disclosed to the named person. Not only is the

named person not shown the information and not permitted to participate in proceedings involving it, but no one but the judge may look at the information with a view to protecting the named person's interests. Why the drafters of the legislation did not provide for special counsel to objectively review the material with a view to protecting the named person's interest, as was formerly done for the review of security certificates by SIRC and is presently done in the United Kingdom, has not been explained. The special counsel system may not be perfect from the named person's perspective, given that special counsel cannot reveal confidential material. But, without compromising security, it better protects the named person's s. 7 interests.

[87] I conclude that the *IRPA*'s procedures for determining whether a certificate is reasonable and for detention review cannot be justified as minimal impairments of the individual's right to a judicial determination on the facts and the law and right to know and meet the case. Mechanisms developed in Canada and abroad illustrate that the government can do more to protect the individual while keeping critical information confidential than it has done in the *IRPA*. Precisely what more should be done is a matter for Parliament to decide. But it is clear that more must be done to meet the requirements of a free and democratic society.

B. Does the Detention of Permanent Residents or Foreign Nationals Under the IRPA Infringe Sections 7, 9, 10(c) or 12 of the Charter, and If So, Are the Infringements Justified Under Section 1 of the Charter?

1. Time Constraints on Review for Foreign Nationals: Breach of Section 9 or Section 10(c)?

[88] Section 9 of the *Charter* guarantees freedom from arbitrary detention. This guarantee expresses one of the most fundamental norms of the rule of law. The state may not detain arbitrarily, but only in accordance with the law. The appellant Mr. Almrei argues that detention under the *IRPA* is arbitrary with respect to foreign nationals, first because it permits their detention without warrant and without regard to their personal circumstances, and second because it prevents review until 120 days after the certificate is confirmed. In both respects, foreign nationals are treated differently than permanent residents. …

[The court rejected the first argument.]

[91] The lack of review for foreign nationals until 120 days after the reasonableness of the certificate has been judicially determined violates the guarantee against arbitrary detention in s. 9 of the *Charter*, a guarantee which encompasses the right to prompt review of detention under s. 10(c)

of the *Charter*. Permanent residents named in certificates are entitled to an automatic review within 48 hours. The same time frame for review of detention applies to both permanent residents and foreign nationals under s. 57 of the *IRPA*. And under the *Criminal Code*, a person who is arrested with or without a warrant is to be brought before a judge within 24 hours, or as soon as possible: s. 503(1). These provisions indicate the seriousness with which the deprivation of liberty is viewed, and offer guidance as to acceptable delays before this deprivation is reviewed.

[92] The government submits that the detention provisions, and more specifically the absence of review for foreign nationals until 120 days after the certificate has been determined to be reasonable, reflect its objective of creating a timely removal process for individuals thought to constitute a danger to national security, and asserts that when the provisions were drafted, it was thought that the removal process would be so fast that there would be no need for review. This is more an admission of the excessiveness of the 120-day period than a justification.

[93] It is clear that there may be a need for some flexibility regarding the period for which a suspected terrorist may be detained. Confronted with a terrorist threat, state officials may need to act immediately, in the absence of a fully documented case. It may take some time to verify and document the threat. Where state officials act expeditiously, the failure to meet an arbitrary target of a fixed number of hours should not mean the automatic release of the person, who may well be dangerous. However, this cannot justify the complete denial of a timely detention review. Permanent residents who pose a danger to national security are also meant to be removed expeditiously. If this objective can be pursued while providing permanent residents with a mandatory detention review within 48 hours, then how can a denial of review for foreign nationals for 120 days after the certificate is confirmed be considered a minimal impairment?

[94] I conclude that the lack of timely review of the detention of foreign nationals violates s. 9 and s. 10(c) and cannot be saved by s. 1.

2. Do Extended Periods of Detention Under the Scheme Violate Section 7 or the Section 12 Guarantee Against Cruel and Unusual Treatment?

[The appellants argued that the IRPA's provisions governing detention fall afoul of the Charter right not to be subjected to cruel and unusual treatment or punishment. The court rejected their argument, noting, first, that the section 12 bar is quite high. If a legislative scheme permits detainees to challenge their detention and have a realistic prospect of release upon satisfaction of reasonable conditions, detention is neither cruel nor unusual. Such is the case here. Second, the court held that the IRPA, properly interpreted, provides sufficient safeguards against indefinite detention.]

[123] [T]he *IRPA*, interpreted in conformity with the *Charter*, permits robust ongoing judicial review of the continued need for and justice of the detainee's detention pending deportation. On this basis, I conclude that extended periods of detention pending deportation under the certificate provisions of the *IRPA* do not violate s. 7 or s. 12 of the *Charter*, provided that reviewing courts adhere to the guidelines set out above. Thus, the *IRPA* procedure itself is not unconstitutional on this ground. However, this does not preclude the possibility of a judge concluding at a certain point that a particular detention constitutes cruel and unusual treatment or is inconsistent with the principles of fundamental justice, and therefore infringes the *Charter* in a manner that is remediable under s. 24(1) of the *Charter*.

[124] These conclusions are consistent with English and American authority. Canada, it goes without saying, is not alone in facing the problem of detention in the immigration context in situations where deportation is difficult or impossible. Courts in the United Kingdom and the United States have suggested that detention in this context can be used only during the period where it is reasonably necessary for deportation purposes. ...

[125] A case raising similar issues is the decision of the House of Lords in *A. v. Secretary of State for the Home Department*, [2005] 3 All E.R. 169, [2004] UKHL 56 ("*Re A*"). This was an appeal brought by nine foreign nationals who were suspected of involvement in terrorism, but were not charged with any crime. The United Kingdom government sought to deport them, but in most cases this was impossible due to a risk of torture. So most of the individuals were detained at Belmarsh Prison under s. 23 of the *Anti-terrorism, Crime and Security Act 2001* (U.K.), 2001, c. 24. This provision empowered the government to detain suspected international terrorists under the provisions governing detention pending deportation, despite the fact that removal from the United Kingdom was temporarily or indefinitely prevented, in derogation from art. 5 of the *European Convention on Human Rights*: see *Chahal*.

[126] The government claimed that this derogation was necessary to combat the national security threat posed by Al-Qaeda terrorists. The House of Lords, by a majority of 8 to 1, accepted that Al-Qaeda terrorism represented a serious threat to the life of the nation, but seven of the eight Lords who accepted this premise nevertheless concluded that s. 23 was not strictly required by the exigencies of the situation. These same seven Lords also concluded that s. 23 was

incompatible with art. 14 of the *European Convention on Human Rights*, because of the way it discriminated between nationals and non-nationals. The derogation permitting permanent detention of non-nationals treated them more harshly than nationals. Absent the possibility of deportation, it lost its character as an immigration provision, and hence constituted unlawful discrimination.

[127] The finding in *Re A* of breach of the detention norms under the European Convention on Human Rights was predicated on the U.K. Act's authorization of permanent detention. The *IRPA*, unlike the U.K. legislation under consideration in *Re A*, does not authorize indefinite detention and, interpreted as suggested above, provides an effective review process that meets the requirements of Canadian law.

[128] The fairness of the detention review procedure arises as an independent issue. I concluded above that this procedure, like the certificate determination procedure, denies the right to a fair hearing and does so in a way that does not minimally impair the detainee's rights. For the reasons given earlier, Parliament must therefore revisit the provisions for detention review in order to meaningfully protect the procedural rights of detainees.

C. Do the Certificate and Detention Review Procedures Discriminate Between Citizens and Non-Citizens, Contrary to Section 15 of the Charter, and If So, Is the Discrimination Justified Under Section 1 of the Charter?

[The court found that no breach of section 15 was established. There was no evidence that the appellants were detained for purposes unrelated to the goals of deportation undergirding the IRPA.]

D. Are the IRPA Certificate Provisions Inconsistent with the Constitutional Principle of the Rule of Law?

[The appellants argued that the IRPA bars an appeal from a judge's determination of the reasonableness of a security certificate, and that the law allows for a warrant for arrest issued by a member of the political executive or for arrest without a warrant. They argued that these provisions violate the constitutional principle of the rule of law. The court dismissed the argument.]

IV. Conclusion

[138] The scheme set up under Division 9 of Part 1 of the *IRPA* suffers from two defects that are inconsistent with the *Charter*.

[139] The first is that s. 78(*g*) allows for the use of evidence that is never disclosed to the named person without providing adequate measures to compensate for this

non-disclosure and the constitutional problems it causes. It is clear from approaches adopted in other democracies, and in Canada itself in other security situations, that solutions can be devised that protect confidential security information and at the same time are less intrusive on the person's rights. It follows that the *IRPA*'s procedure for the judicial confirmation of certificates and review of detention violates s. 7 of the *Charter* and has not been shown to be justified under s. 1 of the *Charter*. I would declare the procedure to be inconsistent with the *Charter*, and hence of no force or effect.

[140] However, in order to give Parliament time to amend the law, I would suspend this declaration for one year from the date of this judgment. If the government chooses to go forward with the proceedings to have the reasonableness of Mr. Charkaoui's certificate determined during the one-year suspension period, the existing process under the *IRPA* will apply. After one year, the certificates of Mr. Harkat and Mr. Almrei (and of any other individuals whose certificates have been deemed reasonable) will lose the "reasonable" status that has been conferred on them, and it will be open to them to apply to have the certificates quashed. If the government intends to employ a certificate after the one-year delay, it will need to seek a fresh determination of reasonableness under the new process devised by Parliament. Likewise, any detention review occurring after the delay will be subject to the new process.

[141] The second defect is found in s. 84(2) of the *IRPA*, which denies a prompt hearing to foreign nationals by imposing a 120-day embargo, after confirmation of the certificate, on applications for release. Counsel for the ministers submitted in oral argument that if this Court were to find that s. 84(2) violates the *Charter*, the appropriate remedy would be to strike s. 84(2) and read foreign nationals into s. 83. This is a good first step, but it does not provide a complete solution, since s. 83 deals with detention review only *until the certificate has been determined to be reasonable*, whereas s. 84(2) deals with detention review *after it has been determined to be reasonable*. Striking s. 84(2) would therefore leave no provision for review of detention of foreign nationals once the certificate has been deemed reasonable.

[142] Accordingly, I conclude that the appropriate remedy is to strike s. 84(2) as well as to read foreign nationals into s. 83 and to strike the words "until a determination is made under subsection 80(1)" from s. 83(2).

R. v. Patrick, 2009

An old English proverb, that a man's home is his castle, captures the sense that everyone should enjoy a private space that is safe from the prying eyes of others. In Pierre Trudeau's edgier version, uttered during a debate on criminal law reform in the 1960s, "the state has no place in the bedrooms of the nation." Privacy is a prime principle of liberal democracies, since the liberal regime is dedicated to safeguarding the legal and physical room for persons to live their lives as they wish.

But private spaces, including bedrooms, are precisely where mischief can be wrought, and so even liberal democracies must accommodate the need for police to enter the private realm to gather evidence, pursue suspects, and make arrests. Section 8 of the Charter protects everyone not against search and seizure, but against *unreasonable* search and seizure. Put in somewhat different terms, section 8 protects not privacy, but the *reasonable expectation* of privacy.[1] Where and when one has such an expectation depends on a variety of variables, ranging from the timing of the search to the historical use one has made of the space being searched.[2]

The courts have expanded the realm of privacy far beyond bedrooms and homes. In 1988 in *R. v. Dyment*, Justice La Forest, known for his zealous regard for privacy rights, wrote that "privacy is at the heart of liberty in a modern state. ... Grounded in man's physical and moral autonomy, privacy is essential for the well-being of the individual. For this reason alone, it is worthy of constitutional protection, but it also has profound significance for the public order. The restraints imposed on government to pry into the lives of the citizen go to the essence of a democratic state."[3] While, for centuries, the common law protected property from trespass, La Forest suggested that the protection of property was really a means to the protection of personal privacy. Section 8 protections follow the individual; they are not confined to his or her property or place of residence.

It is well established that searches generally require warrants—prior judicial authorizations obtained by police who demonstrate that they have reasonable and probable grounds for believing that a search of a specific premises for specific evidence will produce evidence of illegal conduct.[4] But not all searches and seizures require a warrant. Police can seize evidence "in plain view"; they can enter premises while in hot pursuit; they can gather evidence to prevent its destruction; they can conduct bodily searches incident to an arrest, and so on.

A line of cases concerns whether police can gather without a warrant evidence of illegal conduct that emanates from private places. In an early Charter case, police, acting on a tip

---

1 *Hunter et al. v. Southam Inc.*, [1984] 2 S.C.R. 145.

2 *R. v. Edwards*, [1996] 1 S.C.R. 128.

3 *R. v. Dyment*, [1988] 2 S.C.R. 417 at para. 17.

4 *Hunter v. Southam, supra* note 1.

that a house was being used as a grow-op, examined local utility power records and learned that it was consuming four times the usual amount of power. They then conducted a "perimeter search" of the house and gathered enough evidence to obtain a warrant that led to a conviction on narcotics charges. The Supreme Court ruled that the perimeter search violated section 8, but that the evidence from the power bills was gathered, not seized;[5] however, the court noted that when evidence emanating from a private space contains personal biographical information in which a person has a reasonable expectation of privacy, warrantless searches constitute a Charter violation.

There is a significant distinction between evidence that is released for the easy detection of others and evidence so released that reveals personal information about its owner. Consider garbage—trash to one, treasure to another. On the one hand, garbage is one's used, soiled, discarded stuff, which is one's property until it is abandoned and made available for pickup and disposal at a landfill site. On the other hand, it is not just junk; it is a record of one's habits, purchases, thoughts, and conduct that one is likely to wish to keep private. Most of us throw away trash that reveals much about us, but we do not expect others to sift through it for their own purposes. Context is important. It is one thing to throw a tissue into a bin after one has blown one's nose; it is another to do so while in police custody and after one has declared that police are not to collect any of one's bodily fluids. One abandons one's reasonable expectation of privacy in the former case, but not in the latter.[6]

In *R. v. Patrick*, police had reason to think that a house was being used to manufacture an illegal drug, and so had looked through the resident's garbage to discover incriminating evidence that would establish reasonable and probable grounds for obtaining a warrant to search the house. The accused claimed his section 8 right was infringed because the garbage was placed for pickup in a container on his side of the property line. Accordingly, he argued that he did not abandon the garbage to the police. The Supreme Court sided with the police, but the decision rests on fine distinctions with which reasonable people can disagree. In fact, Justice Abella's concurrence reads more like a dissent, and she leaves dangling the question whether police can go on fishing expeditions for evidence or whether they must have some demonstrable grounds for believing someone's trash contains incriminating evidence. ⌁

Discussion Questions

1. The Supreme Court points to a distinction between the abandonment of objects versus the abandonment to the purview of others the biographical information contained in objects. One may abandon one, but not the other. Is this distinction tenable? Can a reasonable person assume that his or her garbage, and the personal information it contains, will *not* be seen by others once it is abandoned? Should it matter whether the garbage bag is opaque rather than clear?

2. An issue for the Supreme Court in this case was the balance between high constitutional principle and practical enforceability of the law by police in the field. Did the court get the balance right in this case? Is this a balance that should even be attempted?

---

5 *R. v. Plant* , [1993] 3 S.C.R. 281.

6 *R. v. Stillman,* [1997] 1 S.C.R. 607.

R. v. PATRICK
2009 SCC 17, [2009] 1 S.C.R. 579

Hearing: October 10, 2008; Judgment: April 9, 2009.

Present: McLachlin C.J. and Binnie, LeBel, Fish, Abella, Charron, and Rothstein JJ.

Interveners: Attorney General of Ontario, Attorney General of British Columbia, Attorney General of Alberta, Canadian Civil Liberties Association and Criminal Lawyers' Association (Ontario).

The judgment of McLachlin C.J. and Binnie, LeBel, Fish, Abella, Charron, and Rothstein JJ. was delivered by

BINNIE J.:

[1] The appellant was convicted of unlawfully producing, possessing and trafficking in a controlled substance (Ecstasy) based in part on evidence gathered by the police from the appellant's garbage. The items of interest to the police, including drug-making paraphernalia, provided the primary basis for a search warrant of his dwelling. The appellant contends that the police inspection of his garbage amounted to a search and seizure and was unreasonable within the meaning of s. 8 of the *Canadian Charter of Rights and Freedoms*. Further, he says the evidence taken from the garbage, and other evidence obtained under the subsequent search warrant, should be excluded on the basis that its admission would bring the administration of justice into disrepute.

[2] In my view, the appellant's initial privacy interest in the evidence was abandoned when he placed the bags for collection as garbage from a stand indented in the back fence of his Calgary home adjacent to a public alleyway, to which any passing member of the public had ready access. The police had no greater access in this regard than the public, but their access was no less. At that point, the appellant had done everything required to rid himself of the contents including whatever private information was embedded therein, and this conduct, I believe, was inconsistent with the continued assertion of a constitutionally protected privacy interest. I would therefore dismiss the appeal.

I. Facts

[3] Police investigators suspected that the appellant was operating an ecstasy lab in his home located in southeast Calgary. On several occasions, they grabbed bags located inside garbage cans placed on a stand (without lids) just inside his property line. The fence was located approximately 17 metres to the rear of his house, parallel to and contiguous to a back alleyway. It was constructed so that the garbage was

visible from the alley but shielded from the sight of persons in the appellant's house or back garden. The stand did not have any doors. Nonetheless, the officers did have to reach through the airspace over the property line in order to retrieve the bags. The items seized by the police included torn-up papers containing chemical recipes and instructions, gloves, used duct tape, paper towel sheets, packaging for rubber gloves, packaging for a digital scale, a product card for a vacuum pump, a balloon, a receipt for muriatic acid and an empty clear plastic bag with residue inside. Some of the items bore a detectable odour of sassafras oil and some were found to be contaminated with ecstasy. ...

III. Issues

[12] At issue is whether the police breached the appellant's s. 8 *Charter* protected right to be free from unreasonable search and seizure, specifically:

(a) whether the appellant had a reasonable expectation of territorial privacy with respect to his dwelling-house, its perimeter and the garbage bags stored thereon; and

(b) whether the appellant had a reasonable expectation of informational privacy with respect to the garbage bags and the information stored therein.

(c) If the police breached the appellant's s. 8 *Charter* right, whether the evidence seized by the police from the search of the appellant's dwelling-house and garage, and a second dwelling-house should be excluded pursuant to s. 24(2) of the *Charter* on the basis that its admission would bring the administration of justice into disrepute.

IV. Analysis

[13] Labels are sometimes misleading. To describe something as "garbage" tends to presuppose the point in issue, namely whether the homeowner had any continuing privacy interest in it. It is possible that the homeowner might have no further interest in physical possession but a very strong interest in keeping private the information embedded in the contents. In that case, the question is whether he or she has so dealt with the items put out for collection in such a way as to forfeit any reasonable expectation (*objectively* speaking) of keeping the contents confidential.

[14] "Expectation of privacy is a normative rather than a descriptive standard" (*Tessling*, [*R. v.*, [2004] 3 S.C.R. 432] at para. 42). A government that increases its snooping on the lives of citizens, and thereby makes them suspicious and reduces their expectation of privacy, will not thereby succeed in unilaterally reducing their constitutional entitlement to

privacy protection. Equally, however, while a disembarking passenger at the Toronto airport might feel entitled to privacy when emptying his bowels after an intercontinental flight, the obligation to make use of a "drug loo facility" under the supervision of the authorities was upheld in the context of border formalities in *R. v. Monney*, [1999] 1 S.C.R. 652. Privacy analysis is laden with value judgments which are made from the independent perspective of the reasonable and informed person who is concerned about the long-term consequences of government action for the protection of privacy. This is inherent in the "assessment" called for by Dickson J. (as he then was) in *Hunter v. Southam Inc.*, [1984] 2 S.C.R. 145, at pp. 159-60:

> This limitation on the right guaranteed by s. 8, whether it is expressed negatively as freedom from "unreasonable" search and seizure, or positively as an entitlement to a "reasonable" expectation of privacy, indicates that an assessment must be made as to whether in a particular situation the public's interest in being left alone by government must give way to the government's interest in intruding on the individual's privacy in order to advance its goals, notably those of law enforcement. ...

[20] The concept of abandonment is about whether a presumed *subjective* privacy interest of the householder in trash put out for collection is one that an independent and informed observer, viewing the matter *objectively*, would consider reasonable in the totality of the circumstances (*Edwards*, [*R. v.*, [1996] 1 S.C.R. 128] at para. 45, and *Tessling*, at para. 19) having regard firstly to the need to balance "societal interests in protecting individual dignity, integrity and autonomy with effective law enforcement" (*R. v. Plant*, [1993] 3 S.C.R. 281, at p. 293); secondly, whether an accused has conducted himself in a manner that is inconsistent with the *reasonable* continued assertion of a privacy interest and, thirdly, the long-term consequences for the due protection of privacy interests in our society.

[21] As emphasized by the Attorney General of Ontario, the police practice of looking through garbage has in the past been an important source of probative evidence for the courts in the search for truth. ...

A. The Issue of Abandonment

...

[25] Abandonment is ... an issue of fact. The question is whether the claimant to s. 8 protection has acted in relation to the subject matter of his privacy claim in such a manner as to lead a reasonable and independent observer to conclude that his continued assertion of a privacy interest is unreasonable in the totality of the circumstances.

B. The Totality of the Circumstances

[26] It was established in *Edwards* (para. 45), and affirmed in *Tessling* (para. 19), that in assessing the reasonableness of a claimed privacy interest, the Court is to look at the "totality of the circumstances," and this is so whether the claim involves aspects of personal privacy, territorial privacy or informational privacy. Frequently the claimant will assert overlapping interests. The assessment always requires close attention to context. Nevertheless, some analytical framework is helpful. The trial judge organized his analysis around the *Tessling* (para. 32) factors and, for ease of reference, I set them out (adapted to the circumstances) here.

(1) Did the Appellant Have a Reasonable Expectation of Privacy?

[27] On the facts of this case, we need to address:

1. What was the nature or subject matter of the evidence gathered by the police?
2. Did the appellant have a direct interest in the contents?
3. Did the appellant have a *subjective* expectation of privacy in the informational content of the garbage?
4. If so, was the expectation *objectively* reasonable? In this respect, regard must be had to:
   a. the place where the alleged "search" occurred; in particular, did the police trespass on the appellant's property and, if so, what is the impact of such a finding on the privacy analysis?
   b. whether the informational content of the subject matter was in public view;
   c. whether the informational content of the subject matter had been abandoned;
   d. whether such information was already in the hands of third parties; if so, was it subject to an obligation of confidentiality?
   e. whether the police technique was intrusive in relation to the privacy interest;
   f. whether the use of this evidence gathering technique was itself objectively unreasonable;
   g. whether the informational content exposed any intimate details of the appellant's lifestyle, or information of a biographic nature.

(2) If There Was a Reasonable Expectation of Privacy in This Case, Was It Violated by the Police Conduct?

[28] The second question is only reached if the first question is answered in the affirmative.

C. Did the Appellant Have a Reasonable Expectation of Privacy in this Case?

(1) The Subject Matter of the Alleged "Search"

...

[30] The Attorneys General characterize the subject matter here as "garbage" but, without more, this oversimplification misses (or assumes away) the point in issue. Residential waste includes an enormous amount of personal information about what is going on in our homes, including a lot of DNA on household tissues, highly personal records (e.g., love letters, overdue bills and tax returns) and hidden vices (pill bottles, syringes, sexual paraphernalia, etc.). As it was put by counsel for the Canadian Civil Liberties Association, a garbage bag may more accurately be described as a bag of "information" whose contents, viewed in their entirety, paint a fairly accurate and complete picture of the householder's activities and lifestyle. Many of us may not wish to disclose these things to the public generally or to the police in particular.

[31] The appellant had a direct interest not only in the garbage itself but, in particular, its informational content.

(2) Concealing Illegal Objects

[32] The majority in the Alberta Court of Appeal seems to state ... that because the items of interest located by the police revealed involvement in criminal activity they cannot "constitute intimate details of lifestyle or core biographical details to which privacy protection ought to be extended," ... The issue is not whether the appellant had a legitimate privacy interest in the concealment of drug paraphernalia, but whether people generally have a privacy interest in the concealed contents of an opaque and sealed "bag of information." I believe that they do. The focus is on "the person, place or thing searched and the purpose for which the search is undertaken" (*A.M.*, at para. 72). A warrantless search of a private place cannot be justified by the after-the-fact discovery of evidence of a crime. ...

(3) A Subjective Expectation of Privacy

...

[37] ... The question is whether the appellant had, or is presumed to have had, an expectation of privacy in the information content of the bags. This is not a high hurdle. As mentioned, in the case of information about activities taking place in the home, such an expectation is presumed in the appellant's favour. It is possible that the appellant (who did not testify on this point) may never have ceased to have a subjective expectation, reasonable or not. The "reasonableness" of an individual's belief in the totality of the circumstances of a particular case is to be tested at the second *objective* branch of the privacy analysis.

(4) Was the Appellant's Expectation of Privacy Objectively Reasonable?

[38] The reasonable expectation of privacy "can vary with the nature of the matter sought to be protected, the circumstances in which and the place where state intrusion occurs, and the purposes of the intrusion": *R. v. Colarusso*, [1994] 1 S.C.R. 20, at p. 53; see also *R. v. Buhay*, 2003 SCC 30, [2003] 1 S.C.R. 631, at paras. 22, 23 and 24.

[39] Four factual elements are of prime importance in the appeal: (i) the garbage was put out by the appellant for collection in the customary location for removal, (ii) that location was at or near the property line, (iii) there was no manifestation (such as a locked receptacle) of any continuing assertion of privacy or control, and (iv) the police took the bags to search for information about activities within the home as part of a continuing criminal investigation.

[40] I acknowledge, however, that apart from the key issue of abandonment, the circumstances in this case favour the appellant. The police were trying to find out what was "happening inside a private dwelling, the most private of places" (*Plant*, at p. 302). The contents of the opaque sealed bags were not in public view. There is no evidence that the information was already in the hands of third parties. The gathering up of the contents of the bags by the police provided them with a window into the appellant's private life.

(5) The Place Where the Alleged "Search" Occurred

[41] In this case, the long arm of the law reached across the property line and collected the bags. On the basis of their examination of the contents of four of the bags and other evidence, the police obtained a search warrant. Conrad J.A., noting that the prosecution was built on the initial garbage seizure, emphasized *territorial* privacy.

[42] The distinctions between personal, territorial and informational privacy provide a useful analytical tool but, as noted, in many instances the categories overlap. I would not draw as strict a distinction as Conrad J.A. did between territorial privacy and informational privacy. I regard the gravamen of the appellant's complaint as the intrusion by the police into activities taking place inside his home rather than the fact that the police invaded the airspace at the foot of his garden by reaching across the lot line for the bags. If, for example, the appellant had been unloading sealed bags from his truck in the back alley, temporarily placing them on public property, I do not think the police could grab the bags on the basis that the bags had not yet reached the sanctuary of a residential lot. That is the implication of focussing privacy protection on "people, not places." In the circumstances of unloading a vehicle, there could be no suggestion of abandonment.

[43] I also do not think constitutional protection should turn on whether the bags were placed a few inches inside the property line or a few inches outside it. The point is that the garbage was at the property line, accessible to passers-by. ...

[45] The point here, I believe, is that while territorial privacy is implicated in this case, the *physical* intrusion by the police was relatively peripheral, and viewed in context, it is better considered as part of the totality of circumstances in a claim that is preferably framed in terms of information privacy.

(6) This Was Not a Perimeter Search

[The court discusses "perimeter searches": warrantless entries onto private property to look inside a dwelling or sniff for odours in order to gather evidence to substantiate a judicial warrant for a more intrusive search inside the dwelling.]

[52] Nothing said in these reasons should throw any doubt on the rulings on perimeter searches in *Kokesch* [*R. v.*, [1990] 3 S.C.R. 3]; *Grant* [*R. v.*, [1993] 3 S.C.R. 223]; *Wiley* [*R. v.*, [1993] 3 S.C.R. 263]; *Evans* [*R. v.*, [1996] 1 S.C.R. 8] and *Plant*. I do not believe that what we have in this case amounts to a "perimeter search." The prohibition laid down in those cases is simply inapplicable to the facts of this case.

(7) Whether the Subject Matter of the Alleged Search Was in Public View

[53] Of course the garbage bags were in plain view but the appellant asserts no privacy interest in the outside surface of the bags. His concern, as was the concern of the police, was with the concealed contents of the bags, which were clearly not in public view.

(8) Whether the Subject Matter of the Alleged "Search" Had Been Abandoned

[54] Clearly, the appellant intended to abandon his proprietary interest in the physical objects themselves. The question is whether he had a reasonable continuing privacy interest in the information which the contents revealed to the police. There was some discussion at the bar that a privacy interest does not cease until garbage becomes "anonymous," but as Conrad J.A. noted, much garbage never becomes anonymous, e.g. addressed envelopes, personal letters and so on. In this case, the garbage included invoices for the purchase of chemicals used in the preparation of the drug Ecstasy. The idea that s. 8 protects an individual's privacy in garbage until the last unpaid bill rots into dust, or the incriminating letters turn into muck and are no longer decipherable, is to my mind too extravagant to contemplate. It would require the entire

municipal disposal system to be regarded as an extension, in terms of privacy, of the dwelling-house. Yet if there is to be a reasonable cut-off point, where is it to be located? The line must be easily intelligible to both police and homeowners. Logically, because abandonment is a conclusion inferred from the conduct of the individual claiming the s. 8 right, the reasonableness line must relate to the conduct of that individual and not to anything done or not done by the garbage collectors, the police or anyone else involved in the subsequent collection and treatment of the "bag of information."

[55] *Stillman* [*R. v.*, [1997] 1 S.C.R. 607] (at para. 62) and *Tessling* (at paras. 40-41) identified garbage as a "classic" instance of abandonment. Here, I believe, abandonment occurred when the appellant placed his garbage bags for collection in the open container at the back of his property adjacent to the lot line. He had done everything required of him to commit his rubbish to the municipal collection system. The bags were unprotected and within easy reach of anyone walking by in a public alleyway, including street people, bottle pickers, urban foragers, nosey neighbours and mischievous children, not to mention dogs and assorted wildlife, as well as the garbage collectors and the police. This conclusion is in general accord with the jurisprudence. ...

[62] Nevertheless, until the garbage is placed at or within reach of the lot line, the householder retains an element of control over its disposition and cannot be said to have unequivocally abandoned it, particularly if it is placed on a porch or in a garage or within the immediate vicinity of the dwelling where the principles set out in the "perimeter" cases such as *Kokesch*, *Grant* and *Wiley* apply.

[63] In municipalities (if there are any left) where garbage collectors come to the garage or porch and carry the garbage to the street, they are operating under (at least) an implied licence from the householder to come onto the property. The licence does not extend to the police. However, when the garbage is placed at the lot line for collection, I believe the householder has sufficiently abandoned his interest and control to eliminate any objectively reasonable privacy interest.

[64] Given the "totality of the circumstances" test, little would be gained by an essay on different variations of garbage disposal. To take a few common examples, however, the rural people who take their garbage to a dump and abandon it to the pickers and the seagulls, the apartment dweller who unloads garbage down a chute to the potential scrutiny of a curious building superintendent, and the householder who takes surreptitious advantage of a conveniently located dumpster to rid himself or herself of the "bag of information" are all acting in a manner inconsistent with the reasonable assertion of a continuing privacy interest, in my view.

(9) Whether the Information Was Already in the Hands of Third Parties; if so, Was it Subject to an Obligation of Confidentiality

[65] It was contended that the appellant retained an objectively reasonable privacy interest in the contents of the garbage bags at least until the bags were actually collected by the municipal employees. In this case, the bags were taken by police before the garbage collectors arrived.

[66] I do not believe it is necessary to defer a finding of abandonment until the further step of the taking of the bags by garbage collectors, as this further step does not depend on any act of the claimant. Further, it would add little in the way of protection as the garbage collector could be accompanied by a police officer and simply hand the bags to the police forthwith on collection, a type of co-operation evident in *Krist* [*R. v.*, 100 C.C.C. (3d) 58]. ...

(10) Was the Police Conduct Intrusive in Relation to the Privacy Interest?

[69] Given that the act of abandonment occurred prior to the police gathering the garbage bags, there was no privacy interest in existence at the time of the police intervention, which therefore did not constitute an intrusion into a subsisting privacy interest.

(11) Was the Policy [sic] Technique Objectively Unreasonable?

[70] Much has been written in the privacy cases about police techniques that undermine privacy and have the potential to make social life in this country intolerable (e.g. the use of electronic recordings of private conversations in *R. v. Duarte*, [1990] 1 S.C.R. 30). This is not one of those cases. There is always, as *Hunter v. Southam* established, a realistic balance that must be struck between privacy and the legitimate demands of law enforcement and criminal investigation. In this case, the appellant's conduct was, in my view, inconsistent with preservation of the former and tipped the balance in favour of the latter.

(12) Whether the Gathering of this Evidence Exposed Intimate Details of the Appellant's Lifestyle or Information of a Biographical Nature

[71] Lifestyle and biographical information was exposed but the effective cause of the exposure was the act of abandonment by the appellant, not an intrusion by the police into a subsisting privacy interest.

D. If the Appellant Had a Reasonable Expectation of Privacy in This Case, Was It Violated by the Police Conduct?

[72] In the absence of a subsisting privacy interest at the time the police gathered the bags, there was no violation. ...

The following are the reasons delivered by

ABELLA J.:

[76] What we inelegantly call "garbage" may contain the most intensely personal and private information about ourselves. Brennan J., in his dissent in *California v. Greenwood*, 486 U.S. 35 (1988), illuminated the issue as follows:

> A single bag of trash testifies eloquently to the eating, reading, and recreational habits of the person who produced it. A search of trash, like a search of the bedroom, can relate intimate details about sexual practices, health, and personal hygiene. Like rifling through desk drawers or intercepting phone calls, rummaging through trash can divulge the target's financial and professional status, political affiliations and inclinations, private thoughts, personal relationships, and romantic interests. [p. 50]

[77] As Binnie J. emphasizes, the main question in this appeal is whether there exists an objectively reasonable expectation of privacy in household waste put out for collection near one's home. While I agree with him that there is no violation of the *Canadian Charter of Rights and Freedoms* in this case, in my view, with respect, the privacy of personal information emanating from the home, which has been transformed into household waste and put out for disposal, is entitled to protection from indiscriminate state intrusion. Such information should not be seen to automatically lose its "private" character simply because it is put outside for garbage disposal. Before the state can rummage through the personal information from this ultimate zone of privacy, there should be, at the very least, a reasonable suspicion that a crime has been or is likely to be committed. ...

[82] In this case, the privacy interest is primarily informational. In *R. v. Plant*, [1993] 3 S.C.R. 281, at p. 293, Sopinka J. described an individual's informational privacy interest as "a biographical core of personal information which individuals in a free and democratic society would wish to maintain and control from dissemination to the state." Further, "[t]his would include information which tends to reveal intimate details of the lifestyle and personal choices of the individual" (p. 293).

[83] What, then, are the reasonable expectations of an individual regarding the information that emanates from the home? Do individuals knowingly and voluntarily choose to part with private information when it is left out for collection? I think that when one considers the kind of medical, financial or other personal information that is potentially exposed, the answer is that most people retain an intention that the information stay private.

[84] But as Binnie J. notes, a key countervailing factor in this appeal is the fact that the subject matter of the search, household waste, was technically "abandoned." Binnie J. acknowledges that except for this factor of the *Tessling* analysis, most indicators in this case point towards a reasonable expectation of privacy.

[85] Abandonment is merely one factor under the *Tessling* analysis. In my view, other factors, including whether the search exposed intimate details of an individual's life and the location of the search at or in close proximity to the property line, militate in favour of finding a reasonable expectation of privacy in such information. Abandonment can be seen more as relating to the *objects* contained in the waste, rather than to the information they reveal or to one's privacy interest in that information. It seems to me to be reasonable to infer that most individuals do not intend that that personal information will *ever* be disclosed without a countervailing legitimate state interest. ...

[88] ... [T]he fact that someone has chosen to "abandon" their household waste for the specific purpose of disposal does not thereby mean that they "abandon" their informational privacy.

[89] Individuals who put out their household waste as "garbage" expect that it will reach the waste disposal system:

nothing more, nothing less. No one would reasonably expect the personal information contained in their household waste to be publicly available for random scrutiny by anyone, let alone the state, before it reaches its intended destination. Household waste, it is true, is composed of abandoned items that the occupant of the household may no longer wish to keep in his or her home. In my view, however, it is a further and unwarranted step to conclude that these individuals have abandoned the expectation, reasonable in my view, that the personal information emanating from their home will remain private.

[90] While personal information may be obtained by searching through household waste that is left at or in close proximity to the property line for collection, on the other hand the individual disposing of the waste has indicated an intention to part with the objects contained in it. From a balancing of the *Tessling* factors, this leads to a conclusion that we are dealing with a diminished expectation of privacy, not unlike the reduced expectation at border crossings (see, for example, *R. v. Simmons*, [1988] 2 S.C.R. 495, and *R. v. Monney*, [1999] 1 S.C.R. 652). This does not mean that the state can arbitrarily search through the information. Barring exigent circumstances, there should at least be a threshold of reasonable suspicion about the possibility of a criminal offence before household waste left for collection is searched. (See *Litchfield v. State*, 824 N.E.2d 356 (Ind. 2005).)

[91] In this case, the police had ample evidence on which to base a reasonable suspicion that a crime had been committed by Mr. Patrick. They were therefore entitled to search the household waste left for disposal.

[92] I therefore agree with Binnie J. that there is no *Charter* violation and would, like him, dismiss the appeal.

R. v N.S., 2012

At issue in this case was whether a witness who wears a niqab for religious reasons is required to remove the niqab when testifying in a criminal trial. N.S is a Muslim woman who wears a niqab (a veil covering the face and head that exposes only the eyes). She was the complainant in a sexual assault trial. The accused were her cousin and uncle who sought a court order requiring her to remove her niqab when testifying. She testified that her religious belief required her to wear a niqab in public where men (other than certain close family members) might see her. After admitting she had removed her niqab for the photo on her driver's licence (taken by a female photographer) and that if required, she would remove it for a security check at a border crossing, the trial judge ordered her to remove it. She objected, after which the preliminary hearing was adjourned and the issue was appealed, eventually landing before the Supreme Court.

The court characterized this as a case of having to balance competing rights—those of freedom of religion and an accused's right to a fair trial, and the common law presumption that this requires seeing a witness's face in order for cross-examination and assessing credibility to take place.

The judgment reflected three distinct positions on how to balance these competing rights.

The majority judgment (McLachlin, Deschamps, Fish, and Cromwell) ruled that the issue should be determined on a case-by-case basis, and formulated four questions that a trial judge should ask when ascertaining how to balance the conflicting rights in question: (1) does the requirement to remove the niqab interfere with a sincere religious belief; (2) would permitting the witness to wear the niqab while testifying create a serious risk to trial fairness; (3) are there alternative measures that would accommodate the conflicting rights at stake; and (4) where accommodation is not possible, do the salutary effects of requiring the witness to remove the niqab outweigh the deleterious effects of so doing? The majority held that in situations where evidence is uncontested, not being able to see the witness's face will not impinge on trial fairness, and thus a witness who wishes to wear a niqab for sincere religious reasons may do so. However, where this is not the case and where a witness's evidence and credibility are core factors, the judge must be particularly mindful of the possibility of a wrongful conviction when determining whether the salutary effects of requiring the witness to remove the niqab outweigh the deleterious effects of so doing. Since cross-examination is essential for the exercise of the right to make full answer and defence, the balancing act must emphasize the rights of the accused.

Two judges (LeBel and Rothstein) characterized the idea of a case-by-case approach to this issue as problematic and emphasized the importance of having a clear rule in place. They disagreed that it was appropriate to ever permit the wearing of a niqab, which they considered to be inconsistent with the principle of an open trial process.

One judge (Justice Abella) agreed with a case by case approach but thought the majority placed insufficient weight on the harmful effects that forcing a woman to remove her niqab would have on her religious freedom. She also thought the majority had placed too much emphasis on the impact that wearing a niqab would have on assessing a witness's demeanour. Unless the witness's face is directly relevant to the case as a matter of identity, she should not be required to remove her niqab. Justice Abella was particularly critical of the impact of the majority ruling on matters of sexual assault (which was the issue in this case), because evidence will inevitably be contested, which forces a woman to choose between laying a complaint and wearing a niqab, which, in her words, "may be no meaningful choice at all."

Some have criticized the court for not undertaking a sufficiently "gendered" analysis of the issue, which they say could discourage Muslim women from pursuing allegations of sexual assault because of the likelihood that they would have to choose between pressing charges and complying with their religious beliefs. When the preliminary inquiry resumed, the trial judge order N.S. to remove her niqab.[1] ～

Discussion Questions

1. Which of the three positions do you find most compelling on how to balance the conflicting rights at stake, and why?

2. To what extent does judicial 'balancing' likely reflect individual judicial philosophies and values?

3. What do you think of the minority position of the importance of having a clear rule, rather than address the issue on a case by case basis?

---

1   Ontario Women's Justice Network, "Competing Rights: *R. v. N.S.* 2012, Supreme Court Decides About Right to Wear Niqab While Testifying," November 2013, online: owjn.org/ owjn_2009/component/content/article/56-criminal-law/358-competing-rights-r-v-ns-2012.

R. v. N.S.
2012 SCC 72, [2012] 3 S.C.R. 726

Hearing: December 8, 2011; Judgment: December 20, 2012.

Present: McLachlin C.J. and LeBel, Deschamps, Fish, Abella, Rothstein, and Cromwell JJ.

Interveners: Ontario Human Rights Commission, Barbra Schlifer Commemorative Clinic, Criminal Lawyers' Association (Ontario), Muslim Canadian Congress, South Asian Legal Clinic of Ontario, Barreau du Québec, Canadian Civil Liberties Association, Women's Legal Education and Action Fund and Canadian Council on American-Islamic Relations.

The judgment of McLachlin C.J. and Deschamps, Fish, and Cromwell JJ. was delivered by

THE CHIEF JUSTICE:

I. Introduction

[1] How should the state respond to a witness whose sincerely held religious belief requires her to wear a niqab that covers her face, except for her eyes, while testifying in a criminal proceeding? One response is to say she must always remove her niqab on the ground that the courtroom is a neutral space where religion has no place. Another response is to say the justice system should respect the witness's freedom of religion and always permit her to testify with the niqab on. In my view, both of these extremes must be rejected in favour of a third option: allowing the witness to testify with her face covered unless this unjustifiably impinges on the accused's fair trial rights.

[2] A secular response that requires witnesses to park their religion at the courtroom door is inconsistent with the jurisprudence and Canadian tradition, and limits freedom of religion where no limit can be justified. On the other hand, a response that says a witness can always testify with her face covered may render a trial unfair and lead to wrongful conviction. What is required is an approach that balances the vital rights protecting freedom of religion and trial fairness when they conflict. The long-standing practice in Canadian courts is to respect and accommodate the religious convictions of

witnesses, unless they pose a significant or serious risk to a fair trial. The *Canadian Charter of Rights and Freedoms*, which protects both freedom of religion and trial fairness, demands no less.

[3] For the reasons that follow, I conclude that a witness who for sincere religious reasons wishes to wear the niqab while testifying in a criminal proceeding will be required to remove it if:

(a) requiring the witness to remove the niqab is necessary to prevent a serious risk to the fairness of the trial, because reasonably available alternative measures will not prevent the risk; *and*

(b) the salutary effects of requiring her to remove the niqab, including the effects on trial fairness, outweigh the deleterious effects of doing so, including the effects on freedom of religion.

II. The Background

[4] The facts may be briefly stated. M—-d S. and M—-l S. stand charged with having sexually assaulted N.S. The accused are N.S.'s cousin and uncle, respectively. The prosecution called N.S. as a witness at the preliminary inquiry. N.S., who is a Muslim, wished to testify wearing her niqab. M—-d S. and his co-accused, M—-l S., sought an order requiring N.S. to remove her niqab when testifying. The preliminary inquiry judge held a *voir dire*, during which N.S. wore her niqab. N.S. testified that her religious belief required her to wear a niqab in public where men (other than certain close family members) might see her. She admitted that she had removed her niqab for the photo on her driver's licence, which was taken by a female photographer, and that, if required, she would remove it for a security check at a border crossing. The judge concluded that N.S.'s religious belief was "not that strong" and ordered her to remove her niqab. N.S. objected. The preliminary inquiry was adjourned. N.S. applied to the Superior Court of Justice to quash the order of the preliminary inquiry judge and to permit her to testify wearing the niqab. ...

III. The Issues

[7] The issue is when, if ever, a witness who wears a niqab for religious reasons can be required to remove it while testifying. Two sets of *Charter* rights are potentially engaged—the witness's freedom of religion (protected under s. 2(*a*)) and the accused's fair trial rights, including the right to make full answer and defence (protected under ss. 7 and 11(*d*)). This Court set out the framework for identifying and resolving rights conflicts that arise at common law in *Dagenais v. Canadian Broadcasting Corp.*, [1994] 3 S.C.R. 835. This approach was further refined in *R. v. Mentuck*, 2001 SCC 76, [2001] 3

S.C.R. 442. The framework was developed in the context of publication bans, but its principles have broader application.

[8] The first task under a *Dagenais/Mentuck*-type inquiry is to determine whether, in the case at hand, allowing the witness to testify in a niqab is necessary to protect her freedom of religion. The second task is to determine whether requiring the witness to testify without the niqab is necessary in order to protect the fairness of the trial. This involves considering whether there are alternative measures for protecting trial fairness that would also allow the witness to exercise her religious practice. Finally, if there is a true conflict that cannot be avoided, it is necessary to assess the competing harms and determine whether the salutary effects of requiring the witness to remove the niqab (for example, reducing the risk of a wrongful conviction) outweigh the deleterious effects of doing so (for example, the harm from interfering with the witness's sincerely held religious belief) ... .

[9] Applying this framework involves answering four questions:

1. Would requiring the witness to remove the niqab while testifying interfere with her religious freedom?
2. Would permitting the witness to wear the niqab while testifying create a serious risk to trial fairness?
3. Is there a way to accommodate both rights and avoid the conflict between them?
4. If no accommodation is possible, do the salutary effects of requiring the witness to remove the niqab outweigh the deleterious effects of doing so?

IV. Would Requiring the Witness to Remove the Niqab While Testifying Interfere With Her Religious Freedom?

[10] N.S. bases her claim to wear a niqab while testifying on the guarantee of freedom of religion in s. 2(*a*) of the *Charter*.

> **2.** Everyone has the following fundamental freedoms:
> (*a*) freedom of conscience and religion;

[11] In order to rely on s. 2(*a*), she must show that her wish to wear the niqab in court is based on a sincere religious belief ... .

[12] The preliminary inquiry judge failed to conduct an adequate inquiry into whether N.S.'s refusal to remove her niqab was based on a sincere religious belief. Based on the fact that N.S. removed the niqab for her driver's licence photo and said she would do so for a security check, the preliminary inquiry judge seems to have concluded that her beliefs were not sufficiently "strong."

[13] This was not an appropriate determination of whether N.S. has a *prima facie* religious claim. First, the question of whether she has a claim focuses on sincerity of belief rather than its strength. ... Second, inconsistent adherence to a religious practice may suggest lack of sincere belief, but it does not necessarily do so. A sincere believer may occasionally lapse, her beliefs may change over time or her belief may permit exceptions to the practice in particular situations. Departures from the practice in the past should also be viewed in context; a witness should not be denied the right to raise s. 2(*a*) merely because she has made what seemed to be a compromise in the past in order to participate in some facet of society. The preliminary inquiry judge did not explore these possibilities. I therefore agree with the Court of Appeal that the matter must be returned to the preliminary inquiry judge for full consideration of whether N.S.'s desire to wear a niqab is based on sincere religious belief.

[14] The balance of my reasons proceeds on the assumption that N.S. has established a sincere religious belief that she must wear a niqab while testifying in a public criminal proceeding. In such circumstances, can the judge order that the niqab be removed on the basis that it will adversely affect the accused's fair trial interests?

V. Would Permitting the Witness to Wear the Niqab While Testifying Create a Serious Risk to Trial Fairness?

[15] M—-d S. submits that permitting N.S. to wear the niqab while testifying would infringe his fair trial rights. ... The right to a fair trial in s. 11(*d*) encompasses a right to make full answer and defence: *R. v. Mills*, [1999] 3 S.C.R. 668, at para. 69. More broadly, s. 7 of the *Charter* provides that a person cannot be deprived of his liberty except "in accordance with the principles of fundamental justice." Those principles include the right to a fair trial and to make full answer and defence. The principles of fundamental justice in s. 7 and the requirements of s. 11(*d*) are "inextricably intertwined." ...

[17] We have no expert evidence in this case on the importance of seeing a witness's face to effective cross-examination and accurate assessment of a witness's credibility. All we have are arguments and several legal and social science articles submitted by the parties as authorities.

[18] M—-d S. and the Crown argue that the link is clear. Communication involves not only words, but facial cues. A facial gesture may reveal uncertainty or deception. The cross-examiner may pick up on non-verbal cues and use them to uncover the truth. Credibility assessment is equally dependent not only on what a witness says, but on how she says it. Effective cross-examination and accurate credibility assessment are central to a fair trial. It follows, they argue, that permitting a witness to wear a niqab while testifying may deny an accused's fair trial rights.

[19] N.S. and supporting interveners, on the other hand, argue that the importance of seeing a witness's face has been greatly exaggerated. They submit that untrained individuals cannot use facial expressions to detect deception. Moreover, to the extent that non-verbal cues are useful at all, a niqab-wearing witness's eyes, tone of voice and cadence of speech remain available to the cross-examiner and trier of fact.

[20] The record sheds little light on the question of whether seeing a witness's face is important to effective cross-examination and credibility assessment and hence to trial fairness. ...

[21] This much, however, can be said. The common law, supported by provisions of the *Criminal Code*, R.S.C. 1985, c. C-46, and judicial pronouncements, proceeds on the basis that the ability to see a witness's face is an important feature of a fair trial. While not conclusive, in the absence of negating evidence this common law assumption cannot be disregarded lightly.

[22] As a general rule, witnesses in common law criminal courts are required to testify in open court, with their faces visible to counsel, the judge and the jury. Face-to-face confrontation is the norm, although not an independent constitutional right. ...

[23] In recent years, Parliament and this Court have confirmed the common law assumption that the accused, the judge and the jury should be able to see the witness as she testifies. To protect child witnesses from trauma, Parliament has passed legislation permitting children to testify via closed-circuit television or from behind a screen so that they cannot see the accused ... . This Court has upheld these testimonial aids, relying on the fact that they do not prevent the accused from seeing the witness ... . Before a witness is permitted to testify by audio link, the *Criminal Code* expressly requires that the judge consider "any potential prejudice to either of the parties caused by the fact that the witness would not be seen by them": ss. 714.3(*d*) and 714.4(*b*). This, too, suggests that not seeing a witness's face during testimony may limit the fairness of a trial.

[24] Covering the face of a witness may impede cross-examination ... . Effective cross-examination is integral to the conduct of a fair trial and a meaningful application of the presumption of innocence ... . Unwarranted constraints may undermine the fairness of the trial ... . Non-verbal communication can provide the cross-examiner with valuable insights that may uncover uncertainty or deception, and assist in getting at the truth.

[25] Covering a witness's face may also impede credibility assessment by the trier of fact, be it judge or jury. It is a settled

axiom of appellate review that deference should be shown to the trier of fact on issues of credibility because trial judges (and juries) have the "overwhelming advantage" of seeing and hearing the witness—an advantage that a written transcript cannot replicate … . This advantage is described as stemming from the ability to assess the demeanour of the witness, that is, to *see* how the witness gives her evidence and responds to cross-examination.

[26] Changes in a witness's demeanour can be highly instructive … .

[27] On the record before us, I conclude that there is a strong connection between the ability to see the face of a witness and a fair trial. Being able to see the face of a witness is not the only—or indeed perhaps the most important—factor in cross-examination or accurate credibility assessment. But its importance is too deeply rooted in our criminal justice system to be set aside absent compelling evidence.

[28] However, whether the ability to observe a witness's face impacts trial fairness in any particular case will depend on the evidence that the witness is to provide. Where evidence is uncontested, credibility assessment and cross-examination are not in issue; therefore, being unable to see the witness's face will not impinge on the accused's fair trial rights … .

[29] If wearing the niqab poses no serious risk to trial fairness, a witness who wishes to wear it for sincere religious reasons may do so.

VI. Is There a Way to Accommodate Both Rights and Avoid the Conflict Between Them?

[30] If both freedom of religion and trial fairness are engaged on the facts, the question is how a judge should reconcile these rights.

[31] … The answer is not to ban religion from the courtroom, transforming the courtroom into a "neutral" space where witnesses must park their religious convictions at the door. Nor does it lie in ignoring the ancient and persistent connection the law has postulated between seeing a witness's face and trial fairness, and holding that a witness may always wear her niqab while testifying. Rather, the answer lies in a just and proportionate balance between freedom of religion on the one hand, and trial fairness on the other, based on the particular case before the Court.

[32] Under the *Dagenais/Mentuck* framework, once a judge is satisfied that both sets of competing interests are actually engaged on the facts, he or she must try to resolve the claims in a way that will preserve both rights. *Dagenais* refers to this as the requirement to consider whether "reasonably available alternative measures" would avoid the conflict altogether (p. 878). We also call this "accommodation." We find a

way to go forward that satisfies each right and each party. Both rights are respected, and the conflict is averted.

[33] When the matter returns to the preliminary inquiry judge, the parties should be able to place before the court evidence relating to possible options for accommodation of the potentially conflicting claims. This is the first step in the reconciliation process. The question is whether there is a reasonably available alternative that would conform to the witness's religious convictions while still preventing a serious risk to trial fairness. On the facts of this case, it may be that no accommodation is possible; excluding men from the courtroom would have implications for the open court principle, the right of the accused to be present at his trial, and potentially his right to counsel of his choice. Testifying without the niqab via closed-circuit television or behind a one-way screen may not satisfy N.S.'s religious obligations. However, when this case is reheard, the preliminary inquiry judge must consider the possibility of accommodation based on the evidence presented by the parties.

VII. Do the Salutary Effects of Requiring the Witness to Remove the Niqab Outweigh the Deleterious Effects of Doing So?

[34] If there is no reasonably available alternative that would avoid a serious risk to trial fairness while conforming to the witness's religious belief, the analysis moves to the next step in the *Dagenais/Mentuck* framework. The question is whether the salutary effects of requiring the witness to remove the niqab, including the effects on trial fairness, outweigh the deleterious effects of doing so, including the effects on freedom of religion … .

[35] As *Dagenais* makes clear, this is a proportionality inquiry, akin to the final part of the test in *R. v. Oakes*, [1986] 1 S.C.R. 103. The effect of insisting that the witness remove the niqab if she is to testify must be weighed against the effect of permitting her to wear the niqab on the stand.

[36] In terms of the deleterious effects of requiring the witness to remove her niqab while testifying, the judge must look at the harm that would be done by limiting the sincerely held religious practice. … The value of adherence does not depend on whether a religious practice is a voluntary expression of faith or a mandatory obligation under religious doctrine … . However, certain considerations may be helpful. How important is the practice to the claimant? What is the degree of state interference with the religious practice? … How does the actual situation in the courtroom—the people present and any measures that can be put in place to limit facial exposure—affect the harm to the claimant of limiting her religious practice? These are but some considerations that

may be relevant to determining the impact of an order to remove the niqab on the witness's right to freedom of religion.

[37] The judge should also consider the broader societal harms of requiring a witness to remove the niqab in order to testify. N.S. and supporting interveners argue that if niqab-wearing women are required to remove the niqab while testifying against their sincere religious belief they will be reluctant to report offences and pursue their prosecution, or to otherwise participate in the justice system. The wrongs done to them will remain unredressed. They will effectively be denied justice. The perpetrators of crimes against them will go unpunished, immune from legal consequences. These considerations may be especially weighty in a sexual assault case such as this one. In recent decades the justice system, recognizing the seriousness of sexual assault and the extent to which it is under-reported, has vigorously pursued those who commit this crime. Laws have been changed to encourage women and children to come forward to testify. Myths that once stood in the way of conviction have been set aside.

[38] Having considered the deleterious effects of requiring the witness to remove the niqab, the judge must also consider the salutary effects of doing so. These include preventing harm to the fair trial interest of the accused and safeguarding the repute of the administration of justice. An important consideration will be the extent to which effective cross-examination and credibility assessment on this witness's testimony is central to the case. On an individual level, the cost of an unfair trial is severe. The right to a fair trial is a fundamental pillar without which the edifice of the rule of law would crumble. No less is at stake than an individual's liberty—his right to live in freedom unless the state proves beyond a reasonable doubt that he committed a crime meriting imprisonment. This is of critical importance not only to the individual on trial, but to public confidence in the justice system.

[39] The nature of the proceeding may also be a relevant factor in assessing the harm to the fair trial interest of the accused if the witness is permitted to testify wearing the niqab ... . For example, determining whether evidence is admissible on a *voir dire* might not raise the same concerns for getting at the truth through cross-examination and credibility assessment as would determining a central factual element of the Crown's case. ...

[43] Another factor to consider is the nature of the evidence to be given by the witness. ... [I]f the witness's evidence is uncontested, the accused's trial fairness interests are not put at risk by the witness wearing a niqab. ...

[44] ... Future cases will doubtless raise other factors, and scientific exploration of the importance of seeing a witness's face to cross-examination and credibility assessment may enhance or diminish the force of the arguments made in this case. At this point, however, it may be ventured that where the liberty of the accused is at stake, the witness's evidence is central to the case and her credibility vital, the possibility of a wrongful conviction must weigh heavily in the balance, favouring removal of the niqab.

[45] The judge must assess all these factors and determine whether, in the case at hand, the salutary effects of requiring the witness to remove the niqab outweigh the deleterious effects of doing so.

VIII. The Alternatives

...

[47] ... Some argue that a witness should always be permitted to wear a niqab in court, while others argue that she should never be permitted to cover her face in court. In my respectful view, while both positions offer the advantage of a clear rule, neither can be sustained. ...

[52] First, as already discussed, our jurisprudence teaches that clashes between rights should be approached by reconciling the rights through accommodation if possible, and in the end, if a conflict cannot be avoided, by case-by-case balancing. ...

[53] Second, to remove religion from the courtroom is not in the Canadian tradition. Canadians have since the country's inception taken oaths based on holy books—be they the Bible, the Koran or some other sacred text. ...

[54] Third, the Canadian approach in the last 60 years to potential conflicts between freedom of religion and other values has been to respect the individual's religious belief and accommodate it if at all possible. ...

[56] This brings me to the final reason for rejecting an approach that would never allow a witness to testify while wearing a religious facial covering. It does not comport with the fundamental premise underlying the *Charter* that rights should be limited only to the extent that the limits are shown to be justifiable. ... A total ban on religious face coverings for all evidence given by all witnesses in the courtroom would mean that freedom of religion is being limited in situations where there is no good reason for the limit. As discussed above, uncontested and uncontroversial evidence does not engage the fair trial interest. A total ban that would permit the state to intrude on freedom of religion where it cannot be justified is not consistent with the premise on which the *Charter* is based—a generous approach to defining the scope of the rights it confers, coupled with the need to justify intrusions on those rights because of conflicting interests or the public good.

IX. Conclusion

[57] I would dismiss the appeal. The matter should be remitted to the preliminary inquiry judge to be decided in accordance with these reasons.

The reasons of LeBel and Rothstein JJ. were delivered by

LeBEL J.:

I. Introduction

[58] The Chief Justice proposes to dismiss the appeal of N.S. I agree with her conclusion. However, she crafts a rule that would allow witnesses to wear niqabs in certain circumstances. I have reservations about her approach and will propose a different rule. ...

II. Conflict Between Religious Rights and the Criminal Justice Process

...

[63] In the instant case, this Court must resolve a conflict between two protected constitutional rights within the framework established by the constitutional system. It is not a question of reconciling a constitutional right, the guarantee of freedom of religion, with a mere common law right, the right to cross-examine a witness, the complainant. As found in the jurisprudence, the right to cross-examine is a component of the constitutional right of the accused to make full answer and defence to the charges against him or her. ...

[68] ... [T]he Court is ... tasked with resolving a problem of balancing of rights, which both enjoy constitutional protection. I agree, in this respect, with the reasons of the Chief Justice that, when the issue involves the credibility of a key witness in respect of the core questions raised by a charge, the rights of the accused must be protected. Since cross-examination is a necessary tool for the exercise of the right to make full answer and defence, the consequences of restrictions on the rights in question weigh more heavily on the accused, and the balancing process works in his favour. A defence that is unduly and improperly constrained might impact on the determination of his guilt or innocence. As a result, the witness, the complainant in this case, must be asked to remove her veil while giving evidence at the preliminary inquiry and at trial.

III. The Niqab—Some Practical Aspects of the Conduct of the Trial

[69] But this does not mean that I agree with the solution the Chief Justice proposes to the problem of a witness wearing a niqab while testifying. In her view, whether a witness will be allowed to wear a niqab would depend on the nature or the importance of the evidence. The application of these criteria looks highly problematic. First, their application could trigger new motions, and possibly another type of "*voir dire*" that would add a new layer of complexity to a trial process that is not always a model of simplicity. We should not forget that a trial is itself a dynamic chain of events. It can often be difficult to foresee which evidence might be considered non-contentious or important at a specific point in a trial. The solution may vary at different stages of a trial, and also with what is known about the evidence. What looked unchallengeable one day might appear slightly dicey a week later. Given the nature of the trial process itself, the niqab should be allowed either in all cases or not at all when a witness testifies. In my opinion, a clear rule should be chosen. Because of its impact on the rights of the defence, in the context of the underlying values of the Canadian justice system, the wearing of a niqab should not be allowed. ...

The following are the reasons delivered by

ABELLA J. (dissenting):

Introduction

...

[81] N.S., the complainant, is alleging that she was repeatedly sexually assaulted by the accused while she was a child. She asserts that her religious beliefs require her to wear a niqab—a veil which covers her face but not her eyes—while testifying in front of any man who is not a direct family member. The accused argues that his right to a fair trial requires that he, his counsel, and the judge be able to see N.S.'s face during her testimony and cross-examination. The issue, therefore, is weighing the competing harms.

[82] I concede without reservation that seeing more of a witness' facial expressions is better than seeing less. What I am not willing to concede, however, is that seeing less is so impairing of a judge's or an accused's ability to assess the credibility of a witness, that the complainant will have to choose between her religious rights and her ability to bear witness against an alleged aggressor. This also has the potential to impair the rights of an accused, who may find herself having to choose between her religious rights and giving evidence in her own defence. The court system has many examples of accepting evidence from witnesses who are unable to testify under ideal circumstances because of visual, oral, or aural impediments. I am unable to see why witnesses who wear niqabs should be treated any differently.

[83] I would, however, make an exception in cases where the accused can demonstrate that the witness' face is directly relevant to the case, such as where the witness' identity is in issue. In such cases, seeing the witness' face is central to the

issues at trial, rather than merely being a part of the assessment of demeanour.

Analysis

...

[86] The crux of this case ... is whether the impact of not having full access to the usual "demeanour assessment package" can be said to so materially harm trial fairness that the religious right must yield. In my view, with very limited exceptions, the harm to a complainant of requiring her to remove her niqab while testifying will generally outweigh any harm to trial fairness.

[87] This Court has adopted a low threshold when it comes to establishing sincerity of belief. Inquiries into sincerity are to be "as limited as possible," intended "only to ensure that a presently asserted religious belief is in good faith, neither fictitious nor capricious, and that it is not an artifice" ... . As a result, sincerity of belief is only the first step through the gate in the discussion regarding a claimant's freedom of religion. ...

[88] ... The record shows that N.S. has worn her niqab for five years in sincere religious observance. In my view, she met the sincerity threshold.

[89] With great respect, however, I disagree with the majority that the "strength" of a witness' belief, while not relevant in assessing the witness' *prima facie* religious claim, *is* nonetheless somehow relevant when balancing that claim against trial fairness. It is unclear to me how a claimant's "strength" of belief—particularly given the highly subjective and imprecise nature of the freedom of religion analysis—affects the protection a claimant should be afforded under the *Charter*. Such an approach, in my respectful view, risks re-entering into inappropriate inquiries into a claimant's past practices, or into the extent to which a claimant's practices follow a religion's orthodox traditions.

[90] The next stage of the analysis is to ask whether permitting the witness to wear the niqab while testifying creates a serious risk to trial fairness. The accused argues that allowing N.S. to testify with her face covered by a niqab violates his right to a fair trial both by preventing effective cross-examination and by presenting an obstacle to the trier of fact's ability to assess her credibility. This brings us to the heart of the issue.

[91] There can be no doubt that the assessment of a witness' demeanour is easier if it is based on being able to scrutinize the whole demeanour package—face, body language, voice, etc. Nor is there any doubt that historically and ideally, we *expect* to see a witness' face when he or she is testifying. That, however, is different from concluding that unless the entire package is available for scrutiny, a witness' credibility cannot adequately be weighed.

[92] To start, while I think it is clear that witnesses in common law criminal courts are expected to testify with their faces visible to counsel and the trier of fact, it does not follow that if they are unable to do so, they cannot testify. A general expectation is not the same as a general rule, and there is no need to enshrine an historic practice into a "common law" requirement. Canada's justice journey has absorbed and accommodated an evolutionary recognition that while history assists in understanding the past, it need not necessarily command the future. That is why we have come to use screens for children, interpreters for those without facility in our official languages, and a myriad of other means to facilitate a witness' ability to give evidence in the courtroom. As this case demonstrates, courts are engaged in a constant process of reconciling historic expectations and practices with the *Charter*'s vision.

[93] A number of interests are engaged when a witness is not permitted to wear her niqab while testifying. First, she is prevented from being able to act in accordance with her religious beliefs. ...

[94] This has the effect of forcing a witness to choose between her religious beliefs and her ability to participate in the justice system. ... As a result, as the majority notes, complainants who sincerely believe that their religion requires them to wear the niqab in public, may choose not to bring charges for crimes they allege have been committed against them, or, more generally, may resist being a witness in someone else's trial. It is worth pointing out as well that where the witness is the accused, she will be unable to give evidence in her own defence. To those affected, this is like hanging a sign over the courtroom door saying "Religious minorities not welcome."

[95] ... Creating a judicial environment where victims are further inhibited by being asked to choose between their religious rights and their right to seek justice, undermines the public perception of fairness not only of the trial, but of the justice system itself.

[96] The majority's conclusion that being unable to see the witness' face is acceptable from a fair trial perspective if the evidence is "uncontested," essentially means that sexual assault complainants, whose evidence will inevitably be contested, will be forced to choose between laying a complaint and wearing a niqab, which, as previously noted, may be no meaningful choice at all.

[97] This brings us to the extent to which N.S., by exercising her freedom of religion in wearing a niqab, harms the accused's fair trial rights. The right to a fair trial is crucial to the presumption of innocence and maintaining confidence in the criminal justice system. While I agree that witnesses generally and ideally testify with their faces uncovered in open

court, abridgements of this "ideal" often occur in practice yet are almost always tolerated. ...

[99] ... [W]hile the ability to assess a witness' demeanour is an important component of trial fairness, many courts have noted its limitations for drawing accurate inferences about credibility. ...

[103] A witness may ... have physical or medical limitations that affect a judge's or lawyer's ability to assess demeanour. A stroke may interfere with facial expressions; an illness may affect body movements; and a speech impairment may affect the manner of speaking. All of these are departures from the demeanour ideal, yet none has ever been held to disqualify the witness from giving his or her evidence on the grounds that the accused's fair trial rights are thereby impaired. ...

[106] Wearing a niqab presents only a partial obstacle to the assessment of demeanour. A witness wearing a niqab may still express herself through her eyes, body language, and gestures. Moreover, the niqab has no effect on the witness' verbal testimony, including the tone and inflection of her voice, the cadence of her speech, or, most significantly, the substance of the answers she gives. Unlike out-of-court statements, defence counsel still has the opportunity to rigorously cross-examine N.S. on the witness stand.

[107] It is clear from all of this that trial fairness cannot reasonably expect ideal testimony from an ideal witness in every case, and that demeanour itself represents only one factor in the assessment of a witness' credibility. ...

[108] And since, realistically, not being able to see a witness' whole face is only a partial interference with what is, in any event, only one part of an imprecise measuring tool of credibility, we are left to wonder why we demand full "demeanour access" where religious belief prevents it.

[109] In my view, therefore, the harmful effects of requiring a witness to remove her niqab, with the result that she will likely not testify, bring charges in the first place, or, if she is the accused, be unable to testify in her own defence, is a significantly more harmful consequence than not being able to see a witness' whole face.

[110] Since, in my view, N.S.'s sincerity has been established, I see no reason to require her to remove her niqab. I would therefore allow the appeal and remit the matter to the preliminary inquiry for continuation, directing that N.S. be permitted to wear her niqab throughout both the preliminary inquiry and any trial that may follow.

R. v. Nur, 2015

When do mandatory minimum sentences for criminal offences unjustifiably infringe the Charter's section 12 prohibition of "cruel and unusual" punishment? This question was first addressed by the Supreme Court in the early Charter case of *Smith*,[1] which concerned a minimum sentence of seven years for importing narcotics. After striking down that provision, the court upheld all other challenged mandatory minimums until *Nur*,[2] when it invalidated sentences for possessing restricted and prohibited firearms.

Firearms issues were important for Stephen Harper's Conservative government. On the one hand, that government famously abolished the criminally enforced requirement to register legal "long guns" (the kinds of shotguns and rifles used by hunters). On the other hand, it cracked down on restricted and prohibited weapons,[3] raising the previous mandatory minimum sentence of one year for possessing such firearms to three years for a first offence (the situation of Hussein Nur) and five for a subsequent offence (the situation of Sydney Charles, Nur's co-litigant).[4]

Both sides of the Conservative firearms policy generated constitutional litigation, but with different outcomes in the Supreme Court. Regarding the abolished long-gun registry, Quebec unsuccessfully challenged the federal government's decision to destroy the relevant registration records, which the province wanted to use to establish its own registry.[5] By contrast, Nur, Charles, and their supporting interveners persuaded the court to strike down the increased mandatory minimum sentences for possessing restricted and prohibited firearms.

Significantly, Nur and Charles did not argue—and the court did not think—that the minimum sentences were unconstitutional as applied to them. Rather, they claimed that the sentences would be unconstitutional if applied to the reasonably foreseeable circumstances of hypothetical others. This approach had been taken in *Smith*, which struck down a seven-year mandatory minimum because it would be "cruel and unusual" for a hypothetical young person driving home to Canada from the United States with "his or her first

---

1 *R. v. Smith (Edward Dewey)*, [1987] 1 S.C.R. 1045.

2 Kent Roach, "Searching for Smith: The Constitutionality of Mandatory Sentences" (2001) 39 *Osgoode Hall Law Journal* 2/3; Debra Parkes, "From Smith to Smickle: The Charter's Minimal Impact on Mandatory Minimum Sentences" (2012) 57 *The Supreme Court Law Review: Osgoode's Annual Constitutional Cases Conference* article 7.

3 Prohibited firearms include short-barrelled handguns, sawed-off long guns, and automatic firearms. Restricted firearms include non-prohibited handguns and semi-automatic firearms.

4 As will be explained in more detail below, these mandatory minimums applied only if the Crown proceeded by indictment rather than by summary conviction.

5 *Quebec (Attorney General) v. Canada (Attorney General)*, 2015 SCC 14, [2015] 1 S.C.R. 693.

'joint of grass,'" not for Edward Smith himself, who had been sentenced to eight years for importing illegal drugs with a "'street value' ... between $126,000 and $168,000."[6]

Chief Justice McLachlin's majority opinion in *Nur* employed the same "reasonable hypothetical" approach to strike down the firearm-possession minimums. Because it was possible in some cases to be licensed to possess prohibited or restricted firearms, subject to strict controls concerning their storage and transportation, Justice McLachlin posited a "licensed and responsible gun owner who stores his unloaded firearm safely with ammunition nearby, but makes a mistake as to where it can be stored." For Justice McLachlin, "a three-year sentence is [as] grossly disproportionate" to this hypothetical circumstance as the seven-year sentence was to the imagined first-joint offender in *Smith*. In her view, both hypotheticals illustrate how the "blunt instrument" of mandatory minimums interferes with the "normal" judicial discretion "to tailor proportionate sentences."

The use of hypotheticals aroused judicial controversy in both *Smith* and *Nur*. Justice McIntyre's dissenting opinion in *Smith* acknowledged that hypotheticals were appropriate when "there may never be a better party,"[7] meaning a party whose circumstances directly involve the alleged infringement of the Constitution. However, Justice McIntyre saw no reason to think that there would "never be a better party" than Smith to raise the issue of applying a seven-year minimum sentence to someone importing a first joint. The issue would arise if and when charges were actually laid for a first-joint transgression. "Under s. 12 of the *Charter*," wrote Justice McIntyre, "individuals should be confined to arguing that *their* punishment is cruel and unusual and not be heard to argue that the punishment is cruel and unusual for some hypothetical third party."[8]

The objection to hypotheticals was somewhat different in *Nur*, where Justice Moldaver in his dissent (joined by Justices Rothstein and Wagner) accepted that *Smith* had been properly decided because a conviction under the relevant law necessarily entailed a disproportionate sentence in the hypothetical first-joint case. *Nur*, however, concerned a so-called hybrid offence, which allowed prosecutors to proceed by either "indictment" (in which case the mandatory minimums applied) or "summary conviction" (which involved no minimum sentence and only a one-year maximum[9]). For Justice Moldaver, the summary-conviction option was a "safety valve" that prevented disproportionate sentences for the minor licensing offences that concerned Justice McLachlin. He could not join the majority "in treating these licensing-type cases as *reasonable* hypotheticals." In his view, they "strain the bounds of credulity [and] are not grounded in experience or common sense."

But what if prosecutors do "strain the bounds of credibility" by electing to indict someone for a minor licensing offence? For Justice Moldaver, the answer lay not in striking down the mandatory minimum, but in remedying the prosecutorial "abuse of process" if and when it occurred. Chief Justice McLachlin's response to this proposal was scathing. Treating it as "a radical departure" from the established "constitutional framework" concerning mandatory minimums, she insisted that it offered "scant protection from grossly disproportionate sentences being imposed on offenders." Justice Moldaver replied that "far from

---

6   *R. v. Smith (Edward Dewey)*, *supra* note 1 at paras. 2, 79.

7   *Ibid.* at para. 80.

8   *Ibid.* at para. 79.

9   The maximum when proceeding by indictment was ten years.

offering *scant* protection, [his] proposal offer[ed] *total* protection from grossly dispropor-tionate sentences." And how, he wondered, can an approach emphasizing the features of "hybrid offences" be a "radical departure" from a "constitutional framework" that had never considered their relevance?

In *R. v. Lloyd*,[10] decided a year after *Nur*, the Supreme Court struck down a mandatory minimum sentence of one year for drug trafficking (or possession for the purpose of traf-ficking). In this case, too, Chief Justice McLachlin, again writing for a six-judge majority, found the law to be "cruel and unusual" as applied to hypothetical offenders rather than to Lloyd himself. And again, her implementation of this approach attracted a three-judge dissent (jointly authored by Justices Wagner, Gascon, and Brown).

For the *Lloyd* majority, the mandatory minimum caught "not only the serious drug trafficking that is its proper aim, but conduct that is much less blameworthy."[11] McLachlin's hypotheticals were meant to illustrate the "less blameworthy" category. For the dissenters, by contrast, "this mandatory minimum simply does not cover a 'wide range' of conduct. It is, rather, carefully tailored to catch only harmful and highly blameworthy conduct."[12] The hypotheticals posed by the majority did not persuade the dissenters. Intriguingly, two judges who participated in *Nur* seemed to switch sides in *Lloyd*. Justice Moldaver, who wrote the strong dissent in *Nur*, joined the Chief Justice in *Lloyd*, while Justice Gascon, part of the *Nur* majority, was among the *Lloyd* dissenters. ⌒

Discussion Questions

1. Justices McLachlin and Moldaver strenuously debate the relevance and significance of discretionary summary-conviction proceedings. Whom do you find most persuasive?

2. Should legislated mandatory minimums ever limit the judicial discretion to tailor indi-vidually proportionate sentences? What about mandatory maximums?

3. Can you determine how often Justices McLachlin and Moldaver revised their opinions in response to each other's arguments?

---

10 *R. v. Lloyd*, 2016 SCC 13, [2016] 1 S.C.R. 130.

11 *Ibid.* at para. 27.

12 *Ibid.* at para. 85.

R. v. NUR
2015 SCC 15, [2015] 1 S.C.R. 773

Hearing: November 7, 2014; Judgment: April 14, 2015.

Present: McLachlin C.J. and LeBel, Abella, Rothstein, Cromwell, Moldaver, Karakatsanis, Wagner, and Gascon JJ.

Interveners: Attorney General of Quebec, Attorney General of British Columbia, Attorney General of Alberta, Pivot Legal Society, John Howard Society of Canada, Canadian Civil Liberties Association, British Columbia Civil Liberties

Association, Advocates' Society, Canadian Bar Association, Canada's National Firearms Association, Canadian Association for Community Living, African Canadian Legal Clinic.

The judgment of McLachlin C.J. and LeBel, Abella, Cromwell, Karakatsanis, and Gascon JJ. was delivered by

THE CHIEF JUSTICE:

...

[1] Gun-related crime poses grave danger to Canadians. Parliament has therefore chosen to prohibit some weapons

outright, while restricting the possession of others. The *Criminal Code*, R.S.C. 1985, c. C-46, imposes severe penalties for violations of these laws.

[2] Section 95(2)(*a*) imposes mandatory minimum sentences for the offence of possessing prohibited or restricted firearms when the firearm is loaded or kept with readily accessible ammunition (s. 95(1))—three years for a first offence and five years for a second or subsequent offence. ...

[8] Anyone who wishes to possess a firearm must obtain a licence under the *Firearms Act*. Although one can obtain licences that authorize the possession of prohibited or restricted firearms, stringent criteria must be met: *Firearms Act*, ss. 7(2) and 12. The *Firearms Act* imposes controls on places where a person who has a licence can possess the restricted or prohibited firearms. ...

[12] Section 95 is a hybrid offence punishable by a maximum of 10 years' imprisonment if the Crown proceeds by way of indictment. When the provision was first introduced by Parliament, the offence carried a one-year minimum sentence if the Crown proceeded by indictment, and a one-year maximum penalty if the Crown proceeded summarily. In May 2008, Parliament increased the minimum term of imprisonment to three years for a first offence and five years for a subsequent offence if the Crown proceeded by indictment .... But Parliament did not change the one-year maximum sentence if the Crown proceeded summarily. ...

[44] Mandatory minimum sentences, by their very nature, have the potential to depart from the principle of proportionality in sentencing. They emphasize denunciation, general deterrence and retribution at the expense of what is a fit sentence for the gravity of the offence, the blameworthiness of the offender, and the harm caused by the crime. They function as a blunt instrument that may deprive courts of the ability to tailor proportionate sentences at the lower end of a sentencing range. They may, in extreme cases, impose unjust sentences, because they shift the focus from the offender during the sentencing process in a way that violates the principle of proportionality. They modify the general process of sentencing which relies on the review of all relevant factors in order to reach a proportionate result. They affect the outcome of the sentence by changing the normal judicial process of sentencing. ...

[46] ... [A] challenge to a mandatory minimum sentencing provision on the ground it constitutes cruel and unusual punishment under s. 12 of the *Charter* involves two steps. First, the court must determine what constitutes a proportionate sentence for the offence having regard to the objectives and principles of sentencing in the *Criminal Code*. Then, the court must ask whether the mandatory minimum requires the judge to impose a sentence that is grossly disproportionate

to the fit and proportionate sentence. If the answer is yes, the mandatory minimum provision is inconsistent with s. 12 and will fall unless justified under s. 1 of the *Charter*. ...

[48] Nur and Charles do not argue that the mandatory minimum terms of imprisonment in s. 95(2) are grossly disproportionate as applied to them. Rather, they argue that these mandatory minimum terms of imprisonment violate s. 12 as they apply to other offenders. Against this, the Attorney General of Ontario, supported by other Attorneys General, argues for a test that puts the primary or exclusive focus on the offender before the court. ...

[51] ... This Court has consistently held that a challenge to a law under s. 52 of the *Constitution Act, 1982* does not require that the impugned provision contravene the rights of the claimant .... This is because "[i]t is the nature of the law, not the status of the accused, that is in issue": *Big M* [*Drug Mart Ltd., R. v.*, [1985] 1 S.C.R. 295], at p. 314, per Dickson J. Section 52 of the *Constitution Act, 1982* entrenches not only the supremacy of the Constitution but also commands that "any law that is inconsistent with the provisions of the Constitution is, to the extent of the inconsistency, of no force or effect." If the only way to challenge an unconstitutional law were on the basis of the precise facts before the court, bad laws might remain on the books indefinitely. This violates the rule of law. No one should be subjected to an unconstitutional law: *Big M*, at p. 313. This reflects the principle that the Constitution belongs to all citizens, who share a right to the constitutional application of the laws of Canada.

[52] The argument that the focus should be mainly or exclusively on the offender before the court is also inconsistent with the jurisprudence of the Court on the review of mandatory minimum sentences under s. 12 of the *Charter*. The cases have sometimes referred to this review as proceeding on "reasonable hypotheticals." ...

[53] The first case to consider the question was *Smith* [*R. v.*, [1987] 1 S.C.R. 1045]. The majority of the Court, per Lamer J. (as he then was) struck down a seven-year mandatory minimum sentence for importing narcotics on the basis that the law could catch a student driving home to Canada from the United States with her first joint of grass. ...

[54] A few years later in *R. v. Goltz*, [1991] 3 S.C.R. 485, the Court, per Gonthier J. for the majority, confirmed that a s. 12 review of mandatory minimum sentencing laws may look at cases other than that of the offender .... The Court upheld a minimum sentence of seven days' imprisonment for driving while prohibited.

[55] Once again, in *Morrisey* [*R. v.*, 2000 SCC 39, [2000] 2 S.C.R. 90], the majority of the Court, per Gonthier J., stressed that the "reasonableness of the hypothetical cannot be overstated": para. 30. The Court upheld a four-year

mandatory minimum sentence for criminal negligence causing death by using a firearm. ...

[62] The inquiry into cases that the mandatory minimum provision may reasonably be expected to capture must be grounded in judicial experience and common sense. ... Fanciful or remote situations must be excluded: *Goltz*, at p. 506. ...

[78] ... [In Nur's case], [t]he question is whether the three-year minimum sentence imposed by s. 95(2)(*a*)(i) will result in grossly disproportionate sentences in reasonably foreseeable cases. ...

[82] Section 95(1) casts its net over a wide range of potential conduct. Most cases within the range may well merit a sentence of three years or more, but conduct at the far end of the range may not. At one end of the range ... "stands the outlaw who carries a loaded prohibited or restricted firearm in public places as a tool of his or her criminal trade. ... [T]his person is engaged in truly criminal conduct and poses a real and immediate danger to the public ... . At this end of the range—indeed for the vast majority of offences—a three-year sentence may be appropriate. A little further along the spectrum stands the person whose conduct is less serious and poses less danger; for these offenders three years' imprisonment may be disproportionate, but not grossly so. At the far end of the range, stands the licensed and responsible gun owner who stores his unloaded firearm safely with ammunition nearby, but makes a mistake as to where it can be stored. For this offender, a three-year sentence is grossly disproportionate. ...

[83] ... The bottom line is that s. 95(1) foreseeably catches licensing offences which involve little or no moral fault and little or no danger to the public. For these offences three years' imprisonment is grossly disproportionate to a fit and fair sentence. ... I conclude that s. 95(2)(*a*)(i) breaches s. 12 of the *Charter*. ...

[85] The Attorneys General of Canada and Ontario argue that the Court of Appeal erred by not taking into account the Crown's ability to elect to proceed summarily and thereby avoid the mandatory minimum sentence in the indictable offence. They argue that the hybrid nature of the offence should be taken into account as a factor when assessing the likelihood that a general application of the offence would result in a grossly disproportionate sentence being imposed. Put differently, they contend that the Crown's election to proceed summarily and thereby avoid a mandatory minimum prevents s. 95 from being grossly disproportionate when the conduct is at the less serious end of the spectrum.

[86] I cannot agree. To accept this argument would result in replacing a public hearing on the constitutionality of s. 95 before an independent and impartial court with the discretionary decision of a Crown prosecutor, who is in an adversarial role to the accused.

[87] Sentencing is inherently a judicial function. It is the courts that are directed by Parliament to impose a mandatory minimum term of imprisonment, and it is the duty of the courts to scrutinize the constitutionality of the provision. The Crown's submission is in effect an invitation to delegate the courts' constitutional obligation to the prosecutors employed by the state, leaving the threat of a grossly disproportionate sentence hanging over an accused's head. ...

[89] This Court recently considered the distinction between the prosecution's function in exercising its discretion to proceed summarily or by way of indictment and the courts' sentencing function in *R. v. Anderson*, 2014 SCC 41, [2014] 2 S.C.R. 167. The Court emphasized that sentencing is a judicial function, and opined that the fact a mandatory regime may require a judge to impose a disproportionate sentence does not alter the prosecutorial function in electing the mode of trial. As Moldaver J. explained for a unanimous Court:

> Mr. Anderson's argument in effect equates the duty of the judge and the prosecutor, *but there is no basis in law to support equating their distinct roles in the sentencing process.* It is *the judge's* responsibility to impose sentence; likewise, it is <u>the judge's</u> responsibility, within the applicable legal parameters, to craft a proportionate sentence. If a mandatory minimum regime requires a judge to impose a disproportionate sentence, the regime should be challenged. [[Emphasis] added [underlining in original]; para. 25.]

[90] This is not to say that the Crown election to proceed summarily is in itself problematic. It is entirely appropriate that the Crown should exercise its discretion in order to screen out some offences at the lower end of the spectrum captured by s. 95(1). Hybrid offences allow the Crown to take into account the variation that exists between cases. They recognize that the same offence can be committed in more and less serious ways, and allows the Crown to take the specific circumstances of each case into account. ...

[91] The argument of the Attorneys General of Canada and Ontario ... is essentially the converse of a constitutional exemption. As I observed on behalf of a unanimous Court in *Ferguson*[*R. v.*, 2008 SCC 6, [2008] 1 S.C.R. 96], "[t]he divergence between the law on the books and the law as applied—and the uncertainty and unpredictability that result—exacts a price paid in the coin of injustice": para. 72. It deprives citizens of the right to know what the law is in advance and to govern their conduct accordingly, and it encourages the uneven and unequal application of the law. To paraphrase *Ferguson*, bad law, fixed up on a case-by-case basis by

prosecutors, does not accord with the role and responsibility of Parliament to enact constitutional laws for the people of Canada: paras. 72-73.

[92] Since writing these reasons, I have had the opportunity to read the reasons of my colleague, Justice Moldaver, who concludes that s. 95(2) does not violate s. 12 of the *Charter* essentially on the ground that the prosecution may elect to proceed by summary conviction where the conduct at issue is such that imposing the mandatory minimum sentence would be grossly disproportionate. I do not agree that *Canada (Attorney General) v. PHS Community Services Society*, 2011 SCC 44, [2011] 3 S.C.R. 134, supports the rule that a mandatory minimum law that imposes grossly disproportionate sentences in foreseeable cases may be saved from unconstitutionality by prosecutorial discretion to proceed by another route.

[93] *PHS* was concerned with the federal Minister of Health's decision not to grant a medical exemption to a safe-injection site from the application of the *Controlled Drugs and Substances Act*, S.C. 1996, c. 19. This was an administrative decision under a statutory exemption that was designed to promote public health. The essence of the challenge before the Court in *PHS* was whether the Minister's administrative law decision was compliant with the *Charter*. But the scenario in *PHS* is a far cry from the proposition ... that the exercise of a prosecutor's discretion as to whether to invoke the mandatory minimum sentence in an adversarial criminal trial can effectively insulate a legislated mandatory minimum term of imprisonment from review under s. 12 of the *Charter*.

[94] I add this about my colleague's proposed framework. The protection it offers against grossly disproportionate punishment is illusory: in practice it would create a situation where the exercise of the prosecutor's discretion is effectively immune from meaningful review. The abuse of discretion standard is a notoriously high bar and has no place in this Court's jurisprudence under s. 12 of the *Charter*. The proposed framework would be a radical departure from the constitutional framework in these cases, and offers scant protection from grossly disproportionate sentences being imposed on offenders.

[95] Two further objections may be raised against the argument that prosecutorial discretion can cure a sentencing provision that violates s. 12 of the *Charter*. The first is that one cannot be certain that the discretion will always be exercised in a way that would avoid an unconstitutional result. Nor can the constitutionality of a statutory provision rest on an expectation that the Crown will act properly: *Lavallee, Rackel & Heintz v. Canada (Attorney General)*, 2002 SCC 61, [2002] 3 S.C.R. 209, at para. 45. As Cory J., for

the majority, stated in *R. v. Bain*, [1992] 1 S.C.R. 91, at pp. 103-4:

> Unfortunately it would seem that whenever the Crown is granted statutory power that can be used abusively then, on occasion, it will indeed be used abusively. The protection of basic rights should not be dependent upon a reliance on the continuous exemplary conduct of the Crown, something that is impossible to monitor or control. Rather the offending statutory provision should be removed.

[96] This leads to a related concern that vesting that much power in the hands of prosecutors endangers the fairness of the criminal process. It gives prosecutors a trump card in plea negotiations, which leads to an unfair power imbalance with the accused and creates an almost irresistible incentive for the accused to plead to a lesser sentence in order to avoid the prospect of a lengthy mandatory minimum term of imprisonment. As a result, the "determination of a fit and appropriate sentence, having regard to all of the circumstances of the offence and offender, may be determined in plea discussions outside of the courtroom by a party to the litigation": R. M. Pomerance, "The New Approach to Sentencing in Canada: Reflections of a Trial Judge" (2013), 17 *Can. Crim. L.R.* 305, at p. 313. We cannot ignore the increased possibility that wrongful convictions could occur under such conditions.

[97] Second ... the exercise of discretion typically occurs before the facts are fully known. An analysis that upholds s. 95(2) on the basis of the summary conviction option "does not come to grips with the timing of the Crown election and the factual basis upon which that election is made": para. 163. The existence of the summary conviction option is therefore not an answer to the respondents' s. 12 claim. As stated in *R. v. Smickle*, 2012 ONSC 602, 110 O.R. (3d) 25, at para. 110:

> The Crown discretion is exercised at an early stage when all of the facts, particularly those favourable to the defence, are often not known. Often, the full facts will not be known until the trial judge delivers his or her reasons or the jury delivers a verdict.

[98] Finally, the Attorney General of Canada, relying on *Morrisey*, argues that parole eligibility reduces the actual impact of the three-year mandatory minimum penalty for an offence. We simply cannot know whether that is in fact the case. Nur correctly argues that parole is a statutory privilege rather than a right. The discretionary decision of the parole board is no substitute for a constitutional law. Canada's submission also misunderstands the role of the parole board—which is to ensure that an offender is safely released into the community, not to ensure that an offender serves a

proportionate sentence. That is the function of one person alone—the sentencing judge.

[Having found that the five-year minimum sentence for second or subsequent offences (section 95(2)(*a*)(ii)) also infringed section 12 of the Charter, Chief Justice McLachlin asked whether the infringements could be justified under section 1 of the Charter. She found that the impugned mandatory minimum terms were "rationally connected" to the pressing and substantial objective of denunciation and retribution, but concluded that they failed the "minimum impairment" component of the *Oakes* test.]

[117] [Regarding minimal impairment,] Parliament could have achieved its objective by drafting an offence with a close correspondence between conduct attracting significant moral blameworthiness—such as those engaged in criminal activity or conduct that poses a danger to others—and the mandatory minimum, rather than a sweeping law that includes in its ambit conduct attracting less blameworthiness for which the mandatory minimum sentence would be grossly disproportionate. The government has not discharged its burden on this branch of the *Oakes* test. There are less harmful means of achieving the legislative goal. ...

[119] I would dismiss the appeals. The mandatory minimum sentences imposed by s. 95(2)(*a*) are inconsistent with s. 12 of the *Charter* and are therefore declared of no force or effect under s. 52 of the *Constitution Act, 1982*.

[120] It remains appropriate for judges to continue to impose weighty sentences in other circumstances, such as those in the cases at bar. For this reason, I would decline to interfere with the sentences that the trial judges imposed on Nur and Charles.

The reasons of Rothstein, Moldaver, and Wagner JJ. were delivered by

MOLDAVER J. (dissenting):

...

[125] In finding s. 95(2) unconstitutional, the majority adopts the "reasonable hypothetical" approach first developed by this Court in *R. v. Smith*, [1987] 1 S.C.R. 1045, and subsequently applied in *R. v. Goltz*, [1991] 3 S.C.R. 485, and *R. v. Morrisey*, 2000 SCC 39, [2000] 2 S.C.R. 90. Tracing through these authorities, the Chief Justice states that reasonable hypotheticals should be "grounded in ... experience and common sense" (para. 62). I agree. She then refers to s. 95(2) and expresses concern about imposing lengthy custodial sentences in certain hypothetical cases, namely "licensing offences which involve little or no moral fault and little or no danger to the public"—a concern which I share (para. 83). Where I

part company with the majority is in treating these licensing-type cases as *reasonable* hypotheticals. With respect, experience and common sense provide proof positive that they are not.

[126] I start with experience. Section 95 was enacted in 1995 and has been in force for nearly two decades. It has always included a mandatory minimum sentence for cases prosecuted by indictment. Since 2008, it has included the present three-year and five-year mandatory minimums. And yet, the respondents Mr. Nur and Mr. Charles are unable to point to a single licensing-type case over its entire history where a mandatory minimum imposed under s. 95(2) could be regarded as grossly disproportionate. Moreover, they cannot identify a single case where an offender who has committed a "licensing offenc[e] ... involv[ing] little or no moral fault and little or no danger to the public" has been prosecuted by indictment, thus attracting a mandatory minimum (para. 83). ...

[129] I turn to common sense. ... The reasonably foreseeable cases advanced by the majority assume that the Crown election is irrelevant. This perspective is at odds with Parliament's deliberate choice to structure s. 95 as a hybrid offence, recognizing its wide ambit and empowering prosecutors to separate licensing-type cases from instances of more serious misconduct. This legislative choice is hardly controversial—hybrid offences abound in the *Criminal Code*. Crown counsel are granted the discretion to make these elections and do so on a daily basis in accordance with their sworn duty to act in the public interest. With respect, an application of the reasonable hypothetical approach that denies this reality—and indeed assumes the opposite—does not accord with common sense. ...

[134] I believe the Chief Justice shares my concern that striking down the impugned mandatory minimums would, to some extent, frustrate Parliament's efforts to denounce and deter gun crime. She identifies an alternative scheme that, in her view, would accomplish Parliament's goals without offending s. 12 of the *Charter*:

> Parliament could have achieved its objective by drafting an offence with a close correspondence between conduct attracting significant moral blameworthiness—such as those engaged in criminal activity or conduct that poses a danger to others—and the mandatory minimum. ... [para. 117]

[135] If I understand the Chief Justice correctly, Parliament could enact the impugned mandatory minimums as part of a revised offence containing an additional element beyond the existing elements of s. 95(1). For example, the offence could be limited to "those engaged in criminal

activity" or to "conduct that poses a danger to others" (para. 117). Respectfully ... this suggestion ... is discordant with Parliament's true objective in creating mandatory minimums for the unlawful *possession* of a loaded or readily loaded prohibited or restricted firearm. ...

[136] Section 95 targets the simple possession of guns that are frequently used in gang-related and other criminal activity: see *R. v. Nur*, 2013 ONCA 677, 117 O.R. (3d) 401, at paras. 54-57. Parliament has concentrated on simple possession for a reason: firearms—and particularly the firearms caught by s. 95—are inherently dangerous. ...

[138] Given this inherent danger, it was open to Parliament to conclude that simple possession of a loaded or readily loaded restricted or prohibited firearm should attract a significant mandatory custodial sentence. ...

[140] ... Parliament chose to punish simple possession with significant custodial penalties, while leaving open the option of summary proceedings for the licensing-type offences about which the majority is rightly concerned. I would respect that legislative choice. ...

[141] Moreover, I am concerned that adding new elements to the offence would render the mandatory minimums under-inclusive. The majority identifies two possible elements that could be added to s. 95. The first would limit the offence to "those engaged in criminal activity" (para. 117). As I understand it, this element would require the Crown to prove that the accused possessed the firearm for a criminal purpose—a high bar for prosecutors to meet. Even on the facts of Mr. Nur's case, it does not appear that the Crown could prove this element beyond a reasonable doubt: *Nur* sentencing reasons, at paras. 61, 66 and 68-69. Incorporating a criminal purpose element could thus exclude cases like Mr. Nur's, where the imposition of a mandatory minimum sentence is uncontroversial.

[142] The second suggestion would limit the offence to "conduct that poses a danger to others" (para. 117). I understand this element to mean something more than the inherent danger posed by all instances of possession contrary to s. 95. The element would therefore require the Crown to prove a *specific* risk of harm. In my view, the addition of this element would again render the offence under-inclusive.

[143] A simple example illustrates this point. A police officer stops a vehicle in a remote, unpopulated area and sees a handgun in plain view on the back seat. The driver is cooperative, but does not have a licence for the firearm. The officer suspects that he may be involved in gang-related activity. In these circumstances, it is unclear whether the Crown could prove, beyond a reasonable doubt, that the driver's possession of the firearm created a specific risk of harm. Yet, this is precisely the type of situation to which the mandatory

minimums in s. 95 are intended to apply. Indeed, the Minister specifically indicated that "increasing numbers of handguns [are being] found in cars," and that "it is very important to have ... higher minimum penalties" to address such situations: *House of Commons Debates*, vol. 141, at pp. 1943 and 1941. ...

[146] As I have explained, the reasonable hypothetical approach does not justify striking down the impugned mandatory minimums. The scenarios contemplated by the majority—sending someone to jail for three years for what amounts to a licensing-type offence—are, in my respectful view, speculative and strain the bounds of credulity. They are not grounded in experience or common sense.

[147] In any event, I believe that a different analytical framework is required here. Why? Because, to date, our s. 12 jurisprudence from *Smith* to *Morrisey* has only considered the constitutionality of mandatory minimum sentences in the context of straight indictable offences. This is the first time we have examined their constitutionality in a hybrid scheme. ...

[153] The majority states that the use of reasonable hypotheticals to evaluate mandatory minimums is settled law and necessarily applies here. It characterizes my proposed framework as "a radical departure from the constitutional framework" that has animated this Court's s. 12 jurisprudence (para. 94). With respect, I disagree with this assessment. Parliament's choice to craft s. 95 as a hybrid offence distinguishes the present context from our previous s. 12 jurisprudence. None of those cases involved a hybrid sentencing scheme that effectively conceded the existence of reasonably foreseeable cases where the mandatory minimum would be grossly disproportionate.

[154] By way of example, s. 95 is markedly different from the offence in *Smith*. In that case, the narcotics importing offence was a straight indictable offence carrying a seven-year mandatory minimum. Like s. 95, it covered a wide array of conduct, from large-scale drug smuggling to the hypothetical "young person who, while driving back into Canada from a winter break in the U.S.A., is caught with ... his or her first 'joint of grass'" (p. 1053). However, unlike s. 95, that offence did not include the option for prosecutors to proceed summarily. Parliament had not turned its mind to the possibility that the offence might catch less serious cases that would not merit a seven-year custodial sentence. Rather, Parliament targeted the problem of narcotics importation with the blunt instrument of a straight indictable offence carrying a long mandatory term of imprisonment. The scheme did not adequately protect against the imposition of grossly disproportionate sentences, and the Court rightly struck it down.

[155] However, if *Smith* had involved a hybrid offence like s. 95, I believe that the Court's analysis would have been different. A hybrid offence would have signalled Parliament's intention to shield the least serious cases from the mandatory minimum. In such circumstances, Lamer J.'s hypothetical would have had little persuasive force. Simply put, it is virtually impossible to imagine Crown counsel proceeding by indictment against a young person caught bringing a single joint of marijuana across the border, especially when he or she would face a minimum penalty of seven years' imprisonment.

[156] In sum, I am not persuaded that the reasonable hypothetical approach is binding or even useful in this context. The legislative intent in enacting a hybrid sentencing scheme points to a different analytical framework. ...

[157] I would adopt a two-stage framework to evaluate whether a mandatory minimum sentence in a hybrid scheme complies with s. 12. First, the court must determine whether the scheme adequately protects against grossly disproportionate sentences *in general*. Second, the court must determine whether the Crown has exercised its discretion in a manner that results in a grossly disproportionate sentence *for the particular offender* before the court.

[158] [The first stage of this analysis—determining whether the scheme protects against grossly disproportionate sentences in general—] has two parts. First, the court must determine the sentencing range for indictable convictions under the sentencing regime that existed prior to the enactment of the impugned mandatory minimum. This is done with reference to actual sentences found in reported cases. The court must then isolate the low end of that sentencing range. By "low end," I do not mean the absolute lowest sentence that can be found in the reported cases. Rather, I refer to the types of sentences that are generally imposed on the least blameworthy offenders in the indictable category. This low end serves as an objective indicator of appropriate sentences for the least serious instances of the offence that would realistically be prosecuted by indictment.

[159] Second, the court must compare the impugned mandatory minimum with the low end of the prior range. If the mandatory minimum is grossly disproportionate to sentences at the low end, then the scheme does not adequately protect against the imposition of grossly disproportionate sentences *in general*. On the contrary, it puts an identifiable set of offenders directly at risk of cruel and unusual punishment in violation of s. 12. The proper remedy here lies under s. 52(1) of the *Constitution Act, 1982*, and the mandatory minimum must be struck down. ...

[160] If the scheme itself is upheld, the court must move on to the second stage and determine whether the Crown has exercised its discretion in a manner that results in a grossly disproportionate sentence for the particular offender before the court. In those rare cases where the Crown's decision to proceed by indictment leads to a grossly disproportionate sentence, a remedy will lie under s. 24(1) of the *Charter*.

[161] As noted, the focus here is on the constitutionality of state action, and not the law itself. Specifically, the state action at issue is the Crown election. The decision to proceed summarily or by indictment is a matter of core prosecutorial discretion, reviewable only for abuse of process: *R. v. Anderson*, 2014 SCC 41, [2014] 2 S.C.R. 167, at paras. 44 and 48. In my view, a decision to prosecute by indictment that would give rise to a grossly disproportionate sentence represents a *per se* abuse of process in violation of s. 12. Generally, the appropriate and just remedy in the circumstances will be a sentence reduction below the mandatory minimum. ...

[167] ... [T]o find an abuse of process under s. 12, I would not require proof of bad faith or malicious intent on the part of the Crown. Rather, an abuse of process will lie, regardless of intent, where the Crown's decision to proceed by indictment "tend[s] to undermine society's expectations of fairness in the administration of justice": *Nixon* [*R. v.*, 2011 SCC 34, [2011] 2 S.C.R. 566], at para. 41.

[168] While proof of bad faith or malicious intent is not necessary, it would certainly suffice to establish an abuse of process under s. 12. For example, if the Crown election was influenced by discriminatory factors such as the race of the offender, this would be an abuse of process: see *Anderson*, at para. 50.

[169] Similarly, an improper use of the mandatory minimum in plea bargaining—a concern raised by the majority, which I share—would also warrant the court's intervention. Thus, if a prosecutor proceeded by indictment in order to use the threat of a mandatory minimum to extort a guilty plea, this would likely qualify as an abuse of process and justify a s. 24(1) remedy: see *Babos* [*R. v.*, [2014] 1 S.C.R. 309], at paras. 58-61. It follows that we do not need to strike down the sentencing scheme to guard against these concerns. To the extent that the majority holds otherwise, I respectfully disagree. ...

[172] For these reasons, I am unable to agree with the majority's assertion that the abuse of process doctrine creates "a notoriously high bar" and "offers scant protection from grossly disproportionate sentences" (para. 94). With respect, this contention misconstrues how the doctrine operates under my proposed framework. Far from offering *scant* protection, my proposal offers *total* protection from grossly disproportionate sentences. If an offender can show that a mandatory minimum would be grossly disproportionate in his or her

case, the judge must declare a *per se* abuse of process and grant a s. 24(1) remedy. ...

[173] In *R. v. Ferguson*, 2008 SCC 6, [2008] 1 S.C.R. 96, this Court held that where a mandatory minimum sentencing scheme is found to violate s. 12, the proper remedy lies under s. 52 and the law must be struck down. The Court expressly rejected the possibility that the law could be saved by granting case-by-case exemptions for any unconstitutional applications.

[174] I agree that constitutional exemptions are not an appropriate response to unconstitutional laws. My proposed framework is consistent with this principle. The remedy it contemplates is *not* a response to an unconstitutional law. Rather, the remedy is a response to a state actor's *exercise of discretion* under a law which a judge has held to be constitutionally compliant at stage one of the framework. As the Chief Justice explained in *Ferguson*:

> Section 24(1) ... is generally used as a remedy, not for unconstitutional laws, but for *unconstitutional government acts committed under the authority of legal regimes which are accepted as fully constitutional...* . The acts of government agents acting under such regimes are not the necessary result or "effect" of the law, *but of the government agent's applying a discretion conferred by the law in an unconstitutional manner.* Section 52(1) is thus not applicable. The appropriate remedy lies under s. 24(1). [Emphasis added; para. 60.]

This logic applies to the acts of prosecutors making an election under s. 95. In my view, once a court has determined that a sentencing scheme itself is constitutional, it is entirely appropriate to guard against its rare unconstitutional application by providing a case-by-case s. 24(1) remedy. ...

[175] The Chief Justice states that reliance on the Crown election to uphold the impugned mandatory minimums effectively "replac[es] a public hearing on the constitutionality of s. 95 before an independent and impartial court with the discretionary decision of a Crown prosecutor" (para. 86). She emphasizes that it is incumbent on courts to scrutinize the constitutionality of the sentencing schemes they apply.

[176] I agree that the responsibility to ensure constitutional compliance rests with judges, and not with prosecutors. The framework I propose places that responsibility squarely in the hands of judges. In this respect, it is consistent with the admonition in *Smith* that "courts are duty bound" to evaluate whether a law is constitutional, and must not "delegate the avoidance of a [*Charter*] violation to the prosecution" (p. 1078).

[177] Specifically, the framework includes two checks to ensure compliance with s. 12, neither of which relies on prosecutorial discretion. First, if the sentencing scheme itself is challenged, the judge may strike it down as unconstitutional. Second, if an offender argues that the mandatory minimum would be grossly disproportionate in his or her case, the judge may find a *per se* abuse of process and grant a sentence reduction under s. 24(1).

[178] I repeat and emphasize that the Crown election under s. 95 does not require prosecutors to go outside the law. Rather, it is a discretion built into the legislative scheme that acts as a safety valve to guard against unconstitutional applications of the law. In my view, any meaningful assessment of the law's constitutionality must take this factor into account: *PHS*, at paras. 109-14. However, in recognizing the relevance of the Crown election, I should not be taken as saying that this safety valve insulates the law from *Charter* scrutiny. Rather, it simply informs *how* that scrutiny should be applied.

[179] Nor does my framework conflate the respective functions of prosecutors and judges. The majority, citing *Anderson*, insists that "sentencing is a judicial function" (para. 89). In its view, the fact that "a mandatory [minimum] regime may require a judge to impose a disproportionate sentence does not alter the prosecutorial function in electing the mode of trial" (*ibid.*). I agree. In prosecuting an accused under a hybrid offence, it is the *Crown's* responsibility to elect a mode of proceedings bearing in mind the gravity of the conduct. Where an election would lead to a grossly disproportionate sentence, it is the *judge's* responsibility to avoid that outcome.

[180] In light of these checks, I cannot accept the majority's suggestion that my framework insulates mandatory minimums from *Charter* scrutiny. With respect, that is just not so. The two checks I have described ensure that judges make the ultimate call as to the constitutionality of the law itself, as well as its application to a particular offender. The majority, relying on *R. v. Bain*, [1992] 1 S.C.R. 91, states that "one cannot be certain that [prosecutorial] discretion will always be exercised in a way that would avoid an unconstitutional result" (para. 95). I agree. It is precisely for this reason that my proposed framework empowers judges to intervene where the Crown election puts an offender at risk of a grossly disproportionate sentence. In my view, this is a full answer to the majority's concerns.

[181] I wish to add one further point. The Chief Justice notes that the Crown election is exercised at an early stage of the proceedings before all of the facts related to an offence have emerged. It follows that the Crown might make an inappropriate election prior to discovering mitigating circumstances. As a result, she contends that "[t]he existence of the summary conviction option is therefore not an answer to the respondents' s. 12 claim" (para. 97).

[182] With respect, I disagree for two reasons. First, if Crown counsel becomes aware of facts suggesting that the initial election was not appropriate, he or she can stay the indictment and initiate summary proceedings: see *Criminal Code*, ss. 579 and 786(2). Second, even if Crown counsel does not re-elect in this manner, it is always open to the judge to find a *per se* abuse of process where the mandatory minimum would be grossly disproportionate for a particular offender. ...

[199] Section 95 represents Parliament's considered response to the pressing problem of gun violence in our communities. Parliament chose to craft a wide-reaching offence to denounce and deter serious criminal activity with lengthy mandatory minimums. At the same time, it provided a safety valve to divert the least serious cases into summary proceedings carrying no minimum sentence. With respect, I see no reason to second-guess Parliament based on hypotheticals that do not accord with experience or common sense. Nor, on my proposed framework, is there any sound basis for disturbing the extensive deliberations of our elected representatives on this important issue. I would allow the appeals, and uphold the constitutional validity of s. 95(2).

E. EVOLVING SCOPE OF SECTION 7

20 Re B.C. Motor Vehicle Act, 1985

The *B.C. Motor Vehicle Reference* is an example of a case that is relatively unimportant with respect to the policy issue at stake, but significant in terms of its impact on constitutional interpretation and development. While the fate of section 94(2) of B.C.'s *Motor Vehicle Act* was quickly forgotten, the Supreme Court's decision in this case has gone on to be one of the court's most frequently cited judgments.

Section 94(1) of B.C.'s *Motor Vehicle Act* made it an offence for a person to drive if his licence had been revoked or he had been legally prohibited from driving. Section 94(2) made it an absolute liability offence—that is, guilt was established by proof of driving, whether or not the driver knew of the prohibition or suspension. The offence was punishable by a fine and a minimum term of imprisonment. Shortly after the adoption of the Charter, the B.C. government had doubts about the compatibility of section 94(2) with the Charter, and so referred the question to the provincial Court of Appeal. The latter found that the provision violated the Charter, and there was an automatic appeal to the Supreme Court of Canada.

At issue was whether the absolute liability provision violated the "principles of fundamental justice" set forth in section 7 of the Charter. The attorney general of British Columbia argued that the meaning of section 7 was limited to "procedural fairness" alone, and that section 7 did not authorize judges to pass judgment on the fairness of the "substance" of impugned legislation.

The notion of "substantive due process" had a long and checkered history in American constitutional law. Between 1900 and 1937, the American Supreme Court had used the due-process clause of the American Constitution to strike down numerous progressive laws that imposed new social and economic regulations on American business. In effect, the American court had used substantive due process to protect the laissez-faire economic system and conservative economic interests from the emerging welfare state. This culminated in the New Deal "court crisis" of 1937, after which the substantive due-process precedents were abandoned and discredited. However, substantive due process re-emerged in American jurisprudence in the 1970s, most notably in the abortion decision.[1] As the Charter was being drafted, the term "fundamental justice" replaced "due process" in order to avoid the substantive connotations the latter term had acquired in American law.

---

1 *Roe v. Wade*, 410 U.S. 113 (1973). See the introduction to *Morgentaler v. The Queen*, case 21.

Speaking for a unanimous court, Justice Lamer rejected a strict dichotomy between "substantive" and "procedural" interpretations of section 7. The two could not be so easily separated. The entire array of procedural safeguards enumerated in sections 8 through 14 of the Charter constitute the substance of principles of fundamental justice articulated in section 7. More to the point, Justice Lamer wrote: "A law that has the potential to convict a person who has not really done anything wrong offends the principles of fundamental justice. ... In other words, absolute liability and imprisonment cannot be combined."

Justice Lamer was well aware that attributing substantive meaning to the concept of principles of fundamental justice could unduly widen the scope of judicial review under section 7, resulting in what he called a "super judicial legislature." To discourage this, he stressed that a substantive interpretation of section 7 was limited to the field of criminal law and legal rights, "the inherent domain of the judiciary," and would not be applied "in the realm of general public policy." However, several subsequent decisions by lower courts extended this doctrine to areas of economic and social policy. The closest the Supreme Court of Canada has come to applying a substantive interpretation of section 7 outside the criminal law area was its decision in *Chaoulli*, where it split, 3 to 3, on whether a ban on private medical insurance for services covered by medicare is "arbitrary" and therefore a violation of section 7.[2] If the Supreme Court were to use section 7 to review the reasonableness of social and economic policy, the scope of the Charter and thus the power of the judges would expand considerably.

Of equal significance was Justice Lamer's handling of the historical evidence of the "framers' intent" to limit section 7 to a narrow procedural meaning. While conceding the admissibility of the framers' intent as relevant to determining the proper interpretation of Charter rights, Justice Lamer cautioned against granting such extrinsic evidence anything more than "minimal weight." To attach any more significance to the "original understanding" of Charter rights, he cautioned, "would in effect be assuming a fact which is nearly impossible of proof, i.e., the intention of the legislative bodies which adopted the *Charter*." Moreover, it would reintroduce the much criticized "frozen concepts" doctrine, as opposed to a "large and liberal" interpretation of the Charter mandated by the frequently cited "living tree" approach.[3]

By freeing constitutional law from the drafters' intentions, the court has granted itself and all other Canadian judges the discretion to read new meaning into the Charter sections other than what the framers' understood and intended those sections to mean. Future litigants can now invoke the symbol of the Charter as a living tree and argue that, even if the meaning they attribute to a Charter right was not part of its original meaning, the judge is still free to add the new meaning.[4]

This aspect of the *B.C. Motor Vehicle Reference* is best illustrated by an anecdote from the *Borowski* anti-abortion case.[5] The very day the Supreme Court handed down its decision

---

2 See case 23.

3 See the Introduction to this book.

4 See *Henrietta Muir Edwards v. Attorney-General for Canada (Persons Case)*, [1930] A.C. 124 (P.C.).

5 Transcript of Appeal Proceedings on October 3 and 4, 1988, *Borowski v. Canada (Attorney General)*, [1989] 1 S.C.R. 342.

in the *Motor Vehicle Reference*—December 17, 1985—pro-life crusader Joe Borowski began his hearing before the Court of Appeal of Saskatchewan. Borowski's lawyer, Morris Schumiatcher, argued that the sections of the *Criminal Code* allowing therapeutic abortions violate the "right to life" of the unborn child/foetus as protected by section 7 of the Charter. The history of the drafting of the Charter clearly indicates that the government rejected requests to include either a right to abortion for women or a right to life for the unborn. The Crown attorney had effectively used this evidence of the framers' intent to rebut Schumiatcher's arguments. The court would be unjustified, the Crown argued, to give a meaning to the Charter that had been explicitly rejected by the people who wrote it.

On the third and last day of the hearing, Schumiatcher was making his closing statement when one of his assistants hurriedly arrived clutching a document. After a brief huddle, Schumiatcher excitedly announced to the court that he had just received a copy of a Supreme Court decision handed down in Ottawa the previous day. The case was the *B.C. Motor Vehicle Reference*. Schumiatcher triumphantly quoted Justice Lamer's comments about the non-binding character of the "original intent." The three judges were now free, Schumiatcher exhorted them, to adopt the living-tree approach and to expand the meaning of section 7 to include the unborn. Ironically, but not surprisingly, Dr. Henry Morgentaler, Borowski's counterpart in the legal battle over Canada's abortion law, subsequently made extensive use of the *B.C. Motor Vehicle* precedent, but for the opposite purpose—to urge the Supreme Court to find a right to abortion in section 7 of the Charter.[6]

Note that the Supreme Court has not been consistent on this matter. In other cases it has relied heavily on the use of the original understanding of Charter text to bolster the authority of its decisions. The most important judicial use of original understanding was the *Quebec Association of Protestant School Boards* decision[7] striking down the education provisions of Bill 101. Referring to the "Canada clause" of section 23 of the Charter, the court declared:

> This set of constitutional provisions was not enacted by the legislator in a vacuum. ... the legislator knew, and clearly had in mind the regimes governing Anglophone and Francophone linguistic minorities in various provinces in Canada ... and their intention was to remedy the perceived defects of these regimes by uniform corrective measures, namely those contained in s. 23 of the *Charter*. ⌢

Discussion Questions

1. What is the difference between a procedural and a substantive interpretation of section 7 of the Charter?

2. How does the court define the principles of fundamental justice?

3. According to the court, what is the relationship between section 7 and section 1?

4. To which types of legal disputes does this reference opinion appear to confine the application of section 7?

6　See case 21.

7　*A.G. (Que.) v. Quebec Protestant School Boards*, [1984] 2 S.C.R. 66.

RE B.C. MOTOR VEHICLE ACT
[1985] 2 S.C.R. 486

Hearing: November 15, 1984; Judgment: December 17, 1985.

Present: Dickson C.J. and Beetz, McIntyre, Chouinard, Lamer, Wilson, and Le Dain JJ.

Interveners: the Attorney General of Canada, the Attorney General for Ontario, the Attorney General for Saskatchewan, the Attorney General for Alberta, the British Columbia Branch of the Canadian Bar Association.

The judgment of Dickson, Beetz, Chouinard, Le Dain, and Lamer JJ. was delivered by

[1] **LAMER J.:**

Introduction

[2] A law that has the potential to convict a person who has not really done anything wrong offends the principles of fundamental justice and, if imprisonment is available as a penalty, such a law then violates a person's right to liberty under s. 7 of the *Charter of Rights and Freedoms* (*Constitution Act, 1982*, as enacted by the *Canada Act 1982*, 1982 (U.K.), c. 11).

[3] In other words, absolute liability and imprisonment cannot be combined.

The Facts

[4] On August 16, 1982, the Lieutenant-Governor in Council of British Columbia referred the following question to the Court of Appeal of that province, by virtue of s. 1 of the *Constitutional Question Act*, R.S.B.C. 1979, c. 63:

Is s. 94(2) of the *Motor Vehicle Act*, R.S.B.C. 1979, as amended by the *Motor Vehicle Amendment Act, 1982*, consistent with the *Canadian Charter of Rights and Freedoms?*

[5] On February 3, 1983, the Court of Appeal handed down reasons in answer to the question in which it stated that s. 94(2) of the *Act* is inconsistent with the *Canadian Charter of Rights and Freedoms* ... .

The Legislation

[6] *Motor Vehicle Act*, R.S.B.C. 1979, c. 288, s. 94, as amended by the *Motor Vehicle Amendment Act, 1982*, 1982 (B.C.), c. 36, s. 19:

94.(1) A person who drives a motor vehicle on a highway or industrial road while

(a) he is prohibited from driving a motor vehicle under sections 90, 91, 92 or 92.1, or

(b) his driver's licence or his right to apply for or obtain a driver's licence is suspended under section 82 or 92 as it was before its repeal and replacement came

into force pursuant to the *Motor Vehicle Amendment Act, 1982*,

commits an offence and is liable,

(c) on a first conviction, to a fine of not less than $300 and not more than $2 000 and to imprisonment for not less than 7 days and not more than 6 months, and

(d) on a subsequent conviction, regardless of when the contravention occurred, to a fine of not less than $300 and not more than $2 000 and to imprisonment for not less than 14 days and not more than one year.

(2) Subsection (1) creates an absolute liability offence in which guilt is established by proof of driving, whether or not the defendant knew of the prohibition or suspension. ...

Section 7

1. Introduction

[10] The issue in this case raises fundamental questions of constitutional theory, including the nature and the very legitimacy of constitutional adjudication under the *Charter* as well as the appropriateness of various techniques of constitutional interpretation. ...

[12] The novel feature of the *Constitution Act* ... is not that it has suddenly empowered courts to consider the content of legislation. This the courts have done for a good many years when adjudicating upon the *vires* of legislation. ...

[13] The truly novel features of the *Constitution Act, 1982* are that it has sanctioned the process of constitutional adjudication and has extended its scope so as to encompass a broader range of values. Content of legislation has always been considered in constitutional adjudication. Content is now to be equally considered as regards new constitutional issues. Indeed, the values subject to constitutional adjudication now pertain to the rights of individuals as well as the distribution of governmental powers. In short, it is the scope of constitutional adjudication which has been altered rather than its nature, at least, as regards the right to consider the content of legislation.

[14] In neither case, be it before or after the *Charter*, have the courts been enabled to decide upon the appropriateness of policies underlying legislative enactments. In both instances, however, the courts are empowered, indeed required, to measure the content of legislation against the guarantees of the Constitution. ...

[15] In this respect, s. 7 is no different than other *Charter* provisions. As the Attorney General for Ontario has noted in his factum:

Section 7, like most of the other sections in the *Charter*, limits the bounds of legislative action. It is the function of the Court to determine whether the challenged legislation has honoured those boundaries. This process necessitates judicial review of the content of the legislation.

Yet, in the context of s. 7, and in particular, of the interpretation of "principles of fundamental justice," there has prevailed in certain quarters an assumption that all but a narrow construction of s. 7 will inexorably lead the courts to "question the wisdom of enactments," to adjudicate upon the merits of public policy.

[16] From this have sprung warnings of the dangers of a judicial "super-legislature" beyond the reach of Parliament, the provincial legislatures and the electorate. The Attorney General for Ontario, in his written argument, stated that,

> ... the judiciary is neither representative of, nor responsive to the electorate on whose behalf, and under whose authority policies are selected and given effect in the laws of the land.

This is an argument which was heard countless times prior to the entrenchment of the *Charter* but which has in truth, for better or for worse, been settled by the very coming into force of the *Constitution Act, 1982.* It ought not to be forgotten that the historic decision to entrench the *Charter* in our Constitution was taken not by the courts but by the elected representatives of the people of Canada. It was those representatives who extended the scope of constitutional adjudication and entrusted the courts with this new and onerous responsibility. Adjudication under the *Charter* must be approached free of any lingering doubts as to its legitimacy.

[17] The concerns with the bounds of constitutional adjudication explain the characterization of the issue in a narrow and restrictive fashion, *i.e.*, whether the term "principles of fundamental justice" has a substantive or merely procedural content. In my view, the characterization of the issue in such fashion preempts an open-minded approach to determining the meaning of "principles of fundamental justice."

[18] The substantive/procedural dichotomy narrows the issue almost to an all-or-nothing proposition. Moreover, it is largely bound up in the American experience with substantive and procedural due process. It imports into the Canadian context American concepts, terminology and jurisprudence, all of which are inextricably linked to problems concerning the nature and legitimacy of adjudication under the U.S. Constitution. That Constitution, it must be remembered, has no s. 52 nor has it the internal checks and balances of ss. 1 and 33. We would, in my view, do our own Constitution a disservice to simply allow the American debate to define the issue for us, all the while ignoring the truly fundamental structural differences between the two constitutions. Finally, the dichotomy creates its own set of difficulties by the attempt to distinguish between two concepts whose outer boundaries are not always clear and often tend to overlap. Such difficulties can and should, when possible, be avoided.

[19] The overriding and legitimate concern that courts ought not to question the wisdom of enactments, and the presumption that the legislator could not have intended same, have to some extent distorted the discussion surrounding the meaning of "principles of fundamental justice." This has led to the spectre of a judicial "super-legislature" without a full consideration of the process of constitutional adjudication and the significance of ss. 1 and 33 of the *Charter* and s. 52 of the *Constitution Act, 1982.* This in turn has also led to a narrow characterization of the issue and to the assumption that only a procedural content to "principles of fundamental justice" can prevent the courts from adjudicating upon the merits or wisdom of enactments. If this assumption is accepted, the inevitable corollary, with which I would have to then agree, is that the legislator intended that the words "principles of fundamental justice" refer to procedure only.

[20] But I do not share that assumption. Since way back in time and even recently the courts have developed the common law beyond procedural safeguards without interfering with the "merits or wisdom" of enactments. ...

[21] The task of the Court is not to choose between substantive or procedural content *per se* but to secure for persons "the full benefit of the *Charter*'s protection" (Dickson J. (as he then was) in *R. v. Big M Drug Mart Ltd.*, [1985] 1 S.C.R. 295, at p. 344), under s. 7, while avoiding adjudication of the merits of public policy. This can only be accomplished by a purposive analysis. ...

[22] I propose therefore to approach the interpretation of s. 7 in the manner set forth by Dickson J. in *Hunter v. Southam Inc.*, [1984] 2 S.C.R. 145, and *R. v. Big M Drug Mart Ltd.*, supra, and by Le Dain J. in *R. v. Therens*, [1985] 1 S.C.R. 613. In *R. v. Big M Drug Mart Ltd.*, Dickson J. wrote at p. 344:

> In *Hunter v. Southam Inc.*, [1984] 2 S.C.R. 145, this Court expressed the view that the proper approach to the definition of the rights and freedoms guaranteed by the *Charter* was a purposive one. The meaning of a right or freedom guaranteed by the *Charter* was to be ascertained by an analysis of the *purpose* of such a guarantee; it was to be understood, in other words, in the light of the interests it was meant to protect. ...

[23] ... [Section 7] states "and the right not to be deprived thereof except in accordance with the principles of fundamental justice." On the facts of this case it is not necessary to decide whether the section gives any greater protection, such as deciding whether, absent a breach of the principles of

fundamental justice, there still can be, given the way the section is structured, a violation of one's rights to life, liberty and security of the person under s. 7. Furthermore, because of the fact that only deprivation of liberty was considered in these proceedings and that no one took issue with the fact that imprisonment is a deprivation of liberty, my analysis of s. 7 will be limited, as was the course taken by all, below and in this Court, to determining the scope of the words "principles of fundamental justice." I will not attempt to give any further content to liberty nor address that of the words life or security of the person.

[24] In the framework of a purposive analysis, designed to ascertain the purpose of the s. 7 guarantee and "the interests it was meant to protect" (*R. v. Big M Drug Mart Ltd.*, *supra*), it is clear to me that the interests which are meant to be protected by the words "and the right not to be deprived thereof except in accordance with the principles of fundamental justice" of s. 7 are the life, liberty and security of the person. The principles of fundamental justice, on the other hand, are not a protected interest, but rather a qualifier of the right not to be deprived of life, liberty and security of the person. …

[26] … As a qualifier, the phrase serves to establish the parameters of the interests but it cannot be interpreted so narrowly as to frustrate or stultify them. For the narrower the meaning given to "principles of fundamental justice" the greater will be the possibility that individuals may be deprived of these most basic rights. …

[26] For these reasons, I am of the view that it would be wrong to interpret the term "fundamental justice" as being synonymous with natural justice as the Attorney General of British Columbia and others have suggested. To do so would strip the protected interests of much, if not most, of their content and leave the "right" to life, liberty and security of the person in a sorely emaciated state. …

[28] Sections 8 to 14 … address specific deprivations of the "right" to life, liberty and security of the person in breach of the principles of fundamental justice, and as such, violations of s. 7. They are designed to protect, in a specific manner and setting, the right to life, liberty and security of the person set forth in s. 7. It would be incongruous to interpret s. 7 more narrowly than the rights in ss. 8 to 14. …

[29] … Clearly, some of those sections embody principles that are beyond what could be characterized as "procedural."

[30] Thus, ss. 8 to 14 provide an invaluable key to the meaning of "principles of fundamental justice." Many have been developed over time as presumptions of the common law, others have found expression in the international conventions on human rights. All have been recognized as essential elements of a system for the administration of justice which is founded upon a belief in "the dignity and worth of the human person" (preamble to the *Canadian Bill of Rights*, R.S.C. 1970, App. III) and on "the rule of law" (preamble to the *Canadian Charter of Rights and Freedoms*).

[31] It is this common thread which, in my view, must guide us in determining the scope and content of "principles of fundamental justice." In other words, the principles of fundamental justice are to be found in the basic tenets of our legal system. They do not lie in the realm of general public policy but in the inherent domain of the judiciary as guardian of the justice system. …

[32] Thus, it seems to me that to replace "fundamental justice" with the term "natural justice" misses the mark entirely. It was, after all, clearly open to the legislator to use the term natural justice, a known term of art, but such was not done. We must, as a general rule, be loath to exchange the terms actually used with terms so obviously avoided.

[33] Whatever may have been the degree of synonymy between the two expressions in the past … as of the last few decades this country has given a precise meaning to the words natural justice for the purpose of delineating the responsibility of adjudicators (in the wide sense of the word) in the field of administrative law.

[34] It is, in my view, that precise and somewhat narrow meaning that the legislator avoided, clearly indicating thereby a will to give greater content to the words "principles of fundamental justice." …

[35] A number of courts have placed emphasis upon the Minutes of the Proceedings and Evidence of the Special Joint Committee of the Senate and of the House of Commons on the Constitution in the interpretation of "principles of fundamental justice." …

[36] In particular, the following passages dealing with the testimony of federal civil servants from the Department of Justice, have been relied upon:

Mr. Strayer (Assistant Deputy Minister, Public Law):
    Mr. Chairman, it was our belief that the words "fundamental justice" would cover the same thing as what is called procedural due process, that is the meaning of due process in relation to requiring fair procedure. However, it in our view does not cover the concept of what is called substantive due process, which would impose substantive requirements as to policy of the law in question.

    This has been most clearly demonstrated in the United States in the area of property, but also in other areas such as the right to life. The term due process has been given the broader concept of meaning both the procedure and substance. Natural justice or fundamental justice in our view does not go beyond the procedural requirements of fairness. …

The term "fundamental justice" appears to us to be essentially the same thing as natural justice.

Mr. Tassé (Deputy Minister) also said of the phrase "principles of fundamental justice" in testimony before the Committee:

We assume that the Court would look at that much like a Court would look at the requirements of natural justice. ...

[37] The Honourable Jean Chrétien, then federal Minister of Justice, also indicated to the Committee that, while he thought "fundamental justice marginally more appropriate than natural justice" in s. 7, either term was acceptable to the Government. ...

[38] The first issue which arises is whether the Minutes of the Proceedings and Evidence of the Special Joint Committee may even be considered admissible as extrinsic aids to the interpretation of *Charter* provisions. Such extrinsic materials were traditionally excluded from consideration in constitutional adjudication. ...

[39] In *Reference re Upper Churchill Water Rights Reversion Act*, [1984] 1 S.C.R. 297, at p. 317, however, McIntyre J. stated that,

The general exclusionary rule formerly considered to be applicable in dealing with the admissibility of extrinsic evidence in constitutional cases has been set aside or at least greatly modified and relaxed.

[40] Indeed, in the reference *Re: Anti-Inflation Act*, [1976] 2 S.C.R. 373, Laskin C.J. stated, at p. 389:

... [N]o general principle of admissibility or inadmissibility can or ought to be propounded by this Court, and ... the questions of resort to extrinsic evidence and what kind of extrinsic evidence may be admitted must depend on the constitutional issues on which it is sought adduce such evidence.

[41] This approach was adopted by Dickson J. in the reference *Re Residential Tenancies Act, 1979* [[1981] 1 S.C.R. 714]. ...

[42] It is to be noted, however, that McIntyre J.'s remarks are in relation to the interpretation of the challenged statutory enactment rather than the interpretation of the Constitution itself. The same is true of the remarks of Laskin C.J. and Dickson J.

[43] With respect to the interpretation of the Constitution, however, such extrinsic materials were considered, in at least two cases, by this Court.

[44] In *Re: Authority of Parliament in relation to the Upper House*, [1980] 1 S.C.R. 54, the Court stated, at p. 66:

It is, we think, proper to consider the historical background which led to the provision which was made in the *Act* for the creation of the Senate as a part of the apparatus for the enactment of federal legislation. In the debates which occurred at the Quebec Conference in 1864, considerable time was occupied in discussing the provisions respecting the Senate. Its important purpose is stated in the following passages in speeches delivered in the debates on Confederation in the parliament of the province of Canada. ...

[45] The other case is *Attorney General of Canada v. Canadian National Transportation, Ltd.*, [1983] 2 S.C.R. 206. Laskin C.J., in that case, referred to the pre-Confederation debates in the course of interpreting ss. 91(27) and 92(14) of the *Constitution Act, 1867* (at p. 225).

[46] I would adopt this approach when interpreting the *Charter*. Consequently, the Minutes of the Proceedings and Evidence of the Special Joint Committee on the Constitution should, in my view, be considered. ...

[47] Having said that, however, I nonetheless believe that the logic underlying the reluctance to allow the use of materials such as speeches in Parliament carries considerable force with respect to the Minutes of the Committee as well.

[48] In *Reference re Upper Churchill Water Rights Reversion Act, supra*, McIntyre J. wrote at p. 319:

... I would say that the speeches and public declarations by prominent figures in the public and political life of Newfoundland on this question should not be received as evidence. They represent, no doubt, the considered views of the speakers at the time they were made, but cannot be said to be expressions of the intent of the Legislative Assembly.

[50] If speeches and declarations by prominent figures are inherently unreliable (*per* McIntyre J. in *Reference re Upper Churchill Water Rights Reversion Act, supra*, at p. 319) and "speeches made in the legislature at the time of enactment of the measure are inadmissible as having little evidential weight" (*per* Dickson J. in the reference *Re: Residential Tenancies Act 1979, supra*, at p. 721), the Minutes of the Proceedings of the Special Joint Committee, though admissible, and granted somewhat more weight than speeches should not be given too much weight. The inherent unreliability of such statements and speeches is not altered by the mere fact that they pertain to the *Charter* rather than a statute.

[51] Moreover, the simple fact remains that the *Charter* is not the product of a few individual public servants, however distinguished, but of a multiplicity of individuals who played major roles in the negotiating, drafting and adoption of the *Charter*. How can one say with any confidence that within this

enormous multiplicity of actors, without forgetting the role of the provinces, the comments of a few federal civil servants can in any way be determinative?

[52] Were this Court to accord any significant weight to this testimony, it would in effect be assuming a fact which is nearly impossible of proof, *i.e.*, the intention of the legislative bodies which adopted the *Charter*. In view of the indeterminate nature of the data, it would in my view be erroneous to give these materials anything but minimal weight.

[53] Another danger with casting the interpretation of s. 7 in terms of the comments made by those heard at the Special Joint Committee Proceedings is that, in so doing, the rights, freedoms and values embodied in the *Charter* in effect become frozen in time to the moment of adoption with little or no possibility of growth, development and adjustment to changing societal needs. ... If the newly planted "living tree" which is the *Charter* is to have the possibility of growth and adjustment over time, care must be taken to ensure that historical materials, such as the Minutes of Proceedings and Evidence of the Special Joint Committee, do not stunt its growth. ...

[54] The appellant states that s. 7 "is a blend of s. 1(*a*) and s. 2(*e*) of the *Canadian Bill of Rights*." Considerable emphasis is then placed upon the case of *Duke v. The Queen*, [1972] S.C.R. 917, in which this Court interpreted the words "principles of fundamental justice" in s. 2(*e*) of the *Canadian Bill of Rights*. Fauteux C.J. noted, at p. 923:

> Without attempting to formulate any final definition of those words, I would take them to mean, generally, that the tribunal which adjudicates upon his rights must act fairly, in good faith, without bias, and in a judicial temper, and must give to him the opportunity adequately to state his case.

[55] However, as Le Dain J. has written in *R. v. Therens*, *supra*, with the implicit support of the majority ...

> In considering the relationship of a decision under the *Canadian Bill of Rights* to an issue arising under the *Charter*, a court cannot, in my respectful opinion, avoid bearing in mind an evident fact of Canadian judicial history, which must be squarely and frankly faced: that on the whole, with some notable exceptions, the courts have felt some uncertainty or ambivalence in the application of the *Canadian Bill of Rights* because it did not reflect a clear constitutional mandate to make judicial decisions having the effect of limiting or qualifying the traditional sovereignty of Parliament. ...

[58] In section 2(*e*) of the *Canadian Bill of Rights*, the words "principles of fundamental justice" were placed explicitly in the context of, and qualify a "right to a fair hearing." Section 7 of the *Charter* does not create the same context. In section 7, the words "principles of fundamental justice" are placed in the context of, and qualify much more fundamental rights, the "right to life, liberty and security of the person." The distinction is important. ...

[66] Whether any given principle may be said to be a principle of fundamental justice within the meaning of s. 7 will rest upon an analysis of the nature, sources, *rationale* and essential role of that principle within the judicial process and in our legal system, as it evolves.

[67] Consequently, those words cannot be given any exhaustive content or simple enumerative definition, but will take on concrete meaning as the courts address alleged violations of s. 7.

[68] I now turn to such an analysis of the principle of *mens rea* and absolute liability offences in order to determine the question which has been put to the Court in the present Reference.

Absolute Liability and Fundamental Justice in Penal Law

[69] It has from time immemorial been part of our system of laws that the innocent not be punished. This principle has long been recognized as an essential element of a system for the administration of justice which is founded upon a belief in the dignity and worth of the human person and on the rule of law. It is so old that its first enunciation was in Latin *actus non facit reum nisi mens sit rea*.

[70] As Glanville Williams said:

> There is no need here to go into the remote history of *mens rea*; suffice it to say that the requirement of a guilty state of mind (at least for the more serious crimes) had been developed by the time of Coke, which is as far back as the modern lawyer needs to go. "If one shoot at any wild fowl upon a tree, and the arrow killeth any reasonable creature afar off, without any evil intent in him, this is *per infortunium*." ...

[72] This view has been adopted by this Court in unmistakable terms in many cases, amongst which the better known are *Beaver v. The Queen*, [1957] S.C.R. 531, and the most recent and often quoted judgment of Dickson J. writing for the Court in *R. v. City of Sault Ste. Marie*, *supra*.

[73] This Court's decision in the latter case is predicated upon a certain number of postulates one of which, given the nature of the rules it elaborates, has to be to the effect that absolute liability in penal law offends the principles of fundamental justice. Those principles are, to use the words of Dickson J., to the effect that "there is a generally held revulsion against punishment of the morally innocent." He also stated

that the argument that absolute liability "violates fundamental principles of penal liability" was the most telling argument against absolute liability and one of greater force than those advanced in support thereof. ...

[75] A law enacting an absolute liability offence will violate s. 7 of the *Charter* only if and to the extent that it has the potential of depriving of life, liberty, or security of the person.

[76] Obviously, imprisonment (including probation orders) deprives persons of their liberty. An offence has that potential as of the moment it is open to the judge to impose imprisonment. There is no need that imprisonment, as in s. 94(2), be made mandatory.

[77] I am therefore of the view that the combination of imprisonment and of absolute liability violates s. 7 of the *Charter* and can only be salvaged if the authorities demonstrate under s. 1 that such a deprivation of liberty in breach of those principles of fundamental justice is, in a free and democratic society, under the circumstances, a justified reasonable limit to one's rights under s. 7. ...

[79] ... I would not want us to be taken by this conclusion as having inferentially decided that absolute liability may not offend s. 7 as long as imprisonment or probation orders are not available as a sentence. The answer to that question is dependant upon the content given to the words "security of the person." That issue was and is a live one. ...

[83] ... In penal law, absolute liability always offends the principles of fundamental justice irrespective of the nature of the offence; it offends s. 7 of the *Charter* if as a result, anyone is deprived of his life, liberty or security of the person, irrespective of the requirement of public interest. In such cases it might only be salvaged for reasons of public interest under s. 1.

[84] In this latter regard, something might be added.

[85] Administrative expediency, absolute liability's main supportive argument, will undoubtedly under s. 1 be invoked and occasionally succeed. Indeed, administrative expediency certainly has its place in administrative law. But when administrative law chooses to call in aid imprisonment through penal law, indeed sometimes criminal law and the added stigma attached to a conviction, exceptional, in my view, will be the case where the liberty or even the security of the person guaranteed under s. 7 should be sacrificed to administrative expediency. Section 1 may, for reasons of administrative expediency, successfully come to the rescue of an otherwise violation of s. 7, but only in cases arising out of exceptional conditions, such as natural disasters, the outbreak of war, epidemics, and the like.

[86] Of course I understand the concern of many as regards corporate offences, specially, as was mentioned by the Court of Appeal, in certain sensitive areas such as the preservation of our vital environment and our natural resources.

This concern might well be dispelled were it to be decided, given the proper case, that s. 7 affords protection to human persons only and does not extend to corporations.

[87] Even if it be decided that s. 7 does extend to corporations, I think the balancing under s. 1 of the public interest against the financial interests of a corporation would give very different results from that of balancing public interest and the liberty or security of the person of a human being.

[88] Indeed, the public interest as regards "air and water pollution offences" requires that the guilty be dealt with firmly, but the seriousness of the offence does not in my respectful view support the proposition that the innocent *human* person be open to conviction, quite the contrary. ...

Section 1

[94] Having found that s. 94(2) offends s. 7 of the *Charter* there remains the question as to whether the appellants have demonstrated that the section is salvaged by the operation of s. 1 of the *Charter*. No evidence was adduced in the Court of Appeal or in this Court. ...

[95] I do not take issue with the fact that it is highly desirable that "bad drivers" be kept off the road. I do not take issue either with the desirability of punishing severely bad drivers who are in contempt of prohibitions against driving. The bottom line of the question to be addressed here is: whether the Government of British Columbia has demonstrated as justifiable that the risk of imprisonment of a few innocent is, given the desirability of ridding the roads of British Columbia of bad drivers, a reasonable limit in a free and democratic society. That result is to be measured against the offence being one of strict liability open to a defence of due diligence, the success of which does nothing more than let those few who did nothing wrong remain free.

[96] As did the Court of Appeal, I find that this demonstration has not been satisfied, indeed, not in the least.

[97] In the result, I would dismiss the appeal and answer the question in the negative, as did the Court of Appeal, albeit for somewhat different reasons, and declare s. 94(2) of the *Motor Vehicle Act*, R.S.B.C. 1979, as amended by the *Motor Vehicle Amendment Act, 1982*, inconsistent with s. 7 of the *Canadian Charter of Rights and Freedoms*.

[98] Having come to this conclusion, I choose, as did the Court of Appeal, not to address whether the section violates the rights guaranteed under ss. 11(*d*) and 12 of the *Charter*.

[Justice McIntyre wrote a short concurring opinion.]

[101] **WILSON J.** (concurring): I agree with my colleague, Mr. Justice Lamer, that s. 94(2) of the *Motor Vehicle Act* violates s. 7 of the *Charter* and is not saved by s. 1. I reach that result, however, by a somewhat different route.

[102] I start with a consideration of statutory "offences." These are divisible into offences for which *mens rea* is required and those for which it is not. Statutory offences are subject to a presumption in favour of a *mens rea* requirement as a matter of interpretation, but the courts have increasingly come to accept the proposition that legislatures may create non *mens rea* offences provided they make it clear that the *actus reus* itself is prohibited. This is typically so in the case of the so-called "regulatory" or "public welfare" offences. There is no moral delinquency involved in these offences. They are simply designed to regulate conduct in the public interest.

[103] Two questions, therefore, have to be answered on this appeal. The first is do absolute liability offences created by statute *per se* offend the *Charter*? The second is, assuming they do not, can they be attended by mandatory imprisonment or can such a sanction only be attached to true *mens rea* offences? Certainly, in the absence of the *Charter*, legislatures are free to create absolute liability offences and to attach to them any sanctions they please. Does s. 7 of the *Charter* circumscribe their power in this regard?

Absolute Liability Offenses

[104] Section 7 affirms the right to life, liberty and security of the person while at the same time indicating that a person may be deprived of such a right if the deprivation is effected "in accordance with the principles of fundamental justice." I do not view the latter part of the section as a qualification on the right to life, liberty and security of the person in the sense that it limits or modifies that right or defines its parameters. Its purpose seems to me to be the very opposite, namely to protect the right against deprivation or impairment unless such deprivation or impairment is effected in accordance with the principles of fundamental justice.

[105] Section 7 does not, however, affirm a right to the principles of fundamental justice *per se*. There must first be found an impairment of the right to life, liberty or security of the person. It must then be determined whether that impairment has been effected in accordance with the principles of fundamental justice. If it has, it passes the threshold test in s. 7 itself but the Court must go on to consider whether it can be sustained under s. 1 as a limit prescribed by law on the s. 7 right which is both reasonable and justified in a free and democratic society. If, however, the limit on the s. 7 right has been effected through a violation of the principles of fundamental justice, the enquiry, in my view, ends there and the limit cannot be sustained under s. 1. I say this because I do not believe that a limit on the s. 7 right which has been imposed in violation of the principles of fundamental justice can be either "reasonable" or "demonstrably justified in a free and democratic society." ...

[106] Assuming that I am correct in my analysis of s. 7 and its relationship to s. 1, an absolute liability offence cannot violate s. 7 unless it impairs the right to life, liberty or security of the person. It cannot violate s. 7 because it offends the principles of fundamental justice because they are not protected by s. 7 absent an impairment of the s. 7 right. Leaving aside for the moment the mandatory imprisonment sanction, I cannot find an interference with life, liberty or security of the person in s. 94 of the *Motor Vehicle Act*. It is true that the section prevents citizens from driving their vehicles when their licences are suspended. Citizens are also prevented from driving on the wrong side of the road. Indeed, all regulatory offences impose some restriction on liberty broadly construed. But I think it would trivialize the *Charter* to sweep all those offences into s. 7 as violations of the right to life, liberty and security of the person even if they can be sustained under s. 1. It would be my view, therefore, that absolute liability offences of this type do not *per se* offend s. 7 of the *Charter*.

2. Absolute Liability Plus Mandatory Imprisonment

[107] The real question, as I see it, is whether s. 7 of the *Charter* is violated by the attachment of a mandatory imprisonment sanction to an absolute liability offence. Clearly a s. 7 right is interfered with here in that a person convicted of such an offence automatically loses his liberty. ... Given that we can have statutory non *mens rea* offences, what is repugnant to fundamental justice in imprisoning someone for their commission? ... I believe we must turn to the theory of punishment for the answer.

3. Punishment and Fundamental Justice

[126] It is now generally accepted among penologists that there are five main objectives of a penal system: see Nigel Walker, *Sentencing in a Rational Society*, 1969. They are:

(1) to protect offenders and suspected offenders against unofficial retaliation;
(2) to reduce the incidence of crime;
(3) to ensure that offenders atone for their offences;
(4) to keep punishment to the minimum necessary to achieve the objectives of the system; and
(5) to express society's abhorrence of crime.

Apart from death, imprisonment is the most severe sentence imposed by the law and is generally viewed as a last resort i.e., *as appropriate only when it can be shown that no other sanction can achieve the objectives of the system.*

[127] The Law Reform Commission of Canada in its Working Paper 11, "Imprisonment and Release," in *Studies on Imprisonment* (1976), states at p. 10:

Justice requires that the sanction of imprisonment not be disproportionate to the offence, and humanity dictates that it must not be heavier than necessary to achieve its objective.

[128] Because of the absolute liability nature of the offence created by s. 94(2) of the *Motor Vehicle Act* a person can be convicted under the section even although he was unaware at the time he was driving that his licence was suspended and was unable to find this out despite the exercise of due diligence. While the legislature may as a matter of government policy make this an offence, and we cannot question its wisdom in this regard, the question is whether it can make it mandatory for the courts to deprive a person convicted of it of his liberty without violating s. 7. This, in turn, depends on whether attaching a mandatory term of imprisonment to an absolute liability offence such as this violates the principles of fundamental justice. I believe that it does. I think the conscience of the court would be shocked and the administration of justice brought into disrepute by such an unreasonable and extravagant penalty. It is totally disproportionate to the offence and quite incompatible with the objective of a penal system referred to in paragraph (4) above.

[129] It is basic to any theory of punishment that the sentence imposed bear some relationship to the offence; it must be a "fit" sentence proportionate to the seriousness of the offence. Only if this is so can the public be satisfied that the offender "deserved" the punishment he received and feel a confidence in the fairness and rationality of the system. This is not to say that there is an inherently appropriate relationship between a particular offence and its punishment but rather that there is a scale of offences and punishments into which the particular offence and punishment must fit. Obviously this cannot be done with mathematical precision and many different factors will go into the assessment of the seriousness of a particular offence for purposes of determining the appropriate punishment but it does provide a workable conventional framework for sentencing. Indeed, judges in the exercise of their sentencing discretion have been employing such a scale for over a hundred years.

[130] I believe that a mandatory term of imprisonment for an offence committed unknowingly and unwittingly and after the exercise of due diligence is grossly excessive and inhumane. It is not required to reduce the incidence of the offence. It is beyond anything required to satisfy the need for "atonement." And society, in my opinion, would not be abhorred by an unintentional and unknowing violation of the section. I believe, therefore, that such a sanction offends the principles of fundamental justice embodied in our penal system. Section 94(2) is accordingly inconsistent with s. 7 of the *Charter* and must, to the extent of the inconsistency, be declared of no force and effect under s. 52.

21   Morgentaler v. The Queen, 1988

Pro-choice crusader Dr. Henry Morgentaler's victory in this case culminated almost 20 years of civil disobedience in protest of Canada's abortion law. In the early 1970s, Morgentaler openly defied the abortion law by performing unauthorized abortions in his Montreal clinic. In three successive trials, juries refused to convict him. However, in 1974, the Quebec Court of Appeal overturned his first jury acquittal and took the unprecedented step of directly convicting him rather than returning the case for retrial. In 1975, the Supreme Court of Canada rejected Morgentaler's appeal, and he was sentenced to 18 months in prison.

Ironically, Morgentaler's legal defeat laid the basis for a subsequent political victory. In response to protests, Parliament amended the *Criminal Code* to withdraw the power to convict from appeal courts. In the light of what was dubbed "the Morgentaler amendment," the federal Attorney General granted Morgentaler a new trial. After his third jury acquittal, Morgentaler was released from prison. The newly elected Parti Québécois government of René Lévesque dropped outstanding charges against Morgentaler, and announced that it would no longer enforce section 251 (the abortion section) of the *Criminal Code* in Quebec. The Lévesque government subsequently supported the creation of community health clinics that included abortion services. By 1980, Morgentaler had achieved his objective of easy and inexpensive access to abortion services in Quebec. In the rest of Canada, however, the section 251 regime still prevailed.

In 1983, Morgentaler renewed his campaign of civil disobedience, opening abortion clinics in Toronto and Winnipeg. Once again he was brought to trial and acquitted by a jury, and once again he saw his acquittal overturned by a court of appeal. This time, however, armed with the new *Canadian Charter of Rights and Freedoms*, Morgentaler prevailed in the Supreme Court.

The court's decision was much narrower than was generally reported. The Supreme Court did not declare a constitutional right to abortion or "freedom of choice." Only Justice Wilson took this position, and even she acknowledged a legitimate state interest in protecting the life of the fetus/unborn child at some point in the second trimester of a pregnancy. The other six carefully and explicitly avoided this "substantive" policy issue.

The two dissenters, McIntyre and La Forest, looked to the framers' understanding of the Charter's meaning. They found that the legislative history of the Charter in 1980-81 indicated that it was intentionally neutral on the abortion issue. They concluded that when the Charter is purposely silent on an issue, so too must be the judges.

The other four judges who ruled against the abortion law did so because they said that it violated the "procedural fairness" required by section 7, not because there is any independent right to abortion. These four further disagreed among themselves on just how serious even the procedural violations were. Two, Dickson and Lamer, suggested that certain elements of the current law—such as removal of the decision-making power for the abortion decision from the pregnant woman—violated the "security of the person." The other two judges—Beetz and Estey—defined the procedural problems more narrowly and thus as remediable. While the current version of certain procedural requirements—such as approval by a therapeutic abortion committee (TAC)—created unfair delays and burdens, a revised version of the TAC might be acceptable. Unlike Dickson and Lamer, Beetz and Estey ruled that in principle there was no legal problem with the requirement of the current law that abortions be permitted only when the continuation of a pregnancy "would threaten the life or health of the mother," or with the requirement that an independent and impartial third party be the judge of this issue. By limiting their ruling to procedural requirements of the criminal law, the majority left the door open for Parliament to respond with an amended abortion law.

Six months later, in July 1988, the Mulroney government introduced a motion in the House of Commons for a reformed abortion law. The motion proposed easy access to abortions during the "early stages" of a pregnancy, but in "subsequent stages" an abortion would be permitted only if two doctors found that continuation of the pregnancy would "endanger the woman's life or seriously endanger her health." After two days of almost around-the-clock debate, the government motion was defeated in a "free vote" (147 to 76). Both "pro-life" and "pro-choice" MPs voted against the compromise measure. Both sides offered their own amendments that would have greatly restricted or eased access to abortion, but these too were defeated. The "pro-life" amendment came closest to adoption, losing 118 to 105.

After the 1988 election, the Mulroney government introduced Bill C-43, yet another attempt to retain some criminal sanction against abortion. Bill C-43 would have made abortion at any time an offence, punishable by up to two years in jail, unless performed by a doctor who was of the opinion that without an abortion the life or health of the pregnant woman would be threatened. The vote on Bill C-43 was not a free vote. It passed the House of Commons by a vote of 140 to 131. But in the Senate, for the first time ever, there was a tied vote, so the Bill died. The Mulroney government had no appetite for reviving it. Indeed, no federal government since has touched this highly divisive issue.[1]

Provinces did touch the issue, however. For example, Nova Scotia acted against free-standing abortion clinics like Morgentaler's. The province prohibited abortions outside of hospitals and denied medical insurance coverage to non-hospital abortions. Morgentaler, not surprisingly, established an abortion clinic in contravention of this law, and when charges were brought against him, he was launched on yet another trip to the Supreme Court. In 1993, the court again found in his favour, though on federalism grounds this time.[2] Although Nova Scotia's law could be characterized as an attempt to prevent private health care within the province's undoubted health care jurisdiction, this was "at best" an incidental concern, said Justice Sopinka on behalf of a unanimous court. The law's true "pith and substance," he wrote, was to "invade" the federal "criminal field by attempting to stiffen, supplement or replace the criminal law ... or to fill perceived defects or gaps therein." In effect, provinces could not re-criminalize what had been decriminalized at the federal level.[3]

---

1   Thomas Flanagan, "The Staying Power of the Status Quo: Collective Choice in Canada's Parliament after Morgentaler" (1999) 30 *Canadian Journal of Political Science* 31.

2   *R. v. Morgentaler*, [1993] 3 S.C.R. 463.

3   As noted in the Introduction to Part I.B of the companion volume, the Supreme Court considers practical concurrency within overlapping jurisdictions to be the "dominant tide of modern federalism." The refusal of *Morgentaler* 1993, *supra* note 2, to find such concurrency stands as an obvious counterexample to this "dominant tide." See Dennis Baker, "The Temptation of Provincial Criminal Law" (2014) 57 *Canadian Public Administration* 2.

The 1988 *Morgentaler* decision pulled the legal rug out from under a parallel challenge to Canada's abortion law brought by Joe Borowski, a former Manitoba Cabinet minister and prominent pro-life activist. Borowski was to Canada's pro-life movement what Morgentaler was to the pro-choice camp—a hero, a symbol, and an opportunity to win in the courts what they could not win in Parliament. Whereas Morgentaler's challenge had emphasized the rights of women to "liberty" and "security of the person" under section 7 of the Charter, Borowski's challenge argued that the human fetus was included in the "everyone" entitled to the section 7 "right to life." While Morgentaler claimed section 251 placed too many restrictions on abortions, Borowski maintained that it too easily permitted them.

Like Morgentaler, Borowski had been travelling the long route to an ultimate Supreme Court decision for many years.[4] When the Supreme Court heard his case in October 1988, however, it had already declared section 251 unconstitutional in *Morgentaler*, creating a serious problem for Borowski. How could he challenge the constitutionality of a law that no longer existed? In legal parlance, Borowski's case had become moot—no longer a live controversy—with the death of section 251. The court dismissed his case for precisely this reason on March 9, 1989. Although the court had agreed to hear Borowski's substantive arguments, it did not address them. To do so, wrote Justice Sopinka for a unanimous court, would be to create a new kind of "private reference," a procedure that would intrude on the prerogative of the executive and possibly pre-empt Parliament's policy options on the abortion issue.

Similar compunctions about mootness did not trouble the Supreme Court in its consideration of another abortion case that burst onto the scene in the summer of 1989, close on the heels of the *Borowski*[5] decision. When Chantal Daigle broke up with her boyfriend, Jean-Guy Tremblay, she decided to abort the fetus she had conceived with him. Tremblay persuaded a Quebec Superior Court judge to issue an injunction preventing the abortion because the fetus was a "human being" protected under the Quebec *Charter of Human Rights*. After this decision was hurriedly confirmed by the Quebec Court of Appeal, the Supreme Court agreed to interrupt its summer vacation to hear an expedited final appeal in August 1989. Before the court could hear Daigle's appeal, however, she slipped across the border to have an abortion in the United States, making her case as moot as Borowski's had been. Nevertheless, the court heard the substantive issues and decided that if the Quebec legislature had intended to include the fetus in the category of "human beings" guaranteed the right to life under the Quebec Charter, it would have done so more explicitly. *Daigle*[6] was based on the Quebec rather than the Canadian charter of rights, but it had obvious implications for the latter and was widely portrayed as a major legal victory for the pro-choice side in the abortion controversy. ∼

Discussion Questions

1. What do you make of the judicial disagreement about the primary objective of the impugned legislation?
2. How would you arrange the four opinions in *Morgentaler* on a spectrum with judicial restraint at one end and judicial activism at the other? Justify your placement of each opinion on the spectrum.

---

4 For a full account of both sagas, see F.L. Morton, *Morgentaler v. Borowski: Abortion, the Charter, and the Courts* (Toronto: McClelland & Stewart, 1992).

5 *Borowski v. Canada (Attorney General)*, [1989] 1 S.C.R. 342.

6 *Tremblay v. Daigle*, [1989] 2 S.C.R. 530.

R v. MORGENTALER
[1988] 1 S.C.R. 30

Hearing: October 7, 8, 9, 10, 1986; Judgment: January 28, 1988.

Present: Dickson C.J. and Beetz, Estey, McIntyre, Lamer, Wilson, and La Forest JJ.

Intervener: The Attorney General of Canada.

The judgment of Dickson C.J. and Lamer J. was delivered by

DICKSON C.J.: The principal issue raised by this appeal is whether the abortion provisions of the *Criminal Code*, R.S.C. 1970, c. C-34, infringe the "right to life, liberty and security of the person and the right not to be deprived thereof except in accordance with the principles of fundamental justice" as formulated in s. 7 of the *Canadian Charter of Rights and Freedoms*. ...

The Criminal Code

251.(1) Every one who, with intent to procure the miscarriage of a female person, whether or not she is pregnant, uses any means for the purpose of carrying out his intention is guilty of an indictable offence and is liable to imprisonment for life.

(2) Every female person who, being pregnant, with intent to procure her own miscarriage, uses any means or permits any means to be used for the purpose of carrying out her intention is guilty of an indictable offence and is liable to imprisonment for two years. ...

(4) Subsections (1) and (2) do not apply to

(*a*) a qualified medical practitioner, other than a member of a therapeutic abortion committee for any hospital, who in good faith uses in an accredited or approved hospital any means for the purpose of carrying out his intention to procure the miscarriage of a female person, or

(*b*) a female person who, being pregnant, permits a qualified medical practitioner to use in an accredited or approved hospital any means described in paragraph (*a*) for the purpose of carrying out her intention to procure her own miscarriage, if, before the use of those means, the therapeutic abortion committee for that accredited or approved hospital, by a majority of the members of the committee and at a meeting of the committee at which the case of such female person has been reviewed,

(*c*) has by certificate in writing stated that in its opinion the continuation of the pregnancy of such female person would or would be likely to endanger her life or health, and

(*d*) has caused a copy of such certificate to be given to the qualified medical practitioner. ...

Section 7 of the Charter

...

In my opinion, it is neither necessary nor wise in this appeal to explore the broadest implications of s. 7 as counsel would wish us to do. ... I will therefore limit my comments to ... only two aspects of s. 7, the right to "security of the person" and "the principles of fundamental justice." ...

... First it is necessary to determine whether s. 251 of the *Criminal Code* impairs the security of the person. ...

The law has long recognized that the human body ought to be protected from interference by others. At common law, for example, any medical procedure carried out on a person without that person's consent is an assault. Only in emergency circumstances does the law allow others to make decisions of this nature. Similarly, art. 19 of the *Civil Code of Lower Canada* provides that "[t]he human person is inviolable" and that "[n]o person may cause harm to the person of another without his consent or without being authorized by law to do so." "Security of the person," in other words, is not a value alien to our legal landscape. With the advent of the *Charter*, security of the person has been elevated to the status of a constitutional norm. This is not to say that the various forms of protection accorded to the human body by the common and civil law occupy a similar status. "Security of the person" must be given content in a manner sensitive to its constitutional position. The above examples are simply illustrative of our respect for individual physical integrity. ...

The case law leads me to the conclusion that state interference with bodily integrity and serious state-imposed psychological stress, at least in the criminal law context, constitute a breach of security of the person. It is not necessary in this case to determine whether the right extends further, to protect either interests central to personal autonomy, such as a right to privacy, or interests unrelated to criminal justice. ...

At the most basic, physical and emotional level, every pregnant woman is told by the section that she cannot submit to a generally safe medical procedure that might be of clear benefit to her unless she meets criteria entirely unrelated to her own priorities and aspirations. Not only does the removal of decision-making power threaten women in a physical sense; the indecision of knowing whether an abortion will be granted inflicts emotional stress. Section 251 clearly interferes with a woman's bodily integrity in both a physical and emotional sense. Forcing a woman, by threat of criminal sanction, to carry a foetus to term unless she meets certain criteria unrelated to her own priorities and aspirations, is a profound interference with a woman's body and thus a violation of security of the person. ...

The ... physical interference caused by the delays created by s. 251, involving a clear risk of damage to the physical well-being of a woman, is sufficient, in my view, to warrant inquiring whether s. 251 comports with the principles of fundamental justice. However, there is yet another infringement of security of the person. It is clear from the evidence that s. 251 harms the psychological integrity of women seeking abortions. A 1985 report of the Canadian Medical Association, discussed in the Powell Report, at p. 15, emphasized that the procedure involved in s. 251, with the concomitant delays, greatly increases the stress levels of patients and that this can lead to more physical complications associated with abortion. ...

In summary, s. 251 is a law which forces women to carry a foetus to term contrary to their own priorities and aspirations and which imposes serious delay causing increased physical and psychological trauma to those women who meet its criteria. It must, therefore, be determined whether that infringement is accomplished in accordance with the principles of fundamental justice, thereby saving s. 251 under the second part of s. 7.

C. The Principles of Fundamental Justice

Although the "principles of fundamental justice" referred to in s. 7 have both a substantive and a procedural component (*Re B.C. Motor Vehicle Act*, [[1985] 2 S.C.R. 486] at p. 499), ... it is not necessary in this appeal to evaluate the substantive content of s. 251 of the Criminal Code. My discussion will therefore be limited to various aspects of the administrative structure and procedure set down in s. 251 for access to therapeutic abortions. ...

... A pregnant woman who desires to have an abortion must apply to the "therapeutic abortion committee" of an "accredited or approved hospital." Such a committee is empowered to issue a certificate in writing stating that in the opinion of a majority of the committee, the continuation of the pregnancy would be likely to endanger the pregnant woman's life or health. Once a copy of the certificate is given to a qualified medical practitioner who is not a member of the therapeutic abortion committee, he or she is permitted to perform an abortion on the pregnant woman and both the doctor and the woman are freed from any criminal liability. ...

As is so often the case in matters of interpretation, however, the straightforward reading of this statutory scheme is not fully revealing. In order to understand the true nature and scope of s. 251, it is necessary to investigate the practical operation of the provisions. ...

The Badgley Report contains a wealth of detailed information which demonstrates ... serious problems with the functioning of s. 251 ... created by procedural and administrative requirements established in the law. ... [For example], the seemingly neutral requirement of s. 251(4) that at least four physicians be available to authorize and to perform an abortion meant in practice that abortions would be absolutely unavailable in almost one quarter of all hospitals in Canada.

Other administrative and procedural requirements of s. 251(4) reduce the availability of therapeutic abortions even further. For the purposes of s. 251, therapeutic abortions can only be performed in "accredited" or "approved" hospitals. As noted above, an "approved" hospital is one which a provincial minister of health has designated as such for the purpose of performing therapeutic abortions. The minister is under no obligation to grant any such approval. Furthermore, an "accredited" hospital must not only be accredited by the Canadian Council on Hospital Accreditation, it must also provide specified services. Many Canadian hospitals do not provide all of the required services, thereby being automatically disqualified from undertaking therapeutic abortions. ...

> Of the total of 1,348 non-military hospitals in Canada in 1976, 789 hospitals, or 58.5 percent, were ineligible in terms of their major treatment functions, the size of their medical staff, or their type of facility to establish therapeutic abortion committees.

Moreover, even if a hospital is eligible to create a therapeutic abortion committee, there is no requirement in s. 251 that the hospital need do so. The Badgley Committee discovered that in 1976, of the 559 general hospitals which met the procedural requirements of s. 251, only 271 hospitals in Canada, or only 20.1 per cent of the total, had actually established a therapeutic abortion committee (p. 105). ...

A further flaw with the administrative system established in s. 251(4) is the failure to provide an adequate standard for therapeutic abortion committees which must determine when a therapeutic abortion should, as a matter of law, be granted. Subsection (4) states simply that a therapeutic abortion committee may grant a certificate when it determines that a continuation of a pregnancy would be likely to endanger the "life or health" of the pregnant woman. ... "[H]ealth" is not defined for the purposes of the section. ...

Various expert doctors testified at trial that therapeutic abortion committees apply widely differing definitions of health. For some committees, psychological health is a justification for therapeutic abortion; for others it is not. Some committees routinely refuse abortions to married women unless they are in physical danger, while for other committees it is possible for a married woman to show that she would suffer psychological harm if she continued with a pregnancy, thereby justifying an abortion. It is not typically possible for women to know in advance what standard of health will be applied by any given committee. ...

When the decision of the therapeutic abortion committee is so directly laden with legal consequences, the absence of any clear legal standard to be applied by the committee in reaching its decision is a serious procedural flaw.

The combined effect of all of these problems with the procedure stipulated in s. 251 for access to therapeutic abortions is a failure to comply with the principles of fundamental justice. In *Re B.C. Motor Vehicle Act*, Lamer J. held, at p. 503, that "the principles of fundamental justice are to be found in the basic tenets of our legal system." One of the basic tenets of our system of criminal justice is that when Parliament creates a defence to a criminal charge, the defence should not be illusory or so difficult to attain as to be practically illusory. The criminal law is a very special form of governmental regulation, for it seeks to express our society's collective disapprobation of certain acts and omissions. When a defence is provided, especially a specifically-tailored defence to a particular charge, it is because the legislator has determined that the disapprobation of society is not warranted when the conditions of the defence are met. ...

The Crown argues in its supplementary factum that women who face difficulties in obtaining abortions at home can simply travel elsewhere in Canada to procure a therapeutic abortion. That submission would not be especially troubling if the difficulties facing women were not in large measure created by the procedural requirements of s. 251 itself. If women were seeking anonymity outside their home town or were simply confronting the reality that it is often difficult to obtain medical services in rural areas, it might be appropriate to say "let them travel." But the evidence establishes convincingly that it is the law itself which in many ways *prevents* access to local therapeutic abortion facilities. ...

... Parliament must be given room to design an appropriate administrative and procedural structure for bringing into operation a particular defence to criminal liability. But if that structure is "so manifestly unfair, having regard to the decisions it is called upon to make, as to violate the principles of *fundamental* justice," that structure must be struck down. In the present case, the structure—the system regulating access to therapeutic abortions—is manifestly unfair. It contains so many potential barriers to its own operation that the defence it creates will in many circumstances be practically unavailable to women who would *prima facie* qualify for the defence, or at least would force such women to travel great distances at substantial expense and inconvenience in order to benefit from a defence that is held out to be generally available.

I conclude that the procedures created in s. 251 of the *Criminal Code* for obtaining a therapeutic abortion do not comport with the principles of fundamental justice. It is not necessary to determine whether s. 7 also contains a substantive content leading to the conclusion that, in some circumstances at least, the deprivation of a pregnant woman's right to security of the person can never comport with fundamental justice. Simply put, assuming Parliament can act, it must do so properly. ...

V. Section 1 Analysis

Section 1 of the *Charter* can potentially be used to "salvage" a legislative provision which breaches s. 7 ... . A statutory provision which infringes any section of the *Charter* can only be saved under s. 1 if the party seeking to uphold the provision can demonstrate first, that the objective of the provision is "of sufficient importance to warrant overriding a constitutionally protected right or freedom" (*R. v. Big M Drug Mart Ltd.*, [[1985] 1 S.C.R. 295] at p. 352) and second, that the means chosen in overriding the right or freedom are reasonable and demonstrably justified in a free and democratic society. This second aspect ensures that the legislative means are proportional to the legislative ends (*Oakes*, [*R. v.*, [1986] 1 S.C.R. 103] at pp. 139-40). In *Oakes*, at p. 139, the Court referred to three considerations which are typically useful in assessing the proportionality of means to ends. First, the means chosen to achieve an important objective should be rational, fair and not arbitrary. Second, the legislative means should impair as little as possible the right or freedom under consideration. Third, the effects of the limitation upon the relevant right or freedom should not be out of proportion to the objective sought to be achieved. ...

... I have no difficulty in concluding that the objective of s. 251 as a whole, namely, to balance the competing interests identified by Parliament, is sufficiently important to meet the requirements of the first step in the *Oakes* inquiry under s. 1. I think the protection of the interests of pregnant women is a valid governmental objective, where life and health can be jeopardized by criminal sanctions. Like Beetz and Wilson JJ., I agree that protection of foetal interests by Parliament is also a valid governmental objective. It follows that balancing these interests, with the lives and health of women a major factor, is clearly an important governmental objective. ...

I am equally convinced, however, that the means chosen to advance the legislative objectives of s. 251 do not satisfy any of the three elements of the proportionality component of *R. v. Oakes*. The evidence has led me to conclude that the infringement of the security of the person of pregnant women caused by s. 251 is not accomplished in accordance with the principles of fundamental justice. ... Indeed, to the extent that

s. 251(4) is designed to protect the life and health of women, the procedures it establishes may actually defeat that objective. The administrative structures of s. 251(4) are so cumbersome that women whose health is endangered by pregnancy may not be able to gain a therapeutic abortion, at least without great trauma, expense and inconvenience.

I conclude, therefore, that the cumbersome structure of subs. (4) not only unduly subordinates the s. 7 rights of pregnant women but may also defeat the value Parliament itself has established as paramount, namely, the life and health of the pregnant woman. As I have noted, counsel for the Crown did contend that one purpose of the procedures required by subs. (4) is to protect the interests of the foetus. State protection of foetal interests may well be deserving of constitutional recognition under s. 1. Still, there can be no escape from the fact that Parliament has failed to establish either a standard or a procedure whereby any such interests might prevail over those of the woman in a fair and non-arbitrary fashion.

Section 251 of the *Criminal Code* cannot be saved, therefore, under s. 1 of the *Charter*. ...

The judgment of Estey and Beetz JJ. was delivered by

BEETZ J.: ...

II. The Right to Security of the Person in s. 7 of the Charter

...

A pregnant woman's person cannot be said to be secure if, when her life or health is in danger, she is faced with a rule of criminal law which precludes her from obtaining effective and timely medical treatment. ...

... [Section] 7 cannot be invoked simply because a woman's pregnancy amounts to a medically dangerous condition. If, however, the delays occasioned by s. 251(4) of the *Criminal Code* result in an additional danger to the pregnant woman's health, then the state has intervened and this intervention constitutes a violation of that woman's security of the person. ...

The evidence reveals that the delays caused by s. 251(4) result in at least three broad types of additional medical risks. The risk of post-operative complications increases with delay. Secondly, there is a risk that the pregnant woman require a more dangerous means of procuring a miscarriage because of the delay. Finally, since a pregnant woman knows her life or health is in danger, the delay created by the s. 251(4) procedure may result in an additional psychological trauma. ...

... The delays mean therefore that the state has intervened in such a manner as to create an additional risk to health, and consequently this intervention constitutes a violation of the woman's security of the person.

IV. The Principles of Fundamental Justice

...

I am of the view ... that certain elements of the procedure for obtaining a therapeutic abortion ... are in fact in accordance with the principles of fundamental justice. ...

I agree with McIntyre J. and the Ontario Court of Appeal that the expression "the continuation of the pregnancy of such female person would or would be likely to endanger her life or health" found in s. 251(4)(*c*) does provide, as a matter of law, a sufficiently precise standard by which therapeutic abortion committees can determine when therapeutic abortions should be granted. ...

[T]he standard is manageable because it is addressed to a panel of doctors exercising medical judgment on a medical question. This being the case, the standard must necessarily be flexible. Flexibility and vagueness are not synonymous. Parliament has set a medical standard to be determined over a limited range of circumstances. ... Evidence has been submitted that many committees fail to apply the standard set by Parliament by requiring the consent of the pregnant woman's spouse, by refusing to authorize second abortions or by refusing all abortions to married women. In so far as these and other requirements fall outside s. 251(4)(*c*), they constitute an unfounded interpretation of the plain terms of the *Criminal Code.* These patent excesses of authority do not, however, mean that the standard of s. 251 is vague. ...

Just as the expression of the standard in s. 251(4)(*c*) does not offend the principles of fundamental justice, the requirement that an independent medical opinion be obtained for a therapeutic abortion to be lawful also cannot be said to constitute a violation of these principles when considered in the context of pregnant women's right to security of the person. ...

Parliament is justified in requiring a reliable, independent and medically sound opinion in order to protect the state interest in the foetus. This is undoubtedly the objective of a rule which requires an independent verification of the practising physician's opinion that the life or health of the pregnant woman is in danger. It cannot be said to be simply a mechanism designed to protect the health of the pregnant woman. While this latter objective clearly explains the requirement that the practising physician be a "qualified medical practitioner" and that the abortion take place in a safe place, it cannot explain the necessary intercession of an in-hospital committee of three physicians from which is excluded the practising physician.

... By requiring an independent medical opinion that the pregnant woman's life or health is in fact endangered, Parliament seeks to ensure that, in any given case, only therapeutic reasons will justify the decision to abort. The amendments to the *Criminal Code* in 1969 amounted to a recognition by Parliament ... that the interest in the life or health of the pregnant woman takes precedence over the interest of the state in the protection of the foetus when the continuation of the pregnancy would or would be likely to endanger the pregnant woman's life or health. Parliament decided that it was necessary to ascertain this from a medical point of view before the law would allow the interest of the pregnant woman to indeed take precedence over that of the foetus and permit an abortion to be performed without criminal sanction.

I do not believe it to be unreasonable to seek independent medical confirmation of the threat to the woman's life or health when such an important and distinct interest hangs in the balance. I note with interest that in a number of foreign jurisdictions, laws which decriminalize abortions require an opinion as to the state of health of the woman independent from the opinion of her own physician. ...

The assertion that an independent medical opinion, distinct from that of the pregnant woman and her practising physician, does not offend the principles of fundamental justice would need to be reevaluated if a right of access to abortion is founded upon the right to "liberty" in s. 7 of the *Charter*. I am of the view that there would still be circumstances in which the state interest in the protection of the foetus would require an independent medical opinion as to the danger to the life or health of the pregnant woman. Assuming without deciding that a right of access to abortion can be founded upon the right to "liberty," there would be a point in time at which the state interest in the foetus would become compelling. From this point in time, Parliament would be entitled to limit abortions to those required for therapeutic reasons and therefore require an independent opinion as to the health exception. The case law reveals a substantial difference of opinion as to the state interest in the protection of the foetus as against the pregnant woman's right to liberty. Wilson J., for example, in her discussion of s. 1 of the *Charter* in the case at bar, notes the following, at p. 183:

> The precise point in the development of the foetus at which the state's interest in its protection becomes "compelling" I leave to the informed judgment of the legislature which is in a position to receive guidance on the subject from all the relevant disciplines. It seems to me, however, that it might fall somewhere in the second trimester. ...
>
> [Similarly] in *Roe* [*v. Wade*, 410 U.S. 113 (1973)], the [US Supreme] Court held that although the State had an important and legitimate interest in protecting potential life, that interest could not become compelling until the point at which the fetus was viable. The difficulty with this analysis is clear: potential life is no less potential in

the first weeks of pregnancy than it is at viability or afterward. At any stage in pregnancy, there is the *potential* for human life. ... The choice of viability as the point at which state interest in potential life becomes compelling is no less arbitrary than choosing any point before viability or any point afterward. Accordingly, I believe that the State's interest in protecting potential human life exists throughout the pregnancy.

... [I]t is nevertheless possible to resolve this appeal without attempting to delineate the right to "liberty" in s. 7 of the *Charter*. The violation of the right to "security of the person" and the relevant principles of fundamental justice are sufficient to invalidate s. 251 of the *Criminal Code*.

Some delay is inevitable in connection with any system which purports to limit to therapeutic reasons the grounds upon which an abortion can be performed lawfully. ... It is only in so far as the administrative structure creates delays which are unnecessary that the structure can be considered to violate the principles of fundamental justice. ...

One ... example of a rule which is unnecessary is the requirement in s. 251(4) that therapeutic abortions must ... take place in accredited or approved hospitals, with at least four physicians ... .

... [M]any first trimester therapeutic abortions may be safely performed in specialized clinics outside of hospitals because the possible complications can be handled, and in some cases better handled, by the facilities of a specialized clinic. ...

... Although the protection of health of the woman is the objective which the in-hospital rule is intended to serve, the requirement that all therapeutic abortions be performed in eligible hospitals is unnecessary to meet that objective in all cases. In this sense, the rule is manifestly unfair and offends the principles of fundamental justice. ...

An objection can also be raised in respect of the requirement that the committee come from the accredited or approved hospital in which the abortion is to be performed. It is difficult to see a connection between this requirement and any of the practical purposes for which s. 251(4) was enacted. It cannot be said to have been adopted in order to promote the safety of therapeutic abortions or the safety of the pregnant woman. Nor is the rule designed to preserve the state interest in the foetus. The integrity of the independent medical opinion is no better served by a committee within the hospital than a committee from outside the hospital as long as the practising physician remains excluded in both circumstances as part of a proper state participation in the choice of the procedure necessary to secure an independent opinion. ...

... [I]t is plain that the requirement that the therapeutic abortion committee come from the hospital in which the abortion will be performed serves no real purpose. The risk resulting from the delay caused by s. 251(4) in this respect is unnecessary. Consequently, this requirement violates the principles of fundamental justice.

Other aspects of the committee requirement in s. 251(4) add to the manifest unfairness of the administrative structure. ... [For example], hospital boards are entitled to appoint committees made up of three or more qualified medical practitioners. [But] if more than three members are appointed, precious time can be lost when quorum cannot be established because members are absent. ...

Similarly, the exclusion of all physicians who practise therapeutic abortions from the committees is exorbitant. ... There are no reasonable grounds to suspect bias from a physician who has no connection with the patient simply because, in the course of his or her medical practice, he or she performs *lawful* abortions. ... Some state control is appropriate to ensure the independence of the opinion. However, this rule as it now stands is excessive and can increase the risk of delay because fewer physicians are qualified to serve on the committees.

The foregoing analysis of the administrative structure of s. 251(4) is by no means a complete catalogue of all the current systems' strengths and failings. It demonstrates, however, that the administrative structure put in place by Parliament has enough shortcomings so that s. 251(4), when considered as a whole, violates the principles of fundamental justice. These shortcomings stem from rules which are not necessary to the purposes for which s. 251(4) was established. These unnecessary rules, because they impose delays which result in an additional risk to women's health, are manifestly unfair.

V. Section 1 of the Charter

...

... With the greatest respect, I believe the Chief Justice incorrectly identifies (at p. 75) the objective of *balancing* foetal interests and those of pregnant women, "with the lives and health of women a major factor," as "sufficiently important to meet the requirements of the first step in the *Oakes* inquiry under s. 1."

The focus in *Oakes* is the objective "which the measures responsible for a limit on a *Charter* right or freedom are designed to serve" (*supra*, at p. 138). In the context of the criminal law of abortion, the objective, which the measures in s. 251 responsible for a limit on the s. 7 *Charter* right are designed to serve, is the protection of the foetus. The narrow aim of s. 251(4) should not be confused with the primary objective of s. 251 as a whole. ...

Does the objective of protecting the foetus in s. 251 relate to concerns which are pressing and substantial in a free and democratic society? The answer to the first step of the *Oakes* test is yes. ...

I turn now to the second test in *Oakes*. ...

... A rule which is unnecessary in respect of Parliament's objectives cannot be said to be "rationally connected" thereto or to be "carefully designed to achieve the objective in question." Furthermore, not only are some of the rules in s. 251 unnecessary to the primary objective of the protection of the foetus and the ancillary objective of the protection of the pregnant woman's life or health, but their practical effect is to undermine the health of the woman which Parliament purports to consider so important. Consequently, s. 251 does not meet the proportionality test in *Oakes*. ...

Given my conclusion in respect of the first component of the proportionality test, it is not necessary to address the questions as to whether the means in s. 251 "impair as little as possible" the s. 7 *Charter* right and whether there is a proportionality between the effects of s. 251 and the objective of protecting the foetus. ...

WILSON J.: ...

... A consideration as to whether or not the procedural requirements for obtaining or performing an abortion comport with fundamental justice is purely academic if such requirements cannot as a constitutional matter be imposed at all. ... Moreover, it would, in my opinion, be an exercise in futility for the legislature to expend its time and energy in attempting to remedy the defects in the procedural requirements unless it has some assurance that this process will, at the end of the day, result in the creation of a valid criminal offence. I turn, therefore, to what I believe is the central issue that must be addressed. ...

It seems to me ... that to commence the analysis with the premise that the s. 7 right encompasses only a right to physical and psychological security and to fail to deal with the right to liberty in the context of "life, liberty and security of the person" begs the central issue in the case. If either the right to liberty or the right to security of the person or a combination of both confers on the pregnant woman the right to decide for herself (with the guidance of her physician) whether or not to have an abortion, then we have to examine the legislative scheme not only from the point of view of fundamental justice in the procedural sense but in the substantive sense as well. ...

The *Charter* is predicated on a particular conception of the place of the individual in society. An individual is not a totally independent entity disconnected from the society in which he or she lives. Neither, however, is the individual a mere cog in an impersonal machine in which his or her values, goals and aspirations are subordinated to those of the collectivity. The individual is a bit of both. The *Charter* reflects this reality by leaving a wide range of activities and decisions open to legitimate government control while at the same time placing limits on the proper scope of that control. Thus, the rights guaranteed in the *Charter* erect around each individual, metaphorically speaking, an invisible fence over which the state will not be allowed to trespass. The role of the courts is to map out, piece by piece, the parameters of the fence.

The *Charter* and the right to individual liberty guaranteed under it are inextricably tied to the concept of human dignity. ...

The idea of human dignity finds expression in almost every right and freedom guaranteed in the *Charter*. Individuals are afforded the right to choose their own religion and their own philosophy of life, the right to choose with whom they will associate and how they will express themselves, the right to choose where they will live and what occupation they will pursue. These are all examples of the basic theory underlying the *Charter*, namely that the state will respect choices made by individuals and, to the greatest extent possible, will avoid subordinating these choices to any one conception of the good life.

Thus, an aspect of the respect for human dignity on which the *Charter* is founded is the right to make fundamental personal decisions without interference from the state. This right is a critical component of the right to liberty. ...

... I would conclude, therefore, that the right to liberty contained in s. 7 guarantees to every individual a degree of personal autonomy over important decisions intimately affecting their private lives.

The question then becomes whether the decision of a woman to terminate her pregnancy falls within this class of protected decisions. I have no doubt that it does. This decision is one that will have profound psychological, economic and social consequences for the pregnant woman. The circumstances giving rise to it can be complex and varied and there may be, and usually are, powerful considerations militating in opposite directions. It is a decision that deeply reflects the way the woman thinks about herself and her relationship to others and to society at large. It is not just a medical decision; it is a profound social and ethical one as well. Her response to it will be the response of the whole person. ...

Given then that the right to liberty guaranteed by s. 7 of the *Charter* gives a woman the right to decide for herself whether or not to terminate her pregnancy, does s. 251 of the *Criminal Code* violate this right? Clearly it does. The purpose of the section is to take the decision away from the woman and give it to a committee. Furthermore, as the Chief Justice correctly points out, at p. 56, the committee bases its decision on "criteria entirely unrelated to [the pregnant woman's] own priorities and aspirations." The fact that the decision whether a woman will be allowed to terminate her pregnancy is in the hands of a committee is just as great a violation of the woman's right to personal autonomy in decisions of an intimate and private nature as it would be if a committee were established to decide whether a woman should be allowed to continue her pregnancy. Both these arrangements violate the woman's right to liberty by deciding for her something that she has the right to decide for herself. ...

Section 7 of the *Charter* also guarantees everyone the right to security of the person. Does this ... extend to the right of control over one's own body?

I agree with the Chief Justice and with Beetz J. that the right to "security of the person" under s. 7 of the *Charter* protects both the physical and psychological integrity of the individual. ... [A]s the Chief Justice and Beetz J. point out, the present legislative scheme for the obtaining of an abortion clearly subjects pregnant women to considerable emotional stress as well as to unnecessary physical risk. I believe, however, that the flaw in the present legislative scheme goes much deeper than that. In essence, what it does is assert that the woman's capacity to reproduce is not to be subject to her own control. It is to be subject to the control of the state. She may not choose whether to exercise her existing capacity or not to exercise it. This is not, in my view, just a matter of interfering with her right to liberty in the sense (already discussed) of her right to personal autonomy in decision-making, it is a direct interference with her physical "person" as well. She is truly being treated as a means—a means to an end which she does not desire but over which she has no control. She is the passive recipient of a decision made by others as to whether her body is to be used to nurture a new life. Can there be anything that comports less with human dignity and self-respect? How can a woman in this position have any sense of security with respect to her person? I believe that s. 251 of the *Criminal Code* deprives the pregnant woman of her right to security of the person as well as her right to liberty.

2. The Scope of Rights Under Section 7

I turn now to a consideration of the degree of personal autonomy the pregnant woman has under s. 7 of the *Charter* when faced with a decision whether or not to have an abortion or, to put it into the legislative context, the degree to which the legislature can deny the pregnant woman access to abortion without violating her s. 7 right. This involves a consideration of the extent to which the legislature can "deprive" her of it under the second part of s. 7 and the extent to which it can put "limits" on it under s. 1.

(a) The Principles of Fundamental Justice

Does section 251 deprive women of their right to liberty and to security of the person "in accordance with the principles of fundamental justice"? ... The question ... is whether the deprivation of the s. 7 right is in accordance not only with procedural fairness (and I agree with the Chief Justice and Beetz J. for the reasons they give that it is not) but also with the fundamental rights and freedoms laid down elsewhere in the *Charter*. ...

In my view, the deprivation of the s. 7 right with which we are concerned in this case offends s. 2(*a*) of the *Charter*. I say this because I believe that the decision whether or not to terminate a pregnancy is essentially a moral decision, a matter of conscience. I do not think there is or can be any dispute about that. ...

Legislation which violates freedom of conscience in this manner cannot, in my view, be in accordance with the principles of fundamental justice within the meaning of s. 7.

(b) Section 1 of the Charter

...

In my view, the primary objective of the impugned legislation must be seen as the protection of the foetus. It undoubtedly has other ancillary objectives, such as the protection of the life and health of pregnant women, but I believe that the main objective advanced to justify a restriction on the pregnant woman's s. 7 right is the protection of the foetus. I think this is a perfectly valid legislative objective.

... The question is: at what point in the pregnancy does the protection of the foetus become such a pressing and substantial concern as to outweigh the fundamental right of the woman to decide whether or not to carry the foetus to term? ...

... It would be my view, and I think it is consistent with the position taken by the United States Supreme Court in *Roe v. Wade* [*supra*], that the value to be placed on the foetus as potential life is directly related to the stage of its development during gestation. The undeveloped foetus starts out as a newly fertilized ovum; the fully developed foetus emerges ultimately as an infant. A developmental progression takes place in between these two extremes and, in my opinion, this progression has a direct bearing on the value of the foetus as potential life. It is a fact of human experience that a miscarriage or spontaneous abortion of the foetus at six months is attended by far greater sorrow and sense of loss than a miscarriage or spontaneous abortion at six days or even six weeks. This is not, of course, to deny that the foetus is potential life from the moment of conception. Indeed, I agree with the observation of O'Connor J., dissenting in *City of Akron v. Akron Center for Reproductive Health, Inc.*, [462 U.S. 416 (1983)], at p. 461, ... that the foetus is potential life from the moment of conception. It is simply to say that in balancing the state's interest in the protection of the foetus as potential life under s. 1 of the *Charter* against the right of the pregnant woman under s. 7 greater weight should be given to the state's interest in the later stages of pregnancy than in the earlier. The foetus should accordingly, for purposes of s. 1, be viewed in differential and developmental terms. ...

... A developmental view of the foetus, on the other hand, supports a permissive approach to abortion in the early stages of pregnancy and a restrictive approach in the later stages. In the early stages the woman's autonomy would be absolute; her decision, reached in consultation with her physician, not to carry the foetus to term would be conclusive. The state would have no business inquiring into her reasons. Her reasons for having an abortion would, however, be the proper subject of inquiry at the later stages of her pregnancy when the state's compelling interest in the protection of the foetus would justify it in prescribing conditions. The precise point in the development of the foetus at which the state's interest in its protection becomes "compelling" I leave to the informed judgment of the legislature which is in a position to receive guidance on the subject from all the relevant disciplines. It seems to me, however, that it might fall somewhere in the second trimester. Indeed, ... a differential abortion policy with a time limit in the second trimester is already in operation in the United States, Great Britain, France, Italy, Sweden, the Soviet Union, China, India, Japan and most of the countries of Eastern Europe although the time limits vary in these countries from the beginning to the end of the second trimester. ...

The judgment of McIntyre and La Forest JJ. was delivered by

McINTYRE J. (dissenting): ... I would say at the outset that it may be thought that this case does not raise the *Charter* issues which were argued and which have been addressed in the reasons of my colleagues. The charge here is one of conspiracy to breach the provisions of s. 251 of the *Criminal Code*. There is no doubt, and it has never been questioned, that the appellants adopted a course which was clearly in defiance of the provisions of the *Code* and it is difficult to see where any infringement of their rights, under s. 7 of the *Charter*, could have occurred. There is no female person involved in the case who has been denied a therapeutic abortion and, as a result, the whole argument on the right to security of the person, under s. 7 of the *Charter*, has been on a hypothetical basis. The case, however, was addressed by all the parties on that basis and the Court has accepted that position. ...

Scope of Judicial Review Under the Charter

Before the adoption of the *Charter*, there was little question of the limits of judicial review of the criminal law. For all practical purposes it was limited to a determination of whether the impugned enactment dealt with a subject which could fall within the criminal law power in s. 91(27) of the *Constitution Act, 1867*. There was no doubt of the power of Parliament to say what was and what was not criminal and to prohibit criminal conduct with penal sanctions, although from 1960 onwards legislation was subject to review under the *Canadian Bill of Rights*: see *Morgentaler (1975), supra*. The adoption of the *Charter* brought a significant change. The power of judicial review of legislation acquired greater scope but, in my view, that scope is not unlimited and should be carefully confined to that which is ordained by the *Charter*. I am well aware that there will be disagreement about what was ordained by the *Charter* and, of course, a measure of interpretation of the *Charter* will be required in order to give substance and reality to its provisions. But the courts must not, in the guise of interpretation, postulate rights and freedoms which do not have a firm and a reasonably identifiable base in the *Charter*. ...

... [T]he courts must confine themselves to such democratic values as are clearly found and expressed in the *Charter* and refrain from imposing or creating other values not so based. ...

The approach, as I understand it, does not mean that judges may not make some policy choices when confronted with competing conceptions of the extent of rights or freedoms. Difficult choices must be made and the personal views of judges will unavoidably be engaged from time to time. The decisions made by judges, however, and the interpretations that they advance or accept must be plausibly inferable from something in the *Charter*. It is not for the courts to manufacture a constitutional right out of whole cloth. I conclude on this question by citing and adopting the following words, although spoken in dissent, from the judgment of Harlan J. in *Reynolds v. Sims*, 377 U.S. 533 (1964), which, in my view, while stemming from the American experience, are equally applicable in a consideration of the Canadian position. Harlan J. commented, at pp. 624-25, on the:

> ... current mistaken view of the Constitution and the constitutional function of this Court. This view, in a nutshell, is that every major social ill in this country can find its cure in some constitutional "principle," and that this Court should "take the lead" in promoting reform when other branches of government fail to act. The Constitution is not a panacea for every blot upon the public welfare, nor should this Court, ordained as a judicial body, be thought of as a general haven for reform movements. The Constitution is an instrument of government, fundamental to which is the premise that in a diffusion of governmental authority lies the greatest promise that this Nation will realize liberty for all its citizens. This Court, limited in function in accordance with that premise, does not serve its high purpose when it exceeds its authority, even to satisfy justified impatience with the slow workings of the political process. For when, in the name of constitutional interpretation, the Court adds something to the Constitution that was deliberately excluded from it, the Court in reality substitutes its view of what should be so for the amending process.

The Right to Abortion and Section 7 of the Charter

The judgment of my colleague, Wilson J., is based upon the proposition that a pregnant woman has a right, under s. 7 of the *Charter*, to have an abortion. The same concept underlies the judgment of the Chief Justice. ...

All laws, it must be noted, have the potential for interference with individual priorities and aspirations. In fact, the very purpose of most legislation is to cause such interference. It is only when such legislation goes beyond interfering with priorities and aspirations, and abridges rights, that courts may intervene. If a law prohibited membership in a lawful association it would be unconstitutional, not because it would interfere with priorities and aspirations, but because of its interference with the guaranteed right of freedom of association under s. 2(d) of the *Charter*. Compliance with the *Income Tax Act* has, no doubt, frequently interfered with priorities and aspirations. The taxing provisions are not, however, on that basis unconstitutional, because the ordinary taxpayer enjoys no right to be tax free. Other illustrations may be found. In my view, it is clear that before it could be concluded that any enactment infringed the concept of security of the person, it would have to infringe some underlying right included in or protected by the concept. For the appellants to succeed here, then, they must show more than an interference with priorities and aspirations; they must show the infringement of a right which is included in the concept of security of the person.

The proposition that women enjoy a constitutional right to have an abortion is devoid of support in the language of s. 7 of the *Charter* or any other section. While some human rights documents ... expressly address the question of abortion, the *Charter* is entirely silent on the point. It may be of some significance that the *Charter* uses specific language in dealing with other topics, such as voting rights, religion, expression and such controversial matters as mobility rights, language rights and minority rights, but remains silent on the question of abortion which, at the time the *Charter* was under consideration, was as much a subject of public controversy as it is today. Furthermore, it would appear that the history of the constitutional text of the *Charter* affords no support for the appellants' proposition. A reference to the Minutes of the Special Joint Committee of Senate and House of Commons on the Constitution of Canada (Proceedings 32nd. Parl., Sess. 1 (1981), vol. 46, p. 43) reveals the following exchange:

> **Mr. Crombie:** ... And I ask you then finally, what effect will the inclusion of the due process clause have on the question of marriage, procreation, or the parental care of children? ...
>
> **Mr. Chrétien:** The point, Mr. Crombie, that it is important to understand the difference is that we pass legislation here on abortion, criminal code, and we pass legislation on capital punishment; parliament [*sic*] has the authority to do that, and the court at this moment, because we do not have the due process of law written there, cannot go and see whether we made the right decision or the wrong decision in Parliament.
>
> If you write down the words, "due process of law" here, the advice I am receiving is the court could go behind our decision and say that their decision on abortion was not the right one, their decision on capital punishment was not the right one, and it is a danger, according to legal advice I am receiving, that it will very much limit the scope of the power of legislation by the Parliament and we do not want that; and it is why we do not want the words "due process of law." These are the two main examples that we should keep in mind.
>
> You can keep speculating on all the things that have never been touched, but these are two very sensitive areas that we have to cope with as legislators and my view is that Parliament has decided a certain law on abortion and a certain law on capital punishment, and it should prevail and we do not want the courts to say that the judgment of Parliament was wrong in using the constitution.

This passage, of course, revolves around the second and not the first limb of s. 7, but it offers no support for the suggestion that it was intended to bring the question of abortion into the *Charter*.

It cannot be said that the history, traditions and underlying philosophies of our society would support the proposition that a right to abortion could be implied in the *Charter*. ...

Procedural Fairness

[Justice McIntyre denied that section 251 infringed the section 7 principle of "fundamental justice" because of procedural unfairness. He, like Justice Beetz, did not consider the standard of "health" used to approve or disapprove abortions to be unconstitutionally vague. As for the studies regarding uneven access to abortion, he preferred to "place principal reliance upon the evidence given under oath in court" on such factual matters. Given that no testifying physician had ever had "an application for a therapeutic abortion on behalf of the patient ultimately refused by an abortion committee," and that "[n]o woman testified that she ... had applied ... and ... been refused" an abortion, Justice McIntyre considered "the extent to which the statutory procedure contributes to the problems connected with procuring an abortion [to be] anything but clear." He concluded that "even if one accepts that it would be contrary to the principles of fundamental justice for Parliament to make available a defence which, by reason of its terms, is illusory or practically so, it cannot, in my view, be said that s. 251 of the *Code* has had that effect."]

Conclusion

Before leaving this case, I wish to make it clear that I express no opinion on the question of whether, or upon what conditions, there should be a right for a pregnant woman to have an abortion free of legal sanction. No valid constitutional objection to s. 251 of the *Criminal Code* has, in my view, been raised and, consequently, if there is to be a change in the law concerning this question it will be for Parliament to make. Questions of public policy touching on this controversial and divisive matter must be resolved by the elected Parliament. It does not fall within the proper jurisdiction of the courts. Parliamentary action on this matter is subject to judicial review but, in my view, nothing in the *Canadian Charter of Rights and Freedoms* gives the Court the power or duty to displace Parliament in this matter involving, as it does, general matters of public policy. ...

... The solution to this question in this country must be left to Parliament. It is for Parliament to pronounce on and to direct social policy. This is not because Parliament can claim all wisdom and knowledge but simply because Parliament is elected for that purpose in a free democracy and, in addition, has the facilities—the exposure to public opinion and information—as well as the political power to make effective its decisions. ...

For all of these reasons, I would dismiss the appeal.

22   Gosselin v. Quebec (Attorney General), 2002

Many who are skeptical about the benefits of the Charter question its relevance for facilitating greater social justice, such as improving the conditions of those who are most in need—the poor who lack adequate housing, food, and other basic necessities. Their skepticism arises from the rights tradition on which the Charter is based—one that allows individuals to invoke rights to constrain the state from interfering with their liberty, but does not generally recognize claims of rights that would compel the state to provide the conditions or resources necessary for those who are economically marginalized in society.

Gosselin v. Quebec (Attorney General) was the first decision where the Supreme Court was required to address the question whether government has a positive obligation under the Charter to ensure that individuals have adequate financial assistance for food, clothing, and housing. At issue was whether judicial review should consider whether the level of social assistance provided by a province violates sections 7 and 15 of the Charter. The majority of the court did not accept the argument that Charter rights are violated by the failure of government to provide adequate levels of social assistance. But the court did not rule out the possibility that one day it might interpret the Charter in this manner.

In 1984, Quebec passed legislation that changed entitlements in its social assistance scheme in a manner that provided young people under 30 substantially lower benefits than those given to others, unless they agreed to participate in either a designated work activity or education program. Initially, the legislation was insulated from Charter review because it was subject to the notwithstanding clause. But this lapsed in 1987. The Charter claim was that, after the expiration of the notwithstanding clause in 1987, the legislation should be declared an unjustifiable restriction of the right to security of the person, since it had the effect of leaving those subject to the reduced levels of assistance in a position of abject poverty that threatened both their physical and psychological integrity. The requested remedy for this violation was reimbursement of all affected welfare recipients for the difference between what they actually received and what they would have received had they been 30 years of age or over for the period after the notwithstanding clause had lapsed, for a total of roughly $389 million plus interest.

The majority and minority disagreed sharply on how to interpret age-based distinctions in the Charter. The majority ruled that the objectives of the legislation are relevant when determining if an age-based distinction constitutes discrimination, whereas the minority indicated that, since age itself is an explicitly prohibited ground of discrimination, any consideration for legislative intent is more appropriately addressed within the context of section 1. But the more interesting issue was how the court responded to the claim that the social assistance scheme violates section 7.

As will be remembered from the *B.C. Motor Vehicle Reference*,[1] the court rejected the argument that section 7 should be interpreted with deference for the framers' intentions, which clearly supported the view that section 7 should have a procedural dimension only and should not authorize judges to evaluate the fairness or substance of legislation. Yet, at the same time, Justice Lamer (as he then was) suggested that the court's decision to engage in a substantive interpretation of section 7 would be limited to the field of criminal law and legal rights, which were, as he stated, "the inherent domain of the judiciary." But it appears that the court no longer feels bound by this earlier self-imposed constraint on how to interpret section 7. Although the majority of the court in *Gosselin* concluded that there was "insufficient evidence" to support what it recognized as a "novel" interpretation of the Charter, it left open the possibility "that a positive obligation to sustain life, liberty, or security of the person may be made out in special circumstances," which it did not define. But two justices thought the case for a positive interpretation of section 7 had been made in this case. Justices Arbour and L'Heureux-Dubé found that the Quebec legislation violated section 7 in a manner not justified under section 1.

The court was also seriously divided on how to characterize the benefits and effects of the workfare scheme in the legislation. The majority thought the legislative objective had been motivated by a genuine intent to improve the conditions of poor, young Quebecers, because it would provide them the remedial education and skills training they lacked, but which were necessary to eventually integrate into the workforce and become self-sufficient. As the majority opined: "Simply handing over a bigger welfare cheque would have done nothing to help welfare recipients under 30 escape from unemployment and its potentially devastating social and psychological consequences above and beyond the short-term loss of income." Thus, the legislative scheme "constituted an affirmation of young people's potential rather than a denial of their dignity." But the minority thought the objective of the legislation was seriously flawed. Justice Arbour held that "[t]he right to a minimum level of social assistance is intimately intertwined with considerations of one's basic health and ... even one's survival." Thus, "[w]ithout the ability to secure the immediate needs of the present, the future is little more than a far-off possibility, remote both in perception and in reality." ∿

Discussion Questions

1. Are Charter skeptics persuasive in their argument that the Charter is of little assistance to those most in need?

2. What are the implications of the court's apparent rejection of Justice Lamer's suggestion, in the *B.C. Motor Vehicle Reference*, that a substantive interpretation of section 7 would be limited to the field of criminal law and legal rights?

3. Is it appropriate for the court to interpret the Charter in a manner that compels the state to provide the conditions or resources necessary for those who are economically marginalized in society?

---

1 Case 20.

GOSSELIN v. QUEBEC
(ATTORNEY GENERAL)
2002 SCC 84, [2002] 4 S.C.R. 429

Hearing: October 29, 2001; Judgment: December 19, 2002.

Present: McLachlin C.J. and L'Heureux-Dubé, Gonthier, Iacobucci, Major, Bastarache, Binnie, Arbour, and LeBel JJ.

Interveners: The Attorney General for Ontario, the Attorney General for New Brunswick, the Attorney General of British Columbia, the Attorney General for Alberta, Rights and Democracy (also known as International Centre for Human Rights and Democratic Development), Commission des droits de la personne et des droits de la jeunesse, the National Association of Women and the Law (NAWL), the Charter Committee on Poverty Issues (CCPI), and the Canadian Association of Statutory Human Rights Agencies (CASHRA).

[The court divided on several issues. A 5-to-4 majority ruled no violation of equality had occurred, with the dissenting judges concluding that equality had been restricted in a manner not justified under section 1; a 7-to-2 majority ruled there was no violation of section 7, with the dissenting judges ruling that section 7 had been restricted and the violation could not be justified under section 1; and a 6-to-1 majority ruled that there was no violation of the Quebec Charter, with two judges indicating there was no need to determine the issue.]

The judgment of McLachlin C.J. and Gonthier, Iacobucci, Major, and Binnie JJ. was delivered by

THE CHIEF JUSTICE:

I. Introduction

[1] Louise Gosselin was born in 1959. She has led a difficult life, complicated by a struggle with psychological problems and drug and alcohol addictions. From time to time she has tried to work, attempting jobs such as cook, waitress, salesperson, and nurse's assistant, among many. But work would wear her down or cause her stress, and she would quit. For most of her adult life, Ms. Gosselin has received social assistance.

[2] In 1984, the Quebec government altered its existing social assistance scheme in an effort to encourage young people to get job training and join the labour force. Under the scheme, which has since been repealed, the base amount payable to welfare recipients under 30 was lower than the base amount payable to those 30 and over. The new feature was that, to receive an amount comparable to that received by older people, recipients under 30 had to participate in a designated work activity or education program.

[3] Ms. Gosselin contends that the lower base amount payable to people under 30 violates: (1) s. 15(1) of the

Canadian Charter of Rights and Freedoms ("*Canadian Charter*"), which guarantees equal treatment without discrimination based on grounds including age; (2) s. 7 of the *Canadian Charter*, which prevents the government from depriving individuals of liberty and security except in accordance with the principles of fundamental justice; and (3) s. 45 of the *Quebec Charter of Human Rights and Freedoms*, R.S.Q., c. C-12 ("*Quebec Charter*"). She further argues that neither of the alleged *Canadian Charter* violations can be demonstrably justified under s. 1.

[4] On this basis, Ms. Gosselin asks this Court to order the Quebec government to pay the difference between the lower and the higher base amounts to all the people who: (1) lived in Quebec and were between the ages of 18 and 30 at any time from 1985 to 1989; (2) received the lower base amount payable to those under 30; and (3) did not participate in the government programs, for whatever reason. On her submissions, this would mean ordering the government to pay almost $389 million in benefits *plus* the interest accrued since 1985. Ms. Gosselin claims this remedy on behalf of over 75 000 unnamed class members, none of whom came forward in support of her claim.

[5] In my view, the evidence fails to support Ms. Gosselin's claim on any of the asserted grounds. Accordingly, I would dismiss the appeal.

II. Facts and Decisions

[6] In 1984, in the face of alarming and growing unemployment among young adults, the Quebec legislature made substantial amendments to the *Social Aid Act*, R.S.Q., c. A-16, creating a new scheme—the scheme at issue in this litigation. Section 29(*a*) of the *Regulation respecting social aid*, R.R.Q. 1981, c. A-16, r. 1, made under the Act continued to cap the base amount of welfare payable to those under 30 at roughly one third of the base amount payable to those 30 and over. However, the 1984 scheme for the first time made it possible for people under 30 to increase their welfare payments, over and above the basic entitlement, to the same (or nearly the same) level as those in the 30-and-over group.

[7] The new scheme was based on the philosophy that the most effective way to encourage and enable young people to join the workforce was to make increased benefits conditional on participation in one of three programs: On-the-job Training, Community Work, or Remedial Education. Participating in either On-the-job Training or Community Work boosted the welfare payment to a person under 30 up to the base amount for those 30 and over; participating in Remedial Education brought an under-30 within $100 of the 30-and-over base amount. The 30-and-over base amount still represented

only 55 percent of the poverty level for a single person. For example, in 1987, non-participating under-30s were entitled to $170 per month, compared to $466 per month for welfare recipients 30 and over. According to Statistics Canada, the poverty level for a single person living in a large metropolitan area was $914 per month in 1987. Long-term dependence on welfare was neither socially desirable nor, realistically speaking, economically feasible. The Quebec scheme was designed to encourage under-30s to get training or basic education, helping them to find permanent employment and avoid developing a habit of relying on social assistance during these formative years.

[8] The government initially made available 30 000 places in the three training programs. The record indicates that the percentage of eligible under-30s who actually participated in the programs averaged around one-third, but it does not explain this participation rate. Although Ms. Gosselin filed a class action on behalf of over 75 000 individuals, she provided no direct evidence of any other young person's experience with the government programs. She alone provided first-hand evidence and testimony as a class member in this case, and she in fact participated in each of the Community Work, Remedial Education and On-the-job Training Programs at various times. She ended up dropping out of virtually every program she started, apparently because of her own personal problems and personality traits. The testimony from one social worker, particularly as his clinic was attached to a psychiatric hospital and therefore received a disproportionate number of welfare recipients who also had serious psychological problems, does not give us a better or more accurate picture of the situation of the other class members, or of the relationship between Ms. Gosselin's personal difficulties and the structure of the welfare program. ...

III. Issues

[12] This case raises the important question of how to determine when the differential provision of government benefits crosses the line that divides appropriate tailoring in light of different groups' circumstances, and discrimination. To what extent does the *Canadian Charter* restrict a government's discretion to extend different kinds of help, and different levels of financial assistance, to different groups of welfare recipients? How much evidence is required to compel a government to retroactively reimburse tens of thousands of people for alleged shortfalls in their welfare payments, arising from a conditional benefits scheme? These issues have implications for the range of options available to governments throughout Canada in tailoring welfare programs to address the particular needs and circumstances of individuals requiring social assistance.

[13] The specific legal issues are found in the stated constitutional questions:

1. Did s. 29(*a*) of the *Regulation respecting social aid*, R.R.Q. 1981, c. A-16, r. 1, adopted under the *Social Aid Act*, R.S.Q., c. A-16, infringe s. 15(1) of the *Canadian Charter of Rights and Freedoms* on the ground that it established a discriminatory distinction based on age with respect to individuals, capable of working, aged 18 to 30 years?
2. If so, is the infringement justified in a free and democratic society under s. 1 of the *Canadian Charter of Rights and Freedoms*?
3. Did s. 29(*a*) of the *Regulation respecting social aid*, R.R.Q. 1981, c. A-16, r. 1, adopted under the *Social Aid Act*, R.S.Q., c. A-16, infringe s. 7 of the *Canadian Charter of Rights and Freedoms* on the ground that it deprived those to whom it applied of their right to security of the person contrary to the principles of fundamental justice?
4. If so, is the infringement justified in a free and democratic society under s. 1 of the *Canadian Charter of Rights and Freedoms*?

[14] A further issue is whether s. 29(*a*) of the Regulation violates s. 45 of the *Quebec Charter*, and if so, whether a remedy is available.

[15] A preliminary issue arises in connection with s. 33 of the *Canadian Charter*—the "notwithstanding clause." By virtue of *An Act respecting the Constitution Act, 1982*, R.S.Q., c. L-4.2, the Quebec legislature withdrew all Quebec laws from the *Canadian Charter* regime for five years from their inception. This means that the Act is immune from *Canadian Charter* scrutiny from June 23, 1982 to June 23, 1987, and the programs part of the scheme is immune from April 4, 1984 to April 4, 1989 (see *An Act to amend the Social Aid Act*, S.Q. 1984, c. 5, ss. 4 and 5). It could be argued, therefore, that the scheme is protected from *Canadian Charter* scrutiny on s. 7 or s. 15(1) grounds for the whole period *except* for the four months from April 4, 1989 to August 1, 1989. This raises the further question of whether evidence on the legislation's impact *outside* the four-month period subject to *Canadian Charter* scrutiny can be used to generate conclusions about compliance with the *Canadian Charter within* the four-month period. In view of my conclusion that the program is constitutional in any event, I need not resolve these issues.

IV. Analysis

... [28] The Regulation at issue made a distinction on the basis of an enumerated ground, age. People under 30 were subject to a different welfare regime than people 30 and over.

The question is whether this distinction in purpose or effect resulted in substantive inequality contrary to s. 15(1)'s purpose of ensuring that governments treat all individuals as equally worthy of concern, respect, and consideration. More precisely, the question is whether a reasonable person in Ms. Gosselin's position would, having regard to all the circumstances and the context of the legislation, conclude that the Regulation in purpose or effect treated welfare recipients under 30 as less worthy of respect than those 30 and over, marginalizing them on the basis of their youth.

[29] To answer this question, we must consider the four factors set out in *Law* [*v. Canada (Minister of Employment and Immigration)*, [1999] 1 S.C.R. 497]. None of these factors is a prerequisite for finding discrimination, and not all factors will apply in every case. The list of factors is neither absolute nor exhaustive. In addition, the factors may overlap, since they are all designed to illuminate the relevant contextual considerations surrounding a challenged distinction. Nonetheless, the four factors provide a useful guide to evaluating an allegation of discrimination, and I will examine each of them in turn.

(a) Pre-existing Disadvantage

[30] A key marker of discrimination and denial of human dignity under s. 15(1) is whether the affected individual or group has suffered from "pre-existing disadvantage, vulnerability, stereotyping, or prejudice": *Law*, at para. 63. ... The contextual factor of pre-existing disadvantage invites us to scrutinize group-based distinctions carefully to ensure that they are not based, either intentionally or unconsciously, on these kinds of unfounded generalizations and stereotypes.

[31] Many of the enumerated grounds correspond to historically disadvantaged groups. For example, it is clear that members of particular racial or religious groups should not be excluded from receiving public benefits on account of their race or religion. However, unlike race, religion, or gender, age is not strongly associated with discrimination and arbitrary denial of privilege. This does not mean that examples of age discrimination do not exist. But age-based distinctions are a common and necessary way of ordering our society. They do not automatically evoke a context of pre-existing disadvantage suggesting discrimination and marginalization under this first contextual factor, in the way that other enumerated or analogous grounds might.

[32] ... Concerns about age-based discrimination typically relate to discrimination against people of advanced age who are presumed to lack abilities that they may in fact possess. ...

[33] Both as a general matter, and based on the evidence and our understanding of society, young adults as a class simply do not seem especially vulnerable or undervalued. There is no reason to believe that individuals between ages 18 and 30 in Quebec are or were particularly susceptible to negative preconceptions. No evidence was adduced to this effect, and I am unable to take judicial notice of such a counter-intuitive proposition. ...

[35] Given the lack of pre-existing disadvantage experienced by young adults, Ms. Gosselin attempts to shift the focus from age to welfare, arguing that *all* welfare recipients suffer from stereotyping and vulnerability. However, this argument does not assist her claim. The ground of discrimination upon which she founds her claim is *age*. ... Re-defining the group as welfare recipients aged 18 to 30 does not help us answer that question, in particular because the 30-and-over group that Ms. Gosselin asks us to use as a basis of comparison also consists entirely of welfare recipients.

[36] I conclude that the appellant has not established that people aged 18 to 30 have suffered historical disadvantage on the basis of their age. There is nothing to suggest that people in this age group have historically been marginalized and treated as less worthy than older people.

(b) Relationship Between Grounds and the Claimant Group's Characteristics or Circumstances

[37] The second contextual factor we must consider in determining whether the distinction is discriminatory in the sense of denying human dignity and equal worth is the relationship between the ground of distinction (age) and the actual characteristics and circumstances of the claimant's group: *Law*, at para. 70. A law that is closely tailored to the reality of the affected group is unlikely to discriminate within the meaning of s. 15(1). By contrast, a law that imposes restrictions or denies benefits on account of presumed or unjustly attributed characteristics is likely to deny essential human worth and to be discriminatory. Both purpose and effect are relevant here, insofar as they would affect the perception of a reasonable person in the claimant's position: see *Law*, at para. 96.

[38] ... The evidence indicates that the purpose of the challenged distinction, far from being stereotypical or arbitrary, corresponded to the actual needs and circumstances of individuals under 30. ... North America experienced a deep recession in the early 1980s, which hit Quebec hard and drove unemployment from a traditional rate hovering around 8 percent to a peak of 14.4 percent of the active population in 1982, and among the young from 6 percent (1966) to 23 percent. At the same time, the federal government tightened eligibility requirements for federal unemployment insurance benefits, and the number of young people entering the job market for the first time surged. These three events caused an unprecedented increase in the number of people capable of working who nevertheless ended up on the welfare rolls.

[39] The situation of young adults was particularly dire. The unemployment rate among young adults was far higher than among the general population. People under 30, capable of working and without any dependants, made up a greater proportion of welfare recipients than ever before. Moreover, this group accounted for the largest—and steadily growing—proportion of *new entrants* into the welfare system: by 1983 fully two-thirds of new welfare recipients were under 30, and half were under the age of 23. In addition to coming onto the welfare rolls in ever greater numbers, younger individuals did so for increasingly lengthy periods of time. In 1975, 60 percent of welfare recipients under 30 not incapable of working left the welfare rolls within six months. By 1983, only 30 percent did so.

[40] Behind these statistics lay a complex picture. The "new economy" emerging in the 1980s offered diminishing prospects for unskilled or under-educated workers. At the same time, a disturbing trend persisted of young Quebecers dropping out of school and trying to join the workforce. The majority of unemployed youths in the early 1980s were school drop-outs. Unemployed youths were, on average, significantly less educated than the general population, and the unemployment rate among young people with fewer than eight years of education stood at 40 percent to 60 percent. Lack of skills and basic education were among the chief causes of youth unemployment.

[41] The government's short-term purpose in the scheme at issue was to get recipients under 30 into work and training programs that would make up for the lower base amount they received while teaching them valuable skills. The differential regime of welfare payments was tailored to help the burgeoning ranks of unemployed youths obtain the skills and basic education they needed to get permanent jobs. The mechanism was straightforward. In order to increase their welfare benefits, people under 30 would be required to participate in On-the-job Training, Community Work or Remedial Education Programs. Participating in the training and community service programs would bring welfare benefits up to the basic level payable to the 30-and-over group, and in the education program to about $100 less.

[42] The government's longer-term purpose was to provide young welfare recipients with precisely the kind of remedial education and skills training they lacked and needed in order eventually to integrate into the workforce and become self-sufficient. This policy reflects the practical wisdom of the old Chinese proverb: "Give a man a fish and you feed him for a day. Teach him how to fish and you feed him for a lifetime." This was not a denial of young people's dignity; it was an affirmation of their potential.

[43] Simply handing over a bigger welfare cheque would have done nothing to help welfare recipients under 30 escape from unemployment and its potentially devastating social and psychological consequences above and beyond the short-term loss of income. Moreover, opposition to the incentive program entirely overlooks the cost to young people of being on welfare during the formative years of their working lives. For young people without significant educational qualifications, skills, or experience, entering into the labour market presents considerable difficulties. A young person who relies on welfare during this crucial initial period is denied those formative experiences which, for those who successfully undertake the transition into the productive workforce, lay the foundation for economic self-sufficiency and autonomy, not to mention self-esteem. The longer a young person stays on welfare, the more difficult it becomes to integrate into the workforce at a later time. In this way, reliance on welfare can contribute to a vicious circle of inability to find work, despair, and increasingly dismal prospects.

[44] Instead of turning a blind eye to these problems, the government sought to tackle them at their roots, designing social assistance measures that might help welfare recipients achieve long-term autonomy. Because federal rules in effect at the time prohibited making participation in the programs mandatory, the province's only real leverage in promoting these programs lay in making participation a prerequisite for increases in welfare. Even if one does not agree with the reasoning of the legislature or with its priorities, one cannot argue based on this record that the legislature's purpose lacked sufficient foundation in reality and common sense to fall within the bounds of permissible discretion in establishing and fine-tuning a complex social assistance scheme. Logic and common sense support the legislature's decision to structure its social assistance programs to give young people, who have a greater potential for long-term insertion into the workforce than older people, the incentive to participate in programs specifically designed to provide them with training and experience. … In this case, far from ignoring the actual circumstances of under-30s, the scheme at issue was designed to address their needs and abilities. A reasonable person in the claimant's circumstances would have taken this into account.

[45] Turning to effect, Ms. Gosselin argues that … notwithstanding the legislature's intentions, the practical consequence of the Regulation was to abandon young welfare recipients, leaving them to survive on a grossly inadequate sum of money. In this way the program did not correspond to their actual needs, she argues, and amounted to discriminatory marginalization of the affected group. …

[47] … There is no indication in the record that any welfare recipient under 30 wanting to participate in one of the programs was refused enrollment. … As the trial judge emphasized, the record contains no first-hand evidence supporting

Ms. Gosselin's claim about the difficulties with the programs, and no indication that Ms. Gosselin can be considered representative of the under-30 class. It is, in my respectful opinion, utterly implausible to ask this Court to find the Quebec government guilty of discrimination under the *Canadian Charter* and order it to pay hundreds of millions of taxpayer dollars to tens of thousands of unidentified people, based on the testimony of a single affected individual. Nor does Ms. Gosselin present sufficient evidence that her own situation was a result of discrimination in violation of s. 15(1). The trial judge did not find evidence indicating a violation, and my review of the record does not reveal any error in this regard. ...

[54] It may well be that some under-30s fell through the cracks of the system and suffered poverty. However, absent concrete evidence, it is difficult to infer from this that the program failed to correspond to the actual needs of under-30s. I find no basis to interfere with the trial judge's conclusion that the record here simply does not support the contention of adverse effect on younger welfare recipients. This makes it difficult to conclude that the effect of the program did not correspond to the actual situation of welfare recipients under 30.

[55] I add two comments. Perfect correspondence between a benefit program and the actual needs and circumstances of the claimant group is not required to find that a challenged provision does not violate the *Canadian Charter*. The situation of those who, for whatever reason, may have been incapable of participating in the programs attracts sympathy. Yet the inability of a given social program to meet the needs of each and every individual does not permit us to conclude that the program failed to correspond to the actual needs and circumstances of the affected group. As Iacobucci J. noted in *Law, supra*, at para. 105, we should not demand "that legislation must always correspond perfectly with social reality in order to comply with s. 15(1) of the *Charter*." Crafting a social assistance plan to meet the needs of young adults is a complex problem, for which there is no perfect solution. No matter what measures the government adopts, there will always be some individuals for whom a different set of measures might have been preferable. The fact that some people may fall through a program's cracks does not show that the law fails to consider the overall needs and circumstances of the group of individuals affected, or that distinctions contained in the law amount to discrimination in the substantive sense intended by s. 15(1).

[56] Second, we cannot infer disparity between the purpose and effect of the scheme and the situation of those affected, from the mere failure of the government to prove that the assumptions upon which it proceeded were correct. ...

[57] A final objection is that the selection of 30 years of age as a cut-off failed to correspond to the actual situation of young adults requiring social assistance. However, all age-based legislative distinctions have an element of this literal kind of "arbitrariness." That does not invalidate them. Provided that the age chosen is reasonably related to the legislative goal, the fact that some might prefer a different age—perhaps 29 for some, 31 for others—does not indicate a lack of sufficient correlation between the distinction and actual needs and circumstances. Here, moreover, there is no evidence that a different cut-off age would have been preferable to the one selected.

[58] I conclude that the record in this case does not establish lack of correlation in purpose or effect between the ground of age and the needs and circumstances of welfare recipients under 30 in Quebec.

(c) The Ameliorative Purpose or Effect of the Impugned Law upon a More Disadvantaged Person or Group in Society

[59] A third factor to be considered in determining whether the group-based devaluation of human worth targeted by s. 15 is established, is whether the challenged distinction was designed to improve the situation of a more disadvantaged group. ...

[62] ... [T]he Regulation was aimed at ameliorating the situation of welfare recipients under 30. A reasonable person in Ms. Gosselin's position would take this into account in determining whether the scheme treated under-30s as less worthy of respect and consideration than those 30 and over.

(d) Nature and Scope of the Interests Affected by the Impugned Law

[63] This factor directs us to consider the impact of the impugned law—how "severe and localized the ... consequences [are] on the affected group": *Egan v. Canada*, [1995] 2 S.C.R. 513, at para. 63, quoted in *Law, supra*, at para. 74. ...

[66] We must decide this case on the evidence before us, not on hypotheticals, or on what we think the evidence ought to show. My assessment of the evidence leads me to conclude that, notwithstanding its possible short-term negative impact on the economic circumstances of some welfare recipients under 30 as compared to those 30 and over, the thrust of the program was to improve the situation of people in this group, and to enhance their dignity and capacity for long-term self-reliance. The nature and scope of the interests affected point not to discrimination but to concern for the situation of welfare recipients under 30. Absent more persuasive evidence to the contrary, I cannot conclude that a reasonable person in the claimant's position would have experienced this scheme as discriminatory, based on the contextual factors and the concern for dignity emphasized in *Law*.

(e) Summary of Contextual Factors Analysis

[67] The question is whether a reasonable welfare recipient under age 30 who takes into account the contextual factors relevant to the claim would conclude that the lower base amount provided to people under 30 treated her, in purpose or effect, as less worthy and less deserving of respect, consideration and opportunity than people 30 and over. On the evidence before us, the answer to this question must be no.

[68] Looking at the four contextual factors set out in *Law*, I cannot conclude that the denial of human dignity fundamental to a finding of discrimination is established. This is not a case where the complainant group suffered from pre-existing disadvantage and stigmatization. Lack of correspondence between the program and the actual circumstances of recipients under 30 is not established, in either purpose or effect. The "ameliorative purpose" factor is neutral with respect to discrimination. Finally, the findings of the trial judge and the evidence do not support the view that the overall impact on the affected individuals undermined their human dignity and their right to be recognized as fully participating members of society, notwithstanding their membership in the class affected by the distinction.

[69] A reasonable welfare recipient under 30 might have concluded that the program was harsh, perhaps even misguided. ... But she would not reasonably have concluded that it treated younger people as less worthy or less deserving of respect in a way that had the purpose or effect of marginalizing or denigrating younger people in our society. If anything, she would have concluded that the program treated young people as more able than older people to benefit from training and education, more able to get and retain a job, and more able to adapt to their situations and become fully participating and contributing members of society.

[70] Far from relying on false stereotypes, the program was calibrated to address the particular needs and circumstances of young adults requiring social assistance, considered from both short-term and long-term perspectives. I do not suggest that stereotypical thinking must always be present for a finding that s. 15 is breached. However, its absence is a factor to be considered. The age-based distinction was made for an ameliorative, non-discriminatory purpose, and its social and economic thrust and impact were directed to enhancing the position of young people in society by placing them in a better position to find employment and live fuller, more independent lives. Nor, on the findings of the trial judge, is it established that the program's effect was to undermine the worth of its members in comparison with older people.

[71] The most compelling way to put the claimant's case is this. We are asked to infer from the apparent lack of widespread participation in programs that some recipients under 30 must at some time have been reduced to utter poverty. From this we are further asked to infer that at least some of these people's human dignity and ability to participate as fully equal members of society were compromised.

[72] The inferences that this argument asks us to draw are problematic. The trial judge, as discussed, was unable to find evidence of actual adverse impact on under-30s as a group. Moreover, the argument rests on a standard of perfection in social programs. As this Court noted in *Law*, that is not the standard to be applied. Some people will always fall through the cracks of social programs. That does not establish denial of human dignity and breach of s. 15. What is required is demonstration that the program as a whole and in the context of *Law*'s four factors in purpose or effect denied human dignity to the affected class, penalizing or marginalizing them simply for being who they were. In this case, that has not been shown. ...

[74] I conclude that the impugned law did not violate the essential human dignity of welfare recipients under 30. We must base our decision on the record before us, not on personal beliefs or hypotheticals. On the facts before us, the law did not discriminate against Ms. Gosselin, either individually or as a member of the group of 18- to 30-year-olds in Quebec. The differential welfare scheme did not breach s. 15(1) of the *Canadian Charter*.

B. Does the Social Assistance Scheme Violate Section 7 of the Canadian Charter?

... [79] In my view, it is both unnecessary and undesirable to attempt to state an exhaustive definition of the administration of justice at this stage, delimiting all circumstances in which the administration of justice might conceivably be implicated. The meaning of the administration of justice, and more broadly the meaning of s. 7, should be allowed to develop incrementally, as heretofore unforeseen issues arise for consideration. The issue here is not whether the administration of justice is implicated—plainly it is not—but whether the Court ought to apply s. 7 despite this fact.

[80] Can s. 7 apply to protect rights or interests wholly unconnected to the administration of justice? The question remains unanswered. ...

[81] Even if s. 7 could be read to encompass economic rights, a further hurdle emerges. Section 7 speaks of the right *not to be deprived* of life, liberty and security of the person, except in accordance with the principles of fundamental justice. Nothing in the jurisprudence thus far suggests that s. 7 places a positive obligation on the state to ensure that each person enjoys life, liberty or security of the person. Rather, s. 7 has been interpreted as restricting the state's ability to *deprive* people of these. Such a deprivation does not exist in the case at bar.

[82] One day s. 7 may be interpreted to include positive obligations. To evoke Lord Sankey's celebrated phrase in *Edwards v. Attorney-General for Canada*, [1930] A.C. 124 (P.C.), at p. 136, the *Canadian Charter* must be viewed as "a living tree capable of growth and expansion within its natural limits" .... The question therefore is not whether s. 7 has ever been—or will ever be—recognized as creating positive rights. Rather, the question is whether the present circumstances warrant a novel application of s. 7 as the basis for a positive state obligation to guarantee adequate living standards.

[83] I conclude that they do not. With due respect for the views of my colleague Arbour J., I do not believe that there is sufficient evidence in this case to support the proposed interpretation of s. 7. I leave open the possibility that a positive obligation to sustain life, liberty, or security of the person may be made out in special circumstances. However, this is not such a case. The impugned program contained compensatory "workfare" provisions and the evidence of actual hardship is wanting. The frail platform provided by the facts of this case cannot support the weight of a positive state obligation of citizen support.

[84] In view of my conclusions under s. 15(1) and s. 7 of the *Canadian Charter*, the issue of justification under s. 1 does not arise. Nor does the issue of *Canadian Charter* remedies arise. ...

[Chief Justice McLachlin indicated she did not accept the view that section 45 of the Quebec Charter invites courts to review the adequacy of Quebec's social assistance regime.]

[Justice L'Heureux-Dubé wrote a dissenting opinion in which she agreed with Justices Arbour, Bastarache, and LeBel that the legislation violated section 15 and could not be upheld under section 1, agreed with Justice Arbour that section 7 had been violated and could not be upheld under section 1, and indicated that the legislation violated section 45 of the Quebec Charter.]

The following are the reasons delivered by

BASTARACHE J. (dissenting):

...

(1) Section 7

... [205] The appellant in this case argues that the statutory framework that reduced benefits for those under 30 infringed her right to security of the person, since it had the effect of leaving her and the members of her class in a position of abject poverty that threatened both their physical and psychological integrity. In order to establish a s. 7 breach, the claimant must first show that she was deprived of her right to life, liberty or security of the person, and then must establish that the state caused such deprivation in a manner that was not in accordance with the principles of fundamental justice.

[206] The protection provided for by s. 7's right to life, liberty and security of the person is reflective of our country's traditional and long-held concern that persons should, in general, be free from the constraints of the state and be treated with dignity and respect. ...

[208] In this case, the appellant has gone to great lengths to demonstrate that the negative effects of living on the reduced level of support were seriously harmful to the physical and psychological well-being of those affected. Certainly, those who, like the appellant, were living on a reduced benefit were not in a very "secure" position. The remaining question at this first stage of the s. 7 analysis is, however, whether this position of insecurity was brought about by the state.

[209] The requirement that the violation of a person's rights under s. 7 must emanate from a particular state action can be found in the wording of the section itself. Section 7 does not grant a right to security of the person, full stop. Rather, the right is protected only insofar as the claimant is deprived of the right to security of the person by the state, in a manner that is contrary to the principles of fundamental justice. The nature of the required nexus between the right and a particular state action has evolved over time.

[210] In *Reference re ss. 193 and 195.1(1)(c) of the Criminal Code (Man.)*, [1990] 1 S.C.R. 1123 ("*Prostitution Reference*"), Lamer J., as he then was, held that s. 7 was not necessarily limited to purely criminal or penal matters (p. 1175). Nonetheless, he did maintain that, given the context of the surrounding rights and the heading "Legal Rights" under which s. 7 is found, it was proper to conclude that "the restrictions on liberty and security of the person that s. 7 is concerned with are those that occur as a result of an individual's interaction with the justice system, and its administration" (p. 1173). ...

[213] [I]n certain exceptional circumstances, this Court has found that s. 7 rights may include situations outside of the traditional criminal context—extending to other areas of judicial competence. In this case, however, there is no link between the harm to the appellant's security of the person and the judicial system or its administration. The appellant was not implicated in any judicial or administrative proceedings, or even in an investigation that would at some point lead to such a proceeding. At the very least, a s. 7 claim must arise as a result of a determinative state action that in and of itself deprives the claimant of the right to life, liberty or security of the person.

[214] Some may find this threshold requirement to be overly formalistic. The appellant, for instance, argues that this Court has found that respect for human dignity underlies most if not all of the rights protected under the *Charter*.

Undoubtedly, I agree that respect for the dignity of all human beings is an important, if not foundational, value in this or any society, and that the interpretation of the *Charter* may be aided by taking such values into account. However, this does not mean that the language of the *Charter* can be totally avoided by proceeding to a general examination of such values or that the court can through the process of judicial interpretation change the nature of the right. As held in *Blencoe* [*v. British Columbia (Human Rights Commission)*, [2000] 2 S.C.R. 307, 2000 SCC 44], "[w]hile notions of dignity and reputation underlie many *Charter* rights, they are not standalone rights that trigger s. 7 in and of themselves" (para. 97). A purposive approach to *Charter* interpretation, while coloured by an overarching concern with human dignity, democracy and other such "*Charter* values," must first and foremost look to the purpose of the section in question. Without some link to the language of the *Charter*, the legitimacy of the entire process of *Charter* adjudication is brought into question.

[215] In the *Charter*, s. 7 is grouped, along with ss. 8 to 14, under the heading "Legal Rights," in French, "*Garanties juridiques.*" Given the wording of this heading, as well as the subject matter of ss. 8 to 14, it is apparent that s. 7 has, as its primary goal, the protection of one's right to life, liberty and security of the person against the coercive power of the state (P. W. Hogg, *Constitutional Law of Canada* (loose-leaf ed.), vol. 2, at p. 44-9; *Prostitution Reference, supra, per* Lamer J.). The judicial nature of the s. 7 rights is also evident from the fact that people may only be deprived of those rights in accordance with the principles of fundamental justice. As Lamer J. held in *Re B.C. Motor Vehicle Act*, [1985] 2 S.C.R. 486, such principles are to be found "in the basic tenets of our legal system. They do not lie in the realm of general public policy but in the inherent domain of the judiciary as guardian of the justice system" (p. 503). It is this strong relationship between the right and the role of the judiciary that leads me to the conclusion that some relationship to the judicial system or its administration must be engaged before s. 7 may be applied.

[216] … [A]t the very least, in order for one to be deprived of a s. 7 right, some determinative state action, analogous to a judicial or administrative process, must be shown to exist. Only then may the process of interpreting the principles of fundamental justice or the analysis of government action be undertaken.

[217] In this case, there has been no engagement with the judicial system or its administration, and thus, the protections of s. 7 are not available. As will be discussed below, I have concluded that s. 29(*a*) of the Regulation, by treating individuals differently on the basis of their age, constitutes an infringement of the appellant's equality rights. However, s. 7

does not have the same comparative characteristics as the s. 15 right. The appellant's situation must be viewed in more absolute terms. In this case, the threat to the appellant's right to security of the person was brought upon her by the vagaries of a weak economy, not by the legislature's decision not to accord her more financial assistance or to require her to participate in several programs in order for her to receive more assistance.

[218] The appellant and several of the interveners made forceful arguments regarding the distinction that is sometimes drawn between negative and positive rights, as well as that which is made between economic and civil rights, arguing that security of the person often requires the positive involvement of government in order for it to be realized. This is true. The right to be tried within a reasonable time, for instance, may require governments to spend more money in order to establish efficient judicial institutions. However, in order for s. 7 to be engaged, the threat to the person's right itself must emanate from the state. …

[220] The appellant also directed our attention to the dissenting statements of Dickson C.J. in *Reference re Public Service Employee Relations Act (Alta.)*, [1987] 1 S.C.R. 313, in which he noted that a conceptual approach in which freedoms are said to involve simply an absence of interference or constraint "may be too narrow since it fails to acknowledge situations where the absence of government intervention may in effect substantially impede the enjoyment of fundamental freedoms" (p. 361). The question of whether a fundamental freedom can be infringed through the lack of government action was canvassed most recently in the case of *Dunmore* [*v. Ontario (Attorney General)*], [2001] 3 S.C.R. 1016, 2001 SCC 94. In that case, I held that legislation that is underinclusive may, in unique circumstances, substantially impact the exercise of a constitutional freedom (para. 22). I explained that in order to meet the requirement that there be some form of government action as prescribed by s. 32 of the *Canadian Charter*, the legislation must have been specifically designed to safeguard the exercise of the fundamental freedom in question. The affected group was required to show that it was substantially incapable of exercising the freedom sought without the protection of the legislation, and that its exclusion from the legislation substantially reinforced the inherent difficulty to exercise the freedom in question. While the existence of the *Social Aid Act* might constitute sufficient government action to engage s. 32, none of the other factors enumerated in *Dunmore* are present in this case.

[221] In *Dunmore*, I found that the Ontario *Labour Relations Act, 1995*, S.O. 1995, c. 1, Sched. A, instantiated the freedom to organize and that without its protection agricultural workers were substantially incapable of exercising their

freedom to associate. The legislation reinforced the already precarious position of agricultural workers in the world of labour relations. In undertaking the underinclusiveness analysis, a complainant must demonstrate that he or she is being deprived of the right itself and not simply the statutory benefit that is being provided to other groups. Here, the *Social Aid Act* seeks to remedy the situation of those persons who find themselves without work or other assistance by providing them with financial support and job training so that they can integrate to the active workforce. As in *Delisle v. Canada (Deputy Attorney General)*, [1999] 2 S.C.R. 989, and *Haig v. Canada*, [1993] 2 S.C.R. 995, the exclusion of people under 30 from the full, unconditional benefit package does not render them substantially incapable of exercising their right to security of the person without government intervention. Leaving aside the possibilities that might exist on the open market, training programs are offered to assist in finding work and to provide additional benefits.

[222] The appellant has failed to demonstrate that there exists an inherent difficulty for young people under 30 to protect their right to security of the person without government intervention. Nor has the existence of a higher base benefit for recipients 30 years of age and over been shown to reduce, on its own, or substantially, the potential of young people to exercise their right to security of the person. The fact that the remedial programs instituted by the reforms of 1984 might not have been designed in a manner that was overly favourable to the appellant does not help the appellant in meeting her burden. My concern here is with the ability of the appellant's group to access the right itself, not to benefit better from the statutory scheme. The appellant has failed to show a substantial incapability of protecting her right to security. She has not demonstrated that the legislation, by excluding her, has reduced her security any more than it would have already been, given market conditions.

[223] For these reasons, I would hold that s. 29(*a*) of the Regulation does not infringe s. 7 of the *Canadian Charter*. The threat to the appellant's security of the person was not related to the administration of justice, nor was it caused by any state action, nor did the underinclusive nature of the Regulation substantially prevent or inhibit the appellant from protecting her own security. Such a result should not be unexpected. As I noted in *Dunmore, supra*, total exclusion of a group from a statutory scheme protecting a certain right may in some limited circumstances engage that right to such an extent that it is in essence the substantive right that has been infringed as opposed to the equality right protected under s. 15(1) of the *Charter*. However, the underinclusiveness of legislation will normally be the province of s. 15(1), and so it is to the equality analysis that we must now turn.

(2) Section 15

... [225] Among the grounds of prohibited discrimination enumerated under s. 15(1), age is the one that tends to cause the most theoretical confusion. The source of such confusion in implementing the s. 15(1) guarantee of age equality is rooted in our understanding of substantive equality. In protecting substantive equality, this Court has recognized that like people should be treated alike and, reciprocally, different people must often be treated differently. Most of the grounds enumerated under s. 15(1) tend to be characteristics that our society has deemed to be "irrelevant" to one's abilities. The problem with age is that because we all, as human beings trapped in the continuum of time, experience the process of aging, it is sometimes difficult to assess discriminative behaviour. ...

[226] Moreover, whereas distinctions based on most other enumerated or analogous grounds may often be said to be using the characteristic as an illegitimate proxy for merit, distinctions based on age as a proxy for merit or ability are often made and viewed as legitimate. This acceptance of distinctions based on age is due to the fact that at different ages people *are* capable of different things. Ten-year-olds, in general, do not make good drivers. The same might be said for the majority of centenarians. It is in recognition of these developmental differences that several laws draw distinctions on the basis of age.

[227] However, despite this apparent recognition that age is of a different sort than the other grounds enumerated in s. 15(1), the fact of the matter is that it was included as a prohibited ground of discrimination in the *Canadian Charter*. ... Legislation that draws a distinction based on such a ground is suspect because it often leads to discrimination and denial of substantive equality. This is the case whether the distinction is based on race, gender or age. While distinctions based on age may often be justified, they are nonetheless equally suspect. While age is a ground that is experienced by all people, it is not necessarily experienced in the same way by all people at all times. Large cohorts may use age to discriminate against smaller, more vulnerable cohorts. A change in economic, historical or political circumstances may mean that presumptions and stereotypes about a certain age group no longer hold true. Moreover, the fact remains that, while one's age is constantly changing, it is a personal characteristic that at any given moment one can do nothing to alter. Accordingly, age falls squarely within the concern of the equality provision that people not be penalized for characteristics they either cannot change or should not be asked to change.

[228] The fact that the Regulation here makes a distinction based on a personal characteristic that is specifically enumerated under s. 15 should therefore raise serious concerns when considering whether such a distinction is in fact

discriminatory. While not creating a presumption of discrimination, a distinction based on an enumerated ground reveals a strong suggestion that the provision in question is discriminatory for the purposes of s. 15. ...

[242] In my view, the treatment of legislative purpose at this stage of the s. 15(1) analysis must not undermine or replace that which will be undertaken when applying s. 1. ...

[244] [G]iving too much weight here to what the government says was its objective in designing the scheme would amount to accepting a s. 1 justification before it is required. ...

[245] ... [T]he legislature's intention is much less important at this stage of the *Law* analysis than the real effects on the claimant. The fundamental question, then, in this case, is not how the legislature viewed the scheme, nor how members of the majority would have viewed it in relation to the claimant group. The approach set out for us by *Law* is to ask how any member of the majority, reasonably informed, would feel in the shoes of the claimant, experiencing the effects of the legislation. This approach is essential: if people whom the legislature views as different are not demonstrably different at all, the measure should not be acceptable. ...

[259] It can be argued that the government could not design a perfect program, and that in a program such as this, some people are bound to fall through the cracks. Indeed, the Chief Justice accepts this argument, noting that a government need not achieve a perfect correspondence between a benefit program and the actual needs and circumstances of the claimant group. But in light of the importance of the interest affected, this should not provide a bar to a finding that Ms. Gosselin's dignity was adversely affected. The severe harm suffered by the appellant as a result of the age-based distinction far exceeds the margin of imperfection Iacobucci J. contemplated in *Law*, *supra*, at para. 105. ... The Chief Justice appears to believe that the appellant has the onus, under s. 15(1), to demonstrate not only that *she* is harmed, but also that the government program allows more than an acceptable number of *other* individuals to fall through the cracks. Given the government's resources, it is much more appropriate to require it to adduce proof of the importance and purpose of the program and its minimal impairment of equality rights in discharging its burden under s. 1. ...

[276] In assessing whether the legislation in place was minimally impairing to the right, the first fact that comes to light is that only 11 percent of social assistance recipients under the age of 30 were in fact enrolled in the employment programs that allowed them to receive the base amount allocated to beneficiaries 30 years of age and over. This in and of itself is not determinative of the fact that the legislation was not minimally impairing, but it does bring to our attention the real possibility that the programs were not designed in a

manner that would infringe upon the appellant's rights as little as is reasonably possible. ...

[290] ... I find that s. 29(*a*) of the Regulation's *Charter* breach should not be upheld as a justified and reasonable limit under s. 1. In the legislative and social context of the legislation, which provided a safety net for those without means to support themselves, a rights-infringing limitation must be carefully crafted. In this case, the programs left too many opportunities for young people to fall through the seams of the legislation. This is borne out to some degree by the low participation rate among beneficiaries under the age of 30 and the fact that there was no basis for the assumption that beneficiaries under 30 were living with their parents and had lesser needs. While the respondent argues that no evidence was presented to show that most if any of the 73 percent of recipients under 30 were not participating in the programs for anything more than personal reasons, I would point out that at the s. 1 stage of analysis, it is the government's responsibility to show that the legislation limits the right as little as reasonably possible. ...

[292] In determining the appropriate remedy in the case of legislation that is found to violate a *Charter* right, courts must walk a fine line between fulfilling their judicial role of protecting rights and intruding on the legislature's role. ...

[299] I would deny the appellant's request for an order for damages pursuant to s. 24(1) of the *Charter*. ...

[Justice Bastarache held that the court has no power to declare any portion of a law invalid due to a conflict with s. 45 of the *Quebec Charter*.]

The following are the reasons delivered by

ARBOUR J. (dissenting):

... [308] I would allow this appeal on the basis of the appellant's s. 7 *Charter* claim. In doing so, I conclude that the s. 7 rights to "life, liberty and security of the person" include a positive dimension. Few would dispute that an advanced modern welfare state like Canada has a positive moral obligation to protect the life, liberty and security of its citizens. There is considerably less agreement, however, as to whether this positive moral obligation translates into a legal one. Some will argue that there are interpretive barriers to the conclusion that s. 7 imposes a positive obligation on the state to offer such basic protection.

[309] In my view these barriers are all less real and substantial than one might assume. This Court has never ruled, nor does the language of the *Charter* itself require, that we must reject any positive claim against the state—as in this case—for the most basic positive protection of life and security. This Court has consistently chosen instead to leave open

the possibility of finding certain positive rights to the basic means of subsistence within s. 7. In my view, far from resisting this conclusion, the language and structure of the *Charter*—and of s. 7 in particular—actually *compel* it. Before demonstrating all of this it will be necessary to deconstruct the various firewalls that are said to exist around s. 7, precluding this Court from reaching in this case what I believe to be an inevitable and just outcome. ...

[311] There was some discussion in the courts below concerning whether s. 7 extends its protection to the class of so-called "economic rights." That discussion gets its impetus from certain dicta of Dickson C.J. in *Irwin Toy Ltd. v. Quebec (Attorney General)*, [1989] 1 S.C.R. 927. In *Irwin Toy*, Dickson C.J. compared the wording of s. 7 to similar provisions in the American *Bill of Rights* and noted the following, at p. 1003:

> The intentional exclusion of property from s. 7, and the substitution therefore of "security of the person" ... leads to a general inference that economic rights as generally encompassed by the term "property" are not within the perimeters of the s. 7 guarantee.

... [312] [T]he rights at issue in this case are so connected to the sorts of interests that fall under s. 7 that it is a gross mischaracterization to attach to them the label of "economic rights." Their only kinship to the economic "property" rights that are *ipso facto* excluded from s. 7 is that they involve some economic value. But if this is sufficient to attract the label "economic right," there are few rights that would not be economic rights. It is in the very nature of rights that they crystallize certain benefits, which can often be quantified in economic terms. What is truly significant, from the standpoint of inclusion under the rubric of s. 7 rights, is not therefore whether a right can be expressed in terms of its economic value, but as Dickson C.J. suggests, whether it "fall[s] within 'security of the person'" or one of the other enumerated rights in that section. It is principally because corporate-commercial "property" rights fail to do so, and not because they contain an economic component *per se*, that they are excluded from s. 7. Conversely, it is because the right to a minimum level of social assistance is clearly connected to "security of the person" and "life" that it distinguishes itself from corporate-commercial rights in being a candidate for s. 7 inclusion.

[313] In my view, this tells decisively against any argument that relies upon a supposed economic rights prohibition within s. 7 of the *Charter*. ...

C. Negative Versus Positive Rights and the Requirement of State Action

[319] There is a suggestion that s. 7 contains only negative rights of non-interference and therefore cannot be implicated absent any positive state action. This is a view that is commonly expressed but rarely examined. It is of course true that in virtually all past s. 7 cases it was possible to identify some definitive act on the part of the state which could be said to constitute an interference with life, liberty or security of the person and consequently ground the claim of a s. 7 violation. It may also be the case that no such definitive state action can be located in the instant appeal, though this will largely depend on how one chooses to define one's terms and, in particular, the phrase "state action." One should first ask, however, whether there is in fact any requirement, in order to ground a s. 7 claim, that there be some affirmative state action interfering with life, liberty or security of the person, or whether s. 7 can impose on the state a duty to act where it has not done so. (I use the terms "affirmative," "definitive" or "positive" to mean an identifiable action in contrast to mere inaction.) No doubt if s. 7 contemplates the existence only of negative rights, which are best described as rights of "non-interference," then active state interference with one's life, liberty or security of the person by way of some definitive act will be necessary in order to engage the protection of that section. But if, instead, s. 7 rights include a positive dimension, such that they are not merely rights of non-interference but also what might be described as rights of "performance," then they may be violable by mere inaction or failure by the state to actively provide the conditions necessary for their fulfilment. We must not sidestep a determination of this issue by assuming from the start that s. 7 includes a requirement of affirmative state action. That would be to beg the very question that needs answering.

[320] It is not often clear whether the theory of negative rights underlying the view that s. 7 can only be invoked in response to a definitive state action is intended to be one of general application, extending to the *Charter* as a whole, or one that applies strictly to s. 7. As a theory of the *Charter* as a whole, any claim that only negative rights are constitutionally recognized is of course patently defective. The rights to vote (s. 3), to trial within a reasonable time (s. 11(*b*)), to be presumed innocent (s. 11(*d*)), to trial by jury in certain cases (s. 11(*f*)), to an interpreter in penal proceedings (s. 14), and minority language education rights (s. 23) to name but some, all impose positive obligations of performance on the state and are therefore best viewed as positive rights (at least in part). By finding that the state has a positive obligation in certain cases to ensure that its labour legislation is properly inclusive, this Court has also found there to be a positive dimension to the s. 2(*d*) right to associate (*Dunmore v. Ontario (Attorney General)*, [2001] 3 S.C.R. 1016, 2001 SCC 94). Finally, decisions like *Schachter v. Canada*, [1992] 2 S.C.R. 679, and *Vriend* [*v. Alberta*, [1998] 1 S.C.R. 493], confirm that

"[i]n some contexts it will be proper to characterize s. 15 as providing positive rights" (*Schachter, supra,* at p. 721). This list is illustrative rather than exhaustive.

[321] Moreover, there is no sense in which the actual language of s. 7 limits its application to circumstances where there has been positive state interference. It is sometimes suggested that the requirement is implicit in the use of the concept of "deprivation" within s. 7. This is highly implausible. ...

[329] The finding that s. 7 may impose positive obligations on the state brings us directly to a frequently expressed objection in the context of claims like the ones at issue in the present case that courts cannot enforce positive rights of an individual to the basic means of basic subsistence. The suggestion is that they cannot do so without being drawn outside their proper judicial role and into the realm of deciding complex matters of social policy better left to legislatures. I turn now to this concern.

D. Justiciability

... [331] ... Questions of resource allocation typically involve delicate matters of policy. Legislatures are better suited than courts to addressing such matters, given that they have the express mandate of the taxpayers as well as the benefits of extensive debate and consultation.

[332] It does not follow, however, that courts are precluded from entertaining a claim such as the present one. While it may be true that courts are ill-equipped to decide policy matters concerning resource allocation—questions of how much the state should spend, and in what manner—this does not support the conclusion that justiciability is a threshold issue barring the consideration of the substantive claim in this case. As indicated above, this case raises altogether a different question: namely, whether the state is under a positive obligation to provide basic means of subsistence to those who cannot provide for themselves. In contrast to the sorts of policy matters expressed in the justiciability concern, this is a question about what kinds of claims individuals can assert against the state. The role of courts as interpreters of the *Charter* and guardians of its fundamental freedoms against legislative or administrative infringements by the state requires them to adjudicate such rights-based claims. One can in principle answer the question of whether a *Charter* right exists— in this case, to a level of welfare sufficient to meet one's basic needs—without addressing how much expenditure by the state is necessary in order to secure that right. It is only the latter question that is, properly speaking, non-justiciable.

[333] Of course, in practice it will often be the case that merely knowing whether the right exists is of little assistance to the claimant. For, unless we also know what is required, or how much expenditure is needed, in order to safeguard the right, it will usually be difficult to know whether the right has been violated. This difficulty does not arise in the present case. Once a right to a level of welfare sufficient to meet one's basic needs is established, there is no question on the facts of this case that the right has been violated. This Court need not enter into the arena of determining what would satisfy such a "basic" level of welfare because that determination has already been made by the legislature, which is itself the competent authority to make it.

[334] Indeed, the very welfare scheme that is challenged here includes provisions that set out the basic amount. Section 23 of the *Regulation respecting social aid,* R.R.Q. 1981, c. A-16, r. 1, provides that the amount receivable is established according to the "ordinary needs" ("*besoins ordinaires*") of the recipients. The bare minimum a single adult aged 30 or over can receive is $466. This is the amount that was deemed by the legislature itself to be sufficient to meet the "ordinary needs" of a single adult. The present case comes before us on the basis that the government failed to provide a level of assistance that, according to its own standards, was necessary to meet the ordinary needs of adults aged 18 to 29. The only outstanding questions are whether this is in fact established and, if so, whether the claimants had a right to the provision of their ordinary needs.

[335] Thus any concern over the justiciability of positive claims against the state has little bearing on this case. At any rate, these issues, to some extent, obscure the real question. At this stage we are less concerned with what, if anything, the state must do in order to bring itself under a positive obligation than with whether s. 7 can support such positive obligations to begin with. I have already indicated several reasons for thinking that it can. I now want to supplement these reasons by means of an interpretive analysis of s. 7. As it turns out, any acceptable approach to *Charter* interpretation—be it textual, contextual, or purposive—quickly makes apparent that interpreting the rights contained in s. 7 as including a positive component is not only possible, but also necessary. ...

[350] Clearly, positive rights are not at odds with the purpose of the *Charter.* Indeed, the *Charter* compels the state to act positively to ensure the protection of a significant number of rights. ... Positive rights are not an exception to the usual application of the *Charter,* but an inherent part of its structure. The *Charter* as a whole can be said to have a positive purpose in that at least some of its constituent parts do. ...

[357] ... In my view, the results are unequivocal: every suitable approach to *Charter* interpretation, including textual analysis, purposive analysis, and contextual analysis, mandates the conclusion that the s. 7 rights of life, liberty and security of the person include a positive dimension. ...

[385] ... Legislative intervention aimed at providing for essential needs touching on the personal security and survival

of indigent members of society is sufficient to satisfy whatever "minimum state action" requirement might be necessary in order to engage s. 32 of the *Charter*. By enacting the *Social Aid Act*, the Quebec government triggered a state obligation to ensure that any differential treatment or underinclusion in the provision of these essential needs did not run afoul of the fundamental rights guaranteed by the *Charter*, and in particular by s. 7. It failed to discharge this obligation. The evidence shows that the underinclusion of welfare recipients aged 18 to 29 under the *Social Aid Act* substantially impeded their ability to exercise their right to personal security (and potentially even their right to life). In the circumstances, I must conclude that this effective lack of government intervention constituted a violation of their s. 7 rights.

IV. The Principles of Fundamental Justice

[386] Under most circumstances, it would now be necessary to determine whether this *prima facie* violation of the appellant's s. 7 rights was "in accordance with the principles of fundamental justice." Such an inquiry appears to have no application to this case for two reasons. First, my analysis indicates that the protection of positive rights is most naturally grounded in the first clause of s. 7, which provides a free-standing right to life, liberty and security of the person and makes no mention of the principles of fundamental justice. Moreover, as Lamer J. observed in *Re B.C. Motor Vehicle Act, supra,* at p. 503 "the principles of fundamental justice are to be found in the basic tenets of our legal system. They do not lie in the realm of general public policy but in the inherent domain of the judiciary as guardian of the justice system." But positive rights, by nature violable by mere inaction on the part of the state, do not bring the justice system into motion by empowering agents of the state to actively curtail the life, liberty and security of the person of individuals. The source of a positive rights violation is in the legislative process, which is of course itself quite distinct from the "inherent domain of the judiciary" and "the justice system" as it has been traditionally conceived. Indeed, the kinds of considerations that would serve to justify the decision to enact one form of protective legislation over another "lie in the realm of ... public policy," which this Court has specifically divorced from the principles of fundamental justice. The principles of fundamental justice therefore have little relevance in the present circumstances, which invoke the inherent domain of the legislature and not that of the justice system.

[387] In view of this, any limitation that might be placed on the s. 7 right asserted in this case—if not in all cases where it is a positive right that is asserted—must be found, not in the principles of fundamental justice, but in the reasonable limits prescribed by law that can be justified in a free and democratic society. Accordingly, it is to s. 1 that we must turn. ...

[391] In this case, the legislated differential treatment, or underinclusion, is purportedly directed at: (1) preventing the attraction of young adults to social assistance; and (2) facilitating their integration into the workforce by encouraging participation in the employment programs. Insofar as either of these "double objectives" is understood as being principally driven by cost considerations, it would fail (barring cases of prohibitive cost) to be pressing and substantial. However, it is possible to frame these objectives in such a way as to ensure that they are properly adapted to the justificatory analysis under s. 1 by focusing instead on their long-term tendency to promote the liberty and inherent dignity of young people. Thus framed, they might indeed satisfy the "pressing and substantial objective" requirement under *Oakes*.

[392] The problem, in my view, is that subsequent stages of the *Oakes* analysis raise doubts concerning the appropriateness of framing the objectives in this manner. For example, it is difficult to accept that denial of the basic means of subsistence is rationally connected to values of promoting the long-term liberty and inherent dignity of young adults. Indeed, the long-term importance of continuing education and integration into the workforce is undermined where those at whom such "help" is directed cannot meet their basic short-term subsistence requirements. Without the ability to secure the immediate needs of the present, the future is little more than a far-off possibility, remote both in perception and in reality. We have already seen, for example, how the inability to afford a telephone, suitable clothes and transportation makes job hunting difficult if not impossible. More drastically, inadequate food and shelter interfere with the capacity both for learning as well as for work itself. There appears, therefore, to be little rational connection between the objectives, as tentatively framed, and the means adopted in pursuit of those objectives. ...

[394] This is sufficient, in my view, to establish that the government has not in this case discharged the always heavy burden of justifying a *prima facie* violation of s. 7 under s. 1. I note in passing that it will be a rare case indeed in which the government can successfully claim that the deleterious effects of denying welfare recipients their most basic requirements are proportional to the salutary effects of doing so in contemplation of long-term benefits, for reasons that are largely encompassed by my discussion of rational connection. This is not that rare case. For this reason among others, I find that the violation of the claimants' right to life, liberty and security of the person is not saved by s. 1. ...

[The dissenting reasons of Justice LeBel are omitted.]

23 Chaoulli v. Quebec (Attorney General), 2005

The *Chaoulli* case involved judicial intervention in a major public policy issue concerning Canada's system of publicly insured health care: did Quebec legislation banning private insurance for services covered by the public health care plan violate the *Canadian Charter of Rights and Freedoms* or the Quebec *Charter of Human Rights and Freedoms*?

The litigation was initiated by George Zeliotis, who had experienced long waiting lists for heart surgery and a hip operation and Jacques Chaoulli, a Montreal physician who had been trying to operate a private hospital. The crux of their case was that the long waiting lists resulting from the public health plan's monopoly of insured medical services violated the right to security of the person under the Canadian Charter and to the inviolability of the person under the Quebec Charter.

The public policy stakes in this case were large. The *Canada Health Act*, which sets out the conditions under which provinces receive federal funding for health services, does not prohibit private insurance for services available through the public plan. However, there is a widespread perception that Canada's system of comprehensive and universal, publicly administered medicare would be jeopardized if private medical insurance became widely available in the country. In addition to Quebec, five other provinces—Alberta, British Columbia, Manitoba, Ontario, and Prince Edward Island—prohibit private insurance for services offered by the public plan. A sixth province, Nova Scotia, has no such ban, but, like Manitoba and Ontario, prohibits physicians operating in the private sector from charging more than physicians receive from the public plan. Only three provinces—New Brunswick, Newfoundland and Labrador, and Saskatchewan—set no limits on what physicians operating outside the public system can charge and have no ban on private medical insurance. But these are smaller provinces with relatively few physicians operating in the private sector. If the Canadian Charter challenge to Quebec's prohibition on private medical insurance were to succeed, similar legislation in provinces containing over 90 percent of Canada's population would be invalid, tipping Canada's health care decisively in the direction of a two-tier system.

Were you to judge the outcome of this case by the media response to the Supreme Court's decision, you would conclude that the challenge had been completely successful and that Quebec's legislation had been found to violate the *Canadian Charter of Rights and Freedoms*, invalidating the ban on private medical insurance all across the country. According to a front page headline in the *Toronto Star*, "The Supreme Court has delivered a hammer-blow to medicare." "The new face of medicare," trumpeted *The Globe and Mail*.[1] But, in fact, the

---

1 Quoted in Peter H. Russell, "Chaoulli: The Political Versus the Legal Life of a Judicial Decision" in Colleen M. Flood, Kent Roach, and Lorne Sossin, eds., *Access to Care, Access to Justice: The Legal Debate over Private Health Insurance in Canada* (Toronto: University of Toronto Press, 2005).

court did not find that the legislation violated the Canadian Charter. The justices split 3 to 3 on that question. The decisive opinion was written by Justice Deschamps, who found that the legislation violated the Quebec Charter. Deschamps did not find it necessary to make a ruling on the Canadian Charter. The three justices—Bastarache, Major, and McLachlin—who did find that the legislation violated the Canadian Charter also found that it violated the Quebec Charter. This means that the common denominator of the court's majority decision was that Quebec's prohibition of private health insurance contravened Quebec's *Charter of Human Rights and Freedoms.* There was no ruling that applied to the rest of Canada. The ban on private health insurance, despite newspaper headlines suggesting the contrary, remained intact elsewhere in the country.

In confining her judgment to the Quebec Charter, Justice Deschamps followed a jurisprudential strategy set down by Justice Jean Beetz in the early years of the Charter when he suggested that it is best, when possible, to decide cases on the basis of rights-protecting laws that do not have the full constitutional weight of the Canadian Charter.[2] Such a strategy Beetz argued will ensure that these statutory, quasi-constitutional instruments continue to play a role in developing the protection of rights and freedoms.

Justice Deschamps accepted the trial judge's finding that the ban on private health care insurance infringed the right to life and security of the person protected in section 7 of the Canadian Charter, and since the right to inviolability of the person in the Quebec Charter is even wider than the right to security of the person, the ban on private insurance must also violate that right. However, Justice Deschamps rejected the trial judge's finding that the Quebec government's rationale for the ban on private insurance satisfies the standard of justification in the Quebec Charter for limiting rights. Justice Deschamps equated that standard of justification with section 1 of the Canadian Charter—except that in her view the burden of proof for meeting the standard is on the government. After reviewing the government's reasons for believing that private health insurance would weaken public medicare, she concluded that the government had failed to prove that its ban on private insurance meets the minimal impairment test—that is, that there are not other ways of protecting public medicare which are less intrusive on the inviolability of the person. Thus, she concludes that the Quebec legislation violates a right guaranteed by the Quebec Charter and is not a reasonable limit on that right.

The real fireworks in this case were set off by a sharp division among the other six justices who focused their opinions on section 7 of the Canadian Charter. Chief Justice McLachlin, Justice Major, and Justice Bastarache found that the ban on private health care violates section 7 and cannot be justified as a reasonable limit under section 1. The other three justices, Binnie, LeBel, and Fish, disagreed. The crux of their disagreement is the interpretation of "principles of fundamental justice" in section 7. All six justices agreed with the trial judge's conclusion that waiting-list delays in the public health system infringe the right to life and security of the person—although the Binnie group underlined that it is some Quebec residents,

---

2   In *Singh v. Minister of Employment and Immigration,* [1985] 1 S.C.R. 177, Justice Beetz and two other justices based their decision that refugee applicants were entitled to a hearing on the statutory *Canadian Bill of Rights.* Three other justices based a similar finding on the *Canadian Charter of Rights and Freedoms.*

not all Quebecers, who experience this deprivation. It is on the second part of section 7 that the judges divided: has the deprivation of the rights been done in a way that breaches "principles of fundamental justice"? The judges agreed that these words require that laws which encroach on the right to life and security must not be "arbitrary," but they differed over what "arbitrary" means. For the chief justice's group, if a law encroaching on a section 7 right cannot be shown to be necessary, it breaches principles of fundamental justice. For the Binnie group, the test is whether the law is related to the objective that lies behind it and does not contradict that objective. The Binnie trio's understanding of "principles of fundamental justice" clearly sets a much lower standard for government to meet than the chief justice trio's test of necessity.

It is evident that much more lies behind this split in the court than a technical point of jurisprudence. The two groups of justices appeared to have profoundly different views on the extent to which Charter-based judicial review should second-guess the policy decisions of democratic governments. The chief justice's group regarded the arguments of government as well as those of the Romanow Commission of Inquiry as unproven assertions of belief. They had confidence in their own assessment of health policy in other jurisdictions, which led them to the observation that public medicare systems can function without prohibitions on private insurance. On that basis they concluded that such a prohibition is unnecessary and therefore arbitrary. The Binnie group was clearly upset by this judicial foray into the field of policy analysis. They were satisfied that the ban on public health insurance is well connected to the government's aim to sustain a high quality, needs-based, public medicare system. They contended that a facts-based debate about the merits of one-tier versus two-tier health systems "does not fit easily within the institutional competence of courts of law."

Echoes of the right-versus-left political debate over medicare can be heard in these conflicting judicial opinions. Justice Deschamps talked somewhat scathingly about the "iconic status" of Canada's medicare program and the emotional way in which its supporters, including her colleagues, Justices Binnie and LeBel, defend it. The chief justice's group talked about the medicare program giving the public plan "a virtual monopoly" that effectively limits access to private medicine to the very rich. The opinion of the Binnie group resonates with an opposing ideology. These justices contended that the beneficiaries of removing the ban on private health insurance would be "the more advantaged members of society" and they recalled the admonition of an earlier chief justice, Brian Dickson, that the Canadian Charter should not become an instrument to be used by the wealthy to "roll back" the benefits of a legislative scheme that helps the poorer members of society.

It would not have been difficult for the Quebec government to bring in legislation overriding this decision. Indeed, this is what the opposition Parti Québécois urged should be done. The Charest Liberal government decided to implement the court's decision—but in a very limited way. It brought in legislation allowing private health insurance for cataract surgery and knee and hip replacements, but imposing strict restrictions on the expansion of private care.[3] ∼

---

3   Rheal Seguin, "Quebec tables bill to expand private health coverage: 'Rigid' checks are to oversee clinic care" *The Globe and Mail* (16 June 2006).

Discussion Questions

1. In what way did media coverage of this decision distort its real legal significance?

2. How and why did McLachlin, Major, and Bastarache differ from Binnie, LeBel, and Fish in their appraisal of the report of the Romanow Commission?

3. If the McLachlin, Major, and Bastarache approach to section 7 became the court's majority position, how would this affect Charter-based judicial review?

CHAOULLI v. QUEBEC (ATTORNEY GENERAL)
2005 SCC 35, [2005] 1 S.C.R. 791

Hearing: June 8, 2004; Judgment: June 9, 2005.*

Present: McLachlin C.J. and Major, Bastarache, Binnie, LeBel, Deschamps, and Fish JJ.

Interveners: Attorney General of Ontario, Attorney General of New Brunswick, Attorney General for Saskatchewan, Augustin Roy, Senator Michael Kirby, Senator Marjory Lebreton, Senator Catherine Callbeck, Senator Joan Cook, Senator Jane Cordy, Senator Joyce Fairbairn, Senator Wilbert Keon, Senator Lucie Pépin, Senator Brenda Robertson and Senator Douglas Roche, Canadian Medical Association and Canadian Orthopaedic Association, Canadian Labour Congress, Charter Committee on Poverty Issues and Canadian Health Coalition, Cambie Surgeries Corp., False Creek Surgical Centre Inc., Delbrook Surgical Centre Inc., Okanagan Plastic Surgery Centre Inc., Specialty MRI Clinics Inc., Fraser Valley MRI Ltd., Image One MRI Clinic Inc., McCallum Surgical Centre Ltd., 4111044 Canada Inc., South Fraser Surgical Centre Inc., Victoria Surgery Ltd., Kamloops Surgery Centre Ltd., Valley Cosmetic Surgery Associates Inc., Surgical Centres Inc., British Columbia Orthopaedic Association, and British Columbia Anesthesiologists Society.

* On August 4, 2005, the Court stayed the judgment for a period of 12 months from the date of the judgment.

English version of the reasons delivered by

[1] **DESCHAMPS J.:** Quebeckers are prohibited from taking out insurance to obtain in the private sector services that are available under Quebec's public health care plan. Is this prohibition justified by the need to preserve the integrity of the plan?

[2] As we enter the 21st century, health care is a constant concern. The public health care system, once a source of national pride, has become the subject of frequent and sometimes bitter criticism. This appeal does not question the appropriateness of the state making health care available to all Quebeckers. On the contrary, all the parties stated that they support this kind of role for the government. Only the state

can make available to all Quebeckers the social safety net consisting of universal and accessible health care. The demand for health care is constantly increasing, and one of the tools used by governments to control this increase has been the management of waiting lists. The choice of waiting lists as a management tool falls within the authority of the state and not of the courts. The appellants do not claim to have a solution that will eliminate waiting lists. Rather, they submit that the delays resulting from waiting lists violate their rights under the *Charter of Human Rights and Freedoms*, R.S.Q., c. C-12 ("*Quebec Charter*"), and the *Canadian Charter of Rights and Freedoms* ("*Canadian Charter*"). They contest the validity of the prohibition in Quebec, as provided for in s. 15 of the *Health Insurance Act*, R.S.Q., c. A-29 ("*HEIA*"), and s. 11 of the *Hospital Insurance Act*, R.S.Q., c. A-28 ("*HOIA*"), on private insurance for health care services that are available in the public system. The appellants contend that the prohibition deprives them of access to health care services that do not come with the wait they face in the public system.

[3] The two sections in issue read as follows:

15. No person shall make or renew a contract of insurance or make a payment under a contract of insurance under which an insured service is furnished or under which all or part of the cost of such a service is paid to a resident or a deemed resident of Québec or to another person on his behalf.

11. (1) No one shall make or renew, or make a payment under a contract under which

(a) a resident is to be provided with or to be reimbursed for the cost of any hospital service that is one of the insured services;

(b) payment is conditional upon the hospitalization of a resident; or

(c) payment is dependent upon the length of time the resident is a patient in a facility maintained by an institution contemplated in section 2.

[4] In essence, the question is whether Quebeckers who are prepared to spend money to get access to health care that is, in practice, not accessible in the public sector because of waiting lists may be validly prevented from doing

so by the state. For the reasons that follow, I find that the prohibition infringes the right to personal inviolability and that it is not justified by a proper regard for democratic values, public order and the general well-being of the citizens of Quebec.

[5] The validity of the prohibition is contested by the appellants, George Zeliotis and Jacques Chaoulli. Over the years, Mr. Zeliotis has experienced a number of health problems and has used medical services that were available in the public system, including heart surgery and a number of operations on his hip. The difficulties he encountered prompted him to speak out against waiting times in the public health care system. Mr. Chaoulli is a physician who has tried unsuccessfully to have his home-delivered medical activities recognized and to obtain a licence to operate an independent private hospital. Mr. Zeliotis and Mr. Chaoulli joined forces to apply to the court by way of motion for a declaration that s. 15 *HEIA* and s. 11 *HOIA* are unconstitutional and invalid. ...

I. Legislative Context

[16] Although the federal government has express jurisdiction over certain matters relating to health, such as quarantine, and the establishment and maintenance of marine hospitals (s. 91(11) of the *Constitution Act, 1867*), it is in practice that it imposes its views on the provincial governments in the health care sphere by means of its spending power. ... In order to receive federal funds, a provincial plan must conform to the principles set out in the *Canada Health Act*, R.S.C. 1985, c. C-6: it must be administered publicly, it must be comprehensive and universal, it must provide for portability from one province to another and it must be accessible to everyone. These broad principles have become the hallmarks of Canadian identity. Any measure that might be perceived as compromising them has a polarizing effect on public opinion. The debate about the effectiveness of public health care has become an emotional one. The Romanow Report stated that the *Canada Health Act* has achieved an iconic status that makes it untouchable by politicians. ... The tone adopted by my colleagues Binnie and LeBel JJ. is indicative of this type of emotional reaction. It leads them to characterize the debate as pitting rich against poor when the case is really about determining whether a specific measure is justified under either the *Quebec Charter* or the *Canadian Charter*. I believe that it is essential to take a step back and consider these various reactions objectively. The *Canada Health Act* does not prohibit private health care services, nor does it provide benchmarks for the length of waiting times that might be regarded as consistent with the principles it lays down, and in particular with the principle of real accessibility.

[17] In reality, a large proportion of health care is delivered by the private sector. First, there are health care services in respect of which the private sector acts, in a sense, as a subcontractor and is paid by the state. There are also many services that are not delivered by the state, such as home care or care provided by professionals other than physicians. In 2001, private sector services not paid for by the state accounted for nearly 30 percent of total health care spending (Canadian Institute for Health Information, *National Health Expenditure Trends, 1975–2003* (2003), at p. 16, Figure 13, "Public and Private Shares of Total Health Expenditure, by Use of Funds, Canada, 2001"). In the case of private sector services that are not covered by the public plan, Quebeckers may take out private insurance without the spectre of the two-tier system being evoked. The *Canada Health Act* is therefore only a general framework that leaves considerable latitude to the provinces. In analysing the justification for the prohibition, I will have occasion to briefly review some of the provisions of Canada's provincial plans. The range of measures shows that there are many ways to deal with the public sector/private sector dynamic without resorting to a ban. ...

III. Priority Given to Arguments Based on the Quebec Charter

[25] The *Canadian Charter* is neither an ordinary statute nor an extraordinary statute like the *Canadian Bill of Rights*, R.S.C. 1985, App. III. It is a part of the Constitution: *Law Society of Upper Canada v. Skapinker*, [1984] 1 S.C.R. 357, at p. 365. As a result, the *Canadian Charter* is different from the *Quebec Charter* in that the *Quebec Charter* is the product of the legislative will of Quebec's National Assembly. In addition, while the *Quebec Charter* has no constitutional dimension, it is also different from ordinary statutes by virtue of its considerably broader purpose: to guarantee respect for human beings (see A. Morel, "La coexistence des Chartes canadienne et québécoise: problèmes d'interaction" (1986), 17 R.D.U.S. 49). The *Quebec Charter* protects not only the fundamental rights and freedoms, but also certain civil, political, economic and social rights. By virtue of s. 52, Quebec courts have the power to review legislation to determine whether it is consistent with the rules set out in the *Quebec Charter*. The *Quebec Charter* has an identity that is independent of the statutes of Quebec.

[26] In the case of a challenge to a Quebec statute, it is appropriate to look first to the rules that apply specifically in Quebec before turning to the *Canadian Charter*, especially where the provisions of the two charters are susceptible of producing cumulative effects, but where the rules are not identical. This is the approach suggested by Beetz J. in *Singh v. Minister of Employment and Immigration*, [1985] 1 S.C.R. 177, at p. 224:

Thus, the *Canadian Bill of Rights* retains all its force and effect, together with the various provincial charters of rights. Because these constitutional or quasi-constitutional instruments are drafted differently, they are susceptible of producing cumulative effects for the better protection of rights and freedoms. But this beneficial result will be lost if these instruments fall into neglect.

[27] In the instant case, s. 7 of the *Canadian Charter* and s. 1 of the *Quebec Charter* have numerous points in common:

Canadian Charter

7. Everyone has the right to life, liberty and security of the person and the right not to be deprived thereof except in accordance with the principles of fundamental justice.

Quebec Charter

1. Every human being has a right to life, and to personal security, inviolability and freedom.

[28] The similarities between these two provisions probably explain in part why the Superior Court and the Court of Appeal considered only the *Canadian Charter* in their decisions. With regard to certain aspects of the two charters, the law is the same. For example, the wording of the right to life and liberty is identical. It is thus appropriate to consider the two together. Distinctions must be made, however, and I believe that it is important to begin by considering the specific protection afforded by the *Quebec Charter* for the reason that it is not identical to the protection afforded by the *Canadian Charter*.

[29] The most obvious distinction is the absence of any reference to the principles of fundamental justice in s. 1 of the *Quebec Charter*. The analysis dictated by s. 7 of the *Canadian Charter* is twofold. Under the approach that is generally taken, the claimant must prove, first, that a deprivation of the right to life, liberty and security of the person has occurred and, second, that the deprivation is not in accordance with the principles of fundamental justice. ...

[30] According to established principles, the onus is on the claimant to prove a violation of constitutional rights: *R. v. Collins*, [1987] 1 S.C.R. 265, and *Rio Hotel Ltd. v. New Brunswick (Liquor Licensing Board)*, [1987] 2 S.C.R. 59; see also Hogg, at p. 44-3. Under s. 7 of the *Canadian Charter*, the claimant would thus have a dual burden. The effect of placing this burden of proof on the claimant is that it makes his or her task more onerous. There is no such dual burden of proof under the *Quebec Charter* because the principles of fundamental justice are not incorporated into s. 1 of the *Quebec Charter*. For this reason, the *Quebec Charter* has a scope that is potentially broader. This characteristic should not be disregarded.

[31] Ruling on the points in issue by applying the *Quebec Charter* enhances an instrument that is specific to Quebec; this approach is also justified by the rules of Canadian constitutional law. ...

V. Infringement of the Rights Protected by Section 1 of the Quebec Charter

[37] The appellant Zeliotis argues that the prohibition infringes Quebeckers' right to life. Some patients die as a result of long waits for treatment in the public system when they could have gained prompt access to care in the private sector. Were it not for s. 11 *HOIA* and s. 15 *HEIA*, they could buy private insurance and receive care in the private sector.

[38] The Superior Court judge stated [TRANSLATION] "that there [are] serious problems in certain sectors of the health care system" (p. 823). The evidence supports that assertion. After meticulously analysing the evidence, she found that the right to life and liberty protected by s. 7 of the *Canadian Charter* had been infringed. As I mentioned above, the right to life and liberty protected by the *Quebec Charter* is the same as the right protected by the *Canadian Charter*. Quebec society is no different from Canadian society when it comes to respect for these two fundamental rights. Accordingly, the trial judge's findings of fact concerning the infringement of the right to life and liberty protected by s. 7 of the *Canadian Charter* apply to the right protected by s. 1 of the *Quebec Charter*.

[39] Not only is it common knowledge that health care in Quebec is subject to waiting times, but a number of witnesses acknowledged that the demand for health care is potentially unlimited and that waiting lists are a more or less implicit form of rationing. ...

[41] The *Quebec Charter* also protects the right to personal inviolability. This is a very broad right. The meaning of "inviolability" is broader than the meaning of the word "security" used in s. 7 of the *Canadian Charter*. In civil liability cases, it has long been recognized in Quebec that personal inviolability includes both physical inviolability and mental or psychological inviolability. ...

[42] In the instant case, Dr. Eric Lenczner, an orthopaedic surgeon, testified that the usual waiting time of one year for patients who require orthopaedic surgery increases the risk that their injuries will become irreparable. Clearly, not everyone on a waiting list is in danger of dying before being treated. According to Dr. Edwin Coffey, people may face a wide variety of problems while waiting. For example, a person with chronic arthritis who is waiting for a hip replacement may experience considerable pain. Dr. Lenczner also stated that many patients on non-urgent waiting lists for orthopaedic surgery are in pain and cannot walk or enjoy any real quality of life.

[43] Canadian jurisprudence shows support for interpreting the right to security of the person generously in relation to delays. In *R. v. Morgentaler*, [1988] 1 S.C.R. 30, at p. 59, Dickson C.J. found, based on the consequences of delays, that the procedure then provided for in s. 251 of the *Criminal Code*, R.S.C. 1970, c. C-34, jeopardized the right to security of the person. Beetz J., at pp. 105-6, with Estey J. concurring, was of the opinion that the delay created an additional risk to health and constituted a violation of the right to security of the person. ... If the evidence establishes that the right to security of the person has been infringed, it supports, *a fortiori*, the finding that the right to the inviolability of the person has been infringed.

[44] In the opinion of my colleagues Binnie and LeBel JJ., there is an internal mechanism that safeguards the public health system. According to them, Quebeckers may go outside the province for treatment where services are not available in Quebec. This possibility is clearly not a solution for the system's deficiencies. The evidence did not bring to light any administrative mechanism that would permit Quebeckers suffering as a result of waiting times to obtain care outside the province. The possibility of obtaining care outside Quebec is case-specific and is limited to crisis situation.

[45] I find that the trial judge did not err in finding that the prohibition on insurance for health care already insured by the state constitutes an infringement of the right to life and security. This finding is no less true in the context of s. 1 of the *Quebec Charter*. Quebeckers are denied a solution that would permit them to avoid waiting lists, which are used as a tool to manage the public plan. I will now consider the justification advanced under s. 9.1 of the *Quebec Charter*.

VI. Justification for the Prohibition

[46] Section 9.1 of the *Quebec Charter* sets out the standard for justification. It reads as follows:

> **9.1.** In exercising his fundamental freedoms and rights, a person shall maintain a proper regard for democratic values, public order and the general well-being of the citizens of Québec.

In this respect, the scope of the freedoms and rights, and limits to their exercise, may be fixed by law.

[47] The Court had occasion to consider the scope of this provision in *Ford v. Quebec (Attorney General)*, [1988] 2 S.C.R. 712. In its view, in the context of the relationship between citizens and the state, the provision is of the same nature as s. 1 of the *Canadian Charter*. ...

[48] The interpretation adopted by the Court in that decision still applies today, and the analytical approach developed in *R. v. Oakes*, [1986] 1 S.C.R. 103, must be followed. This approach is well known. First, the court must determine whether the objective of the legislation is pressing and substantial. Next, it must determine whether the means chosen to attain this legislative end are reasonable and demonstrably justifiable in a free and democratic society. For this second part of the analysis, three tests must be met: (1) the existence of a rational connection between the measure and the aim of the legislation; (2) minimal impairment of the protected right by the measure; and (3) proportionality between the effect of the measure and its objective (*Egan v. Canada*, [1995] 2 S.C.R. 513, at para. 182). It is the minimal impairment analysis that has proven to be the most delicate stage in the instant case. The other stages cannot, however, be bypassed.

A. Purpose of the Statute

[49] The prohibitions are set out in the *HOIA* and the *HEIA*. The general objective of these statutes is to promote health care of the highest possible quality for all Quebeckers regardless of their ability to pay. ...

B. Proportionality

(1) Rational Connection

[57] The next question is whether the prohibition on private insurance has a rational connection with the objective of preserving the public plan. Does this measure assist the state in implementing a public plan that provides high-quality health care services that are accessible to all residents of Quebec?

[58] According to the trial judge, the effect of the measure adopted by the state is to "significantly" limit private health care. Although the effect of a measure is not always indicative of a rational connection between the measure and its objective, in the instant case the consequences show an undeniable connection between the objective and the measure. The public plan is preserved because it has a quasi-monopoly.

(2) Minimal Impairment

[59] The trial judge made certain assertions that suggest she found that the measure met the minimal impairment test. However, her approach was not appropriate to s. 9.1 of the *Quebec Charter*. Her comments must therefore be considered in their context, not only because she failed to address the *Quebec Charter*, but also because she appears to have placed the onus on the appellants to prove that private insurance would provide a solution to the problem of waiting lists. ...

[60] The burden of proof does not rest on the appellants. Under s. 9.1 of the *Quebec Charter*, the onus was on the Attorney General of Quebec to prove that the prohibition is justified. He had to show that the measure met the minimal impairment

test. The trial judge did not consider the evidence on the basis that there was a burden on the Attorney General of Quebec.

[61] To determine whether the Attorney General of Quebec has discharged this burden, I will begin by analysing the expert evidence submitted to the Superior Court. I will then examine the situations in the other provinces of Canada and in certain countries of the Organization for Economic Cooperation and Development ("OECD"). Finally, I will address the deference the Court must show where the government has chosen among a number of measures that may impair protected rights.

(a) The Experts Who Testified at Trial and Whose Evidence Was Accepted by the Superior Court Judge

[62] As can be seen from the evidence, the arguments made in support of the position that the integrity of the public system could be jeopardized by abolishing the prohibition can be divided into two groups. The first group of arguments relates to human reactions of the various people affected by the public plan, while the second group relates to the consequences for the plan itself.

(i) Human Reactions

[63]

1. Some witnesses asserted that the emergence of the private sector would lead to a reduction in popular support in the long term because the people who had private insurance would no longer see any utility for the public plan. ...
2. Some witnesses were of the opinion that the quality of care in the public plan would decline because the most influential people would no longer have any incentive to bring pressure for improvements to the plan. Dr. Bergman cited a study by the World Bank in support of his expert report. Dr. Marmor relied on this argument but confirmed that there is no direct evidence to support this view.
3. There would be a reduction in human resources in the public plan because many physicians and other health care professionals would leave the plan out of a motive for profit: Dr. Charles J. Wright cited a study done in the United Kingdom, but admitted that he had read only a summary and not the study itself. Although Dr. Marmor supported the assertion, he testified that there is really no way to confirm it empirically. In his opinion, it is simply a matter of common sense.
4. An increase in the use of private health care would contribute to an increase in the supply of care for profit and lead to a decline in the professionalism and ethics of physicians working in hospitals. No

study was cited in support of this opinion that seems to be based only on the witnesses' common sense.

[64] It is apparent from this summary that for each threat mentioned, no study was produced or discussed in the Superior Court. ... The evidence that the existence of the health care system would be jeopardized by human reactions to the emergence of a private system carries little weight.

(ii) Impact on the Public Plan

[65]

1. There would be an increase in overall health expenditures: the alleged increase would come primarily from the additional expenditures incurred by individuals who decide to take out private insurance; the rest of the increase in costs would be attributable to the cost of management of the private system by the state.
2. Insurers would reject the most acute patients, leaving the most serious cases to be covered by the public plan.
3. In a private system, physicians would tend to lengthen waiting times in the public sector in order to direct patients to the private sector from which they would derive a profit.

[66] Once again, I am of the opinion that the reaction some witnesses described is highly unlikely in the Quebec context. First, if the increase in overall costs is primarily attributable to the individual cost of insurance, it would be difficult for the state to prevent individuals who wished to pay such costs from choosing how to manage their own finances. Furthermore, because the public plan already handles all the serious cases, I do not see how the situation could be exacerbated if that plan were relieved of the clientele with less serious health problems. ...

[69] There is other evidence in the record that might be of assistance in the justification analysis. In this regard, it is useful to observe the approaches of the other Canadian provinces because they also operate within the financial framework established by the *Canada Health Act.*

(b) Overview of Other Provincial Plans

[70] The approach to the role of the private sector taken by the other nine provinces of Canada is by no means uniform. In addition to Quebec, six other provinces have adopted measures to discourage people from turning to the private sector. The other three, in practice, give their residents free access to the private sector.

[71] Ontario (*Health Care Accessibility Act*, R.S.O. 1990, c. H.3, s. 2), Nova Scotia (*Health Services and Insurance Act,*

R.S.N.S. 1989, c. 197, s. 29(2)) and Manitoba (*Health Services Insurance Act*, R.S.M. 1987, c. H35, s. 95(1)) prohibit non-participating physicians from charging their patients more than what physicians receive from the public plan. In practice, there is no financial incentive to opt for the private sector. It is worth noting that Nova Scotia does not prohibit insurance contracts to cover health care obtained in the private sector. Ontario and Manitoba prohibit insurance contracts but refund amounts paid by patients to non-participating physicians.

[72] Alberta (*Alberta Health Care Insurance Act*, R.S.A. 2000, c. A-20, s. 9(1)), British Columbia (*Medicare Protection Act*, R.S.B.C. 1996, c. 286, s. 18(2)) and Prince Edward Island (*Health Services Payment Act*, R.S.P.E.I. 1988, c. H-2, ss. 10, 10.1 and 14.1) have adopted a very different approach. In those provinces, non-participating physicians are free to set the amount of their fees, but the cost of the services is not refunded and contracts for insurance to cover services offered by the public plan are prohibited. This is the same policy as has been adopted by Quebec.

[73] Saskatchewan (*Saskatchewan Medical Care Insurance Act*, R.S.S. 1978, c. S-29, s. 18(1.1)), New Brunswick (*Medical Services Payment Act*, R.S.N.B. 1973, c. M-7, s. 2.01(a), and *General Regulation—Medical Services Payment Act*, N.B. Reg. 84-20, Sch. 2, para. (n.1)), and Newfoundland and Labrador (*Medical Care Insurance Act*, 1999, S.N.L. 1999, c. M-5.1, s. 10(5), and *Medical Care Insurance Insured Services Regulations*, C.N.L.R. 21/96, s. 3) are open to the private sector. New Brunswick allows physicians to set their own fees. In Saskatchewan, this right is limited to non-participating physicians. The cost is not refunded by the public plan, but patients may purchase insurance to cover those costs. Newfoundland and Labrador agrees to reimburse patients, up to the amount covered by the public plan, for fees paid to non-participating physicians. In Newfoundland and Labrador, patients may subscribe to private insurance to cover the difference.

[74] Even if it were assumed that the prohibition on private insurance could contribute to preserving the integrity of the system, the variety of measures implemented by different provinces shows that prohibiting insurance contracts is by no means the only measure a state can adopt to protect the system's integrity. …

[75] In the context of s. 9.1 of the *Quebec Charter*, I must conclude that a comparison with the plans of the other Canadian provinces does not support the position of the Attorney General of Quebec.

[76] There are also many reports in the record on which to base an overview of current practices in several OECD countries.

(c) Overview of Practices in Certain OECD Countries

[77] Mr. Chaoulli, echoed by at least one of the witnesses (Dr. Coffey), argued that Canada is the only OECD country to prohibit insurance for health care provided by non-participating physicians. This assertion must be clarified as it relates to Canada: it is true of only six provinces. It must also be qualified in the international context: while no such prohibition is found in any other OECD country, it should nonetheless be mentioned that measures to protect the public plan have been implemented in a number of countries, even some of the countries whose health care plans have been provided as models. There is no single model; the approach in Europe is no more uniform than in Canada.

[78] In a number of European countries, there is no insurance paid for directly out of public funds. In Austria, services are funded through decentralized agencies that collect the necessary funds from salaries. People who want to obtain health care in the private sector in addition to the services covered by the mandatory social insurance are free to do so, but private insurance may cover no more than 80 percent of the cost billed by professionals practising in the public sector. The same type of plan exists in Germany and the Netherlands, but people who opt for private insurance are not required to pay for the public plan. Only nine percent of Germans opt for private insurance.

[79] Australia's public system is funded in a manner similar to the Quebec system. However, Australia's system is different in that the private and public sectors coexist, and insurance covering private sector health care is not prohibited. The government attempts to balance access to the two sectors by allowing taxpayers to deduct 30 percent of the cost of private insurance. Insurance rates are regulated to prevent insurers from charging higher premiums for higher-risk individuals (C.H. Tuohy, C.M. Flood and M. Stabile, "How Does Private Finance Affect Public Health Care Systems? Marshaling the Evidence from OECD Nations" (2004), 29 *J. Health Pol.* 359)

[80] The United Kingdom does not restrict access to private insurance for health care (*The Health of Canadians—The Federal Role*, vol. 3, *Health Care Systems in Other Countries*, Interim Report (2002), at p. 38). Nor does the United Kingdom limit a physician's ability to withdraw from the public plan. However, physicians working full-time in public hospitals are limited in the amounts that they may bill in the private sector to supplement income earned in the public sector (p. 40). Only 11.5 percent of Britons had taken out private insurance in 1998 (Tuohy, Flood and Stabile, at p. 374), and only 8 percent of hospital beds in the United Kingdom are private (Quebec and France, *Health Indicators: International Comparisons: 15 years of Evolution: Canada, France, Germany,*

Québec, United Kingdom, United States (1998), at p. 55). New Zealand has a plan similar to that of the United Kingdom with the difference that 40 percent of New Zealanders have private insurance (Tuohy, Flood and Stabile, at p. 363).

[81] Sweden does not prohibit private insurance, and the state does not refund the cost of health care paid for in the private sector. Private insurance accounts for only two percent of total health care expenditures and there are only nine private hospitals. ...

[82] It can be seen from the systems in these various OECD countries that a number of governments have taken measures to protect their public plans from abuse. The measures vary from country to country depending on the nature of their specific systems. For example, in the United Kingdom, there are limits on the amounts physicians may earn in the private sector in addition to what they receive from the public plan. Australia has opted to regulate insurance premiums, but it is alone in this respect. ...

[84] It cannot therefore be concluded from the evidence relating to the Quebec plan or the plans of the other provinces of Canada, or from the evolution of the systems in place in various OECD countries, that the Attorney General of Quebec has discharged his burden of proof under s. 9.1 of the *Quebec Charter*. A number of measures are available to him to protect the integrity of Quebec's health care plan. The choice of prohibiting private insurance contracts is not justified by the evidence. However, is this a case in which the Court should show deference?

(d) Level of Deference Required

... [86] Under the charters, the government is responsible for justifying measures it imposes that impair rights. The courts can consider evidence concerning the historical, social and economic aspects, or any other evidence that may be material.

[87] It cannot be said that the government lacks the necessary resources to show that its legislative action is motivated by a reasonable objective connected with the problem it has undertaken to remedy. The courts are an appropriate forum for a serious and complete debate. As G. Davidov said in "The Paradox of Judicial Deference" (2000-2001), 12 *N.J.C.L.* 133, at p. 143, "[c]ourts do not have to define goals, choose means or come up with ideas. They do not have to create social policies; they just have to understand what the other branches have created. No special expertise is required for such an understanding." In fact, if a court is satisfied that all the evidence has been presented, there is nothing that would justify it in refusing to perform its role on the ground that it should merely defer to the government's position. When the courts are given the tools they need to make a

decision, they should not hesitate to assume their responsibilities. Deference cannot lead the judicial branch to abdicate its role in favour of the legislative branch or the executive branch. ...

[89] The courts have a duty to rise above political debate. They leave it to the legislatures to develop social policy. But when such social policies infringe rights that are protected by the charters, the courts cannot shy away from considering them. The judicial branch plays a role that is not played by the legislative branch. ...

[90] From this perspective, it is through the combined action of legislatures and courts that democratic objectives can be achieved. ...

[91] The court's reasons for showing deference must always reflect the two guiding principles of justification: the measure must be consistent with democratic values and it must be necessary in order to maintain public order and the general well-being of citizens. The variety of circumstances that may be presented to a court is not conducive to the rigidity of an exhaustive list. ...

[97] For many years, the government has failed to act; the situation continues to deteriorate. This is not a case in which missing scientific data would allow for a more informed decision to be made. The principle of prudence that is so popular in matters relating to the environment and to medical research cannot be transposed to this case. Under the Quebec plan, the government can control its human resources in various ways, whether by using the time of professionals who have already reached the maximum for payment by the state, by applying the provision that authorizes it to compel even non-participating physicians to provide services (s. 30 *HEIA*) or by implementing less restrictive measures, like those adopted in the four Canadian provinces that do not prohibit private insurance or in the other OECD countries. While the government has the power to decide what measures to adopt, it cannot choose to do nothing in the face of the violation of Quebeckers' right to security. The government has not given reasons for its failure to act. Inertia cannot be used as an argument to justify deference.

[98] In the instant case, the effectiveness of the prohibition has by no means been established. The government has not proved, by the evidence in the record, that the measure minimally impairs the protected rights. Moreover, the evidence shows that a wide variety of measures are available to governments, as can be seen from the plans of other provinces and other countries.

(3) Proportionality

[99] Having found that s. 15 *HEIA* and s. 11 *HOIA* do not meet the minimal impairment test, I do not need to consider

proportionality. If the prohibition is not minimally impairing, it obviously cannot be regarded as a measure that sufficiently addresses the effect of the measure on the protected rights.

VII. Conclusion

[100] The relief sought by the appellants does not necessarily provide a complete response to the complex problem of waiting lists. However, it was not up to the appellants to find a way to remedy a problem that has persisted for a number of years and for which the solution must come from the state itself. Their only burden was to prove that their right to life and to personal inviolability had been infringed. They have succeeded in proving this. The Attorney General of Quebec, on the other hand, has not proved that the impugned measure, the prohibition on private insurance, was justified under s. 9.1 of the *Quebec Charter*. Given that this finding is sufficient to dispose of the appeal, it is not necessary to answer the other constitutional questions.

[101] For these reasons, I would allow the appeal with costs throughout and would answer the questions relating to the *Quebec Charter* as follows:

Question 1: Does s. 11 of the *Hospital Insurance Act*, R.S.Q., c. A-28, infringe the rights guaranteed by s. 1 of the *Quebec Charter*?

Answer: Yes.

Question 2: If so, is the infringement a reasonable limit prescribed by law as can be demonstrably justified in a free and democratic society under s. 9.1 of the *Quebec Charter*?

Answer: No.

Question 3: Does s. 15 of the *Health Insurance Act*, R.S.Q., c. A-29, infringe the rights guaranteed by s. 1 of the *Quebec Charter*?

Answer: Yes.

Question 4: If so, is the infringement a reasonable limit prescribed by law as can be demonstrably justified in a free and democratic society under s. 9.1 of the *Quebec Charter*?

Answer: No.

The reasons of McLachlin C.J. and Major and Bastarache JJ. were delivered by

[102] **THE CHIEF JUSTICE AND MAJOR J.:** We concur in the conclusion of our colleague Deschamps J. that the prohibition against contracting for private health insurance violates s. 1 of the *Quebec Charter of Human Rights and Freedoms*, R.S.Q., c. C-12, and is not justifiable under s. 9.1. On the

argument that the anti-insurance provision also violates s. 7 of the *Canadian Charter of Rights and Freedoms* ("*Charter*"), we conclude that the provision impermissibly limits the right to life, liberty and security of the person protected by s. 7 of the *Charter* and has not been shown to be justified as a reasonable limit under s. 1 of the *Charter*.

[103] The appellants do not seek an order that the government spend more money on health care, nor do they seek an order that waiting times for treatment under the public health care scheme be reduced. They only seek a ruling that because delays in the public system place their health and security at risk, they should be allowed to take out insurance to permit them to access private services.

[104] The *Charter* does not confer a freestanding constitutional right to health care. However, where the government puts in place a scheme to provide health care, that scheme must comply with the *Charter*. We are of the view that the prohibition on medical insurance in s. 15 of the *Health Insurance Act*, R.S.Q., c. A-29, and s. 11 of the *Hospital Insurance Act*, R.S.Q., c. A-28 (see Appendix), violates s. 7 of the *Charter* because it impinges on the right to life, liberty and security of the person in an arbitrary fashion that fails to conform to the principles of fundamental justice.

[105] The primary objective of the *Canada Health Act*, R.S.C. 1985, c. C-6, is "to protect, promote and restore the physical and mental well-being of residents of Canada and *to facilitate reasonable access* to health services without financial or other barriers" (s. 3). By imposing exclusivity and then failing to provide public health care of a reasonable standard within a reasonable time, the government creates circumstances that trigger the application of s. 7 of the *Charter*.

[106] The *Canada Health Act*, the *Health Insurance Act*, and the *Hospital Insurance Act* do not expressly prohibit private health services. However, they limit access to private health services by removing the ability to contract for private health care insurance to cover the same services covered by public insurance. The result is a virtual monopoly for the public health scheme. The state has effectively limited access to private health care except for the very rich, who can afford private care without need of insurance. This virtual monopoly, on the evidence, results in delays in treatment that adversely affect the citizen's security of the person. Where a law adversely affects life, liberty or security of the person, it must conform to the principles of fundamental justice. This law, in our view, fails to do so. ...

I. Section 7 of the Charter

[109] Section 7 of the *Charter* guarantees that "[e]veryone has the right to life, liberty and security of the person and the right not to be deprived thereof except in accordance

with the principles of fundamental justice." The disposition of this appeal therefore requires us to consider (1) whether the impugned provisions deprive individuals of their life, liberty or security of the person; and (2) if so, whether this deprivation is in accordance with the principles of fundamental justice: see, e.g., *R. v. Malmo-Levine*, [2003] 3 S.C.R. 571, 2003 SCC 74, at para. 83.

A. Deprivation of Life, Liberty, or Security of the Person

[110] The issue at this stage is whether the prohibition on insurance for private medical care deprives individuals of their life, liberty or security of the person protected by s. 7 of the *Charter*.

[111] The appellants have established that many Quebec residents face delays in treatment that adversely affect their security of the person and that they would not sustain but for the prohibition on medical insurance. It is common ground that the effect of the prohibition on insurance is to allow only the very rich, who do not need insurance, to secure private health care in order to avoid the delays in the public system. Given the ban on insurance, most Quebeckers have no choice but to accept delays in the medical system and their adverse physical and psychological consequences.

[112] Delays in the public system are widespread and have serious, sometimes grave, consequences. There was no dispute that there is a waiting list for cardiovascular surgery for life-threatening problems. Dr. Daniel Doyle, a cardiovascular surgeon who teaches and practises in Quebec City, testified that a person with coronary disease is [TRANSLATION] "sitting on a bomb" and can die at any moment. He confirmed, without challenge, that patients die while on waiting lists: A.R., at p. 461. Inevitably, where patients have life-threatening conditions, some will die because of undue delay in awaiting surgery. ...

[116] In addition to threatening the life and the physical security of the person, waiting for critical care may have significant adverse psychological effects. Serious psychological effects may engage s. 7 protection for security of the person. These "need not rise to the level of nervous shock or psychiatric illness, but must be greater than ordinary stress or anxiety": *New Brunswick (Minister of Health and Community Services) v. G.(J.)*, [1999] 3 S.C.R. 46, at para. 60. ...

[124] We conclude, based on the evidence, that prohibiting health insurance that would permit ordinary Canadians to access health care, in circumstances where the government is failing to deliver health care in a reasonable manner, thereby increasing the risk of complications and death, interferes with life and security of the person as protected by s. 7 of the *Charter*.

[125] The remaining question is whether this inference is in accordance with the principles of fundamental justice. "[I]f the state [interferes] with security of the person, the *Charter* requires such interference to conform with the principles of fundamental justice": *Morgentaler*, at p. 54, per Dickson C.J.

B. Deprivation in Accordance with the Principles of Fundamental Justice

[126] Having concluded that the ban on private medical insurance constitutes a deprivation of life and security of the person, we now consider whether that deprivation is in accordance with the principles of fundamental justice. Our colleagues Binnie and LeBel JJ. argue that the record here provides no ground for finding that the deprivation violates the principles of fundamental justice. With respect, we cannot agree. ...

[128] The principle of fundamental justice implicated in this case is that laws that affect the life, liberty or security of the person shall not be arbitrary. We are of the opinion that the evidence before the trial judge supports a finding that the impugned provisions are arbitrary and that the deprivation of life and security of the person that flows from them cannot therefore be said to accord with the principles of fundamental justice.

(1) Laws Shall Not Be Arbitrary: A Principle of Fundamental Justice

[129] It is a well-recognized principle of fundamental justice that laws should not be arbitrary: see, e.g., *Malmo-Levine*, at para. 135; *Rodriguez*, at p. 594. The state is not entitled to arbitrarily limit its citizens' rights to life, liberty and security of the person.

[130] A law is arbitrary where "it bears no relation to, or is inconsistent with, the objective that lies behind [it]." To determine whether this is the case, it is necessary to consider the state interest and societal concerns that the provision is meant to reflect: *Rodriguez*, at pp. 594-95.

[131] In order not to be arbitrary, the limit on life, liberty and security requires not only a theoretical connection between the limit and the legislative goal, but a real connection on the facts. The onus of showing lack of connection in this sense rests with the claimant. The question in every case is whether the measure is arbitrary in the sense of bearing no real relation to the goal and hence being manifestly unfair. The more serious the impingement on the person's liberty and security, the more clear must be the connection. Where the individual's very life may be at stake, the reasonable person would expect a clear connection, in theory and in fact, between the measure that puts life at risk and the legislative goals.

(2) Whether the Prohibition on Private
Medical Insurance Is Arbitrary

... [135] The government argues that the interference with security of the person caused by denying people the right to purchase private health insurance is necessary to providing effective health care under the public health system. It argues that if people can purchase private health insurance, they will seek treatment from private doctors and hospitals, which are not banned under the Act. According to the government's argument, this will divert resources from the public health system into private health facilities, ultimately reducing the quality of public care.

[136] In support of this contention, the government called experts in health administration and policy. Their conclusions were based on the "common sense" proposition that the improvement of health services depends on exclusivity (R.R., at p. 591). They did not profess expertise in waiting times for treatment. Nor did they present economic studies or rely on the experience of other countries. They simply assumed, as a matter of apparent logic, that insurance would make private health services more accessible and that this in turn would undermine the quality of services provided by the public health care system.

[137] The appellants, relying on other health experts, disagreed and offered their own conflicting "common sense" argument for the proposition that prohibiting private health insurance is neither necessary nor related to maintaining high quality in the public health care system. Quality public care, they argue, depends not on a monopoly, but on money and management. They testified that permitting people to buy private insurance would make alternative medical care more accessible and reduce the burden on the public system. The result, they assert, would be better care for all. The appellants reinforce this argument by pointing out that disallowing private insurance precludes the vast majority of Canadians (middle-income and low-income earners) from accessing additional care, while permitting it for the wealthy who can afford to travel abroad or pay for private care in Canada.

[138] To this point, we are confronted with competing but unproven "common sense" arguments, amounting to little more than assertions of belief. We are in the realm of theory. But as discussed above, a theoretically defensible limitation may be arbitrary if in fact the limit lacks a connection to the goal.

[139] This brings us to the evidence called by the appellants at trial on the experience of other developed countries with public health care systems which permit access to private health care. The experience of these countries suggests that there is no real connection in fact between prohibition of health insurance and the goal of a quality public health system.

[140] The evidence adduced at trial establishes that many western democracies that do not impose a monopoly on the delivery of health care have successfully delivered to their citizens medical services that are superior to and more affordable than the services that are presently available in Canada. This demonstrates that a monopoly is not necessary or even related to the provision of quality public health care.

[141] In its report *The Health of Canadians—The Federal Role*, the Standing Senate Committee on Social Affairs, Science and Technology discussed in detail the situations in several countries, including Sweden, Germany and the United Kingdom. The following discussion of the health care systems in these three countries is drawn directly from the findings in volume 3 of that report (*The Health of Canadians—The Federal Role*, vol. 3, *Health Care Systems in Other Countries*, Interim Report (2002) ("Kirby Report")).

[142] In Sweden, as in Canada, access to public health care is universal. The public health care system is financed predominantly by the public sector through a combination of general taxation and social insurance (i.e., employer/employee contributions) and employs a user fee mechanism. Unlike in Canada, private health care insurance that covers the same benefits as public insurance is "legal" in Sweden. However, only a small minority of the population purchase private insurance. The result is a system of public health care coverage that provides quality care on a broader basis than in Canada and encompasses physicians, hospital services, drugs and dental care: Kirby Report, vol. 3, at pp. 29-36. In Sweden, the availability of private health care insurance appears not to have harmed the public health care system.

[143] In Germany, public health care insurance is administered by 453 Sickness Funds—private non-profit organizations structured on a regional task or occupational basis. Sickness Fund membership is compulsory for employees with gross incomes lower than approximately $63,000 Canadian, and voluntary for those with gross incomes above that level. Although all Sickness Funds are regulated at the federal level through what is known as the "Social Code Book," they are essentially run by representatives of employees and employers. As in Sweden, public health care coverage is broader in Germany than in Canada, including physician services, hospitals, prescription drugs, diagnostic services, dental care, rehabilitative care, medical devices, psychotherapists, nursing care at home, medical services by non-physicians (physiotherapists, speech therapists, occupational therapists, etc.) and income support during sick leave: Kirby Report, vol. 3, at p. 14.

[144] In Germany, as in Sweden, private health insurance is available to individuals at a certain income level who may voluntarily opt out of the Sickness Funds. Private coverage is currently offered by 52 private insurance companies

that are obliged to offer an insurance policy with the same benefits as the Sickness Funds at a premium that is no higher than the average maximum contribution to the Sickness Funds. ...

[145] Despite the availability of alternatives, 88 percent of the German population are covered by the public Sickness Funds: this includes 14 percent to whom private insurance is available. Of the remaining 12 percent, only 9 percent are covered by private insurance and less than 1 percent have no health insurance at all. The remaining 2 percent are covered by government insurance for military and other personnel: Kirby Report, vol. 3, at p. 15.

[146] The United Kingdom offers a comprehensive public health care system—the National Health Service (NHS)—while also allowing for private insurance. Unlike Canada, the United Kingdom allows people to purchase private health care insurance that covers the same benefits as the NHS if these services are supplied by providers working outside of the NHS. Despite the existence of private insurance, only 11.5 percent of the population have purchased it: Kirby Report, vol. 3, at pp. 37-44. Again, it appears that the public system has not suffered as a result of the existence of private alternatives.

[147] After reviewing a number of public health care systems, the Standing Senate Committee on Social Affairs, Science and Technology concluded in the Kirby Report that far from undermining public health care, private contributions and insurance improve the breadth and quality of health care for all citizens. ...

[149] In summary, the evidence on the experience of other western democracies refutes the government's theoretical contention that a prohibition on private insurance is linked to maintaining quality public health care.

[150] Binnie and LeBel JJ. suggest that the experience of other countries is of little assistance. With respect, we cannot agree. This evidence was properly placed before the trial judge and, unless discredited, stands as the best guide with respect to the question of whether a ban on private insurance is necessary and relevant to the goal of providing quality public health care.

[151] Binnie and LeBel JJ. also suggest that the government's continued commitment to a monopoly on the provision of health insurance cannot be arbitrary because it is rooted in reliance on "a series of authoritative reports [that analysed] health care in this country and in other countries." ... But the conclusions of other bodies on other material cannot be determinative of this litigation. They cannot relieve the courts of their obligation to review government action for consistency with the *Charter* on the evidence before them.

[152] When we look to the evidence rather than to assumptions, the connection between prohibiting private insurance and maintaining quality public health care vanishes. The evidence before us establishes that where the public system fails to deliver adequate care, the denial of private insurance subjects people to long waiting lists and negatively affects their health and security of the person. The government contends that this is necessary in order to preserve the public health system. The evidence, however, belies that contention.

[153] We conclude that on the evidence adduced in this case, the appellants have established that in the face of delays in treatment that cause psychological and physical suffering, the prohibition on private insurance jeopardizes the right to life, liberty and security of the person of Canadians in an arbitrary manner, and is therefore not in accordance with the principles of fundamental justice.

II. Section 1 of the Charter

[154] Having concluded that the prohibition on private health insurance constitutes a breach of s. 7, we must now consider whether that breach can be justified under s. 1 of the *Charter* as a reasonable limit demonstrably justified in a free and democratic society. The evidence called in this case falls short of demonstrating such justification.

[155] The government undeniably has an interest in protecting the public health regime. However, given the absence of evidence that the prohibition on the purchase and sale of private health insurance protects the health care system, the rational connection between the prohibition and the objective is not made out. Indeed, we question whether an arbitrary provision, which by reason of its arbitrariness cannot further its stated objective, will ever meet the rational connection test under *R. v. Oakes*, [1986] 1 S.C.R. 103.

[156] In addition, the resulting denial of access to timely and effective medical care to those who need it is not proportionate to the beneficial effects of the prohibition on private insurance to the health system as a whole. On the evidence here and for the reasons discussed above, the prohibition goes further than necessary to protect the public system: it is not minimally impairing.

[157] Finally, the benefits of the prohibition do not outweigh the deleterious effects. Prohibiting citizens from obtaining private health care insurance may, as discussed, leave people no choice but to accept excessive delays in the public health system. The physical and psychological suffering and risk of death that may result outweigh whatever benefit (and none has been demonstrated to us here) there may be to the system as a whole.

[158] In sum, the prohibition on obtaining private health insurance, while it might be constitutional in circumstances where health care services are reasonable as to both quality and timeliness, is not constitutional where the public system fails to deliver reasonable services. Life, liberty and security of the

person must prevail. To paraphrase Dickson C.J. in *Morgentaler*, at p. 73, if the government chooses to act, it must do so properly.

[159] We agree with Deschamps J.'s conclusion that the prohibition against contracting for private health insurance violates s. 1 of the *Quebec Charter of Human Rights and Freedoms* and is not justifiable under s. 9.1. We also conclude that this prohibition violates s. 7 of the *Canadian Charter of Rights and Freedoms* and cannot be saved under s. 1.

[160] We would allow the appeal, with costs to the appellants throughout.

The reasons of Binnie, LeBel, and Fish JJ. were delivered by

BINNIE AND LEBEL JJ. (dissenting):

I. Introduction

[161] The question in this appeal is whether the province of Quebec not only has the constitutional authority to establish a comprehensive single-tier health plan, but to discourage a second (private) tier health sector by prohibiting the purchase and sale of private health insurance. The appellants argue that timely access to needed medical service is not being provided in the publicly funded system and that the province cannot therefore deny to those Quebeckers (who can qualify) the right to purchase private insurance to pay for medical services whenever and wherever such services can be obtained for a fee, i.e., in the private sector. This issue has been the subject of protracted debate across Canada through several provincial and federal elections. We are unable to agree with our four colleagues who would allow the appeal that such a debate can or should be resolved as a matter of law by judges. We find that, on the *legal* issues raised, the appeal should be dismissed.

[162] Our colleagues the Chief Justice and Major J. state at para. 105:

> By imposing exclusivity and then failing to provide *public health care of a reasonable standard within a reasonable time*, the government creates circumstances that trigger the application of s. 7 of the [*Canadian*] *Charter*. [Emphasis added.]

[163] The Court recently held in *Auton (Guardian ad litem of) v. British Columbia (Attorney General)*, [2004] 3 S.C.R. 657, 2004 SCC 78, that the government was not required to fund the treatment of autistic children. It did not on that occasion address in constitutional terms the scope and nature of "reasonable" health services. Courts will now have to make that determination. What, then, are constitutionally required "reasonable health services"? What is treatment "within a reasonable time"? What are the benchmarks? How short a waiting list is short enough? How many MRIs does the Constitution require? The majority does not tell us. The majority lays down no manageable constitutional standard. The public cannot know, nor can judges or governments know, how much health care is "reasonable" enough to satisfy s. 7 of the *Canadian Charter of Rights and Freedoms* ("*Canadian Charter*") and s. 1 of the *Charter of Human Rights and Freedoms*, R.S.Q. c. C-12 ("*Quebec Charter*"). It is to be hoped that we will know it when we see it.

[164] The policy of the *Canada Health Act*, R.S.C. 1985, c. C-6, and its provincial counterparts is to provide health care based on need rather than on wealth or status. The evidence certainly established that the public health care system put in place to implement this policy has serious and persistent problems. This does not mean that the courts are well placed to perform the required surgery. The resolution of such a complex fact-laden policy debate does not fit easily within the institutional competence or procedures of courts of law. The courts can use s. 7 of the *Canadian Charter* to pre-empt the ongoing public debate only if the current health plan violates an established "principle of fundamental justice." Our colleagues McLachlin C.J. and Major J. argue that Quebec's enforcement of a single-tier health plan meets this legal test because it is "arbitrary." In our view, with respect, the prohibition against private health insurance is a rational consequence of Quebec's commitment to the goals and objectives of the *Canada Health Act*. ...

[166] The Quebec government views the prohibition against private insurance as essential to preventing the current single-tier health system from disintegrating into a *de facto* two-tier system. The trial judge found, and the evidence demonstrated, that there is good reason for this fear. The trial judge concluded that a private health sector fuelled by private insurance would frustrate achievement of the objectives of the *Canada Health Act*. She thus found no *legal* basis to intervene, and declined to do so. This raises the issue of *who* it is that *should* resolve these important and contentious issues. Commissioner Roy Romanow makes the following observation in his Report:

> Some have described it as a perversion of Canadian values that they cannot use their money to purchase faster treatment from a private provider for their loved ones. I believe it is a far greater perversion of Canadian values to accept a system where money, rather than need, determines who gets access to care.
>
> (*Building on Values: The Future of Health Care in Canada: Final Report* (2002) ("Romanow Report"), at p. xx)

Whether or not one endorses this assessment, his premise is that the debate is about *social* values. It is not about constitutional law. We agree.

[167] We believe our colleagues the Chief Justice and Major J. have extended too far the strands of interpretation under the *Canadian Charter* laid down in some of the earlier cases, in particular the ruling on abortion in *R. v. Morgentaler*, [1988] 1 S.C.R. 30 (which involved criminal liability, not public health policy). We cannot find in the constitutional law of Canada a "principle of fundamental justice" dispositive of the problems of waiting lists in the Quebec health system. In our view, the appellants' case does not rest on constitutional law but on their disagreement with the Quebec government on aspects of its social policy. The proper forum to determine the social policy of Quebec in this matter is the National Assembly. ...

II. Analysis

[177] The appellants' principal argument is that the existence of waiting lists in Quebec and the concurrent prohibition on private health insurance violate s. 7 of the *Canadian Charter*, which guarantees everyone the right to life, liberty and security of the person, and the right not to be deprived thereof except in accordance with the principles of fundamental justice.

[178] The legal question raised by our colleagues the Chief Justice and Major J. under the *Canadian Charter* is whether or not the Quebec health plan violates a principle of fundamental justice and, if so, whether the plan can nevertheless be saved under s. 1.

[179] The reasons of our colleague Deschamps J., on the other hand, are limited to s. 1 of the *Quebec Charter* which protects the right of every human being to life and to personal security, inviolability and freedom. The *Quebec Charter* does not talk explicitly about "principles of fundamental justice." Nevertheless, in our view, the legislative limits fixed by the *Quebec Charter* are no more favourable to the appellants' case than are those fixed by the *Canadian Charter*. Rights under the *Quebec Charter* are to be exercised with "proper" regard to "democratic" values (including those of the electorate) "public order and the general well-being of the citizens of Québec" (including those who cannot afford, or may not qualify for, private health insurance coverage). ...

[180] Our colleagues the Chief Justice and Major J. agree with the appellants that there is a violation of s. 7 of the *Canadian Charter*. As mentioned earlier, their opinion rests in substantial part on observations made by various members of this Court in *Morgentaler*. At issue in that case was the criminal liability of doctors and their patients under s. 251 of the *Criminal Code*, R.S.C. 1970, c. C-34, for performing abortions. The nub of the legal challenge was that in creating the abortion offence Parliament had qualified the charge with a "therapeutic abortion" defence, but the defence was not working. The factual and legal issues raised in that criminal law

problem are, we think, far removed from the debate over a two-tier health system. *Morgentaler* applied a "manifest unfairness" test which has never been adopted by the Court outside the criminal law, and certainly not in the context of the design of social programs. The *Morgentaler* judgment fastened on *internal* inconsistencies in s. 251 of the Code, which find no counterpart here. In our view, with respect, *Morgentaler* provides no support for the appellants in this case, as we discuss commencing at para. 259. ...

B. Canadian Charter of Rights and Freedoms

...

(1) The Application of Section 7 to Matters Not Falling Within the Administration of Justice

... [193] Section 7 gives rise to some of the most difficult issues in *Canadian Charter* litigation. Because s. 7 protects the most basic interests of human beings—life, liberty and security—claimants call on the courts to adjudicate many difficult moral and ethical issues. It is therefore prudent, in our view, to proceed cautiously and incrementally in applying s. 7, particularly in distilling those principles that are so vital to our society's conception of "principles of fundamental justice" as to be constitutionally entrenched. ...

[196] It will likely be a rare case where s. 7 will apply in circumstances entirely unrelated to adjudicative or administrative proceedings. That said, the Court has consistently left open the possibility that s. 7 may apply outside the context of the administration of justice: *Gosselin v. Quebec (Attorney General)*, [2002] 4 S.C.R. 429, 2002 SCC 84, at paras. 78-80 and 414.

[197] The Court has been moving away from a narrow approach to s. 7, which restricted the scope of the section to legal rights to be interpreted in light of the rights enumerated in ss. 8 to 14. ... In *Blencoe v. British Columbia (Human Rights Commission)*, [2000] 2 S.C.R. 307, 2000 SCC 44, the majority held that s. 7 can apply outside of the criminal context. Further, in *Winnipeg Child and Family Services v. K.L.W.*, [2000] 2 S.C.R. 519, 2000 SCC 48, the Court noted that it had held in *B.(R.) v. Children's Aid Society of Metropolitan Toronto*, [1995] 1 S.C.R. 315, that the wardship provisions of the *Child Welfare Act*, R.S.O. 1980, c. 66, denying parents the ability to choose medical treatment for their infants, implicated the s. 7 liberty interests of parents.

[198] Placing s. 7 under the heading "Legal Rights" in the *Canadian Charter* does not narrow or control its scope. Such a result would be unduly formalistic and inconsistent with the large, liberal and purposive interpretation of s. 7 that has been the hallmark of this Court's approach since *Re B.C. Motor Vehicle Act*, [1985] 2 S.C.R. 486. This is evidenced by the

refusal of the majority in that case to restrict "principles of fundamental justice" solely to procedural guarantees. Lamer J. observed that "the principles of fundamental justice are to be found in the basic tenets and principles, *not only of our judicial process*, but also of the other components of our legal system" (p. 512 (emphasis added)).

[199] Claimants whose life, liberty or security of the person is put at risk are entitled to relief only to the extent that their complaint arises from a breach of an identifiable principle of fundamental justice. *The real control over the scope and operation of s. 7 is to be found in the requirement that the applicant identify a violation of a principle of fundamental justice.* The further a challenged state action lies from the traditional adjudicative context, the more difficult it will be for a claimant to make that essential link. As will become clear, that is precisely the difficulty encountered by the claimants here: they are unable to demonstrate that any principle of fundamental justice has been contravened.

(2) Which Section 7 Interests Are Engaged?

[200] Section 7 interests are enumerated as life, liberty and security of the person. As stated, we accept the trial judge's finding that the current state of the Quebec health system, linked to the prohibition against health insurance for insured services, is capable, at least in the cases of *some* individuals on *some* occasions, of putting at risk their life or security of the person.

[201] We do not agree with the appellants, however, that the Quebec Health Plan puts the "liberty" of Quebeckers at risk. The argument that "liberty" includes freedom of contract (in this case to contract for private medical insurance) is novel in Canada, where economic rights are not included in the *Canadian Charter* and discredited in the United States. In that country, the liberty of individuals (mainly employers) to contract out of social and economic programs was endorsed by the Supreme Court in the early decades of the 20th century on the theory that laws that prohibited employers from entering into oppressive contracts with employees violated their "liberty" of contract; see, e.g., *Lochner v. New York*, 198 U.S. 45 (1905), at p. 62:

> ... a prohibition to enter into any contract of labor in a bakery for more than a certain number of hours a week, is, in our judgment, so wholly beside the matter of a proper, reasonable and fair provision, as to run counter to that liberty of person and of free contract provided for in the Federal Constitution.

Of this line of cases, which was not brought to an end until *West Coast Hotel Co. v. Parrish*, 300 U.S. 379 (1937), Professor L.H. Tribe has written that the Supreme Court of the United States:

> ... relied on the Fourteenth Amendment's Due Process Clause to strike down economic legislation that the Court saw as improperly *infringing on contractual liberty*, but in which the Court was widely (even if not always correctly) perceived to be substituting its own judgment, in the absence of any actual constitutional mandate, for that of the legislature. [Emphasis added.]

(*American Constitutional Law* (3rd ed. 2000), vol. 1, at p. 1318)

... [207] As stated, the principal legal hurdle to the appellants' *Canadian Charter* challenge is not the preliminary step of identifying a s. 7 interest potentially affected in the case of *some* Quebeckers in *some* circumstances. The hurdle lies in their failure to find a fundamental principle of justice that is violated by the Quebec health plan so as to justify the Court in striking down the prohibition against private insurance for what the government has identified as "insured services."

C. Principles of Fundamental Justice

[208] For a principle to be one of fundamental justice, it must count among the basic tenets of our *legal* system: *Re B.C. Motor Vehicle Act*, at p. 503. It must generally be accepted as such among reasonable people. As explained by the majority in *Malmo-Levine*, at para. 113:

> The requirement of "general acceptance among reasonable people" enhances the legitimacy of judicial review of state action, and ensures that the values against which state action is measured are not just fundamental "in the eye of the beholder *only*": *Rodriguez*, at pp. 607 and 590. ...

[209] Thus, the formal requirements for a principle of fundamental justice are threefold. First, it must be a *legal* principle. Second, the reasonable person must regard it as vital to our societal notion of justice, which implies a significant *societal consensus*. Third, it must be capable of being *identified with precision* and applied in a manner that yields *predictable results*. These requirements present insurmountable hurdles to the appellants. The aim of "health care of a reasonable standard within a reasonable time" is not a *legal* principle. There is no "societal consensus" about what it means or how to achieve it. It cannot be "identified with precision." As the testimony in this case showed, a level of care that is considered perfectly reasonable by some doctors is denounced by others. ...

[210] Much of the argument pursued by the Chief Justice and Major J., as well as by Deschamps J. in her reasons relating to the *Quebec Charter*, revolves around the vexing issue of waiting lists, which have notoriously fuelled major public debates and controversies.

[211] The case history of the appellant Zeliotis illustrates why rationing of health services is necessary and how it works.

The trial judge, having heard all the evidence, concluded that the delays Mr. Zeliotis experienced in obtaining hip surgery were caused not by excessive waiting lists but by a number of other factors, including his pre-existing depression and his indecision and unfounded medical complaints. ...

(a) There Is No Consensus About What Constitutes "Reasonable" Waiting Times

[212] A review of the expert evidence and the medical literature suggests that there is no consensus regarding guidelines for timely medical treatment. Dr. Wright remarked:

> So the issue of defining what is a reasonable waiting list is a very difficult one because if you have a hundred (100) surgeons, you have a hundred (100) opinions, it's very difficult to come to a consensus on these questions. [A.R., at p. 1186] ...

(b) The Experts Accepted by the Trial Judge Relied on More Than Just "Common Sense"

[214] Our colleagues the Chief Justice and Major J. dismiss the experts accepted by the trial judge as relying on little more than "common sense" (para. 137). Although we agree that the experts offered "common sense," they offered a good deal more. The experts heard by the trial court included Mr. Claude Castonguay, who was Quebec's Minister of Health in 1970 (the [TRANSLATION] "father of Quebec health insurance") and who chaired the Commission of Inquiry on Health and Social Welfare, as well as a number of other public health experts, including Dr. Fernand Turcotte, a professor of medicine at Laval University, who holds degrees from the University of Montreal and Harvard and has been certified by the Royal College of Physicians and Surgeons of Canada as a specialist in community medicine; Dr. Howard Bergman, Chief of the Division of Geriatric Medicine at Montreal's Jewish General Hospital, Director of the Division of Geriatric Medicine and a professor in the departments of Internal Medicine and Family Medicine at McGill University, a fellow of the American Geriatrics Society and an associate professor at the University of Montreal in the department of health administration; Dr. Charles J. Wright, a physician specialized in surgery, Director of the Centre for Clinical Epidemiology & Evaluation at the Vancouver Hospital & Health Sciences Centre, and a faculty member of the University of British Columbia and of the British Columbia Office of Health Technology Assessment; Professor Jean-Louis Denis, a community health doctor of the University of Montreal's [TRANSLATION] "health services organization"; Professor Theodore R. Marmor, a professor of public policy and management and of political science at Yale University, who holds a PhD from Harvard University in politics and history and is a graduate research fellow at Oxford; and Dr. J. Edwin Coffey, a graduate of McGill University in medicine who specializes in obstetrics and gynecology, a fellow of the Royal College of Physicians and Surgeons of Canada and of the American College of Obstetricians and Gynecologists, and a former associate professor in the McGill University Faculty of Medicine. The respondent's experts testified and were cross-examined. The trial judge found them to be credible and reliable. We owe deference to her findings in this respect

[215] The trial judge, having heard the evidence, concluded as follows:

> [TRANSLATION] ... although some of these specialists indicated a desire to be free to obtain private insurance, none of them gave their full and absolute support to the applicants' proposals, as they explained *that it was neither clear nor obvious that a reorganization of the health system with a parallel private system would solve all the existing problems of delays and access.* On the contrary, the specialists who testified remained quite circumspect about this complex and difficult question. [Emphasis added; p. 796.]

The exception to the consensus was the appellants' expert, Dr. Coffey, who stated that in his opinion the development of a private insurance scheme would not affect the public health scheme. This is the argument accepted by our colleagues the Chief Justice and Major J. However on this point the trial judge observed, as on others, [TRANSLATION] "*that Dr. Coffey stood alone in both his expert evaluation and the conclusions he reached*" (p. 808 (emphasis in original)). ...

(c) The Lack of Accurate Data

[217] How serious is the waiting-list problem? No doubt it is serious; but how serious? The first major evidentiary difficulty for the appellants is the lack of accurate data. The major studies concluded that the real picture concerning waiting lists in Canada is subject to contradictory evidence and conflicting claims (Romanow Report, at p. 139, and the Kirby Report, vol. 4, at p. 41, and vol. 6, at pp. 109-10). This can also be seen from the evidence of the experts who testified at trial in the present case. ...

[226] We have similar concerns about the use made by the appellants of various reports in connection with other OECD countries. These "country" reports were included in an *Interim* Kirby Report but not in its final version. The Final Kirby Report's recommendation was to stick with a single-tier system. We think the Court is sufficiently burdened with conflicting evidence about our own health system without attempting a detailed investigation of the merits of trade-offs made in other countries, for their own purposes. ...

[229] We are not to be taken as disputing the undoubted fact that there are serious problems with the single-tier health plan in Canada. Our point is simply that bits of evidence must be put in context. With respect, it is particularly dangerous to venture selectively into aspects of foreign health care systems with which we, as Canadians, have little familiarity. At the very least such information should be filtered and analysed at trial through an expert witness.

[230] Taking the good with the bad, the Final Kirby Report recommended continuation of a single-tier health system (as did the Romanow Report). The authors of the Kirby Report were fully aware of the extracts from their interim report relied upon by our colleagues the Chief Justice and Major J., yet they specifically rejected two-tier health care. …

(2) Arbitrariness

[231] Our colleagues the Chief Justice and Major J. take the view that a law which arbitrarily violates life or security of the person is unconstitutional. We agree that this is a principle of fundamental justice. We do not agree that it applies to the facts of this case.

[232] A deprivation of a right will be arbitrary and will thus infringe s. 7 if it bears no relation to, or is inconsistent with, the state interest that lies behind the legislation. …

[233] We agree with our colleagues the Chief Justice and Major J. that a law is arbitrary if "it bears no relation to, or is inconsistent with, the objective that lies behind [the legislation]" (para. 130). We do not agree with the Chief Justice and Major J. that the prohibition against private health insurance "bears no relation to, or is inconsistent with" the preservation of access to a health system based on need rather than wealth in accordance with the *Canada Health Act*. We also do not agree with our colleagues' expansion of the *Morgentaler* principle to invalidate a prohibition simply because a court believes it to be "unnecessary" for the government's purpose. There must be more than that to sustain a valid objection.

[234] The accepted definition in *Rodriguez* states that a law is arbitrary only where "it bears no relation to, or is inconsistent with, the objective that lies behind the legislation." To substitute the term "unnecessary" for "inconsistent" is to substantively alter the meaning of the term "arbitrary." "Inconsistent" means that the law logically contradicts its objectives, whereas "unnecessary" simply means that the objective could be met by other means. It is quite apparent that the latter is a much broader term that involves a policy choice. If a court were to declare unconstitutional every law impacting "security of the person" that the court considers unnecessary, there would be much greater scope for intervention under s. 7 than has previously been considered by this Court to be acceptable. …

[235] Rejecting the findings in the courts below based on their own reading of the evidence, our colleagues the Chief Justice and Major J. state (at para. 128):

> We are of the opinion that the evidence before the trial judge supports a finding that the impugned provisions are arbitrary and that the deprivation of life and security of the person that flows from them cannot therefore be said to accord with the principles of fundamental justice.

We note that our colleagues refer to the evidence *before* the trial judge rather than the view taken of that evidence *by* the trial judge. The trial judge reached a contrary conclusion on the facts, and deference is due to her view of that evidence; see *Housen v. Nikolaisen*, [2002] 2 S.C.R. 235, 2002 SCC 33. In any event, with respect, we accept the contrary conclusions of the trial judge and the Quebec Court of Appeal. We approach the issue of arbitrariness in three steps:

(i)   What is the "state interest" sought to be protected?

(ii) What is the relationship between the "state interest" thus identified and the prohibition against private health insurance?

(iii) Have the appellants established that the prohibition bears no relation to, or is inconsistent with, the state interest?

We will address each question in turn.

(a) What Is the "State Interest" Sought to Be Protected?

[236] Quebec's legislative objective is to provide high quality health care, at a reasonable cost, for as many people as possible in a manner that is consistent with principles of efficiency, equity and fiscal responsibility. Quebec (along with the other provinces and territories) subscribes to the policy objectives of the *Canada Health Act*, which include (i) the equal provision of medical services to all residents, regardless of status, wealth or personal insurability, and (ii) fiscal responsibility. An overbuilt health system is seen as no more in the larger public interest than a system that on occasion falls short. The legislative task is to strike a balance among competing interests. …

(b) What Is the Relationship Between the "State Interest" Thus Identified and the Prohibition Against Private Health Insurance?

… [239] In *principle*, Quebec wants a health system where access is governed by need rather than wealth or status. Quebec does not want people who are uninsurable to be left behind. To accomplish this objective endorsed by the *Canada Health Act*, Quebec seeks to discourage the growth of private-sector delivery of "insured" services based on wealth and insurability. We believe the prohibition is rationally connected to Quebec's objective and is not inconsistent with it.

[240] In *practical terms*, Quebec bases the prohibition on the view that private insurance, and a consequent major expansion of private health services, would have a harmful effect on the public system. ...

[242] The trial judge considered all the evidence and concluded that the expansion of private health care would undoubtedly have a negative impact on the public health system (at p. 827):

> [TRANSLATION] The evidence has shown that the right of access to a parallel private health care system claimed by the applicants *would have repercussions on the rights of the population as a whole. We cannot bury our heads in the sand. The effect of establishing a parallel private health care system would be to threaten the integrity, proper functioning and viability of the public system.* ...

(vi) Conclusion on "Arbitrariness"

[256] For all these reasons, we agree with the conclusion of the trial judge and the Quebec Court of Appeal that in light of the legislative objectives of the *Canada Health Act* it is not "arbitrary" for Quebec to discourage the growth of private sector health care. Prohibition of private health insurance is directly related to Quebec's interest in promoting a need-based system and in ensuring its viability and efficiency. Prohibition of private insurance is not "inconsistent" with the state interest; still less is it "unrelated" to it.

[257] In short, it cannot be said that the prohibition against private health insurance "bears no relation to, or is inconsistent with" preservation of a health system predominantly based on need rather than wealth or status, as required by the *Rodriguez* test, at pp. 594-95.

[258] As to our colleagues' dismissal of the factual basis for Quebec's legislative choice, the public has invested very large sums of money in a series of authoritative reports to analyse health care in this country and in other countries. The reports uniformly recommend the retention of single-tier medicine. People are free to challenge (as do the appellants) the government's reliance on those reports but such reliance cannot be dismissed as "arbitrary." ...

(4) Conclusion Under Section 7 of the Canadian Charter

[265] For the foregoing reasons, even accepting (as we do) the trial judge's conclusion that the claimants have established a deprivation of the life and security of *some* Quebec residents occasioned in *some* circumstances by waiting list delays, the deprivation would not violate any *legal* principle of fundamental justice within the meaning of s. 7 of the *Canadian Charter*.

On that point, too, we share the opinion of the trial judge and the Quebec Court of Appeal, as previously mentioned.

D. The Appellants' Challenge Under the Quebec Charter

[266] The *Quebec Charter* is a major quasi-constitutional instrument. Our colleague Deschamps J. finds a violation of s. 1. ...

[272] Under s. 1 of the *Quebec Charter*, as at the first stage of a s. 7 analysis, the claimant bears the burden of establishing, on a balance of probabilities, that the impugned law infringes his or her protected rights and interests. If such a claim is made out, the focus of the analysis may shift to s. 9.1 of the *Quebec Charter* in order to determine whether the claimed exercise of the right is made with due regard for "democratic values, public order and the general well-being of the citizens of Québec."

[273] In our view, on the evidence, the exercise by the appellants of their claimed *Quebec Charter* rights to defeat the prohibition against private insurance would not have "proper regard for democratic values" or "public order," as the future of a publicly supported and financed single-tier health plan should be in the hands of elected representatives. Nor would it have proper regard for the "general well-being of the citizens of Québec," who are the designated beneficiaries of the health plan, and in particular for the well-being of the less advantaged Quebeckers.

[274] Those who seek private health insurance are those who can afford it and can qualify for it. They will be the more advantaged members of society. They are differentiated from the general population, not by their health problems, which are found in every group in society, but by their income status. We share the view of Dickson C.J. that the *Canadian Charter* should not become an instrument to be used by the wealthy to "roll back" the benefits of a legislative scheme that helps the poorer members of society. He observed in *Edwards Books*, at p. 779:

> In interpreting and applying the *Charter* I believe that the courts must be cautious to ensure that it does not simply become an instrument of better situated individuals to roll back legislation which has as its object the improvement of the condition of less advantaged persons.

The concern, of course, is that once the health needs of the wealthier members of society are looked after in the "upper tier," they will have less incentive to continue to pressure the government for improvements to the public system as a whole.

[275] The comments of Dickson C.J. are even more relevant to the *Quebec Charter* given its broad scope and its potential application to a wide range of private relationships.

[276] This is not a case, in our view, where the onus of proof determines the outcome. The evidence amply supports the validity of the prohibition of private insurance under the *Quebec Charter*. The objectives are compelling. A rational connection is demonstrated. The decision boils down to an application of the minimal impairment test. In respect of questions of social and economic policy, this test leaves a substantial margin of appreciation to the Quebec legislature. Designing, financing and operating the public health system of a modern democratic society like Quebec remains a challenging task. It calls for difficult choices. In the end, we find that the choice made a generation ago by the National Assembly of Quebec remains within the range of options that are justifiable under s. 9.1. Shifting the design of the health system to the courts is not a wise choice. …

[278] The evidence reviewed above establishes that the impugned provisions were part of a system which is mindful and protective of the interests of all, not only of some.

[279] We would dismiss the appeal.

24 Canada (Attorney General) v. PHS Community Services Society, 2011

"Without effective remedies, the law becomes an empty symbol; full of sound and fury but signifying nothing," so argued Beverley McLachlin, then Justice and soon to be Chief Justice of the Supreme Court.[1] What this quote does not indicate, however, is that determining the nature or scope of remedies is one of the most contentious aspects of judicial review.

The contested nature of remedies was evident in *Canada (Attorney General) v. PHS Community Services Society*, when the Supreme Court ordered the minister of justice (then Tony Clement) to do something he explicitly had earlier opposed: to grant an exemption from criminal prosecution for addicts who use the facilities of Vancouver's safe injection site (Insite) and for those health workers who supervise injections.

Insite was the product of cooperative federalism; the combined efforts of local, provincial, and federal (then Liberal) governments to provide a safe place for supervised drug injections in an urban Vancouver neighbourhood that is notorious for drug-related crimes and deaths from overdoses. Insite is strictly regulated. No drugs are provided. Clients must check in and sign a waiver, and they are closely monitored during and after injection. They are provided with health-care information, counselling, and referrals to service providers or can use an on-site detox centre. What was considered an experimental project has proven successful. Studies indicate that lives have been saved without increasing the incidence of drug use and crime in the surrounding neighbourhood. However, to function, Insite requires the federal minister of justice to grant an exemption from the prohibition against possessing prohibited substances. The initial three-year exemption was granted in 2003.

After the Liberal government was defeated in 2006, then Conservative Health Minister Tony Clement agreed to a temporary extension of the exemption. However, in 2008 he indicated that he was not prepared to grant a further exemption, and told the Standing Committee on Health that he did not approve of the idea of supervised injections. Clement restated his opposition to this idea in public comments that characterized the idea of supervised injection sites as "profoundly disturbing" and called into question the ethics of doctors who support this practice.[2]

With the expiry of the exemption from prosecution looming, and strong indications that Clement was not willing to grant the necessary exception for Insite to function, legal action

---

1 Beverley McLachlin, "The Charter: A New Role for the Judiciary?" (1991) 29 *Alta Law Review* 540 at 548.

2 "Clement Questions MDs Who Favour Safe Injection Sites," CBC News (18 August 2008), online: <http://www.cbc.ca/news/canada/montreal/clement-questions-mds-who-favour-safe-injection-sites-1.731714>.

was taken to try to keep Insite open. The trial judge granted Insite a constitutional exemption that would permit its continued operation. The federal Conservative government was unsuccessful in its appeal of this ruling in the B.C. Court of Appeal.

One of the issues of dispute before the Supreme Court was jurisdictional: are criminal prohibitions on possession and trafficking in the *Controlled Drugs and Substances Act* (CDSA) a valid exercise of federal criminal law power as they relate to a provincial health facility? The court upheld the federal government's jurisdiction. However, it rejected the federal government's argument that if the law is valid from a federalism perspective, provinces do not have the legal authority to provide a safe injection site, and thus no Charter concerns arise.

As for Charter arguments, the federal attorney general unsuccessfully argued that the use of drugs is a personal choice, and therefore the denial of an exemption to enable Insite to function does not constitute a deprivation of the right to life, liberty, and security of the person. The court disagreed with the characterization of drug addiction as a personal choice. In this unanimous ruling, the court ruled that the minister's decision to refuse the exemption for Insite to function would threaten the health and lives of those who benefit from a safe injection site. The court also characterized this ministerial decision not to grant the exemption as arbitrary and grossly disproportionate to any benefit derived from not having this facility, particularly in light of Insite's proven record of saving lives with no discernable negative impact on the public safety and health objectives of Canada.

The Supreme Court had to decide what constitutes an appropriate remedy for this Charter breach. It rejected the claimants' wish to have the relevant prohibition on the possession of banned substances declared invalid, and also decided against issuing a declaration that the minister had erred in refusing to grant a further exemption to Insite, which would return the matter to the minister for reconsideration. In its view, the first option is not appropriate because what is required is an exemption from prosecution, not a new law. The court considered the second option inappropriate because the infringement at stake threatens the lives of the claimants and others like them, and grave consequences could accrue from any lapse in denying an exemption. For the court, the appropriate remedy was to order the minister to grant the exemption. However, the court indicated that this would not preclude this exemption from being withdrawn in the future, should changed circumstances warrant reconsideration.

Neither the ruling nor the Supreme Court's reasons convinced the Harper government to support the creation of new safe injection sites in other large urban centres. In 2015, Parliament passed the *Respect for Communities Act*, which established new criteria that Insite (once its current exemption expired) and any proposed new injection sites would have to satisfy in order to be exempt from prosecution under the *Controlled Drug and Substances Act*. New requirements would give more weight to community opposition to a safe injection site. Among the many critics of the legislation was the Canadian Medical Association, which accused the government's position on the bill as being founded on ideology rather than clinical evidence. The opposition NDP and Liberal parties accused the government of trying to circumvent the 2011 Supreme Court ruling.

Recent years have seen a spike in opioid overdoses in the Vancouver area and elsewhere. In December 2016, new Liberal Minister of Health Jane Philpott introduced Bill C-37 as part of a new strategy to make it easier for safe injection sites to be established. ∼

Discussion Questions

1. What is your assessment of the Conservative government's position that any negative health risks drug users may suffer if Insite is unable to function are not caused by the CDSA's prohibition on possession of illegal drugs, but rather are the consequence of the drug users' decision to use illegal drugs?

2. Do you agree or disagree with the Supreme Court's rejection of the federal government's position that the decision to allow or deny supervised injection is a policy question, and is thus immune from Charter review?

CANADA (ATTORNEY GENERAL) v. PHS COMMUNITY SERVICES SOCIETY
2011 SCC 44, [2011] 3 S.C.R. 134

Hearing: May 12, 2011; Judgment: September 30, 2011.

Present: McLachlin C.J. and Binnie, LeBel, Deschamps, Fish, Abella, Charron, Rothstein, and Cromwell JJ.

Interveners: Attorney General of Quebec, Dr. Peter AIDS Foundation, Vancouver Coastal Health Authority, Canadian Civil Liberties Association, Canadian HIV/AIDS Legal Network, International Harm Reduction Association, CACTUS Montréal, Canadian Nurses Association, Registered Nurses' Association of Ontario, Association of Registered Nurses of British Columbia, Canadian Public Health Association, Canadian Medical Association, British Columbia Civil Liberties Association, British Columbia Nurses' Union, and REAL Women of Canada.

The judgment of the Court was delivered by the **CHIEF JUSTICE:**

[1] Since 2003, the Insite safe injection facility has provided medical services to intravenous drug users in the Downtown Eastside of Vancouver ("DTES"). Local, provincial and federal authorities came together to create a legal framework for a safe injection facility in which clients could inject drugs under medical supervision without fear of arrest and prosecution. Insite was widely hailed as an effective response to the catastrophic spread of infectious diseases such as HIV/AIDS and hepatitis C, and the high rate of deaths from drug overdoses in the DTES.

[2] In 2008, the federal government failed to extend Insite's exemption from the operation of criminal laws in the *Controlled Drugs and Substances Act*, S.C. 1996, c. 19 ("*CDSA*"). Faced with the threat that Insite would have to stop offering services, the claimants brought an action for declarations that the *CDSA* is inapplicable to Insite and that its application to Insite resulted in a violation of the claimants' s. 7 rights under the *Canadian Charter of Rights and Freedoms*, or, in the

alternative, that the federal Minister of Health, in refusing to grant an extension of Insite's exemption, had violated the claimants' s. 7 rights.

[3] The question in this appeal is whether Insite is exempt from the federal criminal laws that prohibit the possession and trafficking of controlled substances, either because Insite is a health facility within the exclusive jurisdiction of the Province, or because the application of the criminal law would violate the *Charter*. For the reasons that follow, we conclude that the *CDSA* is applicable to Insite, and that the scheme of the *CDSA* conforms to the *Charter*. However, the actions of the federal Minister of Health in refusing to extend Insite's exemption under s. 56 of the *CDSA* are in violation of s. 7 of the *Charter*, and cannot be justified under s. 1. Accordingly, we order the Minister to grant Insite an extended exemption, and dismiss the appeal.

I. Introduction and Background

[4] The DTES is home to some of the poorest and most vulnerable people in Canada. Its population includes 4,600 intravenous drug users, which is almost half of the intravenous drug users in the city as a whole. This number belies the size of the DTES. It is in fact a very small area, stretching for a few blocks in each direction from its heart at the intersection of Main and Hastings.

[5] There is no single reason for the concentration of intravenous drug users in this urban neighbourhood. Contributing factors include the presence of several single room occupancy hotels, the de-institutionalization of the mentally ill, the effect of drug enforcement policies over the years, and the availability of illicit narcotics at street level.

[6] The injection drug use problem of the DTES is not hidden. At any given time of day drug transactions can be witnessed in the open air on the very steps of the historic Carnegie Community Centre at Main and Hastings. In alleys steps away, addicts tie rubber bands around their arms to find veins in which to inject heroin and cocaine, or smoke crack from glass pipes.

[7] The residents of the DTES who are intravenous drug users have diverse origins and personal histories, yet familiar themes emerge. Many have histories of physical and sexual abuse as children, family histories of drug abuse, early exposure to serious drug use, and mental illness. Many injection drug users in the DTES have been addicted to heroin for decades, and have been in and out of treatment programmes for years. Many use multiple substances, and suffer from alcoholism. Some engage in street-level survival sex work in order to support their addictions. It should be clear from the above that these people are not engaged in recreational drug use: they are addicted. Injection drug use is both an effect and a cause of a life that is a struggle on a day to day basis.

[8] While some affordable housing is available in the DTES, living conditions there would shock many Canadians. The DTES is one of the few places where Vancouver's poorest people, crippled by disability and addiction, can afford to live. Twenty percent of its population is homeless. Of those who are not homeless, many live in squalid conditions in single-room occupancy hotels. Residents of single-room occupancy hotels live with little in the way of security, privacy or hygienic facilities. The residents of one building often have to share a single bathroom. Single-room occupancy hotels are commonly infested with bedbugs and rats. Existence is bleak.

[9] A survey of approximately 1,000 drug users living in the DTES ... found that:

* those surveyed had been injecting drugs for an average of 15 years;
* the majority (51%) inject heroin and 32% inject cocaine;
* 87% are infected with hepatitis C virus (HCV) and 17% with human immunodeficiency virus (HIV);
* 18% are Aboriginal;
* 20% are homeless and many more live in single resident rooms;
* 80% have been incarcerated;
* 38% are involved in the sex trade;
* 21% are using methadone; and
* 59% reported a non-fatal overdose in their lifetime.

[10] For injection drug users, the nature of addiction makes for a desperate and dangerous existence. Aside from the dangers of the drugs themselves, addicts are vulnerable to a host of other life-threatening practices. Although many users are educated about safe practices, the need for an immediate fix or the fear of police discovering and confiscating drugs can override even ingrained safety habits. Addicts share needles, inject hurriedly in alleyways and dissolve heroin in dirty puddle water before injecting it into their veins. In these back alleyways, users who overdose are often alone and far from medical help. Shared needles transmit HIV and hepatitis C. Unsanitary conditions result in infections. Missing a vein in the rush to inject can mean the development of abscesses. Not taking adequate time to prepare can result in mistakes in measuring proper amounts of the substance being injected. It is not uncommon for injection drug users to develop dangerous infections or endocarditis. These dangers are exacerbated by the fact that injection drug users are a historically marginalized population that has been difficult to bring within the reach of health care providers.

[11] Although injection drug use is by no means a new problem in Vancouver, or for that matter in the rest of the country, in the early 1990s it reached crisis levels in the DTES. In just six years, the number of annual deaths from overdose in Vancouver increased exponentially, from 16 in 1987 to 200 in 1993. In 1996, Vancouver's medical health officer reported an increase in infectious diseases in the DTES, including HIV/AIDS, hepatitis A, B and C, skin and blood-borne infections, endocarditis and septicaemia, as well as fatal and non-fatal overdoses. All were related to injection drug use. The same year, the British Columbia Centre for Excellence in HIV/AIDS reported an HIV/AIDS epidemic in the neighbourhood. The following year, an epidemic of hepatitis C was reported. A public health emergency was declared in the DTES in September 1997.

[12] The decision to implement a supervised safe injection site was the result of years of research, planning, and intergovernmental cooperation. ...

[16] ... Health Canada gave final approval for conditional exemption of the facility from possession and trafficking laws as a pilot research project under s. 56 of the *CDSA* on September 12, 2003.

[17] Insite opened its doors on September 21, 2003. It was North America's first government-sanctioned safe injection facility. ... Its operations are described [as below]:

> Insite is located on East Hastings Street between Carrall and Main Streets. ... The facility is known to DTES residents. Police refer addicts to it. Insite operates under an extensive and detailed operating protocol approved by Health Canada. It is staffed by a combination of PHS, Health Authority and community workers.
>
> Users must be 16 years of age or over, must sign a user agreement, release and consent form, must agree to adhere to a code of conduct, and cannot be accompanied by children. Users must register at each visit to the site and each is asked to identify the substance that will be injected. No substances are provided by staff. It goes without saying that the substances brought to Insite by users have been obtained from a trafficker in an illegal transaction. Users are obviously in possession of their substance en route to Insite. Approximately 60% of the drugs

injected are opioids, of which two-thirds are heroin and one-third morphine or hydromorphone. Approximately 40% of injected drugs are stimulants, approximately 90% of which are cocaine and 10%, methamphetamine.

Insite has 12 injection bays. Users are provided with clean injection equipment which is the only equipment that can be used at the site. Users are monitored by staff during injection. Nurses and paramedical staff provide treatment in the event of overdose and contact a physician and the ambulance service as necessary. Overdoses vary in severity and treatment.

The protocol permits pregnant women to use Insite. They are required to undergo a more intensive assessment than others before being allowed access to the injection room. Those women are also referred to a clinic and child daycare facilities directly managed by the Health Authority, which provides pre- and post-natal care to pregnant women who are actively using illegal substances.

Users who have completed an injection are assessed by staff. They may be discharged to the "chill-out" lounge or treated by a nurse in the treatment room for injection-related conditions. Users requiring extensive or ongoing care are referred to the closest primary care facility, either the Downtown Community Health Centre or the Pender Clinic.

Staff and support workers interact with users at Insite on a one-to-one basis. Users are provided with health care information, counselling and referrals to Health Authority and other service providers. Records indicate that in 2005, 2006 and 2007, staff made 2,270, 1,828, and 2,269 referrals, respectively, to community clinic, hospital emergency, outpatient medical mental health, emergency shelter and community services; and to addiction counselling, housing, withdrawal, methadone treatment, drug recovery, and miscellaneous other services.

Since the fall of 2007, the staff has also been able to refer users to "Onsite," a detox centre located above Insite which permits Insite to provide detox on demand. Onsite is a drug free environment supported by physicians who are addiction specialists and general practitioners, nurses and peers. Users may also be referred to residential detox and additional treatment services. ...

[19] Insite was the product of cooperative federalism. Local, provincial and federal authorities combined their efforts to create it. It was launched as an experiment. The experiment has proven successful. Insite has saved lives and improved health. And it did those things without increasing the incidence of drug use and crime in the surrounding area. The Vancouver police support Insite. The city and provincial government want it to stay open. But continuing the Insite project will be impossible without a federal government

exemption from the laws criminalizing possession of prohibited substances at Insite.

[20] The federal *CDSA* is the federal government's response to the problem of illegal drug use across Canada. By way of the *CDSA*, the federal government has chosen an approach that favours a blanket prohibition on possession and trafficking in illegal drugs. At the same time, Parliament has recognized that there are good reasons to allow the use of illegal substances in certain circumstances. The federal Minister of Health can issue exemptions for medical and scientific purposes under s. 56 of the *CDSA*. Section 55 of the *CDSA* allows for the Governor in Council to make regulations for the medical, scientific and industrial use of illegal substances. In this manner, Parliament has attempted to balance the two competing interests of public safety and public health. In 2008, the federal exemption for Insite from the operation of the criminal drug laws expired. This action was started in an effort to keep Insite open. ...

III. Questions on Appeal

[36] ... The first question is whether ss. 4(1) and 5(1) of the *CDSA* are constitutionally inapplicable to the activities of the staff and clients at Insite by virtue of the division of powers. The second question is whether ss. 4(1) and 5(1) infringe the rights guaranteed by s. 7 of the *Charter*, and if so, whether the infringement is justified under s. 1 of the *Charter*.

[The court discussed division of powers arguments and held that the criminal prohibitions on possession and trafficking in the CDSA are constitutionally valid and applicable to Insite under the division of powers. Moreover, the federal minister alone has the power to determine if an activity should be exempt from the prohibitions in the CDSA.

The federal government argued that if the CDSA is valid federal legislation, then the province has no legal jurisdiction to operate Insite without federal approval. If the provincial government does not have legal authority to provide the safe injection service, there is no valid Charter claim. The Supreme Court rejected this argument.]

VI. Charter Claims

...

(1) Are the Claimants' Section 7 Interests Engaged by the Prohibition on Possession of Drugs in Section 4(1) of the CDSA?

...

[86] I begin with the offence of possession of prohibited-drugs under s. 4(1) of the *CDSA*. The question is whether it engages or limits the s. 7 rights of Insite staff and/or clients.

[87] ... The argument is that the prohibition on possession of proscribed drugs on Insite's premises engages the

liberty interests of the staff of Insite, because it exposes them to the threat of being imprisoned for carrying out their duties. This constitutes a direct limit on the s. 7 rights of staff. ...

[90] The evidence is clear that staff do not buy drugs or assist with their injection. Yet their minimal involvement with clients' drugs may bring them within the legal concept of illegal possession of drugs, contrary to s. 4(1) of the *CDSA*. As such, the availability of a penalty of imprisonment in ss. 4(3) to 4(6) of the *CDSA* engages the liberty interests of staff .... The threat to the liberty of the staff in turn impacts on the s. 7 rights of clients who seek the health services provided by Insite.

[91] The record supports the conclusion that, without an exemption from the application of the *CDSA*, the health professionals who provide the supervised services at Insite will be unable to offer medical supervision and counselling to Insite's clients. This deprives the clients of Insite of potentially lifesaving medical care, thus engaging their rights to life and security of the person. The result is that the limits on the s. 7 rights of staff will in turn result in limits on the s. 7 rights of clients.

[92] The application of s. 4(1) to the clients of Insite also directly engages their s. 7 interests. In order to make use of the lifesaving and health-protecting services offered at Insite, clients must be allowed to be in possession of drugs on the premises. To prohibit possession by drug users *anywhere* engages their liberty interests; to prohibit possession at Insite engages their rights to life and to security of the person. ...

[94] I conclude that s. 4(1) of the *CDSA* limits the s. 7 rights of staff and clients of Insite.

[95] However, I am unable to conclude that the claimants have shown that the prohibition on trafficking in s. 5(1) of the *CDSA* constitutes a limitation of their s. 7 rights to life and security of the person, on the record before us. The clients of Insite are not involved in trafficking. They do not obtain their drugs at the facility, and are not permitted to engage in activities that could be construed as trafficking while they are on the premises.

[96] Nor are the staff of Insite involved in trafficking. Canada concedes that trafficking charges would not lie against the staff of Insite for their legitimate activities on the premises. Staff members do not handle drugs at Insite, except to safely remove and hand over to the police any substances left behind by clients. Delivering leftover drugs to the police does not constitute possession, let alone trafficking. ...

(2) Canada's Arguments on Choice

[97] Canada argues that any negative health risks drug users may suffer if Insite is unable to provide them with health services, are not caused by the *CDSA*'s prohibition on possession of illegal drugs, but rather are the consequence of the drug users' decision to use illegal drugs.

[98] Canada's position, deconstructed, reveals three distinct strands.

[99] The first strand is that from a factual perspective, personal choice, not the law, is the cause of the death and disease Insite prevents. Canada's difficulty is that this assertion contradicts the uncontested factual findings of the trial judge. The trial judge found that addiction is an illness, characterized by a loss of control over the need to consume the substance to which the addiction relates. ...

[102] The second strand of Canada's choice argument is a moral argument that those who commit crimes should be made to suffer the consequences. On this point it suffices to say that whether a law limits a *Charter* right is simply a matter of the purpose and effect of the law that is challenged, not whether the law is right or wrong. The morality of the activity the law regulates is irrelevant at the initial stage of determining whether the law engages a s. 7 right.

[103] The third way to view Canada's choice argument is as a matter of government policy. Canada argues that the decision to allow supervised injection is a policy question, and thus immune from *Charter* review.

[104] The answer, once again, is that policy is not relevant at the stage of determining whether a law or state action limits a *Charter* right. The place for such arguments is when considering the principles of fundamental justice or at the s. 1 stage of justification if a *Charter* breach has been established.

[105] The issue of illegal drug use and addiction is a complex one which attracts a variety of social, political, scientific and moral reactions. There is room for disagreement between reasonable people concerning how addiction should be treated. It is for the relevant governments, not the Court, to make criminal and health policy. However, when a policy is translated into law or state action, those laws and actions are subject to scrutiny under the *Charter* .... The issue before the Court at this point is not whether harm reduction or abstinence-based programmes are the best approach to resolving illegal drug use. It is simply whether Canada has limited the rights of the claimants in a manner that does not comply with the *Charter*.

[106] I conclude that, whatever form it takes, Canada's assertion that choice rather than state conduct is the cause of the health hazards Insite seeks to address and the claimants' resultant deprivation must be rejected.

(3) Is the Deprivation in Accordance With the Principles of Fundamental Justice?

[107] For the reasons just discussed, I conclude that the prohibition on possession in s. 4(1) of the *CDSA* limits the

s. 7 interests of the claimants and others like them. The next question is whether this limitation is in accordance with the principles of fundamental justice.

[108] The claimants argue that the prohibition on possession of illegal drugs in s. 4(1) of the *CDSA* is not in accordance with the principles of fundamental justice because it is arbitrary, disproportionate in its effects, and overbroad. ...

[109] ... If the Act consisted solely of blanket prohibitions with no provision for exemptions for necessary medical or scientific use of drugs, the assertions that it is arbitrary, overbroad and disproportionate in its effects might gain some traction. However, the Act contains not only a prohibition on possession of illegal drugs, but a provision, s. 56, that empowers the Minister to grant exemptions from the prohibition to health service providers like Insite. ...

[110] The scheme of the *CDSA* reveals that it has two purposes: the protection of public health and the maintenance of public safety. The public safety purpose of the Act is achieved by the prohibition on possession and trafficking in listed substances. The public health purpose of the statute is achieved not only by the prohibitions in ss. 4(1) and 5(1), which seek to avert the use of dangerous substances, but also by the provision of regulations guiding exemptions for and the use of listed substances for medical and scientific purposes in ss. 55 and 56 of the Act.

[111] Section 55(1) provides that "[t]he Governor in Council may make regulations for carrying out the purposes and provisions of this Act, including the regulation of the medical, scientific and industrial applications and distribution of controlled substances." There follows a lengthy non-exhaustive list of matters in respect of which regulations may be made, including regulations exempting a person or class of person from the application of the Act. ...

[112] Section 56 gives the Minister of Health a broad discretion to grant exemptions from the application of the Act "if, in the opinion of the Minister, the exemption is necessary for a medical or scientific purpose or is otherwise in the public interest."

[113] The availability of exemptions acts as a safety valve that prevents the *CDSA* from applying where such application would be arbitrary, overbroad or grossly disproportionate in its effects.

[114] I conclude that while s. 4(1) of the *CDSA* engages the s. 7 *Charter* rights of the individual claimants and others like them, it does not violate s. 7. This is because the *CDSA* confers on the Minister the power to grant exemptions from s. 4(1) on the basis, *inter alia*, of health. Indeed, if one were to set out to draft a law that combats drug abuse while respecting *Charter* rights, one might well adopt just this type of scheme—a prohibition combined with the power to grant

exemptions. If there is a *Charter* problem, it lies not in the statute but in the Minister's exercise of the power the statute gives him to grant appropriate exemptions.

[115] The claimants' s. 7 challenge to the *CDSA* accordingly fails.

C. Has the Minister's Decision Violated the Claimants' Section 7 Rights?

[116] ... A preliminary issue arises whether the Court should consider this issue. In the special circumstances of this case, I conclude that it should. The claimants pleaded in the alternative that, if the *CDSA* were valid, the Minister's decision violated their *Charter* rights. The issue was raised at the hearing and the parties afforded an opportunity to address it. It is therefore properly before us and the Attorney General of Canada cannot complain that it would be unfair to deal with it. Most importantly, justice requires us to consider this issue. The claimants have established that their s. 7 rights are at stake. They should not be denied a remedy and sent back for another trial on this point simply because it is the Minister's decision and not the statute that causes the breach when the matter has been pleaded and no unfairness arises.

[117] The discretion vested in the Minister of Health is not absolute: as with all exercises of discretion, the Minister's decisions must conform to the *Charter* ... . If the Minister's decision results in an application of the *CDSA* that limits the s. 7 rights of individuals in a manner that is not in accordance with the *Charter*, then the Minister's discretion has been exercised unconstitutionally. ...

[119] The Attorney General of Canada argues that the Minister has not violated s. 7 because the Minister has not yet made a decision whether to grant a s. 56 exemption to Insite. ...

[120] In my view, the record establishes that the Minister *has* made a decision on the request for an exemption for Insite, and that that decision was to refuse the exemption.

[121] The essential facts are as follows. The first exemption for Insite, which lasted three years, was effective as of September 12, 2003. The Minister granted a temporary extension on September 11, 2006, to expire December 31, 2007. On October 2, 2007, the exemption was extended for another six months to June 30, 2008. In his letters to the VCHA granting the exemption, the Minister stated that the extensions were to be for the purpose of allowing time for additional research on the impact of Insite on prevention, treatment and crime. In the course of the summary trial, on May 2, 2008, the VCHA sent an application to Health Canada formally requesting an extension of the exemption for another three years. The application was supported by the provincial Minister of Health. Health Canada responded on December 19, 2008, after the

trial judge had rendered his judgment. It stated that, in view of the result at trial, an exemption was not required at that time.

[122] However, before December 2008, the Minister indicated that he had decided not to grant the exemption. The then federal Minister of Health, Tony Clement, spoke to the Standing Committee on Health on May 29, 2008. He had at that point received the report of the Expert Advisory Committee, a formal application for a continued exemption, and a statement of support for Insite from the provincial Minister of Health. The federal Minister's comments can be summarized briefly: he approved of the other services Insite was providing, but not supervised injection. He felt that the scientific evidence with respect to its effectiveness was mixed, but that the "public policy is clear," and that "the site itself represents a failure of public policy." ... He disagreed with the experts who saw Insite as a public health success, and stated he intended to appeal the trial judge's decision. These comments, coupled with the failure to accord an exemption, amount to an effective refusal of the application. ...

(3) Does the Minister's Refusal to Grant an Exemption to Insite Accord With the Principles of Fundamental Justice?

[127] ... I conclude that the Minister's refusal to grant Insite a s. 56 exemption was arbitrary and grossly disproportionate in its effects, and hence not in accordance with the principles of fundamental justice. ...

(a) Arbitrariness

[129] When considering whether a law's application is arbitrary, the first step is to identify the law's objectives. Decisions of the Minister under s. 56 of the *CDSA* must target the purpose of the Act. The legitimate state objectives of the *CDSA* ... [are] the protection of health and public safety.

[130] The second step is to identify the relationship between the state interest and the impugned law, or, in this case, the impugned decision of the Minister. ...

[131] The trial judge's key findings in this regard are consistent with the information available to the Minister, and are those on which successive federal Ministers have relied in granting exemption orders over almost five years, including the facts that: (1) traditional criminal law prohibitions have done little to reduce drug use in the DTES; (2) the risk to injection drug users of death and disease is reduced when they inject under the supervision of a health professional; and (3) the presence of Insite did not contribute to increased crime rates, increased incidents of public injection, or relapse rates in injection drug users. On the contrary, Insite was perceived favourably or neutrally by the public; a local business association reported a reduction in crime during the period

Insite was operating; the facility encouraged clients to seek counselling, detoxification and treatment. Most importantly, the staff of Insite had intervened in 336 overdoses since 2006, and no overdose deaths had occurred at the facility. ... These findings suggest not only that exempting Insite from the application of the possession prohibition does not undermine the objectives of public health and safety, but furthers them. ...

(b) Gross Disproportionality

[133] The application of the possession prohibition to Insite is also grossly disproportionate in its effects. Gross disproportionality describes state actions or legislative responses to a problem that are so extreme as to be disproportionate to any legitimate government interest: *Malmo-Levine*, at para. 143. Insite saves lives. Its benefits have been proven. There has been no discernable negative impact on the public safety and health objectives of Canada during its eight years of operation. The effect of denying the services of Insite to the population it serves is grossly disproportionate to any benefit that Canada might derive from presenting a uniform stance on the possession of narcotics.

(c) Overbreadth

[134] Having found the Minister's decision arbitrary and its effects grossly disproportionate, I need not consider this aspect of the argument.

[135] I conclude that, on the basis of the factual findings of the trial judge, the claimants have met the evidentiary burden of showing that the failure of the Minister to grant a s. 56 exemption to Insite is not in accordance with the principles of fundamental justice.

(4) Conclusion on the Challenge to Minister's Decision

[136] The Minister made a decision not to extend the exemption from the application of the federal drug laws to Insite. The effect of that decision, but for the trial judge's interim order, would have been to prevent injection drug users from accessing the health services offered by Insite, threatening the health and indeed the lives of the potential clients. The Minister's decision thus engages the claimants' s. 7 interests and constitutes a limit on their s. 7 rights. Based on the information available to the Minister, this limit is not in accordance with the principles of fundamental justice. It is arbitrary, undermining the very purposes of the *CDSA*, which include public health and safety. It is also grossly disproportionate: the potential denial of health services and the correlative increase in the risk of death and disease to injection drug users outweigh any benefit that might be derived from maintaining an absolute prohibition on possession of illegal drugs on Insite's premises.

Section 1

[137] If a s. 1 analysis were required, a point not argued, no s. 1 justification could succeed. The goals of the *CDSA*, as I have stated, are the maintenance and promotion of public health and safety. The Minister's decision to refuse the exemption bears no relation to these objectives; therefore they cannot justify the infringement of the complainants' s. 7 rights. ...

VII. Remedy

[141] Having found that the Minister's refusal to grant an exemption to Insite violates s. 7 in a manner that cannot be justified under s. 1, we must find the appropriate remedy. ...

[143] The infringement of the claimants' s. 7 rights is ongoing. The federal exemption for Insite expired on June 30, 2008. The application of the federal drug laws to Insite has been suspended in the interim only by judicial intervention. ...

[145] Section 24(1) confers a broad discretion on the Court to craft an appropriate remedy that is responsive to the violation of the respondents' *Charter* rights. ...

[146] One option would be to issue a declaration that the Minister erred in refusing to grant a further exemption to Insite in May 2008, and return the matter to the Minister to reconsider the matter and make a decision that respects the claimants' *Charter* rights.

[147] However, this remedy would be inadequate.

[148] The infringement at stake is serious; it threatens the health, indeed the lives, of the claimants and others like them. The grave consequences that might result from a lapse in the current constitutional exemption for Insite cannot be ignored. These claimants would be cast back into the application process they have tried and failed at, and made to await the Minister's decision based on a reconsideration of the same facts. Litigation might break out anew. A bare declaration is not an acceptable remedy in this case.

[149] Nor is the granting of a permanent constitutional exemption appropriate where the remedy is for a state action, not a law. ...

[150] In the special circumstances of this case, an order in the nature of mandamus is warranted. I would therefore order the Minister to grant an exemption to Insite under s. 56 of the *CDSA* forthwith. (This of course would not affect the Minister's power to withdraw the exemption should the operation of Insite change such that the exemption would no longer be appropriate.) ... The Minister is bound to exercise his discretion under s. 56 in accordance with the *Charter*. On the facts as found here, there can be only one response: to grant the exemption. There is therefore nothing to be gained (and much to be risked) in sending the matter back to the Minister for reconsideration.

[151] This does not fetter the Minister's discretion with respect to future applications for exemptions, whether for other premises, or for Insite. As always, the Minister must exercise that discretion within the constraints imposed by the law and the *Charter*.

[152] The dual purposes of the *CDSA*—public health and public safety—provide some guidance for the Minister. Where the Minister is considering an application for an exemption for a supervised injection facility, he or she will aim to strike the appropriate balance between achieving the public health and public safety goals. Where, as here, the evidence indicates that a supervised injection site will decrease the risk of death and disease, and there is little or no evidence that it will have a negative impact on public safety, the Minister should generally grant an exemption.

[153] The *CDSA* grants the Minister discretion in determining whether to grant exemptions. That discretion must be exercised in accordance with the *Charter*. This requires the Minister to consider whether denying an exemption would cause deprivations of life and security of the person that are not in accordance with the principles of fundamental justice. The factors considered in making the decision on an exemption must include evidence, if any, on the impact of such a facility on crime rates, the local conditions indicating a need for such a supervised injection site, the regulatory structure in place to support the facility, the resources available to support its maintenance, and expressions of community support or opposition.

[The court rejected a cross-appeal by VANDU that challenged the validity of prohibiting the possession of banned drugs to all addicted persons. VANDU's argument was that because addicted persons have no control over the urge to consume addictive substances, they are forced by fear of arrest and prosecution to procure and consume drugs in a manner that threatens their lives and health, and which causes them a high level of psychological stress.]

Canada (Attorney General) v. Bedford, 2013

Prostitution—the exchange of sex for money—has never been illegal in Canada. But many activities associated with it have been subject to criminal regulation. The criminal law has attempted to control or eliminate prostitution by indirect means, making it difficult for prostitutes to carry on their trade. Accepting that prostitution is hard to eliminate in any case, Parliament opted for measures that keep it out of broad public view.

The *Criminal Code* contained three main measures to regulate prostitution. First, the Code prohibited the operation of bawdy houses—that is, places where the sex trade is carried on. Second, the Code banned people from living "on the avails" of prostitution, targeting, in particular, pimps and others who lure people into the trade and then profit from their work. Third, the Code criminalized public communication for the purpose of prostitution. All three provisions targeted the supply side of this industry. They did not go after the demand for prostitution—the johns who seek the services of sex workers.

Municipalities frequently complained that the communications provisions of the Code were not working because public solicitation in downtown neighbourhoods created a nuisance. Meanwhile, upon entrenchment of the Charter and in the face of changing views of prostitution, some argued that the criminalization of communication activities associated with the trade were violations of free speech. By the late 1980s, the courts had declared that economic speech was covered by section 2(b) of the Charter and, the argument went, sex workers should benefit from such an interpretation. While many regard prostitution as inherently exploitive of women, and therefore to be discouraged, others believe that the sex trade is a legitimate activity and that the laws regulating it should make the trade safer, not more dangerous.

This last point is at the heart of the Supreme Court's 2013 decision in *Bedford*. A group of current and former prostitutes brought an action before Ontario courts to have the above three *Criminal Code* provisions declared contrary to section 7 of the Charter. The applicants' main argument is that the criminal laws concerning prostitution make the activity more dangerous for sex-trade workers, not safer. State action should not put purveyors of a legal service in danger. If it does, then a worker's right to security of the person is violated. And if that limitation cannot be accomplished in a manner consistent with the principles of fundamental justice, then a section 7 violation is made out.

The seeds of this account of section 7 are found in the court's 1988 decision in *Morgentaler* (see case 21)[1] There, the issue was the effect of provisions that limited access to lawful abortions. Parliament's objective for section 251 of the Code was to ensure that therapeutic abortions were carried out in facilities able to handle medical emergencies to safeguard the life and health of the mother. But the majority in that case held that the procedures

---

1   *R. v. Morgentaler*, [1988] 1 S.C.R. 30.

mandated to perform lawful therapeutic abortions caused delays and other problems that increased the danger to women. So the law was the cause of a deprivation of a woman's right to security of the person.

In *Bedford*, the chief justice for a unanimous Supreme Court declared that the prostitution provisions put women in greater danger than they would experience in their absence. The ban on bawdy houses meant that prostitutes were confined to "out calls" to premises they neither knew nor could control. The ban on those living on the avails of prostitution meant that sex-trade workers could not hire bodyguards, drivers, and other personnel. And the ban on public communication for the purposes of prostitution meant that potential clients could not be screened in a safe, public setting by means of conversation. Lawful solicitation was forced to isolated areas in the shadows of city life. As a result, the sex-trade workers' right to security of the person was violated.

Is this violation in accordance with the principles of fundamental justice? No, held the chief justice. For a law to be in accord with these, the law must not be arbitrary—that is, there must be a rational connection between the objective of the law and the means used to advance that objective. The law must not be overbroad. It must not catch conduct beyond what the purposes of the law would specify. Finally, the law must not be grossly disproportionate—the deleterious effect of the law on a person must not grossly exceed the good expected to be gained by the law. No one person should have to pay disproportionately for whatever good a law seeks to advance. Here the court found that the bawdy house and communications provisions were grossly disproportionate to the anti-nuisance objective. The ban on living on the avails was overbroad. Here, as in so many section 7 cases, section 1 did not save the section 7 violation.

A wrinkle in the appeal was that the Supreme Court in 1990 issued a reference opinion concerning the constitutionality of the bawdy house and communication provisions of the Code.[2] In that instance, a 5-to-2 majority upheld the provisions against sections 2(b) and 7 attack. What changed in 23 years? And what of the principle of *stare decisis*? The court notes, first, that this case is squarely based on section 7, not section 2(b). Second, section 7 jurisprudence has changed since 1990. The court is not bound by its own prior understanding of section 7. It cites with approval an intervener's remark that the principle of *stare decisis* is subordinate to the Constitution and cannot require it to uphold a law that is unconstitutional. But doesn't this put the cart before the horse? *Stare decisis* is one of the means by which we know whether a law is unconstitutional. In its absence, what other means do we have? On this point the court demurred.

After the decision was rendered, the federal government developed an alternative approach premised on the principle that prostitutes are primarily victims and that they should therefore not be subject to criminal penalties. Instead, the focus shifted to buyers of sexual services; it is now a criminal offence to purchase sexual services. Consistent with the ruling in *Bedford*, the new law allows street solicitation in places where children are unlikely to be present, and persons in "non-exploitive" relationships with prostitutes can make an income from the trade. "In calls" are now also permitted. ~

---

2   *Reference re ss. 193 and 195.1(1)(C) of the criminal code (Man.),* [1990] 1 S.C.R. 1123.

Discussion Questions

1. The attorney general of Canada argued that the danger to prostitutes comes not from the law but from the nature of the profession in which they are engaged. Evaluate this argument.

2. To what extent does this decision signal a shift in societal views of the sex trade? To what extent is exploitation part of the trade? How does your answer affect your view of what is good public policy in this field?

3. The court in *Bedford* struck down laws discouraging the supply of prostitution services. In doing so, it created the legal condition for safer, more efficient, and more satisfying provision of those same services. In the wake of *Bedford*, Parliament has criminalized the purchase of sexual services. Is this policy choice likely to be effective in light of the *Bedford* decision? Should we expect prostitution to decline in Canada?

CANADA (ATTORNEY GENERAL) v. BEDFORD
2013 SCC 72, [2013] 3 S.C.R. 1101

Hearing: June 13, 2014; Judgment: December 20, 2013.

Present: McLachlin C.J. and LeBel, Fish, Abella, Rothstein, Cromwell, Moldaver, Karakatsanis, and Wagner JJ.

The judgment of the Court was delivered by

THE CHIEF JUSTICE:

[1] It is not a crime in Canada to sell sex for money. However, it is a crime to keep a bawdy-house, to live on the avails of prostitution or to communicate in public with respect to a proposed act of prostitution. It is argued that these restrictions on prostitution put the safety and lives of prostitutes at risk, and are therefore unconstitutional.

[2] These appeals and the cross-appeal are not about whether prostitution should be legal or not. They are about whether the laws Parliament has enacted on how prostitution may be carried out pass constitutional muster. I conclude that they do not. I would therefore make a suspended declaration of invalidity, returning the question of how to deal with prostitution to Parliament.

I. The Case

[3] Three applicants, all current or former prostitutes, brought an application seeking declarations that three provisions of the *Criminal Code*, R.S.C. 1985, c. C-46, are unconstitutional.

[4] The three impugned provisions criminalize various activities related to prostitution. They are primarily concerned with preventing public nuisance, as well as the exploitation of prostitutes. Section 210 makes it an offence to be an inmate of a bawdy-house, to be found in a bawdy-house without lawful excuse, or to be an owner, landlord, lessor, tenant, or occupier of a place who knowingly permits it to be used as a bawdy-house. Section 212(1)(*j*) makes it an offence to live on the avails of another's prostitution. Section 213(1)(*c*) makes it an offence to either stop or attempt to stop, or communicate or attempt to communicate with, someone in a public place for the purpose of engaging in prostitution or hiring a prostitute.

[5] However, prostitution itself is not illegal. It is not against the law to exchange sex for money. Under the existing regime, Parliament has confined lawful prostitution to two categories: street prostitution and "out-calls"—where the prostitute goes out and meets the client at a designated location, such as the client's home. This reflects a policy choice on Parliament's part. Parliament is not precluded from imposing limits on where and how prostitution may be conducted, as long as it does so in a way that does not infringe the constitutional rights of prostitutes.

[6] The applicants allege that all three provisions infringe s. 7 of the *Canadian Charter of Rights and Freedoms* by preventing prostitutes from implementing certain safety measures—such as hiring security guards or "screening" potential clients—that could protect them from violent clients. The applicants also allege that s. 213(1)(*c*) infringes s. 2(*b*) of the *Charter*, and that none of the provisions are saved under s. 1.

[The chief justice offers biographical sketches of the three Charter claimants. They are or were prostitutes and have been at times working in fear for their safety. They took steps to make their work and that of other sex-trade workers safer, but these steps potentially brought them into conflict with the *Criminal Code* prohibitions on prostitution-related activity. They have accordingly applied for a declaration that the

Code's prostitution-related provisions violate section 7 of the Charter.]

III. Prior Decisions

[At the Ontario Superior Court of Justice, the judge undertook a detailed examination of the "social fact" evidence associated with the sex trade and concluded that the existing legislative framework increases risks to prostitutes' security of the person. She declared the public communication and living on the avails provisions of the *Criminal Code* to be unconstitutional. She also found the bawdy house provision in relation to prostitution contrary to section 7. She struck the word prostitution from that provision. On appeal, a unanimous Ontario high court declared the bawdy house and living on the avails provisions unconstitutional, but suspended the declaration of invalidity for 12 months. Two of the five justices on the panel would also have struck down the public communication provisions, thereby reversing the Supreme Court's opinion in the 1990 *Prostitution Reference* (*Reference re ss. 193 and 195.1(1)(C) of the Criminal Code (Man.)*, [1990] 1 S.C.R. 1123).]

IV. Discussion

[36] The appellant Attorneys General appeal from the Court of Appeal's declaration that ss. 210 and 212(1)(*j*) of the *Code* are unconstitutional. The respondents cross-appeal on the issue of the constitutionality of s. 213(1)(*c*), and in respect of the Court of Appeal's remedy to resolve the unconstitutionality of s. 210.

[37] Before turning to the *Charter* arguments before us, I will first discuss two preliminary issues: (1) whether the 1990 decision in the *Prostitution Reference*, upholding the bawdy-house and communication prohibitions, is binding on trial judges and this Court; and (2) the degree of deference to be accorded to the application judge's findings on social and legislative facts.

A. Preliminary Issues

(1) Revisiting the Prostitution Reference

[38] Certainty in the law requires that courts follow and apply authoritative precedents. Indeed, this is the foundational principle upon which the common law relies.

[39] The issue of when, if ever, such precedents may be departed from takes two forms. The first "vertical" question is when, if ever, a lower court may depart from a precedent established by a higher court. The second "horizontal" question is when a court such as the Supreme Court of Canada may depart from its own precedents.

[40] In this case, the precedent in question is the Supreme Court of Canada's 1990 advisory opinion in the *Prostitution Reference*, which upheld the constitutionality of the

prohibitions on bawdy-houses and communicating—two of the three provisions challenged in this case. The questions in that case were whether the laws infringed s. 7 or s. 2(*b*) of the *Charter*, and, if so, whether the limit was justified under s. 1. The Court concluded that neither of the impugned laws were inconsistent with s. 7, and that although the communicating law infringed s. 2(*b*), it was a justifiable limit under s. 1 of the *Charter*. ...

[41] The application judge in this case held that she could revisit those conclusions because: the legal issues under s. 7 were different, in light of the evolution of the law in that area; the evidentiary record was richer and provided research not available in 1990; the social, political and economic assumptions underlying the *Prostitution Reference* no longer applied; and the type of expression at issue in that case (commercial expression) differed from the expression at issue in this case (expression promoting safety). The Court of Appeal disagreed with respect to the s. 2(*b*) issue, holding that a trial judge asked to depart from a precedent on the basis of new evidence, or new social, political or economic assumptions, may make findings of fact for consideration by the higher courts, but cannot apply them to arrive at a different conclusion from the previous precedent (at para. 76).

[42] In my view, a trial judge can consider and decide arguments based on *Charter* provisions that were not raised in the earlier case; this constitutes a new legal issue. Similarly, the matter may be revisited if new legal issues are raised as a consequence of significant developments in the law, or if there is a change in the circumstances or evidence that fundamentally shifts the parameters of the debate.

[43] The intervener, the David Asper Centre for Constitutional Rights, argues that the common law principle of *stare decisis* is subordinate to the Constitution and cannot require a court to uphold a law which is unconstitutional. It submits that lower courts should not be limited to acting as "mere scribe[s]," creating a record and findings without conducting a legal analysis (I.F., at para. 25).

[44] I agree. As the David Asper Centre also noted, however, a lower court is not entitled to ignore binding precedent, and the threshold for revisiting a matter is not an easy one to reach. In my view, as discussed above, this threshold is met when a new legal issue is raised, or if there is a significant change in the circumstances or evidence. This balances the need for finality and stability with the recognition that when an appropriate case arises for revisiting precedent, a lower court must be able to perform its full role.

[45] It follows that the application judge in this case was entitled to rule on whether the laws in question violated the security of the person interests under s. 7 of the *Charter*. In the *Prostitution Reference*, the majority decision was based on

the s. 7 physical liberty interest alone. Only Lamer J., writing for himself, touched on security of the person—and then, only in the context of economic interests. Contrary to the submission of the Attorney General of Canada, whether the s. 7 interest at issue is economic liberty or security of the person is *not* "a distinction without a difference" (A.F., at para. 94). The rights protected by s. 7 are "independent interests, each of which must be given independent significance by the Court" (*R. v. Morgentaler*, [1988] 1 S.C.R. 30, at p. 52). Furthermore, the principles of fundamental justice considered in the *Prostitution Reference* dealt with vagueness and the permissibility of indirect criminalization. The principles raised in this case—arbitrariness, overbreadth, and gross disproportionality—have, to a large extent, developed only in the last 20 years.

[46] These considerations do not apply to the question of whether the communication provision is a justified limit on freedom of expression. That issue was decided in the *Prostitution Reference*. Re-characterizing the type of expression alleged to be infringed did not convert this argument into a new legal issue, nor did the more current evidentiary record or the shift in attitudes and perspectives amount to a change in the circumstances or evidence that fundamentally shifted the parameters of the debate.

[47] This brings me to the question of whether this Court should depart from its previous decision on the s. 2(*b*) aspect of this case. At heart, this is a balancing exercise, in which the Court must weigh correctness against certainty (*Canada v. Craig*, 2012 SCC 43, [2012] 2 S.C.R. 489, at para. 27). In this case, however, it is not necessary to determine whether this Court can depart from its s. 2(*b*) conclusion in the *Prostitution Reference*, since it is possible to resolve the case entirely on s. 7 grounds.

(2) Deference to the Application Judge's Findings on Social and Legislative Facts

[48] The Court of Appeal held that the application judge's findings on social and legislative facts—that is, facts about society at large, established by complex social science evidence—were not entitled to deference. With respect, I cannot agree. As this Court stated in *Housen v. Nikolaisen*, 2002 SCC 33, [2002] 2 S.C.R. 235, appellate courts should not interfere with a trial judge's findings of fact, absent a palpable and overriding error.

[49] ... Absent reviewable error in the trial judge's appreciation of the evidence, a court of appeal should not interfere with the trial judge's conclusions on social and legislative facts. This division of labour is basic to our court system. The first instance judge determines the facts; appeal courts review the decision for correctness in law or palpable and overriding error in fact. This applies to social and legislative facts as much

as to findings of fact as to what happened in a particular case. ...

[53] As the Attorney General of Canada points out, this Court's decision in *RJR-MacDonald Inc. v. Canada (Attorney General)*, [1995] 3 S.C.R. 199, suggested that legislative fact findings are owed less deference. However, the use of social science evidence in *Charter* litigation has evolved significantly since *RJR-MacDonald* was decided. In the intervening years, this Court has expressed a preference for social science evidence to be presented through an expert witness (*R. v. Malmo-Levine; R. v. Caine*, 2003 SCC 74, [2003] 3 S.C.R. 571, at paras. 26-28; *R. v. Spence*, 2005 SCC 71, [2005] 3 S.C.R. 458, at para. 68). The assessment of expert evidence relies heavily on the trial judge. ...

B. Section 7 Analysis

...

(1) Is Security of the Person Engaged?

...

[59] Here, the applicants argue that the prohibitions on bawdy-houses, living on the avails of prostitution, and communicating in public for the purposes of prostitution, heighten the risks they face in prostitution—itself a legal activity. The application judge found that the evidence supported this proposition and the Court of Appeal agreed.

[60] ... I am of the same view. The prohibitions at issue do not merely impose conditions on how prostitutes operate. They go a critical step further, by imposing *dangerous* conditions on prostitution; they prevent people engaged in a risky—but legal—activity from taking steps to protect themselves from the risks.

(a) Sections 197 and 210: Keeping a Common Bawdy-House

[61] It is not an offence to sell sex for money. The bawdy-house provisions, however, make it an offence to do so in any "place" that is "kept or occupied" or "resorted to" for the purpose of prostitution (ss. 197 and 210(1) of the *Code*). ...

[62] The practical effect of s. 210 is to confine lawful prostitution to two categories: street prostitution and out-calls (application decision, at para. 385). In-calls, where the john comes to the prostitute's residence, are prohibited. Out-calls, where the prostitute goes out and meets the client at a designated location, such as the client's home, are allowed. Working on the street is also permitted, though the practice of street prostitution is significantly limited by the prohibition on communicating in public (s. 213(1)(*c*)).

[63] The application judge found, on a balance of probabilities, that the safest form of prostitution is working independently from a fixed location (para. 300). She

concluded that indoor work is far less dangerous than street prostitution—a finding that the evidence amply supports. She also concluded that out-call work is not as safe as in-call work, particularly under the current regime where prostitutes are precluded by virtue of the living on the avails provision from hiring a driver or security guard. Since the bawdy-house provision makes the safety-enhancing method of in-call prostitution illegal, the application judge concluded that the bawdy-house prohibition materially increased the risk prostitutes face under the present regime. I agree.

[64] First, the prohibition prevents prostitutes from working in a fixed indoor location, which would be safer than working on the streets or meeting clients at different locations, especially given the current prohibition on hiring drivers or security guards. This, in turn, prevents prostitutes from having a regular clientele and from setting up indoor safeguards like receptionists, assistants, bodyguards and audio room monitoring, which would reduce risks (application decision, at para. 421). Second, it interferes with provision of health checks and preventive health measures. Finally—a point developed in argument before us—the bawdy-house prohibition prevents resort to safe houses, to which prostitutes working on the street can take clients. In Vancouver, for example, "Grandma's House" was established to support street workers in the Downtown Eastside, at about the same time as fears were growing that a serial killer was prowling the streets—fears which materialized in the notorious Robert Pickton. Street prostitutes—who the application judge found are largely the most vulnerable class of prostitutes, and who face an alarming amount of violence (para. 361)—were able to bring clients to Grandma's House. However, charges were laid under s. 210, and although the charges were eventually stayed—four years after they were laid—Grandma's House was shut down ... .

[65] I conclude, therefore, that the bawdy-house provision negatively impacts the security of the person of prostitutes and engages s. 7 of the *Charter*.

(b) Section 212(1)(j): Living on the Avails of Prostitution

[66] Section 212(1)(*j*) criminalizes living on the avails of prostitution of another person, wholly or in part. While targeting parasitic relationships (*R. v. Downey*, [1992] 2 S.C.R. 10), it has a broad reach. As interpreted by the courts, it makes it a crime for anyone to supply a service to a prostitute, because she is a prostitute (*R. v. Grilo* (1991), 2 O.R. (3d) 514 (C.A.); *R. v. Barrow* (2001), 54 O.R. (3d) 417 (C.A.)). In effect, it prevents a prostitute from hiring bodyguards, drivers and receptionists. The application judge found that by denying prostitutes access to these security-enhancing safeguards, the law prevented them from taking steps to reduce the risks they face and negatively impacted their security of the person. ...

(c) Section 213(1)(c): Communicating in a Public Place

[68] Section 213(1)(*c*) prohibits communicating or attempting to communicate for the purpose of engaging in prostitution or obtaining the sexual services of a prostitute, in a public place or a place open to public view. The provision extends to conduct short of verbal communication by prohibiting stopping or attempting to stop any person for those purposes (*R. v. Head* (1987), 59 C.R. (3d) 80 (B.C.C.A.)).

[69] The application judge found that face-to-face communication is an "essential tool" in enhancing street prostitutes' safety (para. 432). Such communication, which the law prohibits, allows prostitutes to screen prospective clients for intoxication or propensity to violence, which can reduce the risks they face (paras. 301 and 421). This conclusion, based on the evidence before her, sufficed to engage security of the person under s. 7.

[70] The application judge also found that the communicating law has had the effect of displacing prostitutes from familiar areas, where they may be supported by friends and regular customers, to more isolated areas, thereby making them more vulnerable (paras. 331 and 502).

[71] On the evidence accepted by the application judge, the law prohibits communication that would allow street prostitutes to increase their safety. By prohibiting communicating in public for the purpose of prostitution, the law prevents prostitutes from screening clients and setting terms for the use of condoms or safe houses. In these ways, it significantly increases the risks they face.

[72] I conclude that the evidence supports the application judge's conclusion that s. 213(1)(*c*) impacts security of the person and engages s. 7.

(2) A Closer Look at Causation

[73] For the reasons discussed above, the application judge concluded—and I agree—that the impugned laws negatively impact and thus engage security of the person rights of prostitutes. However, the appellant Attorneys General contend that s. 7 is not engaged because there is an insufficient causal connection between the laws and the risks faced by prostitutes. First, they argue that the courts below erroneously measured causation by an attenuated standard. Second, they argue that it is the choice of the applicants to engage in prostitution, rather than the law, that is the causal source of the harms they face. These arguments cannot succeed.

(a) The Nature of the Required Causal Connection

[74] Three possible standards for causation are raised for our consideration: (1) "sufficient causal connection," adopted

by the application judge (paras. 287-88); (2) a general "impact" approach, adopted by the Court of Appeal (paras. 108-9); and (3) "active, foreseeable and direct" causal connection, urged by the appellant Attorneys General (A.G. of Canada factum, at para. 65; A.G. of Ontario factum, at paras. 14-15).

[75] I conclude that the "sufficient causal connection" standard should prevail. This is a flexible standard, which allows the circumstances of each particular case to be taken into account. ...

[78] ... [F]rom a practical perspective, a sufficient causal connection represents a fair and workable threshold for engaging s. 7 of the *Charter*. This is the port of entry for s. 7 claims. The claimant bears the burden of establishing this connection. Even if established, it does not end the inquiry, since the claimant must go on to show that the deprivation of her security of the person is not in accordance with the principles of fundamental justice. Although mere speculation will not suffice to establish causation, to set the bar too high risks barring meritorious claims. What is required is a sufficient connection, having regard to the context of the case.

(b) Is the Causal Connection Negated by Choice or the Role of Third Parties?

[79] The Attorneys General of Canada and Ontario argue that prostitutes choose to engage in an inherently risky activity. They can avoid both the risk inherent in prostitution and any increased risk that the laws impose simply by choosing not to engage in this activity. They say that choice—and not the law—is the real cause of their injury. ...

[85] For the following reasons, I cannot accept the argument that it is not the law, but rather prostitutes' choice and third parties, that cause the risks complained of in this case.

[86] First, while some prostitutes may fit the description of persons who freely choose (or at one time chose) to engage in the risky economic activity of prostitution, many prostitutes have no meaningful choice but to do so.... [S]treet prostitutes, with some exceptions, are a particularly marginalized population.... Whether because of financial desperation, drug addictions, mental illness, or compulsion from pimps, they often have little choice but to sell their bodies for money. Realistically, while they may retain some minimal power of choice[,] ... these are not people who can be said to be truly "choosing" a risky line of business (see [*Canada (Attorney General) v.*] *PHS* [*Community Services Society*, 2011 SCC 44, [2011] 3 S.C.R. 134], at paras. 97-101).

[87] Second, even accepting that there are those who freely choose to engage in prostitution, it must be remembered that prostitution—the exchange of sex for money—is not illegal. The causal question is whether the impugned laws make this lawful activity more dangerous. An analogy could be drawn to a law preventing a cyclist from wearing a helmet. That the cyclist chooses to ride her bike does not diminish the causal role of the law in making that activity riskier. The challenged laws relating to prostitution are no different.

[88] Nor is it accurate to say that the claim in this case is a veiled assertion of a positive right to vocational safety. The applicants are not asking the government to put into place measures making prostitution safe. Rather, they are asking this Court to strike down legislative provisions that aggravate the risk of disease, violence and death.

[89] It makes no difference that the conduct of pimps and johns is the immediate source of the harms suffered by prostitutes. The impugned laws deprive people engaged in a risky, but legal, activity of the means to protect themselves against those risks. The violence of a john does not diminish the role of the state in making a prostitute more vulnerable to that violence. ...

(3) Principles of Fundamental Justice

(a) The Applicable Norms

[93] I have concluded that the impugned laws deprive prostitutes of security of the person, engaging s. 7. The remaining step in the s. 7 analysis is to determine whether this deprivation is in accordance with the principles of fundamental justice. If so, s. 7 is not breached. ...

[95] The principles of fundamental justice have significantly evolved since the birth of the *Charter*. Initially, the principles of fundamental justice were thought to refer narrowly to principles of natural justice that define procedural fairness. ...

[96] The *Motor Vehicle Reference* recognized that the principles of fundamental justice are about the basic values underpinning our constitutional order. The s. 7 analysis is concerned with capturing inherently bad laws: that is, laws that take away life, liberty, or security of the person in a way that runs afoul of our basic values. The principles of fundamental justice are an attempt to capture those values. Over the years, the jurisprudence has given shape to the content of these basic values. In this case, we are concerned with the basic values against arbitrariness, overbreadth, and gross disproportionality.

[97] The concepts of arbitrariness, overbreadth, and gross disproportionality evolved organically as courts were faced with novel *Charter* claims.

[98] Arbitrariness was used to describe the situation where there is no connection between the effect and the object of the law. ...

[101] Another way in which laws may violate our basic values is through what the cases have called "overbreadth":

the law goes too far and interferes with some conduct that bears no connection to its objective. In *R. v. Heywood*, [1994] 3 S.C.R. 761, the accused challenged a vagrancy law that prohibited offenders convicted of listed offences from "loitering" in public parks. The majority of the Court found that the law, which aimed to protect children from sexual predators, was overbroad; insofar as the law applied to offenders who did not constitute a danger to children, and insofar as it applied to parks where children were unlikely to be present, it was unrelated to its objective. ...

[103] Laws are also in violation of our basic values when the effect of the law is grossly disproportionate to the state's objective. ...

[104] In *PHS*, this Court found that the Minister's refusal to exempt the safe injection site from drug possession laws was not in accordance with the principles of fundamental justice because the effect of denying health services and increasing the risk of death and disease of injection drug users was grossly disproportionate to the objectives of the drug possession laws, namely public health and safety.

[105] The overarching lesson that emerges from the case law is that laws run afoul of our basic values when the means by which the state seeks to attain its objective is fundamentally flawed, in the sense of being arbitrary, overbroad, or having effects that are grossly disproportionate to the legislative goal. To deprive citizens of life, liberty, or security of the person by laws that violate these norms is not in accordance with the principles of fundamental justice.

[106] As these principles have developed in the jurisprudence, they have not always been applied consistently. ...

[107] Although there is significant overlap between these three principles, and one law may properly be characterized by more than one of them, arbitrariness, overbreadth, and gross disproportionality remain three distinct principles that stem from what Hamish Stewart calls "failures of instrumental rationality"—the situation where the law is "inadequately connected to its objective or in some sense goes too far in seeking to attain it." ...

[111] Arbitrariness asks whether there is a direct connection between the purpose of the law and the impugned effect on the individual, in the sense that the effect on the individual bears some relation to the law's purpose. There must be a rational connection between the object of the measure that causes the s. 7 deprivation, and the limits it imposes on life, liberty, or security of the person .... A law that imposes limits on these interests in a way that bears *no connection* to its objective arbitrarily impinges on those interests. ...

[112] Overbreadth deals with a law that is so broad in scope that it includes *some* conduct that bears no relation to its purpose. In this sense, the law is arbitrary *in part*. At its core, overbreadth addresses the situation where there is no rational connection between the purposes of the law and *some*, but not all, of its impacts. ...

[113] Overbreadth allows courts to recognize that the law is rational in some cases, but that it overreaches in its effect in others. Despite this recognition of the scope of the law as a whole, the focus remains on the individual and whether the effect on the individual is rationally connected to the law's purpose. For example, where a law is drawn broadly and targets some conduct that bears no relation to its purpose in order to make enforcement more practical, there is still no connection between the purpose of the law and its effect on the *specific individual*. Enforcement practicality may be a justification for an overbroad law, to be analyzed under s. 1 of the *Charter*. ...

[118] An ancillary question, which applies to both arbitrariness and overbreadth, concerns how significant the lack of correspondence between the objective of the infringing provision and its effects must be. Questions have arisen as to whether a law is arbitrary or overbroad when its effects are *inconsistent* with its objective, or whether, more broadly, a law is arbitrary or overbroad whenever its effects are *unnecessary* for its objective (see, e.g., *Chaoulli*, at paras. 233-34).

[119] As noted above, the root question is whether the law is inherently bad because there is *no connection*, in whole or in part, between its effects and its purpose. This standard is not easily met. The evidence may, as in *Morgentaler*, show that the effect actually undermines the objective and is therefore "inconsistent" with the objective. Or the evidence may, as in *Chaoulli*, show that there is simply no connection on the facts between the effect and the objective, and the effect is therefore "unnecessary." Regardless of how the judge describes this lack of connection, the ultimate question remains whether the evidence establishes that the law violates basic norms because there is *no connection* between its effect and its purpose. This is a matter to be determined on a case-by-case basis, in light of the evidence.

[120] Gross disproportionality asks a different question from arbitrariness and overbreadth. It targets the second fundamental evil: the law's effects on life, liberty or security of the person are so grossly disproportionate to its purposes that they cannot rationally be supported. The rule against gross disproportionality only applies in extreme cases where the seriousness of the deprivation is totally out of sync with the objective of the measure. This idea is captured by the hypothetical of a law with the purpose of keeping the streets clean that imposes a sentence of life imprisonment for spitting on the sidewalk. The connection between the draconian impact of the law and its object must be entirely outside the norms accepted in our free and democratic society.

[121] Gross disproportionality under s. 7 of the *Charter* does *not* consider the beneficial effects of the law for society. It balances the negative effect on the individual against the purpose of the law, *not* against societal benefit that might flow from the law. ...

[122] Thus, gross disproportionality is not concerned with the number of people who experience grossly disproportionate effects; a grossly disproportionate effect on one person is sufficient to violate the norm.

[123] All three principles—arbitrariness, overbreadth, and gross disproportionality—compare the rights infringement caused by the law with the objective of the law, not with the law's effectiveness. That is, they do not look to how well the law achieves its object, or to how much of the population the law benefits. They do not consider ancillary benefits to the general population. Furthermore, none of the principles measure the percentage of the population that is negatively impacted. The analysis is qualitative, not quantitative. The question under s. 7 is whether *anyone's* life, liberty or security of the person has been denied by a law that is inherently bad; a grossly disproportionate, overbroad, or arbitrary effect on one person is sufficient to establish a breach of s. 7.

(b) The Relationship Between Section 7 and Section 1

[124] This Court has previously identified parallels between the rules against arbitrariness, overbreadth, and gross disproportionality under s. 7 and elements of the s. 1 analysis for justification of laws that violate *Charter* rights. These parallels should not be allowed to obscure the crucial differences between the two sections.

[125] Section 7 and s. 1 ask different questions. The question under s. 7 is whether the law's negative effect on life, liberty, or security of the person is in accordance with the principles of fundamental justice. With respect to the principles of arbitrariness, overbreadth, and gross disproportionality, the specific questions are whether the law's purpose, taken at face value, is connected to its effects and whether the negative effect is grossly disproportionate to the law's purpose. Under s. 1, the question is different—whether the negative impact of a law on the rights of individuals is proportionate to the pressing and substantial goal of the law in furthering the public interest. The question of justification on the basis of an overarching public goal is at the heart of s. 1, but it plays no part in the s. 7 analysis, which is concerned with the narrower question of whether the impugned law infringes individual rights.

[126] As a consequence of the different questions they address, s. 7 and s. 1 work in different ways. Under s. 1, the government bears the burden of showing that a law that breaches an individual's rights can be justified having regard to the government's goal. Because the question is whether the broader public interest justifies the infringement of individual rights, the law's goal must be pressing and substantial. The "rational connection" branch of the s. 1 analysis asks whether the law was a rational means for the legislature to pursue its objective. "Minimal impairment" asks whether the legislature could have designed a law that infringes rights to a lesser extent; it considers the legislature's reasonable alternatives. At the final stage of the s. 1 analysis, the court is required to weigh the negative impact of the law on people's rights against the beneficial impact of the law in terms of achieving its goal for the greater public good. The impacts are judged both qualitatively and quantitatively. Unlike individual claimants, the Crown is well placed to call the social science and expert evidence required to justify the law's impact in terms of society as a whole.

[127] By contrast, under s. 7, the claimant bears the burden of establishing that the law deprives her of life, liberty or security of the person, in a manner that is not connected to the law's object or in a manner that is grossly disproportionate to the law's object. The inquiry into the purpose of the law focuses on the nature of the object, not on its efficacy. The inquiry into the impact on life, liberty or security of the person is not quantitative—for example, how many people are negatively impacted—but qualitative. An arbitrary, overbroad, or grossly disproportionate impact on one person suffices to establish a breach of s. 7. To require s. 7 claimants to establish the efficacy of the law versus its deleterious consequences on members of society as a whole, would impose the government's s. 1 burden on claimants under s. 7. That cannot be right.

[128] In brief, although the concepts under s. 7 and s. 1 are rooted in similar concerns, they are analytically distinct. ...

(4) Do the Impugned Laws Respect the Principles of Fundamental Justice?

(a) Section 210: The Bawdy-House Prohibition

(i) *The Object of the Provision*

...

[131] The appellant Attorneys General argue that the object of this provision, considered alone and in conjunction with the other prohibitions, is to deter prostitution. The record does not support this contention; on the contrary, it is clear from the legislative record that the purpose of the prohibition is to prevent community harms in the nature of nuisance. ...

*(ii) Compliance With the Principles
of Fundamental Justice*

...

[134] ... The application judge found on the evidence that moving to a bawdy-house would improve prostitutes' safety by providing "the safety benefits of proximity to others, familiarity with surroundings, security staff, closed-circuit television and other such monitoring that a permanent indoor location can facilitate." ... Balancing this against the evidence demonstrating that "complaints about nuisance arising from indoor prostitution establishments are rare" ... , she found that the harmful impact of the provision was grossly disproportionate to its purpose.

[The court agrees with this analysis.]

[136] ... Parliament has the power to regulate against nuisances, but not at the cost of the health, safety and lives of prostitutes. A law that prevents street prostitutes from resorting to a safe haven such as Grandma's House while a suspected serial killer prowls the streets, is a law that has lost sight of its purpose.

(b) Section 212(1)(j): Living on the
Avails of Prostitution

(iii) The Object of the Provision

[137] This Court has held ... that the purpose of this provision is to target pimps and the parasitic, exploitative conduct in which they engage. ...

*(iv) Compliance With the Principles
of Fundamental Justice*

[139] The courts below concluded that the living on the avails provision is overbroad insofar as it captures a number of non-exploitative relationships which are not connected to the law's purpose. The courts below also concluded that the provision's negative effect on the security and safety of prostitutes is grossly disproportionate to its objective of protecting prostitutes from harm. ...

[142] ... The law punishes everyone who lives on the avails of prostitution without distinguishing between those who exploit prostitutes (for example, controlling and abusive pimps) and those who could increase the safety and security of prostitutes (for example, legitimate drivers, managers, or bodyguards). It also includes anyone involved in business with a prostitute, such as accountants or receptionists. In these ways, the law includes some conduct that bears no relation to its purpose of preventing the exploitation of prostitutes. The living on the avails provision is therefore overbroad.

[143] The appellant Attorneys General argue that the line between an exploitative pimp and a prostitute's legitimate driver, manager or bodyguard, blurs in the real world. A relationship that begins on a non-exploitative footing may become exploitative over time. If the provision were tailored more narrowly—for example, by reading in "in circumstances of exploitation" as the Court of Appeal did—evidentiary difficulties may lead to exploiters escaping liability. Relationships of exploitation often involve intimidation and manipulation of the kind that make it very difficult for a prostitute to testify. For these reasons, the Attorneys General argue, the provision must be drawn broadly in order to effectively capture those it targets.

[144] This argument is more appropriately addressed under the s. 1 analysis. As stated above, if a law captures conduct that bears no relation to its purpose, the law is overbroad under s. 7; enforcement practicality is one way the government may justify an overbroad law under s. 1 of the *Charter*. ...

(c) Section 213(1)(c): Communicating in
Public for the Purposes of Prostitution

(i) The Object of the Provision

...

[147] ... [T]he purpose of the communicating provision is not to eliminate street prostitution for its own sake, but to take prostitution "off the streets and out of public view" in order to prevent the nuisances that street prostitution can cause. The *Prostitution Reference* belies the Attorneys General's argument that Parliament's overall objective in these provisions is to deter prostitution.

*(ii) Compliance With the Principles
of Fundamental Justice*

[148] The application judge concluded that the harm imposed by the prohibition on communicating in public was grossly disproportionate to the provision's object of removing the nuisance of prostitution from the streets. This was based on evidence that she found established that the ability to screen clients was an "essential tool" to avoiding violent or drunken clients (application decision, at para. 432).

[The Supreme Court agrees with the application judge and rebuts the contrary finding of the appeal court. The prohibition on public communication, the chief justice argues, increases the risk of harm to prostitutes by making it difficult for them to assess and negotiate with clients before the transaction occurs. The ban also forces prostitutes to more isolated, remote locations where the risk of harm is greater.]

[159] In sum, the Court of Appeal wrongly attributed errors in reasoning to the application judge and made a number of errors in considering gross disproportionality. I would restore the application judge's conclusion that s. 213(1)(*c*) is grossly disproportionate. The provision's negative impact on the safety and lives of street prostitutes is a grossly disproportionate response to the possibility of nuisance caused by street prostitution. ...

D. Are the Infringements Justified Under Section 1 of the Charter?

[161] The appellant Attorneys General have not seriously argued that the laws, if found to infringe s. 7, can be justified under s. 1 of the *Charter*. Only the Attorney General of Canada addressed this in his factum, and then, only briefly. I therefore find it unnecessary to engage in a full s. 1 analysis for each of the impugned provisions. However, some of their arguments under s. 7 of the *Charter* are properly addressed at this stage of the analysis.

[162] In particular, the Attorneys General attempt to justify the living on the avails provision on the basis that it must be drafted broadly in order to capture all exploitative relationships, which can be difficult to identify. However, the law not only catches drivers and bodyguards, who may actually be pimps, but it also catches clearly non-exploitative relationships, such as receptionists or accountants who work with prostitutes. The law is therefore not minimally impairing. Nor, at the final stage of the s. 1 inquiry, is the law's effect of preventing prostitutes from taking measures that would increase their safety, and possibly save their lives, outweighed by the law's positive effect of protecting prostitutes from exploitative relationships.

[163] The Attorneys General have not raised any other arguments distinct from those considered under s. 7. I therefore find that the impugned laws are not saved by s. 1 of the *Charter*.

V. Result and Remedy

...

[165] I have concluded that each of the challenged provisions, considered independently, suffers from constitutional infirmities that violate the *Charter*. That does not mean that Parliament is precluded from imposing limits on where and how prostitution may be conducted. ...

[166] This raises the question of whether the declaration of invalidity should be suspended and if so, for how long. ...

[169] The choice between suspending the declaration of invalidity and allowing it to take immediate effect is not an easy one. Neither alternative is without difficulty. However, considering all the interests at stake, I conclude that the declaration of invalidity should be suspended for one year.

26 Carter v. Canada (Attorney General), 2015

The principle of *stare decisis* is a cornerstone of Canada's "judge-made" common law tradition. The term is an abbreviation of the Latin phrase *stare decisis et non quieta movere*, which means to "stand by decisions and not disturb settled matters."[1] Because the Supreme Court of Canada is at the apex of a hierarchical judicial system, the principle of *stare decisis* means that its rulings are binding on all other courts. However, this principle has not prevented the Supreme Court from overruling its own earlier decisions. The case here is one of the court's more notable reversals.

At issue in *Carter v. Canada (Attorney General)* was whether *Criminal Code* provisions prohibiting physician-assisted dying infringe life, liberty, and security of the person in a manner not in accordance with the principles of fundamental justice as provided in section 7 of the Charter and, if so, whether the infringement is justifiable under section 1. The Supreme Court ruled unanimously that section 7 was violated and that the legislation could not be saved under section 1. In so doing, the court overruled its earlier 1993 ruling in *Rodriguez v. British Columbia*[2] in which a majority had upheld the validity of a blanket prohibition on assisted suicide.

In both cases, the Charter claim was made by a woman dying from ALS (amyotrophic lateral sclerosis) who wanted the ability to call on a physician to assist her to die when she considered that her suffering was no longer tolerable. A majority in the earlier *Rodriguez* ruling held that although the ban on physician-assisted suicide denies the right to life, liberty, and security of the person, this denial was consistent with the principles of fundamental justice. However, in *Carter* the court ruled unanimously that the prohibition of section 7 was inconsistent with the principles of fundamental justice and also that this denial could not be justified under section 1.

The federal and Ontario attorneys general each argued that the trial judge was bound by the Supreme Court's position in *Rodriguez* and therefore was not entitled to revisit the constitutionality of the prohibition on assisted suicide. The Supreme Court acknowledged that *stare decisis* "provides certainty while permitting the orderly development of the law in incremental steps." Nevertheless, this principle should not operate as a straitjacket that condemns law to stagnation. Thus, trial courts are entitled to reconsider settled rulings of higher courts in the following two situations: where a new legal issue is raised and where there is a change in the circumstances or evidence that fundamentally shifts the parameters

---

1   As referred to in Joseph J. Arvay, Q.C., Sheila Tucker, and Alison M. Latimer, "*Stare Decisis* and Constitutional Supremacy: Will Our Charter Past Become an Obstacle to Our Charter Future?" (2012) 58 *Supreme Court Law Review* (2d) 61 at 64.

2   *Rodriguez v. British Columbia*, [1993] 3 S.C.R. 519.

of the debate. For the court, both conditions were met in this case. To add additional authority to its new position, the decision was delivered by "The Court."

As frequently occurs, the Supreme Court suspended the effects of its declaration of the law's invalidity for 12 months. The court made clear that it was not prepared to grant a free-standing exemption from prosecution for physician-assisted suicides. In its view, the kind of complex regulatory regime called for is better created by Parliament than by the courts. The Supreme Court indicated that the legislation would need to reconcile the Charter rights of patients and physicians, and also that physicians should not be compelled to provide assistance in dying.

The federal Harper government did little to develop a legislative response to the ruling in its remaining months in office. As the deadline for revised legislation neared, the attorney general of the newly elected Liberal government approached the Supreme Court for additional time to develop a legislative response. Suspended declarations of invalidity can be controversial because they delay the remedial effects of judicial review.[3] By seeking yet more time, a government is effectively asking the court to bear institutional responsibility for further delaying remedies. When federal Justice Department lawyers were seeking an extension of the declaration of invalidity to enact a regulatory framework for physician-assisted suicide, Supreme Court Justice Russell Brown suggested that the government ask Parliament to invoke section 33.[4] Nevertheless, a divided Supreme Court agreed to give Parliament an additional four months.

Despite the extension, time ran out before Parliament passed the government's legislative response to the *Carter* ruling. Bill C-14, introduced in April 2016, amending the *Criminal Code* and other laws relating to medical assistance in dying, was extremely contentious, both in terms of its process (which included closures in debate) and its substance. Critics argued that it was more restrictive than suggested by the Supreme Court's ruling. Many argued that the Bill, if passed, would be challenged and declared unconstitutional, leading to parliamentary pressure on the government to release the legal advice it received with respect to developing and drafting the legislation. The Bill was indeed passed and is likely to be challenged. ⌢

Discussion Questions

1. The federal legislative response was more restrictive than suggested by the Supreme Court. In the event of a subsequent Charter challenge, is this an appropriate issue for judicial deference for Parliament's legislative response? Why or why not?

2. Was a suspended declaration of invalidity an appropriate remedy in this case? Why or why not?

3. Should Parliament enact the notwithstanding clause when more time is required to redress legislative problems identified by the Supreme Court, rather than request additional time?

---

3 Robert Leckey, *Bills of Rights in the Common Law* (Cambridge, UK: Cambridge University Press, 2015).

4 Tonda MacCharles, "Ottawa surprises top court judges by allowing assisted suicide to proceed in Quebec" *Toronto Star* (11 January 2016), online: <http://www.thestar.com/news/canada/2016/01/11/ottawa-surprises-top-court-judges-by-asking-for-more-time-on-assisted-suicide.html>.

CARTER v. CANADA (ATTORNEY GENERAL)
2015 SCC 5, [2015] 1 S.C.R. 331

Hearing: October 15, 2014; Judgment: February 6, 2015.

Present: McLachlin C.J. and LeBel, Abella, Rothstein, Cromwell, Moldaver, Karakatsanis, Wagner, and Gascon JJ.

Interveners: Attorney General of Ontario, Attorney General of Quebec, Council of Canadians with Disabilities, Canadian Association for Community Living, Christian Legal Fellowship, Canadian HIV/AIDS Legal Network, HIV & AIDS Legal Clinic Ontario, Association for Reformed Political Action Canada, Physicians' Alliance against Euthanasia, Evangelical Fellowship of Canada, Christian Medical and Dental Society of Canada, Canadian Federation of Catholic Physicians' Societies, Dying With Dignity, Canadian Medical Association, Catholic Health Alliance of Canada, Criminal Lawyers' Association (Ontario), Farewell Foundation for the Right to Die, Association québécoise pour le droit de mourir dans la dignité, Canadian Civil Liberties Association, Catholic Civil Rights League, Faith and Freedom Alliance, Protection of Conscience Project, Alliance of People With Disabilities Who are Supportive of Legal Assisted Dying Society, Canadian Unitarian Council, Euthanasia Prevention Coalition and Euthanasia Prevention Coalition—British Columbia.

The following is the judgment delivered by **THE COURT:**

I. Introduction

[1] It is a crime in Canada to assist another person in ending her own life. As a result, people who are grievously and irremediably ill cannot seek a physician's assistance in dying and may be condemned to a life of severe and intolerable suffering. A person facing this prospect has two options: she can take her own life prematurely, often by violent or dangerous means, or she can suffer until she dies from natural causes. The choice is cruel.

[2] The question on this appeal is whether the criminal prohibition that puts a person to this choice violates her *Charter* rights to life, liberty and security of the person (s. 7) and to equal treatment by and under the law (s. 15). This is a question that asks us to balance competing values of great importance. On the one hand stands the autonomy and dignity of a competent adult who seeks death as a response to a grievous and irremediable medical condition. On the other stands the sanctity of life and the need to protect the vulnerable. ...

[4] We conclude that the prohibition on physician-assisted dying is void insofar as it deprives a competent adult of such assistance where (1) the person affected clearly consents to the termination of life; and (2) the person has a

grievous and irremediable medical condition (including an illness, disease or disability) that causes enduring suffering that is intolerable to the individual in the circumstances of his or her condition. We therefore allow the appeal.

II. Background

[5] In Canada, aiding or abetting a person to commit suicide is a criminal offence ... . This means that a person cannot seek a physician-assisted death. Twenty-one years ago, this Court upheld this blanket prohibition on assisted suicide by a slim majority ... .

[6] Despite the Court's decision in *Rodriguez*, the debate over physician-assisted dying continued. Between 1991 and 2010, the House of Commons and its committees debated no less than six private member's bills seeking to decriminalize assisted suicide. None was passed. While opponents to legalization emphasized the inadequacy of safeguards and the potential to devalue human life, a vocal minority spoke in favour of reform, highlighting the importance of dignity and autonomy and the limits of palliative care in addressing suffering. The Senate considered the matter as well, issuing a report on assisted suicide and euthanasia in 1995. The majority expressed concerns about the risk of abuse under a permissive regime and the need for respect for life. A minority supported an exemption to the prohibition in some circumstances.

[7] More recent reports have come down in favour of reform. In 2011, the Royal Society of Canada published a report on end-of-life decision-making and recommended that the *Criminal Code* be modified to permit assistance in dying in some circumstances. The Quebec National Assembly's Select Committee on Dying with Dignity issued a report in 2012, recommending amendments to legislation to recognize medical aid in dying as appropriate end-of-life care (now codified in *An Act respecting end-of-life care*, CQLR, c. S-32.0001 (not yet in force)).

[8] The legislative landscape on the issue of physician-assisted death has changed in the two decades since *Rodriguez*. ... By 2010, however, eight jurisdictions permitted some form of assisted dying: the Netherlands, Belgium, Luxembourg, Switzerland, Oregon, Washington, Montana, and Colombia. ... Together, these regimes have produced a body of evidence about the practical and legal workings of physician-assisted death and the efficacy of safeguards for the vulnerable. ...

[10] The debate in the public arena reflects the ongoing debate in the legislative sphere. Some medical practitioners see legal change as a natural extension of the principle of patient autonomy, while others fear derogation from the principles of medical ethics. Some people with disabilities oppose

the legalization of assisted dying, arguing that it implicitly devalues their lives and renders them vulnerable to unwanted assistance in dying, as medical professionals assume that a disabled patient "leans towards death at a sharper angle than the acutely ill—but otherwise non-disabled—patient." ... Other people with disabilities take the opposite view, arguing that a regime which permits control over the manner of one's death respects, rather than threatens, their autonomy and dignity, and that the legalization of physician-assisted suicide will protect them by establishing stronger safeguards and oversight for end-of-life medical care.

[11] The impetus for this case arose in 2009, when Gloria Taylor was diagnosed with a fatal neurodegenerative disease, amyotrophic lateral sclerosis (or ALS), which causes progressive muscle weakness. ALS patients first lose the ability to use their hands and feet, then the ability to walk, chew, swallow, speak and, eventually, breathe. Like Sue Rodriguez before her, Gloria Taylor did "not want to die slowly, piece by piece" or "wracked with pain," and brought a claim before the British Columbia Supreme Court challenging the constitutionality of the *Criminal Code* provisions that prohibit assistance in dying ... . She was joined in her claim by Lee Carter and Hollis Johnson, who had assisted Ms. Carter's mother, Kathleen ("Kay") Carter, in achieving her goal of dying with dignity by taking her to Switzerland to use the services of DIGNITAS, an assisted-suicide clinic; Dr. William Shoichet, a physician from British Columbia who would be willing to participate in physician-assisted dying if it were no longer prohibited; and the British Columbia Civil Liberties Association, which has a long-standing interest in patients' rights and health policy and has conducted advocacy and education with respect to end-of-life choices, including assisted suicide.

[12] By 2010, Ms. Taylor's condition had deteriorated to the point that she required a wheelchair to go more than a short distance and was suffering pain from muscle deterioration. She required home support for assistance with the daily tasks of living, something that she described as an assault on her privacy, dignity, and self-esteem. She continued to pursue an independent life despite her illness, but found that she was steadily losing the ability to participate fully in that life. Ms. Taylor informed her family and friends of a desire to obtain a physician-assisted death. She did not want to "live in a bed-ridden state, stripped of dignity and independence," she said; nor did she want an "ugly death." ...

[13] Ms. Taylor, however, knew she would be unable to request a physician-assisted death when the time came, because of the *Criminal Code* prohibition and the fact that she lacked the financial resources to travel to Switzerland, where assisted suicide is legal and available to non-residents. This left her with what she described as the "cruel choice"

between killing herself while she was still physically capable of doing so, or giving up the ability to exercise any control over the manner and timing of her death. ...

V. Issues on Appeal

[40] The main issue in this case is whether the prohibition on physician-assisted dying found in s. 241(*b*) of the *Criminal Code* violates the claimants' rights under ss. 7 and 15 of the *Charter*. For the purposes of their claim, the appellants use "physician-assisted death" and "physician-assisted dying" to describe the situation where a physician provides or administers medication that intentionally brings about the patient's death, at the request of the patient. The appellants advance two claims: (1) that the prohibition on physician-assisted dying deprives competent adults, who suffer a grievous and irremediable medical condition that causes the person to endure physical or psychological suffering that is intolerable to that person, of their right to life, liberty and security of the person under s. 7 of the *Charter*; and (2) that the prohibition deprives adults who are physically disabled of their right to equal treatment under s. 15 of the *Charter*.

[41] Before turning to the *Charter* claims, two preliminary issues arise: (1) whether this Court's decision in *Rodriguez* can be revisited; and (2) whether the prohibition is beyond Parliament's power because physician-assisted dying lies at the core of the provincial jurisdiction over health.

VI. Was the Trial Judge Bound by Rodriguez?

...

[43] Canada and Ontario argue that the trial judge was bound by *Rodriguez* and not entitled to revisit the constitutionality of the legislation prohibiting assisted suicide. Ontario goes so far as to argue that "vertical *stare decisis*" is a *constitutional* principle that requires all lower courts to rigidly follow this Court's *Charter* precedents unless and until this Court sets them aside.

[44] The doctrine that lower courts must follow the decisions of higher courts is fundamental to our legal system. It provides certainty while permitting the orderly development of the law in incremental steps. However, *stare decisis* is not a straitjacket that condemns the law to stasis. Trial courts may reconsider settled rulings of higher courts in two situations: (1) where a new legal issue is raised; and (2) where there is a change in the circumstances or evidence that "fundamentally shifts the parameters of the debate" (*Canada (Attorney General) v. Bedford*, 2013 SCC 72, [2013] 3 S.C.R. 1101, at para. 42).

[45] Both conditions were met in this case. The trial judge explained her decision to revisit *Rodriguez* by noting the changes in both the legal framework for s. 7 and the evidence

on controlling the risk of abuse associated with assisted suicide.

[46] The argument before the trial judge involved a different legal conception of s. 7 than that prevailing when *Rodriguez* was decided. In particular, the law relating to the principles of overbreadth and gross disproportionality had materially advanced since *Rodriguez*. The majority of this Court in *Rodriguez* acknowledged the argument that the impugned laws were "over-inclusive" when discussing the principles of fundamental justice (see p. 590). However, it did not apply the principle of overbreadth as it is currently understood, but instead asked whether the prohibition was "arbitrary or unfair in that it is unrelated to the state's interest in protecting the vulnerable, and that it lacks a foundation in the legal tradition and societal beliefs which are said to be represented by the prohibition" (p. 595). By contrast, the law on overbreadth, now explicitly recognized as a principle of fundamental justice, asks whether the law interferes with some conduct that has no connection to the law's objectives (*Bedford*, at para. 101). This different question may lead to a different answer. The majority's consideration of overbreadth under s. 1 suffers from the same defect: see *Rodriguez*, at p. 614. Finally, the majority in *Rodriguez* did not consider whether the prohibition was grossly disproportionate.

[47] The matrix of legislative and social facts in this case also differed from the evidence before the Court in *Rodriguez*. The majority in *Rodriguez* relied on evidence of (1) the widespread acceptance of a moral or ethical distinction between passive and active euthanasia (pp. 605-7); (2) the lack of any "halfway measure" that could protect the vulnerable (pp. 613-14); and (3) the "substantial consensus" in Western countries that a blanket prohibition is necessary to protect against the slippery slope (pp. 601-6 and 613). The record before the trial judge in this case contained evidence that, if accepted, was capable of undermining each of these conclusions. ...

VIII. Section 7

...

[55] In order to demonstrate a violation of s. 7, the claimants must first show that the law interferes with, or deprives them of, their life, liberty or security of the person. Once they have established that s. 7 is engaged, they must then show that the deprivation in question is not in accordance with the principles of fundamental justice.

[56] For the reasons below, we conclude that the prohibition on physician-assisted dying infringes the right to life, liberty and security of Ms. Taylor and of persons in her position, and that it does so in a manner that is overbroad and thus is not in accordance with the principles of fundamental justice. It therefore violates s. 7.

A. Does the Law Infringe the Right to Life, Liberty and Security of the Person?

(1) Life

...

[62] This Court has most recently invoked the right to life in *Chaoulli v. Quebec (Attorney General)*, ... where evidence showed that the lack of timely health care could result in death ... and in *PHS*, where the clients of Insite were deprived of potentially lifesaving medical care ... . In each case, the right was only engaged by the threat of death. In short, the case law suggests that the right to life is engaged where the law or state action imposes death or an increased risk of death on a person, either directly or indirectly. Conversely, concerns about autonomy and quality of life have traditionally been treated as liberty and security rights. We see no reason to alter that approach in this case.

[63] This said, we do not agree that the existential formulation of the right to life *requires* an absolute prohibition on assistance in dying, or that individuals cannot "waive" their right to life. This would create a "duty to live," rather than a "right to life," and would call into question the legality of any consent to the withdrawal or refusal of lifesaving or life-sustaining treatment. The sanctity of life is one of our most fundamental societal values. Section 7 is rooted in a profound respect for the value of human life. But s. 7 also encompasses life, liberty and security of the person during the passage to death. It is for this reason that the sanctity of life "is no longer seen to require that all human life be preserved at all costs" (*Rodriguez*, at p. 595, per Sopinka J.). And it is for this reason that the law has come to recognize that, in certain circumstances, an individual's choice about the end of her life is entitled to respect. It is to this fundamental choice that we now turn.

(2) Liberty and Security of the Person

[64] Underlying both of these rights is a concern for the protection of individual autonomy and dignity. Liberty protects "the right to make fundamental personal choices free from state interference." ... Security of the person encompasses "a notion of personal autonomy involving ... control over one's bodily integrity free from state interference" ... and it is engaged by state interference with an individual's physical or psychological integrity, including any state action that causes physical or serious psychological suffering ... . While liberty and security of the person are distinct interests, for the purpose of this appeal they may be considered together. ...

[66] We agree with the trial judge. An individual's response to a grievous and irremediable medical condition is a matter critical to their dignity and autonomy. The law allows

people in this situation to request palliative sedation, refuse artificial nutrition and hydration, or request the removal of life-sustaining medical equipment, but denies them the right to request a physician's assistance in dying. This interferes with their ability to make decisions concerning their bodily integrity and medical care and thus trenches on liberty. And, by leaving people like Ms. Taylor to endure intolerable suffering, it impinges on their security of the person.

[67] The law has long protected patient autonomy in medical decision-making. ... This right to "decide one's own fate" entitles adults to direct the course of their own medical care [and] it is this principle that underlies the concept of "informed consent" and is protected by s. 7's guarantee of liberty and security of the person ... . It is this same principle that is at work in the cases dealing with the right to refuse consent to medical treatment, or to demand that treatment be withdrawn or discontinued ... .

[68] ... [Section] 7 recognizes the value of life, but it also honours the role that autonomy and dignity play at the end of that life. We therefore conclude that ss. 241(*b*) and 14 of the *Criminal Code*, insofar as they prohibit physician-assisted dying for competent adults who seek such assistance as a result of a grievous and irremediable medical condition that causes enduring and intolerable suffering, infringe the rights to liberty and security of the person. ...

(3) Summary on Section 7: Life, Liberty and Security of the Person

[70] For the foregoing reasons, we conclude that the prohibition on physician-assisted dying deprived Ms. Taylor and others suffering from grievous and irremediable medical conditions of the right to life, liberty and security of the person. The remaining question under s. 7 is whether this deprivation was in accordance with the principles of fundamental justice.

B. The Principles of Fundamental Justice

[71] Section 7 does not promise that the state will never interfere with a person's life, liberty or security of the person—laws do this all the time—but rather that the state will not do so in a way that violates the principles of fundamental justice.

[72] Section 7 does not catalogue the principles of fundamental justice to which it refers. Over the course of 32 years of *Charter* adjudication, this Court has worked to define the minimum constitutional requirements that a law that trenches on life, liberty or security of the person must meet ... . While the Court has recognized a number of principles of fundamental justice, three have emerged as central in the recent s. 7 jurisprudence: laws that impinge on life, liberty or security of

the person must not be arbitrary, overbroad, or have consequences that are grossly disproportionate to their object.

[73] ... The first step is ... to identify the object of the prohibition on assisted dying.

[74] The trial judge, relying on *Rodriguez*, concluded that the object of the prohibition was to protect vulnerable persons from being induced to commit suicide at a time of weakness. ... All the parties except Canada accept this formulation of the object.

[75] Canada agrees that the prohibition is intended to protect the vulnerable, but argues that the object of the prohibition should also be defined more broadly as simply "the preservation of life." ... We cannot accept this submission.

[76] First, it is incorrect to say that the majority in *Rodriguez* adopted "the preservation of life" as the object of the prohibition on assisted dying. ...

[77] Second, ... [i]f the object of the prohibition is stated broadly as "the preservation of life," it becomes difficult to say that the means used to further it are overbroad or grossly disproportionate. The outcome is to this extent foreordained.

[78] Finally, the jurisprudence requires the object of the impugned law to be defined precisely for the purposes of s. 7. ... Section 241(*b*) is not directed at preserving life, or even at preventing suicide—attempted suicide is no longer a crime. Yet Canada asks us to posit that the object of the prohibition is to preserve life, whatever the circumstances. This formulation goes beyond the ambit of the provision itself. The direct target of the measure is the narrow goal of preventing vulnerable persons from being induced to commit suicide at a time of weakness.

[79] Before turning to the principles of fundamental justice at play, a general comment is in order. In determining whether the deprivation of life, liberty and security of the person is in accordance with the principles of fundamental justice under s. 7, courts are not concerned with competing social interests or public benefits conferred by the impugned law. These competing moral claims and broad societal benefits are more appropriately considered at the stage of justification under s. 1 of the *Charter* ... .

[80] ... A claimant under s. 7 must show that the state has deprived them of their life, liberty or security of the person and that the deprivation is not in accordance with the principles of fundamental justice. They should not be tasked with also showing that these principles are "not overridden by a valid state or communal interest in these circumstances." ...

[82] This is not to say that such a deprivation cannot be *justified* under s. 1 of the *Charter*. In some cases the government, for practical reasons, may only be able to meet an important objective by means of a law that has some

fundamental flaw. But this does not concern us when considering whether s. 7 of the *Charter* has been breached.

(1) Arbitrariness

[83] The principle of fundamental justice that forbids arbitrariness targets the situation where there is no rational connection between the object of the law and the limit it imposes on life, liberty or security of the person. ... An arbitrary law is one that is not capable of fulfilling its objectives. It exacts a constitutional price in terms of rights, without furthering the public good that is said to be the object of the law.

[84] The object of the prohibition on physician-assisted dying is to protect the vulnerable from ending their life in times of weakness. A total ban on assisted suicide clearly helps achieve this object. Therefore, individuals' rights are not limited arbitrarily.

(2) Overbreadth

[85] The overbreadth inquiry asks whether a law that takes away rights in a way that generally supports the object of the law, goes too far by denying the rights of some individuals in a way that bears no relation to the object. ... The question is not whether Parliament has chosen the least restrictive means, but whether the chosen means infringe life, liberty or security of the person in a way that has no connection with the mischief contemplated by the legislature. The focus is not on broad social impacts, but on the impact of the measure on the individuals whose life, liberty or security of the person is trammelled.

[86] Applying this approach, we conclude that the prohibition on assisted dying is overbroad. ...

[87] Canada argues that it is difficult to conclusively identify the "vulnerable," and that therefore it cannot be said that the prohibition is overbroad. Indeed, Canada asserts, "every person is *potentially* vulnerable" from a legislative perspective ... .

[88] We do not agree. ... [T]hat argument is more appropriately addressed under s. 1 ... .

(3) Gross Disproportionality

[89] This principle is infringed if the impact of the restriction on the individual's life, liberty or security of the person is grossly disproportionate to the object of the measure. As with overbreadth, the focus is not on the impact of the measure on society or the public, which are matters for s. 1, but on its impact on the rights of the claimant. The inquiry into gross disproportionality compares the law's purpose, "taken at face value," with its negative effects on the rights of the claimant, and asks if this impact is completely

out of sync with the object of the law. ... The standard is high: the law's object and its impact may be incommensurate without reaching the standard for *gross* disproportionality ... .

[90] ... [T]he impact of the prohibition is severe: it imposes unnecessary suffering on affected individuals, deprives them of the ability to determine what to do with their bodies and how those bodies will be treated, and may cause those affected to take their own lives sooner than they would were they able to obtain a physician's assistance in dying. Against this it is argued that the object of the prohibition—to protect vulnerable persons from being induced to commit suicide at a time of weakness—is also of high importance. We find it unnecessary to decide whether the prohibition also violates the principle against gross disproportionality, in light of our conclusion that it is overbroad. ...

IX. Does the Prohibition on Assisted Suicide Violate Section 15 of the *Charter*?

[93] Having concluded that the prohibition violates s. 7, it is unnecessary to consider this question.

X. Section 1

[94] In order to justify the infringement of the appellants' s. 7 rights under s. 1 of the *Charter*, Canada must show that the law has a pressing and substantial object and that the means chosen are proportional to that object. ...

[95] It is difficult to justify a s. 7 violation ... . The rights protected by s. 7 are fundamental, and "not easily overridden by competing social interests" ... . And it is hard to justify a law that runs afoul of the principles of fundamental justice and is thus inherently flawed ... . However, in some situations the state may be able to show that the public good—a matter not considered under s. 7, which looks only at the impact on the rights claimants—justifies depriving an individual of life, liberty or security of the person under s. 1 of the *Charter*. More particularly, in cases such as this where the competing societal interests are themselves protected under the *Charter*, a restriction on s. 7 rights may in the end be found to be proportionate to its objective.

[96] Here, the limit is prescribed by law, and the appellants concede that the law has a pressing and substantial objective. The question is whether the government has demonstrated that the prohibition is proportionate.

[97] At this stage of the analysis, the courts must accord the legislature a measure of deference. Proportionality does not require perfection ... . Section 1 only requires that the limits be "reasonable." This Court has emphasized that there may be a number of possible solutions to a particular social problem, and suggested that a "complex regulatory response" to a social ill will garner a high degree of deference ... .

[98] On the one hand ... physician-assisted death involves complex issues of social policy and a number of competing societal values. Parliament faces a difficult task in addressing this issue; it must weigh and balance the perspective of those who might be at risk in a permissive regime against that of those who seek assistance in dying. It follows that a high degree of deference is owed to Parliament's decision to impose an absolute prohibition on assisted death. On the other hand, ... the absolute prohibition could not be described as a "complex regulatory response." ... The degree of deference owed to Parliament, while high, is accordingly reduced.

(1) Rational Connection

[99] ... To establish a rational connection, the government need only show that there is a causal connection between the infringement and the benefit sought "on the basis of reason or logic." ...

[100] ... We ... conclude that there is a rational connection between the prohibition and its objective. ...

(2) Minimal Impairment

...

[103] The question in this case comes down to whether the absolute prohibition on physician-assisted dying ... is the least drastic means of achieving the legislative objective. ...

[104] This question lies at the heart of this case. ...

[114] At trial Canada went into some detail about the risks associated with the legalization of physician-assisted dying. In its view, there are many possible sources of error and many factors that can render a patient "decisionally vulnerable" and thereby give rise to the risk that persons without a rational and considered desire for death will in fact end up dead. It points to cognitive impairment, depression or other mental illness, coercion, undue influence, psychological or emotional manipulation, systemic prejudice (against the elderly or people with disabilities), and the possibility of ambivalence or misdiagnosis as factors that may escape detection or give rise to errors in capacity assessment. Essentially, Canada argues that, given the breadth of this list, there is no reliable way to identify those who are vulnerable and those who are not. As a result, it says, a blanket prohibition is necessary.

[115] The evidence accepted by the trial judge does not support Canada's argument. ...

[117] ... We agree with the trial judge that the risks associated with physician-assisted death can be limited through a carefully designed and monitored system of safeguards.

[118] ... Canada argues that a blanket prohibition should be upheld unless the appellants can demonstrate that an alternative approach eliminates all risk. This effectively reverses the onus under s. 1, requiring the claimant whose rights are infringed to prove less invasive ways of achieving the prohibition's object. The burden of establishing minimal impairment is on the government.

[119] We agree [with the trial judge that Canada had not discharged this burden]. A theoretical or speculative fear cannot justify an absolute prohibition. ... Justification under s. 1 is a process of demonstration, not intuition or automatic deference to the government's assertion of risk. ...

[120] Finally, it is argued that without an absolute prohibition on assisted dying, Canada will descend the slippery slope into euthanasia and condoned murder. Anecdotal examples of controversial cases abroad were cited in support of this argument, only to be countered by anecdotal examples of systems that work well. The resolution of the issue before us falls to be resolved not by competing anecdotes, but by the evidence. ... We should not lightly assume that the regulatory regime will function defectively, nor should we assume that other criminal sanctions against the taking of lives will prove impotent against abuse.

[121] We ... conclude that the absolute prohibition is not minimally impairing.

(3) Deleterious Effects and Salutary Benefits

[122] This stage of the *Oakes* analysis weighs the impact of the law on protected rights against the beneficial effect of the law in terms of the greater public good. Given our conclusion that the law is not minimally impairing, it is not necessary to go on to this step.

[123] We conclude that s. 241(*b*) and s. 14 of the *Criminal Code* are not saved by s. 1 of the *Charter*.

XI. Remedy

...

[126] We have concluded that the laws prohibiting a physician's assistance in terminating life (*Criminal Code*, s. 241(*b*) and s. 14) infringe Ms. Taylor's s. 7 rights to life, liberty and security of the person in a manner that is not in accordance with the principles of fundamental justice, and that the infringement is not justified under s. 1 of the *Charter*. To the extent that the impugned laws deny the s. 7 rights of people like Ms. Taylor they are void by operation of s. 52 of the *Constitution Act, 1982*. It is for Parliament and the provincial legislatures to respond, should they so choose, by enacting legislation consistent with the constitutional parameters set out in these reasons.

[127] The appropriate remedy is therefore a declaration that s. 241(*b*) and s. 14 of the *Criminal Code* are void insofar as they prohibit physician-assisted death for a competent adult person who (1) clearly consents to the termination of

life; and (2) has a grievous and irremediable medical condition (including an illness, disease or disability) that causes enduring suffering that is intolerable to the individual in the circumstances of his or her condition. "Irremediable," it should be added, does not require the patient to undertake treatments that are not acceptable to the individual. The scope of this declaration is intended to respond to the factual circumstances in this case. We make no pronouncement on other situations where physician-assisted dying may be sought.

[128] We would suspend the declaration of invalidity for 12 months. ...

[130] A number of the interveners asked the Court to account for physicians' freedom of conscience and religion when crafting the remedy in this case. ...

[132] In our view, nothing in the declaration of invalidity which we propose to issue would compel physicians to provide assistance in dying. The declaration simply renders the criminal prohibition invalid. What follows is in the hands of the physicians' colleges, Parliament, and the provincial legislatures. However, we note—as did Beetz J. in addressing the topic of physician participation in abortion in *Morgentaler*— that a physician's decision to participate in assisted dying is a matter of conscience and, in some cases, of religious belief (pp. 95-96). In making this observation, we do not wish to pre-empt the legislative and regulatory response to this judgment. Rather, we underline that the *Charter* rights of patients and physicians will need to be reconciled.

F. EQUALITY RIGHTS

Andrews v. Law Society of British Columbia, 1989

*A*ndrews was the first case based exclusively on section 15 to be decided by the Supreme Court. The case arose out of circumstances identical to those of Skapinker, who took the first major Charter case to the Supreme Court, but who had to rely on section 6 "mobility rights" because section 15 had not yet come into effect.[1] Like *Skapinker*, *Andrews* will be remembered not so much for the precise legal issue it settled as for the interpretive orientation it established. Just as *Skapinker* provided the court with the opportunity to indicate the general approach it would take to the Charter, so *Andrews* gave it the opportunity to establish the principles of section 15 jurisprudence. The court's discussion of such terms as "equality" and "discrimination," and of the overall structure of section 15 and its relationship to other parts of the Charter, has become the point of departure for subsequent debate (both in and out of court) about section 15's "equality rights." The pathbreaking importance of this case was recognized by several interest groups who, while not much concerned with the particulars of Andrews's claim, sought and received intervener status in order to persuade the court to lay a foundation for section 15 jurisprudence that was compatible with their section 15 litigation strategies.[2]

Andrews wished to practise law in British Columbia and had met all the standards for admission to the bar except for the requirement of Canadian citizenship contained in section 42(*a*) of the *Barristers and Solicitors Act*. He argued that this legislative discrimination against non-citizens infringed section 15 of the Charter. Because "citizenship" is not one of the prohibited grounds of discrimination explicitly enumerated by section 15, the case raised questions about the reach of that section's open-ended wording. The court unanimously agreed that the citizenship requirement violated section 15 but divided on the question whether it could be saved as a "reasonable limit" under section 1: five members of the six-judge panel[3] concluded that it could not be so defended; Justice McIntyre, who wrote the controlling opinion on most other issues, dissented on this section 1 question.

---

1   See *Law Society of Upper Canada v. Skapinker*, [1984] 1 S.C.R. 357.

2   Intervening on the side of Andrews were the Women's Legal Education and Action Fund (LEAF), the Coalition of Provincial Organizations of the Handicapped, the Canadian Association of University Teachers, and the Ontario Confederation of University Faculty Associations. The Federation of Law Societies of Canada and several provincial attorneys general intervened on the other side.

3   Justice Le Dain was on the panel but took no part in the judgment.

The court was obviously concerned about the potential for the open-ended wording of section 15 to force the judicial evaluation of almost all legislation. This would occur especially if the term "discrimination" were interpreted in a neutral fashion as meaning simply "distinction," and if the open-ended phraseology were taken literally to cover all distinctions. Most laws make distinctions and would, under such an interpretation, violate section 15;[4] they could thus be sustained only as "reasonable limits" under section 1. Although such an interpretation had been suggested by leading commentators, it was too daunting for the court. Justice La Forest, for example, could not "accept that all legislative classifications must be rationally supportable before the courts" because this would involve the judicial assessment of "much economic and social policy-making [that] is simply beyond the institutional competence of the courts." The proper judicial role, he said, "is to protect against incursions on fundamental values, not to second guess policy decisions."

Writing for a unanimous court on this point, Justice McIntyre reduced the potential for violating section 15 by placing two limitations on its scope. First, he held that "discrimination" did not mean merely "distinction," but required the showing of some harm or prejudice. Second, he restricted the reach of the open-ended wording to grounds "analogous" to the enumerated grounds. Both qualifications on the scope of section 15 were designed to ensure that many legislative distinctions will not violate the Charter's equality rights and will thus not have to defend themselves under section 1 as "reasonable limits ... demonstrably justified in a free and democratic society."

Neither qualification applied in this case, however. Justice McIntyre found that non-citizens were harmed by the legislation and that citizenship was an analogous ground because non-citizens "are a good example of a 'discrete and insular minority' who come within the protection of s. 15." Justice Wilson added that discrete and insular minorities were groups "lacking in political power and as such vulnerable to having their interests overlooked and their rights to equal concern and respect violated. They are among 'those groups in society to whose needs and wishes elected officials have no apparent interest in attending.'" This emphasis on section 15's role in protecting groups that lack power and influence is consistent with Chief Justice Dickson's theory, enunciated in both *Edwards Books* and the *Alberta Labour Reference*, that an important purpose of the Charter is to help social and economic "underdogs."[5]

While the court clearly intended to limit the scope of section 15 challenges, the limits are not terribly clear and are likely to generate considerable controversy. For example, the question whether an unlisted group is an "underdog" deserving constitutional protection will not be easy to determine.[6] Nor is the question whether a legislative distinction causes harm likely to be free of difficulty. A further source of ambiguity is introduced by the way in which the court chose to define the term "discrimination." It does not mean just direct,

---

4   Justice McIntyre, following the court below, uses the example of laws forbidding children or drunk persons from driving.

5   See *R. v. Edwards Books and Art Ltd.*, [1986] 2 S.C.R. 713 and *Reference Re Public Service Employee Relations Act (Alta.)*, [1987] 1 S.C.R. 313 (*Alberta Labour Reference*). The case report for the *Alberta Labour Reference* is available in the instructor's supplements package.

6   Consider, for example, the disagreement between Justices Dickson and McIntyre about the power of the labour movement in the *Alberta Labour Reference, ibid.*

intentional discrimination against the enumerated or analogous groups, but also the "disparate impact" on these groups of otherwise neutral policies. This means that classifications not based on an analogous ground will nevertheless be subject to section 15 challenge if they have an unintentional negative "effect" on a group defined by an enumerated or analogous group. For example, war veterans are overwhelmingly male. Does this mean that a "veterans preference," which does not appear to be based on an "analogous ground," is nevertheless open to challenge because its indirect effect is to deny "equal benefit of the law" to women? Justice McIntyre insists that "[a] complainant under s. 15(1) must show not only that he or she is not receiving equal treatment before and under the law or that the law has a differential impact on him or her in the protection or benefit accorded by law but, in addition, must show that the legislative impact of the law is discriminatory [that is, harmful]." He intends this to be a formula for limiting the scope of section 15. In fact, it opens as many interpretive doors as it closes, and the precise scope of section 15 will remain an open question for some time to come. ∼

Discussion Questions

1. How does the approach to equality rights adopted by the court in this case differ from the theory of formal equality?

2. How would you say the court defined unconstitutional discrimination in this case?

3. What alternative approach to equality rights, if any, would you have preferred the court to have taken?

ANDREWS v. LAW SOCIETY OF BRITISH COLUMBIA
[1989] 1 S.C.R. 143

Hearing: October 5, 6, 1987; Judgment: February 2, 1989.

Present: Dickson C.J. and McIntyre, Lamer, Wilson, Le Dain,* La Forest, and L'Heureux-Dubé JJ.

Interveners: The Attorney General for Ontario, the Attorney General of Quebec, the Attorney General of Nova Scotia, the Attorney General for Saskatchewan, the Attorney General for Alberta, the Federation of Law Societies of Canada (for the appellants); the Women's Legal Education and Action Fund, the Coalition of Provincial Organizations of the Handicapped, the Canadian Association of University Teachers, and the Ontario Confederation of University Faculty Associations (for the respondents).

* Le Dain J. took no part in the judgment.

The judgment of Dickson C.J.C. and Wilson and L'Heureux-Dubé JJ. was delivered by

WILSON J.: I have had the benefit of the reasons of my colleague, Justice McIntyre, and I am in complete agreement with him as to the way in which s. 15(1) of the *Canadian Charter*

of Rights and Freedoms should be interpreted and applied. I also agree with my colleague as to the way in which s. 15(1) and s. 1 of the *Charter* interact. I differ from him, however, on the application of s. 1 to this particular case. ...

I agree with my colleague that a rule which bars an entire class of persons from certain forms of employment solely on the ground that they are not Canadian citizens violates the equality rights of that class. I agree with him also that it discriminates against them on the ground of their personal characteristics, i.e., their non-citizen status. I believe, therefore, that they are entitled to the protection of s. 15.

Before turning to s. 1, I would like to add a brief comment to what my colleague has said concerning non-citizens permanently resident in Canada forming the kind of "discrete and insular minority" to which the Supreme Court of the United States referred in *United States v. Carolene Products Co.*, 304 U.S. 144 (1938), at pp. 152-53, n. 4.

Relative to citizens, non-citizens are a group lacking in political power and as such vulnerable to having their interests overlooked and their rights to equal concern and respect violated. They are among "those groups in society to whose needs and wishes elected officials have no apparent interest in attending": see J. H. Ely, Democracy and Distrust (1980), at

p. 151. Non-citizens, to take only the most obvious example, do not have the right to vote. Their vulnerability to becoming a disadvantaged group in our society is captured by John Stuart Mill's observation in Book III of Considerations on Representative Government that "in the absence of its natural defenders, the interests of the excluded is always in danger of being overlooked. ..." I would conclude therefore that non-citizens fall into an analogous category to those specifically enumerated in s. 15. I emphasize, moreover, that this is a determination which is not to be made only in the context of the law which is subject to challenge but rather in the context of the place of the group in the entire social, political and legal fabric of our society. While legislatures must inevitably draw distinctions among the governed, such distinctions should not bring about or reinforce the disadvantage of certain groups and individuals by denying them the rights freely accorded to others.

I believe also that it is important to note that the range of discrete and insular minorities has changed and will continue to change with changing political and social circumstances. For example, Stone J., writing in 1938, was concerned with religious, national and racial minorities. In enumerating the specific grounds in s. 15, the framers of the *Charter* embraced these concerns in 1982 but also addressed themselves to the difficulties experienced by the disadvantaged on the grounds of ethnic origin, colour, sex, age and physical and mental disability. It can be anticipated that the discrete and insular minorities of tomorrow will include groups not recognized as such today. It is consistent with the constitutional status of s. 15 that it be interpreted with sufficient flexibility to ensure the "unremitting protection" of equality rights in the years to come.

While I have emphasized that non-citizens are, in my view, an analogous group to those specifically enumerated in s. 15 and, as such, are entitled to the protection of the section, I agree with my colleague that it is not necessary in this case to determine what limit, if any, there is on the grounds covered by s. 15 and I do not do so. ...

Having found an infringement of s. 15 of the *Charter*, I turn now to the question whether the citizenship requirement for entry into the legal profession in British Columbia constitutes a reasonable limit which can be "demonstrably justified in a free and democratic society" under s. 1.

As my colleague has pointed out, the onus of justifying the infringement rests upon those seeking to uphold the legislation, in this case the Attorney General of British Columbia and the Law Society of British Columbia, and the analysis to be conducted is that set forth by Chief Justice Dickson in *R. v. Oakes*, [1986] 1 S.C.R. 103.

The first hurdle to be crossed in order to override a right guaranteed in the *Charter* is that the objective sought to be achieved by the impugned law must relate to concerns which are "pressing and substantial" in a free and democratic society. ... This, in my view, remains an appropriate standard when it is recognized that not every distinction between individuals and groups will violate s. 15. If every distinction between individuals and groups gave rise to a violation of s. 15, then this standard might well be too stringent for application in all cases and might deny the community at large the benefits associated with sound and desirable social and economic legislation. This is not a concern, however, once the position that every distinction drawn by law constitutes discrimination is rejected as indeed it is in the judgment of my colleague, McIntyre J. Given that s. 15 is designed to protect those groups who suffer social, political and legal disadvantage in our society, the burden resting on government to justify the type of discrimination against such groups is appropriately an onerous one.

The second step in a s. 1 inquiry involves the application of a proportionality test which requires the Court to balance a number of factors. ...

I appreciate the desirability of lawyers being familiar with Canadian institutions and customs but I agree with McLachlin J.A. that the requirement of citizenship is not carefully tailored to achieve that objective and may not even be rationally connected to it. McDonald J. pointed out in *Re Dickenson and Law Society of Alberta* (1978), 84 D.L.R. (3d) 189, at p. 195 that such a requirement affords no assurance that citizens who want to become lawyers are sufficiently familiar with Canadian institutions and "it could be better achieved by an examination of the particular qualifications of the applicant, whether he is a Canadian citizen, a British subject, or something else."

The second justification advanced by the appellants in support of the citizenship requirement is that citizenship evidences a real attachment to Canada. Once again I find myself in agreement with the following observations of McLachlin J.A., at pp. 612-13:

> The second reason for the distinction—that citizenship implies a commitment to Canadian society—fares little better upon close examination. Only those citizens who are not natural-born Canadians can be said to have made a conscious choice to establish themselves here permanently and to opt for full participation in the Canadian social process, including the right to vote and run for public office. While no doubt most citizens, natural-born or otherwise, are committed to Canadian society, citizenship does not ensure that that is the case. Conversely, non-citizens may be deeply committed to our country.

The third ground advanced to justify the requirement relates to the role lawyers are said to play in the governance of our country. McLachlin J.A. disputed the extent to which the practice of law involves the performance of a governmental function. She stated at p. 614:

> While lawyers clearly play an important role in our society, it cannot be contended that the practice of law involves performing a state or government function. In this respect, the role of lawyers may be distinguished from that of legislators, judges, civil servants and policemen. The practice of law is first and foremost a private profession. Some lawyers work in the courts, some do not. Those who work in the courts may represent the Crown or act against it. It is true that all lawyers are officers of the court. That term, in my mind, implies allegiance and certain responsibilities to the institution of the court. But it does not mean that lawyers are part of the process of government.

Although I am in general agreement with her characterization of the role of lawyers *qua* lawyers in our society, my problem with this basis of justification is more fundamental. To my mind, even if lawyers do perform a governmental function, I do not think the requirement that they be citizens provides any guarantee that they will honourably and conscientiously carry out their public duties. They will carry them out, I believe, because they are good lawyers and not because they are Canadian citizens.

In my view, the reasoning advanced in support of the citizenship requirement simply does not meet the tests in *Oakes* for overriding a constitutional right particularly, as in this case, a right designed to protect "discrete and insular minorities" in our society. I would respectfully concur in the view expressed by McLachlin J.A. at p. 617 that the citizenship requirement does not "appear to relate closely to those ends, much less to have been carefully designed to achieve them with minimum impairment of individual rights." …

LA FOREST J.: … My colleague, Justice McIntyre, has set forth the facts and the judicial history of this appeal and it is unnecessary for me to repeat them. Nor need I enter into an extensive examination of the law regarding the meaning of s. 15(1), because in so far as it is relevant to this appeal I am in substantial agreement with the views of my colleague. I hasten to add that the relevant question as I see it is restricted to whether the impugned provision amounts to discrimination in the sense in which my colleague has defined it, i.e., on the basis of "irrelevant personal differences" such as those listed in s. 15 and, traditionally, in human rights legislation.

I am not prepared to accept at this point that the only significance to be attached to the opening words that refer more generally to equality is that the protection afforded by the section is restricted to discrimination through the application of law. It is possible to read s. 15 in this way and I have

no doubt that on any view redress against that kind of discrimination will constitute the bulk of the courts' work under the provision. Moreover, from the manner in which it was drafted, I also have no doubt that it was so intended. However, it can reasonably be argued that the opening words, which take up half the section, seem somewhat excessive to accomplish the modest role attributed to them, particularly having regard to the fact that s. 32 already limits the application of the *Charter* to legislation and governmental activity. It may also be thought to be out of keeping with the broad and generous approach given to other *Charter* rights, not the least of which is s. 7, which like s. 15 is of a generalized character. In the case of s. 7, it will be remembered, the Court has been at pains to give real meaning to each word of the section so as to ensure that the rights to life, liberty and security of the person are separate, if closely related rights. That having been said, I am convinced that it was never intended in enacting s. 15 that it become a tool for the wholesale subjection to judicial scrutiny of variegated legislative choices in no way infringing on values fundamental to a free and democratic society. Like my colleague, I am not prepared to accept that *all* legislative classifications must be rationally supportable before the courts. Much economic and social policy-making is simply beyond the institutional competence of the courts: their role is to protect against incursions on fundamental values, not to second guess policy decisions.

I realize that it is no easy task to distinguish between what is fundamental and what is not and that in this context this may demand consideration of abstruse theories of equality. For example, there may well be legislative or governmental differentiation between individuals or groups that is so grossly unfair to an individual or group and so devoid of any rational relationship to a legitimate state purpose as to offend against the principle of equality before and under the law as to merit intervention pursuant to s. 15. For these reasons I would think it better at this stage of *Charter* development to leave the question open. I am aware that in the United States, where Holmes J. has referred to the equal protection clause there as the "last resort of constitutional arguments" (*Buck v. Bell*, 274 U.S. 200 (1927), at p. 208), the courts have been extremely reluctant to interfere with legislative judgment. Still, as I stated, there may be cases where it is indeed the last constitutional resort to protect the individual from fundamental unfairness. Assuming there is room under s. 15 for judicial intervention beyond the traditionally established and analogous policies against discrimination discussed by my colleague, it bears repeating that considerations of institutional functions and resources should make courts extremely wary about questioning legislative and governmental choices in such areas. As I have indicated, however, this issue does not arise here. For we are concerned in this case with whether or not the legislation amounts to discrimination of a kind similar to those enumerated in s. 15. It was conceded that the impugned legislation does distinguish the respondents from other persons on the basis of a personal characteristic which shares many similarities with those enumerated in s. 15. The characteristic of citizenship is one typically not within the control of the individual and, in this sense, is immutable. Citizenship is, at least temporarily, a characteristic of personhood not alterable by conscious action and in some cases not alterable except on the basis of unacceptable costs.

Moreover, non-citizens are an example without parallel of a group of persons who are relatively powerless politically, and whose interests are likely to be compromised by legislative decisions. History reveals that Canada did not for many years resist the temptation of enacting legislation the animating rationale of which was to limit the number of persons entering into certain employment. Discrimination on the basis of nationality has from early times been an inseparable companion of discrimination on the basis of race and national or ethnic origin, which are listed in s. 15. ...

There is no question that citizenship may, in some circumstances, be properly used as a defining characteristic for certain types of legitimate governmental objectives. I am sensitive to the fact that citizenship is a very special status that not only incorporates rights and duties but serves a highly important symbolic function as a badge identifying people as members of the Canadian polity. Nonetheless, it is, in general, irrelevant to the legitimate work of government in all but a limited number of areas. By and large, the use in legislation of citizenship as a basis for distinguishing between persons, here for the purpose of conditioning access to the practice of a profession, harbours the potential for undermining the essential or underlying values of a free and democratic society that are embodied in s. 15. Our nation has throughout its history drawn strength from the flow of people to our shores. Decisions unfairly premised on citizenship would be likely to "inhibit the sense of those who are discriminated against that Canadian society is not free or democratic as far as they are concerned and ... such persons are likely not to have faith in social and political institutions which enhance the participation of individuals and groups in society, or to have confidence that they can freely and without obstruction by the state pursue their and their families' hopes and expectations of vocational and personal development" (*Kask v. Shimizu*, [1986] 4 W.W.R. 154, at p. 161, per McDonald J. (Alta. Q.B.)).

While it cannot be said that citizenship is a characteristic which "bears no relation to the individual's ability to perform or contribute to society" (*Fontiero v. Richardson*, 411 U.S. 677 (1973), at p. 686), it certainly typically bears an attenuated sense of relevance to these. That is not to say that no legislative conditioning of benefits (for example) on the basis of citizenship is acceptable in the free and democratic society that is Canada, merely that legislation purporting to do so ought to be measured against the touchstone of our Constitution. It requires justification.

I turn then to a consideration of the justifiability, fairness or proportionality of the scheme. I agree with McIntyre J. that any such justification must be found under s. 1 of the *Charter*, essentially because, in matters involving infringements of fundamental rights, it is entirely appropriate that government sustain the constitutionality of its conduct. I am in general agreement with what he has to say about the manner in which legislation must be approached under the latter provision, in particular the need for a proportionality test involving a sensitive balancing of many factors in weighing the legislative objective. If I have any qualifications to make, it is that I prefer to think in terms of a single test for s. 1, but one that is to be applied to vastly differing situations with the flexibility and realism inherent in the word "reasonable" mandated by the Constitution.

The degree to which a free and democratic society such as Canada should tolerate differentiation based on personal characteristics cannot be ascertained by an easy calculus. There will rarely, if ever, be a perfect congruence between means and ends, save where legislation has discriminatory purposes. The matter must, as earlier cases have held, involve a test of proportionality. In cases of this kind, the test must be approached in a flexible manner. The analysis should be functional, focussing on the character of the classification in question, the constitutional and societal importance of the interests adversely affected, the relative importance to the individuals affected of the benefit of which they are deprived, and the importance of the state interest.

With deference, however, I am unable to agree with McIntyre J.'s application of these principles to the present case. I therefore turn to the task of balancing the objectives sought to be accomplished by the legislation against the means sought to achieve that objective. ...

While there is no evidence on this point, the Attorney General offers three purposes sought to be attained by the legislation. These are:

1. Citizenship ensures a familiarity with Canadian institutions and customs;
2. Citizenship implies a commitment to Canadian society;
3. Lawyers play a fundamental role in the Canadian system of democratic government and as such should be citizens. ...

[Like Justice Wilson, Justice La Forest essentially followed the reasoning of McLachlin J.A. in the Court of Appeal on these points.]

The third objective advanced by the Attorney General has more substance. It is that certain state activities should for both symbolic and practical reasons be confined to those who are full members of our political society. The Attorney General reduced his arguments regarding this objective to the following syllogism:

(a) persons who are involved in the processes or structure of government, broadly defined, should be citizens;

(b) lawyers are involved in the processes or structure of government;

(c) lawyers, therefore, should be citizens.

I do not quarrel with the first assertion as a general proposition. The Court of Appeal accepted it, noting that this rationale underlies the common requirement that legislators, voters, judges, police and senior public servants be citizens. However, it rejected the second proposition that lawyers play a vital role in the administration of law and justice and are themselves as much a part of the government processes as are judges, legislators and so on. It rejected the notion that the practice of law itself involved performing a state or government function. ...

I agree. ... It is only in the most unreal sense that it can be said that a lawyer working for a private client plays a role in the administration of justice that would require him or her to be a citizen in order to be allowed to participate therein. Obviously lawyers occupy a position of trust and responsibility in our society, but that is true of all professions, and the members of some of these, like that of chartered accountants, for instance, are privy to matters of the most serious import.

On a more mundane level, the essential purpose behind occupational licensing is to protect the public from unqualified practitioners. But as Lenoir points out ([Robert L., "Citizenship as a Requirement for the Practice of Law in Ontario" (1981) 13 *Ottawa Law Rev.* 527], at p. 547), "Citizenship has not been shown to bear any correlation to one's professional or vocational competency or qualification." Like him, I see no sufficient additional dimension to the lawyer's function to insist on citizenship as a qualification for admission to this profession.

It is not without significance that a requirement of citizenship has not been found to be necessary to the practice of law in either the United States (see *In re Griffiths*, 413 U.S. 717 (1973)), or England (see *Solicitors (Amendment) Act 1974 (U.K.)*, 1974, c. 26, s. 1); see also *Re Howard* [[1976] 1 N.S.W.L.R. 641], at p. 647. The doctrine of privileged communications was pressed into service, but that doctrine exists for the protection of the client. I fail to see what this has to do with the requirement of citizenship.

A requirement of citizenship would be acceptable if limited to Crown Attorneys or lawyers directly employed by government and, therefore, involved in policy-making or administration, so that it could be said that the lawyer was an architect or instrumentality of government policy; see *Reyners v. The Belgian State*, [1974] 2 Common Market Law R. 305. But ordinary lawyers are not privy to government information any more than, say, accountants, and there are rules to restrict lawyers from obtaining confidential governmental information.

I would conclude that although the governmental objectives, as stated, may be defensible, it is simply misplaced *vis-à-vis* the legal profession as a whole. However, even accepting the legitimacy and importance of the legislative objectives, the legislation exacts too high a price on persons wishing to practice law in that it may deprive them, albeit perhaps temporarily, of the "right" to pursue their calling. ...

The judgment of McIntyre and Lamer JJ. was delivered by

McINTYRE J. (dissenting in part): This appeal raises only one question. Does the citizenship requirement for entry into the legal profession contained in s. 42 of the *Barristers and Solicitors Act*, R.S.B.C. 1979, c. 26, (the "*Act*") contravene s. 15(1) of the *Canadian Charter of Rights and Freedoms*? Section 42 provides:

> 42. The benchers may call to the Bar of the Province and admit as a solicitor of the Supreme Court
> (a) a Canadian citizen with respect to whom they are satisfied that he ...

and s. 15 of the *Charter* states:

> **15.** (1) Every individual is equal before and under the law and has the right to the equal protection and equal benefit of the law without discrimination and, in particular, without discrimination based on race, national or ethnic origin, colour, religion, sex, age or mental or physical disability.
> (2) Subsection (1) does not preclude any law, program or activity that has as its object the amelioration of conditions of disadvantaged individuals or groups including those that are disadvantaged because of race, national or ethnic origin, colour, religion, sex, age or mental or physical disability.

The respondent, Andrews, was a British subject permanently resident in Canada at the time these proceedings were commenced. He had taken law degrees at Oxford and had fulfilled all the requirements for admission to the practice of law in British Columbia, except that of Canadian citizenship. He commenced proceedings for a declaration that s. 42 of the *Act* violates the *Charter*. He also sought an order in the nature of mandamus requiring the benchers of the Law Society of British Columbia to consider his application for call to the Bar and admission as a solicitor. His action was dismissed at trial before Taylor J. in the Supreme Court of British Columbia in a judgment reported at (1985), 22 D.L.R. (4th) 9. An appeal was allowed in the Court of Appeal (Hinkson, Craig and McLachlin JJ.A., at (1986), 27 D.L.R. (4th) 600), and this appeal is taken by the Law Society of British Columbia, by leave granted November 27, 1986. Pursuant to an order of this Court on January 28, 1987, Gorel Elizabeth Kinersly, an American citizen who was at the time a permanent resident of Canada articling in the Province of British Columbia, was added as a co-respondent in this appeal. ...

Following the judgment in his favour, the respondent Andrews was called to the Bar and admitted as a solicitor in the Province of British Columbia and is now a Canadian citizen. The co-respondent, Kinersly, who had expressed an intention to become a Canadian citizen, became eligible to do so on March 15, 1988. ...

The Concept of Equality

Section 15(1) of the *Charter* provides for every individual a guarantee of equality before and under the law, as well as the equal protection and equal benefit of the law without discrimination. This is not a general guarantee of equality; it does not provide for equality between individuals or groups within society in a general or abstract sense, nor does it impose on individuals or groups an obligation to accord equal treatment to others. It is concerned with the application of the law. No problem regarding the scope of the word "law," as employed in s. 15(1), can arise in this case because it is an Act of the Legislature which is under attack. Whether other governmental or quasi-governmental regulations, rules, or requirements may be termed laws under s. 15(1) should be left for cases in which the issue arises.

The concept of equality has long been a feature of Western thought. As embodied in s. 15(1) of the *Charter*, it is an elusive concept and, more than any of the other rights and freedoms guaranteed in the *Charter*, it lacks precise definition. As has been stated by John H. Schaar, "Equality of Opportunity and Beyond," in *Nomos IX: Equality*, ed. J. Roland Pennock and John W. Chapman (1967), at p. 228:

> Equality is a protean word. It is one of those political symbols—liberty and fraternity are others—into which men have poured the deepest urgings of their heart. Every

strongly held theory or conception of equality is at once a psychology, an ethic, a theory of social relations, and a vision of the good society.

It is a comparative concept, the condition of which may only be attained or discerned by comparison with the condition of others in the social and political setting in which the question arises. It must be recognized at once, however, that every difference in treatment between individuals under the law will not necessarily result in inequality and, as well, that identical treatment may frequently produce serious inequality. ... The same thought has been expressed in this Court in the context of s. 2(*b*) of the *Charter* in *R. v. Big M Drug Mart Ltd.*, [1985] 1 S.C.R. 295, where Dickson C.J. said at p. 347:

> The equality necessary to support religious freedom does not require identical treatment of all religions. In fact, the interests of true equality may well require differentiation in treatment.

In simple terms, then, it may be said that a law which treats all identically and which provides equality of treatment between "A" and "B" might well cause inequality for "C," depending on differences in personal characteristics and situations. To approach the ideal of full equality before and under the law—and in human affairs an approach is all that can be expected—the main consideration must be the impact of the law on the individual or the group concerned. Recognizing that there will always be an infinite variety of personal characteristics, capacities, entitlements and merits among those subject to a law, there must be accorded, as nearly as may be possible, an equality of benefit and protection and no more of the restrictions, penalties or burdens imposed upon one than another. In other words, the admittedly unattainable ideal should be that a law expressed to bind all should not because of irrelevant personal differences have a more burdensome or less beneficial impact on one than another.

McLachlin J.A. in the Court of Appeal expressed the view, at p. 605, that:

> ... [T]he essential meaning of the constitutional requirement of equal protection and equal benefit is that persons who are "similarly situated be similarly treated" and conversely, that persons who are "differently situated be differently treated." ...

In this, she was adopting and applying as a test a proposition which seems to have been widely accepted with some modifications in both trial and appeal court decisions throughout the country on s. 15(1) of the *Charter*. See, for example, *Reference Re Family Benefits Act* (1986), 75 N.S.R. (2d) 338 (N.S.S.C.A.D.), at p. 351; *Reference Re Use of French in*

Criminal Proceedings in Saskatchewan (1987), 44 D.L.R. (4th) 16 (Sask. C.A.), at p. 46; *Smith, Kline & French Laboratories Ltd. v. Canada (Attorney General)*, [1987] 2 F.C. 359, at p. 366; *R. v. Ertel* (1987), 35 C.C.C. (3d) 398, at p. 419. The reliance on this concept appears to have derived, at least in recent times, from J. T. Tussman and J. tenBroek, "The Equal Protection of Laws" (1949), 37 *Calif. L. Rev.* 341. The similarly situated test is a restatement of the Aristotelian principle of formal equality—that "things that are alike should be treated alike, while things that are unalike should be treated unalike in proportion to their unalikeness" (*Ethica Nichomacea*, trans. W. Ross, Book V3, at p. 1131a-6 (1925)).

The test as stated, however, is seriously deficient in that it excludes any consideration of the nature of the law. If it were to be applied literally, it could be used to justify the Nuremberg laws of Adolf Hitler. Similar treatment was contemplated for all Jews. The similarly situated test would have justified the formalistic separate but equal doctrine of *Plessy v. Ferguson*, 163 U.S. 637 (1896), a doctrine that incidentally was still the law in the United States at the time that Professor Tussman and J. tenBroek wrote their much cited article: see M. David Lepofsky and H. Schwartz "Case Note" (1988), 67 *Can. Bar Rev.* 115, at pp. 119-20. The test, somewhat differently phrased, was applied in the British Columbia Court of Appeal in *R. v. Gonzales* (1962), 132 C.C.C. 237. The Court upheld, under s. 1(*b*) of the *Canadian Bill of Rights*, R.S.C. 1970, App. III, a section of the *Indian Act*, R.S.C. 1970, c. I-6, which made it an offence for an Indian to have intoxicants in his possession off a reserve. In his locality there were no reserves. Tysoe J.A. said that equality before the law could not mean "the same laws for all persons," and defined the right in these words, at p. 243:

> ... [I]n its context s. 1(b) means in a general sense that there has existed and there shall continue to exist in Canada a right in every person to whom a particular law relates or extends no matter what may be a person's race, national origin, colour, religion or sex to stand on an equal footing with every other person to whom that particular law relates or extends and a right to the protection of the law.

This approach was rejected in this Court by Ritchie J. in *R. v. Drybones*, [1970] S.C.R. 282, in a similar case involving a provision of the *Indian Act* making it an offence for an Indian to be intoxicated off a reserve. He said, at p. 297:

> ... I cannot agree with this interpretation pursuant to which it seems to me that the most glaring discriminatory legislation against a racial group would have to be construed as recognizing the right of each of its individual members "to equality before the law," so long as all the

other members are being discriminated against in the same way.

Thus, mere equality of application to similarly situated groups or individuals does not afford a realistic test for a violation of equality rights. For, as has been said, a bad law will not be saved merely because it operates equally upon those to whom it has application. Nor will a law necessarily be bad because it makes distinctions.

A similarly situated test focussing on the equal application of the law to those to whom it has application could lead to results akin to those in *Bliss v. Attorney General of Canada*, [1979] 1 S.C.R. 183. In *Bliss*, a pregnant woman was denied unemployment benefits to which she would have been entitled had she not been pregnant. She claimed that the *Unemployment Insurance Act, 1971*, violated the equality guarantees of the *Canadian Bill of Rights* because it discriminated against her on the basis of her sex. Her claim was dismissed by this Court on the grounds that there was no discrimination on the basis of sex, since the class into which she fell under the *Act* was that of pregnant persons, and within that class, all persons were treated equally. This case, of course, was decided before the advent of the *Charter*. ...

For the reasons outlined above, the test cannot be accepted as a fixed rule or formula for the resolution of equality questions arising under the *Charter*. Consideration must be given to the content of the law, to its purpose, and its impact upon those to whom it applies, and also upon those whom it excludes from its application. The issues which will arise from case to case are such that it would be wrong to attempt to confine these considerations within such a fixed and limited formula.

It is not every distinction or differentiation in treatment at law which will transgress the equality guarantees of s. 15 of the *Charter*. It is, of course, obvious that legislatures may—and to govern effectively—must treat different individuals and groups in different ways. Indeed, such distinctions are one of the main preoccupations of legislatures. The classifying of individuals and groups, the making of different provisions respecting such groups, the application of different rules, regulations, requirements and qualifications to different persons is necessary for the governance of modern society. As noted above, for the accommodation of differences, which is the essence of true equality, it will frequently be necessary to make distinctions. What kinds of distinctions will be acceptable under s. 15(1) and what kinds will violate its provisions?

In seeking an answer to these questions, the provisions of the *Charter* must have their full effect. In *R. v. Big M Drug Mart Ltd.*, this Court emphasized this point at p. 344, where Dickson C.J. stated:

This Court has already, in some measure, set out the basic approach to be taken in interpreting the *Charter*. In *Hunter v. Southam Inc.*, [1984] 2 S.C.R. 145, this Court expressed the view that the proper approach to the definition of the rights and freedoms guaranteed by the *Charter* was a purposive one. The meaning of a right or freedom guaranteed by the *Charter* was to be ascertained by an analysis of the *purpose* of such a guarantee; it was to be understood, in other words, in the light of the interests it was meant to protect.

In my view this analysis is to be undertaken, and the purpose of the right or freedom in question is to be sought by reference to the character and the larger objects of the *Charter* itself, to the language chosen to articulate the specific right or freedom, to the historical origins of the concepts enshrined, and where applicable, to the meaning and purpose of the other specific rights and freedoms with which it is associated within the text of the *Charter*. The interpretation should be, as the judgment in Southam emphasizes, a generous rather than a legalistic one, aimed at fulfilling the purpose of the guarantee and securing for individuals the full benefit of the *Charter*'s protection. At the same time it is important not to overshoot the actual purpose of the right or freedom in question, but to recall that the *Charter* was not enacted in a vacuum, and must therefore, as this Court's decision in *Law Society of Upper Canada v. Skapinker*, [1984] 1 S.C.R. 357, illustrates, be placed in its proper linguistic, philosophic and historical contexts. [Emphasis in original.]

These words are not inconsistent with the view I expressed in *Reference re Public Service Employee Relations Act (Alta.)*, [1987] 1 S.C.R. 313.

The principle of equality before the law has long been recognized as a feature of our constitutional tradition and it found statutory recognition in the *Canadian Bill of Rights*. However, unlike the *Canadian Bill of Rights*, which spoke only of equality before the law, s. 15(1) of the *Charter* provides a much broader protection. Section 15 spells out four basic rights: (1) the right to equality before the law; (2) the right to equality under the law; (3) the right to equal protection of the law; and (4) the right to equal benefit of the law. The inclusion of these last three additional rights in s. 15 of the *Charter* was an attempt to remedy some of the shortcomings of the right to equality in the *Canadian Bill of Rights*. It also reflected the expanded concept of discrimination being developed under the various Human Rights Codes since the enactment of the *Canadian Bill of Rights*. The shortcomings of the *Canadian Bill of Rights* as far as the right to equality is concerned are well known. In *Attorney General of Canada v. Lavell*, [1974] S.C.R. 1349, for example, this Court upheld s. 12(1)(*b*) of the

Indian Act which deprived women, but not men, of their membership in Indian Bands if they married non-Indians. The provision was held not to violate equality *before* the law although it might, the Court said, violate equality *under* the law if such were protected. In *Bliss, supra*, this Court held that the denial of unemployment insurance benefits to women because they were pregnant did not violate the guarantee of equality before the law, because any inequality in the protection and benefit of the law was "not created by legislation but by nature" (p. 190). The case was distinguished from the Court's earlier decision in *Drybones, supra*, as not involving (pp. 191-92) the imposition of a penalty on a racial group to which other citizens are not subjected, but as involving rather "a definition of the qualifications required for entitlement to benefits." It is readily apparent that the language of s. 15 was deliberately chosen in order to remedy some of the perceived defects under the *Canadian Bill of Rights*. The antecedent statute is part of the "linguistic, philosophic and historical context" of s. 15 of the *Charter*.

It is clear that the purpose of s. 15 is to ensure equality in the formulation and application of the law. The promotion of equality entails the promotion of a society in which all are secure in the knowledge that they are recognized at law as human beings equally deserving of concern, respect and consideration. It has a large remedial component. Howland C.J. and Robins J.A. (dissenting in the result but not with respect to this comment) in *Reference re an Act to Amend the Education Act (1986)*, 53 O.R. (2d) 513, attempt to articulate the broad range of values embraced by s. 15. They state at p. 554:

> In our view, s. 15(1) read as a whole constitutes a compendious expression of a positive right to equality in both the substance and the administration of the law. It is an all-encompassing right governing all legislative action. Like the ideals of "equal justice" and "equal access to the law," the right to equal protection and equal benefit of the law now enshrined in the *Charter* rests on the moral and ethical principle fundamental to a truly free and democratic society that all persons should be treated by the law on a footing of equality with equal concern and respect.

It must be recognized, however, as well that the promotion of equality under s. 15 has a much more specific goal than the mere elimination of distinctions. If the *Charter* was intended to eliminate all distinctions, then there would be no place for sections such as 27 (multicultural heritage); 2(*a*) (freedom of conscience and religion); 25 (aboriginal rights and freedoms); and other such provisions designed to safeguard certain distinctions. Moreover, the fact that identical treatment may frequently produce serious inequality is recognized in s. 15(2), which states that the equality rights in s. 15(1) do "not preclude any law, program or activity that has as its object the amelioration of conditions of disadvantaged individuals or groups. ..."

Discrimination

The right to equality before and under the law, and the rights to the equal protection and benefit of the law contained in s. 15, are granted with the direction contained in s. 15 itself that they be without discrimination. Discrimination is unacceptable in a democratic society because it epitomizes the worst effects of the denial of equality, and discrimination reinforced by law is particularly repugnant. The worst oppression will result from discriminatory measures having the force of law. It is against this evil that s. 15 provides a guarantee.

Discrimination as referred to in s. 15 of the *Charter* must be understood in the context of pre-*Charter* history. Prior to the enactment of s. 15(1), the Legislatures of the various provinces and the federal Parliament had passed during the previous fifty years what may be generally referred to as Human Rights Acts. ...

What does discrimination mean? The question has arisen most commonly in a consideration of the Human Rights Acts and the general concept of discrimination under those enactments has been fairly well settled. There is little difficulty, drawing upon the cases in this Court, in isolating an acceptable definition. In *Ontario Human Rights Commission and O'Malley v. Simpsons-Sears Ltd.*, [1985] 2 S.C.R. 536, at p. 551, discrimination (in that case adverse effect discrimination) was described in these terms: "It arises where an employer ... adopts a rule or standard ... which has a discriminatory effect upon a prohibited ground on one employee or group of employees in that it imposes, because of some special characteristic of the employee or group, obligations, penalties, or restrictive conditions not imposed on other members of the work force." It was held in that case, as well, that no intent was required as an element of discrimination, for it is in essence the impact of the discriminatory act or provision upon the person affected which is decisive in considering any complaint. At page 547, this proposition was expressed in these terms:

> The Code aims at the removal of discrimination. This is to state the obvious. Its main approach, however, is not to punish the discriminator, but rather to provide relief for the victims of discrimination. It is the result or the effect of the action complained of which is significant. If it does, in fact, cause discrimination; if its effect is to impose on one person or group of persons obligations, penalties, or restrictive conditions not imposed on other members of the community, it is discriminatory.

In *Canadian National Railway Co. v. Canada (Canadian Human Rights Commission)*, [1987] 1 S.C.R. 1114, better known as the *Action Travail des Femmes* case, where it was alleged that the Canadian National Railway was guilty of discriminatory hiring and promotion practices contrary to s. 10 of the *Canadian Human Rights Act*, S.C. 1976-77, c. 33, in denying employment to women in certain unskilled positions, Dickson C.J. in giving the judgment of the Court said, at pp. 1138-39:

> A thorough study of "systemic discrimination" in Canada is to be found in the Abella Report on equality in employment. The terms of reference of the Royal Commission instructed it "to inquire into the most efficient, effective and equitable means of promoting employment opportunities, eliminating systemic discrimination and assisting individuals to compete for employment opportunities on an equal basis." (Order in Council P.C. 1983-1924 of 24 June 1983). Although Judge Abella chose not to offer a precise definition of systemic discrimination, the essentials may be gleaned from the following comments, found at p. 2 of the Abella Report.
>
> Discrimination ... means practices or attitudes that have, whether by design or impact, the effect of limiting an individual's or a group's right to the opportunities generally available because of attributed rather than actual characteristics. ...
>
> It is not a question of whether this discrimination is motivated by an intentional desire to obstruct someone's potential, or whether it is the accidental by-product of innocently motivated practices or systems. If the barrier is affecting certain groups in a disproportionately negative way, it is a signal that the practices that lead to this adverse impact may be discriminatory.

There are many other statements which have aimed at a short definition of the term discrimination. In general, they are in accord with the statements referred to above. I would say then that discrimination may be described as a distinction, whether intentional or not but based on grounds relating to personal characteristics of the individual or group, which has the effect of imposing burdens, obligations, or disadvantages on such individual or group not imposed upon others, or which withholds or limits access to opportunities, benefits, and advantages available to other members of society. Distinctions based on personal characteristics attributed to an individual solely on the basis of association with a group will rarely escape the charge of discrimination, while those based on an individual's merits and capacities will rarely be so classed.

The Court in the case at bar must address the issue of discrimination as the term is used in s. 15(1) of the *Charter*. In general, it may be said that the principles which have been applied under the Human Rights Acts are equally applicable in considering questions of discrimination under s. 15(1). Certain differences arising from the difference between the *Charter* and the Human Rights Acts must, however, be considered. To begin with, discrimination in s. 15(1) is limited to discrimination caused by the application or operation of law, whereas the Human Rights Acts apply also to private activities. Furthermore, and this is a distinction of more importance, all the Human Rights Acts passed in Canada specifically designate a certain limited number of grounds upon which discrimination is forbidden. Section 15(1) of the *Charter* is not so limited. The enumerated grounds in s. 15(1) are not exclusive and the limits, if any, on grounds for discrimination which may be established in future cases await definition. The enumerated grounds do, however, reflect the most common and probably the most socially destructive and historically practised bases of discrimination and must, in the words of s. 15(1), receive particular attention. Both the enumerated grounds themselves and other possible grounds of discrimination recognized under s. 15(1) must be interpreted in a broad and generous manner, reflecting the fact that they are constitutional provisions not easily repealed or amended but intended to provide a "continuing framework for the legitimate exercise of governmental power" and, at the same time, for "the unremitting protection" of equality rights: see *Hunter v. Southam Inc.*, [1984] 2 S.C.R. 145, at p. 155.

It should be noted as well that when the Human Rights Acts create exemptions or defences, such as a *bona fide* occupational requirement, an exemption for religious and political organizations, or definitional limits on age discrimination, these generally have the effect of completely removing the conduct complained of from the reach of the *Act*. See, for example, exemptions for special interest organizations contained in the *Human Rights Code*, R.S.B.C. 1979, c. 186, as am., s. 22; The *Human Rights Act*, S.M. 1974, c. 65, as am., s. 6(7); and the *Human Rights Code*, 1981, S.O. 1981, c. 53, s. 17. "Age" is often restrictively defined in the Human Rights Acts; in British Columbia, it is defined in s. 1 of the *Code* to mean an age between 45 and 65; in s. 38 of the *Individual's Rights Protection Act*, R.S.A. 1980, c. I-2, it is defined as eighteen and over. For an example of the application of a *bona fide* occupational requirement, see *Bhinder v. Canadian National Railway Co.*, [1985] 2 S.C.R. 561. Where discrimination is forbidden in the Human Rights Acts it is done in absolute terms, and where a defence or exception is allowed it, too, speaks in absolute terms and the discrimination is excused. There is, in this sense, no middle ground. In the *Charter*, however, while s. 15(1), subject always to subs. (2), expresses its prohibition of discrimination in absolute terms, s. 1 makes allowance for a reasonable limit upon the operation of s. 15(1).

A different approach under s. 15(1) is therefore required. While discrimination under s. 15(1) will be of the same nature and in descriptive terms will fit the concept of discrimination developed under the Human Rights Acts, a further step will be required in order to decide whether discriminatory laws can be justified under s. 1. The onus will be on the state to establish this. This is a distinct step called for under the *Charter* which is not found in most Human Rights Acts, because in those Acts justification for or defence to discrimination is generally found in specific exceptions to the substantive rights.

Relationship Between Section 15(1) and Section 1 of the Charter

In determining the extent of the guarantee of equality in s. 15(1) of the *Charter*, special consideration must be given to the relationship between s. 15(1) and s. 1. It is indeed the presence of s. 1 in the *Charter* and the interaction between these sections which has led to the differing approaches to a definition of the s. 15(1) right, and which has made necessary a judicial approach differing from that employed under the *Canadian Bill of Rights*. Under the *Canadian Bill of Rights*, a test was developed to distinguish between justified and unjustified legislative distinctions within the concept of equality before the law itself in the absence of anything equivalent to the s. 1 limit: see *MacKay v. The Queen*, [1980] 2 S.C.R. 370, where it was said, at p. 407:

> ... and whether it is a necessary departure from the general principle of universal application of the law for the attainment of some necessary and desirable social objective. Inequalities created for such purposes may well be acceptable under the *Canadian Bill of Rights*.

It may be noted as well that the 14th Amendment to the American Constitution, which provides that no State shall deny to any person within its jurisdiction the "equal protection of the laws," contains no limiting provisions similar to s. 1 of the *Charter*. As a result, judicial consideration has led to the development of varying standards of scrutiny of alleged violations of the equal protection provision which restrict or limit the equality guarantee within the concept of equal protection itself. Again, article 14 of the *European Convention on Human Rights*, 23 U.N.T.S. 222, which secures the rights guaranteed therein without discrimination, lacks a s. 1 or its equivalent and has also developed a limit within the concept itself. In the *Belgian Linguistic Case (No. 2)* (1968), 1 E.H.R.R. 252, at p. 284, the court enunciated the following test:

> ... [T]he principle of equality of treatment is violated if the distinction has no objective and reasonable justification. The existence of such a justification must be assessed in relation to the aim and effects of the measure under

consideration, regard being had to principles which normally prevail in democratic societies. A difference in treatment in the exercise of a right laid down in the Convention must not only pursue a legitimate aim: Article 14 is likewise violated when it is clearly established that there is no reasonable relationship of proportionality between the means employed and the aim sought to be realised.

The distinguishing feature of the *Charter*, unlike the other enactments, is that consideration of such limiting factors is made under s. 1. This Court has described the analytical approach to the *Charter* in *R. v. Oakes*, [1986] 1 S.C.R. 103; *R. v. Edwards Books and Art Ltd.*, [1986] 2 S.C.R. 713, and other cases, the essential feature of which is that the right guaranteeing sections be kept analytically separate from s. 1. In other words, when confronted with a problem under the *Charter*, the first question which must be answered will be whether or not an infringement of a guaranteed right has occurred. Any justification of an infringement which is found to have occurred must be made, if at all, under the broad provisions of s. 1. It must be admitted at once that the relationship between these two sections may well be difficult to determine on a wholly satisfactory basis. It is, however, important to keep them analytically distinct if for no other reason than the different attribution of the burden of proof. It is for the citizen to establish that his or her *Charter* right has been infringed and for the state to justify the infringement.

Approaches to Section 15(1)

Three main approaches have been adopted in determining the role of s. 15(1), the meaning of discrimination set out in that section, and the relationship of s. 15(1) and s. 1. The first one, which was advanced by Professor Peter Hogg in *Constitutional Law of Canada* (2nd ed. 1985) would treat every distinction drawn by law as discrimination under s. 15(1). There would then follow a consideration of the distinction under the provisions of s. 1 of the *Charter*. He said, at pp. 800-801:

> I conclude that s. 15 should be interpreted as providing for the universal application of every law. When a law draws a distinction between individuals, on any ground, that distinction is sufficient to constitute a breach of s. 15, and to move the constitutional issue to s. 1. The test of validity is that stipulated by s. 1, namely, whether the law comes within the phrase "such reasonable limits prescribed by law as can be demonstrably justified in a free and democratic society."

He reached this conclusion on the basis that, where the *Charter* right is expressed in unqualified terms, s. 1 supplies the standard of justification for any abridgment of the right. He argued that the word "discrimination" in s. 15(1) could be

read as introducing a qualification in the section itself, but he preferred to read the word in a neutral sense because this reading would immediately send the matter to s. 1, which was included in the *Charter* for this purpose.

The second approach put forward by McLachlin J.A. in the Court of Appeal involved a consideration of the reasonableness and fairness of the impugned legislation under s. 15(1). She stated, as has been noted above, at p. 610:

> The ultimate question is whether a fair-minded person, weighing the purposes of legislation against its effects on the individuals adversely affected, and giving due weight to the right of the Legislature to pass laws for the good of all, would conclude that the legislative means adopted are unreasonable or unfair.

She assigned a very minor role to s. 1 which would, it appears, be limited to allowing in times of emergency, war, or other crises the passage of discriminatory legislation which would normally be impermissible.

A third approach, sometimes described as an "enumerated or analogous grounds" approach, adopts the concept that discrimination is generally expressed by the enumerated grounds. Section 15(1) is designed to prevent discrimination based on these and analogous grounds. The approach is similar to that found in human rights and civil rights statutes which have been enacted throughout Canada in recent times. ... The analysis of discrimination in this approach must take place within the context of the enumerated grounds and those analogous to them. The words "without discrimination" require more than a mere finding of distinction between the treatment of groups or individuals. Those words are a form of qualifier built into s. 15 itself and limit those distinctions which are forbidden by the section to those which involve prejudice or disadvantage.

I would accept the criticisms of the first approach made by McLachlin J.A. in the Court of Appeal. She noted that the labelling of every legislative distinction as an infringement of s. 15(1) trivializes the fundamental rights guaranteed by the *Charter* and, secondly, that to interpret "without discrimination" as "without distinction" deprives the notion of discrimination of content. She continued, at p. 607:

> Third, it cannot have been the intention of Parliament that the government be put to the requirement of establishing under s. 1 that all laws which draw distinction between people are "demonstrably justified in a free and democratic society." If weighing of the justifiability of unequal treatment is neither required or permitted under s. 15, the result will be that such universally accepted and manifestly desirable legal distinctions as those prohibiting children or drunk persons from driving motor vehicles

will be viewed as violations of fundamental rights and be required to run the gauntlet of s. 1.

Finally, it may further be contended that to define discrimination under s. 15 as synonymous with unequal treatment on the basis of personal classification will be to elevate s. 15 to the position of subsuming the other rights and freedoms defined by the *Charter*.

In rejecting the Hogg approach, I would say that it draws a straight line from the finding of a distinction to a determination of its validity under s. 1, but my objection would be that it virtually denies any role for s. 15(1).

I would reject, as well, the approach adopted by McLachlin J.A. She seeks to define discrimination under s. 15(1) as an unjustifiable or unreasonable distinction. In so doing she avoids the mere distinction test but also makes a radical departure from the analytical approach to the *Charter* which has been approved by this Court. In the result, the determination would be made under s. 15(1) and virtually no role would be left for s. 1.

The third or "enumerated and analogous grounds" approach most closely accords with the purposes of s. 15 and the definition of discrimination outlined above and leaves questions of justification to s. 1. However, in assessing whether a complainant's rights have been infringed under s. 15(1), it is not enough to focus only on the alleged ground of discrimination and decide whether or not it is an enumerated or analogous ground. The effect of the impugned distinction or classification on the complainant must be considered. Once it is accepted that not all distinctions and differentiations created by law are discriminatory, then a role must be assigned to s. 15(1) which goes beyond the mere recognition of a legal distinction. A complainant under s. 15(1) must show not only that he or she is not receiving equal treatment before and under the law or that the law has a differential impact on him or her in the protection or benefit accorded by law but, in addition, must show that the legislative impact of the law is discriminatory.

Where discrimination is found a breach of s. 15(1) has occurred and—where s. 15(2) is not applicable—any justification, any consideration of the reasonableness of the enactment; indeed, any consideration of factors which could justify the discrimination and support the constitutionality of the impugned enactment would take place under s. 1. This approach would conform with the directions of this Court in earlier decisions concerning the application of s. 1 and at the same time would allow for the screening out of the obviously trivial and vexatious claim. In this, it would provide a workable approach to the problem.

It would seem to me apparent that a legislative distinction has been made by s. 42 of the *Barristers and Solicitors Act*

between citizens and non-citizens with respect to the practice of law. The distinction would deny admission to the practice of law to non-citizens who in all other respects are qualified. Have the respondents, because of s. 42 of the *Act*, been denied equality before and under the law or the equal protection of the law? In practical terms it should be noted that the citizenship requirement affects only those non-citizens who are permanent residents. The permanent resident must wait for a minimum of three years from the date of establishing permanent residence status before citizenship may be acquired. The distinction therefore imposes a burden in the form of some delay on permanent residents who have acquired all or some of their legal training abroad and is, therefore, discriminatory.

The rights guaranteed in s. 15(1) apply to all persons whether citizens or not. A rule which bars an entire class of persons from certain forms of employment, solely on the grounds of a lack of citizenship status and without consideration of educational and professional qualifications or the other attributes or merits of individuals in the group, would, in my view, infringe s. 15 equality rights. Non-citizens, lawfully permanent residents of Canada, are—in the words of the U.S. Supreme Court in *United States v. Carolene Products Co.*, 304 U.S. 144 (1938), at pp. 152-53, n. 4, subsequently affirmed in *Graham v. Richardson*, 403 U.S. 365 (1971), at p. 372—a good example of a "discrete and insular minority" who come within the protection of s. 15.

Section 1

Having accepted the proposition that s. 42 has infringed the right to equality guaranteed in s. 15, it remains to consider whether, under the provisions of s. 1 of the *Charter*, the citizenship requirement which is clearly prescribed by law is a reasonable limit which can be "demonstrably justified in a free and democratic society."

The onus of justifying the infringement of a guaranteed *Charter* right must, of course, rest upon the parties seeking to uphold the limitation, in this case, the Attorney General of British Columbia and the Law Society of British Columbia. As is evident from the decisions of this Court, there are two steps involved in the s. 1 inquiry. First, the importance of the objective underlying the impugned law must be assessed. In *Oakes*, it was held that to override a *Charter* guaranteed right the objective must relate to concerns which are "pressing and substantial" in a free and democratic society. However, given the broad ambit of legislation which must be enacted to cover various aspects of the civil law dealing largely with administrative and regulatory matters and the necessity for the Legislature to make many distinctions between individuals and groups for such purposes, the standard of "pressing and substantial" may be too stringent for application in all cases. To hold otherwise would frequently deny the community-at-large the benefits associated with sound social and economic legislation. In my opinion, in approaching a case such as the one before us, the first question the Court should ask must relate to the nature and the purpose of the enactment, with a view to deciding whether the limitation represents a legitimate exercise of the legislative power for the attainment of a desirable social objective which would warrant overriding constitutionally protected rights. The second step in a s. 1 inquiry involves a proportionality test whereby the Court must attempt to balance a number of factors. The Court must examine the nature of the right, the extent of its infringement, and the degree to which the limitation furthers the attainment of the desirable goal embodied in the legislation. Also involved in the inquiry will be the importance of the right to the individual or group concerned, and the broader social impact of both the impugned law and its alternatives. As the Chief Justice has stated in *R. v. Edwards Books and Art Ltd., supra,* at pp. 768-69:

> Both in articulating the standard of proof and in describing the criteria comprising the proportionality requirement the Court has been careful to avoid rigid and inflexible standards.

I agree with this statement. There is no single test under s. 1; rather, the Court must carefully engage in the balancing of many factors in determining whether an infringement is reasonable and demonstrably justified.

The section 15(1) guarantee is the broadest of all guarantees. It applies to and supports all other rights guaranteed by the *Charter.* However, it must be recognized that Parliament and the Legislatures have a right and a duty to make laws for the whole community: in this process, they must make innumerable legislative distinctions and categorizations in the pursuit of the role of government. When making distinctions between groups and individuals to achieve desirable social goals, it will rarely be possible to say of any legislative distinction that it is clearly the right legislative choice or that it is clearly a wrong one. As stated by the Chief Justice in *R. v. Edwards Books and Art Ltd.,* at pp. 781-82:

> A "reasonable limit" is one which, having regard to the principles enunciated in *Oakes,* it was reasonable for the legislature to impose. The courts are not called upon to substitute judicial opinions for legislative ones as to the place at which to draw a precise line.

In dealing with the many problems that arise legislatures must not be held to the standard of perfection, for in such matters perfection is unattainable. I would repeat the words of my colleague, La Forest J., in *R. v. Edwards Books and Art Ltd.,* at p. 795:

> By the foregoing, I do not mean to suggest that this Court should, as a general rule, defer to legislative judgments when those judgments trench upon rights considered fundamental in a free and democratic society. Quite the contrary, I would have thought the *Charter* established the opposite regime. On the other hand, having accepted the importance of the legislative objective, one must in the present context recognize that if the legislative goal is to be achieved, it will inevitably be achieved to the detriment of some. Moreover, attempts to protect the rights of one group will also inevitably impose burdens on the rights of other groups. There is no perfect scenario in which the rights of all can be equally protected.
>
> In seeking to achieve a goal that is demonstrably justified in a free and democratic society, therefore, a legislature must be given reasonable room to manoeuvre to meet these conflicting pressures.

Disposition

... There is no difficulty in determining that in general terms the *Barristers and Solicitors Act* of British Columbia is a statute enacted for a valid and desirable social purpose, the creation and regulation of the legal profession and the practice of law. The narrower question, however, is whether the requirement that only citizens be admitted to the practice of law in British Columbia serves a desirable social purpose of sufficient importance to warrant overriding the equality guarantee. It is incontestable that the legal profession plays a very significant—in fact, a fundamentally important—role in the administration of justice, both in the criminal and the civil law. I would not attempt to answer the question arising from the judgments below as to whether the function of the profession may be termed judicial or quasi-judicial, but I would observe that in the absence of an independent legal profession, skilled and qualified to play its part in the administration of justice and the judicial process, the whole legal system would be in a parlous state. In the performance of what may be called his private function, that is, in advising on legal matters and in representing clients before the courts and other tribunals, the lawyer is accorded great powers not permitted to other professionals. As pointed out by Taylor J. at first instance, by the use of the subpoena which he alone can procure on behalf of another, he can compel attendance upon examinations before trial and at trial upon pain of legal sanction for refusal. He may, as well, require the production of documents and records for examination and use in the proceedings. He may in some cases require the summoning of jurors, the sittings of courts and, in addition, he may make the fullest inquiry into the matters before the court with a full privilege against actions for slander arising out of his conduct in the court. The solicitor is also bound by the solicitor and client privilege against the disclosure of communications with his client concerning legal matters. This is said to be the only absolute privilege known to the law. Not only may the solicitor decline to disclose solicitor and client communications, the courts will not permit him to do so. This is a privilege against all comers, including the Crown, save where the disclosure of a crime would be involved. The responsibilities involved in its maintenance and in its breach where crimes are concerned are such that citizenship with its commitment to the welfare of the whole community is not an unreasonable requirement for the practice of law. While it may be arguable whether the lawyer exercises a judicial, quasi-judicial, or governmental role, it is clear that at his own discretion he can invoke the full force and authority of the State in procuring and enforcing judgments or other remedial measures which may be obtained. It is equally true that in defending an action he has the burden of protecting his client from the imposition of such state authority and power. By any standard, these powers and duties are vital to the maintenance of order in our society and the due administration of the law in the interest of the whole community.

The lawyer has, as well, what may be termed a public function. Governments at all levels, federal, provincial and municipal, rely extensively upon lawyers, both in technical and policy matters. In the drafting of legislation, regulations, treaties, agreements and other governmental documents and papers lawyers play a major role. In various aspects of this work they are called upon to advise upon legal and constitutional questions which frequently go to the very heart of the governmental role. To discharge these duties, familiarity is required with Canadian history, constitutional law, regional differences and concerns within the country and, in fact, with the whole Canadian governmental and political process. It is entirely reasonable, then, that legislators consider and adopt measures designed to maintain within the legal profession a body of qualified professionals with a commitment to the country and to the fulfilment of the important tasks which fall to it.

McLachlin J.A. was of the view that the citizenship requirement would not ensure familiarity with Canadian institutions and customs, nor would it ensure a commitment to Canada going beyond one involved in the concept of allegiance, as recognized by the taking of an oath of allegiance. I would agree with her that the desired results would not be insured by the citizenship requirement but I would observe, at the same time, that no law will ever ensure anything. To abolish the requirement of citizenship on the basis that it would fail to insure the attainment of its objectives would, in my view, be akin to abolishing the law against theft, for it has certainly not insured the elimination of that crime. Citizenship, however, which requires the taking on of obligations and commitments to the community, difficult sometimes to describe but felt and understood by most citizens, as well as the rejection of past loyalties may reasonably be said to conduce to the desired result.

I would observe, as well, that the comment of McLachlin J.A. that the citizenship requirement was first adopted in British Columbia in 1971 requires some explanation. I do not think that the historical argument should be pushed too far: things need not always remain as once they were although, as noted in *R. v. Big M Drug Mart Ltd.* and *Reference re Public Service Employee Relations Act (Alta.), supra, Charter* construction should be consistent with the history, traditions and social philosophies of our society. The concept of citizenship has been a requirement for entry into the legal profession in British Columbia from its earliest days. When the Law Society was formed in 1874 the profession was open to British subjects. At that time, the idea of a separate Canadian citizenship, as distinct from the general classification of British subject which included Canadians, was scarcely known—though as early as 1910, *Immigration Act*, S.C. 1910, c. 27, the term "Canadian citizen" was defined for the purposes of the *Immigration Act* as a "British subject who has Canadian domicile." The concept of citizenship in those early days was embodied in the expression, British Subject, and thus it was recognized as a requirement for entry into the legal profession in British Columbia. As Canada moved away from its colonial past, a separate identity for Canadians emerged and in 1946 with the passage of *The Canadian Citizenship Act*, S.C. 1946, c. 15, the term, Canadian citizen, was formally recognized, giving effect to what had long been felt and accepted by most Canadians. In adopting the term as a qualification for entry into the legal profession in British Columbia, the Legislature was merely continuing its earlier requirement that the concept of citizenship, as then recognized in the term "British subject," be necessary for entry into the profession.

Public policy, of which the citizenship requirement in the *Barristers and Solicitors Act* is an element, is for the Legislature to establish. The role of the *Charter*, as applied by the courts, is to ensure that in applying public policy the Legislature does not adopt measures which are not sustainable under the *Charter*. It is not, however, for the courts to legislate or to substitute their views on public policy for those of the Legislature. I would repeat for ease of reference the words of the Chief Justice in *R. v. Edwards Books and Art Ltd., supra*, at pp. 781-82:

A "reasonable limit" is one which having regard to the principles enunciated in *Oakes*, it was reasonable for the legislature to impose. The courts are not called upon to substitute judicial opinions for legislative ones as to the place at which to draw a precise line.

The function of the Court is to measure the legislative enactment against the requirements of the *Charter* and where the enactment infringes the *Charter*, in this case the provisions of s. 15(1), and is not sustainable under s. 1, the remedial power of the Court is set out in s. 52 of the *Constitution Act, 1982*: "any law that is inconsistent with the provisions of the Constitution is, to the extent of the inconsistency, of no force or effect."

The essence of s. 1 is found in the expression "reasonable" and it is for the Court to decide if s. 42 of the *Barristers and Solicitors Act* of British Columbia is a reasonable limit. In reaching the conclusion that it is, I would say that the legislative choice in this regard is not one between an answer that is clearly right and one that is clearly wrong. Either position may well be sustainable and, as noted by the Chief Justice, *supra*, the Court is not called upon to substitute its opinion as to where to draw the line. The Legislature in fixing public policy has chosen the citizenship requirement and, unless the Court can find that choice unreasonable, it has no power under the *Charter* to strike it down or, as has been said, no power to invade the legislative field and substitute its views for that of the Legislature. In my view, the citizenship requirement is reasonable and sustainable under s. 1. It is chosen for the achievement of a desirable social goal: one aspect of the due regulation and qualification of the legal profession. This is an objective of importance and the measure is not disproportionate to the object to be attained. The maximum delay imposed upon the non-citizen from the date of acquisition of permanent resident status is three years. It will frequently be less. No impediment is put in the way of obtaining citizenship. In fact, the policy of the Canadian government is to encourage the newcomer to become a citizen. It is reasonable, in my view, to expect that the newcomer who seeks to gain the privileges and status within the land and the right to exercise the great powers that admission to the practice of law will give should accept citizenship and its obligations as well as its advantages and benefits. I would therefore allow the appeal and restore the judgment at trial. ...

28   M. v. H., 1999

The 1999 *M. v. H.* decision represented a significant turning point in terms of state recognition of same-sex partners and their relationships in Canada. The decision had enormous implications for provincial and federal governments because it conveyed the following message: social policies oriented toward spouses that deny recognition or benefits to same-sex partners lack constitutional validity. This decision would have been extremely difficult to anticipate at the time of the Charter's adoption.

When the Charter was debated, lesbian and gay activists had little reason to assume that it would be a useful resource in their efforts to pressure politicians to undertake substantial social policy changes to redress discrimination on the basis of sexual orientation. At the time, both federal and provincial legislation relied heavily on a heterosexual definition of "spouse" that had the effect of denying entitlements or recognition to same-sex partners and their relationships. But legislatures were not the only obstacle in overcoming this form of discrimination. Courts routinely accepted the validity of these legislative distinctions either by using a heterosexual definition of "spouse" or "marriage" or by ruling that, in the absence of a statutory basis for recognizing same-sex spouses, judges were powerless to disagree with legislation. During the entrenchment debate, Jean Chrétien, who was then the federal justice minister, indicated that the federal Liberal government was not prepared to include sexual orientation as a prohibited category of discrimination in the Charter. But he did suggest that, in time, courts might interpret equality in a more expansive manner.

A decade after the equality rights came into force (their application was delayed for three years after the Charter was adopted to allow legislatures to identify and revise legislation that might be inconsistent with equality), the Supreme Court ruled in *Egan v. Canada*[1] that the Charter's equality rights do indeed protect individuals from discrimination on the basis of sexual orientation. However, because the court's ruling was heavily qualified, this decision was not immediately helpful to those hoping for swift legislative changes to redress discrimination against gay men or lesbians. Although the court was unanimous in its conclusion that section 15 equality rights prohibit discrimination on the basis of sexual orientation, it split on the question whether the legislation at issue, the federal *Old Age Security Act* and the allowance it provided for some qualifying spouses of pensioners, actually violated the Charter. Five judges ruled that the heterosexual definition of "spouse" in the Act violated equality, while four judges ruled it did not. But Justice Sopinka, one of the five who ruled that equality was violated, concluded that the legislation imposed a reasonable limit under section 1. He argued that legislatures needed more time to recognize new social relationships because the idea of interpreting "spouse" to include same-sex partners represented a "novel concept" and the legislative changes would have significant fiscal implications. The result

---

1   [1995] 2 S.C.R. 513.

of this section 1 ruling was that a narrow majority upheld the validity of the Act, relieving federal or provincial legislatures of the immediate pressure of having to redress this form of discrimination.

However, it was not long before the court expressed impatience with what it perceived to be inappropriate delays in introducing the necessary social policy reforms. Three years later, the court indicated judicial fatigue with legislative inaction in addressing discrimination on the basis of sexual orientation. In *Vriend v. Alberta*,[2] the court categorically rejected the Alberta government's argument for deference to its explicit decision not to include sexual orientation as a protected ground against discrimination in its provincial human rights code. In *Vriend*, lawyers for the Alberta government argued, unsuccessfully, that the omission of sexual orientation as a prohibited ground of discrimination was justified under section 1, reminding the court that Justice Sopinka had only a few years earlier suggested that legislatures should be given time to develop an incremental approach to reform legislation affecting spouses and families.

M. v. H. was handed down the following year, and this time the court clearly was not prepared to accept legislative inaction on this issue. At issue was the failure in Ontario's *Family Law Act* to recognize same-sex relationships in its processes for resolving property and other issues that arise when family relationships are dissolved. Government lawyers had argued that same-sex partners had options other than statutory ones, such as contract law, and that the differential treatment was therefore acceptable. The court rejected this argument, concluding that the denial of access to the court-enforced and court-protected support system available to others whose relationships have dissolved was not justified under section 1. But it was not simply the lack of equal benefit of the law that troubled the court. The court also ruled that the legislation violated equality because it promoted a view that those in same-sex relationships are less worthy of state recognition and protection than those in heterosexual unions and that this message perpetuates the disadvantages incurred by those in same-sex relationships because of the continued social prejudices they encounter.

Although the legislation had immediate implications for Ontario, it also had important consequences for the federal and other provincial governments because they similarly based legislative entitlements and obligations on a heterosexual definition of "spouse." In Ontario, the Progressive Conservative government of Mike Harris indicated that, although the court's view of family did not correspond with his definition, his government would comply with the court's decision, suggesting that he did not believe that use of the notwithstanding clause was a valid political response to a judicial ruling. But the government's lack of enthusiasm for the legislative changes it introduced was conveyed in the title of its legislation, which suggested grudging acceptance for the ruling: *Amendments Because of the Supreme Court of Canada Decision in M. v. H. Act, 1999*. This legislation amended more than 67 legislative acts by recognizing "same-sex partners" for inclusion in most social policy entitlements. The federal government responded to this ruling in 2000 by introducing the *Modernization of Benefits and Obligations Act*, which introduced a new term, "common-law partner," and expanded the common-law definition of "non-married relationships" to include same-sex partners. The legislation was extremely controversial, as critics argued that it would affect the definition of "marriage." In response to pressure from the Canadian Alliance, the Liberal

---

2 [1998] 1 S.C.R. 493.

government agreed to include a preamble in the legislation, stating that the amendments did not affect the definition of "marriage," which remained "the lawful union of one man and one woman to the exclusion of all others." ∼

Discussion Questions

1. What consequences for social policy flow from the Supreme Court's indication that equality requires not only equal benefit of the law, but also that the law treat same-sex partners with the same degree of respect and recognition given to opposite-sex couples?

2. Was the court justified in its decision that deference is not appropriate when legislatures have failed to redress discrimination in the benefits given to same-sex partners?

3. Was it appropriate for the court to suspend the effects of its ruling? What other remedies were available?

M. v. H.

[1999] 2 S.C.R. 3

Hearing: March 18, 1998; Judgment: May 20, 1999.

Present: Lamer C.J. and L'Heureux-Dubé, Gonthier, Cory, McLachlin, Iacobucci, Major, Bastarache, and Binnie JJ.

Interveners: The Foundation for Equal Families, the Women's Legal Education and Action Fund (LEAF), Equality for Gays and Lesbians Everywhere (EGALE), the Ontario Human Rights Commission, the United Church of Canada, the Evangelical Fellowship of Canada, the Ontario Council of Sikhs, the Islamic Society of North America, Focus on the Family, and REAL Women of Canada.

The judgment of Lamer C.J. and L'Heureux-Dubé, Cory, McLachlin, Iacobucci, and Binnie JJ. was delivered by

CORY AND IACOBUCCI JJ.:

I. Introduction and Overview

[1] The principal issue raised in this appeal is whether the definition of "spouse" in s. 29 of the *Family Law Act*, R.S.O. 1990, c. F.3 ("*FLA*") infringes s. 15(1) of the *Canadian Charter of Rights and Freedoms*, and, if so, whether the legislation is nevertheless saved by s. 1 of the *Charter*. In addition, M. was granted leave to cross-appeal on the issue of the appropriate remedy to be granted and also as to costs.

[2] Our view on this principal issue may be summarized as follows. Section 15(1) of the *Charter* is infringed by the definition of "spouse" in s. 29 of the *FLA*. This definition, which only applies to Part III of the *FLA*, draws a distinction between individuals in conjugal, opposite-sex relationships of

a specific degree of duration and individuals in conjugal, same-sex relationships of a specific degree of duration. ... Essentially, the definition of "spouse" in s. 29 of the *FLA* extends the obligation to provide spousal support, found in Part III of the *FLA*, beyond married persons to include individuals in conjugal opposite-sex relationships of some permanence. Same-sex relationships are capable of being both conjugal and lengthy, but individuals in such relationships are nonetheless denied access to the court-enforced system of support provided by the *FLA*. This differential treatment is on the basis of a personal characteristic, namely sexual orientation, that, in previous jurisprudence, has been found to be analogous to those characteristics specifically enumerated in s. 15(1).

[3] The crux of the issue is that this differential treatment discriminates in a substantive sense by violating the human dignity of individuals in same-sex relationships. As *Law v. Canada (Minister of Employment and Immigration)*, [1999] 1 S.C.R. 497, established, the inquiry into substantive discrimination is to be undertaken in a purposive and contextual manner. In the present appeal, several factors are important to consider. First, individuals in same-sex relationships face significant pre-existing disadvantage and vulnerability, which is exacerbated by the impugned legislation. Second, the legislation at issue fails to take into account the claimant's actual situation. Third, there is no compelling argument that the ameliorative purpose of the legislation does anything to lessen the charge of discrimination in this case. Fourth, the nature of the interest affected is fundamental, namely the ability to meet basic financial needs following the breakdown of a relationship characterized by intimacy and economic dependence. The exclusion of same-sex partners from the benefits of the

spousal support scheme implies that they are judged to be incapable of forming intimate relationships of economic interdependence, without regard to their actual circumstances. Taking these factors into account, it is clear that the human dignity of individuals in same-sex relationships is violated by the definition of "spouse" in s. 29 of the *FLA*.

[4] This infringement is not justified under s.1 of the *Charter* because there is no rational connection between the objectives of the spousal support provisions and the means chosen to further this objective. The objectives were accurately identified by Charron J.A., in the court below, as providing for the equitable resolution of economic disputes when intimate relationships between financially interdependent individuals break down, and alleviating the burden on the public purse to provide for dependent spouses. Neither of these objectives is furthered by the exclusion of individuals in same-sex couples from the spousal support regime. If anything, these goals are undermined by this exclusion.

[5] In this case, the remedy of reading in is inappropriate, as it would unduly recast the legislation, and striking down the *FLA* as a whole is excessive. Therefore the appropriate remedy is to declare s. 29 of no force and effect and to suspend the application of the declaration for a period of six months.

[6] In our elaboration of this position in these joint reasons, Cory J. has addressed the issues of mootness and the breach of s. 15(1) of the *Charter*. Iacobucci J. has addressed s. 1 of the *Charter*, the appropriate remedy, costs and the disposition.

CORY J.:

[7] At the outset, it must be stressed that the questions to be answered are narrow and precise in their scope. The *FLA* provides a means whereby designated persons may apply to the court for support from a spouse or, if unmarried, from a man or woman with whom they lived in an opposite-sex conjugal relationship. The Act specifically extends the obligation for support beyond married persons who, as a result of their married status, have additional rights under the Act.

[8] The question to be resolved is whether the extension of the right to seek support to members of unmarried opposite-sex couples infringes s. 15(1) of the *Charter* by failing to provide the same rights to members of same-sex couples.

II. Factual Background

[9] M. and H. are women who met while on vacation in 1980. It is agreed that in 1982 they started living together in a same-sex relationship that continued for at least five years. ...

[13] By September of 1992, M. and H.'s relationship had deteriorated. ...

[14] The parties did not divide the personal property or household contents. M. alleged that she encountered serious financial problems after the separation. In October 1992, M. sought an order for partition and sale of the house; a declaration that she was the beneficial owner of certain lands and premises owned by H. and by the companies M. named as defendants; and an accounting of the transactions carried out by the companies. By Notice of Cross-Application, H. and the corporate defendants sought damages for slander of title, partition and sale of property, the repayment of certain loans, and other relief. M. then amended her application to include a claim for support pursuant to the provisions of the *FLA*, and served Notice of a Constitutional Question challenging the validity of the definition of "spouse" in s. 29 of the Act. ...

B. Does Section 29 of the FLA Infringe Section 15(1) of the Charter?

[45] The Attorney General for Ontario, displaying great candour, very fairly conceded that s. 29 of the *FLA* contravenes the provisions of s. 15 of the *Charter*. His entire argument was directed at demonstrating that the section was nonetheless justifiable and saved by s. 1 of the *Charter*. The Court is certainly not bound by this concession. Although, in my view, he was correct in taking this position, it would not be appropriate in this appeal to undertake only a s. 1 analysis without considering whether s. 15 has in fact been violated. The s. 15(1) issue in this case is important not only to the parties but also to many Canadians. It was the subject of extensive submissions by the respondent H. and many of the interveners.

1. Approach to Section 15(1)

[46] In the recent decision of this Court in *Law, supra*, Iacobucci J. summarized some of the main guidelines for analysis under s. 15(1) to be derived from the jurisprudence of this Court. He emphasized that these guidelines do not represent a strict test, but rather should be understood as points of reference for a court that is called upon to decide whether a claimant's right to equality without discrimination under the *Charter* has been infringed: see para. 88.

[47] Iacobucci J. explained that the s. 15(1) equality guarantee is to be interpreted and applied in a purposive and contextual manner, in order to permit the realization of the provision's strong remedial purpose, and to avoid the pitfalls of a formalistic or mechanical approach. Following a review of this Court's jurisprudence regarding the fundamental purpose of s. 15(1), he stated this purpose in the following terms, at para. 88:

> In general terms, the purpose of s. 15(1) is to prevent the violation of essential human dignity and freedom through the imposition of disadvantage, stereotyping, or political

or social prejudice, and to promote a society in which all persons enjoy equal recognition at law as human beings or as members of Canadian society, equally capable and equally deserving of concern, respect and consideration.

Iacobucci J. stated that the existence of a conflict between the purpose or effect of an impugned law, on the one hand, and this fundamental purpose of the equality guarantee, on the other, is essential in order to found a discrimination claim.

[48] In *Law*, Iacobucci J. reviewed various articulations of the proper approach to be taken in analyzing a s. 15(1) claim, as expressed in the jurisprudence of this Court. At para. 39, he summarized the basic elements of this Court's approach as involving three broad inquiries, in the following terms:

> In my view, the proper approach to analyzing a claim of discrimination under s. 15(1) of the *Charter* involves a synthesis of these various articulations. Following upon the analysis in *Andrews* [*v. Law Society of British Columbia*], [1989] 1 S.C.R. 143, and the two-step framework set out in *Egan, supra,* and *Miron* [*v. Trudel*, [1995] 2 S.C.R. 418], among other cases, a court that is called upon to determine a discrimination claim under s. 15(1) should make the following three broad inquiries. First, does the impugned law (a) draw a formal distinction between the claimant and others on the basis of one or more personal characteristics, or (b) fail to take into account the claimant's already disadvantaged position within Canadian society resulting in substantively differential treatment between the claimant and others on the basis of one or more personal characteristics? If so, there is differential treatment for the purpose of s. 15(1). Second, was the claimant subject to differential treatment on the basis of one or more of the enumerated and analogous grounds? And third, does the differential treatment discriminate in a substantive sense, bringing into play the *purpose* of s. 15(1) of the *Charter* in remedying such ills as prejudice, stereotyping, and historical disadvantage? [Emphasis in original.]

2. The Structure of the Family Law Act

[49] To begin, it may be useful to review briefly the structure of the *FLA* and the rights and obligations it establishes. First and foremost, it is of critical importance to recognize that the *FLA* contains more than one definition of "spouse." The first definition is set out in s. 1(1) and includes only persons who are actually married, or who have entered into a void or voidable marriage in good faith. This definition applies to *all* parts of the Act.

[50] The second definition is found in s. 29, and extends the meaning of "spouse," but only for certain purposes. Specifically, unmarried opposite-sex couples who have cohabited

for at least three years, or who are the natural or adoptive parents of a child and have also cohabited in a relationship of "some permanence," bear a mutual obligation of support under Part III of the *FLA*. They also have the right to enter into cohabitation agreements to regulate their relationship under Part IV, and may bring a claim for dependants' relief in tort under Part V.

[51] All these rights and obligations are obviously available to married persons as well. However, married persons have additional rights under the *FLA* that are denied common law cohabitants, even those who meet the requirements of s. 29. Under Part I, a husband or wife may apply for an equal share of the wealth generated during the marriage, and of the matrimonial home. Under Part II, both married spouses have a right to possession of the matrimonial home, regardless of who owns the property. Moreover, the ability of the owner of the matrimonial home to sell or encumber the property without the consent of the other spouse is severely restricted. These mutual rights and obligations are denied *all* unmarried opposite-sex cohabitants.

[52] These observations on the structure of the *FLA* serve to emphasize that this appeal has nothing to do with marriage *per se*. Much of the *FLA* is devoted solely to regulating the relationship that exists between married persons, or persons who intend to be married. They alone are guaranteed certain property rights that are not extended to any unmarried persons. In some specific instances—such as Part III dealing with support obligations—the legislature has seen fit to extend the rights and obligations that arise under the *FLA beyond* married persons to include certain *unmarried* persons as well.

[53] In other words, the *FLA* draws a distinction by specifically according rights to individual members of unmarried cohabiting opposite-sex couples, which by omission it fails to accord to individual members of same-sex couples who are living together. It is this distinction that lies at the heart of the s. 15 analysis. The rights and obligations that exist between married persons play no part in this analysis. The legislature did not extend full marital status, for the purposes of all the rights and obligations under the *FLA*, to those unmarried cohabitants included in s. 29 of the Act. Rather, the definition of "spouse" in s. 29 only applies for certain purposes. Specifically, it allows persons who became financially dependent in the course of a lengthy intimate relationship some relief from financial hardship resulting from the breakdown of that relationship. It follows that this provision was designed to reduce the demands on the public welfare system. This will be discussed more fully in the s. 1 analysis below.

[54] ... [T]he legislature drafted s. 29 to allow either a man *or* a woman to apply for support, thereby recognizing that financial dependence can arise in an intimate relationship

in a context entirely unrelated either to child rearing or to any gender-based discrimination existing in our society. ...

[55] [I]n this appeal there is no need to consider whether same-sex couples can marry, or whether same-sex couples must, for all purposes, be treated in the same manner as unmarried opposite-sex couples. The only determination that must be made is whether, in extending the spousal support obligations set out in Part III of the *FLA* to include unmarried men or women in certain opposite-sex relationships, the legislature infringed the equality rights of men or women in similar same-sex relationships, and if so, whether that infringement may be saved by s. 1 of the *Charter*. ...

[57] The definition [of "spouse" in section 29 of the *FLA*] clearly indicates that the legislature decided to extend the obligation to provide spousal support *beyond* married persons. Obligations to provide support were no longer dependent upon marriage. The obligation was extended to include those relationships which:

(i)   exist between a man and a woman;
(ii) have a specific degree of permanence;
(iii) are conjugal.

Only individuals in relationships which meet these minimum criteria may apply for a support order under Part III of the *FLA*.

[58] Same-sex relationships are capable of meeting the last two requirements. Certainly same-sex couples will often form long, lasting, loving and intimate relationships. The choices they make in the context of those relationships may give rise to the financial dependence of one partner on the other. Though it might be argued that same-sex couples do not live together in "conjugal" relationships, in the sense that they cannot "hold themselves out" as husband and wife, on this issue I am in agreement with the reasoning and conclusions of the majority of the Court of Appeal. ...

[60] Certainly an opposite-sex couple may, after many years together, be considered to be in a conjugal relationship although they have neither children nor sexual relations. Obviously the weight to be accorded the various elements or factors to be considered in determining whether an opposite-sex couple is in a conjugal relationship will vary widely and almost infinitely. The same must hold true of same-sex couples. Courts have wisely determined that the approach to determining whether a relationship is conjugal must be flexible. This must be so, for the relationships of all couples will vary widely. ...

[61] Since gay and lesbian individuals are capable of being involved in conjugal relationships, and since their relationships are capable of meeting the *FLA*'s temporal requirements, the distinction of relevance to this appeal is between persons in an opposite-sex, conjugal relationship of some permanence and persons in a same-sex, conjugal relationship of some permanence. In this regard, I must disagree with the dissenting opinion in the court below, which characterized the distinction arising in s. 29 as being between opposite-sex and same-sex *couples*. This conclusion would require that the section be scrutinized for any discriminatory impact it may have on same-sex couples, and not on the individual members of that couple. Section 29 defines "spouse" as "*either* of a man and woman" who meet the other requirements of the section. It follows that the definition could not have been meant to define a couple. Rather it explicitly refers to the *individual* members of the couple. Thus the distinction of relevance must be between individual persons in a same-sex, conjugal relationship of some permanence and individual persons in an opposite-sex, conjugal relationship of some permanence.

[62] Thus it is apparent that the legislation has drawn a formal distinction between the claimant and others, based on personal characteristics. As stated in *Law, supra*, the first broad inquiry in the s. 15(1) analysis determines whether there is differential treatment imposed by the impugned legislation between the claimant and others. It is clear that there is differential treatment here. Under s. 29 of the *FLA*, members of opposite-sex couples who can meet the requirements of the statute are able to gain access to the court-enforced system of support provided by the *FLA*. It is this system that ensures the provision of support to a dependent spouse. Members of same-sex couples are denied access to this system entirely on the basis of their sexual orientation.

4. Sexual Orientation Is an Analogous Ground

[63] Not every legislative distinction is discriminatory. Before it can be found that it gives rise to discrimination, it must be shown that an equality right was denied on the basis of an enumerated or analogous ground, and that this differential treatment discriminates "in a substantive sense, bringing into play the *purpose* of s. 15(1) of the *Charter*": *Law, supra*, at para. 39 (emphasis in original).

[64] In *Egan, supra*, this Court unanimously affirmed that sexual orientation is an analogous ground to those enumerated in s. 15(1). Sexual orientation is "a deeply personal characteristic that is either unchangeable or changeable only at unacceptable personal costs" (para. 5). In addition, a majority of this Court explicitly recognized that gays, lesbians and bisexuals, "whether as individuals or couples, form an identifiable minority who have suffered and continue to suffer serious social, political and economic disadvantage" (para. 175, *per* Cory J.; see also para. 89, *per* L'Heureux-Dubé J.).

5. The Existence of Discrimination in a Purposive Sense

[65] The determination of whether differential treatment imposed by legislation on an enumerated or analogous ground is discriminatory within the meaning of s. 15(1) of the *Charter* is to be undertaken in a purposive and contextual manner. The relevant inquiry is whether the differential treatment imposes a burden upon or withholds a benefit from the claimant in a manner that reflects the stereotypical application of presumed group or personal characteristics, or which otherwise has the effect of perpetuating or promoting the view that the individual is less capable or worthy of recognition or value as a human being or as a member of Canadian society, equally deserving of concern, respect, and consideration: *Law, supra*, at para. 88.

[66] The respondent H. has argued that the differential treatment imposed by s. 29 of the *FLA* does not deny the respondent M. the equal benefit of the law since same-sex spouses are not being denied an economic benefit, but simply the opportunity to gain access to a court-enforced process. Such an analysis takes too narrow a view of "benefit" under the law. It is a view this Court should not adopt. The type of benefit salient to the s. 15(1) analysis cannot encompass only the conferral of an economic benefit. It must also include access to a process that could confer an economic or other benefit: *Egan, supra*, at paras. 158-59; *Vriend v. Alberta*, [1998] 1 S.C.R. 493, at para. 87. Further, the spousal support provisions of the *FLA* help protect the economic interests of individuals in intimate relationships. When a relationship breaks down, the support provisions help to ensure that a member of a couple who has contributed to the couple's welfare in intangible ways will not find himself or herself utterly abandoned. This protective aspect of the spousal support provisions is properly considered in relation to s. 15(1). Thus it is appropriate to conclude that s. 29 of the *FLA* creates a distinction that withholds a benefit from the respondent M. The question is whether this denial of a benefit violates the purpose of s. 15(1).

[67] In *Law*, Iacobucci J. explained that there are a variety of contextual factors that may be referred to by a s. 15(1) claimant in order to demonstrate that legislation demeans his or her dignity. The list of factors is not closed, and there is no specific formula that must be considered in every case. In *Law* itself, Iacobucci J. listed four important contextual factors in particular which may influence the determination of whether s. 15(1) has been infringed. He emphasized, at paras. 59-61, that in examining these contextual factors, a court must adopt the point of view of a reasonable person, in circumstances similar to those of the claimant, who takes into account the contextual factors relevant to the claim.

[68] One factor which may demonstrate that legislation that treats the claimant differently has the effect of demeaning the claimant's dignity is the existence of pre-existing disadvantage, stereotyping, prejudice, or vulnerability experienced by the individual or group at issue. ...

[69] In this case, there is significant pre-existing disadvantage and vulnerability, and these circumstances are exacerbated by the impugned legislation. The legislative provision in question draws a distinction that prevents persons in a same-sex relationship from gaining access to the court-enforced and protected support system. This system clearly provides a benefit to unmarried heterosexual persons who come within the definition set out in s. 29, and thereby provides a measure of protection for their economic interests. This protection is denied to persons in a same-sex relationship who would otherwise meet the statute's requirements, and as a result, a person in the position of the claimant is denied a benefit regarding an important aspect of life in today's society. Neither common law nor equity provides the remedy of maintenance that is made available by the *FLA*. The denial of that potential benefit, which may impose a financial burden on persons in the position of the claimant, contributes to the general vulnerability experienced by individuals in same-sex relationships.

[70] A second contextual factor that was discussed in *Law* as being potentially relevant to the s. 15(1) inquiry is the correspondence, or the lack of it, between the ground on which a claim is based and the actual need, capacity, or circumstances of the claimant or others: para. 70. Iacobucci J. nonetheless cautioned that the mere fact that the impugned legislation takes into account the claimant's actual situation will not necessarily defeat a s. 15(1) claim, as the focus of the inquiry must always remain upon the central question of whether, viewed from the perspective of the claimant, the differential treatment imposed by the legislation has the effect of violating human dignity. However, the legislation at issue in the current appeal fails to take into account the claimant's actual situation. As I have already discussed, access to the court-enforced spousal support regime provided in the *FLA* is given to individuals in conjugal relationships of a specific degree of permanence. Being in a same-sex relationship does not mean that it is an impermanent or a non-conjugal relationship.

[71] A third contextual factor referred to by Iacobucci J. in *Law, supra*, at para. 72, is the question of whether the impugned legislation has an ameliorative purpose or effect for a group historically disadvantaged in the context of the legislation:

An ameliorative purpose or effect which accords with the purpose of s. 15(1) of the *Charter* will likely not violate the human dignity of more advantaged individuals where the exclusion of these more advantaged individuals largely corresponds to the greater need or the different circumstances experienced by the disadvantaged group being targeted by the legislation. I emphasize that this factor will likely only be relevant where the person or group that is excluded from the scope of ameliorative legislation or other state action is more advantaged in a relative sense. Underinclusive ameliorative legislation that excludes from its scope the members of an historically disadvantaged group will rarely escape the charge of discrimination: see *Vriend, supra,* at paras. 94-104, *per* Cory J.

In other words, the existence of an ameliorative purpose or effect may help to establish that human dignity is not violated where the person or group that is excluded is more advantaged with respect to the circumstances addressed by the legislation. Gonthier J. argues that the legislation under scrutiny in the present appeal is just such ameliorative legislation—that it is meant to target women in married or opposite-sex relationships. He proceeds to argue that in this legal context, women in same-sex relationships are not similarly disadvantaged. For the reasons expressed elsewhere, we disagree with this characterization of the legislation. Accordingly, we reject the idea that the allegedly ameliorative purpose of this legislation does anything to lessen the charge of discrimination in this case.

[72] A fourth contextual factor specifically adverted to by Iacobucci J. in *Law,* at para. 74, was the nature of the interest affected by the impugned legislation. Drawing upon the reasons of L'Heureux-Dubé J. in *Egan, supra,* Iacobucci J. stated that the discriminatory calibre of differential treatment cannot be fully appreciated without considering whether the distinction in question restricts access to a fundamental social institution, or affects a basic aspect of full membership in Canadian society, or constitutes a complete non-recognition of a particular group. In the present case, the interest protected by s. 29 of the *FLA* is fundamental, namely the ability to meet basic financial needs following the breakdown of a relationship characterized by intimacy and economic dependence. Members of same-sex couples are entirely ignored by the statute, notwithstanding the undeniable importance to them of the benefits accorded by the statute.

[73] The societal significance of the benefit conferred by the statute cannot be overemphasized. The exclusion of same-sex partners from the benefits of s. 29 of the *FLA* promotes the view that M., and individuals in same-sex relationships generally, are less worthy of recognition and protection. It implies that they are judged to be incapable of forming intimate relationships of economic interdependence as compared to opposite-sex couples, without regard to their actual circumstances. As the intervener EGALE submitted, such exclusion perpetuates the disadvantages suffered by individuals in same-sex relationships and contributes to the erasure of their existence.

[74] Therefore I conclude that an examination of the four factors outlined above, in the context of the present appeal, indicate that the human dignity of individuals in same-sex relationships is violated by the impugned legislation. In light of this, I conclude that the definition of "spouse" in s. 29 of the *FLA* violates s. 15(1).

IACOBUCCI J.:

C. Is Section 29 of the FLA Justified Under Section 1 of the Charter?

1. Stare Decisis and Egan

[75] At the outset, I wish to address the appellant's submission that an independent examination of the s. 1 issues is unnecessary in the present case. The appellant asserts that the principle of *stare decisis* binds this Court to the decision in *Egan, supra,* and that the s. 1 analysis in that case ought to apply with equal force to the case at bar. Although I recognize the fundamental role of precedent in legal analysis, I cannot accept this submission. Granted, *Egan,* like the case now before this Court, was also concerned with the opposite-sex definition of "spouse" in provincial legislation. However, the similar focus of the two cases is not sufficient to bind the Court to the *Egan* decision. The instant case is based on entirely different legislation with its own unique objectives and legislative context. As a result, it must be evaluated on its own merits.

2. Approach to Section 1

[76] The analytical framework for determining whether a law constitutes a "reasonable" limit that can be "demonstrably justified in a free and democratic society" under s. 1 of the *Charter* was first set out by Dickson C.J. in *R. v. Oakes,* [1986] 1 S.C.R. 103. ...

[77] However, it is important not to lose sight of the underlying principles animating this general approach. ...

[78] As noted by this Court in *Vriend, supra,* at para. 134, the introduction of the *Charter* brought about "a redefinition of our democracy." Central to this democratic vision is a dialogue of mutual respect between the courts and the legislatures, which includes the idea that [*Vriend,* at para. 136]:

> In carrying out their duties, courts are not to second-guess legislatures and the executives; they are not to make value judgments on what they regard as the proper policy choice; this is for the other branches. Rather, the courts are to uphold the Constitution and have been expressly

invited to perform that role by the Constitution itself. But respect by the courts for the legislature and executive role is as important as ensuring that the other branches respect each others' role and the role of the courts.

This Court has often stressed the importance of deference to the policy choices of the legislature in the context of determining whether the legislature has discharged its burden of proof under s. 1 of the *Charter*. ... However, it is important to note that deference is not a kind of threshold inquiry under s. 1. As a general matter, the role of the legislature demands deference from the courts to those types of policy decisions that the legislature is best placed to make. The simple or general claim that the infringement of a right is justified under s. 1 is not such a decision. As Cory J. stated in *Vriend, supra*, at para. 54: "The notion of judicial deference to legislative choices should not ... be used to completely immunize certain kinds of legislative decisions from *Charter* scrutiny."

[79] Under s. 1, the burden is on the legislature to prove that the infringement of a right is justified. In attempting to discharge this burden, the legislature will have to provide the court with evidence and arguments to support its general claim of justification. Sometimes this will involve demonstrating why the legislature had to make certain policy choices and why it considered these choices to be reasonable in the circumstances. These policy choices may be of the type that the legislature is in a better position than the court to make, as in the case of difficult policy judgments regarding the claims of competing groups or the evaluation of complex and conflicting social science research: *Irwin Toy, supra*, at p. 993, *per* Dickson C.J. and Lamer and Wilson JJ. Courts must be cautious not to overstep the bounds of their institutional competence in reviewing such decisions. The question of deference, therefore, is intimately tied up with the nature of the particular claim or evidence at issue and not in the general application of the s. 1 test; it can only be discussed in relation to such specific claims or evidence and not at the outset of the analysis.

[80] I therefore agree with my colleague, Bastarache J., that an examination of *context* is essential in determining whether deference is appropriate. It may also be the case that a discussion of context is appropriate at the outset of a s. 1 analysis, depending on the nature of the evidence at issue, for ease of reference when later applying the various steps of s. 1: see, for example, *Thomson Newspapers Co. v. Canada (Attorney General)*, [1998] 1 S.C.R. 877, at para. 88, *per* Bastarache J. However, with respect to his reasons in the present appeal, I am concerned that Bastarache J. implies that the question of *deference* in a general sense should also be determined at the outset of the inquiry. For example, Bastarache J. states that the

question to ask in this case is whether the Court can "rewrite the boundary in order to include that smaller number of individuals [in same-sex relationships] who are in such a position [of dependency], or must it defer to legislative determination of the issue?" (para. 304). The question of rewriting boundaries is, to my mind, at most a question of the appropriate remedy should the rights infringement be unjustified. The question of deference to the role of the legislature certainly enters into any discussion of remedy, as discussed in *Vriend, supra*, and can enter into the discussion of whether the legislature has discharged its burden under any of the steps of the s. 1 test. However, the question of deference is not an issue that can be determined prior to engaging in any of these specific inquiries. Nor should it be determined at the outset of the inquiry, given the court's important role in applying s. 1 of the *Charter* to determine whether the infringement of a guaranteed right can be justified in a free and democratic society.

[81] I will therefore not deal with the question of deference at the outset and will instead discuss it, where appropriate, under the various steps of the s. 1 test.

3. Pressing and Substantial Objective

[82] Section 29 of the *FLA* defines "spouse" as being either of a man and woman who are married to each other or cohabiting within the meaning of the Act. Same-sex couples are necessarily excluded from this definition, thereby giving rise to the charge that the legislation is underinclusive. In *Vriend, supra*, at paras. 109-11, this Court found that where a law violates the *Charter* owing to under-inclusion, the first stage of the s. 1 analysis is properly concerned with the object of the legislation as a whole, the impugned provisions of the Act, and the omission itself. ...

[86] ... There is considerable disagreement between the parties as to the underlying purpose of [the *FLA*]. ...

[93] As I see the matter, the objectives of the impugned spousal support provisions were accurately identified by Charron J.A. in the court below ... [who] identified the objectives of the Part III provisions as both a means to provide "for the equitable resolution of economic disputes that arise when intimate relationships between individuals who have been financially interdependent break down" and to "alleviate the burden on the public purse by shifting the obligation to provide support for needy persons to those parents and spouses who have the capacity to provide support to these individuals" (p. 450). I find support for this position in the legislative debates, the terms of the provisions, as well as the jurisprudence of this Court. ...

[100] ... I turn to the objective of the omission. As I have already stated, when dealing with underinclusive legislation

it is important also to consider the impugned omission when construing the objective. Often legislation does not simply further one goal but rather strikes a balance among several goals, some of which may be in tension. This balancing exercise may only become apparent after asking whether, in the case of underinclusive legislation, there is any objective being furthered by the impugned omission. A consideration of what is omitted from legislation may also lead a court to refine its interpretation of the objectives of the impugned legislation, perhaps reducing its scope. I agree with my colleague, Bastarache J., at para. 329, that if the omission is not taken into account in construing the objective then it is more likely that the omission will cause the impugned legislation to fail the rational connection step of the proportionality analysis.

[101] However, the concerns just outlined do not imply that the court must find that there is a separate objective being furthered by the omission. Even if there is no such objective the omission must still be evaluated as part of the means chosen to further the objective of the specific provision in question, under the proportionality analysis. Otherwise the court risks collapsing the two stages of the *Oakes* test (pressing and substantial objective and proportionality) into a general question regarding the reasonableness of the omission. There may be exceptions to this general approach, such as when there is evidence of a deliberate omission by the legislature that is "on its face the very antithesis of the principles embodied in the legislation as a whole": *Vriend, supra*, at para. 116.

[102] With these concerns in mind, I turn to the present appeal. The appellant does not argue that a separate objective is furthered by the impugned omission. Rather, the argument is that a proper consideration of the exclusion of same-sex couples from the definition of "spouse" in s. 29 of the *FLA* reduces the apparent scope of the objective furthered by that provision. The appellant made two arguments in this regard. First, the appellant argued that the *FLA* is a remedial statute designed to address the power imbalance that continues to exist in many opposite-sex relationships. Thus, it was submitted that the inclusion of same-sex couples in a scheme established to deal with problems that are not typical of their relationships is inappropriate. Further, the appellant asserted that where persons fall outside the rationale for which a benefit was established, the legislature is justified in withholding it from those persons.

[103] With respect, I disagree with these submissions. As I stated above, I do not believe that the purpose of the *FLA* in general, nor Part III in particular, is to remedy the disadvantages suffered by women in opposite-sex relationships.

[104] The second objective for the omission advanced by the appellant is the promotion of opposite-sex relationships to ensure the protection of children. Having found that neither the *FLA* as a whole nor the spousal support provisions in Part III of the Act are primarily concerned with the protection of children, I must also reject the submission that this is part of the objective of s. 29 of the *FLA*.

[105] Finally, I note that Bastarache J. accepts that the rejection of the *Equality Rights Statute Law Amendment Act, 1994* by the Ontario legislature can provide evidence regarding the objective of s. 29 of the *FLA*. In particular, he argues, at para. 349: "It can therefore be inferred that the legislature's purpose was also to exclude all types of relationships not typically characterized by the state of economic dependency apparent in traditional family relationships." With respect, I cannot agree that a failed amendment can provide evidence as to the objective of the legislation that was to have been amended. Section 17 of the *Interpretation Act*, R.S.O. 1990, c. I.11, provides: "The repeal or amendment of an Act shall be deemed not to be or to involve any declaration as to the previous state of the law." If the amendment of an Act may not be used to interpret the meaning of the Act prior to the amendment, then I do not see how a *failed* amendment may be used in this manner.

[106] Therefore I endorse the description of the objectives of the impugned provisions provided by Charron J.A. in the court below. These objectives are consonant with the overall scheme of the *FLA* and are not plausibly reinterpreted through examining the omission of same-sex spouses. Providing for the equitable resolution of economic disputes when intimate relationships between financially interdependent individuals break down, and alleviating the burden on the public purse to provide for dependent spouses, are to my mind pressing and substantial objectives. These objectives promote both social justice and the dignity of individuals— values Dickson C.J. identified in *Oakes, supra*, at p. 136, as values underlying a free and democratic society.

[107] In saying this, I wish to note my disagreement with my colleague, Bastarache J., who argues, at para. 354, that s. 29 of the *FLA* "must be respectful of the equality of status and opportunity of all persons" in order to be consistent with *Charter* values and therefore pass this stage of the s. 1 analysis. While I agree that an objective must be consistent with the principles underlying the *Charter* in order to pass the first stage of the s. 1 analysis, I find Bastarache J.'s approach unnecessarily narrow. It may be that a violation of s. 15(1) can be justified because, although not designed to promote equality, it is designed to promote *other* values and principles of a free and democratic society. This possibility must be left open, as the inquiry into *Charter* values under s. 1 is a broad inquiry into the values and principles that, as Dickson C.J. stated in *Oakes, supra*, at p. 136, "are the *genesis* of the rights and freedoms guaranteed by the *Charter*" (emphasis added).

4. *Proportionality Analysis*

(a) Rational Connection

... [109] ... In my view, it defies logic to suggest that a gender-neutral support system is rationally connected to the goal of improving the economic circumstances of heterosexual women upon relationship breakdown. In addition, I can find no evidence to demonstrate that the exclusion of same-sex couples from the spousal support regime of the *FLA* in any way furthers the objective of assisting heterosexual women. ...

[112] The second of the objectives put forth by the appellant, namely, the protection of children, also fails the rational connection test. The appellant submits that the exclusion of same-sex partners from Part III of the *FLA* is rationally connected to this objective as such couples are far less likely to engage in parenting than opposite-sex couples. ...

[116] If anything, the goals of the legislation are undermined by the impugned exclusion. Indeed, the *inclusion* of same-sex couples in s. 29 of the *FLA* would better achieve the objectives of the legislation while respecting the *Charter* rights of individuals in same-sex relationships. In these circumstances, I conclude that the exclusion of same-sex couples from s. 29 of the Act is simply not rationally connected to the dual objectives of the spousal support provisions of the legislation.

[117] Given this lack of a rational connection, s. 29 of the *FLA* is not saved by s. 1 of the *Charter*. Although it is therefore not strictly necessary to consider the other two branches of the second stage of the *Oakes* test, I will discuss them briefly in order to clarify some fundamental misunderstandings advanced in this appeal.

(b) Minimal Impairment

[118] ... The appellant suggests that the exclusion of same-sex couples from s. 29 of the *FLA* minimally impairs the respondent's s. 15 rights since reasonable alternative remedies are available where economic dependence does occur in such relationships. I cannot accept these submissions.

[119] The appellant's arguments on this point are based on the remedies available under the equitable doctrine of unjust enrichment (e.g. constructive trust) and the law of contract. Turning first to the equitable remedies, the doctrine of unjust enrichment allows claimants to found an action on indirect or non-financial contributions to the acquisition, maintenance, or preservation of an asset held by the other spouse. However, to be successful, the applicant must demonstrate his or her spouse's enrichment, a corresponding personal deprivation and the absence of any juristic reason for the enrichment. ...

[120] Moreover, ... equitable common law remedies such as a constructive trust are proprietary in nature and ... not all relationships will give rise to property claims. Indeed, as

submitted by LEAF, the *FLA* expressly recognizes that entitlement to the division of property is in addition to, and not in lieu of entitlement to support. Thus, it seems to me that compared to awards of spousal support, the equitable remedies are less flexible, impose more onerous requirements on claimants, and are available under far narrower circumstances. I do not accept that they provide an adequate alternative to spousal support under the *FLA*.

[121] In my view, the law of contract is an equally unacceptable alternative to the spousal support scheme under the *FLA*. The appellant emphasizes that the impugned provisions of the Act do not preclude same-sex partners from contracting for mutual support obligations. However, the voluntary assumption of such obligations is not equivalent to a statutory entitlement to apply for a support order. ...

[124] In sum, neither the common law equitable remedies nor the law of contract are adequate substitutes for the *FLA*'s spousal support regime. Indeed, if these remedies were considered satisfactory there would have been no need for the spousal support regime, or its extension to unmarried, opposite-sex couples. It must also be remembered that the exclusion of same-sex partners from this support regime does not simply deny them a certain benefit, but does so in a manner that violates their right to be given equal concern and respect by the government. The alternative regimes just outlined do not address the fact that exclusion from the statutory scheme has moral and societal implications beyond economic ones. ... Therefore the existence of these remedies fails to minimize sufficiently the denial of same-sex partners' constitutionally guaranteed equality rights.

[125] However, the appellant asserts that the circumstances of this case call for a measure of deference to the decision of the Ontario legislature. In this context, it is argued that it was reasonable for the government to conclude that it had impaired the rights of same-sex partners as little as possible.

[126] As I see the matter, the deferential approach advocated by the appellant is inappropriate in the case at bar. This Court has resorted to such an approach where the impugned legislation involves the balancing of claims of competing groups (see, e.g., *Irwin Toy, supra*, at pp. 999-1000; *McKinney v. University of Guelph*, [1990] 3 S.C.R. 229, at pp. 317-19, *per* La Forest J.; and *Egan, supra*, at para. 29, *per* La Forest J. and at paras. 105-8, *per* Sopinka J.). ... This is not such a case. As no group will be disadvantaged by granting members of same-sex couples access to the spousal support scheme under the *FLA*, the notion of deference to legislative choices in the sense of balancing claims of competing groups has no application to this case. ...

[128] In addition, the deferential approach is not warranted, as submitted by the appellant, on the basis that Part III

of the *FLA* and s. 29 thereof are steps in an incremental process of reform of spousal support. As this Court noted in *Vriend, supra,* government incrementalism, or the notion that government ought to be accorded time to amend discriminatory legislation, is generally an inappropriate justification for *Charter* violations. However, even if I were to accept that such a justification might be suitable in the present case, it seems to me that its application to the facts of the case at bar cannot legitimize the continued exclusion of same-sex couples from the *FLA*'s spousal support regime.

[129] ... [T]here is no evidence of any progress with respect to this group since the inception of the spousal support regime. If the legislature refuses to act so as to evolve towards *Charter* compliance then deference as to the timing of reforms loses its *raison d'être.*

[130] Moreover, in contrast to *Egan, supra,* where Sopinka J. relied in part on incrementalism in upholding the impugned legislation under s. 1 of the *Charter,* there is no concern regarding the financial implications of extending benefits to gay men and lesbians in the case at bar. As already pointed out, rather than increasing the strain on the public coffers, the extension will likely go some way toward alleviating those concerns because same-sex couples as a group will be less reliant on government welfare if the support scheme is available to them. Thus, I conclude that government incrementalism cannot constitute a reason to show deference to the legislature in the present case.

[131] Finally, as this Court has emphasized on other occasions, "[d]eference must not be carried to the point of relieving the government of the burden which the *Charter* places upon it of demonstrating that the limits it has imposed on guaranteed rights are reasonable and justifiable": *RJR-MacDonald, supra,* at para. 136, *per* McLachlin J. See also *Eldridge* [*v. British Columbia (Attorney General),* [1997] 3 S.C.R. 624]; *Tétreault-Gadoury v. Canada (Employment and Immigration Commission),* [1991] 2 S.C.R. 22; and *Vriend, supra.*

[132] In the present case, the government has failed to show that it had a reasonable basis for concluding that the rights of same-sex couples were impaired no more than was reasonably necessary to achieve its goals. The exclusion from the s. 29 definition of "spouse," and consequently from the *FLA* spousal support regime, is absolute. No effort has been made to tailor the limiting measure. I conclude that the appellant's case also fails at the minimal impairment stage of the s. 1 analysis.

(c) Proportionality Between the Effect
of the Measure and the Objective

[133] ... The damaging effects engendered by the exclusion of same-sex couples from s. 29 of the *FLA,* as noted by

Cory J., are numerous and severe. Such harms cannot be justified where the statute has not achieved what it set out to do. Where, as here, the impugned measures actually undermine the objectives of the legislation it cannot be said that the deleterious effects of the measures are outweighed by the promotion of any laudable legislative goals, nor by the salutary effects of those measures.

[134] I therefore conclude that the exclusion of same-sex couples from s. 29 of the *FLA* cannot be justified as a reasonable limit on constitutional rights under s. 1 of the *Charter.* Before turning to a discussion of the appropriate remedy, I wish to emphasize, like Cory J., that the sole issue presented by this case is whether the *Charter* mandates that same-sex couples be accorded the right to apply for spousal support under the *FLA.* This appeal does not challenge traditional conceptions of marriage, as s. 29 of the Act expressly applies to *unmarried* opposite-sex couples. That being said, I do not wish to be understood as making any comment on marriage or indeed on related issues. ...

VI. Remedy

[136] ... In the court below, the words "a man and woman" were read out of the definition of "spouse" in s. 29 of the *FLA* and replaced with the words "two persons." The application of the order was suspended for a period of one year. With respect, I am not convinced that that is a suitable remedy in the circumstances of the present case. ...

[141] If the remedy adopted by the court below is allowed to stand, s. 29 of the *FLA* will entitle members of same-sex couples who otherwise qualify under the definition of "spouse" to apply for spousal support. However, any attempt to opt out of this regime by means of a cohabitation agreement provided for in s. 53 or a separation agreement set out in s. 54 would not be recognized under the Act. Both ss. 53 and 54 extend to common-law cohabitants but apply only to agreements entered into between "a man and woman." Any extension of s. 29 of the Act would have no effect upon these Part IV domestic contract provisions of the *FLA,* which do not rely upon the Part III definition of "spouse." Thus, same-sex partners would find themselves in the anomalous position of having no means of opting out of the default system of support rights. As this option is available to opposite-sex couples, and protects the ability of couples to choose to order their own affairs in a manner reflecting their own expectations, reading in would in effect remedy one constitutional wrong only to create another, and thereby fail to ensure the validity of the legislation.

[142] In addition, reading into the definition of "spouse" in s. 29 of the Act will have the effect of including same-sex couples in Part V of the *FLA* (Dependants' Claim for

Damages), as that part of the Act relies upon the definition of "spouse" as it is defined in Part III. In my opinion, where reading in to one part of a statute will have significant repercussions for a separate and distinct scheme under that Act, it is not safe to assume that the legislature would have enacted the statute in its altered form. In such cases, reading in amounts to the making of *ad hoc* choices, which Lamer C.J. in *Schachter* [*v. Canada*, [1992] 2 S.C.R. 679], at p. 707, warned is properly the task of the legislatures, not the courts.

[143] In cases where reading in is inappropriate, the court must choose between striking down the legislation in its entirety and severing only the offending portions of the statute. As noted by Lamer C.J. in *Schachter*, at p. 697, "[w]here the offending portion of a statute can be defined in a limited manner it is consistent with legal principles to declare inoperative only that limited portion. In that way, as much of the legislative purpose as possible may be realized."

[144] In the case at bar, striking down the whole of the *FLA* would be excessive as only the definition of "spouse" in Part III of the Act has been found to violate the *Charter*. This is not a case where the parts of the legislative scheme which do offend the *Charter* are so inextricably bound up with the non-offending portions of the statute that what remains cannot independently survive. As a result, it would be safe to assume that the legislature would have passed the constitutionally sound parts of the statute without the unsound parts. See *Attorney-General for Alberta v. Attorney-General for Canada*, [1947] A.C. 503, at p. 518; *Schachter, supra*, at p. 697.

[145] On the basis of the foregoing, I conclude that severing s. 29 of the Act such that it alone is declared of no force or effect is the most appropriate remedy in the present case. This remedy should be temporarily suspended for a period of six months. ...

[147] ... I note that declaring s. 29 of the *FLA* to be of no force or effect may well affect numerous other statutes that rely upon a similar definition of the term "spouse." The legislature may wish to address the validity of these statutes in light of the unconstitutionality of s. 29 of the *FLA*. On this point, I agree with the majority of the Court of Appeal which noted that if left up to the courts, these issues could only be resolved on a case-by-case basis at great cost to private litigants and the public purse. Thus, I believe the legislature ought to be given some latitude in order to address these issues in a more comprehensive fashion. ...

GONTHIER J. (dissenting): ...

[268] The *Charter* cannot possibly require the Legislative Assembly to revise the *FLA* to exclude non-procreative opposite-sex couples from its scope. As La Forest J. indicated, the legislative and administrative scheme necessary to do so would be highly intrusive and would likely violate *Charter* privacy guarantees. By contrast, exclusion of same-sex couples, who are inherently, rather than situationally, non-procreative, from the *FLA* support regime raises none of these concerns. ...

[270] The entire issue in this appeal is whether the distinction drawn by the Legislative Assembly between cohabiting opposite-sex couples and all other relationships is maintainable. My colleagues' implicit suggestion is that the simplest way to render s. 29 constitutionally viable would be to restrict its application to married couples alone. I see no reason to conclude that the *Charter* operates so restrictively. Here, the Legislative Assembly has made a distinction on the basis of a fundamental biological and social reality to address a unique form of disadvantage specific to opposite-sex couples. On the other hand, if the Legislative Assembly is obliged to address all of the manifestations of economic interdependence between individuals, it is difficult to see how drawing the line to include same-sex couples, but to exclude those relationships which are not conjugal (and which can be similarly distinguished on enumerated or analogous grounds), can itself withstand constitutional challenge.

[271] It may be, of course, that extending the definition of "spouse" to include same-sex couples or other relationships or otherwise providing for support obligations based on dependency would be a prudent or reasonable policy decision. My colleague Iacobucci J.'s view, for example, is that to make this extension would advance what he sees as the purpose of the legislation. However, the wisdom or desirability of such an extension is not itself a matter properly within the consideration of this Court. The legislature itself considered the desirability of extending the scope of s. 29 to same-sex couples, but in the end, decided to the contrary. We must take seriously the contention that the legislation violates the *Charter*. Yet we must be careful not to jump from the assertion that a legislative change would be prudent to the contention that such a change is constitutionally mandated. In my view, my colleagues make that jump. For this reason, I respectfully disagree. ...

[273] One of the fundamental principles in Canadian society is that individuals enjoy freedom and are expected to provide for their own needs. This rule is obviously not absolute. Canadians take pride in our social programs which lend a hand to those who, for differing reasons, cannot provide for themselves. At the same time, these social programs have specific policy goals, and in pursuit of those goals, they target specific groups of people. When the State provides assistance, only those who need the assistance should receive it. In this appeal, the impugned legislation sought to redress a historical fact that individuals in opposite-sex relationships suffer a *systemic* dynamic of dependence, which manifests in a

support obligation that exists not only while the two individuals are in the relationship, but also after the relationship breaks down. Usually, it is the female partner who suffers the greatest burden upon marriage or common-law relationship breakdown: *Moge* [*v. Moge*, [1992] 3 S.C.R. 813]. The legislature has, since 1859, used a variety of legislative tools to alleviate this systemic suffering, which is unique to opposite-sex relationships. The statutory language, the preamble, and the legislative debates reveal that this legislation is one of those tools.

[274] In my view, the s. 15(1) claim in this case fails because s. 29 of the *FLA* seeks to ameliorate a historical and structural disadvantage specific to individuals in certain types of opposite-sex relationships, and in so doing, accurately corresponds with the needs, capacity, and circumstances of the claimant and these opposite-sex couples. Although individuals in same-sex relationships suffer pre-existing disadvantage in many areas of life, it has not been shown that this is one of them. In fact, the contrary has been shown: individuals in same-sex relationships generally exhibit less dependency in the relationship; they do not have a structural wage differential between the partners in the relationship; and they do not exhibit the same gendered division of domestic and child-care responsibilities. Although any of these elements may be present in a same-sex relationship, none will have been created by the structural dynamic of dependence which the legislature has seen fit to address, but rather will be attributable to the individual idiosyncrasies of the claimant.

[275] ... The right to equality in s. 15(1) does not guarantee equality in the abstract; it rests on a comparison with others. This requires us to examine whether the claimant group suffers pre-existing disadvantage, stereotyping, prejudice or vulnerability *as compared with* the selected comparison group, and as related to the subject-matter of the legislation. In this case, individuals in same-sex relationships are not disadvantaged in relation to the dynamic of dependence which the legislation seeks to address. As such, the ameliorative purpose of the *FLA* is not underinclusive of a group which is disadvantaged in relation to that purpose. Moreover, although the claimant is affected by her exclusion from the mandatory support regime, this regime both confers a benefit *and* imposes a burden. Mandatory support restricts personal choice and reduces the concomitant financial advantages. The legislation does not render individuals in same-sex relationships "invisible." They are fully entitled to impose support obligations upon themselves, if they so choose. However, the circumstances unique to individuals in opposite-sex relationships which warrant the reduction of that group's autonomy do not similarly exist in same-sex relationships.

[276] By analysing all of the contextual factors, it is apparent that the claimant's human dignity is not violated by s. 29 of the *FLA*. A reasonable person in the position of the claimant, having taken into account all of the contextual factors relevant to the claim, would not find their human dignity violated by a provision which appropriately takes into account their actual needs, capacity, and circumstances as compared to those of opposite-sex couples subject to the legislation. For these reasons, it is my view that the s. 15(1) claim must fail. ...

[Justices Major and Bastarache wrote separate reasons that concurred with the majority's decision. Justice Major reached the result on a more narrow basis than the majority. Justice Bastarache differed with how the majority interpreted the purpose of the legislation.]

29 Auton v. British Columbia (Attorney General), 2004

An essential purpose of a bill of rights is to protect individuals from legislation, or the conduct of those acting on behalf of the state, where decisions or actions interfere with protected rights. In this sense, the protection offered by bills of rights is most often construed in a negative sense as providing *freedom from* state actions that interfere with rights. But the claim made in *Auton* represented a different view of rights. It rested on a more positive interpretation in the sense that the Charter confers the *right to* receive a social policy entitlement that the legislature had not intended to provide.

The question whether the Charter should protect positive rights is sharply contested. Critics of the idea of interpreting Charter rights in positive terms argue that reasonable, rights-respecting people will disagree about the meaning or scope of these rights or the extent of the state's obligation to provide publicly funded programs or services to facilitate positive rights. For this reason, they believe there is little justification in asking judges to define positive rights, which require value-laden decisions that ultimately have little to do with the legal training or interpretive duties normally associated with judicial review. Moreover, since the recognition of social rights ultimately implicates the full range of a legislature's decisions about how best to allocate limited resources, judgments about allocating social benefits should be made by Parliament so that they can be reviewed and revised to correspond to changes in the nation's circumstances and priorities. In contrast, supporters of justiciable social and economic rights argue that a negative approach to rights is too restrictive and will not provide the necessary conditions for realizing equality. They also suggest that the distinction between negative and positive rights is not as clear as critics of positive rights would suggest. Negative interpretations of rights often have financial implications for the state, particularly if a government incurs substantial costs in order to comply with a judicially authorized remedy. For example, following the Supreme Court's ruling that equality was violated in *M. v. H.*[1] (the equality claim was based on the differential treatment resulting from the interpretation of "spouse" in the Ontario *Family Law Act*), provincial and federal governments incurred financial costs to overhaul hundreds of laws to include same-sex partners in recognition and benefit schemes.

The Supreme Court has been reluctant to recognize social rights under the Charter. Although on several occasions the court has ruled that existing legislation must be modified to address discrimination or other Charter violations, the court has not been prepared to rule that Charter rights are implicated because Parliament or a provincial legislature has failed to introduce legislation that would create new benefits. This reluctance was obvious in this case. The overarching issue in *Auton* was whether a province's public health plan under the *Canada Health Act* is required to provide a particular health treatment beyond

---

1 Case 28.

what is considered a "core" service administered by doctors and hospitals. More specifically, the question was whether the B.C. government's refusal to fund a particular form of therapy for preschool-aged autistic children violates equality. The provincial health plan makes a distinction between "core" services, as required by the *Canada Health Act*, and non-core services, which the government provides at its discretion. Some non-core services that are entitled for partial public funding are those provided by chiropractors, dentists, optometrists, podiatrists, physical therapists, massage therapists, and naturopathic doctors. The treatment in question was designated as a non-core service. This is a controversial and expensive form of behavioural therapy for young autistic children (applied behavioural analysis [ABA] or intensive behavioural intervention [IBI]). Although some limited forms of this treatment were funded, there was no funding for intensive, universal treatment for all autistic children between the ages of three and six.

Those arguing that the province's public health plan discriminates against autistic children believed that an earlier Supreme Court ruling supported their position. This earlier decision was *Eldridge v. British Columbia (Attorney General)*,[2] where the court ruled that the province was required to provide translators for deaf people attempting to access hospital services, even though legislation did not explicitly authorize this. But the court disagreed that *Eldridge* supports the Charter claim made in *Auton*. It characterized the *Eldridge* case as being concerned with unequal access to a benefit that the legislation had conferred, whereas the *Auton* case was said to involve access to a benefit that the legislation had not granted. The court suggested that despite its sympathy for the petitioners it was not for the court to decide "what the public health system should provide," which was a matter for Parliament or the legislature. As the court stated, the health plan "does not promise that any Canadian will receive funding for all medically required treatment. All that is conferred is core funding for services provided by medical practitioners." Funding for non-core services is at the government's discretion and thus the "benefit here claimed—funding for all medically required services—was not provided for by the law." But this explanation did not address an important dimension of the Charter claim made in *Auton*: that discrimination arises from the discretionary legislative decision to provide some non-core services for non-disabled children or adults with mental illness while deciding not to fund ABA/IBI therapy to autistic children. In addressing the argument that the denial of this therapy constitutes a Charter violation, the court advanced a narrow, technical view of how to determine whether discrimination has occurred. Lawyers arguing on behalf of autistic children had argued that the court should compare the services provided to autistic children with those services provided to non-disabled children or to adults with mental illness. But the court disagreed, ruling that the decision about whether discrimination has occurred concerns whether the legislation treats autistic children differently than it does a "non-disabled person or a person suffering a disability other than a mental disability (here autism) seeking or receiving funding for a non-core therapy important for his or her present and future health, which is emergent and only recently becoming recognized as medically required."

The federal and seven provincial attorneys general intervened in the case, no doubt aware of the implications a positive ruling in this case could have had for provincial health budgets. Reaction to the Supreme Court's decision in *Auton* was mixed. While some commentators

---

2 [1997] 3 S.C.R. 624.

approved of the decision, because of apprehension about the fiscal implications this decision would have should the court recognize Charter claims for services under the public health system, others believed that the court's approach to what constitutes discrimination in this case was overly restrictive. ～

Discussion Questions

1. Was the Supreme Court persuasive when explaining why its ruling in *Eldridge* did not support the rights claim made in *Auton*?

2. Should the Charter be interpreted as protecting positive rights? How would interpreting the Charter to recognize positive rights change the judicial role?

3. Is the government justified in its decision to fund some non-core services and yet not fund therapy for autistic children? Whose role is it to decide?

AUTON (GUARDIAN AD LITEM OF) v. BRITISH COLUMBIA (ATTORNEY GENERAL)
2004 SCC 78, [2004] 3 S.C.R. 657

Hearing: June 9, 2004; Judgment: November 19, 2004.

Present: McLachlin C.J. and Major, Bastarache, Binnie, LeBel, Deschamps, and Fish JJ.

Interveners: Attorney General of Canada, Attorney General of Ontario, Attorney General of Quebec, Attorney General of Nova Scotia, Attorney General of New Brunswick, Attorney General of Prince Edward Island, Attorney General of Alberta, Attorney General of Newfoundland and Labrador, Canadian Association for Community Living and Council of Canadians with Disabilities, Women's Legal Education and Action Fund and DisAbled Women's Network Canada, Autism Society Canada, Michelle Dawson, Families for Effective Autism Treatment of Alberta Foundation, Friends of Children with Autism, and Families for Early Autism Treatment of Ontario.

The judgment of the Court was delivered by

THE CHIEF JUSTICE:

I. Introduction

[1] This case raises the issue of whether the Province of British Columbia's refusal to fund a particular treatment for preschool-aged autistic children violates the right to equality under the *Canadian Charter of Rights and Freedoms*. The petitioners are autistic children and their parents. They argue that the government's failure to fund applied behavioral therapy for autism unjustifiably discriminated against them. In the background lies the larger issue of when, if ever, a province's public health plan under the *Canada Health Act*, R.S.C. 1985, c. C-6 ("*CHA*"), is required to provide a particular health treatment outside the "core" services administered by doctors and hospitals.

[2] One sympathizes with the petitioners, and with the decisions below ordering the public health system to pay for their therapy. However, the issue before us is not what the public health system should provide, which is a matter for Parliament and the legislature. The issue is rather whether the British Columbia Government's failure to fund these services under the health plan amounted to an unequal and discriminatory denial of benefits under that plan, contrary to s. 15 of the *Charter*. Despite their forceful argument, the petitioners fail to establish that the denial of benefits violated the *Charter*.

[3] The government must provide the services authorized by law in a non-discriminatory manner. Here, however, discrimination has not been established. First, the claim for discrimination is based on the erroneous assumption that the *CHA* and the relevant British Columbia legislation provided the benefit claimed. Second, on the facts here and applying the appropriate comparator, it is not established that the government excluded autistic children on the basis of disability. For these reasons, the claim fails and the appeal is allowed.

II. History of the Case

[4] The four infant petitioners suffer from autism, a neuro-behavioural syndrome caused by a dysfunction of the central nervous system that impairs social interaction, hinders communication and results in repetitive, stereotyped behaviour. The symptoms and effects of autism vary from mild to severe. Over 90 percent of untreated autistic children end up in group homes or other residential facilities.

[5] The cause and cure of autism remain unknown. However, a 1987 study published by a Texas researcher, Dr. O. Ivar Lovaas, suggested that applied behavioural therapy based on the repetitive use of stimuli and emphasized cues might help

some autistic children between ages three and six. The therapy is intensive and therefore expensive—between $45,000 and $60,000 per year. It is not always successful; the trial judge found only that in "some cases" it may produce "significant results" ((2000), 78 B.C.L.R. (3d) 55, 2000 BCSC 1142, at para. 51). While increasingly accepted, Applied Behavioural Analysis ("ABA") or Intensive Behavioural Intervention ("IBI") therapy is not uncontroversial. Objections range from its reliance in its early years on crude and arguably painful stimuli, to its goal of changing the child's mind and personality. Indeed one of the interveners in this appeal, herself an autistic person, argues against the therapy.

[6] The infant petitioners received Lovaas therapy. Their parents, the adult petitioners, funded the treatment, although Connor Auton's mother ultimately became unable to continue for financial reasons. Until the government forbade it on the ground that new options were being evaluated, some families used funds for support services from the Ministry of Children and Families to help finance Lovaas therapy for their children with the tacit support of Ministry workers in some regions. Over a period of years, the petitioners and others lobbied the Ministers of Health, of Education, and of Children and Families for funding for Lovaas therapy, without success. In 1995, the petitioners commenced this action.

[7] In the years leading up to the trial in 2000, the government funded a number of programs for autistic children and their families. This was done through the Ministry of Children and Families, which in 1997 had been given responsibility for child and youth mental health. The programs included infant development, supported child care, at-home respite, respite relief, contracted respite, occupational therapy, physical therapy, speech and language therapy, homemaker and home support services, hearing services, child care workers and specific behavioural support. Under the latter category, some programs attempted to positively treat autism. The Ministry provided services to autistic children through contracted agencies, some of which employed some behavioural analysis techniques. However, the focus was on teaching families the techniques to enable them to work themselves with the children.

[8] An early intervention ABA/IBI program called LEAP had been established in Ladner but it was underfunded and equipped to serve only six children. Other centres and groups provided some ABA/IBI but the Crown's expert, Dr. Glen Davies, testified that these programs were not intensive, not delivered early enough in the child's development, and were rarely of sufficient duration to maximize the child's development. Finally, in May 1999, the Ministry announced an Autism Action Plan and an Autism Action Implementation Plan, which acknowledged the importance of early

intervention, diagnosis and assessment, but stated that services for autistic children had to be balanced with services to children with other special needs. Moreover, the plan did not specifically target ABA/IBI therapy. As of the date of trial a year or so later, the Ministry had not produced much. No new funding had been provided and a concrete plan for intensive early treatment remained to be developed.

[9] In a nutshell, at the time of trial the government funded a number of programs for young autistic children, and appeared to be moving toward funding some form of early intervention therapy. However, it had not established funding for intensive, universal ABA/IBI therapy available to all autistic children between the ages of three and six.

[10] This delay appears to have been due to a number of factors. The first was the 1997 decision to transfer child and youth mental health from the Ministry of Health to the Ministry of Children and Families, which put a non-medical slant on treatment. The second was financial constraint: in 1998, the deputy ministers of the ministries of Health, Education, and Children and Families informed families that the government was not "in a resource position" to fund ABA/IBI therapy.

[11] A final factor may have been the emergent and somewhat controversial nature of ABA/IBI therapy, although by the time of the trial the evidence was sufficient to convince the trial judge that it was "medically necessary." ...

III. Analysis

... [20] This case engages s. 15's guarantee of "equal benefit of the law without discrimination ... based on ... mental ... disability."

[21] Different cases have formulated the requirements for a successful s. 15(1) claim in different ways. Nevertheless, there is "broad agreement on the general analytic framework": *Eldridge v. British Columbia (Attorney General)*, [1997] 3 S.C.R. 624, at para. 58. In *Andrews v. Law Society of British Columbia*, [1989] 1 S.C.R. 143, at pp. 168 *et seq.*—this Court's seminal statement on the interpretation of s. 15(1)—the s. 15 analysis was described in two steps: first, whether there is unequal treatment under the law; and, second, whether the treatment is discriminatory. ...

[22] The dual requirements of *Andrews, supra*, and *Eldridge, supra*, were broken into three requirements in *Law v. Canada (Minister of Employment and Immigration)*, [1999] 1 S.C.R. 497, at para. 88: (1) differential treatment under the law; (2) on the basis of an enumerated or analogous ground; (3) which constitutes discrimination.

[23] There is no magic in a particular statement of the elements that must be established to prove a claim under s. 15(1). It is the words of the provision that must guide. Different cases will raise different issues. In this case, as will be

discussed, an issue arises as to whether the benefit claimed is one provided by the law. The important thing is to ensure that all the requirements of s. 15(1), as they apply to the case at hand, are met.

[24] A complicating factor is that however one states the requirements for s. 15(1), they inevitably overlap. For example, the nature of the benefit, the enumerated or analogous ground at issue, and the choice of a correct comparator play a role in all three steps: see *Hodge v. Canada (Minister of Human Resources Development)*, [2004] 3 S.C.R. 357, 2004 SCC 65. Frameworks thus do not describe discreet linear steps; rather, they serve as a guide to ensure that the language and purpose of s. 15(1) are respected.

[25] Whatever framework is used, an overly technical approach to s. 15(1) is to be avoided. In *Andrews, supra*, at pp. 168-69, McIntyre J. warned against adopting a narrow, formalistic analytical approach, and stressed the need to look at equality issues substantively and contextually. The Court must look at the reality of the situation and assess whether there has been discriminatory treatment having regard to the purpose of s. 15(1), which is to prevent the perpetuation of pre-existing disadvantage through unequal treatment.

[26] In this case, the following issues arise from an application of the language of s. 15(1) to the facts:

(1) Is the claim for a benefit *provided by law*? If not, what relevant benefit is provided by law?
(2) Was the relevant benefit denied to the claimants while being granted to a comparator group alike in all ways relevant to benefit, except for the personal characteristic associated with an enumerated or analogous ground?
(3) If the claimants succeed on the first two issues, is discrimination established by showing that the distinction denied their equal human worth and human dignity?

(1) Is the Claim for a Benefit Provided by Law?

[27] In order to succeed, the claimants must show unequal treatment under the law—more specifically that they failed to receive a benefit that the law provided, or was saddled with a burden the law did not impose on someone else. The primary and oft-stated goal of s. 15(1) is to combat discrimination and ameliorate the position of disadvantaged groups within society. Its specific promise, however, is confined to benefits and burdens "of the law." Combatting discrimination and ameliorating the position of members of disadvantaged groups is a formidable task and demands a multi-pronged response. Section 15(1) is part of that response. Section 15(2)'s exemption for affirmative action programs is another

prong of the response. Beyond these lie a host of initiatives that governments, organizations and individuals can undertake to ameliorate the position of members of disadvantaged groups.

[28] The specific role of s. 15(1) in achieving this objective is to ensure that when governments choose to enact benefits or burdens, they do so on a non-discriminatory basis. This confines s. 15(1) claims to benefits and burdens imposed by law. ...

[29] Most s. 15(1) claims relate to a clear statutory benefit or burden. Consequently, the need for the benefit claimed or burden imposed to emanate from law has not been much discussed. Nevertheless, the language of s. 15(1) as well as the jurisprudence demand that it be met before a s. 15(1) claim can succeed.

[30] In this case, the issue of whether the benefit claimed is one conferred by law does arise, and must be carefully considered. The claim, as discussed, is for funding for a "medically necessary" treatment. The unequal treatment is said to lie in funding medically required treatments for non-disabled Canadian children or adults with mental illness, while refusing to fund medically required ABA/IBI therapy to autistic children. The decisions under appeal proceeded on this basis. The trial judge, affirmed by the Court of Appeal, ruled that the discrimination lay in denying a "medically necessary" service to a disadvantaged group while providing "medically necessary" services for others. Thus the benefit claimed, in essence, is funding for all medically required treatment.

[31] This raises the question of whether the legislative scheme in fact provides anyone with all medically required treatment. An examination of the scheme shows that it does not. ...

[32] The scheme designates two distinct categories of funded treatment based on service. First, the scheme provides complete funding for services delivered by medical practitioners, referred to as "core" services. This is required by the *CHA*. Many medically necessary or required services, including ABA/IBI therapy for autistic children, fall outside this core.

[33] Secondly, the *CHA* permits the provinces at their discretion to fund non-core medical services—services that are not delivered by physicians. British Columbia does this by naming classes of "health care practitioners" whose services may be partially funded. It then falls to the Medical Services Commission, an administrative body, to designate particular practitioners and procedures within these categories for funding.

[34] It was suggested that the reference by the *Medicare Protection Act*, R.S.B.C. 1996, c. 286 ("*MPA*"), to "medically required" services is an indication that all medically required or necessary non-core services must be funded. However, the Act does not say this. Section 1 uses the phrase "medically

required services" in conjunction with the services of doctors or "medical practitioners" or an "approved diagnostic facility" (s. 1 "benefits," paras. (a) and (c)). Only these services are funded on the basis of being "medically required." "Medically required" in the *MPA* does not touch the services of "health care practitioners" which are funded only if the Province chooses to place a class of health care practitioner on an "enrolled" list by legislation or regulation. ...

[35] In summary, the legislative scheme does not promise that any Canadian will receive funding for all medically required treatment. All that is conferred is core funding for services provided by medical practitioners, with funding for non-core services left to the Province's discretion. Thus, the benefit here claimed—funding for all medically required services—was not provided for by the law.

[36] More specifically, the law did not provide funding for ABA/IBI therapy for autistic children. The British Columbia *MPA* authorized partial funding for the services of the following health care practitioners: chiropractors, dentists, optometrists, podiatrists, physical therapists, massage therapists and naturopathic doctors. In addition, provincial regulations authorized funding for the services of physical therapists, massage therapists and nurses. At the time of trial, the Province had not named providers of ABA/IBI therapy as "health care practitioners," whose services could be funded under the plan.

[37] It followed that the Medical Services Commission, charged with administration of the *MPA*, had no power to order funding for ABA/IBI therapy. The Commission, as an administrative body, had no authority to enlarge the class of "health care practitioners." That could be done only by the government. Since the government had not designated ABA/IBI therapists as "health care practitioners," the Commission was not permitted to list their services for funding. This is how things stood at the time of trial. British Columbia's law governing non-core benefits did not provide the benefit that the petitioners were seeking.

[38] The petitioners rely on *Eldridge* in arguing for equal provision of medical benefits. In *Eldridge*, this Court held that the Province was obliged to provide translators to the deaf so that they could have equal access to core benefits accorded to everyone under the British Columbia medicare scheme. The decision proceeded on the basis that the law provided the benefits at issue—physician-delivered consultation and maternity care. However, by failing to provide translation services for the deaf, the Province effectively denied to one group of disabled people the benefit it had granted by law. *Eldridge* was concerned with unequal access to a benefit that the law conferred and with *applying* a benefit-granting law in a non-discriminatory fashion. By contrast, this case is concerned

with access to a benefit that the law has not conferred. For this reason, *Eldridge* does not assist the petitioners.

[39] However, this does not end the inquiry. Courts should look to the reality of the situation to see whether the claimants have been denied benefits of the legislative scheme other than those they have raised. This brings up the broader issue of whether the legislative scheme is discriminatory, since it provides non-core services to some groups while denying funding for ABA/IBI therapy to autistic children. The allegation is that the scheme is itself discriminatory, by funding some non-core therapies while denying equally necessary ABA/IBI therapy.

[40] ... We must look behind the words and ask whether the statutory definition is itself a means of perpetrating inequality rather than alleviating it. Section 15(1) requires not merely formal equality, but substantive equality: *Andrews, supra*, at p. 166.

[41] It is not open to Parliament or a legislature to enact a law whose policy objectives and provisions single out a disadvantaged group for inferior treatment: *Corbiere v. Canada (Minister of Indian and Northern Affairs)*, [1999] 2 S.C.R. 203. On the other hand, a legislative choice not to accord a particular benefit absent demonstration of discriminatory purpose, policy or effect does not offend this principle and does not give rise to s. 15(1) review. This Court has repeatedly held that the legislature is under no obligation to create a particular benefit. It is free to target the social programs it wishes to fund as a matter of public policy, provided the benefit itself is not conferred in a discriminatory manner: *Granovsky v. Canada (Minister of Employment and Immigration)*, [2000] 1 S.C.R. 703, 2000 SCC 28, at para. 61; *Nova Scotia (Attorney General) v. Walsh*, [2002] 4 S.C.R. 325, 2002 SCC 83, at para. 55; *Hodge, supra*, at para. 16.

[42] A statutory scheme may discriminate either directly, by adopting a discriminatory policy or purpose, or indirectly, by effect. Direct discrimination on the face of a statute or in its policy is readily identifiable and poses little difficulty. Discrimination by effect is more difficult to identify. Where stereotyping of persons belonging to a group is at issue, assessing whether a statutory definition that excludes a group is discriminatory, as opposed to being the legitimate exercise of legislative power in defining a benefit, involves consideration of the purpose of the legislative scheme which confers the benefit and the overall needs it seeks to meet. If a benefit program excludes a particular group in a way that undercuts the overall purpose of the program, then it is likely to be discriminatory: it amounts to an arbitrary exclusion of a particular group. If, on the other hand, the exclusion is consistent with the overarching purpose and scheme of the legislation, it is unlikely to be discriminatory. Thus, the question is

whether the excluded benefit is one that falls within the general scheme of benefits and needs which the legislative scheme is intended to address.

[43] The legislative scheme in the case at bar, namely the *CHA* and the *MPA*, does not have as its purpose the meeting of all medical needs. As discussed, its only promise is to provide full funding for core services, defined as physician-delivered services. Beyond this, the provinces may, within their discretion, offer specified non-core services. It is, by its very terms, a partial health plan. It follows that exclusion of particular non-core services cannot, without more, be viewed as an adverse distinction based on an enumerated ground. Rather, it is an anticipated feature of the legislative scheme. It follows that one cannot infer from the fact of exclusion of ABA/IBI therapy for autistic children from non-core benefits that this amounts to discrimination. There is no discrimination by effect.

[44] The correctness of this conclusion may be tested by considering the consequences to the legislative scheme of obliging provinces to provide non-core medical services required by disabled persons and people associated with other enumerated and analogous grounds, like gender and age. Subject to a finding of no discrimination at the third step, a class of people legally entitled to non-core benefits would be created. This would effectively amend the medicare scheme and extend benefits beyond what it envisions—core physician-provided benefits plus non-core benefits at the discretion of the Province.

[45] Had the situation been different, the petitioners might have attempted to frame their legal action as a claim to the benefit of equal application of the law by the Medical Services Commission. This would not have been a substantive claim for funding for particular medical services, but a procedural claim anchored in the assertion that benefits provided by the law were not distributed in an equal fashion. Such a claim, if made out, would be supported by *Eldridge, supra*. The argument would be that the Medical Services Commission violated s. 15(1) by approving non-core services for non-disabled people, while denying equivalent services to autistic children and their families.

[46] Such a claim depends on a prior showing that there is a benefit provided by law. There can be no administrative duty to distribute non-existent benefits equally. Had the legislature designated ABA/IBI therapists (or a broader group of therapists which included them) as "health care practitioners" under the *MPA* at the time of trial, this would have amounted to a legislated benefit, which the Commission would be charged with implementing. The Commission would then have been obliged to implement that benefit in a non-discriminatory fashion. However, this is not the case. Here,

the legislature had not legislated funding for the benefit in question, and the Commission had no power to deal with it.

[47] I conclude that the benefit claimed, no matter how it is viewed, is not a benefit provided by law. This is sufficient to end the inquiry. However, since this is the first case of this type to reach this Court, it is appropriate to consider whether the petitioners would have succeeded had they established that ABA/IBI therapy was a benefit provided by law, by being designated as a non-core benefit.

(2) Denial of a Benefit Granted to a Comparator Group, on an Enumerated or Analogous Ground

[48] This question first requires us to determine the appropriate comparator group, and then to ask whether, as compared with people in that group, the petitioners have been denied a benefit.

[49] The first task is to determine the appropriate comparator group. The petitioners suggested that they should be compared with non-disabled children and their parents, as well as adult persons with mental illness. A closer look reveals problems with both suggested comparators.

[50] The law pertaining to the choice of comparators ... establishes the following propositions.

[51] First, the choice of the correct comparator is crucial, since the comparison between the claimants and this group permeates every stage of the analysis. "[M]isidentification of the proper comparator group at the outset can doom the outcome of the whole s. 15(1) analysis": *Hodge, supra*, at para. 18.

[52] Second, while the starting point is the comparator chosen by the claimants, the Court must ensure that the comparator is appropriate and should substitute an appropriate comparator if the one chosen by the claimants is not appropriate: *Hodge, supra*, at para. 20.

[53] Third, the comparator group should mirror the characteristics of the claimant or claimant group relevant to the benefit or advantage sought, except for the personal characteristic related to the enumerated or analogous ground raised as the basis for the discrimination: *Hodge, supra*, at para. 23. The comparator must align with both the benefit and the "universe of people potentially entitled" to it and the alleged ground of discrimination: *Hodge*, at paras. 25 and 31.

[54] Fourth, a claimant relying on a personal characteristic related to the enumerated ground of disability may invite comparison with the treatment of those suffering a different type of disability, or a disability of greater severity: *Hodge, supra*, at paras. 28 and 32. Examples of the former include the differential treatment of those suffering mental disability from those suffering physical disability in *Battlefords and District Co-operative Ltd. v. Gibbs*, [1996] 3 S.C.R. 566, and the differential treatment of those suffering chronic pain from

those suffering other workplace injuries in *Nova Scotia (Workers' Compensation Board) v. Martin,* [2003] 2 S.C.R. 504, 2003 SCC 54. An example of the latter is the treatment of persons with temporary disabilities compared with those suffering permanent disabilities in *Granovsky, supra.*

[55] Applying these criteria, I conclude that the appropriate comparator for the petitioners is a non-disabled person or a person suffering a disability other than a mental disability (here autism) seeking or receiving funding for a non-core therapy important for his or her present and future health, which is emergent and only recently becoming recognized as medically required. It will be recalled that in many jurisdictions ABA/IBI therapy remained unfunded at the time of trial. Indeed, it was only in the year preceding the trial that two Canadian provinces had authorized funding for ABA/IBI therapy to autistic children. The comparators, as noted, must be like the claimants in all ways save for characteristics relating to the alleged ground of discrimination. People receiving well-established non-core therapies are not in the same position as people claiming relatively new non-core benefits. Funding may be legitimately denied or delayed because of uncertainty about a program and administrative difficulties related to its recognition and implementation. This has nothing to do with the alleged ground of discrimination. It follows that comparison with those receiving established therapies is inapt.

[56] The petitioners' comparators were deficient in that they focussed on the non-existent medical benefit of medically required care, as discussed above. However, even if I were to assume that the benefit is one provided by law—more particularly, that the B.C. legislation had listed ABA/IBI therapists as "health care practitioners" whose services could be considered funded benefits—the petitioners' comparators would still be deficient, because they have left the recent and emergent nature of ABA/IBI therapy out of the equation. This error was replicated in the decisions below.

[57] The remaining question is whether, applying the appropriate comparator, the claimant or claimant group was denied a benefit made available to the comparator group. Differential treatment having regard to the appropriate comparator may be established either by showing an explicit distinction (direct discrimination) or by showing that the effect of the government action amounted to singling the claimant out for less advantageous treatment on the basis of the alleged ground of discrimination (indirect discrimination). In indirect discrimination, the terms on which the claimants are denied the benefit operate as a proxy for their group status. For example, in *British Columbia (Public Service Employee Relations Commission) v. BCGSEU,* [1999] 3 S.C.R. 3, facially neutral physical requirements for firefighters were set at

aerobic levels not generally attainable by female firefighters—levels, moreover, which were not required for performance of the job. The specified aerobic levels made no mention of gender. On their face, they did not discriminate. Yet, in effect, they excluded women, not on the basis of ability to do the job, but on the basis of gender. The aerobic levels served as a proxy for gender. Hence, they were held to discriminate on the basis of gender.

[58] As discussed, the appropriate comparator in this case is a member of a non-disabled group or a person suffering a disability other than a mental disability that requests or receives funding for non-core therapy important to present and future health, but which is emergent and only recently becoming recognized as medically required. On the evidence adduced here, differential treatment either directly or by effect is not established. There was no evidence of how the Province had responded to requests for new therapies or treatments by non-disabled or otherwise disabled people. We know that it was slow in responding to the demands for ABA/IBI funding for autistic children. But we do not know whether it acted in a similar manner with respect to other new therapies.

[59] Indeed, the conduct of the government considered in the context of the emergent nature of ABA/IBI therapy for autistic children raises doubts about whether there was a real denial or differential treatment of autistic children. The government put in place a number of programs, albeit not intensive ABA/IBI therapy, directed to helping autistic children and their families. In the year before the trial, the government had announced an Autism Action Plan and an Autism Action Implementation Plan which acknowledged the importance of early intervention, diagnosis and assessment. The government's failing was to delay putting in place what was emerging in the late-1990s as the most, indeed the only known, effective therapy for autism, while continuing to fund increasingly discredited treatments.

[60] As discussed earlier, the delay in providing funding for ABA/IBI therapy seems to have been related to three factors. The first was the inauspicious decision to transfer child and youth mental health from the Ministry of Health to the Ministry of Children and Families, which meant that the decision makers lacked medical and psychiatric expertise and viewed autism from a social rather than medical perspective. The second was financial concerns and competing claims on insufficient resources. The third was the emergent nature of the recognition that ABA/IBI therapy was appropriate and medically required.

[61] With hindsight, it is possible to say that the government should have moved more quickly. But on the evidence before us, it is difficult to say that the government in purpose or effect put autistic children and their families "on the back

burner" when compared to non-disabled or otherwise disabled groups seeking emergent therapies. Rather, to use the trial judge's phrase, the government's failing was that its actions to that point did not meet the "gold standard of scientific methodology" ((2000), 78 B.C.L.R. (3d) 55, at para. 66).

[62] The issue, however, is not whether the government met the gold standard of scientific methodology, but whether it denied autistic people benefits it accorded to others in the same situation, save for mental disability. There is no evidence suggesting that the government's approach to ABA/IBI therapy was different than its approach to other comparable, novel therapies for non-disabled persons or persons with a different type of disability. In the absence of such evidence, a finding of discrimination cannot be sustained.

(3) Discrimination

[63] If differential denial of a benefit provided by law on a ground enumerated in s. 15(1) or analogous thereto were established, it would still be necessary to examine whether the distinction was discriminatory in the sense of treating autistic children as second-class citizens and denying their fundamental human dignity. The failure to establish the basis for a claim for discrimination deprives us of the necessary foundation for this final inquiry.

B. Did the Government's Conduct Infringe the Petitioners' Rights Under Section 7 of the Charter?

[64] Section 7 of the *Charter* provides:

Everyone has the right to life, liberty and security of the person and the right not to be deprived thereof except in accordance with the principles of fundamental justice.

... [67] [T]he limited submissions before us do not permit us to conclude that the government's conduct in the case at bar infringed the petitioners' s. 7 rights.

IV. Conclusion

... [69] I would answer the constitutional questions as follows:

1. Do the definitions of "benefits" and "health care practitioner" in s. 1 of the *Medicare Protection Act*, R.S.B.C. 1996, c. 286, and ss. 17-29 of the *Medical and Health Care Services Regulation*, B.C. Reg. 426/97, infringe s. 15(1) of the *Canadian Charter of Rights and Freedoms* by failing to include services for autistic children based on applied behavioural analysis?

    No.

2. If so, is the infringement a reasonable limit prescribed by law as can be demonstrably justified in a free and democratic society under s. 1 of the *Canadian Charter of Rights and Freedoms*?

    It is unnecessary to answer this question.

3. Do the definitions of "benefits" and "health care practitioner" in s. 1 of the *Medicare Protection Act*, R.S.B.C. 1996, c. 286, and ss. 17-29 of the *Medical and Health Care Services Regulation*, B.C. Reg. 426/97, infringe s. 7 of the *Canadian Charter of Rights and Freedoms* by failing to include services for autistic children based on applied behavioural analysis?

    No.

4. If so, is the infringement a reasonable limit prescribed by law as can be demonstrably justified in a free and democratic society under s. 1 of the *Canadian Charter of Rights and Freedoms*?

    It is unnecessary to answer this question.

R. v. Kapp, 2008

While particular B.C. First Nations enjoy a constitutionally protected right to fish,[1] this does not extend to commercial fishing. In 1992, the federal government implemented a program to allow certain B.C. First Nations temporary, exclusive, commercial access to the Fraser River salmon fishery. For 24 hours in August 1998, non-Aboriginal fishers were kept from the river while Aboriginal fishers netted sockeye salmon for commercial sale. The federal program clearly preferred one category of Canadians over another in setting access to a commercial benefit. A coalition of fishers representing a variety of racial and ethnic backgrounds—many of them descendants of persons subject to government-enforced, race-based deprivations earlier in the 20th century—challenged the program on the basis of section 15 of the Charter, arguing that it was a discriminatory, race-based initiative.

What is discrimination? In law, "to discriminate against" means to make a distinction among persons based on an irrelevant criterion, the effect of which is to demean members of the excluded group. For instance, when we deprive pre-teens of the vote, we do discriminate on the basis of age, but this is not considered "discriminatory" because young people are not objects of traditional disadvantage and are widely held to be incapable of exercising the franchise intelligently. We do not think kids are demeaned by being deprived of the vote. But when blacks are deprived of the right to vote, we say this is discriminatory because race is not a relevant reason for the deprivation; blacks as a group have traditionally suffered disadvantage by being considered inferior to others.[2]

It has been difficult to determine whether a law or program is discriminatory, particularly since all laws make distinctions among categories of persons. Formulating the test for finding discrimination has also been a challenge. Section 15 of the Charter was drafted to give courts ample ammunition to attack discriminatory laws. But it has had a turbulent career in the Supreme Court. As the following decision indicates, the court started in *Andrews* in 1989[3] with a relatively clear interpretive approach to section 15, but through the 1990s that consensus broke down. Tact forbade the court in this case from stating the reason, which is that one mercurial justice, Claire L'Heureux-Dubé, throughout the 1990s insisted on an expansive, "dignity-based" approach to section 15, but never attracted many of her colleagues to her

---

1 *R. v. Sparrow,* [1990] 1 S.C.R. 1075.

2 As the Supreme Court insists, sometimes identical treatment—the *failure* to treat different groups differently—can be discriminatory. Think of stairs to a building that are meant to be used by everyone. This identical treatment disadvantages the disabled. The courts have declared for years that equality is in this sense substantive, not formal; it is about attainment of a society in which all persons have their particular attributes respected and accounted for. Equality demands ramps for the disabled.

3 *Andrews v. Law Society of British Columbia,* [1989] 1 S.C.R. 143.

position. In 1999, the Supreme Court in *Law v. Canada*[4] attempted to bolt L'Heureux-Dubé's approach onto the *Andrews* scaffolding, but the resulting structure was hardly able to stand. *R. v. Kapp* became the occasion for a renovation—in essence it was a return to 1989.

But *Kapp* is not merely a return to 1989. The court here had to deal with another dimension of "equality rights": affirmative action programs. Modern governments strive not merely to avoid discriminating against persons in their laws; they also design programs to help designated groups. Programs, for example, may relax university admission standards or provide more financial support for targeted groups. Some think that group-based distinctions of all kinds—whether designed to help or harm—are pernicious. Others believe that, to overcome "traditional disadvantage," it is only just that groups benefit from government programs targeting them for special treatment. In *Kapp*, many fishers of Chinese and Japanese descent argue that a program preferring First Nations over them in the commercial fishery may help the Aboriginal fishers, but is race-based discrimination nonetheless. So, does section 15(2) of the Charter override section 15(1) of the Charter, even when helping some involves harming others? Does the harm to others matter? In this case, the court found no Charter violation: the federal program was ameliorative in design and so did not discriminate against fishers kept from the water that day in 1998.

A final issue in this decision concerns the fact that the impugned federal program was designed to help the First Nations commercial fishery. Access to the river was given to designated Aboriginal communities. The program was also understood to dovetail with Crown obligations to First Nations. A collective right (established by statute, not constitutional law) of First Nations was pitted against the individual rights of non-Aboriginal fishers. For eight members of the panel, the appeal could be disposed by reference entirely to section 15. But for Justice Bastarache, who concurred in the result, the case engages section 25 of the Charter, an interpretive provision that declares that Charter rights are not to be interpreted to conflict with Aboriginal rights, most of which are of a collective character. Justice Bastarache argued that section 25 is a "shield" that protects Aboriginal rights from challenges based on other Charter provisions. The other eight justices distanced themselves from his analysis. *Kapp* thus broaches but does not squarely address a major constitutional issue: to what extent does the Constitution protect collective Aboriginal rights that are in conflict with individual Charter rights? Can an Aboriginal band, for example, use the section 25 shield to maintain punishments on its members that would otherwise violate section 12 of the Charter?[5] ∼

Discussion Questions

1. The Supreme Court asserts that programs *designed* to ameliorate the conditions of protected groups (that is, those groups protected from discrimination under section 15(1)) do not violate the Charter. Do you think it matters whether the *effect* of such programs is to harm groups excluded from the ameliorative programs?

---

4   *Law v. Canada (Minister of Employment and Immigration)*, [1999] 1 S.C.R. 497.

5   See David Milward, *Aboriginal Justice and the Charter: Realizing a Culturally Sensitive Interpretation of Legal Rights* (Vancouver: UBC Press, 2012).

2. Think of two group characteristics that were once thought legitimate bases for legislative distinctions but are now considered discriminatory. Are there any group characteristics once thought discriminatory that are now not thought to be so? What determines whether a distinction is also discriminatory?

R. v. KAPP
2008 SCC 41, [2008] 2 S.C.R. 483

Hearing: December 11, 2007; Judgment: June 27, 2008.

Present: McLachlin C.J. and Bastarache, Binnie, LeBel, Deschamps, Fish, Abella, Charron, and Rothstein JJ.

Interveners: Attorney General of Ontario, Attorney General of Quebec, Attorney General for Saskatchewan, Attorney General of Alberta, Tsawwassen First Nation, Haisla Nation, Songhees Indian Band, Malahat First Nation, T'Sou-ke First Nation, Snaw-naw-as (Nanoose) First Nation and Beecher Bay Indian Band (collectively Te'mexw Nations), Heiltsuk Nation, Musqueam Indian Band, Cowichan Tribes, Sportfishing Defence Alliance, B.C. Seafood Alliance, Pacific Salmon Harvesters Society, Aboriginal Fishing Vessel Owners Association, United Fishermen and Allied Workers Union, Japanese Canadian Fishermens Association, Atlantic Fishing Industry Alliance, Nee Tahi Buhn Indian Band, Tseshaht First Nation and Assembly of First Nations.

The judgment of McLachlin C.J. and Binnie, LeBel, Deschamps, Fish, Abella, Charron, and Rothstein JJ. was delivered by

THE CHIEF JUSTICE AND ABELLA J.:

...

B. Factual and Judicial History

[4] Prior to European contact, aboriginal groups living in the region of the mouth of the Fraser River fished the river for food, social and ceremonial purposes. It is no exaggeration to say that their life centered in large part around the river and its abundant fishery. In the last two decades, court decisions have confirmed that pre-contact fishing practices integral to the culture of aboriginal people translate into a modern-day right to fish for food, social and ceremonial purposes: *R. v. Sparrow*, [1990] 1 S.C.R. 1075. The right is a communal right. It inheres in the community, not the individual, and may be exercised by people who are linked to the ancestral aboriginal community.

[5] The aboriginal right has not been recognized by the courts as extending to fishing for the purpose of sale or commercial fishing: *R. v. Van der Peet*, [1996] 2 S.C.R. 507. The participation of Aboriginals in the commercial fishery was thus left to individual initiative or to negotiation between aboriginal peoples and the government. The federal government determined that aboriginal people should be given a stake in the commercial fishery. The bands tended to be disadvantaged economically, compared to non-Aboriginals. Catching fish for their own tables and ceremonies left many needs unmet.

[6] ... The decision to enhance aboriginal participation in the commercial fishery may also be seen as a response to the directive of this Court in *Sparrow*, at p. 1119, that the government consult with aboriginal groups in the implementation of fishery regulation in order to honour its fiduciary duty to aboriginal communities. ...

[7] ... Introduced in 1992, the Aboriginal Fisheries Strategy has three stated objectives: ensuring the rights recognized by the *Sparrow* decision are respected; providing aboriginal communities with a larger role in fisheries management and increased economic benefits; and minimizing the disruption of non-aboriginal fisheries (1994 Gardner Pinfold Report). In response to consultations with stakeholders carried out since its inception, the Aboriginal Fisheries Strategy has been reviewed and adjusted periodically in order to achieve these goals. A significant part of the Aboriginal Fisheries Strategy was the introduction of three pilot sales programs, one of which resulted in the issuance of the communal fishing licence at issue in this case. The licence was granted pursuant to the *Aboriginal Communal Fishing Licences Regulations*, SOR/93-332 ("*ACFLR*"). The *ACFLR* grants communal licences to "aboriginal organization[s]," defined as including "an Indian band, an Indian band council, a tribal council and an organization that represents a territorially based aboriginal community" (s. 2). The communal licence cannot be granted to individuals, but an aboriginal organization can designate its use to individuals.

[8] The licence with which we are concerned permitted fishers designated by the bands to fish for sockeye salmon between 7:00 a.m on August 19, 1998 and 7:00 a.m. on August 20, 1998, and to use the fish caught for food, social and ceremonial purposes, and for sale. Some of the fishers designated by the bands to fish under the communal fishing licence were also licensed commercial fishers entitled to fish at other openings for commercial fishers.

[9] The appellants are all commercial fishers who were excluded from the fishery during the 24 hours allocated to the aboriginal fishery under the communal fishing licence. Under the auspices of the B.C. Fisheries Survival Coalition, they participated in a protest fishery during the prohibited period, for the purpose of bringing a constitutional challenge to the communal licence. As anticipated, they were charged with fishing at a prohibited time. In defence of the charges, they filed notice of a constitutional question seeking declarations that the communal fishing licence, the *ACFLR* and related regulations and the Aboriginal Fisheries Strategy were unconstitutional.

[The Charter claimants won in the provincial court but lost on two subsequent appeals. They appealed their B.C. Court of Appeal loss to this court.]

C. Analysis

...

1. The Purpose of Section 15

[14] Nearly 20 years have passed since the Court handed down its first s. 15 decision in the case of *Andrews v. Law Society of British Columbia*, [1989] 1 S.C.R. 143. *Andrews* set the template for this Court's commitment to substantive equality—a template which subsequent decisions have enriched but never abandoned.

[15] Substantive equality, as contrasted with formal equality, is grounded in the idea that: "The promotion of equality entails the promotion of a society in which all are secure in the knowledge that they are recognized at law as human beings equally deserving of concern, respect and consideration." ...

[19] A decade later, in *Law*, this Court suggested that discrimination should be defined in terms of the impact of the law or program on the "human dignity" of members of the claimant group, having regard to four contextual factors: (1) pre-existing disadvantage, if any, of the claimant group; (2) degree of correspondence between the differential treatment and the claimant group's reality; (3) whether the law or program has an ameliorative purpose or effect; and (4) the nature of the interest affected (paras. 62-75).

[20] The achievement of *Law* was its success in unifying what had become, since *Andrews*, a division in this Court's approach to s. 15. *Law* accomplished this by reiterating and confirming *Andrews'* interpretation of s. 15 as a guarantee of substantive, and not just formal, equality. Moreover, *Law* made an important contribution to our understanding of the conceptual underpinnings of substantive equality.

[21] At the same time, several difficulties have arisen from the attempt in *Law* to employ human dignity *as a legal test*.

There can be no doubt that human dignity is an essential value underlying the s. 15 equality guarantee. In fact, the protection of all of the rights guaranteed by the *Charter* has as its lodestar the promotion of human dignity. ...

[22] But as critics have pointed out, human dignity is an abstract and subjective notion that, even with the guidance of the four contextual factors, cannot only become confusing and difficult to apply; it has also proven to be an *additional* burden on equality claimants, rather than the philosophical enhancement it was intended to be. Criticism has also accrued for the way *Law* has allowed the formalism of some of the Court's post-*Andrews* jurisprudence to resurface in the form of an artificial comparator analysis focussed on treating likes alike. ...

[25] The central purpose of combatting discrimination, as discussed, underlies both s. 15(1) and s. 15(2). Under s. 15(1), the focus is on *preventing* governments from making distinctions based on the enumerated or analogous grounds that: have the effect of perpetuating group disadvantage and prejudice; or impose disadvantage on the basis of stereotyping. Under s. 15(2), the focus is on *enabling* governments to pro-actively combat existing discrimination through affirmative measures. ...

2. Section 15(2)

[27] Under *Andrews*, as previously noted, s. 15 does not mean identical treatment. McIntyre J. explained that "every difference in treatment between individuals under the law will not necessarily result in inequality," and that "identical treatment may frequently produce serious inequality" (p. 164). McIntyre J. explicitly rejected identical treatment as a *Charter* objective, based in part on the existence of s. 15(2). At p. 171, he stated that "the fact that identical treatment may frequently produce serious inequality is recognized in s. 15(2)." ...

[29] In our view, the appellants have established that they were treated differently based on an enumerated ground, race. Because the government argues that the program ameliorated the conditions of a disadvantaged group, we must take a more detailed look at s. 15(2).

[30] The question that arises is whether the program that targeted the aboriginal bands falls under s. 15(2) in the sense that it is a "law, program or activity that has as its object the amelioration of conditions of disadvantaged individuals or groups." As noted, the communal fishing licence authorizing the three bands to fish for sale on August 19-20 was issued pursuant to an enabling statute and regulations—namely the *ACFLR*. This qualifies as a "law, program or activity" within the meaning of s. 15(2). The more complex issue is whether the program fulfills the remaining criteria of s. 15(2)—that

is, whether the program "has as its object the amelioration of conditions of disadvantaged individuals or groups." ...

[33] In essence, s. 15(2) of the *Charter* seeks to protect efforts by the state to develop and adopt remedial schemes designed to assist disadvantaged groups. This interpretation is confirmed by the language in s. 15(2), "does not preclude." ...

[37] ... [I]f the government can demonstrate that an impugned program meets the criteria of s. 15(2), it may be unnecessary to conduct a s. 15(1) analysis at all. As discussed at the outset of this analysis, s. 15(1) and s. 15(2) should be read as working together to promote substantive equality. The focus of s. 15(1) is on *preventing* governments from making distinctions based on enumerated or analogous grounds that have the effect of perpetuating disadvantage or prejudice or imposing disadvantage on the basis of stereotyping. The focus of s. 15(2) is on *enabling* governments to pro-actively combat discrimination. Read thus, the two sections are confirmatory of each other. Section 15(2) supports a full expression of equality, rather than derogating from it. "Under a substantive definition of equality, different treatment in the service of equity for disadvantaged groups is an expression of equality, not an exception to it": P. W. Hogg, *Constitutional Law of Canada* (5th ed. Supp. 2007), vol. 2, at p. 55-53.

[38] But this confirmatory purpose does not preclude an independent role for s. 15(2). Section 15(2) is more than a hortatory admonition. It tells us, in simple clear language, that s. 15(1) cannot be read in a way that finds an ameliorative program aimed at combatting disadvantage to be discriminatory and in breach of s. 15.

[39] Here the appellants claim discrimination on the basis of s. 15(1). The source of that discrimination—the very essence of their complaint—is a program that may be ameliorative. This leaves but one conclusion: if the government establishes that the program falls under s. 15(2), the appellants' claim must fail.

[40] In other words, once the s. 15 claimant has shown a distinction made on an enumerated or analogous ground, it is open to the government to show that the impugned law, program or activity is ameliorative and, thus, constitutional. This approach has the advantage of avoiding the symbolic problem of finding a program discriminatory before "saving" it as ameliorative, while also giving independent force to a provision that has been written as distinct and separate from s. 15(1). Should the government fail to demonstrate that its program falls under s. 15(2), the program must then receive full scrutiny under s. 15(1) to determine whether its impact is discriminatory.

[41] We would therefore formulate the test under s. 15(2) as follows. A program does not violate the s. 15 equality guarantee if the government can demonstrate that: (1) the program has an ameliorative or remedial purpose; and (2) the program targets a disadvantaged group identified by the enumerated or analogous grounds. In proposing this test, we are mindful that future cases may demand some adjustment to the framework in order to meet the litigants' particular circumstances. However, at this early stage in the development of the law surrounding s. 15(2), the test we have described provides a basic starting point—one that is adequate for determining the issues before us on this appeal, but leaves open the possibility for future refinement.

[42] We build our analysis of s. 15(2) and its operation around three key phrases in the provision. The subsection protects "any law, program or activity that *has as its object* the *amelioration* of conditions of *disadvantaged* individuals or groups." While there is some overlap in the considerations raised by each of these terms, it may be useful to consider each of them individually.

(a) "Has as Its Object"

[43] In interpreting this phrase, two issues arise. The first is whether courts should look to the *purpose* or to the *effect* of legislation. The second is whether, in order to qualify for s. 15(2) protection, a program must have an ameliorative purpose as its sole object, or whether having such a goal as one of several objectives is sufficient.

[44] The language of s. 15(2) suggests that legislative goal rather than actual effect is the paramount consideration in determining whether or not a program qualifies for s. 15(2) protection. Michael Peirce defends this view, which he refers to as the "subjective" approach, because it adheres more closely to the language of the provision and avoids potentially inappropriate judicial intervention in government programs ("A Progressive Interpretation of Subsection 15(2) of the *Charter*" (1993), 57 *Sask. L. Rev.* 263). Scholars have nonetheless disagreed about the appropriate approach, often using the "subjective" (goal-based) and "objective" (effect-based) language.

[The justices cite a number of academics who believe that the effects, not just the purpose, must be evaluated by a program under section 15(2) analysis. Otherwise, a government could erode rights simply by declaring a program with discriminatory effects to have the purpose of benefitting a particular group.]

[46] In our opinion, this concern can be easily addressed. There is nothing to suggest that a test focussed on the goal of legislation must slavishly accept the government's characterization of its purpose. Courts could well examine legislation to ensure that the declared purpose is genuine. Courts confronted with a s. 15(2) claim have done just that. ...

[47] In that vein, proponents of the approach that focusses on the ameliorative goal of the program, rather than its effect, argue that doing so will prevent courts from unduly interfering in ameliorative programs created by the legislature. They note that Canadian *Charter* drafters wished to avoid the American experience, whereby judges overturned affirmative action programs under the banner of equality. The purpose-driven approach also reflects the language of the provision itself, which focusses on the "object" of the program, law or activity rather than its impact. Moreover, the effects of a program in its fledgling stages cannot always be easily ascertained. The law or program may be experimental. If the sincere purpose is to promote equality by ameliorating the conditions of a disadvantaged group, the government should be given some leeway to adopt innovative programs, even though some may ultimately prove to be unsuccessful. The government may learn from such failures and revise equality-enhancing programs to make them more effective.

[48] Given the language of the provision and its goal of enabling governments to pro-actively combat discrimination, we believe the "purpose"-based approach is more appropriate than the "effect"-based approach: where a law, program or activity creates a distinction based on an enumerated or analogous ground, was the government's goal in creating that distinction to improve the conditions of a group that is disadvantaged? In examining purpose, courts may therefore find it necessary to consider not only statements made by the drafters of the program but also whether the legislature chose means rationally related to that ameliorative purpose, in the sense that it appears at least plausible that the program may indeed advance the stated goal of combatting disadvantage. ...

[49] Analysing the means employed by the government can easily turn into assessing the *effect* of the program. As a result, to preserve an intent-based analysis, courts could be encouraged to frame the analysis as follows: Was it rational for the state to conclude that the means chosen to reach its ameliorative goal would contribute to that purpose? For the distinction to be rational, there must be a correlation between the program and the disadvantage suffered by the target group. Such a standard permits significant deference to the legislature but allows judicial review where a program nominally seeks to serve the disadvantaged but in practice serves other non-remedial objectives.

[The justices argue that a program can be saved under section 15(2) even if only one of its objectives is ameliorative.]

(b) "Amelioration"

...

[54] ... [L]aws designed to restrict or punish behaviour would not qualify for s. 15(2) protection. Nor, as already discussed, should the focus be on the effect of the law. This said, the fact that a law has no plausible or predictable ameliorative effect may render suspect the state's ameliorative purpose. Governments, as discussed above, are not permitted to protect discriminatory programs on colourable pretexts.

(c) "Disadvantaged"

[55] ... "Disadvantage" under s. 15 connotes vulnerability, prejudice and negative social characterization. Section 15(2)'s purpose is to protect government programs targeting the conditions of a specific and identifiable disadvantaged group, as contrasted with broad societal legislation, such as social assistance programs. Not all members of the group need to be disadvantaged, as long as the group as a whole has experienced discrimination.

3. Application of Section 15(2) to This Case

...

[58] The first issue is whether the program that excluded Mr. Kapp and other non-band fishers from the fishery had an ameliorative or remedial purpose. The Crown describes numerous objectives for the impugned pilot sales program. These include negotiating solutions to aboriginal fishing rights claims, providing economic opportunities to native bands and supporting their progress towards self-sufficiency. The impugned fishing licence relates to all of these goals. The pilot sales program was part of an attempt—albeit a small part—to negotiate a solution to aboriginal fishing rights claims. The communal fishing licence provided economic opportunities, through sale or trade, to the bands. Through these endeavours, the government was pursuing the goal of promoting band self-sufficiency. In these ways, the government was hoping to redress the social and economic disadvantage of the targeted bands. The means chosen to achieve the purpose (special fishing privileges for aboriginal communities, constituting a benefit) are rationally related to serving that purpose. It follows that the Crown has established a credible ameliorative purpose for the program.

[59] The government's aims correlate to the actual economic and social disadvantage suffered by members of the three aboriginal bands. The disadvantage of aboriginal people is indisputable. ...

[60] Mr. Kapp suggests that the focus must be on the particular forms of disadvantage suffered by the bands who received the benefit, and argues that this program did not offer a benefit that effectively tackled the problems faced by these bands. As discussed above, what is required is a correlation between the program and the disadvantage suffered by the target group. If the target group is socially and economically disadvantaged, as is the case here, and the program may

rationally address that disadvantage, then the necessary correspondence is established.

[61] We conclude that the government program here at issue is protected by s. 15(2) as a program that "has as its object the amelioration of conditions of disadvantaged individuals or groups." It follows that the program does not violate the equality guarantee of s. 15 of the *Charter*.

4. Section 25 of the Charter

[62] Having concluded that a breach of s. 15 is not established, it is unnecessary to consider whether s. 25 of the *Charter* would bar the appellants' claim. However, we wish to signal our concerns with aspects of the reasoning of Bastarache J. and of Kirkpatrick J.A., both of whom would have dismissed the appeal solely on the basis of s. 25.

[63] An initial concern is whether the communal fishing licence at issue in this case lies within s. 25's compass. In our view, the wording of s. 25 and the examples given therein—aboriginal rights, treaty rights, and "other rights or freedoms," such as rights derived from the *Royal Proclamation* or from land claims agreements—suggest that not every aboriginal interest or program falls within the provision's scope. Rather, only rights of a constitutional character are likely to benefit from s. 25. If so, we would question, without deciding, whether the fishing licence is a s. 25 right or freedom.

[64] A second concern is whether, even if the fishing licence does fall under s. 25, the result would constitute an absolute bar to the appellants' s. 15 claim, as distinguished from an interpretive provision informing the construction of potentially conflicting *Charter* rights.

[65] These issues raise complex questions of the utmost importance to the peaceful reconciliation of aboriginal entitlements with the interests of all Canadians. In our view, prudence suggests that these issues are best left for resolution on a case-by-case basis as they arise before the Court.

D. Conclusion

[66] We would dismiss the appeal on the ground that breach of the s. 15 equality guarantee has not been established.

The following are the reasons delivered by

BASTARACHE J.:

. . .

2. Analysis

[76] … I am of the view that s. 25 of the *Charter* provides a complete answer to the question posed in this appeal. I will initially address the role and effect of s. 25, then outline the scope of the provision. Finally, I will propose an analytical approach to be followed when s. 25 is engaged and apply that approach to the present matter.

[77] There is no need for me to engage in a full analysis of the application of s. 15 of the *Charter*. It is sufficient for me to establish the existence of a potential conflict between the pilot sales program and s. 15. This said, I want to state clearly that I am in complete agreement with the restatement of the test for the application of s. 15 that is adopted by the Chief Justice and Abella J. in their reasons for judgment.

2.1 Role and Effect of Section 25

[78] The enactment of the *Charter* undoubtedly heralded a new era for individual rights in Canada. Nevertheless, the document also expressly recognizes rights more aptly described as collective or group rights. The manner in which collective rights can exist with the liberal paradigm otherwise established by the *Charter* remains a source of ongoing tension within the jurisprudence and the literature. This tension comes to a head in the aboriginal context in s. 25.

[79] Most authors believe that s. 25 is an interpretative provision and does not create new rights. B. H. Wildsmith outlines the two modes of interpretation most commonly posited:

> Under one mode of interpreting section 25, the section admonishes the decision maker to construe the Charter right or freedom so as to give effect to it, if possible, without an adverse impact on section 25 rights or freedoms. If it is not possible to so construe the Charter right or freedom so as to avoid a negative impact on native rights, then the force of section 25 is spent. Effect is given to the Charter right or freedom despite the [negative] impact on native rights. Under the second mode of interpreting section 25, the conflict between Charter rights and section 25 rights, if irreconcilable, would be resolved by giving effect to the section 25 rights and freedoms. In short, native rights remain inviolable and unaffected by the rights or freedoms guaranteed by the Charter.

([Bruce H. Wildsmith,] *Aboriginal Peoples & Section 25 of the Canadian Charter of Rights and Freedoms* ([Saskatoon: University of Saskatchewan Native Law Centre,] 1988), at pp. 10-11)

[80] The first mode has been described in the literature as an interpretative prism or a mere canon of interpretation. The second method is most commonly referred to as a shield. Wildsmith provides an example (at pp. 11-12) that is highly reminiscent of the present matter to demonstrate that there is a serious difficulty in finding that s. 25 is a mere canon of interpretation. If a provincial Act were to establish that "[n]o Indian shall hunt (or fish) except for his own personal consumption

unless he has first obtained a licence," and that no treaty or aboriginal right to this exemption existed, then a non-Indian hunter or fisherman would say that the statute violated s. 15(1) of the *Charter*. Indians would have a right to hunt or fish for personal consumption denied to others. The statutory right given to the Indians would be an "other righ[t] or freedo[m]" under s. 25. The court would then be forced to choose between vindicating the equality right or the right protected by s. 25. If the real effect of s. 25 is to protect native rights and freedoms from erosion based on the *Charter*, the conflict should be resolved by refusing to apply s. 15 in these circumstances.

[81] I agree that giving primacy to s. 25 is what was clearly intended. As will be seen, this is consistent with the wording and history of the provision. It is also consistent with the declarations of the then Deputy Minister of Justice, Roger Tassé, and with those of the Minister of Justice at the time of the 1983 amendment, Justice Minister Mark MacGuigan.

[Justice Bastarache devotes a long section of his reasons to suggesting that the "shield" interpretation of section 25 is supported by the text of the provision, the legislative history of the Charter, and academic commentary.]

2.1.5 Limitations on the Shield

[97] Is this shield absolute? Obviously not. First, it is restricted by s. 28 of the *Charter* which provides for gender equality "[n]otwithstanding anything in this Charter." Second, it is restricted to its object, placing *Charter* rights and freedoms in juxtaposition to aboriginal rights and freedoms. ... This means in essence that only laws that actually impair native rights will be considered, not those that simply have incidental effects on natives.

[98] There is some uncertainty concerning what rights and freedoms are contemplated in s. 25. Most concerns have been with self-government issues. Are all of the laws adopted by bands under the authority of the *Indian Act*, R.S.C. 1985, c. I-5, protected? Wildsmith suggests that this is possibly the case because their source is in s. 91(24) of the *Constitution Act, 1867*, which is clearly associated with the concept of Indianness (p. 33). He nevertheless says that the power in question would not be unrestrained because the courts would read in the need for "reasonableness" as they did for the exercise of municipal powers, and because the *Canadian Bill of Rights* would continue to apply. (The courts would of course have to deal with the *Lavell* precedent to make this avenue useful.) Wildsmith, at pp. 25-26 suggests that the court may want to apply a proportionality test similar to that in *Oakes* in order to determine whether an Act would truly abrogate an aboriginal right or freedom (*R. v. Oakes*, [1986] 1 S.C.R. 103). He argues at p. 37 that *Charter* rights would still be available to Indians who would want to attack federal legislation giving preferential treatment to other Indians.

[99] There is no reason to believe that s. 25 has taken Aboriginals out of the *Charter* protection scheme. One aboriginal group can ask to be given the same benefit as another aboriginal group under s. 15(1). Sections 2 and 3 of the *Charter* apply to Aboriginals. Macklem, at pp. 225-27, suggests that the courts should distinguish between external and internal restrictions on aboriginal laws that clash with the *Charter* and that in the case of internal restrictions, aboriginal communities should be required to satisfy the *Oakes* test to resist a challenge. It could also be argued that it would be contrary to the purpose of s. 25 to prevent an Aboriginal from invoking those sections to attack an Act passed by a band council. It is not at all obvious in my view that it is necessary to constrain the individual rights of Aboriginals in order to recognize collective rights under s. 25. ...

2.2 Scope of Section 25 Protection

[101] In this case, what is significant about the scope of s. 25 protection is the meaning of the words "other rights or freedoms." ...

[103] I believe that the reference to "aboriginal and treaty rights" suggests that the focus of the provision is the uniqueness of those persons or communities mentioned in the Constitution; the rights protected are those that are unique to them because of their special status. As argued by Macklem, s. 25 "protects federal, provincial and Aboriginal initiatives that seek to further interests associated with indigenous difference from Charter scrutiny": see p. 225. Accordingly, legislation that distinguishes between aboriginal and non-aboriginal people in order to protect interests associated with aboriginal culture, territory, sovereignty or the treaty process deserves to be shielded from *Charter* scrutiny. ...

[105] Laws adopted under the s. 91(24) power would normally fall into this category, the power being in relation to the aboriginal peoples as such, but not laws that fall under s. 88 of the *Indian Act*, because they are by definition laws of general application. "[O]ther rights or freedoms" comprise statutory rights which seek to protect interests associated with aboriginal culture, territory, self-government, as mentioned above, and settlement agreements that are a replacement for treaty and aboriginal rights. But private rights of individual Indians held in a private capacity as ordinary Canadian citizens would not be protected.

[106] The inclusion of statutory rights and settlement agreements pertaining to the treaty process and pertaining to indigenous difference is consistent with the jurisprudence of this Court. ...

2.3 Approach to Section 25

[108] One important issue is to determine when s. 25 is triggered. ... What has to be determined is whether there is a real conflict.

[109] I do not think it is reasonable to invoke s. 25 once a *Charter* violation is established. One reason for this position is that there would be no rationale for invoking s. 25 in the case of a finding of discrimination that could not be justified under s. 1, simply because, in the context of s. 15, as in this case for instance, considerations that serve to justify that an Act is not discriminatory would have to be relitigated under the terms of s. 25. Another reason is that a true interpretative section would serve to define the substantive guarantee. Section 25 is meant to preserve some distinctions, which are inconsistent with weighing equality rights and native rights. What is called for, in essence, is a contextualized interpretation that takes into account the cultural needs and aspirations of natives. Dan Russell (*A People's Dream: Aboriginal Self-Government in Canada* ([Vancouver: UBC Press,] 2000), at p. 100) gives an example of this based on s. 3 of the *Charter*: he says that the right to vote should be reinterpreted in the context of band elections to reflect the particularities of the clan system. This, I believe, is tantamount to saying natives do not have the same rights as other Canadians, rather than saying they are protected like all other Canadians from interference with their individual rights as guaranteed by the *Charter*. W. F. Pentney (*The Aboriginal Rights Provisions in the Constitution Act, 1982* ([Saskatoon: University of Saskatchewan Native Law Centre,] 1987)), takes the same approach by suggesting that the *Charter* be interpreted through a native prism. I do not believe there are distinct *Charter* rights for aboriginal individuals and non-aboriginal individuals, or that it is feasible to take into account the specific cultural experience of Aboriginals in defining rights guaranteed by the *Charter*. The rights are the same for everyone; their application is a matter of justification according to context.

[110] I also think it is contrary to the scheme of the *Charter* to invoke s. 25 as a factor in applying s. 1. Section 1 does not apply to s. 25 as such because s. 25 does not create rights; to incorporate s. 25 is inconceivable in that context. Section 1 already takes into account the aboriginal perspective in the right case. Section 25 is protective and its function must be preserved. Section 25 was not meant to provide for balancing *Charter* rights against aboriginal rights. There should be no reading down of s. 25 while our jurisprudence establishes that aboriginal rights must be given a broad and generous application, and that where there is uncertainty, every effort should be made to give priority to the aboriginal perspective. It seems to me that the only reason for wanting to consider s. 25 within the framework of s. 15(1) is the fear mentioned earlier that individual rights will possibly be compromised. Another fear that is revealed by some pleadings in this case is that rights falling under s. 25 will be constitutionalized; this fear is totally unfounded. Section 25 does not create or constitutionalize rights.

2.4 Application in This Case

[111] There are three steps in the application of s. 25. The first step requires an evaluation of the claim in order to establish the nature of the substantive *Charter* right and whether the claim is made out, *prima facie*. The second step requires an evaluation of the native right to establish whether it falls under s. 25. The third step requires a determination of the existence of a true conflict between the *Charter* right and the native right.

2.4.1 The Nature of the Claim

[112] The appellants claim that aboriginal fishers have been given the right to fish in exclusivity, for one day, prior to the opening of the general commercial fishery in which they participate, and that this right gives rise to a benefit that is denied to non-Aboriginals on the basis of race. They argue that the fact that communal licences are given to a number of bands which then authorize specific fishers to fish is irrelevant, membership in bands not being a valid proxy that is functionally relevant to the regulation of the public fishery. ...

[116] There is in my view a *prima facie* case of discrimination pursuant to s. 15(1). There is no need to proceed further in the analysis or to invoke s. 1. The potential for conflict is established.

2.4.2 The Native Right

[117] The Minister issued licences to Aboriginals in application of a discretion given by the *Fisheries Act* and the *Aboriginal Communal Fishing Licences Regulations*. The respondent argues that these licences do not constitute a right or freedom as prescribed by s. 25 of the *Charter*. He says that only those rights and freedoms that "are vital to maintaining the distinctiveness of aboriginal cultures within the larger Canadian polity ... have the potential to fall within s. 25 " (factum, at para. 131), and adds that "[i]t follows that to be afforded protection under s. 25, an 'other right or freedom' must: (1) be of sufficient magnitude to warrant overriding a *Charter* right or freedom; (2) manifest a strong degree of permanence; and, (3) be intimately related to the protection and affirmation of aboriginal distinctiveness.["] The licence in question does not satisfy these criteria. The licence permitting sale was simply an exercise of administrative discretion, subject to numerous

conditions and of brief duration. It was only effective for twenty-four hours. The agreement entered into with the Musqueam, Burrard and Tsawwassen bands expressly stated that it did not create any aboriginal rights. The conclusion of Brenner C.J.S.C. that the licence did not create a right under s. 25 was correct" (paras. 137-38).

[118] The first comment that I would make is that the criterion of magnitude is simply inconsistent with the actual terms of s. 25. That section simply speaks of rights that pertain to the aboriginal peoples of Canada, i.e., any rights that advance the distinctive position of aboriginal peoples. The same is true with regard to the criterion of permanence; as mentioned earlier in these reasons, "other rights or freedoms" necessarily refers to statutory rights, which can be abolished at any time. The fact that the agreements with the named bands stated that they did not create any aboriginal rights is of no moment. Section 25 does not create any rights.

[119] ... At para. 101 of his factum, the respondent speaks of the unique relationship between British Columbia aboriginal communities and the fishery. This should be enough to draw a link between the right to fish given to Aboriginals pursuant to the pilot sales program and the rights contemplated by s. 25. The right to fish has consistently been the object of claims based on aboriginal rights and treaty rights, the enumerated terms in the provisions. ...

[121] Finally, in my opinion, the right in this case is totally dependent on the exercise of powers given to Parliament under s. 91(24) of the *Constitution Act, 1867* which deals with a class of persons, Indians. Here again it is interesting to note the parallel made between s. 93 and s. 91(24) of the *Constitution Act, 1867* by Estey J. in *Reference re Bill 30*, at p. 1206, where he says: "In this sense, s. 93 is a provincial counterpart of s. 91(24) (Indians, and lands reserved for Indians) which authorizes the Parliament of Canada to legislate for the benefit of the Indian population in a preferential, discriminatory, or distinctive fashion *vis-à-vis* others." To argue that according these licences is not a right but an exercise of ministerial discretion is to privilege form over substance. The *Charter* cannot be interpreted as rendering unconstitutional the exercise of powers consistent with the purposes of s. 91(24), nor is it rational to believe that every exercise of the s. 91(24) jurisdiction requires a justification under s. 1. Section 25 is a necessary partner to s. 35(1); it protects s. 35(1) purposes and enlarges the reach of measures needed to fulfill the promise of reconciliation.

2.4.3 Potential Conflict

[122] I think it is established, in this case, that the right given by the pilot sales program is limited to Aboriginals and has a detrimental effect on non-aboriginal commercial fishers who operate in the same region as the beneficiaries of the program. It is also clear that the disadvantage is related to racial differences. Section 15 of the *Charter* is *prima facie* engaged. The right to equality afforded to every individual under s. 15 is not capable of application consistently with the rights of aboriginal fishers holding licences under the pilot sales program. There is a real conflict.

3. Conclusion

[123] Section 25 of the *Charter* applies in the present situation and provides a full answer to the claim. For this reason, I would dismiss the appeal.

Appeal dismissed.

G. LANGUAGE RIGHTS

 Mahe v. Alberta, 1990

The *Constitution Act, 1867* contains only two sections explicitly recognizing rights. These sections confer rights on groups rather than individuals. These are section 93, which sets out school rights for the Protestant minority in Quebec and the Roman Catholic minority in other provinces, and section 133, which sets out rights to use French in the federal Parliament and courts and reciprocal rights to use English in the Quebec legislature and courts. When Manitoba became a province of Canada, a similar provision enshrined the right to use English and French in its legislature and courts. These rights sections in Canada's founding Constitution are specific to the Canadian historical experience. They reflect the accommodation of European cultures upon which Confederation was based.

Section 93 guaranteed that Quebec Protestants would have the same rights to separate schools that Catholics enjoyed in Ontario. It protected not only any school rights enjoyed by Protestant and Catholic minorities in any province at the time of Confederation but any rights that might be established thereafter. This guarantee of denominational schools was varied slightly for the prairie provinces when they became part of Canada and a more extensive guarantee was included in Newfoundland's terms of union in 1949.

The provisions of section 93 show how little the Fathers of Confederation looked to the courts to enforce constitutional rights. Appeals against provinces for denying section 93 rights were to go to the federal Cabinet, and if a province failed to comply with the federal government's instructions, the federal Parliament could pass remedial legislation. The first and only time a federal government threatened to use these remedial powers was when Charles Tupper introduced a Remedial Bill in response to an appeal by Manitoba Catholics in 1895. The proposed Remedial Bill was a major reason for defeat of Tupper's Conservative government by Wilfrid Laurier's Liberals in the 1896 federal election. Laurier favoured provincial rights over the rights of Manitoba's Catholic minority. Since then, appeals against denials of section 93 rights have been dealt with in the courts.

In the years when the most important section 93 cases were heard, Canada's highest court was the Judicial Committee of the Privy Council (JCPC), and it was remarkably restrained in interpreting section 93. In 1892, it reversed the Supreme Court of Canada and upheld Manitoba legislation establishing a secular school system and withdrawing public funding for Roman Catholic separate schools.[1] In 1917, it upheld an Ontario regulation prohibiting the use of French in all schools, including Roman Catholic separate schools, even though

---

1 *Barrett v. The City of Winnipeg* (1892), A.C. 445.

in some parts of the province most of the separate school students at that time were French-speaking.[2] These JCPC decisions were a major factor in preventing Canada west of Quebec from developing along bicultural lines.

Section 29 of the Charter stipulates that nothing in the Charter can abrogate the historic section 93 denominational school rights. In 1984, the Supreme Court rejected a section 15 Charter challenge to Ontario legislation extending public funding to the full secondary-school program of the province's Roman Catholic Separate Schools.[3] The court based its decision not so much on section 29 of the Charter as on the plenary authority section 93 gives provinces to develop a system of denominational schools.

Section 93 came up in a peripheral way in *Mahe*. The central issues in the case were whether the right to minority-language education facilities included the minority's right to manage and control its educational facilities, and whether that right to management and control could be met in Edmonton by including minority-language trustees on the city's Roman Catholic Separate School Board. This raised the side issue whether the denominational school rights would be violated by this arrangement. The court ruled that because the Separate School Board would lose no power over religious aspects of its schools, there was no abrogation of denominational school rights.

Although the Supreme Court has made it clear that the "new Constitution" is not to invalidate fundamental provisions of the "old Constitution," the rights sections of the old Constitution have been changing, reflecting the secularization of Canadian society and an emphasis on minority language rights over minority faith-based rights. In 1997, in response to a unanimous resolution of Quebec's National Assembly, the federal Parliament supported a constitutional amendment making the section 93 guarantee of denominational school rights inapplicable in Quebec. This amendment reflects the desire of English-speaking and French-speaking Quebecers to organize their schools around language communities rather than religious communities. The following year, Newfoundlanders voted by a 73 percent majority to scrap their faith-based school system.[4]

Fundamental to Pierre Trudeau and his government in pressing for a charter of rights was a vision of Canada in which French-speaking Canadians would feel at home in all parts of the country and English-speaking Canadians would feel secure in Quebec. This vision is reflected in sections 16 to 23 of the Charter. The fact that the Charter's legislative override clause does not apply to these sections is indicative of their importance to the Charter's framers. These sections of the Charter extend the language rights in section 133 of the Constitution in four ways. First, section 16 states, for the first time, that English and French are "the official languages of Canada." Second, the right to use English or French is extended to communications with all federal head offices and all other offices "where there is significant demand." Third, New Brunswick becomes Canada's first province in which English and French are official languages, and the right to use both languages is extended to its legislature, provincial courts, and governmental services. Fourth, section 23 establishes a complex set of minority-language education rights. This section gives citizens who are

---

2 *Ottawa Roman Catholic Separate School v. Mackell* (1917), A.C. 62.

3 *Reference Re Bill 30, An Act to Amend the Education Act (Ont.)*, [1987] 1 S.C.R. 1148.

4 For details, see Peter H. Russell, *Constitutional Odyssey: Can Canadians Become a Sovereign People?*, 3rd ed. (Toronto: University of Toronto Press, 2004) at 249.

members of the English-speaking minority in Quebec or the French-speaking minority in the other provinces the right to have their children receive their primary- and secondary-school instruction in the minority language in that province. The minority-language instruction is to be supported by public funds where numbers warrant. A similar numbers-warrant qualification applies to the right to have the instruction provided through "minority language educational facilities."

In interpreting constitutional language rights, the Supreme Court's performance has been virtually the polar opposite of the Judicial Committee's treatment of denominational school rights. With one notable exception, it has given these rights, both the old rights in the *Constitution Act, 1867* and the new rights in the Charter, a broad and liberal interpretation. This trend was evident before the Charter in 1979 when, after decades in which there was virtually no litigation based on the historic language rights, two cases came before the court. *Blaikie*[5] involved a collision between Bill 101, Quebec's *Charter of the French Language*, the most important legislative initiative of Quebec's recently elected Parti Québécois government, and section 133 in the *Constitution Act, 1867*. The other case, *Forest*,[6] involved a challenge, based on Manitoba's equivalent of section 133, to that province's *Official Language Act*, which had been enacted nearly a century earlier, and which had made English the official language of Manitoba.

The Supreme Court vigorously applied the constitutional guarantees in both the 1979 cases. In *Blaikie*, the court held that the provision in section 133 that the acts of Quebec's legislature "shall be printed and published in both English and French" required more than providing an English translation of Quebec's laws. It required that the legislation be actually enacted in both languages so that, contrary to Bill 101, the English version had the same legal status as the French version. Moreover, the court required that not just acts, but all regulations and subordinate legislation be available in English as well as French, and that the right to use both languages in the courts of Quebec apply to all administrative agencies exercising adjudicative responsibilities. The court applied similar guarantees of bilingualism just as vigorously in *Forest*—except that here it was applying them to a regime that had been much more extreme in its unilingualism than Quebec has ever been. The 1890 Manitoba act actually forbade the use of French in the records and journals of the legislature and in court proceedings and provided that acts of the legislature be printed and published in English only. This legislation had remained in force since its enactment—despite several *successful* challenges at the lower-court level. Now it was found to be unconstitutional by Canada's highest court and in an era when judicial decisions, no matter how challenging and counter-majoritarian they may be, cannot simply be ignored.

There was a remarkable sequel to *Forest*. Even with a brigade of translators, 90 years of legislation cannot be translated overnight. Are statutes and regulations that have not been translated into French unconstitutional? In 1985, this question was referred to the Supreme Court in a highly charged political context. In 1983, a referendum in the city of Winnipeg, where over half of Manitoba's population live, resulted in a 4-to-1 majority against proceeding with a constitutional amendment that would give the province time to translate its laws. In the 1985 reference case, the Supreme Court seemed to be between a rock and a hard

---

5   *Att. Gen. of Quebec v. Blaikie et al.*, [1979] 2 S.C.R. 1016.

6   *Attorney General of Manitoba v. Forest*, [1979] 2 S.C.R. 1032.

place.[7] If it ruled that Manitoba's English-only laws were valid, it would make a mockery of its decision in *Forest*. If it made the opposite ruling and rendered nearly the entire provincial statute book null and void, it would plunge the province into the dark sea of legal anarchy. The court's solution was to draw on international experience in upholding the laws of unconstitutional regimes and in order to safeguard the rule of law give temporary validity to the English-only laws while they were being translated into French. "The Constitution," said the court, "will not suffer a province without laws." It gave Manitoba five years to get the job done, and it gave the world a new contribution to constitutional theory.

One of the Supreme Court's very first Charter decisions was the Association of Quebec Protestant School Boards' Charter-based challenge to Quebec's Bill 101.[8] In effect, the case pitted the "Quebec Clause" in Bill 101 against the Charter's "Canada Clause." Sections 72 and 73 of Bill 101 restricted access to publicly funded English-language schools to the children of Anglophone parents already living in Quebec. It was called the "Quebec Clause" because it was designed to stem the growth of English-speaking Quebec. Section 23(1)(*b*) of the Charter gave the right to instruction in English to children of parents who had received their primary education in English outside Quebec and at any time in the future moved to Quebec.[9] It applied in a reciprocal way to French-speaking Quebecers who moved to other provinces. It was called the "Canada Clause" because it was designed to enable English-speaking and French-speaking Canadians to move anywhere in Canada with assurance that their children could be educated in their parents' mother tongue. In a unanimous unsigned *per curiam* decision, the court struck down sections 72 and 73 of Bill 101. It refused to consider the section 1 arguments advanced by Quebec showing demographic data about the decline in the percentage of French speakers in the province. Because the "Quebec Clause," in the judges' view, was a complete denial of the Charter right, it could not be considered as a reasonable limit. In no subsequent case has the court made this distinction between a denial of a right and a limit on a right. Coming on the heels of Quebec's loss in the *Quebec Veto* case,[10] this decision contributed to Quebec's sense of alienation from the rest of Canada and fueled its agitation for constitutional change.

In a trio of cases decided in 1986, the Supreme Court seemed to be applying the brakes to its language-rights express. Two of the cases, one from Quebec[11] and the other from Manitoba,[12] involved challenges to unilingual summonses issued for traffic violations. In both cases, the court's majority rejected the challenge on the ground that section 133 states that English or French "may be used" in any process issuing from a court in these provinces

---

7   *Reference re Manitoba Language Rights*, [1985] 2 S.C.R. 347.

8   *A.G. (Que) v. Quebec Protestant School Boards*, [1984] 2 S.C.R. 66.

9   Section 23(1)(*a*) confers the right to minority-language education to new Canadians whose first language is English or French. As a last minute concession to Quebec, section 59 was added to the *Constitution Act, 1982*, suspending the enforcement of section 23(1)(*a*) until such time as the legislative assembly or government of Quebec brings it into force.

10   *Re: Objection by Quebec to a Resolution to amend the Constitution*, [1982] 2 S.C.R. 793 (the *Quebec Veto* case), available in the instructor's supplements package.

11   *MacDonald v. City of Montreal*, [1986] 1 S.C.R. 460.

12   *Bilodeau v. A.G. (Man.)*, [1986] 1 S.C.R. 449.

so that in this context the minority language is optional, not mandatory. The third case[13] was initiated by New Brunswick Acadians who sought a ruling that their right to use French in New Brunswick's courts implied a right to be understood in French. Again, the court's majority, which included all of the court's francophone justices, rejected the language-rights claim. Justice Beetz's majority opinion recognized that there is a common law right to be heard and understood in court, which, as one aspect of a universal right to a fair hearing, should be interpreted in a broad and liberal way. But, he argued, the language rights in Canada's Constitution are founded on political compromise and should be interpreted narrowly. The development of such a right should be left primarily to legislatures and the political process. Justice Wilson took the opposite view, contending that there was a "principle of growth" in the language-rights provisions of the Constitution and that, if these rights are to be developed to their full potential, courts must go beyond the literal words of these provisions.

The *Mahe* case was the culmination of a struggle by French-speaking minority communities across Canada, in the words of Michael Behiels, to "infuse s. 23 (of the *Charter*) with real power."[14] On the other side of the struggle were provincial governments (five of them were interveners in the case) concerned that their control over education might be diluted by judicial interpretation of the Charter's section 23. The key issue in the case was whether the right to receive instruction in "minority language education facilities" includes the right to control and manage such facilities. The court, in a unanimous opinion written by Chief Justice Dickson, answered this question in the affirmative.

While the case was certainly seen as a victory for the various associations of francophone parents that brought it on, the court did not give them all that they were after. In their submissions, these groups argued that the management and control of minority education facilities required that the direction of such facilities be exercised by an independent francophone school board. Justice Dickson did not think that the number of students likely to attend francophone schools in Edmonton was sufficient to justify such an independent board. It would suffice to guarantee francophone representation on the separate school board and give these representatives full control over all aspects of French-language instruction. He put forward the idea of a sliding scale of entitlement based on the number of children who qualify for minority-language education as the methodology for applying section 23(3). One additional point that he granted to the francophone parents was to hold that an Alberta education regulation requiring no less than 300 minutes per week of instruction in the English language in all schools, including francophone schools, infringed section 23 and was invalid until and unless such a limitation was justified under section 1 of the Charter.

Three years later, in *Reference re Public School Act (Man.), s. 79(3), (4) and (7)*,[15] the Supreme Court struck down Manitoba legislation respecting French-language schools because it made no provision for francophone parents to control and manage French-language

---

13   *Société des Acadiens v. Association of Parents*, [1986] 1 S.C.R. 549.

14   Michael D. Behiels, *Canada's Francophone Minority Communities: Constitutional Renewal and the Winning of School Governance* (Montreal and Kingston: McGill-Queen's University Press, 2004) at 169.

15   [1993] 1 S.C.R. 839.

education. In a 2000 case, the court ruled that Prince Edward Island must provide a school in the community of Summerside for the 49 students enrolled there for French-language education, rather than bus those students to a French-language school 28 kilometres away.[16] The court's liberal and vigorous treatment of the Charter's language of education rights has certainly qualified the province's exclusive jurisdiction over education much more than the denominational education rights in section 93 ever did. Indeed, this may be the Charter's most significant impact on the federal division of powers. ∿

Discussion Questions

1. Do you agree with the Supreme Court's approach to the issue of "where numbers warrant"?

2. Which side of the following judicial debates is more persuasive? (1) Language rights in Canada's Constitution are founded on political compromise and should be interpreted narrowly, where the development of the right should be left primarily to legislatures and the political process, or (2) a "principle of growth" should guide judicial approaches, and thus if these rights are to be developed to their full potential, courts must go beyond the literal words of these provisions.

---

16 *Arsenault-Cameron v. Prince Edward Island*, 2000 SCC 1, [2000] 1 S.C.R. 3.

MAHE v. ALBERTA
[1990] 1 S.C.R. 342

Hearing: June 14, 1989; Judgment: March 15, 1990.

Present: Dickson C.J. and Wilson, La Forest, L'Heureux-Dubé, Sopinka, Gonthier, and Cory JJ.

Interveners: The Attorney General of Canada, the Attorney General for Ontario, the Attorney General of Quebec, the Attorney General for New Brunswick, the Attorney General of Manitoba, the Attorney General of Manitoba, the Attorney General for Saskatchewan, the Association canadienne-française de l'Alberta, the Commissioner of Official Languages for Canada, Alliance Quebec, Alliance for Languages Communities in Quebec, the Association canadienne-française de l'Ontario, the Association française des conseils scolaires de l'Ontario, the Association des enseignantes et des enseignantes franco-ontariens, the Quebec Association of Protestant School Boards, the Edmonton Roman Catholic Separate School District No. 7, and the Alberta School Trustees' Association.

The judgment of the Court was delivered by

THE CHIEF JUSTICE: In this appeal the Court is asked to determine whether the educational system in the city of Edmonton satisfies the demands of s. 23 of the *Canadian Charter of Rights and Freedoms*. ...

Section 23 is one component in Canada's constitutional protection of the official languages. The section is especially important in this regard, however, because of the vital role of education in preserving and encouraging linguistic and cultural vitality. It thus represents a linchpin in this nation's commitment to the values of bilingualism and biculturalism. ...

Constitutional Questions

The following constitutional questions, stated by order of the Court, indicate the range of the issues which this appeal raises:

1. Have the rights of the linguistic minority population in metropolitan Edmonton to minority language educational facilities pursuant to s. 23(3)(*b*) of the *Canadian Charter of Rights and Freedoms* been infringed or denied?

2. Does the right to minority language instruction and educational facilities pursuant to s. 23(3)(*a*) and s. 23(3)(*b*) of the *Charter* include management and control by the minority of:
   (a) the instruction?
   (b) the educational facilities?
      If so, what is the nature and extent of such management and control?

3. (a) Are the *School Act*, R.S.A. 1980, c. S-3, and the regulations passed thereunder inconsistent with or in contravention of s. 23 of the *Charter*?

   (b) If so, is such inconsistency or contravention justified under s. 1 of the *Charter*?

4. Are the rights guaranteed by s. 23 of the *Charter* affected by the provisions of s. 93 of the *Constitution Act, 1867*, s. 29 of the *Charter* and s. 17 of the *Alberta Act*? If so, how?

The Parties and Interveners

The appellants Jean-Claude Mahe and Paul Dubé are parents whose first language learned and still understood is French. The appellant Angeline Martel is a parent who received her primary school instruction in French. All three have school age children, and thus qualify under s. 23(1) of the *Charter* as persons who, subject to certain limitations, "have the right to have their children receive primary and secondary school instruction" in the language of the linguistic minority population of the province—in this case, the French language. They may therefore conveniently be called "s. 23 parents," and their children "s. 23 students." The fourth appellant, the Association de l'école Georges et Julia Bugnet, is an incorporated society whose prime objective is the encouragement of French language education in the province of Alberta. ...

Facts

The appellants were and still are dissatisfied with the provision of French language education in Alberta, particularly in Edmonton. In 1982 they forwarded a proposal to the Minister of Education of Alberta for a new French-language public elementary school in Edmonton, which would have the following features: (1) it would instruct Francophone children exclusively in the French language and in a totally "French" environment; (2) it would be administered by a Committee of Parents under the structure of an autonomous French School Board; and (3) it would have a programme reflecting the French linguistic culture.

The appellants were advised that it was a policy of the Province, acting through the Department of Education, to *not* create any French school jurisdictions. The appellants were encouraged to take their proposal to either the Edmonton Roman Catholic Separate School Board or to the Edmonton Public School Board. The appellants did this, but both Boards rejected their proposal. The Roman Catholic Separate School Board did decide to conduct a study with respect to whether the needs of Francophone students in Edmonton were being met. As a result of that study, in June of 1983 the Roman Catholic Separate School Board directed that a Francophone school, École Maurice Lavallée, be established

in September of 1984 under the direction of the Edmonton Roman Catholic Separate School District No. 7. ...

At École Maurice Lavallée, French is the language of instruction and administration, the personnel are all Francophone, and the stated aim of the school is "to primarily reflect the cultural heritage of the French linguistic minority in Alberta." The government emphasized in its argument that the school is not a French immersion school. The respondent also pointed out that non-residents are granted admission to the school if they qualify under s. 23 of the *Charter* and that the school has a Parent Advisory Committee which is incorporated pursuant to the *Societies Act*, R.S.A. 1980, c. S-18, and which acts as an advisory body to the Board of Trustees.

As a result of the failure of the government to accede to all of their requests, the appellants commenced the action which has culminated in the present appeal. ...

At the heart of this appeal is the claim of the appellants that the term "minority language educational facilities" referred to in s. 23(3)(*b*) includes administration by distinct school boards. The respondent takes the position that the word "facilities" means a school building. The respondent submits that the rights of the Francophone minority in metropolitan Edmonton have not been denied because those rights are being met with current Francophone educational facilities. ...

Analysis

The primary issue raised by this appeal is the degree, if any, of "management and control" of a French language school which should be accorded to s. 23 parents in Edmonton. (The phrase "management and control," it should be noted, is not a term of art: it appears to have been introduced in earlier s. 23 cases and has now gained such currency that it was utilized by all the groups in this appeal.) The appellants appear to accept that, with a few exceptions, the government has provided whatever other services or rights might be mandated in Edmonton under s. 23: their fundamental complaint is that they do not have the exclusive management and control of the existing Francophone schools. The other issues raised by the appellants in their statement of claim are either consequent upon or secondary to this primary issue. ...

(1) The Purpose of Section 23

...

In my view the appellants are fully justified in submitting that "history reveals that s. 23 was designed to correct, on a national scale, the progressive erosion of minority official language groups and to give effect to the concept of the 'equal partnership' of the two official language groups in the context of education."

The remedial aspect of s. 23 was indirectly questioned by the respondent and several of the interveners in an argument which they put forward for a "narrow construction" of s. 23. The following statements by Beetz J. in a case dealing with s. 16 of the *Charter*, *Société des Acadiens du Nouveau-Brunswick Inc. v. Association of Parents for Fairness in Education*, [1986] 1 S.C.R. 549, at p. 578, were relied upon in support of this argument:

> Unlike language rights which are based on political compromise, legal rights tend to be seminal in nature because they are rooted in principle. Some of them, such as the one expressed in s. 7 of the *Charter*, are so broad as to call for frequent judicial determination.
>
> Language rights, on the other hand, although some of them have been enlarged and incorporated into the *Charter*, remain nonetheless founded on political compromise.
>
> This essential difference between the two types of rights dictates a distinct judicial approach with respect to each. More particularly, the courts should pause before they decide to act as instruments of change with respect to language rights. This is not to say that language rights provisions are cast in stone and should remain immune altogether from judicial interpretation. But, in my opinion, the courts should approach them with more restraint than they would in construing legal rights.

I do not believe that these words support the proposition that s. 23 should be given a particularly narrow construction, or that its remedial purpose should be ignored. ...
... Beetz J.'s warning that courts should be careful in interpreting language rights is a sound one. Section 23 provides a perfect example of why such caution is advisable. The provision provides for a novel form of legal right, quite different from the type of legal rights which courts have traditionally dealt with. Both its genesis and its form are evidence of the unusual nature of s. 23. Section 23 confers upon a group a right which places positive obligations on government to alter or develop major institutional structures. Careful interpretation of such a section is wise: however, this does not mean that courts should not "breathe life" into the expressed purpose of the section, or avoid implementing the possibly novel remedies needed to achieve that purpose.

(2) The Context of Section 23(3)(b): An Overview of Section 23

The proper way of interpreting s. 23, in my opinion, is to view the section as providing a general right to minority language instruction. Paragraphs (*a*) and (*b*) of subs. (3) qualify this general right: para. (*a*) adds that the right to instruction is only guaranteed where the "number of children" warrants, while para. (*b*) further qualifies the general right to instruction by adding that where numbers warrant it includes a right to "minority language educational facilities." In my view, subs. (3)(*b*) is included in order to indicate the upper range of possible institutional requirements which may be mandated by s. 23 (the government may, of course, provide more than the minimum required by s. 23).

Another way of expressing the above interpretation of s. 23 is to say that s. 23 should be viewed as encompassing a "sliding scale" of requirement, with subs. (3)(*b*) indicating the upper level of this range and the term "instruction" in subs. (3)(*a*) indicating the lower level. ...

The sliding scale approach can be contrasted with that which views s. 23 as only encompassing two rights—one with respect to instruction and one with respect to facilities—each providing a certain level of services appropriate for one of two numerical thresholds. On this interpretation of s. 23, which could be called the "separate rights" approach, a specified number of s. 23 students would trigger a particular level of instruction, while a greater, specified number of students would require, in addition, a particular level of minority language educational facilities. Where the number of students fell between the two threshold numbers, only the lower level of instruction would be required.

The sliding scale approach is preferable to the separate rights approach, not only because it accords with the text of s. 23, but also because it is consistent with the purpose of s. 23. The sliding scale approach ensures that the minority group receives the full amount of protection that its numbers warrant. ...

(4) Management and Control: The Text of Section 23(3)(b)

In my view, the words of s. 23(3)(*b*) are consistent with and supportive of the conclusion that s. 23 mandates, where the numbers warrant, a measure of management and control. ... If the term "minority language educational facilities" is not viewed as encompassing a degree of management and control, then there would not appear to be any purpose in including it in s. 23. This common sense conclusion militates against interpreting "facilities" as a reference to physical structures. Indeed, once the sliding scale approach is accepted it becomes unnecessary to focus too intently upon the word "facilities." Rather, the text of s. 23 supports viewing the entire term "minority language educational facilities" as setting out an upper level of management and control. ...

(6) The Meaning of the Phrase "Management and Control"

...

The appellants argue for a completely independent Francophone school board. Much is to be said in support of this position and indeed it may be said to reflect the ideal. ...

Historically, separate or denominational boards have been the principal bulwarks of minority language education in the absence of any provision for minority representation and authority within public or common school boards. Such independent boards constitute, for the minority, institutions which it can consider its own with all this entails in terms of opportunity of working in its own language and of sharing a common culture, interests and understanding and being afforded the fullest measure of representation and control. These are particularly important in setting overall priorities and responding to the special educational needs of the minority.

In some circumstances an independent Francophone school board is necessary to meet the purpose of s. 23. However, where the number of students enrolled in minority schools is relatively small, the ability of an independent board to fulfill this purpose may be reduced and other approaches may be appropriate whereby the minority is able to identify with the school but has the benefit of participating in a larger organization through representation and a certain exclusive authority within the majority school board. Under these circumstances, such an arrangement avoids the isolation of an independent school district from the physical resources which the majority school district enjoys and facilitates the sharing of resources with the majority board, something which can be crucial for smaller minority schools. By virtue of having a larger student population, it can be expected that the majority board would have greater access to new educational developments and resources. Where the number of s. 23 students is not sufficiently large, a complete isolation of the minority schools would tend to frustrate the purpose of s. 23 because, in the long run, it would contribute to a decline in the status of the minority language group and its educational facilities. Graduates of the minority schools would be less well-prepared (thus hindering career opportunities for the minority) and potential students would be disinclined to enter minority language schools. ...

In my view, the measure of management and control required by s. 23 of the *Charter* may, depending on the numbers of students to be served, warrant an independent school board. Where numbers do not warrant granting this maximum level of management and control, however, they may nonetheless be sufficient to require linguistic minority representation on an existing school board. ...

... I think it should be self-evident that in situations where the above degree of management and control is warranted the quality of education provided to the minority should in principle be on a basis of equality with the majority. ... However,

the specific form of educational system provided to the minority need not be identical to that provided to the majority. The different circumstances under which various schools find themselves, as well as the demands of a minority language education itself, make such a requirement impractical and undesirable. It should be stressed that the funds allocated for the minority language schools must be at least equivalent on a per student basis to the funds allocated to the majority schools. Special circumstances may warrant an allocation for minority language schools that exceeds the per capita allocation for majority schools. I am confident that this will be taken into account not only in the enabling legislation, but in budgetary discussions of the board. ...

... [T]he next step is to determine what degree the numbers in Edmonton warrant granting. Before I approach this task, however, it will be convenient at this point to consider the issue of denominational rights.

(7) Denominational Schools' Rights

Under the terms of s. 29 of the *Charter* any interpretation of s. 23 must be consistent with the rights and privileges of denominational schools. Section 29 reads:

> **29.** Nothing in this *Charter* abrogates or derogates from any rights or privileges guaranteed by or under the Constitution of Canada in respect of denominational, separate or dissentient schools.

The rights of denominational, separate or dissentient schools referred to in s. 29 are generally provided for in s. 93(1) of the *Constitution Act, 1867*:

> **93.** In and for each Province the Legislature may exclusively make Laws in relation to Education, subject and according to the following Provisions:
>
> (1) Nothing in any such Law shall prejudicially affect any Right or Privilege with respect to Denominational Schools which any Class of Persons have by Law in the Province at the Union:

The province of Alberta is governed by a slightly different provision. When Alberta became a province in 1905, it adopted s. 93 of the *British North America Act, 1867* (later renamed the *Constitution Act, 1867*), but with an amendment to s. 93(1). The amendment is set out in s. 17 of the *Alberta Act*:

> Section 93 of the *Constitution Act, 1867*, shall apply to the said province, with the substitution for paragraph (1) of the said section 93, of the following paragraph:
>
> "(1) Nothing in any such law shall prejudicially affect any right or privilege with respect to separate schools which any class of persons have at the date of the passing of this *Act*, under the terms of chapters 29 and 30 of the

Ordinances of the North-west Territories, passed in the year 1901, or with respect to religious instruction in any public or separate school as provided for in the said ordinances." ...

... [T]he powers of management and control which s. 23 would accord to minority language groups under the interpretation proposed would not affect any rights in respect of the denominational aspects of education or related non-denominational aspects. The minority language trustees on a denominational school board who are to be given powers over management and control will be, at the same time, denominational trustees: in such instances, the denominational board is not required to cede powers to a non-denominational group of persons, it is only required to give certain of its members authority over minority language education. The proposed regulation would not remove a denominational board's power to manage and control, or alter its denominational character.

The transfer of the powers in respect of management and control thus amounts to the *regulation* of a non-denominational aspect of education, namely, the language of instruction, a form of regulation which the courts have long held to be valid. ...

(8) The "Numbers Warrant" Provision

What is being considered when a court addresses the "numbers warrant" question—existing demand, potential demand, or something else? The appellants' position was that the *existing* demand for Francophone services is not a reliable indicator of demand because the demand for any service will to some extent follow the provision of that service. The respondent, on the other hand, argued that the courts cannot simply use the total number of *potential* s. 23 students as a gauge, since it is highly unlikely that all of these students will take advantage of a proposed service. ... In my view, the relevant figure for s. 23 purposes is the number of persons who will eventually take advantage of the contemplated programme or facility. It will normally be impossible to know this figure exactly, yet it can be roughly estimated by considering the parameters within which it must fall—the known demand for the service and the total number of persons who potentially could take advantage of the service.

The numbers warrant provision requires, in general, that two factors be taken into account in determining what s. 23 demands: (1) the services appropriate, in pedagogical terms, for the numbers of students involved; and (2) the cost of the contemplated services. The first, pedagogical requirements, recognizes that a threshold number of students is required before certain programmes or facilities can operate effectively.

There is no point, for example, in having a school for only ten students in an urban centre. ...

Cost, the second factor, is not usually explicitly taken into account in determining whether or not an individual is to be accorded a right under the *Charter*. In the case of s. 23, however, such a consideration is mandated. Section 23 does not, like some other provisions, create an absolute right. Rather, it grants a right which must be subject to financial constraints, for it is financially impractical to accord to every group of minority language students, no matter how small, the same services which a large group of s. 23 students are accorded. I note, however, that in most cases pedagogical requirements will prevent the imposition of unrealistic financial demands upon the state. Moreover, the remedial nature of s. 23 suggests that pedagogical considerations will have more weight than financial requirements in determining whether numbers warrant.

In my view, the phrase "where numbers warrant" does not provide an explicit standard which courts can use to determine the appropriate instruction and facilities (in light of the aforementioned considerations) in every given situation. The standard will have to be worked out over time by examining the particular facts of each situation which comes before the courts, but, in general, the inquiry must be guided by the purpose of s. 23. In particular, the fact that s. 23 is a remedial section is significant, indicating that the section does not aim at merely guaranteeing the status quo.

Thus, a number of complex and subtle factors must be taken into account beyond simply counting the number of students. For example, what is appropriate may differ between rural and urban areas. Another factor to consider is that s. 23 speaks of "wherever in the province" the "numbers warrant." This means that the calculation of the relevant numbers is not restricted to existing school boundaries (although the redrawing of school boundaries will often involve a certain cost which must be taken into account). ...

(9) The Situation in Edmonton

We can now examine the facts underlying this appeal to determine whether s. 23 parents in Edmonton should be accorded a measure of management and control as contemplated by s. 23.

At the time of the trial, there were approximately 2,948 citizens in Edmonton whose first language learned and still understood was French and who, therefore, qualified under s. 23 of the *Charter*. These citizens had approximately 4,127 children from birth to age 19, of whom 3,750 were between five and 19 years of age. The vast majority of these parents were separate school supporters. The enrollment at the existing Francophone school, École Maurice Lavallée was 242 students from kindergarten to grade 6, with room for more. No one has been turned away for lack of space. The capacity of the school is 720 students. At the time of trial there were 315 in attendance, of whom 73 were in grades 7 and 8 immersion programme.

It does not appear that any financial or pedagogical problems have accompanied the operation of the existing Francophone school, École Maurice Lavallée. In view of the substantial numbers of students involved I do not think that such problems would be likely. It is, no doubt, slightly more expensive on a per student basis to operate a school with 242 students as compared to a school with 1,000 students. However, the remedial nature of s. 23 means that such differences in cost, if not unreasonable, must be accepted. It seems clear that even at the present level of demand, there are sufficient students to justify in both pedagogical and financial terms the creation of an independent school, such as the one presently existing as well as providing for a continuing course of primary and secondary schooling. A recognition of this fact appeared to be common ground between all of the parties involved in this appeal, as well as by both of the Alberta courts.

Having established that the existing Francophone school in Edmonton is required in order to comply with s. 23, I believe it is reasonable to require, in addition, that the minority language parents enjoy the right to representation on the separate school board and the degree of management and control that this entails (as specified above). ... Because a Francophone school already exists in Edmonton, the pedagogical and financial effects of granting management and control in the case at hand are not likely to be great. ...

In Edmonton there were approximately 116,788 students enrolled in the public and separate school systems in some nine school jurisdictions. Five of these districts had less than 5,000 students (specifically, the numbers of students in these districts were 4,187, 3,043, 2,600, 758, and 381).

... Overall, I think it clear that the numbers described above show that requiring a Francophone school, together with a degree of management and control to the parents, is, in respect of a group of students who, at a minimum, number at least 242, a reasonable requirement. At the same time, I am not satisfied on the basis of present evidence that it has been established that numbers of students likely to attend Francophone schools in Edmonton are sufficient to mandate under s. 23 the establishment of an independent Francophone school board. ... If actual experience reveals a larger than anticipated demand, however, it may be necessary to reconsider whether the appropriate degree of management and control mandates the establishment of an independent minority language school board.

To conclude: the numbers of minority language students in Edmonton warrant as a minimum the provision of s. 23 rights by way of minority language representation on school boards administering minority language schools in the manner and with the authority above described. These rights are not provided at the present time. The Province must enact legislation (and regulations, if necessary) that are in all respects consistent with the provisions of s. 23 of the *Charter*.

Remedies

...

... There are several factors to consider when deciding whether this situation should lead to a declaration of invalidity.

First, the effect of a declaration of invalidity should be considered. In this case, as it is impossible for the Court to rewrite the impugned legislation, the result of a declaration of invalidity would be to create a legislative vacuum. This result would not help the position of the appellants. Indeed, the appellants might be worse off, because if the above legislation is invalidated the public authorities in Alberta would presumably be temporarily precluded from exercising their powers so as to change the existing system in order to comply with s. 23.

The second factor is that the right which the appellants possess under s. 23 is not a right to any particular legislative scheme, it is a right to a certain type of educational system. What is significant under s. 23 is that the appellants receive the appropriate services and powers; how they receive these services and powers is not directly at issue in determining if the appellants have been accorded their s. 23 rights. ... [I]t is not clear that the existing legislation in Alberta is a bar to the realization of the appellants' rights. The real obstacle is the inaction of the public authorities. The government could implement a scheme within the existing legislation to ensure that these s. 23 parents and other s. 23 parents in the province receive what is due to them. The problem is that they have not done so.

For these reasons I think it best if the Court restricts itself in this appeal to making a declaration in respect of the concrete rights which are due to the minority language parents in Edmonton under s. 23. ... The government should have the widest possible discretion in selection the institutional means by which its s. 23 obligations are to be met .... To date, the legislature of Alberta has failed to discharge that obligation. It must delay no longer in putting into place the appropriate minority language education scheme. ...

Regulation 490/82 ... mandates that a minimum of approximately 20 per cent of class time be spent on English language education. ... In their statement of claim the appellants asked for a declaration to the effect that 100 per cent of their children's instruction should be in French. The appellants' position is that the regulation directly contradicts s. 23. I agree that Regulation 490/82 may impede the achievement of the purpose of s. 23. The appellants' rights under s. 23 include a general right for their children to be instructed entirely in the French language. However, by virtue of s. 1 of the *Charter*, "reasonable" limitations of *Charter* rights are permitted. Both of the Alberta courts held that if Regulation 490/82 does in fact infringe s. 23, it could nevertheless be upheld as a reasonable limitation on s. 23 rights. In support of this finding they referred to evidence that a knowledge of English is required for any student in Alberta.

I am prepared to agree with the Alberta courts that a certain amount of mandatory English language instruction is a reasonable limitation on s. 23. It seems indisputable that some English language education is important for all students in Alberta. It is not self-evident, however, that a full 300 minutes a week of English instruction is necessary in Francophone schools. It is for the respondent to prove that this limit infringes the s. 23 right no more than is necessary, and in the absence of such a demonstration I conclude that the Regulation is not saved by s. 1. This conclusion does not, of course, preclude the respondent from attempting in the future to prove that some mandatory English instruction, perhaps even 300 minutes per week, is a reasonable limit under s. 1.

Conclusion

In order to comply with s. 23 of the Charter, minority language parents in Edmonton should be granted management and control over minority language instruction and facilities in Edmonton in accordance with the following principles:

(1) The representation of the linguistic minority on local boards or other public authorities which administer minority language instruction or facilities should be guaranteed;

(2) The number of minority language representatives on the board should be, at a minimum, proportional to the number of minority language students in the school district, i.e., the number of minority language students for whom the board is responsible;

(3) The minority language representatives should have exclusive authority to make decisions relating to the minority language instruction and facilities, including:

    (a) expenditures of funds provided for such instruction and facilities;

    (b) appointment and direction of those responsible for the administration of such instruction and facilities;

    (c) establishment of programs of instruction;

    (d) recruitment and assignment of teachers and other personnel; and

    (e) making of agreements for education and services for minority language pupils.

To the above declaration I add that, as I explained earlier, the quality of education provided to the minority language group in Edmonton should be on a basis of reasonable equality with the majority, although it need not be identical, and public funding adequate for this purpose must be provided.

32 Doucet-Boudreau v. Nova Scotia, 2003

Having found Nova Scotia in violation of its constitutional duty to provide minority language education, the trial judge in this case directed the creation of new facilities and programs by a specified date. He also retained jurisdiction over the case to monitor the government's compliance with his order. Was this retention of jurisdiction an appropriate judicial function or did it encroach on public administration, thus breaching the constitutional separation of powers? The Supreme Court divided 5-to-4 in answering this question. Although a variety of other issues were considered,[1] the excerpts below focus on this central disagreement.

Both sides agreed that Canada had a separation of powers between the executive, legislative, and judicial branches of government. It was not a "watertight" separation;[2] the boundaries were often "blurred." They were not so blurred as to be non-existent, however, and it remained important not to overstep them. This meant, wrote Justices Iacobucci and Arbour for the five-judge majority, that "courts must be sensitive to their role as judicial arbiters and not fashion remedies which usurp the role of the other branches of governance by taking on tasks to which other persons or bodies are better suited." On behalf of the four dissenters, Justices LeBel and Deschamps said that courts should avoid "administrative functions that properly lie in the sphere of the executive," because the "judiciary is ill equipped to make polycentric choices or to evaluate the wide-ranging consequences that flow from policy implementation." The boundary was sketched out by both opinions in remarkably similar language; had the trial judge's retention of jurisdiction transgressed it? Here the two sides parted company, with the majority finding that Justice LeBlanc had appropriately "encourage[d] the Province's prompt construction of school facilities, without drawing the court outside its proper role," while the dissenters thought he had illegitimately "intervene[d] … in matters of administration properly entrusted to the executive."

Part of the disagreement concerned the availability of more traditionally judicial alternatives to a trial judge retaining jurisdiction. "If the claimants felt that the government was not complying with any part of the order," wrote the dissenters, "then they could have

---

1 For example, the court elected to decide the appeal even though it had become moot because "the schools at issue have been built" (*Doucet-Boudreau*, para. 17). It also considered whether the trial judge's order was too vague to be fair.

2 The idea of a "watertight" separation of powers is something of a red herring. Even the stronger U.S. separation of powers has, from the beginning (and by intention), involved what James Madison called the "partial agency" of the branches in each other's affairs. See Dennis Baker, *Not Quite Supreme: The Courts and Coordinate Constitutional Interpretation* (Montreal & Kingston: McGill-Queen's University Press, 2010), especially ch. 4. Baker's book contains an extensive discussion of *Doucet-Boudreau* in ch. 7.

brought an application for contempt." This did not impress the majority, which argued that contempt proceedings, while certainly available, would not as effectively reduce "the risk that the minority language education rights would be smothered in additional procedural delay." The dissenters replied that "expedited applications are possible" in contempt proceedings. They also worried that if the point of retaining jurisdiction was mainly to allow the trial judge to "hold 'the Province's feet to the fire,'" this was an essentially political rather than judicial function. The two sides obviously engaged directly and vigorously with each other's arguments; their point–counterpoint debate repays close attention. ∼

Discussion Questions

1. Does the judicial disagreement in this case have anything in common with the disagreement in *Saskatchewan Federation of Labour* (see case 11)?

2. Does it matter whether the trial judge retained jurisdiction to make further judicial orders if needed, or only to put persuasive pressure on the government?

DOUCET-BOUDREAU v. NOVA SCOTIA (MINISTER OF EDUCATION)
2003 SCC 62, [2003] 3 S.C.R. 3

Hearing: October 4, 2002; Judgment: November 6, 2003.

Present: McLachlin C.J. and Gonthier, Iacobucci, Major, Bastarache, Binnie, Arbour, LeBel, and Deschamps JJ.

Interveners: Attorney General of Canada, Attorney General of Ontario, Attorney General of New Brunswick, Attorney General of Newfoundland and Labrador, Commissioner of Official Languages for Canada, Fédération nationale des conseillères et conseillers scolaires francophones, Fédération des associations de juristes d'expression française de Common Law Inc. (FAJEFCL) and Conseil scolaire acadien provincial (CSAP).

The judgment of McLachlin C.J. and Gonthier, Iacobucci, Bastarache, and Arbour JJ. was delivered by

IACOBUCCI AND ARBOUR JJ.:

[1] This appeal involves the nature of remedies available under s. 24(1) of the *Canadian Charter of Rights and Freedoms* for the realization of the minority language education rights protected by s. 23 of the *Charter*. The specific issue is whether a trial judge may, after ordering that a provincial government use its best efforts to build French-language school facilities by given dates, retain jurisdiction to hear reports on the progress of those efforts. ...

[4] It is conceded in this appeal that s. 23 of the *Charter* entitles the appellant parents to publicly funded French-language educational facilities for their children. For some

time, Francophone parents in ... Nova Scotia had been urging their provincial government to provide homogeneous French-language schools at the secondary level in addition to the existing primary level facilities. The government of Nova Scotia, for its part, agreed: it did not dispute that the number of students warranted the facilities demanded. The government amended the *Education Act*, S.N.S. 1995-96, c. 1, ss. 11-16, in 1996 to create the Conseil scolaire acadien provincial (the "Conseil"), a province-wide French-language school board, with a view to realizing the *Charter's* minority language education rights. However, while s. 11(1) empowered the Conseil to deliver and administer all French-language programs, only the Minister, with the approval of the Governor in Council, could construct, furnish and equip schools (see s. 88(1)). Although the government eventually announced the construction of the new French-language school facilities, construction of the promised schools never began. So in 1998, 16 years after the right was entrenched in the Constitution, the appellant parents applied to the Supreme Court of Nova Scotia for an order directing the Province and the Conseil to provide, out of public funds, homogeneous French-language facilities and programs at the secondary school level. ...

[7] [The trial judge] LeBlanc J. considered the state of school programs and facilities, including the progress that had already been made toward complying with s. 23 of the *Charter* .... . He directed the Province, which, through the Department of Education, is responsible for providing school facilities, and the Conseil, which is responsible for program provision, to build schools and provide programs by more and less specific deadlines. LeBlanc J. required that the

respondents use their "best efforts" to comply with his order. Finally, he retained jurisdiction to hear reports from the respondents on their compliance. ...

[8] ... LeBlanc J. presided over several of these "reporting hearings" between July 27, 2000, and March 23, 2001. Prior to each reporting session the trial judge directed the Province to file an affidavit from the appropriate official at the Department of Education, setting out the Department's progress in complying with the trial judge's decision. The trial judge permitted the respondent and Conseil to adduce evidence, including rebuttal evidence on various matters relating to compliance with the best efforts order. The Attorney General of Nova Scotia, on behalf of the Department of Education, appealed the part of the order in which LeBlanc J. retained his jurisdiction to hear reports. ...

[14] LeBlanc J.'s order was designed to remedy a breach of s. 23 of the *Charter* which provides:

23.(1) Citizens of Canada

(*a*) whose first language learned and still understood is that of the English or French linguistic minority population of the province in which they reside, or

(*b*) who have received their primary school instruction in Canada in English or French and reside in a province where the language in which they received that instruction is the language of the English or French linguistic minority population of the province,

have the right to have their children receive primary and secondary school instruction in that language in that province.

(2) Citizens of Canada of whom any child has received or is receiving primary or secondary school instruction in English or French in Canada, have the right to have all their children receive primary and secondary school instruction in the same language.

(3) The right of citizens of Canada under subsections (1) and (2) to have their children receive primary and secondary school instruction in the language of the English or French linguistic minority population of a province

(*a*) applies wherever in the province the number of children of citizens who have such a right is sufficient to warrant the provision to them out of public funds of minority language instruction; and

(*b*) includes, where the number of those children so warrants, the right to have them receive that instruction in minority language educational facilities provided out of public funds.

[15] LeBlanc J. ordered the remedy challenged in this case pursuant to s. 24(1) of the *Charter* which provides:

24.(1) Anyone whose rights or freedoms, as guaranteed by this Charter, have been infringed or denied may apply to a court of competent jurisdiction to obtain such remedy as the court considers appropriate and just in the circumstances. ...

[28] The minority language education rights protected under s. 23 of the *Charter* are unique. They are distinctively Canadian, representing "a linchpin in this nation's commitment to the values of bilingualism and biculturalism" (*Mahe* [*v. Alberta*, [1990] 1 S.C.R. 342], at p. 350). Section 23 places positive obligations on governments to mobilize resources and enact legislation for the development of major institutional structures (*Mahe*, at p. 389). While the rights are granted to individuals (*Schools Reference* [*Reference re Public Schools Act (Man.)*, s. 79(3), (4) and (7), [1993] 1 S.C.R. 839], at p. 865), they apply only if the "numbers warrant," and the specific programs or facilities that the government is required to provide varies depending on the number of students who can potentially be expected to participate (*Mahe, supra*, at p. 366; *Schools Reference, supra*, at p. 850; *Arsenault-Cameron* [*v. Prince Edward Island*, [2000] 1 S.C.R. 3], at para. 38). This requirement gives the exercise of minority language education rights a unique collective aspect even though the rights are granted to individuals.

[29] Another distinctive feature of the right in s. 23 is that the "numbers warrant" requirement leaves minority language education rights particularly vulnerable to government delay or inaction. For every school year that governments do not meet their obligations under s. 23, there is an increased likelihood of assimilation which carries the risk that numbers might cease to "warrant." Thus, particular entitlements afforded under s. 23 can be suspended, for so long as the numbers cease to warrant, by the very cultural erosion against which s. 23 was designed to guard. In practical, though not legal, terms, such suspensions may well be permanent. If delay is tolerated, governments could potentially avoid the duties imposed upon them by s. 23 through their own failure to implement the rights vigilantly. The affirmative promise contained in s. 23 of the *Charter* and the critical need for timely compliance will sometimes require courts to order affirmative remedies to guarantee that language rights are meaningfully, and therefore necessarily promptly, protected. ...

[32] Fortunately, Canada has had a remarkable history of compliance with court decisions by private parties and by all institutions of government. That history of compliance has become a fundamentally cherished value of our constitutional democracy; we must never take it for granted but always be careful to respect and protect its importance, otherwise the seeds of tyranny can take root.

[33] This tradition of compliance takes on a particular significance in the constitutional law context, where courts must ensure that government behaviour conforms with constitutional norms but in doing so must also be sensitive to the separation of function among the legislative, judicial and executive branches. While our Constitution does not expressly provide for the separation of powers (see *Re Residential Tenancies Act, 1979*, [1981] 1 S.C.R. 714, at p. 728; *Douglas/Kwantlen Faculty Assn. v. Douglas College*, [1990] 3 S.C.R. 570, at p. 601; *Reference re Secession of Quebec*, [1998] 2 S.C.R. 217, at para. 15), the functional separation among the executive, legislative and judicial branches of governance has frequently been noted. (See, for example, *Fraser v. Public Service Staff Relations Board*, [1985] 2 S.C.R. 455, at pp. 469-70.) In *New Brunswick Broadcasting Co. v. Nova Scotia (Speaker of the House of Assembly)*, [1993] 1 S.C.R. 319, McLachlin J. (as she then was) stated, at p. 389:

> Our democratic government consists of several branches: the Crown, as represented by the Governor General and the provincial counterparts of that office; the legislative body; the executive; and the courts. It is fundamental to the working of government as a whole that all these parts play their proper role. It is equally fundamental that no one of them overstep its bounds, that each show proper deference for the legitimate sphere of activity of the other.

[34] In other words, in the context of constitutional remedies, courts must be sensitive to their role as judicial arbiters and not fashion remedies which usurp the role of the other branches of governance by taking on tasks to which other persons or bodies are better suited. Concern for the limits of the judicial role is interwoven throughout the law. The development of the doctrines of justiciability, and to a great extent mootness, standing, and ripeness resulted from concerns about the courts overstepping the bounds of the judicial function and their role *vis-à-vis* other branches of government.

[35] In addition, it is unsurprising, given how the *Charter* changed the nature of our constitutional structure by requiring that all laws and government action conform to the *Charter*, that concerns about the limits of the judicial role have animated much of the *Charter* jurisprudence and commentary surrounding it (see, for example, K. Roach, *The Supreme Court on Trial: Judicial Activism or Democratic Dialogue* (2001); C. P. Manfredi, *Judicial Power and the Charter: Canada and the Paradox of Liberal Constitutionalism* (1993); F. L. Morton and R. Knopff, *The Charter Revolution and the Court Party* (2000); A. Petter, "The Politics of the Charter" (1986), 8 *Supreme Court L.R.* 473). Thus, in *Vriend*, [*v. Alberta*, [1998] 1 S.C.R. 493], this Court stated, at para. 136:

In carrying out their duties, courts are not to second-guess legislatures and the executives; they are not to make value judgments on what they regard as the proper policy choice; this is for the other branches. Rather, the courts are to uphold the Constitution and have been expressly invited to perform that role by the Constitution itself. But respect by the courts for the legislature and executive role is as important as ensuring that the other branches respect each others' role and the role of the courts.

[36] Deference ends, however, where the constitutional rights that the courts are charged with protecting begin. As McLachlin J. stated in *RJR-MacDonald Inc. v. Canada (Attorney General)*, [1995] 3 S.C.R. 199, at para. 136:

> Parliament has its role: to choose the appropriate response to social problems within the limiting framework of the Constitution. But the courts also have a role: to determine, objectively and impartially, whether Parliament's choice falls within the limiting framework of the Constitution. The courts are no more permitted to abdicate their responsibility than is Parliament.

Determining the boundaries of the courts' proper role, however, cannot be reduced to a simple test or formula; it will vary according to the right at issue and the context of each case.

[37] Returning to this appeal, we believe that LeBlanc J. was duly guided by historical and contextual factors in crafting a remedy that would meaningfully protect, indeed implement, the applicants' rights to minority official language education for their children while maintaining appropriate respect for the proper roles of the executive and legislative branches. ...

[43] A remedy under s. 24(1) is available where there is some government action, beyond the enactment of an unconstitutional statute or provision, that infringes a person's *Charter* rights (see *Schachter v. Canada*, [1992] 2 S.C.R. 679, at pp. 719-20). In the present appeal, the difficulty does not lie with the legislation: no provision or omission in the *Education Act* prevented the government from providing minority language education as required by the *Constitution Act, 1982*. On the contrary, the *Education Act*, as amended in 1996, establishes a French-language school board to provide homogeneous French-language education to children of s. 23 entitled parents. Neither is the problem rooted in any particular government action; rather, the problem was *inaction* on the part of the provincial government, particularly its failure to mobilize resources to provide school facilities in a timely fashion, as required by s. 23 of the *Charter*. Section 24(1) is available to remedy this failure.

[44] To repeat its text, s. 24(1) of the *Charter* provides:

> Anyone whose rights or freedoms, as guaranteed by this Charter, have been infringed or denied may apply

to a court of competent jurisdiction to obtain such remedy as the court considers appropriate and just in the circumstances. ...

[52] What, then, is meant in s. 24(1) by the words "appropriate and just in the circumstances"? Clearly, the task of giving these words meaning in particular cases will fall to the courts ordering the remedies since s. 24(1) specifies that the remedy should be such as *the court considers* appropriate and just. Deciding on an appropriate and just remedy in particular circumstances calls on the judge to exercise a discretion based on his or her careful perception of the nature of the right and of the infringement, the facts of the case, and the application of the relevant legal principles. ...

[54] While it would be unwise at this point to attempt to define, in detail, the words "appropriate and just" or to draw a rigid distinction between the two terms, there are some broad considerations that judges should bear in mind when evaluating the appropriateness and justice of a potential remedy. These general principles may be informed by jurisprudence relating to remedies outside the *Charter* context, such as cases discussing the doctrine of *functus* and overly vague remedies, although, as we have said, that jurisprudence does not apply strictly to orders made under s. 24(1).

[55] First, an appropriate and just remedy in the circumstances of a *Charter* claim is one that meaningfully vindicates the rights and freedoms of the claimants. Naturally, this will take account of the nature of the right that has been violated and the situation of the claimant. A meaningful remedy must be relevant to the experience of the claimant and must address the circumstances in which the right was infringed or denied. An ineffective remedy, or one which was "smothered in procedural delays and difficulties," is not a meaningful vindication of the right and therefore not appropriate and just (see *Dunedin* [*R. v. 974649 Ontario Inc.*, [2001] 3 S.C.R. 575], at para. 20, McLachlin C.J. citing *Mills* [*v. The Queen*, [1986] 1 S.C.R. 863], at p. 882, *per* Lamer J. (as he then was)).

[56] Second, an appropriate and just remedy must employ means that are legitimate within the framework of our constitutional democracy. As discussed above, a court ordering a *Charter* remedy must strive to respect the relationships with and separation of functions among the legislature, the executive and the judiciary. This is not to say that there is a bright line separating these functions in all cases. A remedy may be appropriate and just notwithstanding that it might touch on functions that are principally assigned to the executive. The essential point is that the courts must not, in making orders under s. 24(1), depart unduly or unnecessarily from their role of adjudicating disputes and granting remedies that address the matter of those disputes.

[57] Third, an appropriate and just remedy is a judicial one which vindicates the right while invoking the function and powers of a court. It will not be appropriate for a court to leap into the kinds of decisions and functions for which its design and expertise are manifestly unsuited. The capacities and competence of courts can be inferred, in part, from the tasks with which they are normally charged and for which they have developed procedures and precedent.

[58] Fourth, an appropriate and just remedy is one that, after ensuring that the right of the claimant is fully vindicated, is also fair to the party against whom the order is made. The remedy should not impose substantial hardships that are unrelated to securing the right.

[59] Finally, it must be remembered that s. 24 is part of a constitutional scheme for the vindication of fundamental rights and freedoms enshrined in the *Charter*. As such, s. 24, because of its broad language and the myriad of roles it may play in cases, should be allowed to evolve to meet the challenges and circumstances of those cases. That evolution may require novel and creative features when compared to traditional and historical remedial practice because tradition and history cannot be barriers to what reasoned and compelling notions of appropriate and just remedies demand. In short, the judicial approach to remedies must remain flexible and responsive to the needs of a given case. ...

[64] Our colleagues LeBel and Deschamps JJ. state at para. 140 of their reasons that the trial judge was not faced with a government which had understood its obligations but refused to comply with them. Our colleagues suggest that there was some issue as to what s. 23 demanded in the situation. With respect, this portrayal is directly at odds with the findings of fact made by the trial judge. ...

[65] ... According to the trial judge, the government did not deny the existence or content of the s. 23 rights of the parents but rather failed to prioritize those rights and delayed fulfilling its obligations. The government "did not give sufficient priority to the serious rate of assimilation occurring among Acadians and Francophones in Nova Scotia and the fact that rights established in s. 23 are individual rights" (para. 204) despite clear reports showing that assimilation was "reaching critical levels" (para. 215). These are the findings of fact which can only be made by a judge who has heard all the evidence at trial. These findings are not on appeal and it is not open for appellate judges to reverse these findings without proper justification. LeBlanc J. properly took account of the factual circumstances within which he exercised his discretion to select a remedy which was appropriate and just. ...

[67] Our colleagues LeBel and Deschamps JJ. suggest that the reporting order in this case was not called for since any violation of a simple declaratory remedy could be dealt with

in contempt proceedings against the Crown. We do not doubt that contempt proceedings may be available in appropriate cases. The threat of contempt proceedings is not, in our view, inherently more respectful of the executive than simple reporting hearings in which a linguistic minority could discover in a timely way what progress was being made towards the fulfilment of their s. 23 rights. More importantly, given the critical rate of assimilation found by the trial judge, it was appropriate for him to grant a remedy that would in his view lead to prompt compliance. Viewed in this light, LeBlanc J. selected a remedy that reduced the risk that the minority language education rights would be smothered in additional procedural delay. ...

[71] Although it may not be common in the context of *Charter* remedies, the reporting order issued by LeBlanc J. was judicial in the sense that it called on the functions and powers known to courts. In several different contexts, courts order remedies that involve their continuing involvement in the relations between the parties (see R. J. Sharpe, *Injunctions and Specific Performance* (2nd ed. (loose-leaf)), at paras. 1.260-1.490). Superior courts, which under the Judicature Acts possess the powers of common law courts and courts of equity, have "assumed active and even managerial roles in the exercise of their traditional equitable powers" (K. Roach, *Constitutional Remedies in Canada* (loose-leaf), at para. 13.60). A panoply of equitable remedies are now available to courts in support of the litigation process and the final adjudication of disputes. For example, prejudgment remedies developed in such cases as *Mareva Compania Naviera S.A. v. International Bulkcarriers S.A.*, [1975] 2 Lloyd's Rep. 509 (C.A.), and *Anton Piller KG v. Manufacturing Processes Ltd.*, [1976] 1 Ch. 55 (C.A.), involve the court in the preservation of evidence and the management of parties' assets prior to trial. In bankruptcy and receivership matters, courts may be called on to supervise fairly complex and ongoing commercial transactions relating to debtors' assets. Court-appointed receivers may report to and seek guidance from the courts and in some cases must seek the permission of the courts before disposing of property (see *Bennett on Receiverships* (2nd ed. 1999), at pp. 21-37, 443-45). Similarly, the courts' jurisdiction in respect of trusts and estates may sometimes entail detailed and continuing supervision and support of their administration (see D. W. M. Waters, *Law of Trusts in Canada* (2nd ed. 1984), at pp. 904-9; *Oosterhoff on Wills and Succession* (5th ed. 2001), at pp. 27-28). Courts may also retain an ongoing jurisdiction in family law cases to order alterations in maintenance payments or parenting arrangements as circumstances change. Finally, this Court has in the past remained seized of a matter so as to facilitate the implementation of constitutional language rights: see *Reference re Manitoba Language Rights*, [1985] 1 S.C.R. 721; *Re Manitoba Language Rights Order*, [1985] 2 S.C.R. 347; *Re Manitoba Language Rights Order*, [1990] 3 S.C.R. 1417; *Reference re Manitoba Language Rights*, [1992] 1 S.C.R. 212. Lower courts have also retained jurisdiction in s. 23 cases: *British Columbia (Association des parents francophones) v. British Columbia* (1996), 139 D.L.R. (4th) 356 (B.C.S.C.), at p. 380; *Lavoie [v. Nova Scotia (Attorney-General) (1988), 47 D.L.R. (4th) 586 (N.S.S.C.)]*, at pp. 593-95; *Société des Acadiens du Nouveau-Brunswick Inc. v. Minority Language School Board No. 50* (1983), 48 N.B.R. (2d) 361 (Q.B.), at para. 109.

[72] The difficulties of ongoing supervision of parties by the courts have sometimes been advanced as a reason that orders for specific performance and mandatory injunctions should not be awarded. Nonetheless, courts of equity have long accepted and overcome this difficulty of supervision where the situations demanded such remedies (see Sharpe, *supra*, at paras. 1.260-1.380; *Attorney-General v. Birmingham, Tame, and Rea District Drainage Board*, [1910] 1 Ch. 48 (C.A.), aff'd [1912] A.C. 788 (H.L.); *Kennard v. Cory Brothers and Co.*, [1922] 1 Ch. 265, aff'd [1922] 2 Ch. 1 (C.A.)).

[73] As academic commentators have pointed out, the range of remedial orders available to courts in civil proceedings demonstrates that constitutional remedies involving some degree of ongoing supervision do not represent a radical break with the past practices of courts (see W. A. Bogart, "'Appropriate and Just': Section 24 of the Canadian Charter of Rights and Freedoms and the Question of Judicial Legitimacy" (1986), 10 *Dalhousie L.J.* 81, at pp. 92-94; N. Gillespie, "Charter Remedies: The Structural Injunction" (1989-90), 11 *Advocates' Q.* 190, at pp. 217-18; Roach, *Constitutional Remedies in Canada*, [(Aurora, Ont.: Canada Law Book, 1994) (loose-leaf updated October 2002, release 9)], at paras. 13.50-13.80; Sharpe, [*Injunctions and Specific Performance*, 2nd ed. (Aurora, Ont.: Canada Law Book, 1992) (loose-leaf updated November 2002, release 10)], at paras. 1.260-1.490). The change announced by s. 24 of the *Charter* is that the flexibility inherent in an equitable remedial jurisdiction may be applied to orders addressed to government to vindicate constitutionally entrenched rights.

[74] The order in this case was in no way inconsistent with the judicial function. There was never any suggestion in this case that the court would, for example, improperly take over the detailed management and co-ordination of the construction projects. Hearing evidence and supervising cross-examinations on progress reports about the construction of schools are not beyond the normal capacities of courts. ...

[87] Section 24(1) of the *Charter* requires that courts issue effective, responsive remedies that guarantee full and meaningful protection of *Charter* rights and freedoms. The meaningful protection of *Charter* rights, and in particular

the enforcement of s. 23 rights, may in some cases require the introduction of novel remedies. A superior court may craft any remedy that it considers appropriate and just in the circumstances. In doing so, courts should be mindful of their roles as constitutional arbiters and the limits of their institutional capacities. Reviewing courts, for their part, must show considerable deference to trial judges' choice of remedy, and should refrain from using hindsight to perfect a remedy. A reviewing court should only interfere where the trial judge has committed an error of law or principle.

[88] The remedy crafted by LeBlanc J. meaningfully vindicated the rights of the appellant parents by encouraging the Province's prompt construction of school facilities, without drawing the court outside its proper role. ...

The reasons of Major, Binnie, LeBel, and Deschamps JJ. were delivered by

LeBEL AND DESCHAMPS JJ. (dissenting):

[91] ... Courts should not unduly encroach on areas which should remain the responsibility of public administration and should avoid turning themselves into managers of the public service. Judicial interventions should end when and where the case of which a judge is seized is brought to a close.

[92] In our respectful view, without putting in any doubt the desire of the trial judge to fashion an effective remedy to address the consequences of a long history of neglect of the rights of the Francophone minority in Nova Scotia, the drafting of his so-called reporting order was seriously flawed. It ... assumed that the judge could retain jurisdiction at will, after he had finally disposed of the matter of which he had been seized, thereby breaching the constitutional principle of separation of powers. ...

[107] ... It is true that Canadians have never adopted a watertight system of separation of judicial, legislative and executive functions. In the discharge of their functions, courts have had to strike down laws, regulations or administrative decisions. They have imposed liability on the Crown or public bodies and have awarded damages against them. Forms of administrative justice or adjudication have grown out of the development of executive functions (*Ocean Port Hotel Ltd. v. British Columbia (General Manager, Liquor Control and Licensing Branch)*, [2001] 2 S.C.R. 781; *Bell Canada v. Canadian Telephone Employees Association*, [2003] 1 S.C.R. 884). Such developments may be said to have blurred theoretical distinctions between government functions. Nevertheless, in a broad sense, a separation of powers is now entrenched as a cornerstone of our constitutional regime. ...

[109] Our Court has strongly emphasized and vigorously applied the principle of separation of powers in order to uphold the independence of the judiciary (see for example: *Provincial Court Judges Reference [Reference re Remuneration of Judges of the Provincial Court of Prince Edward Island*, [1997] 3 S.C.R. 3]; see also *Mackin v. New Brunswick (Minister of Finance)*, [2002] 1 S.C.R. 405). In that context, the principle was viewed as a shield designed to protect the judiciary in order to allow it to discharge its duties under the Constitution with complete independence and impartiality. Nothing less was required to maintain the normative ordering of the Canadian legal system.

[110] However, the principle of separation of powers has an obverse side as well, which equally reflects the appropriate position of the judiciary within the Canadian legal system. Aside from their duties to supervise administrative tribunals created by the executive and to act as vigilant guardians of constitutional rights and the rule of law, courts should, as a general rule, avoid interfering in the management of public administration.

[111] More specifically, once they have rendered judgment, courts should resist the temptation to directly oversee or supervise the administration of their orders. They should generally operate under a presumption that judgments of courts will be executed with reasonable diligence and good faith. Once they have declared what the law is, issued their orders and granted such relief as they think is warranted by circumstances and relevant legal rules, courts should take care not to unnecessarily invade the province of public administration. To do otherwise could upset the balance that has been struck between our three branches of government. ...

[117] ... In our view, if a court intervenes, as here, in matters of administration properly entrusted to the executive, it exceeds its proper sphere and thereby breaches the separation of powers. By crossing the boundary between judicial acts and administrative oversight, it acts illegitimately and without jurisdiction. Such a crossing of the boundary cannot be characterized as relief that is "appropriate and just in the circumstances" within the meaning of s. 24(1) of the *Charter.* ...

[119] ... [T]he trial judge equivocated on the question of whether his purported retention of jurisdiction empowered him to make further orders.

[At paragraph 101, Justices LeBel and Deschamps observe that, at the hearing sessions, Justice LeBlanc initially "appeared to lean towards the view that those hearings were regular sessions of the court, that he had not issued a final order and that additional relief could be requested," but that "at the last hearing ... he commented that he could not grant further relief," and that "the sessions had a solely informational purpose."]

Regardless of which position is taken, the separation of powers was still breached. ...

[120] ... By purporting to be able to make subsequent orders, the trial judge would have assumed a supervisory role which included administrative functions that properly lie in the sphere of the executive. These functions are beyond the capacities of courts. The judiciary is ill equipped to make polycentric choices or to evaluate the wide-ranging consequences that flow from policy implementation. This Court has recognized that courts possess neither the expertise nor the resources to undertake public administration. ...

[125] Thus, if the trial judge's initial suggestion that he could continue to make orders, and thereby effectively engage in administrative supervision and decision making accurately characterizes the nature of the reporting sessions, the order for reporting sessions breached the constitutional principle of separation of powers. ...

[126] If, however, the trial judge's statement in the last session that he could not make further orders correctly characterized his remedial order, then he breached the separation of powers in another way. ...

[127] The appellants argued that the trial judge retained jurisdiction *only* to hear reports, and that these hearings had purely "suasive" value. They also argued that the hearings were designed to hold "the Province's feet to the fire" (SCC hearing transcripts). They further suggested that the threat of having to report to the trial judge functioned as an incentive for the government to comply with the best efforts order. In the words of the appellants:

Is it a coincidence that, after a nine month delay (October 1999 to July 2000) the Province called for tenders eight days before the reporting hearing and "fast tracked" the school? The Province knew that it would have to report on July 27. The Province ensured that a call for tenders and a construction schedule were in place for July 27.

[128] If this characterization of the trial judge's activity is accurate, then the order for reporting sessions did not result in the exercise of adjudicative, or any other, functions that traditionally define the ambit of a court's proper sphere. Moreover, it resulted in activity that can be characterized as political. According to the appellants' characterization, a primary purpose of the hearings was to put public pressure on the government to act. This kind of pressure is paradigmatically associated with political actors. ...

[130] In *Provincial Court Judges Reference, supra*, Lamer C.J. described the separation of powers as providing that "the relationships between the different branches of government should have a particular *character*" (para. 139 (emphasis in original)). In particular, according to him, the

separation of powers doctrine requires that these relationships be *depoliticized* (para. 140 (emphasis in original)).

[131] In that case, Lamer C.J. remarked that the legislature and the executive cannot exert, and cannot appear to exert political pressure on the judiciary (para. 140). The reciprocal proposition applies to the immediate case. With the reporting hearings, the trial judge may have sought to exert political or public pressure on the executive, and at least appeared to do so. In our view, such action would tend to politicize the relationship between the executive and the judiciary.

[132] If the reporting hearings were intended to hold "the Province's feet to the fire," the character of the relationship between the judiciary and the executive was improperly altered and, as per the *Provincial Court Judges Reference*, the constitutional principle of separation of powers was breached. ...

[135] One might argue that such a breach is appropriate where it is the only way that a claimant's rights can be vindicated. Alternatively, one might suggest that if a government has ignored previous, less intrusive judicial measures, and thereby put into question their efficacy, a court might be justified in abandoning the presumption of governmental good will that we referred to above. In our view, the present case gave rise to neither of these arguments.

[136] Turning to the first argument, if the hearings were aimed at ensuring the vindication of the claimants' rights by providing them with the opportunity to enforce or alter the remedy, there were alternatives available. If the claimants felt that the government was not complying with any part of the order, then they could have brought an application for contempt. The majority seems to suggest that contempt proceedings would have been less effective in this case in ensuring timely performance of the order, without being any more respectful of the separation of powers. However, we would note that expedited applications are possible in Nova Scotia and other jurisdictions to deal with cases quickly and efficiently. In addition, the reporting order at issue in this case precluded applying to any other judge for relief and was, in this way, even more limiting than a contempt proceeding. Most importantly, contempt proceedings are more consistent with our adversarial system, which is based on the common law norm of giving the parties primary control over the proceedings (see J. I. H. Jacob, *The Fabric of English Civil Justice* (1987), at p. 13). In contrast, the present order for reporting sessions placed the trial judge in an inappropriate, ongoing supervisory and investigative role despite the availability of the equally effective, well-established, and minimally intrusive alternative of contempt relief.

[137] Consequently, it is clear that the order for reporting hearings was not the only means of vindicating the claimants'

rights, and that recourse to a readily available alternative would have been consistent with a defining feature of our legal system. Recourse to this alternative would not have resulted in an interpretation of the court's remedial powers that was so broad as to purport to endow the court with powers that it was "never intended to exercise" (*Dunedin, supra,* at para. 22). It is important to stress that in the present case, it is not clear that actual recourse to a contempt application would have been necessary. The point is simply that if judicial enforcement of the deadlines in question were necessary, recourse to this alternative would not have overextended the court's powers. ...

[139] The second argument is simply not applicable in this case. The facts here do not require us to decide whether previous government non-compliance can ever justify remedial orders that breach principles of procedural fairness and the separation of powers. The Government of Nova Scotia did not refuse to comply with either a prior remedial order or a declaration with respect to its particular obligations in the fact-situation at hand. No such order was made and it is impossible to determine whether the government would have responded in the present case to either a declaration of rights, or the injunction to meet the deadline as these measures were combined with the order purporting to retain jurisdiction to oversee the reporting sessions. Therefore, it cannot be asserted that the trial judge's order has succeeded where less intrusive remedial measures failed.

[140] Moreover, what was required by the Government of Nova Scotia to comply with its obligations pursuant to s. 23 was not self-evident at trial. The trial judge was not faced with a government which was cognizant of how it should fulfill its obligations, but refused to do so. Indeed, at issue before the trial judge was precisely the question of what compliance with s. 23 involved. The present order, therefore, did not overcome governmental recalcitrance in the face of a clear understanding of what s. 23 required in the circumstances of the case. Remedies must be chosen in light of the nature and structure of the Canadian constitutional order, an important feature of which is the presumption of co-operation between the branches of government. Therefore, unless it is established that this constitutional balance has been upset by the executive's clear defiance of a directly applicable judicial order, increased judicial intervention in public administration will rarely be appropriate. ...

[143] In the present case, refusing superior courts the power to order reporting hearings clearly would not deny claimants' access to a recognized *Charter* remedy, as such an order is entirely idiosyncratic. More importantly, refusing superior courts this power would not deprive claimants of access to that which they are guaranteed by s. 23, namely, the timely provision of minority language instruction facilities. Indeed, if the appellants' characterization of the reporting hearings' purpose is correct, it is difficult to see how they could have been more effective than the construction deadline coupled with the possibility of a contempt order. In our view, the availability of this legal sanction for non-compliance with the order to meet the construction deadline would have provided at least as much incentive for the government to remedy the s. 23 breach as would have reporting hearings, in which the presiding judge was without the power to make further orders. Moreover, at the level of constitutional principle, because this incentive is legal in nature, it would not have led to the improper politicization of the relationship between the judiciary and the executive.

H. REMEDIES

33 R. v. Askov, 1990

Section 11(*b*) of the Charter gives any person charged with a criminal offence the right "to be tried within a reasonable time." This right embodies the fundamental precept that "justice delayed is justice denied." Fundamental as this right is to the criminal justice system, it requires some authority to define the length of time that is reasonable to allow in bringing an accused person to trial. If elected legislators decline to set standards of reasonableness, by default the responsibility for doing so ends up entirely in the hands of the judiciary. That is what has happened in giving guidance on the practical meaning of section 11(*b*) of the Charter. In taking on this responsibility, the courts in effect developed judicial legislation to guide those who administer the justice system. The Supreme Court's decision in *Askov* was a milestone in the Supreme Court of Canada's struggle to establish a coherent set of rules and principles on the right to be tried within a reasonable time.

On November 5, 1983, a police surveillance team apprehended Elijah Anton Askov and three other men who were brandishing a sawed-off shotgun and a knife at Peter Belmont, the operator of an "exotic" dancers service, in an attempt to extort money from him. The four men were charged with conspiracy to commit extortion. Askov and two of the men were held in custody until bail was granted on May 7, 1984. Their preliminary hearing took place on September 21, 1984. It took two more years for their trial to begin, and when it did, on September 2, 1986, their lawyer asked for a stay of proceedings on the ground that the trial had been unreasonably delayed. The trial judge granted the stay, but her order was set aside by the Ontario Court of Appeal. That is the decision the Supreme Court reviewed and reversed in *Askov*.

In *Mills*,[1] the court's first decision on section 11(*b*), rendered in 1986, Chief Justice Dickson and Justice Lamer wrote a lengthy opinion on how courts should interpret the right. But their opinion did not win the support of other justices. In a series of section 11(*b*) cases following *Mills*, the court dealt with various factors to be taken into account in interpreting section 11(*b*). There was general agreement on the need for a flexible approach to the reasonable time requirement. The different degrees of complexity in criminal cases rule out a standard time for all cases. In each case, the cause of delay must be considered—did the delay result from actions or lack of action by the prosecutors, or from delaying tactics of the accused? There was agreement that an accused could waive the right to a speedy trial

---

1 *Mills v. The Queen*, [1986] 1 S.C.R. 863.

but that such a waiver cannot be simply inferred from a failure to complain about delay. But there was a lack of consensus on several other issues. In interpreting the right, what weight should be given to society's interest in seeing accused persons brought to justice quickly and having fair trials that are not jeopardized by witnesses' fading memories? What weight should be given to how much the delay has caused prejudice and hardship to the accused? And—a key issue in *Askov*—how should the institutional resources of the court system be taken into account?

Justice Cory's opinion in *Askov*, concurred in by Chief Justice Dickson, Justices La Forest, L'Heureux-Dubé, and Gonthier, and on most of its main points by Justices Lamer, Wilson, Sopinka, and McLachlin, brought the court much closer to a consensus on the interpretation of section 11(*b*). The justices were in agreement that the cause of the two-year delay between the preliminary hearing and the trial was institutional—a lack of adequate court resources—and that two years was an unreasonable length of time for a delay of this kind. In reaching this conclusion the court relied on the research of Professor Carl Baar, a leading scholar in the field of judicial studies, showing that in Brampton, in Ontario's Peel District where the Askov trial was to be heard, time spent awaiting trial was significantly longer for similar types of cases than in other Canadian and U.S. jurisdictions. Baar described the *Askov* case as representing one of the worst delays in the worst district, not only in Canada but "anywhere north of the Rio Grande." Sifting through the comparative data on time spent awaiting trial, Justice Cory went on to conclude "that a period of delay in a range of some six to eight months between committal and trial might be deemed to be the outside limit of what is reasonable." This conclusion was supported by all nine justices. The court was unanimous in finding that Askov's and his co-accused's right to a trial within a reasonable time had been violated, and that there was no basis on which such a violation could be justified.

The justices were also unanimous in their choice of remedy—they directed a stay of proceedings. This meant that Askov and his co-accused would walk. Justice Cory acknowledged that the charges against the accused were serious and threatening to the community. But the infringement of the accused persons' rights in this case was also serious. In the court's view, any other remedy, such as moving the trial to another venue or recognizing a transitional period to provide time to bolster the system's resources, would render the right to a trial in a reasonable time meaningless.

The *Askov* decision broke like a bombshell on the Ontario government. The government responded on two fronts. It moved rapidly to appoint judges to the Provincial Court. Fortunately, Ontario had a pool of well-qualified candidates selected by its Judicial Appointments Advisory Committee ready for appointment. The decision had the effect of enabling the province's attorney general to secure more funds for the court system.[2] That was the good news. But on the prosecutorial side, the news was shocking. The attorney general announced that thousands of cases in the province's criminal justice system had no chance of meeting the *Askov* time requirement, and would therefore have to be terminated, allowing the accused, many of whom were charged with serious crimes, to go free. Between October 22, 1990 and September 6, 1991, 47,000 charges were stayed. When account is taken of cases

---

2   Peter H. Russell, "Canadian Constraints on Judicialization From Without" (1993) *International Political Science Review* 170. Russell also chaired Ontario's Judicial Appointments Advisory Committee at this time.

in which there were multiple charges, this amounts to the termination of approximately 25,000 criminal cases.[3]

The *Askov* ruling caused considerable consternation for trial judges faced with the challenge of applying it. The ruling indicated that six to eight months was the outside limit for the period from "committal" to trial. Committal in this context means the finding of the preliminary inquiry judge that the prosecution has enough evidence to justify committing the accused to trial. But what about summary conviction cases, where there is no preliminary hearing? And how should the ruling in *Askov* be related to previous cases, which had considered that the relevant period for assessing reasonable time was from the laying of charges to trial? When Justice Cory, at a conference of judges and lawyers in the United Kingdom in August 1991, expressed shock at the rigidity with which the *Askov* rule was being interpreted and surprise at the extent of the decision's impact, Ontario's Attorney General Howard Hampton called for a review of the decision.[4]

Ontario's Attorney General did not have to wait long for the review. In March 1992, the Supreme Court released its decision in *Morin*,[5] an Ontario case involving a delay of 14½ months in bringing a person charged with driving while impaired to trial. In *Morin*, while the court did not repudiate its decision in *Askov*, it considerably softened its approach to section 11(*b*). Justice Sopinka, who wrote the main opinion for the court, said that the provincial courts could take 8 to 10 months from committal to trial as an "administrative guideline" for not unreasonable institutional delay between committal and trial. He emphasized that this was a guideline, not a rigid rule, and acknowledged that, in addition to the time from committal to trial, there would have to be allowance for time between laying the charge and committal. The court now gave more weight to the need for the accused to demonstrate prejudice caused by the delay. In upholding the Ontario Court of Appeal's decision that 14½ months was not an unreasonable time for Morin to wait after she was charged to be brought to trial, Justice Sopinka took into account the burgeoning population and increase in criminal caseloads in the district where the trial was to take place.

The Supreme Court's performance in *Askov* was not one of its shining hours in the Charter era. After the decision, Professor Baar revealed how the court had drawn mistaken inferences from his comparative data.[6] When social science evidence is used in determining factual matters that are relevant to constitutional rights, it is best submitted in the lower courts where it can be subject to thorough examination. The decision also had a tone of moral outrage that indicated a lack of sufficient sensitivity to its practical consequences. Moreover, Canadians may well continue to ask why the Supreme Court regards the termination of proceedings as the only possible remedy for a breach of section 11(*b*). When an accused is held in custody for a long time while waiting for trial, a judicial order to speed up the trial date seems to be a remedy that is both sensible and just.[7]

---

3 For an account of the public reaction to *Askov*, see Kent Roach, *The Supreme Court on Trial: Judicial Activism or Democratic Dialogue* (Toronto: Irwin Law, 2001) 180-82.

4 "Hampton calls for review of ruling in Askov" *The Globe and Mail* (17 July 1991) A5.

5 *R. v. Morin*, [1992] 1 S.C.R. 771.

6 Carl Baar, "Criminal Court Delay and the Charter" (1993) 72 *Canadian Bar Review* 305.

7 For a discussion of these options, see Anthony G. Amsterdam, "Speedy Criminal Trial: Rights and Remedies" (1975) 27 *Stanford Law Review* 525.

Askov also raises questions about the performance of the political branches. The case exposed shameful conditions in the administration of justice that the Ontario government had allowed to develop in the Peel District of the province. A more alert and responsible government could have done much more to reduce delays in Peel by pushing Crown prosecutors to screen charges more carefully, to disclose more of their case to defence lawyers, and to be more open to negotiating pleas—defence lawyers referred to the district as "no deal Peel."[8] And it should not have needed the shock of *Askov* to wake up the government to the need to appoint more judges. In the United States, a number of states have enacted legislation setting standards for speedy trials. In Canada, where the federal Parliament has exclusive jurisdiction over criminal law and procedure, this option was considered by federal legislators in the early 1980s, but then dropped.

In the Charter era, legislative responsibilities that elected legislators decline to accept are apt to be taken up by the judiciary. Although the legislative effort of the Supreme Court in *Askov* was clumsy, at least the justices recognized its inadequacies and began the process of correcting their work in *Morin*. The process of refining time standards for bringing accused persons to trial continues. James Kelly reports that in the 12 years following *Askov*, the Supreme Court considered trial delay in 22 cases, and that the average time accepted as reasonable in these cases was 16 months.[9] ∼

Discussion Questions

1. What can we learn from this case about the use of statistical data in judicial decisions interpreting the constitution?

2. How was the court's interpretation of section 11(*b*) modified in subsequent judicial decisions?

3. How would you assess the impact of judicial decisions on section 11(*b*) on the administration of criminal justice in Canada?

---

8 Kent Roach, *supra* note 3 at 181.

9 James Kelly, *Governing with the Charter: Legislative and Judicial Activism and Framers' Intent* (Vancouver: University of British Columbia Press, 2005) 130.

R. v. ASKOV
[1990] 2 S.C.R. 1199

Hearing: March 23, 1990; Judgment: October 18, 1990.

Present: Dickson C.J.* and Lamer C.J.** and Wilson, La Forest, L'Heureux-Dubé, Sopinka, Gonthier, Cory, and McLachlin JJ.

 * Chief Justice at the time of hearing.

** Chief Justice at the time of judgment.

[This is the most important case the court has rendered on section 11(*b*) of the Charter, guaranteeing the right to a trial within a reasonable time. Justice Cory's opinion provides for

the first time a clear majority position on the factors to be taken into account in determining whether this right has been violated. The court found that the accused's rights were violated primarily because Ontario had failed to provide adequate court resources in the Peel area. Within three months, more than 12,000 cases in Ontario had been either stayed by judges or had charges withdrawn by the Crown for failing to meet the standard established in the *Askov* case, which has generally been interpreted to require a trial between six to eight months after a charge has been laid.]

The judgment of Dickson C.J. and La Forest, L'Heureux-Dubé, Gonthier, and Cory JJ. was delivered by

CORY J.: Section 11(*b*) of the *Canadian Charter of Rights and Freedoms* provides that any person charged with an offence has the right to be tried within a reasonable time. What constitutes an unreasonable delay of a trial must be determined on this appeal. In order to reach a conclusion it will be necessary to consider and apply criteria or factors which should be used to ascertain if a delay is unreasonable and in particular, to consider the consequences of so-called institutional delays.

Factual Background

All the appellants, Askov, Hussey, Melo and Gugliotta, were charged with conspiracy to commit extortion against Peter Belmont. As well, Askov, Hussey and Melo were jointly charged with the offences of possession of a prohibited weapon, possession of a weapon for a purpose dangerous to the public peace, pointing a firearm and assault with a weapon. Hussey was also charged with criminal negligence in the operation of a motor vehicle. ...

[Askov and Melo were arrested on November 12, 1983, Hussey on November 14, and Gugliotta on November 30.]

It is necessary to set out the proceedings following the arrest in some detail. The appellants Melo, Askov and Hussey were initially denied bail. They were detained in custody for almost six months. On May 7, 1984, they were each ordered to be released on a recognizance of $50,000. Gugliotta was released on December 2, 1983 shortly after his arrest on a recognizance of $20,000. The terms of release for all the appellants involved reporting to the police and abstention from communicating with their co-accused. These conditions were varied from time to time to permit more freedom of movement for the appellants. All the applications which were made for more lenient bail conditions were granted. Nonetheless, the appellants remained under considerable restraint.

Askov was re-arrested on an unrelated charge on October 1, 1984.

With three of the accused in custody, the Crown, in a commendable manner, was prepared as soon as December 1983 to set an early date for the preliminary hearing. However, at the request of the appellants the matter was put over to February 14, 1984 when all counsel agreed on a date in the first week of July for the preliminary hearing to be held. At this time it was specifically indicated that an earlier date could be arranged if a request was made by the appellants, but none was forthcoming. When the preliminary hearing commenced on July 4, 1984, it could not be completed because another preliminary had been set for a later day in the same week. As a result, the preliminary hearing could not be completed until September 21, 1984, some ten months after the arrests.

On October 1, 1984, the appellants appeared before Judge Keenan presiding in the assignment court. A trial date was set for the first available date which was October 15, 1985, more than a year away and nearly two years from the date of the initial arrests. Despite what seems far too lengthy a delay, an earlier date could not be set due to other cases which had priority either because the accused was in custody or because the offence date was earlier than that of the case at bar. On October 25, 1985, when it was apparent that the case simply could not be heard during that session, counsel for all the appellants and the Crown appeared and the case was put over for trial to September 2, 1986. When the trial finally began on that date, counsel for the appellants moved to stay the proceedings on the grounds that the trial had been unreasonably delayed. The stay was granted by order of Judge Bolan, the senior judge of the District Court of the Judicial District of Peel. The Crown appealed the order of Bolan Dist. Ct. J. to the Court of Appeal, which set aside the stay and directed that the trial proceed. ...

The United States

In the United States the Sixth Amendment ensures that "[i]n all criminal prosecutions, the accused shall enjoy the right to a speedy and public trial." The United States Supreme Court considered the issue in *Barker v. Wingo*, 407 U.S. 514 (1972). In that case Barker, who was charged with murder, was brought to trial five years after the murder was committed. The delay was caused by the necessity of trying an accomplice beforehand. This prerequisite trial was extremely complicated; the accomplice was tried no less than six times. During this ongoing process, Barker initially had agreed to continuances or adjournments. He only began to assert his right to a speedy trial three and one-half years after the charges were laid.

The court held that a flexible approach should be taken to cases involving delay and that the multiple purposes or aims of the Sixth Amendment must be appreciated. Powell J., giving the reasons for the court, recognized the general concern that all persons accused with crimes should be treated according to fair and decent procedures. He particularly noted that there were three individual interests which the right was designed to protect. They were:

(i) to prevent oppressive pre-trial incarceration;
(ii) to minimize the anxiety and concern of the accused; and
(iii) to limit the possibility that the defence will be impaired or prejudiced.

However, Powell J. went on to observe that unlike other constitutional rights which only have an individual interest, the right to a speedy trial involved the added dimension of a societal interest. He found that a delay could result in increased financial cost to society and as well, could have a negative effect upon the credibility of the justice system. Further, it was noted that a delay could work to the advantage of the accused. ...

In order to balance the individual right and the communal aspect of the Sixth Amendment, the U.S. Supreme Court adopted an approach of *ad hoc* balancing "in which the conduct of both the prosecution and the defendant are weighed" (p. 530). The balancing is undertaken by reference to four factors identified by Powell J. as the test for infringement of the right to a "speedy trial." They are as follows:

(i) the length of the delay;
(ii) the reason for the delay;
(ii) the accused's assertion of the right; and
(iv) prejudice to the accused.

The first factor is the triggering mechanism or threshold determination of the excessiveness of the delay. If that delay appears *prima facie* excessive, the Court must then consider the three remaining factors to determine whether the accused has been deprived of the Sixth Amendment right.

Position in Canada Subsequent to the Passing of the Charter

Immediately following the passage of the *Charter*, the approach taken by the U.S. Supreme Court in *Barker v. Wingo, supra,* was widely approved and adopted. ...

The issue was first considered by this Court in *Mills v. The Queen, supra.* Lamer J. in his dissenting reasons called into question the appropriateness of adopting the American approach in the Canadian setting. ... Although he favoured a flexible balancing test, he rejected the approach taken in *Barker v. Wingo, supra.* His difference with the reasoning in that case was grounded on the proposition that in the context of the Canadian *Charter*, the s. 11(*b*) right was by its very nature an individual right and that the provision did not have a collective or societal dimension. ...

Since there was no need to balance any interest of society, the test did not need to take into account the conduct of the parties, particularly that of the accused. As well, actual prejudice to the accused did not need to be considered, as actual prejudice is also a component of society's interest in a fair trial. ...

The Court next examined the application of s. 11(*b*) in *R. v. Rahey* [[1987] 1 S.C.R. 588]. Rahey was charged with six counts of making false returns in his income tax forms and one count of wilful income tax evasion. His trial before a provincial court judge began six months after he was charged. In the eleven-month period which followed the closing of the

Crown's case there were no fewer than nineteen adjournments, all initiated by the trial judge. For nine of these adjournments, Rahey made no objection. When the judge ordered further adjournments, he contended that they constituted a violation of his s. 11(*b*) *Charter* rights. He brought an application to stay before the Supreme Court of Nova Scotia and later an appeal to this Court where a stay of proceedings was granted.

Four judges delivered written reasons. Lamer J., with Dickson C.J. concurring, restated his position in *Mills*, but extended the "transitional period" to include the period up to the issuance of the reasons in *Rahey*. Wilson J., with Estey J. concurring, maintained her position set forth in *Mills* and referred again to the necessity of focussing on the prejudice resulting from the unreasonable delay and not upon the prejudice flowing from the charge. Le Dain J., with Beetz J. concurring, supported the approach taken by the U.S. Supreme Court in *Barker v. Wingo.* ...

In *R. v. Conway,* [1989] 1 S.C.R. 1659, Conway sought to obtain from this Court a stay of proceedings to prevent a third trial which would take place more than five years after the initial charge of murder had been laid.

Conway was charged with first degree murder in connection with the stabbing death. Some sixteen months after he was charged, the accused was tried and convicted of the included offence of second degree murder. An appeal was taken and one year later a new trial was directed by the Court of Appeal. It was agreed that there was no time lost during the period from the launching of the appeal until the order was given by the Court of Appeal directing a new trial. Conway then had difficulty finding a counsel to represent him at the second trial. It was conceded that the problem arose in no small part from Conway's own actions. ...

L'Heureux-Dubé J., writing for the majority of a panel of five judges, which included Dickson C.J. and La Forest J., dismissed the appeal and rejected the stay. She held that the overall delay did not prevent the accused from obtaining a fair trial. ... The critical factor in the decision was the conduct of the accused Conway who was responsible for much of the delay. It was held that the rest of the delay was justified by the inherent time requirements of the case. Further, it was noted that it was impossible to conclude that the accused had been prejudiced. ...

The facts in *R. v. Smith,* [1989] 2 S.C.R. 1120, are relatively straightforward. Smith was charged with theft. The preliminary inquiry could not be scheduled until over a year had passed from the time he was charged. The institutional reasons which caused this delay arose from the scheduling of the preliminary hearing for four days in August, at a time when the provincial court judges were on holiday. The preliminary hearing could not be rescheduled until late in December because the investigating officer was unavailable before that date. Once again the scheduled December date came within a holiday period for provincial court judges and a further adjournment was required. When the case finally came to trial, an application was brought for a stay which was granted.

In this Court, Sopinka J., writing for all members of the Court, upheld the stay. He recognized that there was still a considerable disagreement as to the factors that should be taken into account on the balancing process and also with regard to the composition of the constituent components of the prejudice issue. However, he was of the view that the problem did not have to be dealt with in light of the facts of the case. ...

On the facts of *Smith*, Sopinka J. determined that the length of time was longer than could be justified particularly in light of the cause of the delays. ...

Purpose of Section 11(b)

I agree with the position taken by Lamer J. that s. 11(*b*) explicitly focusses upon the individual interest of liberty and security of the person. Like other specific guarantees provided by s. 11, this paragraph is primarily concerned with an aspect of fundamental justice guaranteed by s. 7 of the *Charter*. There could be no greater frustration imaginable for innocent persons charged with an offence than to be denied the opportunity of demonstrating their innocence for an unconscionable time as a result of unreasonable delays in their trial. The time awaiting trial must be exquisite agony for accused persons and their immediate family. It is a fundamental precept of our criminal law that every individual is presumed to be innocent until proven guilty. It follows that on the same fundamental level of importance, all accused persons, each one of whom is presumed to be innocent, should be given the opportunity to defend themselves against the charges they face and to have their name cleared and reputation re-established at the earliest possible time.

Although the primary aim of s. 11(*b*) is the protection of the individual's rights and the provision of fundamental justice for the accused, nonetheless there is, in my view, at least by inference, a community or societal interest implicit in s. 11(*b*). That community interest has a dual dimension. First, there is a collective interest in ensuring that those who transgress the law are brought to trial and dealt with according to the law. Second, those individuals on trial must be treated fairly and justly. Speedy trials strengthen both those aspects of the community interest. A trial held within a reasonable time must benefit the individual accused as the prejudice which results from criminal proceedings is bound to be minimized. If the accused is in custody, the custodial time awaiting trial will be kept to a minimum. If the accused is at liberty

on bail and subject to conditions, then the curtailments on the liberty of the accused will be kept to a minimum. From the point of view of the community interest, in those cases where the accused is detained in custody awaiting trial, society will benefit by the quick resolution of the case either by reintegrating into society the accused found to be innocent or if found guilty by dealing with the accused according to the law. ...

There are as well important practical benefits which flow from a quick resolution of the charges. There can be no doubt that memories fade with time. Witnesses are likely to be more reliable testifying to events in the immediate past as opposed to events that transpired many months or even years before the trial. Not only is there an erosion of the witnesses' memory with the passage of time, but there is bound to be an erosion of the witnesses themselves. Witnesses are people; they are moved out of the country by their employer; or for reasons related to family or work they move from the east coast to the west coast; they become sick and unable to testify in court; they are involved in debilitating accidents; they die and their testimony is forever lost. Witnesses too are concerned that their evidence be taken as quickly as possible. Testifying is often thought to be an ordeal. It is something that weighs on the minds of witnesses and is a source of worry and frustration for them until they have given their testimony.

It can never be forgotten that the victims may be devastated by criminal acts. They have a special interest and good reason to expect that criminal trials take place within a reasonable time. From a wider point of view, it is fair to say that all crime disturbs the community and that serious crime alarms the community. All members of the community are thus entitled to see that the justice system works fairly, efficiently and with reasonable dispatch. The very reasonable concern and alarm of the community which naturally arises from acts of crime cannot be assuaged until the trial has taken place. The trial not only resolves the guilt or innocence of the individual, but acts as a reassurance to the community that serious crimes are investigated and that those implicated are brought to trial and dealt with according to the law.

The failure of the justice system to deal fairly, quickly and efficiently with criminal trials inevitably leads to the community's frustration with the judicial system and eventually to a feeling of contempt for court procedures. When a trial takes place without unreasonable delay, with all witnesses available and memories fresh, it is far more certain that the guilty parties who committed the crimes will be convicted and punished and those that did not, will be acquitted and vindicated. It is no exaggeration to say that a fair and balanced criminal justice system simply cannot exist without the support of the community. Continued community support for our system will not endure in the face of lengthy and unreasonable delays.

Further, implicit support for the concept that there is a societal aspect to s. 11(*b*) can be derived from the observation that the last thing that some wish for is a speedy trial. There is no doubt that many accused earnestly hope that the memory of a witness will fail and that other witnesses will become unavailable. ...

I believe the inferred societal interest should be considered in conjunction with the main and primary concept of the protection of the individual's right to fundamental justice. This is closer to the views expressed by Wilson J. in *Mills, supra*. At some level, the conduct of and prejudice to the accused must be examined. Although it must be recognized that the primary goal of s. 11(*b*) is the protection of the individual's interest in fundamental justice, nevertheless that same section contains a secondary and inferred societal interest that should not be ignored. If the recognition of both the primary individual interest and the inferred society interest is accepted as the true aim of s. 11(*b*), then I think the various factors which should be taken into consideration in determining whether there has been an unreasonable delay can be clarified and set forth in a consistent test.

Factors to Be Taken into Account in Determining Whether or Not There Has Been an Infringement of Section 11(b)

(i) The Length of the Delay

It is clear that the longer the delay, the more difficult it should be for a court to excuse it. This is not a threshold requirement as in the United States, but rather is a factor to be balanced along with the others. However, very lengthy delays may be such that they cannot be justified for any reason.

(ii) Explanation for the Delay

This category referred to by Sopinka J. in *Smith, supra*, may be usefully subdivided with the aspects of systemic delay and conduct of the accused amplified.

(a) The Conduct of the Crown (or Delay Attributable to the Crown)

Generally speaking, this category will comprise all of the potential factors causing delay which flow from the nature of the case, the conduct of the Crown, including officers of the state, and the inherent time requirements of the case. Delays attributable to the actions of the Crown or its officers will weigh in favour of the accused. For example, the nineteen adjournments initiated by the trial judge in *Rahey* or the unavailability of judges because of holidays in *Smith* are examples where the actions or the lack of actions of Crown officers weighed against the state in the assessment of the reasonableness of the delay.

It is under this heading that the complexity of the case should be taken into account. Complex cases which require longer time for preparation, a greater expenditure of resources by Crown officers and the longer use of institutional facilities will justify delays longer than those that would be acceptable in simple cases.

(b) Systemic or Institutional Delays

On a more specific level, the question of delays caused by systemic or institutional limitations should also be discussed under the heading of delays attributable to the Crown. This factor will often be the most difficult to assess. A careful and sensitive balancing will be required in order to properly assess the significance of this aspect of delay. First, let us consider the problem from the point of view of society. Section 11(*b*) applies to all Canadians in every part of our land. In a country as vast and diverse as ours, the institutional problems are bound to differ greatly from province to province and from district to district within each province. Differences of climate, terrain, population and financial resources will require different solutions for the problem of providing adequate facilities and personnel. Lack of financial resources may require imaginative answers to difficult problems, including the provision of temporary facilities. The problems presented and the solutions required will vary between heavily populated centres such as Toronto and Montréal and the sparsely populated districts bordering on Hudson Bay.

Wise political decisions will be required with regard to the allocation of scarce funds. Due deference will have to be given to those political decisions as the provisions of courtroom facilities and Crown Attorneys must, for example, be balanced against the provision of health care and highways. Yet solutions must be found as indeed they have been in many jurisdictions outside Ontario. Similarly situated communities can provide a rough comparison and some guidance as to what time period constitutes an unreasonable delay of the trial of an accused person. That comparison should always be made with the more efficient of the comparable jurisdictions.

The right guaranteed by s. 11(*b*) is of such fundamental importance to the individual and of such significance to the community as a whole that the lack of institutional resources cannot be employed to justify a continuing unreasonable postponement of trials. ...

Where inordinate delays do occur, it is those who are responsible for the lack of facilities who should bear the public criticism that is bound to arise as a result of the staying of proceedings which must be the inevitable consequence of unreasonable delays. Members of the community will not and should not condone or accept a situation where those alleged to have committed serious crimes are never brought to trial

solely as a result of unduly long delays. It is a serious consequence with potentially dangerous overtones for the community. It is right and proper that there be criticism of the
situation when it occurs.

The response to the question of "how long is too long" as
it applies to institutional delay will always be difficult to fashion in our country. The question must be answered in light of
the particular facts of each case. There can be no certain standard of a fixed time which will be applicable in every region
of the country. Nonetheless, an inquiry into what is reasonable
in any region should not be taken in isolation and must, of
necessity, involve a comparison with other jurisdictions. Consideration must be given to the geography, the population and
the material resources of the province and district. The comparison of similar and thus comparable districts must always
be made with the better districts and not with the worst. ...

To summarize, when considering delays occasioned by
inadequate institutional resources, the question of how long
a delay is too long may be resolved by comparing the questioned jurisdiction to the standard maintained by the best
comparable jurisdiction in the country. The comparison need
not be too precise or exact. Rather, it should look to the appropriate ranges of delay to determine what is a reasonable limit.
In all cases it will be incumbent upon the Crown to show that
the institutional delay in question is justifiable.

(c) The Conduct of the Accused
(or Delay Attributable to the Accused)

As Lamer J. so cogently observed in *Mills*, it is a fundamental
precept of our criminal justice system that it is the responsibility of the Crown to bring the accused to trial. Further, the right
to be tried within a reasonable time is an aspect of fundamental justice protected by s. 7 of the *Charter*. It follows that any
inquiry into the conduct of the accused should in no way
absolve the Crown from its responsibility to bring the accused
to trial. Nonetheless, there is a societal interest in preventing an
accused from using the guarantee as a means of escaping trial.
It should be emphasized that an inquiry into the actions of the
accused should be restricted to discovering those situations
where the accused's acts either directly caused the delay (as in
Conway), or the acts of the accused are shown to be a deliberate and calculated tactic employed to delay the trial. ...

In addition, since the protection of the right of the individual is the primary aim of s. 11(*b*), the burden of proving
that the direct acts of the accused caused the delay must fall
upon the Crown. This would be true except in those cases
where the effects of the accused's action are so clear and readily apparent that the intent of the accused to cause a delay is
the inference that must be drawn from the record of his or
her actions.

(iii) Waiver

While the question of waiver could be discussed under factor
(ii)(c) above (Delay Attributable to the Accused), for reasons
of clarity, I prefer to examine the issue separately.

The accused should not be required to assert the explicitly
protected individual right to trial within a reasonable time. It
is now well established that any waiver of a *Charter* right must
be "clear and unequivocal ... with full knowledge of the rights
the procedure was enacted to protect and of the effect the
waiver will have on those rights in the process." See *Korponay
v. Attorney General of Canada*, [1982] 1 S.C.R. 41, at p. 49. The
failure of an accused to assert the right does not give the
Crown licence to proceed with an unfair trial. Failure to assert
the right would be insufficient in itself to impugn the motives
of the accused as might be the case with regard to other s. 11
rights. Rather there must be something in the conduct of the
accused that is sufficient to give rise to an inference that the
accused has understood that he or she had a s. 11(*b*) guarantee, understood its nature and has waived the right provided
by that guarantee. Although no particular magical incantation
of words is required to waive a right, nevertheless the waiver
must be expressed in some manner. Silence or lack of objection cannot constitute a lawful waiver. ...

In sum, the burden always rests with the Crown to bring
the case to trial. Further, the mere silence of the accused is not
sufficient to indicate a waiver of a *Charter* right; rather, the
accused must undertake some direct action from which a consent to delay can be properly inferred. The onus rests upon the
Crown to establish on a balance of probabilities that the
actions of the accused constitute a waiver of his or her rights.

(iv) Prejudice to the Accused

The different positions taken by Members of the Court with
regard to the prejudice suffered by an accused as a result of a
delayed trial are set forth in *Mills* and *Rahey*. Perhaps the differences can be resolved in this manner. It should be inferred
that a very long and unreasonable delay has prejudiced the
accused. ... Nevertheless, it will be open to the Crown to
attempt to demonstrate that the accused has not been prejudiced. This would preserve the societal interest by providing
that a trial would proceed in those cases where despite a long
delay no resulting damage had been suffered by the accused. ...

Application of the Principles to the Case at Bar

As the disposition of this case will ultimately turn on the
factors headed (ii) Explanation for the Delay, particularly (b)
Systemic or Institutional Delay and (c) Delays Attributable to
the Accused; and (iii) Waiver, I need but briefly deal with the
factors titled (i) The Length of the Delay and (iv) Prejudice
to the Accused.

(i) The Length of the Delay

No matter what standard of measure is used or what test is applied, the trial in this case has been inordinately delayed. ... The experienced trial judge who has presided for many years in Peel District described the delay as "clearly excessive and unreasonable." It is interesting to note that the delay at issue in *Mills* was nineteen months, in *Rahey* eleven months, and in *Smith* one year. Although the period of delay in *Conway* is comparable to that of this case, it must be remembered that in that case the delay was directly attributable to the actions of Conway.

The period of delay in the case at bar is so lengthy that unless there is some very strong basis for justifying the delay, which becomes clear from an examination of the other factors, then it would be impossible for a court to tolerate such a delay.

(ii) Prejudice to the Accused

The trial judge found that the appellants had been prejudiced by the delay. In support, he noted the lengthy period of incarceration for three of the appellants and the restrictions contained in the bail terms. Those conditions of bail included curfews, a direction not to associate with the co-accused and a system of regular reporting to the police. There has been no attack on these findings. Consequently, it is impossible to say that the Crown discharged the burden that rested upon it to show that the delay caused no prejudice to the appellants. As a result, the prejudice suffered by the appellants weighs against the Crown and cannot be used to excuse the length of delay.

(iii) Explanation for the Delay

(a) Delays Attributable to the Crown

It is clear that delays cannot be attributable to any action of the Crown. At no time did the Crown make any requests for adjournments or take any step that delayed the trial of the action in any way.

There is nothing in the case that is so complex or inherently difficult that it would justify a lengthy delay. ...

(b) Systemic or Institutional Delay

This trial was to be heard in Brampton, in the District of Peel in Ontario. This district has long been notorious for the inordinate length of time required to obtain a trial date. The delays are said to be caused by lack of facilities. The evidence submitted contains a study done by Prof. Carl Baar, Director of the Judicial Administration Program at Brock University. From the research and comparative studies that he has undertaken, Professor Baar has concluded that the Peel District (referred to as Brampton by Professor Baar) experiences extremely long delays that are out of the ordinary compared to the rest of Ontario, the rest of Canada or the United States. He notes that the situation has arisen partly as a result of rapid urban growth and the presence of a very large international airport which generates a great many drug-related offences. He also finds that a shortage of court space and judges are significant factors which contribute to the lengthy delays. His research indicates that comparatively speaking it is without doubt one of the worst districts in Canada, if not the worst, in terms of delays between committal and trial. Ontario can take no pride in this situation and must indeed bear the responsibility for it. ...

It is apparent that the situation in Peel District has been in a deplorable state for many years. Something is terribly wrong. As Justice Zuber noted the situation is "enormously complex" and there is no "magic solution" or "quick fix." Nonetheless, something must be done. Urgent attention to the situation is required. The response of the Government of Ontario has been neither overwhelming nor particularly successful. A program known as the Delay Reduction Initiative instituted by the Government is summarized in the Chaloner affidavit. ...

The most recent statistics set forth in the Chaloner affidavit for the period from October 1988 to December 1989 clearly indicate that in four of the six target areas, including Peel District, there is no visible long-term trend towards improvement of the mean average time of case delays. ...

The only conclusion which can be drawn from an analysis of the material filed is that the problem of systemic delay in Peel has not and cannot be resolved simply by introducing a more efficient caseflow management system. More resources must be supplied to this district perhaps by way of additional Crown Attorneys and courtrooms. This conclusion cannot come as a surprise. The problem has existed for many years, back at least as far as 1981. ...

The extent and gravity of the problem in Peel is brought home by reference to the comparative study done in 1987 by Professor Baar. The study illustrated that in Canada, New Brunswick and Quebec were best able to bring their cases to trial within the thirty to ninety-day range. In terms of the time taken to completely dispose of a case from committal to disposition, the median total time in New Brunswick's lower courts (provincial courts) was 152 days. The median total time in upper courts (s. 96 courts) was 72 days. By comparison, in Ontario the best district was London with a median total time of 239 days and the median upper court time of 105 days. Toronto, Ottawa and St. Catherines were all close together with median total times of between 315 and 349 days, and upper court times between 133 and 144 days.

Professor Baar wrote that "[b]y all measures used in the study, Brampton District Court was significantly slower than any other location studied: median total time was 607 days and median upper court time was 423 days." Nor can any comfort be drawn by comparison to the United States. Professor Baar concluded that the Peel District is generally substantially slower than the slowest United States jurisdictions. Further, he noted that the delay in the present case was longer than ninety per cent of all cases in terms of median total time among those heard even in Peel District. This case therefore represents one of the worst from the point of view of delay in the worst district not only in Canada, but so far as the studies indicate, anywhere north of the Rio Grande.

If it should be argued that the statistics from New Brunswick cannot represent a basis for comparison, then surely those from Quebec can and do provide a guide for comparison. A review of the recent statistics kept by the courts in Montréal, Longueuil and Terrebonne by comparison reveals how very unsatisfactory and intolerable is the state of affairs in Peel.

At Montréal, for the 5½ month period beginning January 8, 1990, the delay between the date of remitting a case for trial at the next assize and the date of trial is 82½ days. This figure includes the time for all trials save one which was remitted by the Court of Appeal for a second trial. If from this figure are deducted those cases where the defence either requested an adjournment or brought a motion such as *certiorari*, the time was 60 days.

In the District of Terrebonne, taking into account all the cases before the Superior Court, the delay between remission for trial and trial is 91.5 days. If one case with exceptional circumstances is deleted, the waiting period drops to 86 days.

In the District of Longueuil, the waiting period for trial is 90.5 days. Once again, if the exceptional cases are deleted, the waiting period drops to 66.75 days.

The average time in the three districts to commence a trial is 84.3 days and if from the total there is deducted those cases where a second trial was directed or the defence requested an adjournment, the waiting period is only 63.5 days.

Making a very rough comparison and more than doubling the longest waiting period to make every allowance for the special circumstances in Peel would indicate that a period of delay in a range of some six to eight months between committal and trial might be deemed to be the outside limit of what is reasonable. The usual delays in Peel are more than four times as long as those of busy metropolitan districts in the province of Quebec and the delay in this case is more than eight times as long. The figures from the comparable districts demonstrate that the Peel District situation is unreasonable and intolerable.

The delay in this case is such that it is impossible to come to any other conclusion than that the s. 11(*b*) *Charter* rights guaranteed to the individual accused have been infringed. As well, the societal interest in ensuring that these accused be brought to trial within a reasonable time has been grossly offended and denigrated. Indeed the delay is of such an inordinate length that public confidence in the administration of justice must be shaken. ... Yet, that trial can only be undertaken if the *Charter* right to trial within a reasonable time has not been infringed. In this case that right has been grievously infringed and the sad result is that a stay of proceedings must be entered. To conclude otherwise would render meaningless a right enshrined in the *Charter* as the supreme law of the land. ...

This conclusion should not be taken as a direction to build an expensive courthouse at a time of fiscal restraint. Rather, it is a recognition that this situation is unacceptable and can no longer be tolerated. Surely an imaginative solution could be found that would rectify the problem. For example, courtroom space might be found in other nearby government buildings. Or perhaps an interim solution could be achieved by the installation of portable structures similar to those used in the school system. If the children who represent the most precious resource of the nation can be taught in portable classrooms, then as a temporary solution trials can take place in similar accommodation.

Arguments can always be raised as to why interim solutions should not be used. Yet, imaginative cooperation can surely resolve these problems. If temporary structures cannot be used for criminal cases for reasons of security, then the criminal trials might proceed in the courthouse while the civil cases are heard in the nearby government buildings or portable buildings.

Another temporary solution might be to encourage changes of venue. ...

These tentative suggestions may very well be unworkable. But some solution must be found to eradicate this malignant growth of unreasonable trial delay that constitutes such an unacceptable blight upon the administration of justice in Peel District.

(c) Delay Attributable to the Accused

In order to consider this factor, it is necessary to examine the conduct of the accused in order to ascertain whether it was such that it excused the delay by in effect bringing it about. At the outset, I would repeat that in this case it is clear that there was no direct action on the part of the appellants which resulted in any delay apart from that which occurred prior to the preliminary hearing. ...

The complete transcript also reveals that there was no evidence to even support a finding that the appellants had a concealed plan to wait until the delay was unreasonable before complaining or bringing a motion. ...

(iv) Waiver

... On the facts of this case there was no explicit waiver of their rights by the appellants. ...

The silence of the appellants or their failure to raise an objection to a long delay is certainly not enough in the circumstances to infer waiver. Rather, the onus rests upon the Crown to demonstrate that the actions of the accused amounted to an agreement to the delay or waiver of their right.

In summary, the appellants did not specifically waive their s. 11(*b*) rights. Neither can it be inferred from their actions that they waived those rights.

The foregoing review indicates that there is no basis upon which this delay can be justified and as a result, a stay of proceedings must be directed. Courts may frequently be requested to take such a step. Fortunately, Professor Baar's work indicates that most regions of this country are operating within reasonable and acceptable time limits with the result that such relief will be infrequently granted. However, in situations such as this where the delay is extensive and beyond justification there is no alternative but to direct a stay of proceedings.

The following are the reasons delivered by

LAMER C.J.: I agree with Justice Cory's resolution of this appeal and with most of his reasons. However, with respect, I am unable to accept his position that one of the objectives of s. 11(*b*) of the *Canadian Charter of Rights and Freedoms* is the protection of a societal interest in speedy trials. I also respectfully disagree that prejudice suffered by the accused resulting from the delay is a factor to be considered when determining the "reasonableness" of the delay.

Societal Interest

As I stated in my reasons in *Mills v. The Queen*, [1986] 1 S.C.R. 863, at pp. 917-18, reasons in which Dickson C.J. and Wilson J. concurred, and in which I still firmly believe, while society may have an interest in the efficient functioning of the criminal justice system, this interest is not what s. 11(*b*) is designed to protect. ...

Prejudice

Cory J. adopts the consideration of "prejudice" from Wilson J.'s position in *Mills*, at p. 967:

> There may, indeed, be an irrebuttable presumption in favour of prejudice flowing from the fact of an accused's being charged with a criminal offence but that is not protected by s. 11(*b*) of the *Charter*. The prejudice arising from anxiety, stress and stigmatization by family and friends also exists where the accused is tried within a reasonable time. What the accused has to demonstrate

under s. 11(*b*), in my opinion, is that he has suffered an impairment of his liberty and security interests as a result of the Crown's failure to bring him to trial within a reasonable time, not as a result of the Crown's having charged him.

In *Mills*, I took the position that because of the very nature of our criminal justice system, a certain degree of prejudice, including, at p. 920, "stigmatization of the accused, loss of privacy, stress and anxiety resulting from a multitude of factors, including possible disruption of family, social life and work, legal costs, uncertainty as to the outcome and sanction," will inevitably be imposed upon an individual charged with a criminal offence and will thereby infringe the rights of liberty and security of the person. Therefore, there exists an irrebuttable presumption of prejudice from the moment the charge is laid. ...

Making prejudice affecting the fairness of the trial a relevant consideration for s. 11(*b*) sets a precedent which could have dangerous consequences for the scope of other *Charter* rights. For example, s. 10(*b*) of the *Charter* guarantees the right, upon arrest or detention, to be informed of the right to retain and instruct counsel without delay. Suppose an individual is arrested and there is considerable delay in advising him or her of the right to retain counsel. Even if the individual later states that had he or she been promptly informed of the right to retain and instruct counsel, he or she would not have done so because of financial considerations, the rights guaranteed under s. 10(*b*) have still been restricted. This person may not have suffered any prejudice, but surely his or her rights have been infringed. Of course, lack of prejudice would be a consideration when fashioning a remedy under s. 24(1) or when applying s. 24(2). But the absence or presence of prejudice is not, in my respectful view, in any way relevant to the initial issue of *Charter* breach.

The following are the reasons delivered by

WILSON J.: ...

[Justice Wilson concurred with Chief Justice Lamer on whether section 11(*b*) protects a societal as well as an individual interest. On the issue of the relevance of prejudice to the accused, she sided with the Cory majority—an accused should bear the onus of proving that the delay harmed his or her interests.]

The following are the reasons delivered by

SOPINKA J.: I have had the benefit of reading the reasons for judgment prepared in this appeal by Chief Justice Lamer and Justice Cory. I am of the view that this appeal must be allowed for the reasons given by Cory J., with the exception of his reference to a societal interest. In this respect, I agree with Lamer C.J.'s comments concerning the purported societal interest in s. 11(*b*) of the *Canadian Charter of Rights and Freedoms*.

The following are the reasons delivered by

McLACHLIN J.: I agree in substance and result with the reasons of Justice Cory. I wish to add only the following comments relevant to the process of determining whether a trial has unreasonably been delayed.

Like Cory J., I see s. 11(*b*) of the *Canadian Charter of Rights and Freedoms* as designed to serve both the interests of the accused and the interests of the prosecution, as well as the interests of society generally. This requires adoption of a balancing approach such as that which has prevailed in the United States, "in which the conduct of both the prosecution and the defendant are weighed": *Barker v. Wingo*, 407 U.S. 514 (1972), *per* Powell J., at p. 530.

Two elements must be assessed under s. 11(*b*). The first is the length of the delay. The second is its reasonableness.

The length of the delay is to be determined by the norms usually prevailing in similar jurisdictions, as Cory J. suggests. The question at this stage is whether the delay is *prima facie* excessive. If it is not, it is unnecessary to pursue the analysis further. If it is, it is necessary to go on to consider whether the delay is reasonable, notwithstanding its length.

The reasonableness of the delay may depend on a variety of factors. ... The ultimate question in each case is whether, after considering all relevant factors, the *prima facie* excessive delay can be justified as reasonable.

The factors to be considered will often pull in opposite directions. Thus, it is impossible to dictate in advance how the balancing is to be done in each case. Yet certain parameters can be suggested. The accused will rarely be entitled to the benefit of s. 11(*b*) where the Crown can show that the accused caused the delay or has suffered no prejudice as a consequence of the delay. On the other hand, lengthy and avoidable delay caused entirely by the Crown's sloppiness or inattention, or by unjustified delays in the legal system, will frequently entitle an accused to the benefit of s. 11(*b*).

In this case, the delay is *prima facie* excessive; indeed it is grossly excessive. We must therefore proceed to the second stage of the analysis to ask whether it is reasonable. The trial judge found that the accused had been prejudiced by the delay. As for the cause of the delay, the defence neither caused the delay nor agreed to it; I agree with Cory J. that failure to protest the delay should not be determinative against the accused in this case. Here the prosecution caused the delay. That delay was not due to inherent difficulties in the case but to systemic or institutional causes. Notwithstanding ample time since the advent of the *Charter* to increase the ability of the courts in Peel County to process their heavy trial lists within a reasonable time, this has not been done. Taking these factors together, the result is clear. The delay cannot be justified; it is unreasonable.

I would allow the appeal and direct a stay of proceedings.

34 Canada (Attorney General) v. Hislop, 2007

A central issue for the Supreme Court was how far back should remedies for discriminatory treatment be extended. In *Hislop*, the court had to confront the issue of whether a remedy should be prospective (applying only to the future and not providing relief or compensation for earlier Charter violations) or instead should be retroactive. If the latter, should the remedy reach back to 1985, when equality rights first came into force?

The case arose from a class action lawsuit that challenged federal government amendments to the Canada Pension Plan. The amendments, passed in 2000, were introduced in response to the Supreme Court's earlier ruling in *M. v. H.* (case 28), which ruled that the opposite-sex definition of spouse was unconstitutional.

The changes to the Canada Pension Plan would make same-sex partners eligible for CPP, thus addressing the discriminatory effects of the CPP's earlier reliance on an exclusively opposite-sex definition of spouse. However, the amendments restricted eligibility to survivors of same-sex relationships who died on or after January 1, 1998 and entitlement to benefits was delayed until July 1, 2000 (the month the amendments came into force). After that time, both same-sex and opposite-sex partners would be subject to a general rule that limits survivors' eligibility for arrears to not more than 12 months prior to the month in which an application is received.

This limit on retroactive arrears was challenged for discriminating against same-sex partners, because they were able to apply benefits only as of July 2000. The class action suit argued that same-sex survivors should be eligible for benefits dating back to 1985, the date that section 15 equality rights first came into effect.

Although the court agreed that equality rights had been violated in a manner not justified under section 1, it was not prepared to grant retroactive remedies dating back to 1985. The court held that where the law changes because of "judicial intervention" (in this case, the court's ruling in *M. v. H.* that social policies violate equality rights when they do not include, or recognize the validity of, same-sex spousal relationships), it might be appropriate to limit the retroactive effect of remedies. Other factors that can justify limiting the retroactive nature of remedies are whether government has acted in good faith despite approving legislation that has subsequently been found to violate rights; whether a retroactive remedy unduly interferes with the constitutional role of Parliament; and whether denial of a retroactive remedy would affect fairness for the litigant.

In this case, the Supreme Court ruled that the government had not acted in bad faith by denying same-sex survivor benefits and in fact had attempted to correct this denial soon after it was discovered. Moreover, granting a retroactive remedy to 1985 would not only overlook the evolution in the jurisprudence on same-sex equality rights but would also fail to recognize the appropriate balance between fairness to individual litigants and respect for Parliament's legislative role.

Some question the court's theoretical explanation for determining the nature of remedies. The majority opinion indicated that the retroactive effect of a constitutional declaration of invalidity is grounded in the 18th-century writings of jurist William Blackstone.[1] According to Blackstone, under the "declaratory approach," judges do not create law but merely discover it, whereas legislatures "fashion new laws for the future." Since judges are simply rediscovering "rules which are deemed to have already existed," it is appropriate for a court to grant retroactive effect to a declaration of invalidity. Based on this argument, the majority said that where courts are "articulating new legal principles rather than applying the existing law, it may be appropriate for the court to issue a prospective rather than retroactive remedy.[2] However, critics argue that the court's explanation relies on "a questionable distinction" between "discovering" the law and "creating" new law, because "[v]irtually all cases that reach the Supreme Court of Canada involve some significant creative legal element."[3] ∼

Discussion Questions

1. What arguments can be made to justify or disagree with the Supreme Court's refusal to extend the remedial effects of its ruling to 1985 when equality rights came into force?

2. Is the Supreme Court on shaky ground when grounding its approach to remedies on the distinction between articulating new legal principles and applying existing law?

---

1   William Blackstone, *Commentaries on the Laws of England*, vol. 1 (Oxford: Clarendon Press, 1765).

2   *Canada (Attorney General) v. Hislop*, 2007 SCC 10, [2007] 1 S.C.R. 429 at paras. 84-86 (extracted below).

3   See, for example, Patrick J. Monahan and James Gotowiec, "Constitutional Cases 2007: An Overview" (2008) 42 *Supreme Court Law Review* (2d) at pp. 7-8.

CANADA (ATTORNEY GENERAL) v. HISLOP
2007 SCC 10, [2007] 1 S.C.R. 429

Hearing: May 16, 2006; Judgment: March 1, 2007.

Present: McLachlin C.J. and Bastarache, Binnie, LeBel, Deschamps, Abella, and Rothstein JJ.

Interveners: Attorney General of Ontario, Attorney General of Quebec, Attorney General of Alberta, and Egale Canada Inc.

The judgment of McLachlin C.J. and Binnie, LeBel, Deschamps, Abella, and Rothstein JJ. was delivered by

LeBEL and ROTHSTEIN JJ.:

I. Introduction

[1]   This is an appeal by the Attorney General of Canada ("government") from a decision of the Ontario Court of Appeal upholding in part the decision of the Ontario Superior Court of Justice and a cross-appeal by the respondents ("Hislop class"). The government appeals the finding of unconstitutionality of ss. 44(1.1) and 72(2) of the *Canada Pension Plan* ("*CPP*"), ... as enacted by the *Modernization of Benefits and Obligations Act*. The Hislop class cross-appeals the finding of constitutionality of ss. 72(1) and 60(2) of the *CPP* and the denial of a remedy with respect thereto. We propose to dismiss both the appeal and the cross-appeal.

II. Overview

[2]   Under the *CPP*, the spouse of a contributor was entitled to apply for a survivor's pension after the death of the contributor. If the survivor's pension was approved, it would be payable for each month following the death of the contributor. ...

[4]   Until July 2000, for purposes of entitlement to a survivor's pension under the *CPP*, the survivor had to have been married to the contributor or had to be a person of the

opposite sex who was cohabiting with the contributor in a conjugal relationship at the time of the contributor's death. Same-sex conjugal relationships were not recognized and the survivor of a same-sex conjugal relationship was not eligible to receive a survivorship pension under the *CPP*.

[5] In *M. v. H.*, [1999] 2 S.C.R. 3, this Court struck down the opposite-sex definition of spouse in the *Family Law Act* ... as contrary to s. 15(1) of the *Canadian Charter of Rights and Freedoms*. The declaration of invalidity was suspended for six months to give the Ontario government time to review the legislation. As a consequence of *M. v. H.*, the federal government and the governments of other provinces also amended a number of their statutes to address the constitutional deficiency. The federal government enacted the *MBOA*, which amended 68 pieces of legislation. This appeal involves a constitutional challenge to remedial amendments made to the *CPP* by the *MBOA* to recognize same-sex conjugal relationships for the purpose of entitlement to survivor's pensions under the *CPP*.

[6] The Hislop class commenced a class action claiming that the *MBOA's* remedial amendments to the *CPP* were contrary to s. 15(1) of the *Charter*. ... The Hislop class argued that survivors of contributing partners of same-sex conjugal relationships who died anytime after s. 15(1) of the *Charter* became effective (April 17, 1985) should be eligible to make an application for *CPP* survivorship benefits. The Ontario Court of Appeal agreed with the Hislop class and found that the *eligibility* restriction violated s. 15(1) of the *Charter* and that the restriction could not be justified under s. 1. In other words, survivors of same-sex conjugal relationships in which the contributors died any time after April 17, 1985 should be eligible to receive survivor's pensions. We agree with that conclusion. ...

[8] The Hislop class argued that survivors of same-sex conjugal relationships should be entitled to retroactive benefits from the time of death of the same-sex conjugal contributing partner. The Ontario Court of Appeal dismissed the Hislop class's claim for retroactive benefits.

[The Supreme Court characterized the third and fourth issues raised as having "less pervasive significance," and dealt with whether the lack of failure to grant same-sex survivors 12 months of arrears (the same for which opposite-sex partners are entitled) violated the Charter and also whether the estates of same-sex survivors have legal standing to claim a remedy for a breach of section 15(1).]

[13] By a series of other *MBOA* amendments to the *CPP*, survivors of same-sex conjugal relationships became entitled to receive benefits under the *CPP*. However, by s. 45(2) of the *MBOA*, s. 44(1.1) of the *CPP* was added whereby no survivorship pension would be payable to survivors of same-sex conjugal relationships unless they became survivors on or after January 1, 1998. In other words, if the partner of the same-sex survivor died before January 1, 1998, the survivor would not be eligible for a survivorship pension under the *CPP*. ...

[14] A second provision added by the *MBOA* was s. 72(2) of the *CPP*. Section 72(2) operated to preclude payments to same-sex survivors for any month before July 2000, the month s. 72(2) came into force. ...

[15] The effect of s. 72(2) was to entirely preclude retroactive pension benefits to same-sex survivors. The Hislop class's position is that same-sex survivors should be entitled to retroactive benefits to the month following the death of their same-sex conjugal partner. ...

VI. Analysis

[33] The *MBOA* was enacted in response to this Court's decision in *M. v. H.* The Act seeks to eliminate from federal legislation distinctions based on sexual orientation. ... [T]he gender of the parties to a conjugal relationship is now irrelevant in the survivorship provisions of the *CPP*. Even though the *MBOA* is remedial legislation, the complaint is that the relief granted by the *MBOA* does not go far enough, in that it fails to confer eligibility on survivors whose same-sex partner died prior to January 1, 1998 and fails to grant retroactive relief.

A. Section 44(1.1)

...

[37] ... Throughout this litigation, the government has argued that s. 44(1.1) draws a temporal distinction only. The government's position is that the provisions of the *MBOA* do not differentiate between same-sex couples and opposite-sex couples, but rather, between two groups of survivors of same-sex relationships, based on the date their relationships ended as a result of one partner's death. It cannot, therefore, violate s. 15(1) because a temporal basis for a distinction is not an enumerated or recognized analogous ground of discrimination. In our opinion, the courts below were correct in rejecting this argument.

[38] To frame the comparator group in terms of the express distinction made in s. 44(1.1) between survivors whose partners died before January 1, 1998 and those whose partners died on or after that date would be to miss the fundamental reason for the enactment of the *MBOA*. ...The *MBOA* was expressly intended to extend equal treatment to same-sex partners in a wide range of statutes. ... What must be compared is the subset of same-sex survivors that remains excluded from the *CPP* survivor's benefits, i.e., those whose partners died before January 1, 1998, and similarly situated

opposite-sex survivors. The appropriate comparator group in respect of the s. 44(1.1) analysis is survivors of opposite-sex conjugal relationships whose partners died before January 1, 1998.

[39] ... When the government enacts remedial legislation, that legislation may still violate s. 15(1) requirements. The fact that it is remedial legislation does not immunize it from *Charter* review. ...

[41] The government cursorily argued that the *Charter* should be interpreted in a manner recognizing the evolution of societal opinions and the incremental recognition of analogous grounds. The government says the *MBOA* amendments restricting eligibility to survivors whose partners died on or after January 1, 1998 are consistent with that evolution. With respect, we do not see how the evolution of societal opinions and the incremental recognition of analogous grounds bear on whether s. 44(1.1) continues the discrimination which the *MBOA* amendments are intended to remedy. The question is not whether there was recognition of same-sex discrimination prior to 1998. Rather, the question is whether the prior discrimination which was recognized by the *MBOA* is or is not now being remedied. If survivors of same-sex conjugal relationships whose partners died before 1998 continue to be ineligible for *CPP* survivorship pensions, the prior discrimination that has been recognized by Parliament in enacting the *MBOA* continues for such survivors. For these reasons, we do not accept the government's evolution argument as a valid response to the s. 15(1) claim in respect of s. 44(1.1). ...

(2) Section 1

...

[44] The framework for a s. 1 analysis is the well-known *Oakes* test ... . The four tests ask the following questions:

(1) Is the objective of the legislation pressing and substantial?
(2) Is there a rational connection between the government's legislation and its objective?
(3) Does the government's legislation minimally impair the *Charter* right or freedom at stake?
(4) Is the deleterious effect of the *Charter* breach outweighed by the salutary effect of the legislation?

[45] As the *MBOA* was the legislative response to this Court's decision in *M. v. H.*, the Act obviously has a pressing and substantial purpose. However, in *M. v. H.*, the Court also held that "when dealing with underinclusive legislation it is important also to consider the impugned omission when construing the objective" (para. 100).

[46] It is therefore necessary to consider whether the objective of s. 44(1.1) is pressing and substantial. The effect

of s. 44(1.1) is to limit eligibility for *CPP* survivorship pensions in the case of survivors of same-sex conjugal relationships. No survivorship pension is payable where the partner died prior to January 1, 1998. ...

[49] We acknowledge that there may be cases in which the pressing and substantial objective of legislation and the impugned provisions are obvious and may be deduced from the legislation itself. However, in the majority of cases, in order to satisfy the pressing and substantial objective test, the government must adduce some evidence to support its argument. ...

[55] More than a vague argument raised for the first time in this Court by the government will be necessary if a s. 1 argument is to succeed. It cannot succeed in this case. Because the government has failed to establish the pressing and substantial objective of the provision, its rational connection to its objective and that it minimally impairs the Hislop class's *Charter* rights, its argument fails in respect of s. 44(1.1) of the *CPP*.

B. Section 72(2)

...

[59] The government makes the same "comparator group" argument in respect of s. 72(2) as it did in respect of s. 44(1.1). It says the *MBOA* amendments did not differentiate between same-sex and opposite-sex couples but rather between two groups of survivors of same-sex relationships based on the date on which the relationship ended as a result of the death of one of the partners.

[60] ... For the reasons we have expressed in our analysis of the s. 15(1) arguments in respect of s. 44(1.1), we do not find merit in the government's submissions in respect of s. 72(2).

[61] With respect to s. 1, the government seems to make two arguments in support of s. 72(2). One is that the general principle is that legislation operates from the time of enactment forward and that this approach is consistent with prior amendments to the *CPP*. The other is that the focus was to fix the liability of the *CPP* as of July 2000. ...

[64] We recognize that costs may be a factor in a s. 1 analysis. The government says that July 2000 was selected in order to fix the liability of the *CPP* as of that date. However, as of July 2000, the *CPP* had to anticipate up to 12 months of arrears liability arising from opposite-sex relationships. The government did not refer to evidence to suggest that cost was the reason to deny same-sex survivors up to 12 months of benefit arrears during the transitional period.

[65] We are not persuaded that, in the circumstances of this case, s. 72(2) is justified under s. 1 of the *Charter*. ... Here, there is an absence of evidence of cost justifying the provision.

In the circumstances, we cannot find there is a rational connection between s. 72(2) and its objective, or indeed, that s. 72(2) minimally impairs the *Charter* rights of the Hislop class. ...

C. Section 72(1)

[67] Because we have found that s. 72(2) violates s. 15(1) and is not saved by s. 1 of the *Charter*, same-sex survivors will be entitled to up to 12 months of pension arrears for the period from August 1999 to July 2000, pursuant to s. 72(1).

[68] However, the Hislop class takes issue with s. 72(1) itself. ... Based upon s. 44(1.1) and s. 72(2) being struck down, it is argued that same-sex survivors should be entitled to claim retroactive benefits from the time they became survivors after April 17, 1985 when s. 15(1) of the *Charter* came into force. For example, if an individual became a survivor of a same-sex relationship in 1995, the survivor should be entitled to a lump sum of benefits for the period from 1995 to the time the application was received. ...

[69] ... What the Hislop class is seeking is retroactive *Charter* relief. Their request for a constitutional exemption from the limitation on arrears in s. 72(1) is, in effect, a request for a remedy in respect of their exclusion from the survivors' benefits by the pre-*MBOA CPP* between 1985 and 2000. As will be explained hereafter, this Court has been explicit in restricting entitlement to retroactive *Charter* relief of this nature. ...

[The Hislop class argued that estates should be able to apply for the benefits to which survivors would have been entitled, which was precluded by section 60(2). The Supreme Court accepted the government's argument that estates are not individuals, but artificial entities incapable of having their human dignity infringed. In this sense, section 15 rights die with the individual. However, Mr. Hislop's individual situation is different. Although he died between the time his notice of appeal was filed in this court and the hearing of this appeal, he obtained judgment while he was still alive. Thus, the estate of any class member who was alive on the date that argument concluded in the Ontario Superior Court, and who otherwise met the requirements under the Canada Pension Plan, is entitled to the benefit of this judgment.]

E. Remedies

[78] We now turn to the question of remedy. In challenging s. 72(1) of the *CPP*, the appellants seek a fully retroactive remedy. They argue that a declaration of invalidity under s. 52 of the *Constitution Act, 1982* necessarily operates back to the coming into force of s. 15 of the *Charter*. ...

[80] The supremacy clause, now enshrined at s. 52, is silent about the remedies which may flow from a declaration

of nullity. Does it mean that such a declaration is always both prospective and retroactive? This does not appear to have been the position of our Court throughout the incremental development of the law of constitutional remedies after the adoption of the *Charter*. A body of jurisprudence now accepts the legitimacy of limiting the retroactive effect of a declaration of nullity and of fashioning prospective remedies in appropriate circumstances.

(1) Retroactive and Prospective Remedies Under the Charter

[81] The Constitution empowers courts to issue constitutional remedies with *both* retroactive and prospective effects. ...

[82] Section 52(1) instructs courts to declare unconstitutional legislation of no force or effect. When a court issues a declaration of invalidity, it declares that, henceforth, the unconstitutional law cannot be enforced. The nullification of a law is thus prospective. However, s. 52(1) may also operate retroactively so far as the parties are concerned, reaching into the past to annul the effects of the unconstitutional law: see, e.g., *Miron v. Trudel*, [1995] 2 S.C.R. 418.

[83] This Court has applied in many cases the "declaratory approach" to constitutional remedies, which implies that s. 52(1) remedies are often given retroactive effect. ... On this view, s. 52(1) remedies are deemed to be fully retroactive because the legislature never had the authority to enact an unconstitutional law. ... If the law was invalid from the outset, then any government action taken pursuant to that law is also invalid, and consequently, those affected by it have a right to redress which reaches back into the past.

[84] ... [T]he declaratory approach is derived from Blackstone's [Blackstone, William, *Commentaries on the Laws of England*, vol. 1 (Oxford: Clarendon Press, 1765)] famous aphorism that judges do not create law but merely discover it. ... It reflects a traditional and widespread understanding of the role of the judiciary in a democratic state governed by strong principles of separation of powers between courts, legislatures and executives. In this perspective, courts grant retroactive relief applying existing law or rediscovered rules which are deemed to have always existed. On the other hand, legislators fashion new laws for the future.

[85] Blackstone's declaratory approach has not remained unchallenged in modern law. Commentators and courts have pointed out that judges fulfill a legitimate law-making function. Judges do not merely declare law; they also make law. These critics argue that Blackstone's view is a fiction as judges make law, especially in the common law world. ...

[86] However, this acknowledgement does not require abandoning Blackstone's declaratory approach altogether.

The critique of the Blackstonian approach applies only to situations in which judges are fashioning new legal rules or principles and not when they are applying the existing law. In instances where courts apply pre-existing legal doctrine to a new set of facts, Blackstone's declaratory approach remains appropriate and remedies are necessarily retroactive. Because courts are adjudicative bodies that, in the usual course of things, are called upon to decide the legal consequences of past happenings, they generally grant remedies that are retroactive to the extent necessary to ensure that successful litigants will have the benefit of the ruling. ... There is, however, an important difference between saying that judicial decisions are *generally* retroactive and that they are *necessarily* retroactive. When the law changes through judicial intervention, courts operate outside of the Blackstonian paradigm. In those situations, it may be appropriate for the court to issue a prospective rather than a retroactive remedy. The question then becomes what kind of change and which conditions will justify the crafting of judicial prospective remedies. ...

[88] ... Despite this Court's endorsement of the Blackstonian declaratory approach, in its development of the law of constitutional remedies, it has frequently seen fit to temper the retroactive effect of s. 52(1) remedies. ...

[89] ... [T]he the fact that this Court has occasionally prescribed transition periods, intended to give a s. 52(1) remedy prospective effect only, suggests that this Court is not wedded to the declaratory approach in all *Charter* cases.

[90] In another type of situation, which arises more frequently, the Court has held that providing immediate and retroactive judicial remedies may be "inappropriate" when "doing so would create a lacuna in the regime before Parliament would have a chance to act." ... In such cases, the Court has temporarily suspended the declaration of invalidity of the unconstitutional legislation to avoid creating a "legal vacuum" or "legal chaos" before Parliament or the legislature has the opportunity to enact something in place of the unconstitutional legislation. ... In *Schachter* [*v. Canada*, [1992] 2 S.C.R. 679], this Court held that the suspended declaration of invalidity was appropriate when giving immediate retroactive effect to the Court's declaration of invalidity would (a) "pose a danger to the public"; (b) "threaten the rule of law"; or (c) "result in the deprivation of benefits from deserving persons", such as when the legislation was "deemed unconstitutional because of underinclusiveness rather than overbreadth": *Schachter*, at p. 719.

[91] Like transition periods and other purely prospective remedies, the suspended declaration of invalidity is not fully consistent with the declaratory approach. By suspending the declaration of invalidity, the Court allows the constitutional infirmity to continue temporarily so that the legislature can fix the problem. In other words, the Court extends the life of a law which, on the Blackstonian view, never existed.

[92] Although if the legislature fails to comply with the Court's order within the period of suspension, the Court's declaration would apply retroactively, the purpose of a suspended declaration of invalidity can be to facilitate the legislature's function in crafting a prospective remedy. The temporal delay in striking down the law also has the effect of extending the life of an unconstitutional law. In such cases, to allow the claimants to recover concurrent retroactive relief would be at cross-purposes with the Court's decision to grant a suspended declaration of invalidity: *Schachter*, at p. 720. ...

[94] The approach which our Court has adopted in respect of the crafting of constitutional remedies also flows from its understanding of the process of constitutional interpretation, which the "living tree" metaphor neatly describes. ... This Court has often stated that the Canadian Constitution should not be viewed as a static document but as an instrument capable of adapting with the times by way of a process of evolutionary interpretation, within the natural limits of the text, which "accommodates and addresses the realities of modern life." ...

[95] It is true that the "living tree" doctrine is not wedded to a particular model of the judicial function. At times, its application may reflect the fact that, in a case, the Court is merely declaring the law of the country as it has stood and that a retroactive remedy is then generally appropriate. In other circumstances, its use recognizes that the law has changed, that the change must be acknowledged and that, from a given point in time, the new law or the new understanding of some legal principle will prevail.

[96] The question is no longer the legitimacy of prospective remedies, but rather when, why and how judges may rule prospectively or restrict the retroactive effect of their decisions in constitutional matters. The key question becomes the nature and effect of the legal change at issue in order to determine whether a prospective remedy is appropriate. The legitimacy of its use turns on the answer to this question. ...

[99] Change in the law occurs in many ways. "Clear break with the past" catches some of its diversity. It can be best identified with those situations where, in Canadian law, the Supreme Court departs from its own jurisprudence by expressly overruling or implicitly repudiating a prior decision. Such clear situations would justify recourse to prospective remedies in a proper context. But other forms of substantial change may be as relevant, especially in constitutional adjudication, where courts must give content to broad, but previously undefined, rights, principles or norms. The definition

of a yet undetermined standard or the recognition that a situation is now covered by a constitutional guarantee also often expresses a substantial change in the law. The right may have been there, but it finds an expression in a new or newly recognized technological or social environment. Such a legal response to these developments properly grounds the use of prospective remedies, when the appropriate circumstances are met. A substantial change in the law is necessary, not sufficient, to justify purely prospective remedies. Hence, we must now turn to what else must be considered once legal change has been established.

[100] Although the list of such factors should not be considered as closed, some of them appear more clearly compelling. They may include reasonable or in good faith reliance by governments … or the fairness of the limitation of the retroactivity of the remedy to the litigants. Courts ought also consider whether a retroactive remedy would unduly interfere with the constitutional role of legislatures and democratic governments in the allocation of public resources (*Benner* [*v. Canada (Secretary of State)*, [1997] 1 S.C.R. 358], at para. 103; *Schachter*, at p. 710).

[101] A careful consideration of reliance interests is critical to this analytical process. … Fully retroactive remedies might prove highly disruptive in respect of government action, which, on the basis of settled or broadly held views of the law as it stood, framed budgets or attempted to design social programs. Persons and public authorities could then become liable under a new legal norm. Neither governments nor citizens could be reasonably assured of the legal consequences of their actions at the time they are taken. …

[103] People generally conduct their affairs based on their understanding of what the law requires. Governments in this country are no different. Every law they pass or administrative action they take must be performed with an eye to what the Constitution requires. Just as ignorance of the law is no excuse for an individual who breaks the law, ignorance of the Constitution is no excuse for governments. But where a judicial ruling changes the existing law or creates new law, it may, under certain conditions, be inappropriate to hold the government retroactively liable. An approach to constitutional interpretation that makes it possible to identify, in appropriate cases, a point in time when the law changed, makes it easier to ensure that persons and legislatures who relied on the former legal rule while it prevailed will be protected. In this way, a balance is struck between the legitimate reliance interests of actors who make decisions based on a reasonable assessment of the state of the law at the relevant time on one hand and the need to allow constitutional jurisprudence to evolve over time on the other. …

(2) The Appropriate Remedy in This Case

(a) Limits on the Retroactive Effect of the Remedy in the Context of This Case

[109] Same-sex equality jurisprudence since 1985 is illustrative of the sort of legal shift that gives rise to new law and justifies consideration of prospective remedies. The factors mentioned above also weigh in favour of limiting the retroactive effect of the remedy in the context of this case.

(i) The Substantial Change in the Law

[110] This Court's decision in *M. v. H.* marked a departure from pre-existing jurisprudence on same-sex equality rights. …

(ii) Reasonable Reliance

[112] Given the state of the jurisprudence prior to *M. v. H.*, the exclusion of same-sex partners from the former *CPP* was based on a reasonable understanding of the state of s. 15(1) jurisprudence as it existed after *Egan* and before *M. v. H.* …

[114] … The inviolability of the Constitution ensures that our nation's most cherished values are preserved, while the role of the courts in applying the Constitution ensures that the law is sufficiently flexible to change over time to reflect advances in human understanding. But it also means that the Constitution, at any snapshot in time, is only as robust as the court interpreting it. If the judiciary errs or is slow to recognize that previous interpretations of the Constitution no longer correspond to social realities, it must change the law. However, in breaking with the past, the Court does not create an automatic right to redress for the Court's prior ruling. Where the government's reliance on the unconstitutional law was reasonable because it was relying on this Court's jurisprudence, it will be less likely that a right to retroactive relief will flow from a subsequent declaration of invalidity of the unconstitutional law.

(iii) Good Faith

[115] Our comments above indicate that the government did not act in bad faith in failing to extend survivors' benefits to same-sex couples prior to *M. v. H.* It is significant that the survivors' benefit scheme under the former *CPP* was never struck down by a court of competent jurisdiction. Rather, recognizing the likely implications of this Court's ruling in *M. v. H.* for that scheme, Parliament endeavoured to pre-emptively correct the constitutional deficiencies therein by enacting remedial legislation. Because the government acted in good faith by attempting pre-emptively to correct a constitutional infirmity soon after it was discovered, it would be

inappropriate to reach back further in time and impose a retroactive remedy.

(iv) Fairness to Litigants

[116] In seeking payment of arrears back as far as 1985, the Hislop class effectively asks this Court to overlook the evolution in the jurisprudence of same-sex equality rights that has taken place and to declare that the understanding to which we have come over that period of time was in fact the law in 1985. This position cannot be sustained. Although *M. v. H.* declares what the Constitution requires, it does not give rise to an automatic right to every government benefit that might have been paid out had the Court always interpreted the Constitution in accordance with its present-day understanding of it. ...

(v) Respecting Parliament's Role

[117] Achieving an appropriate balance between fairness to individual litigants and respecting the legislative role of Parliament may mean that *Charter* remedies will be directed more toward government action in the future and less toward the correction of past wrongs. In the present case, the Hislop class's claim for a retroactive remedy is tantamount to a claim for compensatory damages flowing from the underinclusiveness of the former *CPP*. Imposing that sort of liability on the government, absent bad faith, unreasonable reliance or conduct that is clearly wrong, would undermine the important balance between the protection of constitutional rights and the need for effective government that is struck by the general rule of qualified immunity. A retroactive remedy in the instant case would encroach unduly on the inherently legislative domain of the distribution of government resources and of policy making in respect of this process.

(vi) Conclusion

[118] For the foregoing reasons, the retroactive relief sought by the Hislop class is unavailable under the law applicable to constitutional remedies. It is not therefore necessary to carry out a s. 15(1) analysis in respect of s. 72(1).

(b) Remedies Arising From the Specific Provisions: Sections 44(1.1) and 72(2)

[119] We turn now to a consideration of the appropriate remedy for the specific constitutional violations that have been identified in this case. ...

[121] In the present case, ss. 44(1.1) and 72(2), although found within remedial legislation, restrict the availability of that legislation to a marginalized group. The extent of the inconsistency with the equality guarantee is co-extensive with the scope of these two provisions. As such, the inconsistency can be cured without distorting or interfering with the rest of the legislative scheme. A declaration that ss. 44(1.1) and 72(2) are of no force and effect is in keeping with the scheme and obvious purpose of the *MBOA* to extend the survivors' benefit to same-sex survivors. Finally, a temporary suspension of the declaration of invalidity is not appropriate in the present case. ... Suspensions should only be used where striking down the legislation without enacting something in its place would pose a danger to the public, threaten the rule of law or where it would result in the deprivation of benefits from deserving persons without benefiting the rights claimant ([*Schachter*,] p. 719). None of these factors are present in the case at bar.

[122] Throughout these proceedings, the Crown has taken the position that the specific provisions are constitutionally unassailable because they merely ensure that the remedial provisions in the *MBOA* apply prospectively (i.e., not retroactively) from the time of the enactment. Further, the Crown has relied on the argument that same-sex equality rights, as they are understood today, are not what they were in 1985. In effect, it is the Crown's position that striking down the specific provisions would be tantamount to applying today's legal understanding of equality rights to past situations.

[123] As we have explained above, the specific provisions violate s. 15(1) and cannot be justified under s. 1. The constitutional analysis related to these provisions does not depend on any particular conception of the equality rights of same-sex survivors prior to the enactment of the *MBOA*. The specific provisions, as applied to same-sex survivors *today*, are discriminatory.

[124] Any concerns about retroactivity in respect of s. 44(1.1) are misplaced because they mistakenly construe the survivor's benefit as a payment in respect of a past event, namely the death of the survivor's spouse or common law partner, rather than the ongoing status of being a survivor. ...

[133] The analysis in relation to s. 72(2) is somewhat different. Prior to the enactment of the *MBOA*, it is true that same-sex survivors had no right to the survivor's benefit. Striking down s. 72(2) admittedly alters the legal consequences of having been a survivor (a past situation) in the 12 months preceding July 2000, when the *MBOA* came into force. To the extent that this involves a retroactive change in the law, it flows necessarily from the fact that Parliament has included in the *CPP* a right to up to 12 months of arrears. It is clearly open to Parliament to legislate retroactively, which it has done in s. 72(1). The *Charter* simply requires that same-sex survivors receive equal treatment as their opposite-sex counterparts. To the extent that s. 72(2) withholds from same-sex survivors a

right to arrears to which similarly situated opposite-sex survivors are entitled, it is of no force and effect.

[134] In conclusion, class members who were precluded by s. 44(1.1) or s. 72(2) from receiving the survivor's benefit, and who otherwise meet the eligibility requirements, will be entitled to payment of that benefit. In the circumstances, the relevant date for the purpose of that payment is the date on which application was received or where no application was made because of the unconstitutional provisions, the date on which the statement of claim was filed. In no event are benefits payable in respect of a month prior to August 1999, which is the earliest month in respect of which a class member who applied for the survivor's benefit on the day the *MBOA* came into force could have been eligible.

VII. Interest

[135] … [W]e reject the government's contention that pre-judgment interest is not available in the instant case. …

8. If so, is the infringement a reasonable limit prescribed by law as can be demonstrably justified in a free and democratic society under s. 1 of the *Canadian Charter of Rights and Freedoms*?

It is not necessary to answer this question.

[Justice Bastarache provided separate reasons that, while agreeing with the outcome, disagreed with the approach taken to the question of retroactive constitutional remedies.]

35   R. v. Grant, 2009

Section 9 of the Charter guarantees "the right not to be arbitrarily detained." If one *is* detained by the police, one has the right under section 10 "to retain and instruct counsel without delay and to be informed of that right." Does every stop by a police officer constitute a detention that triggers the right to counsel? Of course not. Think of the officer controlling and stopping movement at an accident or crime scene. As the majority opinion[1] in this case puts it, "reasonable people" in such circumstances "understand that the police are not constraining individual choices but rather helping people or gathering information."

What about the beat cop establishing a neighbourhood presence as part of a crime prevention strategy? Is it a "detention" whenever he or she stops and questions people, even for investigative purposes? Again, the Supreme Court answers no:

> Section 9 of the *Charter* does not require that police abstain from interacting with members of the public until they have specific grounds to connect the individual to the commission of a crime. Nor does s. 10 require that the police advise everyone at the outset of any encounter that they have no obligation to speak to them and are entitled to legal counsel.

What if, as in this case, a young man being questioned starts nervously adjusting his clothing, and is told to "keep his hands in front of him"? Again, the majority thinks the officer should be permitted this "precautionary directive" without immediately advising the right to counsel.

Finally—coming to the full facts of *R. v. Grant*—what if two plainclothes officers, also observing the nervous behaviour, hustle over to assist the uniformed beat cop, whose subsequent questioning leads to the discovery of a loaded revolver? This, says the court, *does* involve the kind of detention at stake in sections 9 and 10 of the Charter.

Grant's detention started as soon as the plainclothes officers arrived and the additional questioning began. It was "arbitrary detention" because "the police lacked legal grounds to detain the appellant." The infringement of section 9 was compounded, moreover, by the failure to inform Grant about his section 10 right to counsel before proceeding with questions.

But what to do with the gun? It was reliable evidence of a crime, to be sure, but it was "conscripted" from the accused through the infringement of his rights, and would likely have gone undiscovered had those rights been respected. Should the gun be excluded from evidence under section 24(2) of the Charter—thus effectively obviating any firearms charges—because its admission "would bring the administration of justice into disrepute"? That might have been the result under existing jurisprudence, which established an "all-but-automatic

---

1   Justices Binnie and Deschamps each wrote partially concurring opinions. For reasons of space, we provide excerpts only from the majority opinion.

exclusionary rule for non-discoverable conscriptive evidence." Instead of accepting this outcome, the court chose to revise the test for excluding evidence to better balance all the relevant circumstances. In Grant's case, for example, the Charter infringement, which "weighs strongly in favour of excluding the gun," had to be balanced against "the public interest in the adjudication of the case on its merits," which "weighs strongly in favour of its admission." Because the police officers had not engaged in "egregious" conduct and "were operating in circumstances of considerable legal uncertainty," the gun could safely be admitted into evidence without bringing "the administration of justice into disrepute."[2] ∼

Discussion Questions

1. Was the Supreme Court right in abandoning the "all-but-automatic exclusionary rule for non-discoverable conscriptive evidence"?

2. The Supreme Court allowed the unlawfully secured gun to be admitted as evidence in this case because the officers proceeded in good faith on their understanding of ambiguous law. By contrast, in a 1985 case, very early in the Charter's history, the court excluded evidence arguably secured because of good faith understanding of an ambiguous legal situation.[3] Which is the right approach? What might/should the court do in a subsequent case that exhibits a fact situation similar to the one in *Grant*?

---

2   Although all seven of the Supreme Court judges who sat on the case came to the same bottom-line conclusions, (1) that the police had infringed Grant's Charter rights, and (2) that the gun discovered as a result should be admitted into evidence, Justices Binnie and Deschamps arrived at these conclusions by somewhat different routes, sometimes disagreeing with the analytical approach of the majority.

3   *R. v. Therens*, [1985] 1 S.C.R. 613. See especially the dissenting opinion of Justice LeDain on the good faith actions of the police in that case.

R. v. GRANT
2009 SCC 32, [2009] 2 S.C.R. 353

Hearing: April 24, 2008; Judgment: July 17, 2009.

Present: McLachlin C.J. and Binnie, LeBel, Deschamps, Fish, Abella, and Charron JJ.

Interveners: Director of Public Prosecutions of Canada, Attorney General of British Columbia, Canadian Civil Liberties Association and Criminal Lawyers' Association (Ontario).

The judgment of McLachlin C.J. and LeBel, Fish, Abella, and Charron JJ. was delivered by

THE CHIEF JUSTICE AND CHARRON J.:

[1] Mr. Grant appeals his convictions on a series of firearms offences, relating to a gun seized by police during an encounter on a Toronto sidewalk. The gun was entered as evidence against Mr. Grant and formed the basis of his convictions. The question on this appeal is whether that evidence was obtained in breach of Mr. Grant's *Charter* rights, and if so, whether the evidence should have been excluded under s. 24(2) of the *Canadian Charter of Rights and Freedoms*.

[2] Resolving these questions requires us to revisit two important and contentious areas of criminal law *Charter* jurisprudence. The first is the definition of "detention" under ss. 9 and 10 of the *Charter*. The second is the test for exclusion of evidence obtained in violation of the *Charter* pursuant to s. 24(2). ...

[4] The encounter at the centre of this appeal occurred at mid-day on November 17, 2003, in the Greenwood and Danforth area of Toronto. With four schools in the area and a history of student assaults, robberies, and drug offences occurring over the lunch hour, the three officers involved in

the encounter were on patrol for the purposes of monitoring the area and maintaining a safe student environment. Two of the officers, Constables Worrell and Forde, were dressed in plainclothes and driving an unmarked car. Although on patrol, their primary task was to visit the various schools to determine if there were persons on school property who should not have been there—either non-students or students from another school. The third officer, Constable Gomes, was in uniform and driving a marked police car. On "directed patrol," he had been tasked with maintaining a visible police presence in the area in order to provide student reassurance and to deter crime during the high school lunch period.

[5] Mr. Grant, a young black man, was walking northbound on Greenwood Avenue when he came to the attention of Constables Worrell and Forde. As the two officers drove past, Cst. Worrell testified that the appellant "stared" at them in an unusually intense manner and continued to do so as they proceeded down the street, while at the same time "fidgeting" with his coat and pants in a way that aroused their suspicions. Given their purpose for being in the area and based on what he had just seen, Cst. Worrell decided that "maybe we should have a chat with this guy and see what's up with him." Cst. Worrell wanted to know whether Mr. Grant was a student at one of the schools they were assigned to monitor, and, if he was not, whether he was headed to one of the schools anyway. Noticing Cst. Gomes parked on the street ahead of Mr. Grant, and in light of his uniformed attire, the two plainclothes officers suggested to Cst. Gomes that he "have a chat" with the approaching appellant to determine if there was any need for concern.

[6] Cst. Gomes then got out of his car and initiated an exchange with Mr. Grant, while standing on the sidewalk directly in his intended path. The officer asked the appellant "what was going on," and requested his name and address. In response, the appellant provided a provincial health card. At one point, the appellant, behaving nervously, adjusted his jacket, prompting the officer to ask him to "keep his hands in front of him." By this point, the two other officers had returned and parked on the side of the street.

[7] Cst. Worrell testified on cross-examination that he and Cst. Forde pulled up because he got a funny feeling based on Mr. Grant's way of looking over at them, looking around "all over the place," and adjusting himself. On direct examination he said that "[h]e still seemed to be, I don't know, looking a bit nervous the way he was looking around, looking at us, looking around when speaking to Officer Gomes. And at this time, I suggested to my partner, you know, I don't think it would hurt if we just go up to Officer Gomes and just stand by, just to make sure everything was okay." Thus, after a brief period observing the exchange from their car, the two officers

approached the pair on the sidewalk, identified themselves to the appellant as police officers by flashing their badges, and took up positions behind Cst. Gomes, obstructing the way forward. The exchange between Cst. Gomes and Mr. Grant subsequent to the arrival of the two officers was as follows:

Q. Have you ever been arrested before?

A. I got into some trouble about three years ago.

Q. Do you have anything on you that you shouldn't?

A. No. Well, I got a small bag of weed.

Q. Where is it?

A. It's in my pocket.

Q. Is that it?

A. (Male puts his head down.) Yeah. Well, no.

Q. Do you have other drugs on you?

A. No, I just have the weed, that's it.

Q. Well, what is it that you have?

A. I have a firearm.

[8] At this point, the officers arrested and searched the appellant, seizing the marijuana and a loaded revolver. They then advised Mr. Grant of his right to counsel and took him to the police station. ...

A. Breach of the Charter

[11] The first issue in this case is whether the evidence of the gun was obtained in a manner that breached Mr. Grant's rights under the *Charter*. Mr. Grant argues that the police breached his *Charter* rights by arbitrarily detaining him contrary to s. 9 and by failing to advise him of his right to speak to a lawyer contrary to s. 10(*b*), before the questioning that led to the discovery of the firearm that is the subject of these charges. ...

[12] The threshold question is whether the appellant was detained before he produced the firearm and was arrested. If he was detained, the detention was arbitrary; all parties are agreed that the police lacked legal grounds to detain the appellant. Further, if detained, Mr. Grant was entitled to be advised of the right to counsel at that point, which would establish breach of s. 10(*b*) of the *Charter*. ...

[28] The general principle that determines detention for *Charter* purposes was set out in *Therens* [*R. v.*, [1985] 1 S.C.R. 613]: a person is detained where he or she "submits or acquiesces in the deprivation of liberty and reasonably believes that the choice to do otherwise does not exist" (*per* Le Dain J., at

p. 644). This principle is consistent with the notion of choice that underlies our conception of liberty and, as such, shapes our interpretation of ss. 9 and 10 of the *Charter*. When detention removes the "choice to do otherwise" but comply with a police direction, s. 10(*b*) serves an indispensable purpose. It protects, among other interests, the detainee's ability to choose whether to cooperate with the investigation by giving a statement. The ambit of detention for constitutional purposes is informed by the need to safeguard this choice without impairing effective law enforcement. ...

[30] Moving on from the fundamental principle of the right to choose, we find that psychological constraint amounting to detention has been recognized in two situations. The first is where the subject is legally required to comply with a direction or demand, as in the case of a roadside breath sample. The second is where there is no legal obligation to comply with a restrictive or coercive demand, but a reasonable person in the subject's position would feel so obligated. ...

[31] This second form of psychological detention— where no legal compulsion exists—has proven difficult to define consistently. The question is whether the police conduct would cause a reasonable person to conclude that he or she was not free to go and had to comply with the police direction or demand. ...

[33] In most cases, it will be readily apparent whether or not an encounter between the police and an individual results in a detention. Making the task easier is the fact that what would reasonably be understood by all concerned is often informed by generally understood legal rights and duties, as a few examples illustrate.

[34] At one end of the spectrum of possibilities, detention overlaps with arrest or imprisonment and the *Charter* will clearly apply. Similarly, a legal obligation to comply with a police demand or direction, such as a breath sample demand at the roadside, clearly denotes s. 9 detention. As Le Dain J. observed in *Therens*, "[i]t is not realistic to speak of a person who is liable to arrest and prosecution for refusal to comply with a demand which a peace officer is empowered by statute to make as being free to refuse to comply" (p. 643).

[35] At the other end of the spectrum lie encounters between individual and police where it would be clear to a reasonable person that the individual is not being deprived of a meaningful choice whether or not to cooperate with a police demand or directive and hence not detained.

[36] We may rule out at the outset situations where the police are acting in a non-adversarial role and assisting members of the public in circumstances commonly accepted as lacking the essential character of a detention. In many common situations, reasonable people understand that the police are not constraining individual choices, but rather helping people or gathering information. For instance, the reasonable person would understand that a police officer who attends at a medical emergency on a 911 call is not detaining the individuals he or she encounters. This is so even if the police, in taking control of the situation, effectively interfere with an individual's freedom of movement. Such deprivations of liberty will not be significant enough to attract *Charter* scrutiny because they do not attract legal consequences for the concerned individuals.

[37] Another often-discussed situation is when police officers approach bystanders in the wake of an accident or crime, to determine if they witnessed the event and obtain information that may assist in their investigation. While many people may be happy to assist the police, the law is clear that, subject to specific provisions that may exceptionally govern, the citizen is free to walk away: *R. v. Grafe* (1987), 36 C.C.C. (3d) 267 (Ont. C.A.). Given the existence of such a generally understood right in such circumstances, a reasonable person would not conclude that his or her right to choose whether to cooperate with them has been taken away. This conclusion holds true even if the person may feel compelled to cooperate with the police out of a sense of moral or civic duty. The Ontario Court of Appeal adverted to this concept in *Grafe*, where Krever J.A. wrote, at p. 271:

> The law has long recognized that although there is no legal duty there is a moral or social duty on the part of every citizen to answer questions put to him or her by the police and, in that way to assist the police: see, for example, *Rice v. Connolly*, [1966] 2 All E.R. 649 at p. 652, *per* Lord Parker C.J. Implicit in that moral or social duty is the right of a police officer to ask questions even, in my opinion, when he or she has no belief that an offence has been committed. To be asked questions, in these circumstances, cannot be said to be a deprivation of liberty or security.

[38] In the context of investigating an accident or a crime, the police, unbeknownst to them at that point in time, may find themselves asking questions of a person who is implicated in the occurrence and, consequently, is at risk of self-incrimination. This does not preclude the police from continuing to question the person in the pursuit of their investigation. Section 9 of the *Charter* does not require that police abstain from interacting with members of the public until they have specific grounds to connect the individual to the commission of a crime. Nor does s. 10 require that the police advise everyone at the outset of any encounter that they have no obligation to speak to them and are entitled to legal counsel.

[39] Effective law enforcement is highly dependent on the cooperation of members of the public. The police must be

able to act in a manner that fosters this cooperation, not discourage it. However, police investigative powers are not without limits. The notion of psychological detention recognizes the reality that police tactics, even in the absence of exercising actual physical restraint, may be coercive enough to effectively remove the individual's choice to walk away from the police. This creates the risk that the person may reasonably feel compelled to incriminate himself or herself. Where that is the case, the police are no longer entitled simply to expect cooperation from an individual. Unless, as stated earlier, the police inform the person that he or she is under no obligation to answer questions and is free to go, a detention may well crystallize and, when it does, the police must provide the subject with his or her s. 10(*b*) rights. ...

[47] [Coming to the case at hand], [t]he encounter began with Cst. Gomes approaching Mr. Grant (stepping in his path) and making general inquiries. Such preliminary questioning is a legitimate exercise of police powers. At this stage, a reasonable person would not have concluded he or she was being deprived of the right to choose how to act, and for that reason there was no detention.

[48] Cst. Gomes then told the appellant to "keep his hands in front of him." This act, viewed in isolation, might be insufficient to indicate detention, on the ground that it was simply a precautionary directive. However, consideration of the entire context of what transpired from this point forward leads to the conclusion that Mr. Grant was detained.

[49] Two other officers approached, flashing their badges and taking tactical adversarial positions behind Cst. Gomes. The encounter developed into one where Mr. Grant was singled out as the object of particularized suspicion, as evidenced by the conduct of the officers. The nature of the questioning changed from ascertaining the appellant's identity to determining whether he "had anything that he should not." At this point the encounter took on the character of an interrogation, going from general neighbourhood policing to a situation where the police had effectively taken control over the appellant and were attempting to elicit incriminating information.

[50] Although Cst. Gomes was respectful in his questioning, the encounter was inherently intimidating. The power imbalance was obviously exacerbated by Mr. Grant's youth and inexperience. Mr. Grant did not testify, so we do not know what his perceptions of the interaction actually were. However, because the test is an objective one, this is not fatal to his argument that there was a detention. ... In our view, the evidence supports Mr. Grant's contention that a reasonable person in his position (18 years old, alone, faced by three physically larger policemen in adversarial positions) would conclude that his or her right to choose how to act had been removed by the police, given their conduct.

[51] The police conduct that gave rise to an impression of control was not fleeting. The direction to Mr. Grant to keep his hands in front, in itself inconclusive, was followed by the appearance of two other officers flashing their badges and by questioning driven by focussed suspicion of Mr. Grant. The sustained and restrictive tenor of the conduct after the direction to Mr. Grant to keep his hands in front of him reasonably supports the conclusion that the officers were putting him under their control and depriving him of his choice as to how to respond.

[52] We conclude that Mr. Grant was detained when Cst. Gomes told him to keep his hands in front of him, the other two officers moved into position behind Cst. Gomes, and Cst. Gomes embarked on a pointed line of questioning. At this point, Mr. Grant's liberty was clearly constrained and he was in need of the *Charter* protections associated with detention. ...

[58] In *R. v. Suberu*, 2009 SCC 33, [2009] 2 S.C.R. 460, we conclude that the s. 10(*b*) right to counsel arises immediately upon detention, whether or not the detention is solely for investigative purposes. That being the case, s. 10(*b*) of the *Charter* required the police to advise Mr. Grant that he had the right to speak to a lawyer, and to give him a reasonable opportunity to obtain legal advice if he so chose, before proceeding to elicit incriminating information from him. ... The breach of s. 10(*b*) is established.

B. Exclusion of Evidence

[59] When must evidence obtained in violation of a person's *Charter* rights be excluded? Section 24(2) of the *Charter* provides the following answer:

> Where, in proceedings under subsection (1), a court concludes that evidence was obtained in a manner that infringed or denied any rights or freedoms guaranteed by this Charter, the evidence shall be excluded if it is established that, *having regard to all the circumstances, the admission of it in the proceedings would bring the administration of justice into disrepute.*

[60] The test set out in s. 24(2)—what would bring the administration of justice into disrepute having regard to all the circumstances—is broad and imprecise. The question is what considerations enter into making this determination. In *Collins* [*R. v.*, [1987] 1 S.C.R. 265] and in *R. v. Stillman*, [1997] 1 S.C.R. 607, this Court endeavoured to answer this question. The *Collins/Stillman* framework, as interpreted and applied in subsequent decisions, has brought a measure of certainty to the s. 24(2) inquiry. Yet the analytical method it imposes and the results it sometimes produces have been criticized as inconsistent with the language and objectives of s. 24(2). ...

[The *Collins/Stillman* framework grouped "the factors to be considered under s. 24(2) into three categories: (1) whether the evidence will undermine the fairness of the trial by effectively conscripting the accused against himself or herself; (2) the seriousness of the Charter breach; and (3) the effect of excluding the evidence on the long-term repute of the administration of justice." For Justices McLachlin and Charron, this framework, as it had evolved over time, had become too procrustean, undermining the direction in section 24 to have "regard to all the circumstances." Especially problematic was *Stillman*'s treatment of "conscriptive evidence," namely, evidence secured when "an accused, in violation of his *Charter* rights, is compelled to incriminate himself at the behest of the state by means of a statement, the use of the body or the production of bodily samples." Such conscripted evidence included so-called "derivative evidence" or "real evidence discovered as a result of an unlawfully conscripted statement," like the loaded gun in the possession of Grant. Under *Stillman*, said Justices McLachlin and Charron, conscriptive evidence, including derivative real evidence, "is generally inadmissible ... unless if it would have been independently discovered;" that is, unless it would have been discovered independently of the "unlawfully conscripted statement." For them, this "all-but-automatic exclusionary rule for non-discoverable conscriptive evidence" went "against the requirement of s. 24(2) that the court determining admissibility must consider 'all the circumstances.'" They thus proposed a revised framework that would be more flexible and balanced. For the three categories of the *Collins/Stillman* framework, they substituted three new "avenues of inquiry."]

[71] ... When faced with an application for exclusion under s. 24(2), a court must assess and balance the effect of admitting the evidence on society's confidence in the justice system having regard to: (1) the seriousness of the *Charter*-infringing state conduct (admission may send the message the justice system condones serious state misconduct), (2) the impact of the breach on the *Charter*-protected interests of the accused (admission may send the message that individual rights count for little), and (3) society's interest in the adjudication of the case on its merits. ...

[74] [First, s]tate conduct resulting in *Charter* violations varies in seriousness. At one end of the spectrum, admission of evidence obtained through inadvertent or minor violations of the *Charter* may minimally undermine public confidence in the rule of law. At the other end of the spectrum, admitting evidence obtained through a wilful or reckless disregard of *Charter* rights will inevitably have a negative effect on the public confidence in the rule of law, and risk bringing the administration of justice into disrepute. ...

[76] [The second] inquiry focusses on the seriousness of the impact of the *Charter* breach on the *Charter*-protected interests of the accused. It calls for an evaluation of the extent to which the breach actually undermined the interests protected by the right infringed. The impact of a *Charter* breach may range from fleeting and technical to profoundly intrusive. The more serious the impact on the accused's protected interests, the greater the risk that admission of the evidence may signal to the public that *Charter* rights, however high-sounding, are of little actual avail to the citizen, breeding public cynicism and bringing the administration of justice into disrepute. ...

[79] Society generally expects that a criminal allegation will be adjudicated on its merits. Accordingly, the third line of inquiry relevant to the s. 24(2) analysis asks whether the truth-seeking function of the criminal trial process would be better served by admission of the evidence, or by its exclusion. This inquiry reflects society's "collective interest in ensuring that those who transgress the law are brought to trial and dealt with according to the law." ...

[81] ... The reliability of the evidence is an important factor in this line of inquiry. ... The admission of unreliable evidence serves neither the accused's interest in a fair trial nor the public interest in uncovering the truth. Conversely, exclusion of relevant and reliable evidence may undermine the truth-seeking function of the justice system and render the trial unfair from the public perspective, thus bringing the administration of justice into disrepute. ...

[83] The importance of the evidence to the prosecution's case is another factor that may be considered in this line of inquiry. ... The admission of evidence of questionable reliability is more likely to bring the administration of justice into disrepute where it forms the entirety of the case against the accused. Conversely, the exclusion of highly reliable evidence may impact more negatively on the repute of the administration of justice where the remedy effectively guts the prosecution.

[84] It has been suggested that the judge should also, under this line of inquiry, consider the seriousness of the offence at issue. Indeed, Deschamps J. views this factor as very important, arguing that the more serious the offence, the greater society's interest in its prosecution (para. 226). In our view, while the seriousness of the alleged offence may be a valid consideration, it has the potential to cut both ways. Failure to effectively prosecute a serious charge due to excluded evidence may have an immediate impact on how people view the justice system. Yet ... it is the long-term repute of the justice system that is s. 24(2)'s focus. ... The short-term public clamour for a conviction in a particular case must not deafen the s. 24(2) judge to the longer-term repute of the

administration of justice. Moreover, while the public has a heightened interest in seeing a determination on the merits where the offence charged is serious, it also has a vital interest in having a justice system that is above reproach, particularly where the penal stakes for the accused are high.

[85] To review, the three lines of inquiry identified above— the seriousness of the *Charter*-infringing state conduct, the impact of the breach on the *Charter*-protected interests of the accused, and the societal interest in an adjudication on the merits—reflect what the s. 24(2) judge must consider in assessing the effect of admission of the evidence on the repute of the administration of justice. Having made these inquiries, which encapsulate consideration of "all the circumstances" of the case, the judge must then determine whether, on balance, the admission of the evidence obtained by *Charter* breach would bring the administration of justice into disrepute.

[86] In all cases, it is the task of the trial judge to weigh the various indications. No overarching rule governs how the balance is to be struck. Mathematical precision is obviously not possible. However, the preceding analysis creates a decision tree, albeit more flexible than the *Stillman* self-incrimination test. We believe this to be required by the words of s. 24(2). We also take comfort in the fact that patterns emerge with respect to particular types of evidence. These patterns serve as guides to judges faced with s. 24(2) applications in future cases. …

[Justices McLachlin and Charron examined the "patterns" involved in four "types of evidence": (1) statements by the accused, (2) bodily evidence, (3) non-bodily physical evidence, and (4) derivative evidence.]

[92] [Regarding statements by the accused, t]he three lines of inquiry described above support the presumptive general, although not automatic, exclusion of statements obtained in breach of the *Charter*.

[93] The first inquiry focusses on whether admission of the evidence would harm the repute of justice by associating the courts with illegal police conduct. Police conduct in obtaining statements has long been strongly constrained. The preservation of public confidence in the justice system requires that the police adhere to the *Charter* in obtaining statements from a detained accused.

[94] The negative impact on the justice system of admitting evidence obtained through police misconduct varies with the seriousness of the violation. The impression that courts condone serious police misconduct is more harmful to the repute of the justice system than the acceptance of minor or inadvertent slips.

[95] The second inquiry considers the extent to which the breach actually undermined the interests protected by the right infringed. Again, the potential to harm the repute of the justice system varies with the seriousness of the impingement on the individual's protected interests. As noted, the right violated by unlawfully obtained statements is often the right to counsel under s. 10(*b*). The failure to advise of the right to counsel undermines the detainee's right to make a meaningful and informed choice whether to speak, the related right to silence, and, most fundamentally, the protection against testimonial self-incrimination. These rights protect the individual's interest in liberty and autonomy. Violation of these fundamental rights tends to militate in favour of excluding the statement.

[96] This said, particular circumstances may attenuate the impact of a *Charter* breach on the protected interests of the accused from whom a statement is obtained in breach of the *Charter*. For instance, if an individual is clearly informed of his or her choice to speak to the police, but compliance with s. 10(*b*) was technically defective at either the informational or implementational stage, the impact on the liberty and autonomy interests of the accused in making an informed choice may be reduced. Likewise, when a statement is made spontaneously following a *Charter* breach, or in the exceptional circumstances where it can confidently be said that the statement in question would have been made notwithstanding the *Charter* breach (see *R. v. Harper*, [1994] 3 S.C.R. 343), the impact of the breach on the accused's protected interest in informed choice may be less. Absent such circumstances, the analysis under this line of inquiry supports the general exclusion of statements taken in breach of the *Charter*.

[97] The third inquiry focusses on the public interest in having the case tried fairly on its merits. This may lead to consideration of the reliability of the evidence. Just as involuntary confessions are suspect on grounds of reliability, so may, on occasion, be statements taken in contravention of the *Charter*. Detained by the police and without a lawyer, a suspect may make statements that are based more on a misconceived idea of how to get out of his or her predicament than on the truth. This danger, where present, undercuts the argument that the illegally obtained statement is necessary for a trial of the merits.

[98] In summary, the heightened concern with proper police conduct in obtaining statements from suspects and the centrality of the protected interests affected will in most cases favour exclusion of statements taken in breach of the *Charter*, while the third factor, obtaining a decision on the merits, may be attenuated by lack of reliability. This, together with the common law's historic tendency to treat statements of the

accused differently from other evidence, explains why such statements tend to be excluded under s. 24(2). ...

[108] [Regarding bodily evidence, t]he first inquiry informing the s. 24(2) analysis—the seriousness of the *Charter*-infringing conduct—is fact-specific. Admission of evidence obtained by deliberate and egregious police conduct that disregards the rights of the accused may lead the public to conclude that the court implicitly condones such conduct, undermining respect for the administration of justice. On the other hand, where the breach was committed in good faith, admission of the evidence may have little adverse effect on the repute of the court process.

[109] The second inquiry ... requires the judge to look at the seriousness of the breach on the accused's protected interests. In the context of bodily evidence obtained in violation of s. 8, this inquiry requires the court to examine the degree to which the search and seizure intruded upon the privacy, bodily integrity and human dignity of the accused. The seriousness of the intrusion on the accused may vary greatly. At one end of the spectrum, one finds the forcible taking of blood samples or dental impressions (as in *Stillman*). At the other end of the spectrum lie relatively innocuous procedures such as fingerprinting or iris-recognition technology. The greater the intrusion on these interests, the more important it is that a court exclude the evidence in order to substantiate the *Charter* rights of the accused.

[110] The third line of inquiry—the effect of admitting the evidence on the public interest in having a case adjudicated on its merits—will usually favour admission in cases involving bodily samples. Unlike compelled statements, evidence obtained from the accused's body is generally reliable, and the risk of error inherent in depriving the trier of fact of the evidence may well tip the balance in favour of admission.

[111] While each case must be considered on its own facts, it may be ventured in general that where an intrusion on bodily integrity is deliberately inflicted and the impact on the accused's privacy, bodily integrity and dignity is high, bodily evidence will be excluded, notwithstanding its relevance and reliability. On the other hand, where the violation is less egregious and the intrusion is less severe in terms of privacy, bodily integrity and dignity, reliable evidence obtained from the accused's body may be admitted. For example, this will often be the case with breath sample evidence, whose method of collection is relatively non-intrusive. ...

[112] [Regarding non-bodily physical evidence,] under the first inquiry, the seriousness of the *Charter*-infringing conduct will be a fact-specific determination. The degree to which this inquiry militates in favour of excluding the bodily evidence will depend on the extent to which the conduct can be characterized as deliberate or egregious.

[113] With respect to the second inquiry, the *Charter* breach most often associated with non-bodily physical evidence is the s. 8 protection against unreasonable search and seizure: see, e.g., *Buhay* [*R. v.*, 2003 SCC 30, [2003] 1 S.C.R. 631]. Privacy is the principal interest involved in such cases. The jurisprudence offers guidance in evaluating the extent to which the accused's reasonable expectation of privacy was infringed. For example, a dwelling house attracts a higher expectation of privacy than a place of business or an automobile. An illegal search of a house will therefore be seen as more serious at this stage of the analysis.

[114] Other interests, such as human dignity, may also be affected by search and seizure of such evidence. The question is how seriously the *Charter* breach impacted on these interests. For instance, an unjustified strip search or body cavity search is demeaning to the suspect's human dignity and will be viewed as extremely serious on that account: *R. v. Simmons*, [1988] 2 S.C.R. 495, at pp. 516-17, *per* Dickson C.J.; *R. v. Golden*, 2001 SCC 83, [2001] 3 S.C.R. 679. The fact that the evidence thereby obtained is not itself a bodily sample cannot be seen to diminish the seriousness of the intrusion.

[115] The third inquiry, whether the admission of the evidence would serve society's interest in having a case adjudicated on its merits, like the others, engages the facts of the particular case. Reliability issues with physical evidence will not generally be related to the *Charter* breach. Therefore, this consideration tends to weigh in favour of admission. ...

[116] The class of evidence that presents the greatest difficulty is evidence that combines aspects of both statements and physical evidence—physical evidence discovered as a result of an unlawfully obtained statement. The cases refer to this evidence as derivative evidence. This is the type of evidence at issue in this case. ...

[124] The first inquiry concerns the police conduct in obtaining the statement that led to the real evidence. Once again, the extent to which this inquiry favours exclusion will depend on the factual circumstances of the breach: the more serious the state conduct, the more the admission of the evidence derived from it tends to undermine public confidence in the rule of law. Were the police deliberately and systematically flouting the accused's *Charter* rights? Or were the officers acting in good faith, pursuant to what they thought were legitimate policing policies?

[125] The second inquiry focusses on the impact of the breach on the *Charter*-protected interests of the accused. Where a statement is unconstitutionally obtained, in many

cases the *Charter* right breached is the s. 10(*b*) right to counsel, which protects the accused's interest in making an informed choice whether or not to speak to authorities. The relevant consideration at this stage will be the extent to which the *Charter* breach impinged upon that interest in a free and informed choice. Where that interest was significantly compromised by the breach, this factor will strongly favour exclusion. In determining the impact of the breach, the discoverability of the derivative evidence may also be important as a factor strengthening or attenuating the self-incriminatory character of the evidence. If the derivative evidence was independently discoverable, the impact of the breach on the accused is lessened and admission is more likely.

[126] The third inquiry in determining whether admission of the derivative evidence would bring the administration into disrepute relates to society's interest in having the case adjudicated on its merits. Since evidence in this category is real or physical, there is usually less concern as to the reliability of the evidence. Thus, the public interest in having a trial adjudicated on its merits will usually favour admission of the derivative evidence.

[127] The weighing process and balancing of these concerns is one for the trial judge in each case. Provided the judge has considered the correct factors, considerable deference should be accorded to his or her decision. As a general rule, however, it can be ventured that where reliable evidence is discovered as a result of a good faith infringement that did not greatly undermine the accused's protected interests, the trial judge may conclude that it should be admitted under s. 24(2). On the other hand, deliberate and egregious police conduct that severely impacted the accused's protected interests may result in exclusion, notwithstanding that the evidence may be reliable.

[128] The s. 24(2) judge must remain sensitive to the concern that a more flexible rule may encourage police to improperly obtain statements that they know will be inadmissible, in order to find derivative evidence which they believe may be admissible. The judge should refuse to admit evidence where there is reason to believe the police deliberately abused their power to obtain a statement which might lead them to such evidence. Where derivative evidence is obtained by way of a deliberate or flagrant *Charter* breach, its admission would bring the administration of justice into further disrepute and the evidence should be excluded. ...

[133] [Turning to the case at hand, we] consider first the seriousness of the improper police conduct that led to the discovery of the gun. The police conduct here, while not in conformity with the *Charter*, was not abusive. There was no suggestion that Mr. Grant was the target of racial profiling or other discriminatory police practices. The officers went too far in detaining the accused and asking him questions. However, the point at which an encounter becomes a detention is not always clear, and is something with which courts have struggled. Though we have concluded that the police were in error in detaining the appellant when they did, the mistake is an understandable one. Having been under a mistaken view that they had not detained the appellant, the officers' failure to advise him of his right to counsel was similarly erroneous but understandable. It therefore cannot be characterized as having been in bad faith. Given that the police conduct in committing the *Charter* breach was neither deliberate nor egregious, we conclude that the effect of admitting the evidence would not greatly undermine public confidence in the rule of law. We add that the Court's decision in this case will be to render similar conduct less justifiable going forward. While police are not expected to engage in judicial reflection on conflicting precedents, they are rightly expected to know what the law is.

[134] The second inquiry ... focusses on the impact of the breach on the accused's protected interests. ...

[135] The initial *Charter* violation was arbitrary detention under s. 9 of the *Charter*, curtailing Mr. Grant's liberty interest. ... [W]hile not severe, [it] was more than minimal.

[136] The second *Charter* violation was breach of Mr. Grant's s. 10(*b*) right to counsel. ...

[137] As discussed, discoverability remains a factor in assessing the impact of *Charter* breaches on *Charter* rights. The investigating officers testified that they would not have searched or arrested Mr. Grant but for his self-incriminatory statements. Nor would they have had any legal grounds to do so. Accordingly, the fact that the evidence was non-discoverable aggravates the impact of the breach on Mr. Grant's interest in being able to make an informed choice to talk to the police. He was in "immediate need of legal advice" (*Brydges* [*R. v.*, [1990] 1 S.C.R. 190], at p. 206) and had no opportunity to seek it. ...

[139] The third and final concern is the effect of admitting the gun on the public interest in having a case adjudicated on its merits. The gun is highly reliable evidence. It is essential to a determination on the merits. The Crown also argues that the seriousness of the offence weighs in favour of admitting the evidence of the gun, so that the matter may be decided on its merits, asserting that gun crime is a societal scourge, that offences of this nature raise major public safety concerns and that the gun is the main evidence in the case. ...

[140] To sum up, the police conduct was not egregious. The impact of the *Charter* breach on the accused's protected interests was significant, although not at the most serious end

of the scale. Finally, the value of the evidence is considerable. ... The significant impact of the breach on Mr. Grant's *Charter*-protected rights weighs strongly in favour of excluding the gun, while the public interest in the adjudication of the case on its merits weighs strongly in favour of its admission. Unlike the situation in *R. v. Harrison*, 2009 SCC 34, [2009] 2 S.C.R. 494, the police officers here were operating in circumstances of considerable legal uncertainty. In our view, this tips the balance in favour of admission, suggesting that the repute of the justice system would not suffer from allowing the gun to be admitted in evidence against the appellant.

36 Canada (Prime Minister) v. Khadr, 2010

In the aftermath of the terrorist attacks of September 11, 2001, the U.S. military invaded Afghanistan and sought to dislodge both the Taliban and al Qaeda. This war on terror was not a conventional interstate conflict but rather an asymmetric contest between the military power of the United States and its coalition allies (including Canada) and the supple, shadowy forces of decentralized Islamist terrorist groups whose operatives engage in suicide missions and target civilians. Warfare in these new conditions involved the creation of a category of captive outside the terms of the Geneva Conventions ("unlawful enemy combatants"), the construction of the Guantanamo Bay detention facility on Cuban soil, and the use of "aggressive interrogation techniques" to extract valuable information from captives. To try those charged with war crimes, the U.S. government created "military commissions" by executive fiat with relaxed rules of procedure: no right to *habeus corpus*, no right to a lawyer of one's choice, no disclosure to the defence of evidence in the prosecutors' possession, and the use of methods of interrogation that, for many, were simply torture. Legal challenges to several of these features of the war on terror succeeded, but at time of writing Guantanamo Bay still operates.

Omar Khadr was subject to the Guantanamo process. On July 27, 2002, the 15-year-old was in an Afghanistan compound when it came under fire from coalition forces. All occupants were killed but him. One American soldier was also killed in the firefight. Khadr was treated for his severe injuries and later charged with the murder of the soldier and with aiding terrorism. (The factual basis for his role in the soldier's death is murky.) He was questioned in Afghanistan, then transferred to Guantanamo and subjected to many of the indignities for which Guantanamo is notorious. On October 13, 2010, he pleaded guilty to the charges and in 2012 was released to serve his sentence in Canada. He is appealing his conviction and is also suing the Canadian government for $20 million for its role in his alleged mistreatment.

Khadr was born in Canada to parents who travelled frequently to Afghanistan and Pakistan, ostensibly to run a charitable organization in the region, but who also became intimately acquainted with al Qaeda leaders, including Osama bin Laden. Omar's mother and sister were candid in media interviews about their support both for the aims of Islamist terror organizations and for Omar's bravery in fighting for his "right."[1] Undoubtedly the Khadrs' reputation affected perceptions of Khadr's status at Guantanamo. But of course,

---

1 Michelle Shepherd, *Guantanamo's Child: The Untold Story of Omar Khadr* (Mississauga: John Wiley & Sons, 2008) ch. 7.

"[t]hat some regard him or his family as 'bad' citizens does not alter the fact that Omar is a citizen in Canadian law."[2]

The following decision concerns the obligations of the Canadian government when one of its nationals is confined in another state's territory and subject to another state's laws. Normally, the Charter has no extraterritorial effect: it applies to Canadian officials and Canadian laws, and when a Canadian travels to another state, he or she is subject to that state's laws and justice system. But in this case, Canadian intelligence officials travelled to Guantanamo Bay, interviewed Khadr, and shared the fruits of those interviews with American officials. Further, the evidentiary and other procedural rules for trials at Guantanamo were found by American courts to violate international treaties to which Canada is a signatory.

Building on an earlier case in which Omar Khadr used section 7 of the Charter to force Canadian officials to disclose to him records of his interviews with them that were then passed on to the Americans,[3] Khadr in a subsequent action argued that the Charter applies to his case because Canadian officials are subject to the Charter whether they are on Canadian soil or not and that they are accountable for the use to which their evidence is put by Guantanamo officials. Further, when the procedures under which the evidence is used are themselves violations of Khadr's human rights, the officials are implicated in these breaches. In a unanimous judgment, the Supreme Court agreed.

Where there is a right, there is a remedy for the violation of that right. What relief could Khadr expect from the court? Here things become more complicated. This is because, as a parliamentary democracy on the Westminster model, the government of the day—that is, the Cabinet—exercises a residue of Crown prerogative power. In areas of foreign policy and the conduct of war, Cabinet has untrammelled constitutional authority. The royal prerogative thus clashes with the post-1982 principle that all governmental authority is subject to the Charter and thus to judicial review. In an early decision, the Supreme Court declared that the Charter governs Cabinet decisions in relation to foreign policy.[4] In Khadr's case, the court is more tentative and finds it difficult, as paragraph 37 of the decision indicates, to reconcile Charter supremacy with the royal prerogative. In the end, it took the unusual and uncharacteristically restrained step of declaring that Khadr's section 7 Charter rights were violated, but refused to order the government to remedy that breach by requesting Khadr's repatriation to Canada. One wonders whether it held back for fear of being openly ignored by the government in a politically volatile case. The decision, however, was not without effect. In February 2010, the government sent a diplomatic note asking that the evidence given to Canadian interrogators not be used in the trial against Khadr. ∿

---

2 Audrey Macklin, "The Rule of Law, the Force of Law, and the Rule of Force" in Janice Williamson, ed., *Omar Khadr, Oh Canada* (Montreal and Kingston: McGill-Queen's University Press, 2012) at 232.

3 *Canada (Justice) v. Khadr*, 2008 SCC 28, [2008] 2 S.C.R. 125.

4 *Operation Dismantle Inc. v. The Queen*, [1985] 1 S.C.R. 441.

Discussion Questions

1. Was the Supreme Court's discussion of the remedy persuasive? Should it have ordered a remedy? If so, what remedy?

2. The Supreme Court here was certain that the use to which Canadian officials' evidence was put was nefarious, and that Canadian officials are accountable for the entanglement of that evidence in rights violations. Should this be a categorical rule, or should Canadian officials be able to suggest on the one hand that they did know about the circumstance of the use of evidence or on the other that they cannot be accountable for what others do with their evidence? In other words, how far into the bowels of foreign government should the Charter reach?

CANADA (PRIME MINISTER) v. KHADR
2010 SCC 3, [2010] 1 S.C.R. 44

Hearing: November 13, 2009; Judgment: January 29, 2010.

Present: McLachlin C.J. and Binnie, LeBel, Deschamps, Fish, Abella, Charron, Rothstein, and Cromwell JJ.

Interveners: Amnesty International (Canadian Section, English Branch), Human Rights Watch, University of Toronto, Faculty of Law—International Human Rights Program, David Asper Centre for Constitutional Rights, Canadian Coalition for the Rights of Children, Justice for Children and Youth, British Columbia Civil Liberties Association, Criminal Lawyers' Association (Ontario), Canadian Bar Association, Lawyers Without Borders Canada, Barreau du Québec, Groupe d'étude en droits et libertés de la Faculté de droit de l'Université Laval, Canadian Civil Liberties Association, and National Council for the Protection of Canadians Abroad.

The following is the judgment delivered by

THE COURT: ...

II. Background

[3] Mr. Khadr was 15 years old when he was taken prisoner on July 27, 2002, by U.S. forces in Afghanistan. He was alleged to have thrown a grenade that killed an American soldier in the battle in which he was captured. About three months later, he was transferred to the U.S. military installation at Guantanamo Bay. He was placed in adult detention facilities.

[4] On September 7, 2004, Mr. Khadr was brought before a Combatant Status Review Tribunal which affirmed a previous determination that he was an "enemy combatant." He was subsequently charged with war crimes and held for trial before a military commission. In light of a number of procedural delays and setbacks, that trial is still pending.

[5] In February and September 2003, agents from the Canadian Security Intelligence Service ("CSIS") and the Foreign Intelligence Division of the Department of Foreign Affairs and International Trade ("DFAIT") questioned Mr. Khadr on matters connected to the charges pending against him and shared the product of these interviews with U.S. authorities. In March 2004, a DFAIT official interviewed Mr. Khadr again, with the knowledge that he had been subjected by U.S. authorities to a sleep deprivation technique, known as the "frequent flyer program," in an effort to make him less resistant to interrogation. During this interview, Mr. Khadr refused to answer questions. In 2005, von Finckenstein J. of the Federal Court issued an interim injunction preventing CSIS and DFAIT agents from further interviewing Mr. Khadr in order "to prevent a potential grave injustice" from occurring: *Khadr v. Canada*, 2005 FC 1076, [2006] 2 F.C.R. 505, at para. 46. In 2008, this Court ordered the Canadian government to disclose to Mr. Khadr the transcripts of the interviews he had given to CSIS and DFAIT in Guantanamo Bay, under s. 7 of the *Charter*: *Canada (Justice) v. Khadr*, 2008 SCC 28, [2008] 2 S.C.R. 125 ("*Khadr 2008*").

[6] Mr. Khadr has repeatedly requested that the Government of Canada ask the United States to return him to Canada ... .

[7] The Prime Minister announced his decision not to request Mr. Khadr's repatriation on July 10, 2008, during a media interview. The Prime Minister provided the following response to a journalist's question, posed in French, regarding whether the government would seek repatriation:

> [TRANSLATION] The answer is no, as I said the former Government, and our Government with the notification of the Minister of Justice had considered all these issues and the situation remains the same. ... We keep on looking for [assurances] of good treatment of Mr. Khadr. ...

[8] On August 8, 2008, Mr. Khadr applied to the Federal Court for judicial review of the government's "ongoing decision and policy" not to seek his repatriation ... . He alleged that the decision and policy infringed his rights under s. 7 of the Charter ... .

[The Supreme Court reviewed the lower court decision. The Federal Court found a section 7 violation and ordered that the government request repatriation. A 2-to-1 majority of the Federal Court of Appeal dismissed the government's appeal. Notably, the dissenter in the appeal decision was Marc Nadon, whose opinion is widely thought to be the signal of a judicial conservatism that led the prime minister to nominate him for the Supreme Court in 2013.]

III. The Issues

...

A. Was There a Breach of Section 7 of the Charter?

1. Does the Canadian Charter Apply to the Conduct of the Canadian State Officials Alleged to Have Infringed Mr. Khadr's Section 7 Charter Rights?

[14] As a general rule, Canadians abroad are bound by the law of the country in which they find themselves and cannot avail themselves of their rights under the *Charter*. International customary law and the principle of comity of nations generally prevent the *Charter* from applying to the actions of Canadian officials operating outside of Canada .... The jurisprudence leaves the door open to an exception in the case of Canadian participation in activities of a foreign state or its agents that are contrary to Canada's international obligations or fundamental human rights norms ... .

[15] The question before us, then, is whether the rule against the extraterritorial application of the *Charter* prevents the *Charter* from applying to the actions of Canadian officials at Guantanamo Bay.

[16] This question was addressed in *Khadr 2008*, in which this Court held that the *Charter* applied to the actions of Canadian officials operating at Guantanamo Bay who handed the fruits of their interviews over to U.S. authorities. This Court held, at para. 26, that "the principles of international law and comity that might otherwise preclude application of the *Charter* to Canadian officials acting abroad do not apply to the assistance they gave to U.S. authorities at Guantanamo Bay," given holdings of the Supreme Court of the United States that the military commission regime then in place constituted a clear violation of fundamental human rights protected by international law: see *Khadr 2008*, at para. 24; *Rasul v. Bush*, 542 U.S. 466 (2004), and *Hamdan v. Rumsfeld*, 548 U.S. 557 (2006). The principles of fundamental justice thus required the Canadian officials who had interrogated Mr. Khadr to disclose to him the contents of the statements he had given them. The Canadian government complied with this Court's order.

[17] We note that the regime under which Mr. Khadr is currently detained has changed significantly in recent years.

The U.S. Congress has legislated and the U.S. courts have acted with the aim of bringing the military processes at Guantanamo Bay in line with international law. ...

[18] Though the process to which Mr. Khadr is subject has changed, his claim is based upon the same underlying series of events at Guantanamo Bay (the interviews and evidence-sharing of 2003 and 2004) that we considered in *Khadr 2008*. We are satisfied that the rationale in *Khadr 2008* for applying the *Charter* to the actions of Canadian officials at Guantanamo Bay governs this case as well.

2. Does the Conduct of the Canadian Government Deprive Mr. Khadr of the Right to Life, Liberty or Security of the Person?

[19] The United States is holding Mr. Khadr for the purpose of trying him on charges of war crimes. The United States is thus the primary source of the deprivation of Mr. Khadr's liberty and security of the person. However, the allegation on which his claim rests is that Canada has also contributed to his past and continuing deprivation of liberty. To satisfy the requirements of s. 7, as stated by this Court in *Suresh v. Canada (Minister of Citizenship and Immigration)*, 2002 SCC 1, [2002] 1 S.C.R. 3, there must be "a sufficient causal connection between [the Canadian] government's participation and the deprivation [of liberty and security of the person] ultimately effected" (para. 54).

[20] The record suggests that the interviews conducted by CSIS and DFAIT provided significant evidence in relation to these charges. During the February and September 2003 interrogations, CSIS officials repeatedly questioned Mr. Khadr about the central events at issue in his prosecution, extracting statements from him that could potentially prove inculpatory in the U.S. proceedings against him .... A report of the Security Intelligence Review Committee titled *CSIS's Role in the Matter of Omar Khadr* (July 8, 2009), further indicated that CSIS assessed the interrogations of Mr. Khadr as being "highly successful, as evidenced by the quality intelligence information" elicited from Mr. Khadr (p. 13). These statements were shared with U.S. authorities and were summarized in U.S. investigative reports ... . Pursuant to the relaxed rules of evidence under the U.S. *Military Commissions Act of 2006*, Mr. Khadr's statements to Canadian officials are potentially admissible against him in the U.S. proceedings, notwithstanding the oppressive circumstances under which they were obtained ... . The above interrogations also provided the context for the March 2004 interrogation, when a DFAIT official, knowing that Mr. Khadr had been subjected to the "frequent flyer program" to make him less resistant to interrogations, nevertheless proceeded with the interrogation of Mr. Khadr ... .

[21] ... [W]e conclude on the record before us that Canada's active participation in what was at the time an illegal regime has contributed and continues to contribute to Mr. Khadr's current detention, which is the subject of his current claim. The causal connection ... between Canadian conduct and the deprivation of liberty and security of person is established.

3. Does the Deprivation Accord With the Principles of Fundamental Justice?

...

[23] The principles of fundamental justice "are to be found in the basic tenets of our legal system": *Re B.C. Motor Vehicle Act*, [1985] 2 S.C.R. 486, at p. 503. They are informed by Canadian experience and jurisprudence, and take into account Canada's obligations and values, as expressed in the various sources of international human rights law by which Canada is bound. In *R. v. D.B.*, 2008 SCC 25, [2008] 2 S.C.R. 3, at para. 46, the Court (Abella J. for the majority) restated the criteria for identifying a new principle of fundamental justice in the following manner:

(1) It must be a legal principle.
(2) There must be a consensus that the rule or principle is fundamental to the way in which the legal system ought fairly to operate.
(3) It must be identified with sufficient precision to yield a manageable standard against which to measure deprivations of life, liberty or security of the person.

[24] We conclude that Canadian conduct in connection with Mr. Khadr's case did not conform to the principles of fundamental justice. That conduct may be briefly reviewed. The statements taken by CSIS and DFAIT were obtained through participation in a regime which was known at the time to have refused detainees the right to challenge the legality of detention by way of *habeas corpus*. It was also known that Mr. Khadr was 16 years old at the time and that he had not had access to counsel or to any adult who had his best interests in mind. As held by this Court in *Khadr 2008*, Canada's participation in the illegal process in place at Guantanamo Bay clearly violated Canada's binding international obligations (*Khadr 2008*, at paras. 23-25; *Hamdan v. Rumsfeld*). In conducting their interviews, CSIS officials had control over the questions asked and the subject matter of the interviews ... . Canadian officials also knew that the U.S. authorities would have full access to the contents of the interrogations (as Canadian officials sought no restrictions on their use) by virtue of their audio and video recording (*CSIS's Role in the Matter of Omar Khadr*, at pp. 11-12). The purpose of the interviews was for intelligence gathering and not criminal investigation. While in some contexts there may be an important distinction between those interviews conducted for the purpose of intelligence gathering and those conducted in criminal investigations, here, the distinction loses its significance. Canadian officials questioned Mr. Khadr on matters that may have provided important evidence relating to his criminal proceedings, in circumstances where they knew that Mr. Khadr was being indefinitely detained, was a young person and was alone during the interrogations. Further, the March 2004 interview, where Mr. Khadr refused to answer questions, was conducted knowing that Mr. Khadr had been subjected to three weeks of scheduled sleep deprivation, a measure described by the U.S. Military Commission in [*United States of America v.*] *Jawad* [Military Commission, September 24, 2008] as designed to "make [detainees] more compliant and break down their resistance to interrogation" (para. 4).

[25] This conduct establishes Canadian participation in state conduct that violates the principles of fundamental justice. Interrogation of a youth, to elicit statements about the most serious criminal charges while detained in these conditions and without access to counsel, and while knowing that the fruits of the interrogations would be shared with the U.S. prosecutors, offends the most basic Canadian standards about the treatment of detained youth suspects.

[26] We conclude that Mr. Khadr has established that Canada violated his rights under s. 7 of the *Charter*.

B. Is the Remedy Sought Appropriate and Just in All the Circumstances?

[27] In previous proceedings (*Khadr 2008*), Mr. Khadr obtained the remedy of disclosure of the material gathered by Canadian officials against him through the interviews at Guantanamo Bay. The issue on this appeal is whether the breach of s. 7 of the *Charter* entitles Mr. Khadr to the remedy of an order that Canada request of the United States that he be returned to Canada. Two questions arise at this stage: (1) Is the remedy sought sufficiently connected to the breach? and (2) Is the remedy sought precluded by the fact that it touches on the Crown prerogative power over foreign affairs?

[28] The judge at first instance held that the remedy sought was open to him. The Federal Court of Appeal held that he did not abuse his remedial discretion. On the basis of our answer to the second of the foregoing questions, we conclude that the trial judge, on the record before us, erred in the exercise of his discretion in granting the remedy sought.

[29] First, is the remedy sought sufficiently connected to the breach? We have concluded that the Canadian government breached Mr. Khadr's s. 7 rights in 2003 and 2004 through its participation in the then-illegal military regime at Guantanamo Bay. The question at this point is whether the remedy now being sought—an order that the Canadian government

ask the United States to return Mr. Khadr to Canada—is appropriate and just in the circumstances.

[30] An appropriate and just remedy is "one that meaningfully vindicates the rights and freedoms of the claimants": *Doucet-Boudreau v. Nova Scotia (Minister of Education)*, 2003 SCC 62, [2003] 3 S.C.R. 3, at para. 55. The first hurdle facing Mr. Khadr, therefore, is to establish a sufficient connection between the breaches of s. 7 that occurred in 2003 and 2004 and the order sought in these judicial review proceedings. In our view, the sufficiency of this connection is established by the continuing effect of these breaches into the present. Mr. Khadr's *Charter* rights were breached when Canadian officials contributed to his detention by virtue of their interrogations at Guantanamo Bay knowing Mr. Khadr was a youth, did not have access to legal counsel or *habeas corpus* at that time and, at the time of the interview in March 2004, had been subjected to improper treatment by the U.S. authorities. As the information obtained by Canadian officials during the course of their interrogations may be used in the U.S. proceedings against Mr. Khadr, the effect of the breaches cannot be said to have been spent. It continues to this day. As discussed earlier, the material that Canadian officials gathered and turned over to the U.S. military authorities may form part of the case upon which he is currently being held. The evidence before us suggests that the material produced was relevant and useful. There has been no suggestion that it does not form part of the case against Mr. Khadr or that it will not be put forward at his ultimate trial. We therefore find that the breach of Mr. Khadr's s. 7 *Charter* rights remains ongoing and that the remedy sought could potentially vindicate those rights.

[31] The acts that perpetrated the *Charter* breaches relied on in this appeal lie in the past. But their impact on Mr. Khadr's liberty and security continue to this day and may redound into the future. The impact of the breaches is thus perpetuated into the present. When past acts violate present liberties, a present remedy may be required.

[32] We conclude that the necessary connection between the breaches of s. 7 and the remedy sought has been established for the purpose of these judicial review proceedings.

[33] Second, is the remedy sought precluded by the fact that it touches on the Crown prerogative over foreign affairs? A connection between the remedy and the breach is not the only consideration. As stated in *Doucet-Boudreau*, an appropriate and just remedy is also one that "must employ means that are legitimate within the framework of our constitutional democracy" (para. 56) and must be a "judicial one which vindicates the right while invoking the function and powers of a court" (para. 57). The government argues that courts have no power under the Constitution of Canada to require the executive branch of government to do anything in the area of foreign policy. It submits that the decision not to request the

repatriation of Mr. Khadr falls directly within the prerogative powers of the Crown to conduct foreign relations, including the right to speak freely with a foreign state on all such matters: P. W. Hogg, *Constitutional Law of Canada* (5th ed. Supp.), at p. 1-19.

[34] The prerogative power is the "residue of discretionary or arbitrary authority, which at any given time is legally left in the hands of the Crown": *Reference as to the Effect of the Exercise of the Royal Prerogative of Mercy Upon Deportation Proceedings*, [1933] S.C.R. 269, at p. 272, *per* Duff C.J., quoting A. V. Dicey, *Introduction to the Study of the Law of the Constitution* (8th ed. 1915), at p. 420. It is a limited source of non-statutory administrative power accorded by the common law to the Crown: Hogg, at p. 1-17.

[35] The prerogative power over foreign affairs has not been displaced by s. 10 of the *Department of Foreign Affairs and International Trade Act*, R.S.C. 1985, c. E-22 , and continues to be exercised by the federal government. The Crown prerogative in foreign affairs includes the making of representations to a foreign government: *Black v. Canada (Prime Minister)* (2001), 199 D.L.R. (4th) 228 (Ont. C.A.). We therefore agree with O'Reilly J.'s implicit finding (paras. 39, 40 and 49) that the decision not to request Mr. Khadr's repatriation was made in the exercise of the prerogative over foreign relations.

[36] In exercising its common law powers under the royal prerogative, the executive is not exempt from constitutional scrutiny: *Operation Dismantle v. The Queen*, [1985] 1 S.C.R. 441. It is for the executive and not the courts to decide whether and how to exercise its powers, but the courts clearly have the jurisdiction and the duty to determine whether a prerogative power asserted by the Crown does in fact exist and, if so, whether its exercise infringes the *Charter* (*Operation Dismantle*) or other constitutional norms (*Air Canada v. British Columbia (Attorney General)*, [1986] 2 S.C.R. 539).

[37] The limited power of the courts to review exercises of the prerogative power for constitutionality reflects the fact that in a constitutional democracy, all government power must be exercised in accordance with the Constitution. This said, judicial review of the exercise of the prerogative power for constitutionality remains sensitive to the fact that the executive branch of government is responsible for decisions under this power, and that the executive is better placed to make such decisions within a range of constitutional options. The government must have flexibility in deciding how its duties under the power are to be discharged: see, e.g., *Reference re Secession of Quebec*, [1998] 2 S.C.R. 217, at paras. 101-2. But it is for the courts to determine the legal and constitutional limits within which such decisions are to be taken. It follows that in the case of refusal by a government to abide by constitutional constraints, courts are empowered to make orders ensuring that the government's foreign affairs prerogative is exercised in

accordance with the constitution: *United States v. Burns*, 2001 SCC 7, [2001] 1 S.C.R. 283.

[38] Having concluded that the courts possess a narrow power to review and intervene on matters of foreign affairs to ensure the constitutionality of executive action, the final question is whether O'Reilly J. misdirected himself in exercising that power in the circumstances of this case (*R. v. Bjelland*, 2009 SCC 38, [2009] 2 S.C.R. 651, at para. 15; *R. v. Regan*, 2002 SCC 12, [2002] 1 S.C.R. 297, at paras. 117-18). (In fairness to the trial judge, we note that the government proposed no alternative (trial judge's reasons, at para. 78).) If the record and legal principle support his decision, deference requires we not interfere. However, in our view that is not the case.

[39] Our first concern is that the remedy ordered below gives too little weight to the constitutional responsibility of the executive to make decisions on matters of foreign affairs in the context of complex and ever-changing circumstances, taking into account Canada's broader national interests. For the following reasons, we conclude that the appropriate remedy is to declare that, on the record before the Court, Canada infringed Mr. Khadr's s. 7 rights, and to leave it to the government to decide how best to respond to this judgment in light of current information, its responsibility for foreign affairs, and in conformity with the *Charter*.

[40] As discussed, the conduct of foreign affairs lies with the executive branch of government. The courts, however, are charged with adjudicating the claims of individuals who claim that their *Charter* rights have been or will be violated by the exercise of the government's discretionary powers: *Operation Dismantle*.

[41] In some situations, courts may give specific directions to the executive branch of the government on matters touching foreign policy. For example, in *Burns*, the Court held that it would offend s. 7 to extradite a fugitive from Canada without seeking and obtaining assurances from the requesting state that the death penalty would not be imposed. The Court gave due weight to the fact that seeking and obtaining those assurances were matters of Canadian foreign relations. Nevertheless, it ordered that the government seek them.

[42] The specific facts in *Burns* justified a more specific remedy. The fugitives were under the control of Canadian officials. It was clear that assurances would provide effective protection against the prospective *Charter* breaches: it was entirely within Canada's power to protect the fugitives against possible execution. Moreover, the Court noted that no public purpose would be served by extradition without assurances that would not be substantially served by extradition with assurances, and that there was nothing to suggest that seeking such assurances would undermine Canada's good relations with other states: *Burns*, at paras. 125 and 136.

[43] The present case differs from *Burns*. Mr. Khadr is not under the control of the Canadian government; the likelihood that the proposed remedy will be effective is unclear; and the impact on Canadian foreign relations of a repatriation request cannot be properly assessed by the Court.

[44] This brings us to our second concern: the inadequacy of the record. The record before us gives a necessarily incomplete picture of the range of considerations currently faced by the government in assessing Mr. Khadr's request. We do not know what negotiations may have taken place, or will take place, between the U.S. and Canadian governments over the fate of Mr. Khadr. As observed by Chaskalson C.J. in *Kaunda v. President of the Republic of South Africa*, [2004] ZACC 5, 136 I.L.R. 452, at para. 77: "The timing of representations if they are to be made, the language in which they should be couched, and the sanctions (if any) which should follow if such representations are rejected are matters with which courts are ill-equipped to deal." It follows that in these circumstances, it would not be appropriate for the Court to give direction as to the diplomatic steps necessary to address the breaches of Mr. Khadr's *Charter* rights.

[45] Though Mr. Khadr has not been moved from Guantanamo Bay in over seven years, his legal predicament continues to evolve. During the hearing of this appeal, we were advised by counsel that the U.S. Department of Justice had decided that Mr. Khadr will continue to face trial by military commission, though other Guantanamo detainees will now be tried in a federal court in New York. How this latest development will affect Mr. Khadr's situation and any ongoing negotiations between the United States and Canada over his possible repatriation is unknown. But it signals caution in the exercise of the Court's remedial jurisdiction.

[46] In this case, the evidentiary uncertainties, the limitations of the Court's institutional competence, and the need to respect the prerogative powers of the executive, lead us to conclude that the proper remedy is declaratory relief. A declaration of unconstitutionality is a discretionary remedy: *Operation Dismantle*, at p. 481, citing *Solosky v. The Queen*, [1980] 1 S.C.R. 821. It has been recognized by this Court as "an effective and flexible remedy for the settlement of real disputes": *R. v. Gamble*, [1988] 2 S.C.R. 595, at p. 649. A court can properly issue a declaratory remedy so long as it has the jurisdiction over the issue at bar, the question before the court is real and not theoretical, and the person raising it has a real interest to raise it. Such is the case here.

[47] The prudent course at this point, respectful of the responsibilities of the executive and the courts, is for this Court to allow Mr. Khadr's application for judicial review in part and to grant him a declaration advising the government of its opinion on the records before it which, in turn, will provide the legal framework for the executive to exercise its functions and to consider what actions to take in respect of Mr. Khadr, in conformity with the *Charter*.

APPENDIX
The Constitution Act, 1982

Schedule B
Constitution Act, 1982

Enacted as Schedule B to the *Canada Act 1982*, (U.K.) 1982,
c. 11, which came into force on April 17, 1982

PART I

Canadian Charter of Rights and Freedoms

Whereas Canada is founded upon principles that recognize the supremacy of God and the rule of law:

Guarantee of Rights and Freedoms

1. The *Canadian Charter of Rights and Freedoms* guarantees the rights and freedoms set out in it subject only to such reasonable limits prescribed by law as can be demonstrably justified in a free and democratic society.

Rights and freedoms in Canada

Fundamental Freedoms

2. Everyone has the following fundamental freedoms:

Fundamental freedoms

(*a*) freedom of conscience and religion;

(*b*) freedom of thought, belief, opinion and expression, including freedom of the press and other media of communication;

(*c*) freedom of peaceful assembly; and

(*d*) freedom of association.

Democratic Rights

3. Every citizen of Canada has the right to vote in an election of members of the House of Commons or of a legislative assembly and to be qualified for membership therein.

Democratic rights of citizens

4. (1) No House of Commons and no legislative assembly shall continue for longer than five years from the date fixed for the return of the writs of a general election of its members.

Maximum duration of legislative bodies

(2) In time of real or apprehended war, invasion or insurrection, a House of Commons may be continued by Parliament and a legislative assembly may be continued by the legislature beyond five years if such continuation is not opposed by the votes of more than one-third of the members of the House of Commons or the legislative assembly, as the case may be.

Continuation in special circumstances

Annual sitting of legislative bodies

5. There shall be a sitting of Parliament and of each legislature at least once every twelve months.

Mobility Rights

Mobility of citizens

6. (1) Every citizen of Canada has the right to enter, remain in and leave Canada.

Rights to move and gain livelihood

(2) Every citizen of Canada and every person who has the status of a permanent resident of Canada has the right

(*a*) to move to and take up residence in any province; and

(*b*) to pursue the gaining of a livelihood in any province.

Limitation

(3) The rights specified in subsection (2) are subject to

(*a*) any laws or practices of general application in force in a province other than those that discriminate among persons primarily on the basis of province of present or previous residence; and

(*b*) any laws providing for reasonable residency requirements as a qualification for the receipt of publicly provided social services.

Affirmative action programs

(4) Subsections (2) and (3) do not preclude any law, program or activity that has as its object the amelioration in a province of conditions of individuals in that province who are socially or economically disadvantaged if the rate of employment in that province is below the rate of employment in Canada.

Legal Rights

Life, liberty and security of person

7. Everyone has the right to life, liberty and security of the person and the right not to be deprived thereof except in accordance with the principles of fundamental justice.

Search or seizure

8. Everyone has the right to be secure against unreasonable search or seizure.

Detention or imprisonment

9. Everyone has the right not to be arbitrarily detained or imprisoned.

Arrest or detention

10. Everyone has the right on arrest or detention

(*a*) to be informed promptly of the reasons therefor;

(*b*) to retain and instruct counsel without delay and to be informed of that right; and

(*c*) to have the validity of the detention determined by way of *habeas corpus* and to be released if the detention is not lawful.

Proceedings in criminal and penal matters

11. Any person charged with an offence has the right

(*a*) to be informed without unreasonable delay of the specific offence;

(*b*) to be tried within a reasonable time;

(*c*) not to be compelled to be a witness in proceedings against that person in respect of the offence;

(*d*) to be presumed innocent until proven guilty according to law in a fair and public hearing by an independent and impartial tribunal;

(*e*) not to be denied reasonable bail without just cause;

(*f*) except in the case of an offence under military law tried before a military tribunal, to the benefit of trial by jury where the maximum punishment for the offence is imprisonment for five years or a more severe punishment;

(*g*) not to be found guilty on account of any act or omission unless, at the time of the act or omission, it constituted an offence under Canadian or international law or was criminal according to the general principles of law recognized by the community of nations;

(*h*) if finally acquitted of the offence, not to be tried for it again and, if finally found guilty and punished for the offence, not to be tried or punished for it again; and

(*i*) if found guilty of the offence and if the punishment for the offence has been varied between the time of commission and the time of sentencing, to the benefit of the lesser punishment.

12. Everyone has the right not to be subjected to any cruel and unusual treatment or punishment.

Treatment or punishment

13. A witness who testifies in any proceedings has the right not to have any incriminating evidence so given used to incriminate that witness in any other proceedings, except in a prosecution for perjury or for the giving of contradictory evidence.

Self-crimination

14. A party or witness in any proceedings who does not understand or speak the language in which the proceedings are conducted or who is deaf has the right to the assistance of an interpreter.

Interpreter

Equality Rights

15. (1) Every individual is equal before and under the law and has the right to the equal protection and equal benefit of the law without discrimination and, in particular, without discrimination based on race, national or ethnic origin, colour, religion, sex, age or mental or physical disability.

Equality before and under law and equal protection and benefit of law

(2) Subsection (1) does not preclude any law, program or activity that has as its object the amelioration of conditions of disadvantaged individuals or groups including those that are disadvantaged because of race, national or ethnic origin, colour, religion, sex, age or mental or physical disability.

Affirmative action programs

Official Languages of Canada

16. (1) English and French are the official languages of Canada and have equality of status and equal rights and privileges as to their use in all institutions of the Parliament and government of Canada.

Official languages of Canada

(2) English and French are the official languages of New Brunswick and have equality of status and equal rights and privileges as to their use in all institutions of the legislature and government of New Brunswick.

Official languages of New Brunswick

(3) Nothing in this Charter limits the authority of Parliament or a legislature to advance the equality of status or use of English and French.

Advancement of status and use

16.1. (1) The English linguistic community and the French linguistic community in New Brunswick have equality of status and equal rights and privileges, including the right to distinct educational institutions and such distinct cultural institutions as are necessary for the preservation and promotion of those communities.

English and French linguistic communities in New Brunswick

(2) The role of the legislature and government of New Brunswick to preserve and promote the status, rights and privileges referred to in subsection (1) is affirmed.

Role of the legislature and government of New Brunswick

Proceedings of Parliament

17. (1) Everyone has the right to use English or French in any debates and other proceedings of Parliament.

Proceedings of New
Brunswick legislature

(2) Everyone has the right to use English or French in any debates and other proceedings of the legislature of New Brunswick.

Parliamentary statutes
and records

18. (1) The statutes, records and journals of Parliament shall be printed and published in English and French and both language versions are equally authoritative.

New Brunswick statutes
and records

(2) The statutes, records and journals of the legislature of New Brunswick shall be printed and published in English and French and both language versions are equally authoritative.

Proceedings in courts
established by Parliament

19. (1) Either English or French may be used by any person in, or in any pleading in or process issuing from, any court established by Parliament.

Proceedings in New
Brunswick courts

(2) Either English or French may be used by any person in, or in any pleading in or process issuing from, any court of New Brunswick.

Communications by public
with federal institutions

20. (1) Any member of the public in Canada has the right to communicate with, and to receive available services from, any head or central office of an institution of the Parliament or government of Canada in English or French, and has the same right with respect to any other office of any such institution where

(*a*) there is a significant demand for communications with and services from that office in such language; or

(*b*) due to the nature of the office, it is reasonable that communications with and services from that office be available in both English and French.

Communications by public
with New Brunswick
institutions

(2) Any member of the public in New Brunswick has the right to communicate with, and to receive available services from, any office of an institution of the legislature or government of New Brunswick in English or French.

Continuation of existing
constitutional provisions

21. Nothing in sections 16 to 20 abrogates or derogates from any right, privilege or obligation with respect to the English and French languages, or either of them, that exists or is continued by virtue of any other provision of the Constitution of Canada.

Rights and privileges
preserved

22. Nothing in sections 16 to 20 abrogates or derogates from any legal or customary right or privilege acquired or enjoyed either before or after the coming into force of this Charter with respect to any language that is not English or French.

Minority Language Educational Rights

Language of instruction

23. (1) Citizens of Canada

(*a*) whose first language learned and still understood is that of the English or French linguistic minority population of the province in which they reside, or

(*b*) who have received their primary school instruction in Canada in English or French and reside in a province where the language in which they received that instruction is the language of the English or French linguistic minority population of the province,

have the right to have their children receive primary and secondary school instruction in that language in that province.

Continuity of language
instruction

(2) Citizens of Canada of whom any child has received or is receiving primary or secondary school instruction in English or French in Canada, have the right to have all their children receive primary and secondary school instruction in the same language.

(3) The right of citizens of Canada under subsections (1) and (2) to have their children receive primary and secondary school instruction in the language of the English or French linguistic minority population of a province

(*a*) applies wherever in the province the number of children of citizens who have such a right is sufficient to warrant the provision to them out of public funds of minority language instruction; and

(*b*) includes, where the number of those children so warrants, the right to have them receive that instruction in minority language educational facilities provided out of public funds.

Application where numbers warrant

Enforcement

24. (1) Anyone whose rights or freedoms, as guaranteed by this Charter, have been infringed or denied may apply to a court of competent jurisdiction to obtain such remedy as the court considers appropriate and just in the circumstances.

Enforcement of guaranteed rights and freedoms

(2) Where, in proceedings under subsection (1), a court concludes that evidence was obtained in a manner that infringed or denied any rights or freedoms guaranteed by this Charter, the evidence shall be excluded if it is established that, having regard to all the circumstances, the admission of it in the proceedings would bring the administration of justice into disrepute.

Exclusion of evidence bringing administration of justice into disrepute

General

25. The guarantee in this Charter of certain rights and freedoms shall not be construed so as to abrogate or derogate from any aboriginal, treaty or other rights or freedoms that pertain to the aboriginal peoples of Canada including

Aboriginal rights and freedoms not affected by Charter

(*a*) any rights or freedoms that have been recognized by the Royal Proclamation of October 7, 1763; and

(*b*) any rights or freedoms that now exist by way of land claims agreements or may be so acquired.

26. The guarantee in this Charter of certain rights and freedoms shall not be construed as denying the existence of any other rights or freedoms that exist in Canada.

Other rights and freedoms not affected by Charter

27. This Charter shall be interpreted in a manner consistent with the preservation and enhancement of the multicultural heritage of Canadians.

Multicultural heritage

28. Notwithstanding anything in this Charter, the rights and freedoms referred to in it are guaranteed equally to male and female persons.

Rights guaranteed equally to both sexes

29. Nothing in this Charter abrogates or derogates from any rights or privileges guaranteed by or under the Constitution of Canada in respect of denominational, separate or dissentient schools.

Rights respecting certain schools preserved

30. A reference in this Charter to a Province or to the legislative assembly or legislature of a province shall be deemed to include a reference to the Yukon Territory and the Northwest Territories, or to the appropriate legislative authority thereof, as the case may be.

Application to territories and territorial authorities

31. Nothing in this Charter extends the legislative powers of any body or authority.

Legislative powers not extended

Application of Charter

Application of Charter

32. (1) This Charter applies

(*a*) to the Parliament and government of Canada in respect of all matters within the authority of Parliament including all matters relating to the Yukon Territory and Northwest Territories; and

(*b*) to the legislature and government of each province in respect of all matters within the authority of the legislature of each province.

Exception

(2) Notwithstanding subsection (1), section 15 shall not have effect until three years after this section comes into force.

Exception where express declaration

33. (1) Parliament or the legislature of a province may expressly declare in an Act of Parliament or of the legislature, as the case may be, that the Act or a provision thereof shall operate notwithstanding a provision included in section 2 or sections 7 to 15 of this Charter.

Operation of exception

(2) An Act or a provision of an Act in respect of which a declaration made under this section is in effect shall have such operation as it would have but for the provision of this Charter referred to in the declaration.

Five year limitation

(3) A declaration made under subsection (1) shall cease to have effect five years after it comes into force or on such earlier date as may be specified in the declaration.

Re-enactment

(4) Parliament or the legislature of a province may re-enact a declaration made under subsection (1).

Five year limitation

(5) Subsection (3) applies in respect of a re-enactment made under subsection (4).

Citation

Citation

34. This Part may be cited as the *Canadian Charter of Rights and Freedoms*.

Suggestions for Further Reading

Baker, Dennis, and Rainer Knopff. "Charter Checks and Parliamentary Balances" (2007) 16 *Constitutional Forum* 71.

Baker, Dennis, and Rainer Knopff. "Daviault Dialogue: The Strange Journey of Canada's Intoxication Defence" (2014) 19:1 *Review of Constitutional Studies* 35.

Baker, Dennis, and Rainer Knopff. "Minority Retort: A Parliamentary Power to Resolve Judicial Disagreement in Close Cases" (2002) 21 *Windsor Yearbook of Access to Justice* 348.

Bayefsky, Anne F., and Mary Eberts, eds. *Equality Rights and the Canadian Charter of Rights and Freedoms* (Toronto: Carswell, 1985).

Beckton, Clare F., and A. Wayne Mackay. *The Courts and the Charter* (Toronto: University of Toronto Press, 1985).

Brodie, Ian. *Friends of the Court: The Privileging of Interest Group Litigants in Canada* (Albany, NY: State University of New York Press, 2002).

Cairns, Alan C. *Charter versus Federalism: The Dilemmas of Constitutional Reform* (Montreal and Kingston: McGill-Queen's University Press, 1992).

Cavalluzzo, Paul. "Judicial Review and the Bill of Rights: Drybones and Its Aftermath" (1971) 9 *Osgoode Hall Law Journal* 511.

Choudhry, Sujit, and Claire E. Hunter. "Measuring Judicial Activism on the Supreme Court of Canada: A Comment on Newfoundland (Treasury Board) v. NAPE" (2003) 48 *McGill Law Journal* 525.

Choudhry, Sujit. "So What Is the Real Legacy of Oakes? Two Decades of Proportionality Analysis Under the Canadian Charter's Section 1" (2006) 34 *Supreme Court Law Review* (2d) 501.

Clarke, Jeremy. "Beyond the Democratic Dialogue, and Towards a Federalist One: Provincial Arguments and Supreme Court Responses in Charter Litigation" (2006) 39 *Canadian Journal of Political Science* 293.

Epp, Charles R. *The Rights Revolution* (Chicago: University of Chicago Press, 1998).

Fudge, Judy. "Legally Speaking: Courts, Democracy, and the Market" (2003) 19 *Supreme Court Law Review* (2d) 111.

Gaudreault-Desbiens, Jean-François. "La Charte canadienne des droits et libertés et le fédéralisme: Quelques remarques sur les vingt premières années d'une relation amigugé" (2003) *Revue du Barreau* 271.

Harding, Mark, and Rainer Knopff. "Charter Values vs. Charter Dialogue" (2013) 31 *National Journal of Constitutional Law* 161.

———. "Constitutionalizing Everything: The Role of 'Charter Values.'" (2013) 18:2 *Review of Constitutional Studies* 141.

Hennigar, Mathew. "Expanding the 'Dialogue' Debate: Canadian Federal Government Responses to Lower Court Charter Decisions" (2004) 37 *Canadian Journal of Political Science* 3.

Hiebert, Janet L. *Charter Conflicts: What Is Parliament's Role?* (Montreal and Kingston: McGill-Queen's University Press, 2002).

———. "Compromise and the Notwithstanding Clause: Why the Dominant Narrative Distorts Our Understanding" in James B. Kelly and Christopher P. Manfredi, eds., *Contested Constitutionalism: Reflections on the Canadian Charter of Rights and Freedoms* (Vancouver: University of British Columbia Press, 2009).

———. *Limiting Rights: The Dilemma of Judicial Review* (Montreal and Kingston: McGill-Queen's University Press, 1996).

———. "The Notwithstanding Clause and Charter Compliance: Why Infrequent Use Should Not Be Equated with Charter Compliance" in Nathalie Des Rosiers, Patrick Macklem, and Peter Oliver, eds., *Oxford Handbook of the Canadian Constitution* (Oxford: Oxford University Press, 2017).

Hirschl, Ran. *Towards Juristocracy: The Origins and Consequences of the New Constitutionalism* (Cambridge, MA: Harvard University Press, 2004).

Hogg, Peter W., and A.A. Bushell. "The Charter Dialogue Between Courts and Legislatures (Or Perhaps the Charter of Rights Isn't Such a Bad Thing After All)" (1997) 35 *Osgoode Hall Law Journal* 75.

Howe, Paul, and Peter H. Russell, eds. *Judicial Power and Canadian Democracy* (Montreal and Kingston: McGill-Queen's University Press, 2001).

Huscroft, Grant A. " 'Thank God We're Here': Judicial Exclusivity in Charter Interpretation and Its Consequences" (2004) 25 *Supreme Court Law Review* (2d) 239.

Hutchinson, Allan, and Andrew Petter. "Private Rights/Public Wrongs: The Liberal Lie of the Charter" (1988) 38 *University of Toronto Law Journal* 278.

James, Patrick, Donald E. Abelson, and Michael Lusztig, eds. *The Myth of the Sacred: The Charter, the Courts, and the Politics of the Constitution in Canada* (Montreal and Kingston: McGill-Queen's University Press, 2002).

Kahana, Tsvi. "The Notwithstanding Mechanism and Public Discussion: Lessons from the Ignored Practice of Section 33 of the Charter" (2001) 44 *Canadian Public Administration* 255.

Kelly, James B. "Bureaucratic Activism and the Charter of Rights and Freedoms: The Department of Justice and Its Entry into the Centre of Government" (1999) 42 *Canadian Public Administration* 476.

———. *Governing with the Charter: Legislative and Judicial Activism and Framers' Intent* (Vancouver: University of British Columbia Press, 2005).

Kelly, James B. and Christopher Manfredi, eds. *Contested Constitutionalism: Reflections on the Charter of Rights and Freedoms* (Vancouver: University of British Columbia Press, 2009) at 102-28.

Knopff, Rainer. "Charter Reconsiderations" (2012) 21:2 *National Magazine* 38-41.

———. "How Democratic Is the Charter? And Does It Matter?" (2003) 19 *Supreme Court Law Review* (2d) 199.

———. "Populism and the Politics of Rights: The Dual Attack on Representative Democracy" (1998) 31 *Canadian Journal of Political Science* 683.

———. "What Do Constitutional Equality Rights Protect Canadians Against?" (1987) 20 *Canadian Journal of Political Science* 265.

Knopff, Rainer, Rhonda Evans, Dennis Baker, and Dave Snow. "Dialogue: Clarified and Reconsidered" (2017) 54:2 *Osgoode Hall Law Journal* (forthcoming).

Knopff, Rainer, and F.L. Morton. *Charter Politics* (Scarborough, ON: Nelson Canada, 1992).

LaSelva, Samuel V. *The Moral Foundations of Canadian Federalism* (Montreal and Kingston: McGill-Queen's University Press, 1996).

Laskin, Bora. "Our Civil Liberties—The Role of the Supreme Court" (1955) 41 *Queen's Quarterly* 445.

Leeson, Howard. "Section 33, The Notwithstanding Clause: A Paper Tiger?" in Paul Howe and Peter H. Russell, eds., *Judicial Power and Canadian Democracy* (Montreal and Kingston: McGill-Queen's University Press, 2001).

Lemmens, Trudo, Andrew Flavelle Martin, Cheryl Milne, and Ian B. Lee, eds. *Regulating Creation: The Law, Ethics, and Policy of Assisted Human Reproduction* (Toronto: University of Toronto Press, 2017).

MacIvor, Heather. *Canadian Politics and Government in the Charter Era* (Toronto: Thomson-Nelson, 2006).

———. "The Charter of Rights and Party Politics" (2004) 10 *Choices* 1.

MacLennan, Christopher. *Toward the Charter: Canadians and the Demand for a National Bill of Rights, 1929-1960* (Montreal and Kingston: McGill-Queen's University Press, 2003).

Manfredi, Christopher P. "The Day the Dialogue Died: A Comment on Sauvé v. Canada" (2007) 45 *Osgoode Hall Law Journal* 105.

———. *Feminist Activism in the Supreme Court* (Vancouver: University of British Columbia Press, 2004).

———. *Judicial Power and the Charter: Canada and the Paradox of Liberal Constitutionalism*, 2d ed. (Don Mills, ON: Oxford University Press, 2001).

———. "Same-Sex Marriage and the Notwithstanding Clause" (October 2003) 24:9 *Policy Options* 21.

Manfredi, Christopher, and Mark Rush. *Judging Democracy* (Peterborough, ON: Broadview Press, 2008).

McCormick, Peter J. *The End of the Charter Revolution: Looking Back From the New Normal* (Toronto: University of Toronto Press, 2015).

Morton, F.L. "Dialogue or Monologue" in Paul Howe and Peter H. Russell, eds., *Judicial Power and Canadian Democracy* (Montreal and Kingston: McGill-Queen's University Press, 2001).

———. "The Political Impact of the Canadian Charter of Rights and Freedoms" (1987) 20 *Canadian Journal of Political Science* 31.

————. "The Politics of Rights: What Canadians Should Know About the American Bill of Rights" (1988) 1 *Windsor Review of Legal and Social Issues* 61.

Morton, F.L., and Rainer Knopff. *The Charter Revolution and the Court Party* (Peterborough, ON: Broadview Press, 2000).

Morton, F.L., Peter H. Russell, and Troy Riddell. "The Canadian Charter of Rights and Freedoms: A Descriptive Analysis of the First Decade, 1982-1992" (1995) 5 *National Journal of Constitutional Law* 1.

Petter, Andrew. "The Politics of the Charter" (1986) 8 *Supreme Court Law Review* 473.

————. "Taking Dialogue Theory Much Too Seriously (Or Perhaps Charter Dialogue Isn't Such a Good Thing After All" (2007) 45 *Osgoode Hall Law Journal* 147.

Pinard, Danielle. "Une Malheureuse celebration de la Charte des droits et libertés de la personne par la Cour suprême du Canada: L'arrête Chaoulli" in *La Charter Québécoise: Origines, enjeux et perspectives,* Revue du Barreau du Québec 2006.

Roach, Kent. *The Supreme Court on Trial: Judicial Activism or Democratic Dialogue?* (Toronto: Irwin Law, 2001).

Russell, Peter H. "The Political Purposes of the Canadian Charter of Rights and Freedoms" (1983) 61 *Canadian Bar Review* 30.

————. "Standing Up for Notwithstanding" (1991) 29 *Alberta Law Review* 293.

Schmeiser, D.A. *Civil Liberties in Canada* (Toronto: Oxford University Press, 1964).

Scott, F.R. *Civil Liberties and Canadian Federalism* (Toronto: University of Toronto Press, 1959).

————. "The Privy Council and Minority Rights" (1930) *Queen's Quarterly* 668.

Sharpe, Robert J. *Charter Litigation* (Toronto: Butterworths, 1987).

Smith, Miriam. *Lesbian and Gay Rights in Canada: Social Movements and Equality-Seeking, 1971-1995* (Toronto: University of Toronto Press, 1999).

————. *Political Institutions and Lesbian and Gay Rights in the United States and Canada* (New York: Routledge, 2008).

Sniderman, Paul M., Joseph F. Fletcher, Peter H. Russell, and Philip E. Tetlock. *The Clash of Rights: Liberty, Equality and Legitimacy in Pluralist Democracy* (New Haven, CT: Yale University Press, 1997).

Strayer, Barry. "Life Under the Charter: Adjusting the Balance Between Legislatures and Courts" (1988) *Public Law* 347.

Stuart, Don. *Charter Justice in Canadian Criminal Law*, 4th ed. (Toronto: Thomson Carswell, 2005).

Tarnopolsky, W.S. *The Canadian Bill of Rights* (Toronto: McClelland & Stewart, 1975).

Weiler, Paul. "Rights and Judges in a Democracy: A New Canadian Version" (1984) 18 *University of Michigan Journal of Law Reform* 51.

Whyte, John D. "On Not Standing for Notwithstanding" (1990) 28 *Alberta Law Review* 347.

Wilson, Bertha. "The Making of a Constitution: Approaches to Judicial Interpretation" (1988) *Public Law* 370.